COLLECTED  WORKS OF

BERNARD LONERGAN

VOLUME 1

GRACE AND FREEDOM:

OPERATIVE GRACE IN THE THOUGHT OF

ST THOMAS AQUINAS

COLLECTED WORKS
OF BERNARD

LONERGAN

GRACE AND FREEDOM:
OPERATIVE GRACE IN THE
THOUGHT OF
ST THOMAS AQUINAS
edited by
Frederick E. Crowe and
Robert M. Doran

Published for Lonergan Research Institute
of Regis College, Toronto
by University of Toronto Press
Toronto Buffalo London

ISBN 0-8020-4799-8 (cloth)
ISBN 0-8020-8337-4 (paper)

Reprinted 2005, 2009, 2013

Printed on acid-free paper

Canadian Cataloguing in Publication Data

Lonergan, Bernard J.F. (Bernard Joseph Francis), 1904–1984
    Collected works of Bernard Lonergan

    Partial contents: v. 1. Grace and freedom: operative grace in the thought of St. Thomas Aquinas / edited by Frederick E. Crowe and Robert M. Doran. Includes bibliographical references and index.
    ISBN 0-8020-4799-8 (v. 1: bound)   ISBN 0-8020-8337-4 (v. 1: pbk.)

    1. Theology – 20th century.   2. Catholic Church.   I. Crowe, Frederick E.
    II. Doran, Robert M., 1939–   .   III. Lonergan Research Institute.
    IV. Title.

    BX891.L595 1988   230   C88-093328-3

The Lonergan Research Institute gratefully acknowledges the generous contribution of the MALLINER CHARITABLE FOUNDATION, which has made possible the production of this entire series.

The Lonergan Research Institute gratefully acknowledges the financial assistance of the JESUITS OF HALIFAX toward the publication of this volume of the Collected Works of Bernard Lonergan.

University of Toronto Press acknowledges the financial support for its publishing activities of the Government of Canada through the Book Publishing Industry Development Program (BPIDP).

Contents

General Editors' Preface to Collected Works of Bernard Lonergan

The project of publishing the Collected Works of Bernard Lonergan (CWL) was conceived while Lonergan was still alive, though he was no longer able to take any active role in its execution. The Trustees of his Estate, however, gave the project enthusiastic backing, designated the works to be included, appointed General Editors, and commissioned the Lonergan Research Institute as agent publisher. The Institute in turn engaged the services of the University of Toronto Press, which has continued to turn out handsomely printed volumes, as well as reprints of works published earlier that will be included only later in our CWL series.

The title of the series is Collected Works, not The Collected Works, by which we wish to indicate that it is not our purpose to include all the works of Lonergan in the familiar style of an Opera Omnia. Nevertheless, the collection will include the vast majority of his works, enough to permit a thorough study of all the main elements of his thought; and references to archival material will enable researchers to pursue their quest beyond these volumes for minutiae, fragments, sketches, memos, and so on not included here.

The order of the first dozen volumes as numbered (though not as appearing in print) will follow the main steps of Lonergan's public career in chronological order and so will start with his doctoral dissertation of 1940; later we will abandon chronology in order to go back and include works of his student days and of his early teaching years that throw significant light on the major works, as well as to collect scattered reviews, responses to questions, and other items of a less developed character, and to follow the development in his courses and institutes on method.

Our editing policy is frankly conservative, taking it as our ideal to publish exactly what Lonergan said or wrote. The ideal, of course, is in many cases unattainable; for one simple example, we have sometimes had to reproduce what previous editors have given us, without knowing how much their editing changed the text; for another much more important example, we have often had to transcribe recordings of lectures that were never meant for publication and had to be rewritten (as Lonergan himself once requested) for the reading public. The mechanics of publishing a collection of over twenty volumes also required a good many minor changes, and so we have adopted a uniform spelling and punctuation, taking as our authorities for the most part the *Oxford American Dictionary* and *The Chicago Manual of Style.*

Still, the conservative principle has been dominant. There was no question, then, of changing language that would now be regarded as non-inclusive, or of removing statements that are less ecumenical in tone than we would wish, or even of 'correcting' some of Lonergan's outdated language. This has a more important basis than mere fussiness; Lonergan had a lifelong concern for history, and the history of his own development is crucial to the interpretation of his ideas. Our decision, then, has been to leave intact whatever may help readers to locate a work in his history; if his earlier writing shows a preference for English usage and his later writing a preference for American, that is part of his history; if he spoke of 'gramophones,' that too points to his personal history.

For the rest we may conclude with all possible brevity. We have often added numbering and subtitles for his divisions (always recording that fact). We have translated in text or footnotes Lonergan's Latin and Greek quotations, words, and phrases, and have provided a lexicon for handy reference to them. We have checked his footnote references wherever possible, and have here and there provided editorial notes of our own.

As we go to press with this volume we are not quite halfway through the original project. We have incurred many debts of gratitude in these fifteen years and expect to incur many more as the work progresses. Since it is not possible to name all future collaborators and this Preface is meant to introduce the whole series, we have to be content at this point with a general 'Thank you' to those who have contributed and/or will contribute to our task: translating Lonergan's Latin, transcribing tapes, editing lectures, checking references, and performing the many office tasks associated with publishing. Here we may mention especially others who have accepted responsibility for editing certain volumes, and as well the staffs of the Lonergan Research Institute and of the University of Toronto Press.

Finally we acknowledge the financial help we have received from the sponsors of particular volumes; it was clear from the beginning that we would have to subsidize the series; we appealed for financial help, and it was given promptly, generously, and so joyfully that it seemed that we were the benefactors of those donating the subsidies rather than the reverse.

FREDERICK E. CROWE
ROBERT M. DORAN

Editors' Preface

The two works presented here are sufficiently distinct to be called two works, but enough of a unity to be included together in one volume. The second work in the volume was the first to be written: Lonergan's doctoral dissertation, completed in May 1940 at the Gregorian University in Rome under the title *Gratia Operans: A Study of the Speculative Development in the Writings of St. Thomas of Aquin.* The first work in the volume was a publication of that dissertation in what Lonergan called a 'condensed and abbreviated' form in four articles in *Theological Studies* (1941–42) under the title 'St. Thomas' Thought on *Gratia Operans.*'[1] Some thirty years later the four articles were collected and published in book form under the title *Grace and Freedom: Operative Grace in the Thought of St. Thomas Aquinas.*[2] We retain the book and dissertation titles for parts one and two respectively of the present volume and as well have usurped the book title for this whole volume which is number one in the Collected Works of Bernard Lonergan.

Such in a paragraph is the brief history of CWL 1; it may be worth our while to see it in greater detail.

Lonergan's religious superiors had sent him to Rome in 1933 with the intention that, after his basic theological studies, he should obtain a doctor-

---

1 Bernard Lonergan, 'St. Thomas' Thought on *Gratia Operans,*' *Theological Studies* 2 (1941) 289–324, 3 (1942) 69–88, 375–402, 533–78. Note that in this series the title of the third article was given as 'St. Thomas' Theory of Operation.'

2 Bernard J.F. Lonergan, *Grace and Freedom: Operative Grace in the Thought of St. Thomas Aquinas,* ed. J. Patout Burns (London: Darton, Longman & Todd, and New York, Herder and Herder, 1971).

ate in philosophy.[3] This expectation oriented Lonergan's spare-time reading and writing for the next five years, during which he completed the regular program of studies and formation for Jesuit scholastics. He had even focused his personal thought on philosophy of history and had study of this as a distant goal right up to August 1938.[4]

At this time, however, on the eve of his return to Rome for doctoral studies, his superiors, planning now to keep him in Rome on the faculty of the Gregorian University, decided to switch him from philosophy to theology, on the ground of the large number of English-speaking students in that faculty.[5]

This dislocation of his plans meant that Lonergan arrived in Rome in the late fall of 1938 without plans or proposals for the topic of his doctoral dissertation. He had, however, made inquiries in France about possible directors, and had been told Charles Boyer, then Prefect of Studies at the Gregorian University, was an intelligent person; so Lonergan asked him to be his director.[6] Boyer agreed, and they discussed a number of different topics, only to set them aside. Finally Boyer reached for his copy of Thomas Aquinas's *Prima secundae*, pointed to an article that he himself had difficulty in interpreting, and suggested that Lonergan make a study of that article in itself, of its *loca parallela*, and of its historical sources.[7] Thus, by a simple accident of history, Lonergan was led to concentrated study of Thomas

3 Perhaps with a view that he should join the faculty of the Jesuits' newly opened house for philosophical studies in Toronto.
4 Letter to Henry Keane, his Provincial Superior, 10 August 1938; File 713 in his unpublished papers, especially the writings of 1937–38 (Archives, Lonergan Research Institute, Toronto).
5 Letter of Vincent McCormick to Henry Keane; Lonergan's account thirty-five years later: 'The following September [that is, in 1938] I had a letter from Fr Vincent McCormick informing me that most of the English-speaking students at the Gregorian were in theology and that I, accordingly, was to do a biennium in theology.' Bernard Lonergan, '*Insight* Revisited,' in *A Second Collection*, ed. William F.J. Ryan and Bernard J. Tyrrell (London: Darton, Longman & Todd, 1974, and Philadelphia: Westminster, 1975; repr. Toronto: University of Toronto Press, 1996) 263–78, at 266.
6 Information received from Fred Lawrence and Richard Renshaw (the latter in an interview with Lonergan, 18 January 1973 – Archives) on the choice of Boyer for director; see also the notes Lonergan made in 1943, in preparation for the defense of his thesis, College of the Immaculate Conception, Montreal (Archives, Batch I-A, Folder 16; A51 in the catalogue made by Robert Doran; these very extensive notes are a valuable resource for study of various points in the dissertation).
7 Archives, as in preceding note.

Aquinas, beginning what would be an eleven-year apprenticeship,[8] and proposed as his topic, duly listed in the university records as accepted, 'A history of St. Thomas's thought on operative grace.'

There is hardly any information on the actual writing of the dissertation, but we do know that he shed his Molinist views very quickly: 'Within a month or so it was completely evident to me that Molinism had no contribution to make to an understanding of Aquinas.'[9] My interview with Boyer over thirty years later yielded only meager results.[10] The dissertation itself shows a quite remarkable amount of research, and some work notes that remain give us a glimpse of Lonergan at work. As we shall see, there is reason to believe that Lonergan was persuaded to rush the completion of his task. It is, in any case, something of a *tour de force* to write a doctoral thesis in the 'biennium' that was then the normal amount of time available to doctoral candidates, and Lonergan submitted the typed work (ix and 338 pages, plus bibliography of ix pages), on 1 May 1940, less than seventeen months from the date of his topic approval.[11]

The oddity that the doctorate was awarded only in 1946 brings up a curious bit of history in regard to fulfilment of the doctoral requirements and has its interest for the dissertation itself, the last chapter of which shows evidence of a hastier composition.[12] In fact the war broke out as Lonergan began the second year of his 'biennium,' and was raging furiously as he awaited the defense of his dissertation. It is highly probable that there was pressure on him to finish the written work, fulfil the further requirements for the doctorate, and get back to Canada while there was still time. The date originally set for the defense of his thesis, which I presume would

8 1938–49; Lonergan's letter of 3 March 1980, to F. Crowe. I borrow from William Mathews the use of 'apprenticeship.' Much later Lonergan attributed the choice of his thesis topic to luck (*Curiosity at the Center of One's Life: Statements and Questions of R. Eric O'Connor*, ed. J. Martin O'Hara [Montreal: Thomas More Institute, 1984] 375–76, in the interview of 25 February 1969); one must remember that for him 'luck,' like 'fate,' was the created component of divine providence.
9 Bernard J.F. Lonergan, *Method in Theology*, 2nd ed. (London: Darton, Longman & Todd; New York: Herder and Herder, 1972; reprint Toronto: University of Toronto Press, 1996) 163, note 5.
10 In 1973. Boyer remembered directing Lonergan's thesis, but had little information on the details of its composition.
11 The Gregorian University Catalogus IV gives this information about Lonergan's thesis. Catalogus I, entry 615, thema approbatum, 6.xii.38; Catalogus II, entry 793, dissertatio scripta, 1.v.40; Catalogus III, entry 479, dissertatio typis edita, 23.xii.46.
12 Typos uncorrected, pagination added by hand, etc.

normally have been in June or even July, was advanced to mid-May, but then just two days before the new date he was told to take ship from Italy, and so he arrived home without his doctorate.[13] Years later, Lonergan still showed his displeasure at the way he was pushed around, but in retrospect we have to say providence was at work; it is frightening to think of this Canadian citizen holed up in the four walls of the Gregorian University, where he would enjoy Vatican protection from the 'enemy,' till the liberation of Rome in 1944.[14]

The next steps followed slowly. As the war dragged on and Lonergan was still without his doctorate, his Provincial Superior, Thomas J. Mullally, pressed on Rome the anomaly of the situation, to the good effect that an examination board of 'Magistri Aggregati' of the Gregorian University (a degree held by several professors at the College of the Immaculate Conception, not now in use) was set up in Montreal and Lonergan duly presented his 'Lectio coram' there on 27 May 1943, and defended his thesis two weeks later on 8 June.[15]

One requirement remained. To obtain the doctorate, candidates must 'publish' their thesis or 'excerpta' from it, where 'publishing' meant providing fifty copies for the Gregorian University. This had to be delayed till

13 Sketchy notes of a conversation with Lonergan over thirty years later enable us to deduce the following sequence. The exam was set for Friday, 17 May, to enable Lonergan to take ship on the *Washington*, sailing from Naples Saturday, 18 May. Then it was discovered that there was no room on the *Washington*, and so on 15 May, two days before the date assigned for his defense, Lonergan was sent to Genoa, where he embarked on the *Conti di Savoia*, and arrived in New York on 24 May 1940.
    Worth noting is a little flurry of bureaucratic activity that May, both at the Gregorian and at the Jesuit Curia, which gave Lonergan's case unusual attention. At the University the advanced date was arranged by Joseph Filograssi (Dean of Theology) when neither Charles Boyer (his Director) nor Vincent McCormick (the Rector) favored the hurry-up. At the Jesuit Curia, Fr Lodimir Ledochowski, the Superior General, was against the move, but it was pushed by Adelard Dugré, a member of the French-Canadian Jesuit Province, and Assistant to the Superior General in Rome for the region covering Canada; Dugré, it seems, had his own agenda and wished to transfer Lonergan to the faculty of the College of the Immaculate Conception in Montreal. – Quite a fuss of top administrators over a doctoral examination, but the times were chaotic!
14 Italy became an 'enemy' country for Canada on 10 June 1940, but the signs of approaching hostilities were already clear shortly after Lonergan submitted his thesis.
15 *The News-Letter: Province of Upper Canada* 18:6 (June 1943) 45: '[T]he Gregorian University delegated the theological faculty' of Immaculate Conception College to hear the examinations.

the war was over, and Lonergan then fulfilled the requirement by supplying fifty copies of his fourth *Theological Studies* article, adding a prefatory note (published here in an appendix) and a table of contents of the four articles. It was an arrangement that would probably be frowned on today, but was wisely accepted in the chaos of the 1940s, and Lonergan was finally granted his doctorate on 23 December 1946. The Gregorian *Liber Annualis* duly recorded the fact in its 1948 volume (for the years 1946–47).[16]

Meanwhile, as this curious history was unfolding and prior to most of it, Lonergan had written for *Theological Studies* the 'contracta et abbreviata' account of his dissertation in the four articles mentioned above. Some thirty years later, J. Patout Burns, then a student at Regis College, Willowdale (Toronto), edited the articles and published them in book form as *Grace and Freedom: Operative Grace in the Thought of St. Thomas Aquinas*. His 'Editor's Foreword' lists the editorial work involved: stylistic modifications to divide the four articles into six chapters, significant changes in the mode of making references, addition of Bekker numbers for references to Aristotle, the Quaracchi editions for the works of Peter Lombard, St Bonaventure, and Duns Scotus, the Borgnet edition for St Albert, the Marietti numbers for their editions of St Thomas, and so on. The foreword also mentions Lonergan's expansion of some of the notes and his elimination of a small number of references that in the new context would be pedantic; it concludes by saying: 'Fr. Lonergan's own advice has been invaluable' – a remark that gains weight from the fact that Burns and Lonergan were both resident at Regis College in 1970 during the work of editing.

In the context of that last remark, the editors of this Collected Works edition of *Grace and Freedom* are happy in their turn to acknowledge that the work of Professor Burns has been invaluable to them. We have taken over and incorporated his work in specifying references, particularly in his use of the Marietti numbers for several works of Aquinas and his list of loci in Aristotle and Thomas; we have added to that list the further loci in the dissertation, but we have not included the loci in Augustine, Peter Lombard, Albert, and Bonaventure.

The dissertation, however, presented its own problems. We worked from Lonergan's copy, which is a carbon (probably a second carbon). Lonergan

16 The 'excerpta' records the 'Vidimus et approbamus' of the Gregorian readers (Charles Boyer and Joseph de Guibert) as given 8 June 1943, the date of the defense at Montreal, and the 'Nihil obstat' (Alex. Carter, 'censor ad hoc') and 'Imprimatur' (Philippe Perrier) of the Montreal Archdiocese as given 21 May 1946.

clearly was his own typist, and made his own typos, though they were fewer than was normally the case in getting English texts typed professionally in Rome, and were easily corrected. But he also wrote in the margins, presumably after submitting the good copy (or copies), often adding further references to Aquinas; anyone who has worked on Aquinas will recognize the syndrome: further texts noticed that pertain to a point made in the original; that is an endless process, but we have noted them when they seemed more important.

Chapter 1 of the thesis (II-1 in this volume) is a special case, with a good deal of sidelining, underlining, marginal ticking, and so on. Some of this is done in Lonergan's style, and could be explained as preparation for his doctoral defense, first for the aborted defense of 1940 and then for the actual defense of 1943.[17] But some of the markings are not his, as when a note asks whether Melchior Cano is meant.[18]

One further curiosity remains in this already curious history. At the end of his own bound copy of the dissertation Lonergan included 71 pages (numbered in his hand and concluding at 70, but he missed a page at 28–29) of what are obviously work notes for chapter 3 of the dissertation. The section numbers show they were drafted (and sometimes drafted twice) as developments of various topics: Aristotle's cosmic views, his hierarchy of movers, Thomas's theory of motion, causation by intellect, the idea of application, and so on. If these various drafts have any unity in themselves, it is probably to be found under the heading of God as an agent 'per intellectum agens,' and the advance made by Thomas over Aristotle under that heading. The editors, after some debate, decided not to add these notes to an already oversize volume, but they have no doubt about the value of the notes; Lonergan himself saw reason to bind them in his personal copy of the dissertation, and they remain to be studied by some future researcher.

We conclude with our usual word regarding the editorial conventions we have adopted: the use of the *Oxford American Dictionary* and the *Chicago*

---

17 One intriguing notation occurs on p. 430 below, on the word 'trahuntur,' quoted from Aquinas on chapter 6 of John's Gospel, on our being drawn by the Father. The notation is 'S. Aug., Homilia, Fer. iv, Oct. Pentecost.' Pentecost in 1940 was on 12 May, feria 4 would be a Wednesday, but Matins and Lauds were regularly anticipated the evening before, and Lonergan could have made this notation after reading Matins on Tuesday, the eve of his departure for Genoa – sheer speculation, but an intriguing possibility nevertheless.

18 P. 11 of the dissertation MS.

Manual of Style as guides to the minutiae of editing; the addition of a lexicon of Latin and Greek phrases (longer passages are translated in the text or the accompanying footnote); a list of the editions of Thomas that we consulted. *PL* is our abbreviation for references to Migne's *Patrologia latina. DB* and *DS* are used for Denzinger's *Enchiridion Symbolorum.* Lonergan's English quotations from scripture remain as he gave them, but we rely on the *New Revised Standard Version* for our own translations, so that correspondence with the Latin is at times in the sense rather than in the letter. No attempt is made to soften the sometimes unecumenical tone of his remarks, even where we believe he would have written differently in later years. Nor have we attempted to correct his non-inclusive language.

Finally, besides our already acknowledged debt to J. Patout Burns, we have other debts of gratitude to pay: to Marcela Dayao, who typed *Grace and Freedom* (the present first part) onto computer, and Elaine MacMillan, who did the same for a good part of the dissertation (here the second part), completing a task begun by Robert Doran; to Richard Tetreau and Barbara Geiger, Librarians at Regis College, who allowed us the great convenience of long-term loans from the Regis Library while we were checking Lonergan's work; to Giovanni Sala and Michael Stebbins, who provided helpful corrections to Lonergan's references; to Gene Merz, s.j., and the Marquette University Jesuit community for the hospitality accorded Robert Doran in the semester he spent with them editing the volume; and to the librarians at Marquette University for the kind and gracious assistance they gave to Robert Doran in that same semester.

FREDERICK E. CROWE
(for the editors)

PART ONE

Grace and Freedom:
Operative Grace in the Thought of
St Thomas Aquinas

I-1

Historical Background

The differences that have been observed between St Thomas's earlier and later expositions of *gratia operans* can hardly be understood without some prior account of the thought of his predecessors. Accordingly, the present chapter, after an introductory note on St Augustine's *De gratia et libero arbitrio*, turns to the work of compiling and focusing some of the results of recent research. In addition to the monographs of Dr Schupp on the *Gnadenlehre* of Peter Lombard and of Dr Doms on that of St Albert the Great, there are two important series of articles: with great thoroughness Dr Landgraf has investigated several aspects of the general movement of speculation on grace prior to Aquinas, and Dom Lottin, o.s.b., has furnished what from our point of view is a complementary study of contemporary theories of liberty. Together these labors constitute clearly enough an introduction to St Thomas's thought on *gratia operans*, and our task will be so to exploit this wealth of information that the state of the question when St Thomas began to write may become apparent.[1]

---

1 Fr Norbert del Prado in his three-volume work, *De gratia et libero arbitrio* (Fribourg: Ex Typis Consociationis Sancti Pauli, 1907), laid great stress on St Thomas's idea of *gratia operans*. Fr Lange, in his treatise *De gratia* [Hermann Lange, *De gratia tractatus dogmaticus* (Freiburg: Herder, 1929) 472–74, §§590–99], objected that more probably St Thomas attached little importance to the idea; *gratia operans* was an old term on which something had to be said; it is treated three times (*Super II Sententiarum*, d. 26, q. 1, a. 5; *De veritate*, q. 27, a. 5, ad 1m; *Summa theologiae*, 1-2, q. 111, a. 2) yet never twice in the same fashion. These variations we believe to be of the greatest interest in the history of speculation on grace.

It may not be amiss to make plain that we are engaged not in the history of dogma but in the history of theological speculation. *Non affirmando sed coniectando* is a fairly frequent phrase in the old writers: it is a signal that they are not enunciating their faith but trying to elaborate its speculative coherence. At any time such work is difficult enough, but it was particularly so in its initial phases when essential theorems were still in process of finding formulation. Thus there is a real difference between the continuity of the history of dogma and the succession of theses and antitheses which characterize the human effort of *fides quaerens intellectum*; and precisely because there is this real difference, speculative failure is not the same as heresy: indeed, such failure was inevitable through the whole period in which theological speculation was groping through trial and error towards the discovery of its proper method and technique.

1   St Augustine's *De Gratia et Libero Arbitrio*

The division of grace into operative and cooperative arose not from a detached love of systematization but to meet the exigencies of a controversy. Like more recent strategists, the Pelagians did not defend a rigidly coherent line but rather an elastic set of positions arranged in depth. They agreed with the Stoics that man asked the gods not for virtue but only for fortune: that was their citadel; their battlefront was anywhere. If grace existed, then it was not necessary. If necessary, then it was the law, or knowledge of the law, or nature, or free will, or the remission of sins. If none of these would do, then it was given man according to his merits. If forced to admit that the merit of good deeds presupposes the gift of grace, there were those who would reply that the grace that causes good deeds is meted out according to the previous merit of good will.[2]

> 2 Augustine, *De gratia et libero arbitrio*, c. 14, §27, *PL* 44, 897: '"Etsi non datur [gratia] secundum merita bonorum operum, quia per ipsam bene operamur; tamen secundum merita bonae voluntatis datur: quia bona voluntas," inquiunt, "praecedit orantis, quam praecessit voluntas credentis, ut secundum haec merita gratia sequatur exaudientis Dei"'[Although (grace) is not given according to the merits of our good works, for it is through grace that we are able to do good works, nevertheless it is given according to the merits of good will, because, they say, the good will of a person praying precedes (grace), and is itself preceded by the will of a person believing, so that according to these merits the grace of the God who hears follows]. The semi-Pelagians added to the above list of alternatives the view that the *initium fidei* sometimes was due to grace and sometimes to free will.

The last of these Pelagian evasions, based on the familiar distinction between good will and good performance, St Augustine countered with a parallel distinction between divine operation and divine cooperation. It was a complete and perfect answer. God cooperates with good will to give it good performance; but alone he operates on bad will to make it good; so that good will itself no less than good performance is to be attributed to the divine gift of grace. To pluck out our heart of stone and substitute a heart of flesh is, indeed, a divine operation; and since our heart of stone neither desires nor deserves such a transformation, *Deus sine nobis operatur*. But when once we have willed to be good, we are not straightway saints and martyrs; we are not like St Peter when on an inverted cross he showed that his good will had grown great and strong; we are like him when at the Last Supper he boasted his fidelity and then in the courtyard thrice denied his Lord. We have our weak and imperfect good will only to pray for strength and spiritual growth; and when in answer to our prayers God enables us to will so firmly that we do perform, *nobiscum cooperatur*. Thus God operates to initiate us in the spiritual life, and he cooperates to bring us to perfection; alone he works to give us good desires, and together with our good desires he labors to give us good performance.[3]

It is to be observed that this operation and cooperation is a division neither of habitual grace nor of actual grace; it is a division simply of grace. Only in the course of the thirteenth century was the idea of habitual grace firmly established,[4] while the correlative concept of actual grace seems a corollary to the development of the idea of the habit.[5] But, in any case, St

---

3 Ibid. cc. 14–17, §§ 27–33, 897–901.
4 Contrast Clement v (*DB* 483 [*DS* 904]) with Innocent III (*DB* 410 [*DS* 780]). [*DS* gives 1201 as the date for § 780, 1312 for § 904.]
5 Dr Landgraf affirms that the term *gratia actualis* does not occur in the whole of early Scholasticism and that a host of terms such as *gratia operans, praeveniens*, etc., uniformly refer to justification. See Artur M. Landgraf, 'Die Erkenntnis der helfenden Gnade in der Frühscholastik,' *Zeitschrift für katholische Theologie* 55 (1931) 177–238, 403–37, 562–91, at 179–81. [Most of the Landgraf articles referred to by Lonergan were rewritten for Artur Michael Landgraf, *Dogmengeschichte der Frühscholastik*, Erster Teil, *Die Gnadenlehre*, Band 1 (Regensburg: Verlag Friedrich Pustet, 1952). At times the revisions are extensive; what is given little space in the earlier article is sometimes expanded; what was given more space is sometimes shortened. Hence the discrepancy the reader will find in the number of pages assigned for different references. The revision of the present article appears on pp. 51–140, and the material relevant to the present issue is on p. 51 (henceforth in the form *DFG* 51).] See below, p. 19, note 89; p. 20, note 90; p. 42, note 66.

Augustine in the work we are examining does not pay the slightest attention to this future development. Grace is any gratuitous gift of God: it is a vocation to the life of the celibate[6] or the most efficacious vocation of St Paul;[7] it is forgiveness, regeneration, justification,[8] but also it is the power to avoid sins in future;[9] it is being a child of God, and, as well, it is being moved by the Spirit of God;[10] it is creation in Christ Jesus in whom all things are made new,[11] and no less is it his aid without which we can do nothing;[12] it is faith operating through charity,[13] but above all it is charity itself.[14] Habitual and actual graces are not distinguished.

This fact eliminates not a little of the surprise that we experience in finding the ideas of justification and of liberation from sin in the foreground when St Augustine attempts to reconcile divine operation and human liberty. For he has no doubt that the will is free, not only when God cooperates with its good desires, but even when he operates good will itself, when he removes the heart of stone and inserts a heart of flesh. The prophet Ezekiel recounts, indeed, the divine promise to pluck out Israel's heart of stone, but no less does he deliver the divine command that Israel harden not its heart. How, Augustine asks, can God say both *dabo vobis* and *facite vobis?* Why does he give, if man is to be the maker? Or why does he command, if he himself is to be the giver? To this the answer is the celebrated paradox: the will of man is always free but not always good: either it is free from justice, and then it is evil; or it is liberated from sin, and then it is good.[15]

In a sense this disjunction is a major Augustinian problem, but in a more fundamental sense it is not a problem at all. For a problem exists only if there is an intelligibility to be discovered, and to assert a problem of interpretation here involves the assumption that the *mens Augustini* was a speculative system on the nature of grace and liberty. Now certainly this view has no support in the work with which we are dealing, for the *De gratia et libero arbitrio* was concerned not with speculation but with dogma. It was

6 Augustine, *De gratia et libero arbitrio,* c. 4, §7, 886.
7 Ibid. c. 5, §12, 888–89.
8 Ibid. cc. 5–6, §§12–14, 889–90; c.12, §24, 895–96.
9 Ibid. c. 13, §26, 896–97.
10 Ibid. c. 11, §23, 895.
11 Ibid. c. 8, §20, 892–93.
12 Ibid. c. 5, §10, 888; c. 6, §13, 890.
13 Ibid. c. 7, §18, 892.
14 Ibid. cc. 17–19, §§34–40, 902–905.
15 Ibid. cc. 14–15, §§29–31, 898–900 (Ezekiel 11.19–20; 18.31–32; 36.22–27).

written because the prototypes of exaggerated Augustinianism, certain monks at Hadrumetum, so extolled the grace of God as to deny human liberty.[16] It was addressed not to their understanding but to their faith; and if they failed to understand what they were to believe, they were not to dispute but to pray for light.[17] The concepts employed were not the specialized products of abstract reflection but common notions to be found in scripture and, indeed, familiar to all. There are no definitions, nor are any distinctions drawn except implicitly by the mere juxtaposition of complementary passages of Holy Writ.[18] There is argument, indeed, but not philosophic argument nor any scientific ordering of thought, just triumphant rhetoric marshaling such an array of texts that the claim is obviously true, 'Not I, but scripture itself has argued with you.'[19] The existence of human liberty is proved from revelation;[20] Pelagian ideas on grace are refuted in the same manner;[21] and when the ultimate problem of reconciliation is faced, St Augustine is fully content to exclaim *O altitudo* with St Paul.[22]

Still, despite the essentially dogmatic character of the work before us, it cannot be denied that the disjunction of freedom from justice and liberation from sin is speculative in nature and intention. However abrupt, brief, and paradoxical, it does aim at explaining; and similarly, throughout Augustine's many writings on grace, there is not only positive theology but also such a penetration of thought and understanding that one must affirm the development of speculative theology already to have begun. But, while we think this to be true, we also are inclined to assert that the most legitimate commentary on this initial speculation, the commentary most free from the endless vices of anachronism, is simply the history of subsequent speculation.

2   St Anselm

'Once there were proud men who placed the whole efficacy of the virtues in freedom alone; in our times there are many who utterly despair of the

16 Letter 214, § 1, *PL* 44, 875–76.
17 Ibid. § 7, 877–78; *De gratia et libero arbitrio*, c. 1, § 1, 881; c. 24, § 46, 911–12.
18 For example, ibid. cc. 14–15, §§ 29–31, 898–900.
19 Ibid. c. 20, § 41, 905–906: '... sic disputasse ut non magis ego quam divina ipsa Scriptura vobiscum locuta sit' [(I believe I) have so argued that not I but rather divine scripture itself has spoken to you].
20 Ibid. c. 2, § 2, 882: 'Revelavit autem nobis per Scripturas suas sanctas, esse in homine liberum voluntatis arbitrium' [(God) has revealed to us through his holy scriptures that there is free choice of will in man].
21 Ibid. cc. 4–19, §§ 6–40, 885–905.
22 Ibid. cc. 22–23, §§ 44–45, 909–11.

existence of freedom.'[23] Thus St Anselm expresses the contrast between his own day and that of St Augustine. He was faced not with the Pelagian denial of grace, nor yet with the denial of freedom made by the simple-minded monks of Hadrumetum, but with the deeper problem of reconciliation. He felt no need to prove from scripture either the necessity of grace or the existence of freedom, for both were taken for granted by the age of faith. But he was driven by the imperious impulse of *fides quaerens intellectum* to try and construct a mode of conception that would lend coherence to the mystery. The brilliance of his work is a monument to his genius; its almost complete unsatisfactoriness is an illuminating instance of the difficulty there was in evolving the method and technique of theological speculation.

In the synthetic sweep[24] of his thought the fundamental concept is rectitude. Truth is the rectitude that mind alone perceives.[25] Justice is rectitude of will maintained for its own sake.[26] Freedom is the capacity of maintaining rectitude of will for the sake of rectitude.[27] Grace, finally, is the cause of rectitude of will: prevenient grace is the sole cause of its emergence, and the same grace as subsequent is the main cause of its preservation.[28] Thus, grace and freedom are the causes of justice,[29] and justice is the ground of salvation.[30]

23 Anselm, *Tractatus de concordia praescientiae et praedestinationis nec non gratiae cum libero arbitrio*, c. 11, *PL* 158, 522: ['... fuerunt quidam superbi, qui totam virtutum efficaciam in sola libertate arbitrii consistere sunt arbitrati: et sunt nostro tempore multi, qui liberum arbitrium esse aliquid penitus desperant.' See also *S. Anselmi Cantuariensis Archiepiscopi Opera Omnia*, ed. Franciscus Salesius Schmitt, o.s.b. (Edinburgh: Thomas Nelson and Sons, 1946), vol. 2, p. 264. We will give the Schmitt references (in the format Schmitt 2: 264) as well as *PL*, but will use the latter as our text. Differences in the texts are minor. All Schmitt references are from volumes 1 and 2.]

24 Anselm, *De casu diaboli*, c. 12, *PL* 158, 341 [Schmitt 1: 252]: '... opus est ut tu ea, quae dicam, non sis contentus singula tantum intelligere, sed omnia simul memoria quasi sub uno intuitu colligere' [it is necessary that you not be content to understand just singly the things I am saying, but that you gather them all together in your memory as if under one comprehension].

25 Anselm, *De veritate*, c. 11, *PL* 158, 480 [Schmitt 1: 191]: '... veritas est rectitudo sola mente perceptibilis' [truth is rectitude perceived by mind alone].

26 Ibid. c. 12, 482 [Schmitt 1: 194]: 'Justitia ... est rectitudo voluntatis propter se servata' [Justice ... is rectitude of the will maintained for its own sake]. See Anselm, *De conceptu virginali*, c. 4, *PL* 158, 436–38 [Schmitt 2: 143–45].

27 Anselm, *De libero arbitrio*, c. 3, *PL* 158, 494 [Schmitt 1: 212]: '... illa libertas arbitrii est potestas servandi rectitudinem voluntatis propter ipsam rectitudinem' [that liberty of will is the power of preserving rectitude of will for the sake of rectitude itself].

28 Anselm, *Tractatus de concordia*, c. 14, 524–25 [Schmitt 2: 267–68].

29 Ibid.

30 Ibid. c. 12, 522–23 [Schmitt 2: 264], and passim.

The necessity of grace is, first, a dogma to be believed but second, almost a theorem to be demonstrated. For the will can obtain rightness neither from itself nor from any other creature. Not from itself, for right acts of will are not a cause but an effect of rightness of will. Not from any other creature, for as no creature can confer salvation, so no creature can confer the ground of salvation.[31]

On the other hand, the idea of freedom is obtained not by philosophic inquiry but rather as a theological conclusion. The *Dialogus de libero arbitrio* begins by showing that freedom cannot be the capacity to sin or not sin, for then neither God nor the blessed would be free. It adds that the capacity to sin cannot be even a part of freedom, for sin is servitude, and freedom cannot be constituted by the possibility of its opposite.[32] This, as is plain, immediately creates a problem of freedom in sinful acts. With regard to the sin of the angels and of Adam, it is maintained that they sinned not of necessity but of their own accord for they did so by a choice that was free; still it was not by the freedom of their choice that they sinned but rather by their capacity of servitude.[33] With regard to those already in the state of sin, there is no question of their doing what is right for they have lost their rectitude of will; the solution of the difficulty was to affirm that nonetheless they are truly free, truly able to maintain a rectitude of will they do not possess, just as a man bound and blindfold in a dungeon is truly able to see.[34]

In this it is easy to discern a dialectical unfolding of St Augustine's disjunction: either the will is free from justice and then it is evil, or it is liberated from sin and then it is good. Indeed, to escape this dilemma it was necessary to insert an ideal middle term between the two extremes, to place *natura pura* between *natura lapsa* and *natura elevata*, and so, with speculation released by this metaphysical perspective, to study the data of psychology on freedom and the data of revelation on grace. But it is not hard to be wise after the event, and in fact St Anselm was prevented from adopting such a course both by the exigencies of his age and by the unsolved problem of theological method.

There were the exigencies of the age. One has only to read over the titles of Anselm's treatises and dialogues to see that his interest lay in all the

31 Ibid. c. 13, 523–24 [Schmitt 2: 266]. See the argument in *De casu diaboli*, c. 1, 325–28 [Schmitt 1: 233–35] and c. 12, 341–44 [Schmitt 1: 251–55].
32 Anselm, *De libero arbitrio*, c. 1, 489–91 [Schmitt 1: 207–209].
33 Ibid. c. 2, 491–92 [Schmitt 1: 209–10].
34 Ibid. cc. 3–4, 492–96 [Schmitt 1: 210–14].

profoundest problems of theology. The Trinity, the end of the Incarnation, the fall of the angels, original sin, divine foreknowledge and predestination, grace and liberty – only what is difficult seems to his taste. Yet this is not a merely personal matter, for the objective logic of development should seem to play the more fundamental role. Not only are the questions St Anselm treated the most difficult; they also are the most obviously problems, the most apt to excite wonder and to impose the necessity of speculative thought in the medieval re-creation of culture and civilization. Thus, perhaps, the real issue that he faced and settled was the most general one of all: Is speculation possible and is it worth while? The strong words he used to describe his contemporaries – *penitus desperant* – show that this issue was real. The exuberance of speculation in the twelfth and thirteenth centuries may be the measure of the prestige of his example and the success of his effort.

From this viewpoint the problem of method falls into second place, for *primum est esse*. Still, this problem is simultaneous with existence, and it must be acknowledged that St Anselm in no way solved it. Naturally enough his canon of procedure is the Augustinian *crede ut intelligas*, a canon which, if it insists on faith, fails to point out that there are two standards for the understanding: natural truths can be reduced eventually to perfect coherence, but the truths of faith have the apex of their intelligibility hidden in the transcendence of God. Without this basic rule, defined by Vatican Council I, speculation risks perpetually a twofold error: it may reduce mystery to the level of natural truth, as did Peter Abelard and Gilbert de la Porrée; but it may also make the mistake of elevating natural problems to the order of mystery, and this seems to have been St Anselm's tendency. He makes such a mystery of human liberty that, by the logic of his position, he can afford to conceive grace as the cause of a state of will and to identify this state with the justice of justification. Thus, because baptism is accompanied by no act of will in an infant, he distinguishes between justice and the remission of sins; the infant is not justified but its sins are remitted, and this, together with the justice of Christ and of the church, opens to it the gates of heaven.[35] The effects of this strange, explicitly speculative, position on subsequent thought have been studied by the indefatigable Dr Landgraf.[36] Its cause would seem to lie in the then unformulated problem of speculative method.

35 Anselm, *De conceptu virginali*, c. 29, 462–64 [Schmitt 2: 172–73].
36 A.M. Landgraf, 'Der Gerechtigkeitsbegriff des hl. Anselm v. Canterbury und seine Bedeutung für die Theologie der Frühscholastik,' *Divus Thomas* (Fribourg) 5 (1927) 155–77 [DFG 37–50].

3   Peter Lombard

Between the bold genius of St Anselm and the timid positivism of the *Glossa ordinaria*,[37] the *Sentences* of Peter Lombard struck a golden mean. They cover the whole field of theology, as it then was known, not by any premature attempt at unattainable synthesis but, in the spirit of Aristotelian dialectic, by collecting, arranging, and discussing scriptural texts, patristic affirmations, and the more notable of contemporary opinions. Quite naturally this work, very solid and not very brilliant, became the basis of lectures in theology and, for centuries, the starting point of speculative commentaries. It was as though the Lombard had assembled the basic data and then left it to posterity to work out their coherence.[38]

Perhaps the best way to present the position of the *Sentences* on *gratia operans* will be to give a crude outline and then indicate the forces at work towards a transposition of the whole problem. Basically and essentially, thought is still in the Anselmian phase, grace and liberty are correlatives, with freedom an effect of grace and grace what makes freedom free. But while St Anselm tried to make this coherent by force of subtlety, the Lombard innocently lays bare the incoherence and, as well, unconsciously suggests the lines along which deliverance was to be found.

Fundamental in an outline are the four states of human liberty: the earthly paradise, fallen man, man redeemed, and heaven. In the first there is no difficulty in doing good and no impulsion to evil. In the second we find the startling alternative of *posse peccare et non posse non peccare etiam damnabiliter*. In the third, man can avoid mortal sin but also can commit it. In the fourth confirmation in grace gives impeccability.[39]

---

37 *PL* 113–14. On authorship see Beryl Smalley, 'Gilbertus Universalis, Bishop of London (1128–34), and the Problem of the "Glossa Ordinaria,"' *Recherches de théologie ancienne et médiévale* 7 (1935) 235–62; 8 (1936) 24–60.

38 See Franz Pelster, 'Die Bedeutung der Sentenzenvorlesung für die theologische Spekulation des Mittelalters. Ein Zeugnis aus der ältesten Oxforder Dominikanerschule,' *Scholastik* 2 (1927) 250–55. [*Scholastik* has become *Theologie und Philosophie*.]

39 Peter Lombard, *Libri IV Sententiarum* [henceforth, *Sententiae*], 2, d. 25, cc. 5–6. [Lonergan's bibliography for his thesis indicates that he used the Ad Claras Aquas (Quaracchi) edition of 1916 (Petri Lombardi, *Libri IV Sententiarum*, secunda editio, Ad Claras Aquas prope Florentiam, Ex Typographia Collegii S. Bonaventurae, 1916). In the articles in *Theological Studies* the edition is referred to as Quaracchi, and page numbers are given. We use the same edition, calling it *QL*, and also give the page numbers: here *QL* 1: 431.] This scheme had its origin in Augustine (*De correptione et gratia*, §§ 33–35, *PL* 44, 936–38; *De civitate Dei* 22, c. 30, *PL* 41, 801–804) and

Grace, operative and cooperative, is defined with reference to this scheme of the states of liberty: it is what makes the difference between the second and the third, between *non posse non peccare* and *posse non peccare*, between the liberty of nature which St Paul describes with *velle adiacet mihi, perficere autem non invenio* and, on the other hand, the liberty of grace which is efficacious and brings forth fruit in good deeds.[40]

Grace is operative inasmuch as it causes this efficacious good will, making what already was a will into a good and right will.[41] It is cooperative inasmuch as it aids good will to execute good intentions.[42] But, probably enough, operative and cooperative grace are not two things but one, for grace is not inert but grows and increases.[43]

This grace which cures and liberates man's free choice would seem to be a virtue. But whether a virtue is an internal act of the soul, as opposed to external, corporeal acts, or else some quality or form that combines with the will after the fashion that rain combines with earth and seed, is a disputed point. The testimonies of the saints can be cited for both sides.[44]

Operative grace, which prevents and prepares good will, is faith with charity, justifying faith, faith in Christ.[45] Does this cause surprise? It could not surprise the Lombard's contemporaries, for they all held approximately the same view.[46] And it throws not a little light on the fact that St Thomas always included habitual grace among operative graces.

So much for the crude outline. It now is necessary to point out other features that lead to an entirely new conception of the issue. For in the *Sentences* there is a real, though often incoherent, tendency to think of grace in terms of merit and to think of liberty in terms of nature. In other words, there is a direction of thought that only has to be pushed to its logical conclusion and the theorems regarding the supernatural will be elaborated inevitably.

Thus in the twenty-fourth distinction one finds what was termed the 'theological' definition of liberty: free will is what does what is right with the aid of grace and, without grace, does evil. Of itself, the will is efficacious in

---

reached its final form in Peter Lombard. See Landgraf, 'Die Erkenntnis der helfenden Gnade ...' [see above, note 5] 422 [*DFG* 99].

40 Peter Lombard, *Sententiae*, 2, d. 25, c. 9 (*QL* 1: 435–36); see ibid. d. 26, c. 1 (*QL* 1: 436–37).

41 Peter Lombard, *Sententiae*, 2, d. 26, c. 1 (*QL* 1: 436–37).

42 Ibid.

43 Ibid. d. 27, c. 1 (*QL* 1: 444).

44 Ibid. cc. 6 (*QL* 1: 447) and 12 (*QL* 1: 451–52).

45 Ibid. d. 26, c. 3 (*QL* 1: 439).

46 Landgraf, 'Die Erkenntnis der helfenden Gnade ...' 179–81 [*DFG* 51].

evil but in good slight and inconsiderable.[47] This view fits with the distinction between *libertas naturae* and *libertas gratiae*, where the former is illustrated by St Paul's *velle adiacet mihi*.[48] It squares with the definition of operative grace as the liberation of free choice.[49] It squares with the cruel lot of fallen man, *posse peccare et non posse non peccare etiam damnabiliter*, as this is mitigated by the assertion that some good acts are possible without grace[50] and by the contradictory, though very useful, affirmation *hominem semper et peccare et non peccare posse*.[51]

But the Lombard also was interested in the philosophers' definition of liberty, and he makes a distinct effort to work it into his theory of grace. He accepts *liberum de voluntate iudicium*, provided this does not involve indifference to good and evil,[52] but simply means that the will, without coercion or necessity, desires and elects what reason decides.[53] Again, besides the fourfold chronological scheme of the states of liberty, he also gives the threefold analytic scheme: *libertas a necessitate* which always exists; *libertas a peccato* which in our present state presupposes grace; and *libertas a miseria* which is the harmony of the earthly paradise and still more of heaven.[54] Finally, there is an attempt to distinguish between *naturalia* and *gratuita*.[55] Still, one must not leap to conclusions, for all this represents no more than an effort, a direction. Ultimately, a very real antinomy remains.

47 Peter Lombard, *Sententiae*, 2, d. 24, c. 3 (*QL* 1: 421). On the origin of this definition, see Dom Odon Lottin, o.s.b., 'Les définitions du libre arbitre au douzième siècle,' *Revue thomiste* (nouvelle série) 10 (1927) 104–20, 214–30, at 116–17. [This article is found again in Lottin, *La théorie du libre arbitre depuis s. Anselme jusqu'à saint Thomas d'Aquin* (Saint-Maximum, France: École de Théologie, and Louvain: Abbaye du Mont-César, 1929) 1–34; the corresponding pp. are 13–14.]

48 Peter Lombard, *Sententiae*, 2, d. 25, c. 9 (*QL* 1: 435–36).

49 Ibid. d. 26, c. 1 (*QL* 1: 436–37).

50 Ibid. c. 7 (*QL* 1: 443).

51 [man is always able to sin and not to sin] Ibid. d. 28, c. 4 (*QL* 1: 456). [Editorial note supplied by J. Patout Burns: This phrase is quoted in a section which the Lombard attributes to Jerome under the title *Explanatione fidei catholicae ad Damasum papam*. The work had also been attributed to Augustine as Sermon 191, but is now listed among the inauthentic sermons, 236, *PL* 39, 2181–83. Actually the cited section is from Pelagius's *Libellus fidei ad Innocentium* and is to be found among the documents relating to the Pelagian controversy, *PL* 45, 1718, § 15. See Martin von Schanz, *Geschichte der römischen Litteratur*, vol. 4, part 2 (Munich: Beck, 1920) 506.]

52 Peter Lombard, *Sententiae*, 2, d. 25, cc. 1–3 (*QL* 1: 428–30).

53 Ibid. c. 4 [ad fin.] (*QL* 1: 431).

54 Ibid. c. 8 (*QL* 1: 432–35).

55 Ibid. c. 7 (*QL* 1: 432).

Yet even this antinomy is not without its promise of solution. If in the fundamental passages grace is what frees free will, at least twice in meeting difficulties the Lombard has recourse to another function of grace, namely, as the ground of merit with respect to eternal life. Thus, against the position that prevenient grace is justifying faith, he objects that *bona cogitatio praecedit fidem* and consequently that good will precedes prevenient grace. His answer is that such a *bona cogitatio* does indeed precede but does not suffice for salvation since it does not spring from the virtue *qua recte vivitur.*[56] Later he affirms that there are many good acts prior to prevenient or operative grace, and that these acts are due either to grace and free choice or even to free choice alone; but by them man merits neither justification nor eternal life.[57] However, one must not suppose that the Lombard generalizes the significance of merit, for with regard to Adam's position his thought is most anomalous. In virtue of creation Adam had *posse stare* but needed grace for *posse proficere;* he could resist temptation without grace but he could not merit eternal life.[58] This is perfectly sound, but to the objection that resistance to temptation is meritorious, the Lombard answers not in terms of the gratuitous character of merit but that the merit of resistance is proportionate to the difficulty; in Eden there was no difficulty.[59]

Perhaps enough has been said to indicate that though the Anselmian position had not been transcended, still there were forces at work making for a vast development.

4   The Transition

Between Peter Lombard and St Albert the Great there emerged the idea of the supernatural habit.[60] It is necessary to illustrate the precise nature of this *emergence.*

56 Ibid. d. 26, cc. 4–5 (*QL* 1: 440–42).
57 Ibid. c. 7 (*QL* 1: 443).
58 [Ibid. d. 24, c. 1 (*QL* 1: 419).] For contemporary opinions: Landgraf, 'Die Erkenntnis der helfenden Gnade ...' 403–22 [*DFG* 82–99].
59 Peter Lombard, *Sententiae*, 2, d. 24, c. 1 (*QL* 1: 419–21).
60 St Albert conceived *gratia operans* as the *forma gratiae* in the will, *gratia cooperans* as the *forma meriti* in the free act. See *Commentarium in II Sententiarum* [henceforth *In II Sententiarum*], d. 26, a. 6 [vol. 27 in B. Alberti Magni Opera Omnia, ed. S.C.A. Borgnet (Paris: Vivès, 1894) 453 (henceforth in the form *BA* 27: 453)]. Not only is this line of thought quite unknown to the Lombard, but also the Lombard's seems to have been extremely mystifying to St Albert; see, for instance, his discussion of the Lombard's view that merit presupposes difficulty (*In II Sententiarum*, d. 24, a. 4 [*BA* 27: 400]).

Everyone is familiar with the common notion of *going faster*. Few understand what you mean when you explain that an acceleration is the second derivative of a continuous function of distance and time. To apprehend *going faster* one has only to drop from a sufficient height. To apprehend *acceleration* one has to master the somewhat difficult notions underlying the differential calculus. Both *going faster* and *acceleration* apprehend the same fact, but the former merely apprehends, while the latter adds to apprehension acts of analysis and generalization, of deduction and systematic correlation. For *acceleration* is *going faster*, but analyzed as d^2s/dt^2, generalized to include *going slower*, enriched with all the implications of the second derivative of a function, and given a significant place in systematic thought on quantitative motion.

Now in the writings of St Albert or St Thomas, the *supernatural* is a scientific theorem: it has an exact philosophic definition; its implications are worked out and faced; and this set of abstract correlations gives the mere apprehension a significant, indeed a fundamental, position in an explanatory account of the nature of grace. But just as one can apprehend *going faster* without understanding the calculus, so also the theologians of the twelfth century and earlier could apprehend globally the supernatural character of grace without suspecting the theorem that regards the relations of grace and nature. Thus, from the writings of Peter Lombard, Dr Schupp has been able to list nineteen different expressions referring to the supernatural,[61] while the masterly articles of Dr Landgraf, 'Studien zur Erkenntnis des Übernatürlichen in der Frühscholastik,' bear witness to the fact that the idea seems in many writers to be just around the corner.[62]

Accordingly, the development with which we are concerned was not dogmatic but speculative, and our immediate point will be to illustrate the magnitude of the release which formulation of the theorem effected. In the first place, then, without the idea of the supernatural there can be no satisfactory definition of grace. The dogmatic issue is indeed secure, and all repeated that grace was God's free gift beyond all desert of man. But the difficulty was to explain why everything was not grace; after all, what is there that is not a free gift of God? This question more than puzzled Cardinal Laborans who, defining grace in the strict sense, *veri nominis*, affirmed it to

---

61 Johann Schupp, *Die Gnadenlehre des Petrus Lombardus* (Freiburg im Breisgau: Herder & Co., 1932) 20–22. [While Lonergan says 'nineteen different expressions,' Schupp actually lists twenty-two.]

62 Artur Landgraf, 'Studien zur Erkenntnis des Übernatürlichen in der Frühscholastik,' *Scholastik* 4 (1929) 1–37, 189–220, 352–89 [DFG 141–201].

include everything man either has at birth or receives after birth. Feeling that this definition did not square with common notions, he next attempted to indicate two narrower senses of the term; yet even in this he was scarcely more fortunate, for he took grace to mean more specifically everything that the elect have at birth or receive afterwards, and still more specifically the virtues of the elect.[63]

This difficulty with the idea of grace naturally involves an even greater difficulty with the distinction between *naturalia* and *gratuita*. The distinction was a commonplace, but what could it mean? An extreme position was taken by Radulphus Ardens when he affirmed that before the fall all the virtues were natural but now, because of the fall, they are gratuitous.[64] A more common tendency was to depress nature: Peter Abelard asserted the disjunction between charity and cupidity, and St Bernard of Clairvaux added that nature in itself was crooked;[65] even as late as the beginning of the thirteenth century a writer can be found to maintain that without divine charity there can be no virtues at all.[66]

Again, the doctrine of merit tended to hang in mid air. It followed that the need of grace in the angels and in our first parents was accompanied with endless difficulties.[67] On the other hand, the need of grace in fallen man was regarded, in the main, as a need of liberating liberty: sin darkened the understanding and weakened the will; grace illuminated the understanding and strengthened the will.[68] This psychological conception resulted in difficulties, already observed in Peter Lombard, both with regard to habitual grace and with regard to liberty, and it is not too surprising to find Petrus Pictaviensis, a pupil of the Lombard, explicitly distinguishing the theologians' and philosophers' definitions of liberty.[69]

But, with the thirteenth century, the dawn. Stephen Langton noted the connection between *gratuitum* and *meritum* to give significance to *gratum faciens*.[70] Praepositinus placed the distinction between *gratuita* and *naturalia* on a solid basis by pointing out that reason is the highest thing in nature,

63 Ibid. 20–21 [*DFG* 159–60].
64 Ibid. 212 [*DFG* 180].
65 Ibid. 195, 374; see whole section, 352–89 [*DFG* 164–65, 194, whole section, 183–201].
66 Ibid. 191 [*DFG* 163–64].
67 Landgraf, 'Die Erkenntnis der helfenden Gnade ...' 403–22 [*DFG* 82–99].
68 Artur Landgraf, 'Die Erkenntnis der heiligmachenden Gnade in der Frühscholastik,' *Scholastik* 3 (1928) 29–39 [*DFG* 202–205].
69 See Lottin, 'Les définitions du libre arbitre ...' [see above, note 47] 224–25, note 4 [*La théorie du libre arbitre* ... 28–29, note 4; see *PL* 211, 1031].
70 Landgraf, 'Studien zur Erkenntnis des Übernatürlichen ...' 214–15 [*DFG* 181].

yet faith is above reason.[71] The final steps were taken by Philip, Chancellor
of the University of Paris from 1218 to 1230. Against St Bernard and Hugh
of St Victor,[72] he reaffirmed William of Auxerre's affirmation of a natural
amor amicitiae erga Deum quite distinct from charity, the meritorious love of
God. He then presented the theory of two orders, entitatively dispropor-
tionate: not only was there the familiar series of grace, faith, charity, and
merit, but also nature, reason, and the natural love of God.[73]

We have already suggested that the best commentary on Augustine's
speculation lies in the subsequent speculative movement. Now the twelfth-
century theologians were steeped in Augustine, yet their unceasing efforts
with a material which must have seemed hopelessly refractory terminated in
the idea of the supernatural. The anachronistic thinkers of a much later
age attempted to reverse that decision, but it is difficult to esteem them
without being completely ignorant of the evolution of medieval thought.
Especially is this so when one succeeds in grasping that the idea of the
supernatural is a theorem, that it no more adds to the data of the problem
than the Lorentz transformation puts a new constellation in the heavens.
What Philip the Chancellor systematically posited was not the supernatural
character of grace, for that was already known and acknowledged, but the
validity of a line of reference termed nature. In the long term and in the
concrete the real alternatives remain charity and cupidity, the elect and the
massa damnata. But the whole problem lies in the abstract, in human
thinking: the fallacy in early thought had been an unconscious confusion of
the metaphysical abstraction 'nature' with concrete data which do not quite
correspond; Philip's achievement was the creation of a mental perspective,
the introduction of a set of coordinates, that eliminated the basic fallacy
and its attendant host of anomalies.

Still, this assertion of dogmatic continuity must not obscure the existence
of a 'Copernican revolution' in theory: the center of the whole issue shifted
violently; certain developments were released at once; others followed in a
series of intervals, change implying further change, till the genius of St
Thomas Aquinas mastered the situation. It is necessary to grasp the logic of
this movement if St Thomas's thought is to be understood.

Philip himself presented the idea of sanctifying grace. The idea of the
divine virtues, *quibus recte vivitur*, was a commonplace out of Augustine, but
it was difficult to define their quality of *divine* as long as men doubted with

71 Ibid. 214 [*DFG* 180].
72 Ibid. 374, 377 [*DFG* 194, 197].
73 Ibid. 381–84 [*DFG* 197–99; see 182].

the Lombard[74] whether a virtue was a qualitative form or an internal act. Further, there was the concrete question of the effect of infant baptism. In this matter many followed St Anselm and affirmed that the Holy Spirit is given in two manners: to infants by the remission of sins; to adults by the bestowal of the virtues.[75] This view, given priority of place in a Brief of Innocent III,[76] rested both on the difficulty of conceiving justifying faith as anything but an act[77] and on the tendency to conceive grace as a psychological liberation of the will.[78] However, the study of Aristotle, the reaction against the obviously heretical demand of Waldenses and Cathari for the rebaptism of those baptized in infancy, and finally the shift in the theory of grace, enabled Philip to make a closer study of the doctrine of our life in Christ. The result was a fourfold distinction: *vivificari* or sanctifying grace; *illuminari* or faith; *uniri* or charity; *rectificari* or justice.[79] This position spread rapidly, was profoundly developed by St Albert,[80] and as the more probable view received approbation from the Council of Vienne.[81]

The development of the theory of liberty is more obscure. In strict logic there could hardly be any theory of liberty as long as grace was conceived psychologically to the practical neglect of the idea of merit. But strict logic does not rule even the exercise of thought, and it is easy enough to justify an investigation in which one is interested by making a distinction to which one is not entitled. By and large, however, it should seem that the theorem of the supernatural did release speculation on the nature of liberty. Dom Lottin, who has studied the period in all its arid detail, speaks of the twelfth-century writers as defining liberty,[82] of the first third of the thirteenth as evolving theories,[83] and of the period subsequent to Philip as writing

---

74 Peter Lombard, *Sententiae*, 2, d. 27, cc. 6 (*QL* 1: 447) and 12 (*QL* 1: 451–52).
75 Landgraf, 'Die Erkenntnis der heiligmachenden Gnade ...' [see above, note 68] 45–46 [*DFG* 207–14].
76 *Maiores Ecclesiae causas*, A.D. 1201; see *DB* 410 [*DS* 780].
77 Landgraf, 'Der Gerechtigkeitsbegriff des hl. Anselm ...' [see above, note 36] 169; also, 'Grundlagen für ein Verständnis der Busslehre der Früh- und Hochscholastik,' *Zeitschrift für katholische Theologie* 51 (1927) 186.
78 Landgraf, 'Die Erkenntnis der heiligmachenden Gnade ...' 31–39 [*DFG* 203–205].
79 Ibid. 42, 56–62, 64 [*DFG* 207, 212–19].
80 Herbert Doms, *Die Gnadenlehre des sel. Albertus Magnus* (Breslau: Müller & Seiffert, 1929), chapters 1–9, pp. 8–162.
81 *DB* 483 [*DS* 904].
82 Lottin, 'Les définitions du libre arbitre ...' [see above, note 47].
83 Dom Odon Lottin, 'La théorie du libre arbitre pendant le premier tiers du XIIIe siècle,' *Revue thomiste* (nouvelle série) 10 (1927) 350–82. [This article is reprinted in Lottin, *La théorie du libre arbitre* ... (see above, note 47) 35–67.]

treatises.[84] He credits Philip with putting the questions that were discussed by Alexander of Hales, Odo Rigaldi, St Albert, and St Bonaventure, and to the latter galaxy he attributes the initial stages of a philosophic doctrine of freedom.[85]

A more complex movement results from the theorem of the supernatural displacing the fourfold scheme of the states of human liberty. In the early period the necessity of grace was in terms of the liberation of liberty; but the new analysis explains this necessity in terms of human finality, so that one cannot be surprised to find in the commentaries on the *Sentences* of St Albert and of St Thomas a vigorous rejection of *non posse non peccare* both in the name of the supernatural and in the name of a coherent idea of freedom.[86] Still, this is only the first phase of the movement. The dogmatic data force a revision of the solution: the old *non posse non peccare*, which had been a line of reference for the whole of grace, returns in its proper perspective as the moral impotence of the sinner;[87] and the scheme of the states of liberty reappears in the transposed form of the states of human nature.[88]

Finally, superposed on this complexity, comes the whole question of actual grace.[89] As long as grace was simply grace, it was possible to say that

84 Dom Odon Lottin, 'Le traité du libre arbitre depuis le chancelier Philippe jusqu'à saint Thomas d'Aquin,' *Revue thomiste* (nouvelle série) 10 (1927) 446–72; 12 (1929) 234–69. [This article is also reprinted in Lottin, *La théorie du libre arbitre* ... 68–128].

85 Ibid. 12 (1929) 266–67.

86 St Albert, *Summa de creaturis*, 2, q. 70, a. 5 [*BA* 35: 588]; *In II Sententiarum*, d. 25, a. 6 [*BA* 27: 433–34]; Thomas Aquinas, *Super II Sententiarum*, d. 28, q. 1, a. 2.

87 Albert, *Summa theologica*, 2, q. 100, mem. 2–4 [*BA* 33: 246–52]; Thomas Aquinas, *De veritate*, q. 24, a. 12.

88 Thomas Aquinas, *Summa theologiae*, 1–2, q. 109.

89 See Lange's chapter on 'Praeparatio ad gratiam,' in his *De gratia*; Artur Landgraf, 'Die Vorbereitung auf die Rechtfertigung und die Eingiessung der heiligmachenden Gnade in der Frühscholastik,' *Scholastik* 6 (1931) 42–62, 222–47, 354–80, 481–504 [*DFG*, with title 'Die Vorbereitung auf die Rechtfertigung und die Eingiessung der Rechtfertigenden Gnade,' 238–302]; and Landgraf, 'Die Erkenntnis der helfenden Gnade in der Frühscholastik.' [There is no chapter called 'Praeparatio ad gratiam' in the 1929 edition of Lange's *De gratia*, which is the edition that Lonergan cites in the bibliography of his thesis. However, J. Patout Burns mentions pages from an earlier edition (Valkenburg: Limburg, 1926, pp. 173–88) which, while not having this title, present a thesis (11) which seems to correspond to the material to which Lonergan refers in this note. The same thesis 11 appears in the 1929 edition on pp. 230–50: 'Ad iustificationem adultus debet se disponere per actus salutares, ad quod praeter alios pertinet fides dogmatica, non vero fides fiducialis Protestantium.']

‚race is one or many or the equivalent many of an increasing one. But the elaboration of the idea of sanctifying grace, which seems to have absorbed most of St Albert's attention,[90] was not without a strange influence on wider aspects of the issue. Thus in both the commentary on the *Sentences* and the *De veritate* St Thomas asked: Is there but one grace in each individual? In the earlier work[91] only the number of habitual graces seems to be considered. In the later[92] the question really is whether there are graces that are not habitual; indeed one may even discern an attempt to formulate the difference between general providence and such nonhabitual graces.[93]

5   Conclusion

Since any further examination of St Thomas's thought lies outside the scope of an introduction, we may at once conclude. The pivotal moment in the history of *gratia operans* was Philip the Chancellor's formulation of the idea of the supernatural habit. Earlier writers did not possess the distinctions necessary to treat satisfactorily the problem whose existence St Augustine had established. On the other hand, the transposition of the issue effected by Philip only gradually worked towards a new synthesis, and the period of transition, with all its fluidity, was still dominant when Aquinas came on the scene. Accordingly, there is a notable antecedent probability that in the development of St Thomas's thought on grace[94] great importance is to be attached to variations in his treatment of *gratia operans*.[95]

90 Doms, *Die Gnadenlehre des sel. Albertus Magnus* 163–68.
91 *Super II Sententiarum*, d. 26, q. 1, a. 6.
92 *De veritate*, q. 27, a. 5.
93 Ibid. q. 27, a. 5 [ad 3m]; q. 24, aa. 14–15. See *Summa theologiae*, 1-2, q. 109.
94 The existence of some development in St Thomas's thought on grace has, perhaps, always been known: Capreolus, *Defensiones theologiae divi Thomae, In II Sententiarum*, d. 28, q. 1. a. 3, § 4 in fine; Didacus Deza Hispalensis, *In II Sententiarum*, d. 28, q. 1, a. 3, not. 1 in fine; Cajetan, *In summam theologiae*, 1-2, q. 109, a. 6 [in the Leonine ed. of Thomas's *Opera omnia* (henceforth *LT*), vol. 7: 300–301]; and Dominicus Soto, *De natura et gratia*, lib. 2, c. 3. [The source of these references seems to be Lange, *De gratia* 91 note 2, and 146 note 1. See below, p. 159, note 1. Elsewhere Lonergan refers to Lange, *De gratia* 140–52, but the exact pages are 141–47; see below, p. 238, note 151. The Didacus Deza Hispalensis reference appears in *TS* (and in the thesis) but not in the 1971 *Grace and Freedom*.]
95 See *Super II Sententiarum*, d. 26, q. 1, a. 6, ad 2m; a. 5; *De veritate*, q. 27, a. 5, ad 1m; *Summa theologiae*, 1-2, q. 111, a. 2.

I-2

The General Movement of
Aquinas's Thought

Philip the Chancellor's formulation of the supernatural habit resolved justification into a twofold operation: as supernatural, grace effected the meritoriousness of human acts, elevating them above the merely human level; as a habit or virtue, grace operated psychologically, effecting the moral goodness of the will. This line of thought dominates in the three great commentaries on the *Sentences*: St Albert's, St Bonaventure's, and St Thomas's.

Next, Peter Lombard's error in identifying *gratia operans* with *gratia cooperans* was discovered. It had passed unperceived in the midst of the labor of developing the idea of the supernatural. But St Thomas in his *De veritate* came face to face with the fact that St Augustine was speaking of two graces: one that initiates us in the spiritual life by giving good will, another that enables us to translate our good intentions into good performance. This forced a broadening of the category *gratia gratum faciens* and stimulated attention to what we term actual grace.

Finally, this attention brought to light another datum. Grace is needed not only after justification that we may persevere; it is also needed before justification that we may prepare for it. That this earlier grace must be internal, a divine operation within the will, was first formulated in St Thomas's *Quodlibetum primum*. Clearly, it gives an actual grace that is *operans* to combine with the *De veritate*'s actual grace that is *cooperans*. Thus we find in the *Summa theologiae* the first expression of his final position: grace is divided into habitual and actual; each is subdivided into operative and cooperative.

Our purpose is to present this general movement of thought, to set forth a series of different positions, to provide a sketch of broad contours under six headings.

1   The Unity of *Gratia Gratum Faciens*

Sanctifying grace, the principle of transcendental value that consistently had slipped through the fingers of earlier analysis, became an accepted and established notion in the first half of the thirteenth century. As usual, however, this general agreement only covered over a number of subsidiary issues on which unanimity was not obtained. Was sanctifying grace to be identified with the infused virtues? If distinct, was it radicated in the substance of the soul or in its faculties? In either case, was it to be conceived as some single grace or as a common property of many graces? Of these questions, the most fundamental was the last. It will be sufficient for our purpose if we outline how it was treated in St Bonaventure's commentary on the *Sentences*[1] and in St Thomas's,[2] for such an outline will explain how the unity of sanctifying grace obscured the multiplicity of divine operation and divine cooperation.

St Bonaventure had no doubt that sanctifying grace was one. Grace was God's image in the soul: an image of the One must be one. It was the life of the soul: one living being has only one life. It was the principle of merit and divine acceptance: but God either accepts or rejects. It was the seed of eternal glory: but one fruit springs from a single seed.[3] Accordingly, when we read in the *Glossa* that a single grace does not suffice for sanctity, that there is a prevenient grace giving love and knowledge of God and then a

1 Mandonnet has affirmed that St Bonaventure was a *baccalaureus sententiarius* in the years 1250–52. See *Bulletin thomiste* 3 (1926) [96].
2 Commonly attributed to 1254–56. On the subject of grace I have not come across any internal evidence that would imply a revision of St Thomas's commentary on the *Sentences* subsequent to the *De veritate*. On this question, see André Hayen, 'Saint Thomas a-t-il édité deux fois son Commentaire sur le livre des Sentences?' *Recherches de théologie ancienne et médiévale* 9 (1937) 219–36.
3 *S. Bonaventurae Opera Omnia*, ed. PP. Collegii a S. Bonaventura (Ad Claras Aquas [Quaracchi] prope Florentinum, 1985), vol. 2, *In Secundum Librum Sententiarum* (henceforth *In II Sententiarum*), d. 27, a. 1, q. 1, pp. 654–55 (henceforth in the form [*QB* 2: 654–55]). [Lonergan used the Vivès edition, *S. Bonaventurae Opera Omnia*, ed. A.C. Peltier. The pertinent volume is vol. 3, at pp. 266–68. We will give both references, the Vivès first (here *VB* 3: 266–68), then the Quaracchi. We follow the Quaracchi text where there are textual variants; but see note 27 below.]

subsequent grace preserving us in purity, this cannot mean that there are many sanctifying graces. It can only mean that one sanctifying grace has many effects.[4]

Now, this one grace is, as it were, located in the faculties of the soul and not in its substance; not only does reason lead to this conclusion but also the authority of St Augustine. For did he not say that grace is to free choice as the rider to the horse? and is not his whole account of divine operation in terms of good will?[5] On the other hand, though in the faculties, sanctifying grace is not to be identified with the virtues. For then either of two errors follows: one mortal sin completely destroys all the virtues; or else one mortal sin does not completely destroy sanctifying grace.[6] Hence grace and the virtues must be distinct as are light and color. Without light color is invisible; yet one light illuminates all colors. Similarly sanctifying grace is distinct from the virtues yet one grace informs them all.[7]

It is in terms of this discussion that St Thomas asked, *Utrum gratia sit multiplex in anima?*[8] He points out that if grace is identified with the virtues, there must be many graces really distinct. Next, he denies the utility of any analogy from light and color: one light informs many colors only insofar as the many colors are on a single continuous surface; but the virtues are in different faculties, and grace, informing these many subjects, necessarily becomes many. Further, he rejects a similar view based on the analogy of light: grace is one at its source and center in the substance of the soul, but its many rays inform the different virtues. Finally, he gives the opinion he favors: grace and the virtues are essentially distinct; the virtues are said to be informed by grace not because grace is in them but it is their origin; accordingly, grace is one.

As to the objection, 'Grace must be many, for it is both prevenient and subsequent,' St Thomas gives the same solution as had St Bonaventure. One and the same grace is prevenient and subsequent, operative and cooperative. The differences implicit in these distinctions are not the differences of many graces but of the many effects of one grace.[9]

---

4 Ibid. ob. 1 and ad 1m [*VB* 3: 265, 267; *QB* 2: 653, 654].
5 Ibid. d. 26, a. 1, q. 5 [*VB* 3: 253; *QB* 2: 643].
6 Ibid. d. 27, a. 1, q. 2 [*VB* 3: 269; *QB* 2: 657]. Note that the argument would not hold against the Scotist identification of grace with charity.
7 Ibid. [*VB* 3: 269–70; *QB* 2: 657–58].
8 [Whether grace is multiple in the soul] Thomas Aquinas, *Super II Sententiarum*, d. 26, q. 1, a. 6.
9 Ibid. ad 2m.

2   The Ambiguities of *Gratia Gratis Data*

In St Thomas's *Summa theologiae* and ever since it was written, *gratia gratis data* has denoted graces of public utility such as inspiration and thaumaturgy. On the other hand, in Peter Lombard's *Sentences* it denoted the grace of justification and stood in opposition to *gratia gratis dans*, the uncreated grace that is God himself.[10] But between these two periods of definite meaning there was a time when *gratia gratis data* was more a sweeping gesture than an exact concept, more a catalogue than a category; *gratia gratum faciens* came to denote the essential feature of justification, and the other term was left with a roving commission. This ambiguity naturally conspired with the problems outlined above to conceal the real difference between operative and cooperative graces.

Thus Dr Doms has drawn up a list of eight senses of *gratia gratis data* in the writings of St Albert the Great: (1) rational nature and its faculties; (2) natural moral goodness; (3) Adam's preternatural gifts before the fall; (4) unformed habits, servile fear, imperfect movements towards salvation; (5) inspiration, miracles, and the like; (6) the assistance of the angels; (7) the indelible character received in baptism, confirmation, and orders; (8) the divine activity, which not only conserves in being and moves to action but also conserves in goodness and moves to good action.[11]

St Bonaventure's commentary on the *Sentences* marks an advance, for *gratia gratis data* is clearly distinguished both from human nature[12] and from general *concursus*.[13] Still, the latter categories are understood in quite a narrow sense, and so great is the field left for *gratia gratis data* that St Bonaventure himself finds it hard to suppose that any adult is ever without it.[14] Not only does it include the gifts of the Spirit enumerated by St

---

10 Peter Lombard, *Sententiae*, 2, d. 27, c. 7 [*QL* 1: 448].

11 Doms, *Die Gnadenlehre des sel. Albertus Magnus* [see above, p. 18, note 80] 167–68.

12 For instance, Bonaventure, *In II Sententiarum*, d. 27, dub. 1 [*VB* 3: 262; *QB* 2: 669]: 'Accipitur enim gratia uno modo largissime, et sic comprehendit dona naturalia et dona gratuita ... Alio modo accipitur gratia minus communiter, et sic comprehendit gratiam gratis datam et gratum facientem' [For grace in one way is taken very broadly, and then it includes natural gifts and gratuitous gifts ... In another way grace is taken less widely, and then it includes grace given freely and making one pleasing].

13 See, for instance, ibid. d. 37, a. 1, q. 1, ad 6m, ad 5m [*VB* 3: 493; *QB* 2: 863]; d. 28, a. 2, q. 3 [*VB* 3: 302; *QB* 2: 689].

14 Ibid. d. 28, a. 2, q. 1 conc. [*VB* 3: 295; *QB* 2: 682]: 'Sine hac quidem gratia gratis data vix aut numquam aliquis habens usum liberi arbitrii reperitur ...' [Without this freely given grace hardly ever or not at all is anyone found having use of free will].

Paul,[15] but also anything whatever that may be conceived as added to nature: it may be like a habit, as servile fear or an inborn tendency to piety; or it may be actual, as any appeal or speech by which God awakens the soul of man.[16]

In his commentary on the *Sentences* and up to the twenty-seventh question of the *De veritate* St Thomas never seems to presuppose that any definite meaning can be assigned to *gratia gratis data*. Whenever the matter comes up, alternative possible meanings are discussed. However, it is clear that the alternatives cover a wide field: he attributes the conversion that prepares for justification to any occasion – an admonishing voice, loss of health, or anything of the sort;[17] he goes so far as to insist that the light which shone

15 1 Corinthians 12.8.
16 Bonaventure, *In II Sententiarum*, d. 28, a. 2, q. 1 conc. [*VB* 3: 295; *QB* 2: 682]: '... vocatur hic gratia gratis data, quidquid illud sit, quod superadditum est naturalibus, adiuvans aliquo modo et praeparans voluntatem ad habitum vel usum gratiae, sive illud gratis datum sit habitus, sicut timor servilis, vel pietas aliquorum visceribus inserta ab infantia, sive sit etiam aliquis actus, sicut aliqua vocatio vel locutio, qua Deus excitat animam hominis, ut se requirat [or: praeparet (*VB*)]' [that is here called grace freely given, what-ever it be, which is added over and above things in the natural order, assist-ing in some way and preparing the will for the habit or the use of grace, whether that freely given thing be a habit, as is servile fear, or the piety inserted into the interior of some from their infancy, or whether it be also some act, such as a call or a word, by which God arouses the human soul to place demands on (or: prepare) itself]. On the whole question, see Franz Mitzka, 'Die Lehre des hl. Bonaventura von der Vorbereitung auf die heiligmachenden Gnade,' *Zeitschrift für katholische Theologie* 50 (1926) 27–72, 220–52.
17 *Super II Sententiarum*, d. 28, q. 1, a. 4 c. Fr Stufler has discussed the point in an article, 'Die entfernte Vorbereitung auf die Rechtfertigung nach dem hl. Thomas,' *Zeitschrift für katholische Theologie* 47 (1923) 1–23, 161–83. For lists of discussions of Fr Stufler, see *Bulletin thomiste* 2 (1925) 217–19; 3 (1926) 188–89. Interesting because independent are: P. DeVooght, 'A propos de la grâce actuelle dans la théologie de saint Thomas,' *Divus Thomas* (Piacenza) 31 (1928) 386–416, and E. Neveut's many articles in *Divus Thomas* (Piacen-za). A radical criticism of all this discussion is that it makes no pretence to historical perspective. If anything is evident, it is the fundamental necessity of such perspective. [The last sentence of this paragraph is in Lonergan's article in *Theological Studies*, but not in *Grace and Freedom*. What follows in this note is in *Grace and Freedom*, but not in *Theological Studies*.]
   There has been raised a related but quite different question of possibility: Could St Thomas teach that the *auxilium Dei moventis*, given prior to the infusion of supernatural habits, results in entitatively supernatural acts? Note I raise only the question of possibility. The question of fact is far more complicated, and the evidence will emerge in due course.
   On the question of possibility, Henri Bouillard correctly observes that St Thomas knows nothing of a transient *gratia elevans*. From this he concludes that acts preparatory of justification cannot be entitatively supernatural. See

round St Paul on the way to Damascus was a corporeal and external, not an internal, light.[18]

So much for the fact of an ambiguous *gratia gratis data*. As is apparent, the whole treatise on grace was in process of formation. In consequence of this fluidity, of the unity of *gratia gratum faciens* and the ambiguities of *gratia gratis data*, we shall find that in their commentaries on the *Sentences* St Albert, St Bonaventure, and St Thomas conceive operative grace to denote the habitual graces infused at the instant of justification.

3   *Gratia Operans* in the Three Great Commentaries

According to St Albert's commentary on the *Sentences* operative grace is what makes meritorious action possible.[19] This operation is not efficient but formal causality, for its effect is not something distinct from grace but rather the diffusion of grace itself by the activity known as information.[20] As

---

Bouillard, *Conversion et grâce chez s. Thomas d'Aquin* (Paris: Aubier, 1944) 74, 196.

This conclusion would be quite valid if St Thomas held the later doctrine of vital or immanent act, namely, that such acts are produced by the faculty in which they are received. Only a supernaturally elevated faculty is proportionate to producing a supernatural act.

However, I do not believe that St Thomas held the later doctrine on vital or immanent act; see my *Verbum: Word and Idea in Aquinas* (now CWL 2, ed. Frederick E. Crowe and Robert M. Doran [Toronto: University of Toronto Press, 1997]) 140–43, for an array of instances in which *sentire, intelligere, velle* are not produced by but simply received in their respective faculties.

Finally, it cannot be advanced that a faculty has to be elevated to receive a supernatural act, for then, *a pari*, the faculty would have to be elevated to receive the supernatural elevation, and an infinite regress would result.

18 *Super II Sententiarum*, d. 28, q. 1, a. 4, ad 3m.
19 Albert, *In II Sententiarum*, d. 26, a. 6 [*BA* 27: 453]: '... gratia praeveniens est quae omne nostrum meritum praevenit, et haec est quae operatur esse bonum in voluntate per informationem voluntatis: oportet enim voluntatem habitualem informatam esse gratia, antequam bonus actus meritorius eliciatur ex illa' [prevenient grace is that which is prior to all our merit, and this it is which operates good in the will by informing the will; for habitual will has to be informed by grace before a good and meritorious act is elicited from it].
20 St Albert asks, What does operative grace operate? It cannot produce itself; there is no use saying it produces the will, which already exists; and if you suggest that it produces the goodness of the will, that only means that it informs the will, produces itself in the will. He answers as follows (*In II Sententiarum*, d. 26, a. 7 [*BA* 27: 455]): 'Dicendum ad primum, quod operans dicitur, quia operatur esse bonum in voluntate: et dicitur operari sicut forma facit esse, non sicut efficiens. Hoc autem facere quod est formae, non

operative grace gives the possibility of merit, so cooperative grace makes good acts actually meritorious: the meritorious act is conceived as a compound of matter and form, with the matter proceeding from free will and the form of merit coming from grace.[21]

In this cooperation the respective provinces of the two factors are so beautifully demarcated that a problem of grace and freedom does not arise. This remains true, even though free choice is the subordinate member of the partnership, as long as this subordination has no other basis than the fact of matter's dependence on form.[22] However, St Albert recognizes

---

est nisi diffusio sui in formato. Et ideo bene concedo, quod forma absolute accepta actu formae non efficientis facit se in formato: sed nihil facit se secundum eamdem considerationem acceptum: et efficiens non facit se etiam in diversis considerationibus acceptum: sed quia forma non proprie facit, sed dat, et suum dare est diffusio sui et informatio, ideo forma dat esse quod est actus illius formae, et operatur, et hoc [quod operatur] est esse suum in formato. Primae autem obiectiones procedebant quasi gratia esset operans per modum efficientis, et non formae' [To the first point it has to be said that it is called operative because it operates good in the will, and it is said to operate in the way form makes being, not in the way an efficient (cause) does. But this making which belongs to form is nothing but a diffusion of itself in what is formed. And therefore I readily concede that form taken absolutely, by the act of a form and not the act of an efficient (cause), makes itself in what is formed: but nothing makes itself when we take (the self) under the same aspect: and an efficient (cause) does not make itself even when we take (the self) under different aspects: but because a form does not properly make, but gives, and its giving is a diffusion of itself and an information, therefore form gives the being which is the act of that form, and operates, and this (which it operates) is its being in what is formed. But the earlier objections proceeded as if grace were operative in the way of an efficient (cause) and not in the way of a form]. Compare Thomas Aquinas, *Super II Sententiarum*, d. 26, q. 1, a. 5, ad 2m [see below, notes 35 and 37]; *Summa theologiae*, 1-2, q. 111, a. 2, ad 1m. [The addition in square brackets in the quoted Latin text is Lonergan's.]

21 Albert, *In II Sententiarum*, d. 26, a. 6 [*BA* 27: 453]: 'Subsequens autem invenitur primo in ea [voluntate] quae meretur: quia habitum immediate sequitur actus: et ideo dicitur cooperans, quia libero arbitrio [liberum arbitrium?] in merito ministrat materiam actus: sed formam per quam est efficacia meriti, dat gratia quae est in anima et libero arbitrio' [But subsequent (grace) is found first in that (will?) which merits, because act follows habit immediately; and it is called cooperative on this account that in merit free will provides the matter of the act, but the form by which merit has efficacy is given by grace, which is in the soul and in free will]. [The additions in square brackets in the Latin text are Lonergan's.] Compare Thomas Aquinas, *Super II Sententiarum*, d. 26, q. 1, a. 5, ad 4m [see below, note 38].

22 See the second of the three reasons in note 24 below.

another ground of subordination, and this, though not analyzed as *operans* and *cooperans*, is in terms of efficient causality. Grace, he asserts, rules free will to make free will like an obedient beast.[23] It is a *primum movens*, a habitual form that causes motion as do natural forms of weight and the like.[24] Finally, as Scotus was later to maintain, this influence transcends the division of motions into natural and violent: the habitual form in question is a *habitus voluntarius*, an inclination or spontaneity within the will itself.[25]

In St Bonaventure's commentary on the *Sentences* the same ideas recur in a somewhat broader setting and with grace as an efficient cause receiving more attention. Six senses are assigned the couplet *praeveniens et subsequens*;

23 See the third of the three reasons in note 24 below.

24 Albert, *In II Sententiarum*, d. 26, a. 7 [*BA* 27: 455]: '... et bene concedo, quod liberum arbitrium est secundarium in opere illo tribus de causis: quarum una est, quia gratia est primum movens, sicut habitus movet in modum inclinantis naturae ad impetum actus alicuius, ut grave inclinat deorsum. Secunda est: quia ipsa non dat proprietatem sive accidentalem formam, sed formam substantialem meriti, a qua est tota meriti efficacia: ita ut actus sine forma illa, non est meritorius, nec valeret vitam aeternam. Tertia causa est quam tangit Augustinus, quia regit liberum arbitrium: et liberum arbitrium est ut iumentum obediens' [and for three reasons I readily concede that free will is secondary in that operation. One of these is that grace is a first mover, as habit moves after the manner of nature inclining towards the impetus of some act, as a heavy object turns downward. The second is that it (grace) does not give a property or accidental form, but the substantial form of merit, from which comes the entire efficacy of merit, so that an act without that form is not meritorious, nor would it have any value for eternal life. The third cause is one that Augustine touches on, that (grace) governs free will, and free will is like an obedient beast of burden].

25 Ibid. [*BA* 27: 454–55]: 'Si dicas, quod gratia movet et excitat liberum arbitrium ad agendum: et ideo est principalior. Tunc quaeritur, Utrum moveat naturaliter vel violenter? ... Dicendum, quod nulla est divisio: quia voluntarius motus, nec naturalis, nec violentus est: et ipsa [gratia] movet ut perfectio voluntatis. Sed verum est, quia movet in modum naturae, sicut dicit Tullius de virtute. Tamen est habitus voluntarius: et ideo in talibus innati sumus suscipere [perfectionem?], et perfectio est ab assuetudine in virtute civili: sed in gratia perfectio est ab infusore gratiae' [If you say that grace moves and inspires free will to act, and is therefore the more important (factor): then the question is, Does it move naturally or violently? ... It has to be said that there is no division there, because a voluntary motion is neither natural nor violent, and it (grace) moves as a perfection of the will. But it is true that it moves after the manner of a nature, as even Tullius says of virtue. Still, it is a voluntary habit; and therefore in such matters it is natural for us to receive (a perfection?); and in civil virtue the perfection comes from habituation; but in grace the perfection comes from the one who infuses grace]. [The additions in square brackets in the Latin text are Lonergan's.]

they arise from the different meanings assigned the term 'grace' and from the different effects of grace; the list reveals the fluid state of thought at the time; it contains elements we shall meet again in St Thomas.

Grace, then, may mean every gift from God: in this sense St Gregory in his *Moralia* makes natural gifts prevenient and gratuitous gifts subsequent. It may be restricted to *gratia gratis data* and *gratia gratum faciens*: then the former is prevenient and the latter subsequent. Again, it may be confined to sanctifying grace, which is prevenient, and eternal glory, which is subsequent. However, in the strict sense, grace is sanctifying grace, *gratia gratum faciens*, and this is divided into prevenient and subsequent according to its different effects. Thus, it overcomes evil and makes for good: so we read *gratia praeveniens hominis voluntatem liberat et praeparat, subsequens vero inquantum eandem adiuvat*. Next, it makes for good in two ways, as a principle of information and as a principle of motion: hence *gratia praeveniens praevenit voluntatem ut sanemur, et subsequitur ut sanati vegetemur.*[26] Finally, as a principle of motion, it both initiates us in good will and makes good will effective: accordingly, *gratia praevenit voluntatem ut velit, et subsequitur ne frustra velit.*[27]

To the last form of the distinction St Bonaventure devotes a special question, *An gratia comparetur ad animam in ratione motoris?* Though by grace is meant sanctifying grace, still there is no difficulty in establishing an affirmative answer; as the reader may suspect, the secret of this facility is that he neglects to consider actual grace; all dogmatic sources on grace are assumed to refer to habitual grace.[28] The difficulty for St Bonaventure was to explain how grace, an accident in the potencies, can be conceived as moving its own subjects. Two solutions were known, and both are accepted, the one to account for operative, the other for cooperative grace.

The first solution we have already seen indicated in St Albert. Grace moves after the fashion of a disposition or tendency. Just as weight disposes

---

26 Observe that the Augustinian *gratia sanans* is interpreted as a *gratia elevans*. The same procedure is to be found in St Thomas, *Super II Sententiarum*, d. 26, q. 1, a. 5 c.

27 [prevenient grace liberates and prepares the human will, but grace is subsequent insofar as it assists the same will ... prevenient grace precedes the will that we may be healed, and follows that being healed we may flourish ... grace precedes the will that it may will, and follows that it may not will in vain] Bonaventure, *In II Sententiarum*, d. 27, dub. 1 [*VB* 3: 261–63; *QB* 2: 668–70; for the first of these quotations, *VB*, the text that Lonergan used, has 'inquantum eadem adiuvat': insofar as the same grace assists].

28 [Is grace compared to the soul under the heading of motor?] Ibid. d. 26, a. 1, q. 6 [*VB* 3: 254–56; *QB* 2: 644–46].

corporeal objects to their motions, so grace is a spiritual weight pulling the soul towards God. More precisely, free choice is self-moving, both mover and moved; grace acts upon it as mover, making it move itself the more excellently. This solution regards grace as cooperating with free will.

The second solution points out that one must take into consideration not only the subject in which an accident inheres but also the subject by which it is produced. Thus, light is not only an accident inhering in the air but also an operation of the sun upon the air. Similarly, grace is not only an accident in the will cooperating with the will; it also is an operation which God effects upon the will. In this sense grace is operative, and it prevents free choice.[29]

This brief indication of the positions of St Albert and St Bonaventure naturally leads to the position of St Thomas, who combines the former's insistence on the principle of information with the latter's on the principle of motion in his article, *Utrum gratia dividatur convenienter in gratiam operantem et cooperantem.*[30] In the context, grace uniformly means sanctifying grace.[31] The response to the article may be paraphrased as follows.

> Grace produces in us a number of effects which follow one upon the other. First, it gives a participation of divine reality; second, it causes the meritoriousness of our acts; third, there is the reward of merit, eternal life, which is the final effect of grace. Again, one human act follows on another: first, there is the internal operation of the will; second, there is external action, which is a complement to willing.
>
> Now these sequences seem to be the reason why St Augustine gives various meanings to the terms 'prevenient' and 'subsequent.' Thus, the sequence of merit and reward leads him to name the principle of merit a prevenient grace and eternal glory a subsequent grace: *gratia praevenit ut pie vivamus et subsequitur ut semper cum illo vivamus; et nunc praevenit ut vocemur, et tunc subsequitur ut glorificemur.*
>
> Again, the sequence of internal and external acts leads him to say that prevenient grace causes the motion of a good will while subse-

29 Ibid. conc. [*VB* 3: 255–56; *QB* 2: 645–46].
30 [Whether grace is conveniently divided into operative and cooperative grace] *Super II Sententiarum*, d. 26, q. 1, a. 5.
31 The articles of the single question of the twenty-sixth distinction ask: Is grace a creature? Is it an accident? Is it in the soul or in its faculties? Is it a virtue? Is it divided into operative and cooperative? Is it multiple? Throughout, St Thomas speaks of habitual grace, and in the last article he admits only one grace.

quent grace is the principle of its completion by an external deed: *praevenit voluntatem ut velit bonum; subsequitur ut compleat.* In fact this seems to be his meaning in nearly all the texts cited by the Lombard.[32]

Finally, the sequence of *esse* and *operatio* appears when he attributes to prevenient grace the healthy state of the soul and to subsequent grace its meritorious acts: *praevenit ut sanemur et subsequitur ut sanati negotiemur.*

So much for the distinction between grace as prevenient and as subsequent. The couplet *operans et cooperans,* since obviously it refers only to the present life, can have only two of the three senses above defined. These are:

Uno modo ut per gratiam operantem significetur ipsa gratia, prout esse divinum in anima operatur, secundum quod gratum facit habentem; et per gratiam cooperantem significetur ipsa gratia secundum quod opus meritorium causat, prout opus hominis gratum reddit.

Alio modo secundum quod gratia operans dicitur prout causat voluntatis actum; et cooperans secundum quod causat exteriorem actum in quo voluntas completur vel[33] perseverantiam in illo.[34]

This passage is clarified by reference to the objections. The basic distinction is between grace as a formal cause and grace as an efficient cause: in the

---

32 [grace precedes that we may live piously and follows that we may live always with him; and precedes now that we may be called and follows then that we may be glorified ... precedes the will that it may will the good, follows that it may complete (the act) ... precedes that we may be healed, and follows that being healed we may carry on life] Observe St Thomas's close attention to the positive data. He has observed that nearly all the Lombard's citations refer to the distinction between good will and good performance. This he tries to express by a distinction between internal and external acts.

33 The Parma edition gives 'per' [*Sancti Thomae Aquinatis Opera Omnia* (New York: Musurgia Publishers, 1948), vol. 6, p. 625].

34 [(But operative and cooperative grace can be distinguished in two ways.) In one way so that by operative grace there is signified grace as it operates divine being in the soul, according as it makes pleasing the one who has it; and by cooperative grace there is signified grace according as it causes a meritorious deed, as making a human deed pleasing.

Another way (of making the distinction) is to understand operative grace as it causes an act of will; and to understand cooperative grace according as it causes the external act in which the will is completed, or causes perseverance in that (act)] *Super II Sententiarum,* d. 26, q. 1, a. 5 c.

former sense, grace makes a man acceptable to God the way whiteness makes a wall white; in the latter, inasmuch as a habit or virtue is the efficient cause of an act, grace by means of the virtues, *mediante virtute*, effects the meritorious motion of the will.[35] Thus the scheme of the division is

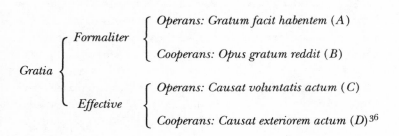

$$
Gratia
\begin{cases}
Formaliter
\begin{cases}
Operans: Gratum\ facit\ habentem\ (A)\\[2ex]
Cooperans: Opus\ gratum\ reddit\ (B)
\end{cases}\\[4ex]
Effective
\begin{cases}
Operans: Causat\ voluntatis\ actum\ (C)\\[2ex]
Cooperans: Causat\ exteriorem\ actum\ (D)^{36}
\end{cases}
\end{cases}
$$

The first member (*A*) offers no difficulty. Sanctifying grace makes a man acceptable to God; in this operation it is a formal cause.[37]

The second member (*B*) is understood as it was by St Albert: the meritorious act is a compound of matter and form; free choice gives the matter, and grace supplies the form.[38]

35 Ibid. ad 2m: 'Ad secundum dicendum, quod gratia operans secundum unam acceptionem dicitur operari in anima, non effective, sed formaliter, secundum quod quaelibet forma facit esse aliquod in subiecto, sicut albedo facit esse album; unde per hunc modum gratia dicitur operans, quia formaliter hominem Deo gratum facit. Secundum vero aliam acceptionem dicitur operans effective, secundum quod habitus effective causat opus; ita enim gratia motum meritorium voluntatis operatur eliciendo ipsum, licet mediante virtute, propter quod operans dicitur' [To the second objection it has to be said that operative grace, according to one understanding, is said to operate in the soul, not effectively but formally, in the way that any form at all gives a certain being in the subject, as whiteness makes white being; and so in this way grace is called operative, because it formally makes man pleasing to God. But according to another understanding it is called operative effectively, in the way a habit causes a work effectively; for in this way grace operates a meritorious movement of the will, eliciting the movement, even if a virtue is mediator, and on this account it is called operative].
36 [Grace formally operative makes pleasing the one who has it (*A*). Grace formally cooperative makes the deed pleasing (*B*). Grace effectively operative causes the act of will (*C*). Grace effectively cooperative causes the external act (*D*).]
37 Ibid. ad 2m: '... sicut albedo facit esse album' [as whiteness makes white being]; ibid. ad 3m: '... albedo formaliter facit album parietem ...' [whiteness formally makes a wall white]. See Albert, above, note 20.
38 Thomas Aquinas, *Super II Sententiarum*, d. 26, q. 1, a. 5, ad 4m: '... liberum arbitrium ministrat substantiam actus, et a gratia est forma per quam meritorius est; unde illud quod gratia ministrat est sicut ultimum com-

The third member (C) turns on a notion already familiar from our study of St Albert and St Bonaventure. A virtue acts as a natural principle, *per modum naturae*, so that grace in causing the virtues moves the will, just as the form of weight moves a body downwards.[39] However, St Albert had not attempted to say whether this influence was operative or cooperative, and St Bonaventure had understood it as cooperative. In the *De veritate* and the *Prima secundae* St Thomas will adopt the latter view, but here he advances the anomalous opinion that grace operates efficiently by cooperating with free will.[40]

The fourth member (D) indicates the origin of this anomaly. Neither St Albert nor St Bonaventure had attempted to take into account the fact that St Augustine had based his distinction between divine operation and divine cooperation on the difference between good will and good performance. St Thomas had noted the prominence of that difference in the texts cited by

---

plementum: et propter hoc dicitur cooperans, quasi complens illud quod per liberum arbitrium ut praeiacens exhibetur' [free will provides the substance of the act, and from grace comes the form through which it is meritorious; and so that which grace provides is like an ultimate complement, and on this account it is called cooperative, as if completing that which is presented through free will as antecedent]. See Albert, above, note 21.

39 Thomas Aquinas, *Super II Sententiarum*, d. 26, q. 1, a. 5, ad 3m: '... inclinat in talem actum per modum cuiusdam naturae ... sicut gravitas dicitur operari motum deorsum' [it inclines to such an act in the way of a certain nature ... as gravity is said to operate a downward movement]. See Albert, above, note 25.

40 Thomas Aquinas, *Super II Sententiarum*, d. 26, q. 1, a. 5, ad 3m: 'Ad tertium dicendum, quod si accipiatur gratia operans secundum primam acceptionem, tunc planum est quod effectus quos operatur formaliter, ipsa sola operatur; sicut enim sola albedo formaliter facit album parietem, ita sola gratia formaliter gratum facit. Sed secundum aliam acceptionem verum est quod ipse motus voluntatis non est a gratia sine libero arbitrio; et tamen quia se habet gratia ut principale, quia inclinat in talem actum per modum cuiusdam naturae, ideo ipsa sola talem actum dicitur operari, non quod sine libero arbitrio operetur, sed quia est principalior causa, sicut gravitas dicitur operari motum deorsum' [To the third objection it has to be said that, if grace is considered operative according to the first understanding, then it is plain that it alone operates the effects which it operates formally; for as whiteness alone formally makes a wall white, so grace alone formally makes one pleasing. But according to the other understanding it is true that this movement of the will is not from grace without free will; and nevertheless, because grace has the principal role, because it inclines to such an act in the way of a certain nature, therefore it alone is said to operate such an act, not that it operates without free will, but because it is the principal cause, as gravity is said to operate a downward movement].

Peter Lombard, and he expresses it in terms of the distinction between external and internal acts. Since Aristotle had remarked that in moral matters the internal act is more important than the external, St Thomas suggests that grace may suitably be divided into *operans* and *cooperans* according as it causes the principal or internal act and the subordinate or external act.[41]

Finally, the four members do not denote four graces but one and the same grace which has different effects.

> ... quocumque modo distinguatur [gratia], maxime quantum ad duas distinctiones, operans et cooperans, praeveniens et subsequens, non differunt essentia sed ratione tantum; una enim forma est quae dat esse, et quae est principium operis; unus etiam habitus est qui elicit actum extrinsecum et intrinsecum; unde eadem gratia est operans et cooperans. Nec dicitur praeveniens et subsequens propter ordinem gratiae ad gratiam, sed propter ordinem effectus ad effectum.[42]

Closely connected with this position is the obscurity enshrouding the division of graces. St Thomas had just said:

> ... Apostolus large accipit gratiam pro quolibet dono quod nobis gratis a Deo confertur; et haec quidem dona plura et divisa sunt. Sed

41 Ibid. ad 4m: '... dicitur cooperans non propter principalitatem liberi arbitrii ad gratiam, sed propter principalitatem actus ad actum; actus enim interiores in moralibus potiores sunt exterioribus, ut in x *Ethic.*, cap. xii, Philosophus dicit; unde convenienter gratia secundum quod causat principalem actum, dicitur operans; et secundum quod causat secundarium, dicitur cooperans' [it is called cooperative not because of the principal role of free will with regard to grace, but because of the principal role of one act with regard to another; for in moral matters internal acts prevail over external, as the Philosopher says in *Ethics* x, c. 12; and so grace is suitably called operative according as it causes the principal act, and is called cooperative according as it causes the secondary act].

42 [whatever way (grace) is distinguished, most especially in regard to the two distinctions, operative and cooperative, prevenient and subsequent, there is no real distinction but only a mental one; for it is one form which gives being and which is the principle of the work; also it is one habit which elicits the extrinsic (act) and the intrinsic; and therefore the same grace is both operative and cooperative. Nor is it called prevenient and subsequent because of the order of grace to grace, but because of the order of effect to effect] Ibid. d. 26, q. 1, a. 6, ad 2m.

nos hic loquimur de gratia prout est primum donum, gratam faciens animam.[43]

4   The Multiplicity of *Gratia Gratum Faciens*

In the article just cited of the commentary on the *Sentences*, St Thomas had answered negatively the question, *Utrum gratia sit multiplex in anima?*[44] The same question under a different form reappears in the *De veritate*; he asks, *Utrum in uno homine sit una tantum gratia gratum faciens?*[45] The extremely significant answer runs more or less as follows.

> Grace is either *gratis data* or *gratum faciens*. The former denotes such gifts as inspiration and thaumaturgy: obviously it is multiple. The latter denotes either the gratuitous will of God or else a created gift that perfects man formally and makes him worthy of eternal life.
>
> Now if you mean by grace this created gift, then grace cannot but be one in each individual. God accepts the individual and only consequently the individual's acts: *respexit Deus ad Abel et ad munera eius*.
>
> If, however, you mean by grace the gratuitous will of God, then plainly grace is one not only with regard to each individual but also with regard to all of them together. God is simplicity.
>
> The one possibility of many graces arises if you term every effect of gratuitous divine will a *gratia gratum faciens*, if for instance you call good thoughts and pious desires sanctifying graces. More fully:
>
> … ex parte autem effectuum divinorum [gratia] potest esse multiplex; ut dicamus omnem effectum quem Deus facit in nobis ex gratuita sua voluntate, qua nos in suum regnum acceptat, pertinere ad gratiam gratum facientem; sicut quod immittat nobis bonas cogitationes et sanctas affectiones.
>
> Sic igitur gratia, secundum quod est quoddam donum habituale in nobis, est una tantum, secundum autem quod dicit effectum

---

43 [the Apostle takes grace in a broad sense for any gift which is freely conferred on us by God; and these gifts are many and distinct. But here we are speaking of grace insofar as it is the first gift, making the soul pleasing] Ibid. ad 1m.

44 [Whether grace is multiple in the soul] Ibid. c.

45 [Whether in one person there is only one grace that makes the person pleasing] *De veritate*, q. 27, a. 5.

aliquem Dei in nobis ordinatum ad nostram salutem, possunt dici
multae gratiae in nobis.[46]

The awkwardness of the division is palpable. The many graces seem to
come in as an afterthought; asserted tentatively with an *ut dicamus* and a
possunt dici, they are characterized none too happily as the effects of the
gratuitous divine will by which God accepts us into his kingdom. In the
Contra Gentiles the division will be given a new basis; divine acceptance will
give way to the divine aid necessary for man to attain a transcendent
finality.[47] And in the *Summa theologiae* synthesis appears: grace denotes the
special love God has for those whom he is leading to eternal life; it denotes
this love in itself, as when we speak of the grace of predestination; or it
denotes this love in its effects, as when we speak of supernatural entities in
the soul – motions or habits[48] – fitting man for his last end.[49]

On the other hand, one has only to read earlier attempts at the division
of graces, especially the commentary on the *Sentences*, 2, d. 28, q. 1, aa. 1–4,
and *De veritate*, q. 24, aa. 14–15, to realize that the awkward cross-division[50]
of the article we are discussing marks the turning point in a long effort to
get things in order. What, then, was the immediate cause of this assertion of
a multiplicity in *gratia gratum faciens*?

I think the answer admits little doubt: the immediate cause of the development was a hitherto unnoticed point in St Augustine. In treating the
unity of sanctifying grace both St Bonaventure[51] and St Thomas[52] in their
commentaries on the *Sentences* had raised the objection that grace was both
operative and cooperative, both prevenient and subsequent. The answer

---

46 [but (grace) can be multiple on the side of the divine effects; as we might
say that every effect that God works in us from his gratuitous will, by which
he accepts us into his kingdom, pertains to the grace that makes one pleasing; for example, that he sends us good thoughts and holy desires. In this
way, then, according as grace is a certain habitual gift in us, it is only one;
but according as it means some effect of God in us that is ordered to our
salvation, the graces in us can be called many] Ibid. c.

47 *Summa contra Gentiles*, 3, cc. 52, 147, 150–53.

48 *Summa theologiae*, 1-2, q. 110, a. 2.

49 Ibid. a. 1.

50 Habitual grace appears twice: first, in opposition to the gratuitous will of
God; second, among the effects of that will.

51 Bonaventure, *In II Sententiarum*, d. 27, a. 1, q. 1, ob. 1 [*VB* 3: 265; *QB* 2: 653].

52 Thomas Aquinas, *Super II Sententiarum*, d. 26, q. 1, a. 6, ob. 2. [Neither
Bonaventure (note 51) nor Thomas uses the terms *operans* and *cooperans* in
these references, only *praeveniens* and *subsequens*. But all four terms appear
in St Thomas's response to the objection.]

they gave was that this distinction did not imply a multiplicity of graces but only a multiplicity of effects from one and the same sanctifying grace. Now in the *De veritate*, in the very article under consideration, this objection is repeated in a variety of ways to receive uniformly a new answer. The most significant of these is, perhaps, as follows.

> 3. Praeterea, nullus habet necesse petere id quod iam habet. Sed habens gratiam praevenientem necesse habet petere subsequentem, secundum Augustinum. Ergo non est una gratia praeveniens et subsequens ...
>
> Ad tertium dicendum, quod quantumcumque homo habeat habitum gratiae, semper tamen indiget divina operatione ... Et ideo habens gratiam necesse habet petere divinum auxilium, quod ad *gratiam cooperantem* pertinet.[53]

Plainly, this objection was decisive against the earlier view, for one cannot pray for something that is only notionally distinct from what one already has received. A real distinction had to be introduced between operative and cooperative, prevenient and subsequent grace. To introduce such a distinction the category of grace in its strict sense, *gratia gratum faciens*, had to be enlarged.

5   *Gratia Operans* in the *De Veritate*

The fundamental text, with the addition of a phrase dropped in some manuscripts and in the printed editions,[54] runs as follows.

---

53 [Besides, no one needs to ask for what he already has. But one who has prevenient grace needs to ask for subsequent, according to Augustine. Therefore prevenient and subsequent grace are not one grace ... To the third objection it has to be said that no matter to what extent one has the habit of grace, still one always needs the divine operation ... And therefore one who has grace needs to ask the divine help, which pertains to cooperative grace] *De veritate*, q. 27, a. 5, ob. 3 and ad 3m. [Emphasis in the Latin text is Lonergan's.]

54 Ibid. ob. 1 and ad 1m. The line in italic type is not found in the printed editions (Parma, Marietti, etc.). The internal evidence for its inclusion seems overwhelming. Not only is the omission easily explained by homoioteleuton, but without it the sentence in which it stands lacks both balance and sense and is contradicted immediately by St Thomas in three distinct phrases: first and second, when he states that *operans* (A) and *operans* (C)

Quinto quaeritur utrum in uno homine sit una tantum gratia gratum faciens: et videtur quod non. Nihil enim contra se ipsum dividitur per operantem et cooperantem. Ergo diversae sunt gratiae, operans scilicet et cooperans; et sic in uno homine est non una tantum gratia gratum faciens ...

Ad primum ergo dicendum quod gratia operans et cooperans potest distingui et ex parte ipsius gratuitae Dei voluntatis et ex parte doni nobis collati.

Operans enim dicitur gratia respectu illius effectus quem sola *efficit; cooperans dicitur respectu illius effectus quem sola* non efficit, sed cum libero arbitrio cooperante. Ex parte vero gratuitae Dei voluntatis gratia operans (*A*) dicetur ipsa iustificatio impii, quae fit ipsius doni gratuiti infusione. Hoc enim donum sola gratuita divina voluntas causat in nobis, nec aliquo modo eius causa est liberum arbitrium, nisi per modum dispositionis sufficientis.

Ex parte vero eiusdem gratia cooperans (*B*) dicetur secundum quod in libero arbitrio operatur, motum eius causando, et exterioris actus executionem expediendo, et perseverantiam praebendo, in quibus omnibus aliquid agit liberum arbitrium. Et sic constat quod aliud est gratia operans et cooperans.

Ex parte vero doni gratuiti eadem gratia per essentiam dicetur operans et cooperans: operans (*C*) quidem, secundum quod informat animam; ut operans formaliter intelligatur per modum loquendi quo dicimus quod albedo facit album parietem; hoc enim nullo modo est actus liberi arbitrii; cooperans (*D*) vero dicetur secundum quod inclinat ad actum intrinsecum et extrinsecum, et

---

are *operans* because free will does nothing; third, when he explains *cooperans* (*B*) by pointing out that free will does something. Nor is there any lack of external evidence: with minor variations our reading is found in *Cod. Vat. Ottob.*, 204, 208, 214, 187; *Urb.*, 134; it is missing in *Cod. Vat. Lat.*, 781, 785, 786, *Reg.*, 1883, but one must recall that the autograph part of *Lat.*, 781, ends with *De veritate*, q. 22, a. 11. For the MSS references I am indebted to the President of the Commission for the Leonine Edition, R.P. Suermondt, O.P. [The later Marietti edition that we are using for this edition has the phrase, with a slight difference in wording (and a misprint). The Leonine edition has: 'Operans enim dicitur gratia respectu illius effectus quem voluntas Dei in nobis efficit, cooperans vero respectu, etc.' The need for correction was pointed out in *Bulletin thomiste* 5 (1937–39), note 77, pp. 58–59. Lonergan's manuscript references could not be checked, and so are listed simply as he gave them.]

secundum quod praestat facultatem perseverandi usque in finem.[55]

The underlying division of grace has already been discussed in the preceding section: grace is either a habitual gift or any effect of the gratuitous will of God accepting us into his kingdom. Thus the scheme of the subdivisions is as follows.

> *Gratia ut quilibet effectus divinae voluntatis gratuitae:*
> A. *Operans: Iustificatio impii.*
> B. *Cooperans: Operatio Dei in libero arbitrio, etc.*
> *Gratia ut donum habituale:*
> C. *Operans: Animam informans.*
> D. *Cooperans: Inclinans ad actum intrinsecum, etc.*[56]

55   [Fifthly it is asked whether in one man there is only one grace making him pleasing; and it seems the answer is no. For nothing is divided against itself by operative and cooperative. Therefore, there are distinct graces, namely, operative and cooperative; and thus in one man there is not just one grace making him pleasing ...

To the first objection it must be said that operative and cooperative grace can be distinguished both from the side of the gratuitous will of God himself, and from the side of the gift bestowed on us.

For grace is called operative in regard to that effect *which it operates alone, but cooperative with regard to that effect* which it does not operate alone but with the cooperation of free will.

But from the side of the gratuitous will of God, operative grace will be called the justification itself of the wicked, which is effected by the infusion of this gratuitous gift; for the gratuitous will alone of God causes this gift in us, nor is free will in any way its cause unless by way of a sufficient disposition.

But from the side of the same (gratuitous will of God) grace will be called cooperative according as it operates in free will, causing its movement, and expediting the execution of an external act, and granting perseverance, in all of which free will does something. And so it is clear that operative grace is other than cooperative.

But from the side of the gratuitous gift essentially the same grace will be called operative and cooperative. It is operative as informing the soul – the way operative is formally understood in the manner of speaking in which we say that whiteness makes a wall white – for in no way is this the act of free will. But it will be called operative as inclining to an intrinsic or extrinsic act, and as furnishing the power of persevering to the end] *De veritate,* q. 27, a. 5, ob. 1 and ad 1m.

56   [Grace as any effect whatever of the divine gratuitous will: *A.* Operative: Justification of the wicked. *B.* Cooperative: The operation of God in free will, etc.

Grace as a habitual gift: *C.* Operative: Informing the soul. *D.* Cooperative: Inclining to an intrinsic act, etc.]

The first subdivision, *A* and *B*, is of graces really distinct.[57] The second subdivision, *C* and *D*, is of graces notionally distinct.[58] Further, there is not a real distinction between *operans* (*A*) and *operans* (*C*), an oddity that results from the basic cross-division.

We are already familiar with the distinction between the formal and the efficient causality of habitual grace. But while in the commentary on the *Sentences* St Thomas divided each of these into *operans* and *cooperans*, here the formal causality of the habit is said to be *operans* (*C*) and its efficient causality to be *cooperans* (*D*). Essentially this is an improvement to be retained in the *Summa theologiae*,[59] for it eliminates the anomaly of the commentary on the *Sentences*, where an operative grace cooperates with free will.[60] Still, this improvement is at the expense of sacrificing the Augustinian connection of operation with good will and cooperation with good performance: where the commentary on the *Sentences* attributed internal acts to operative grace and external to cooperative, we now find both internal and external attributed to cooperative, *B* and *D*.

The great advance of the *De veritate* is to be found in the first pair, *operans* (*A*) and *cooperans* (*B*). Here we find the enlarged category of *gratia gratum faciens*. But *operans* (*A*) calls for no comment: it is the justification of the sinner in which free acts are no more than disposing causes. On the other hand, nothing can be added at this stage of our inquiry to what has already been said on *cooperans* (*B*): it is the grace for which one has to pray no matter how much habitual grace one has received;[61] it is illustrated by the divine gift of good thoughts and holy aspirations;[62] it is defined as any effect, apart from habitual grace, by which God gratuitously accepts us into his kingdom.

6   *Gratia Operans* in the *Summa Theologiae*

In the *De veritate* operative grace was discussed incidentally. In the *Summa*

---

57 *De veritate*, q. 27, a. 5, ad 1m: 'Et sic constat quod aliud est gratia operans et cooperans' [And so it is clear that operative grace is other than cooperative].
58 Ibid.: 'Ex parte vero doni gratuiti eadem gratia per essentiam dicetur operans et cooperans' [But from the side of the gratuitous gift essentially the same grace will be called operative and cooperative].
59 *Summa theologiae*, 1-2, q. 111, a. 2.
60 *Super II Sententiarum*, d. 26, q. 1, a. 5, ad 3m. Cited above, note 40.
61 *De veritate*, q. 27, a. 5, ad 3m.
62 Ibid. c.: '... sicut quod immittat nobis bonas cogitationes et sanctas affectiones' [for example, that he sends us good thoughts and holy desires].

theologiae, as in the commentary on the *Sentences*, a separate article is devoted to the issue. The response may be summarized as follows.

> A grace may be either a habit or a motion, but both habits and motions may be operative, and both may be cooperative. For grace operates inasmuch as the soul is purely passive; it cooperates inasmuch as the soul is both passive and active.
>
> Now there are two kinds of human acts, interior and exterior. With regard to the former, the will is purely passive, notably when a will, formerly evil, is made good; with regard to the latter, the will is not only passive but also active, and so grace cooperates. In this fashion, grace as a motion is divided into operative and cooperative.
>
> On the other hand, habitual grace like any other form has two effects: *esse* and *operari*. Accordingly, inasmuch as habitual grace cures or justifies the soul or makes it acceptable to God, it is said to be operative. But inasmuch as it is a principle of meritorious acts, it is cooperative.[63] Thus we have as a final scheme of division:

$$
Gratia
\begin{cases}
Motus
\begin{cases}
Operans: Actus\ interior \\
Cooperans: Actus\ exterior
\end{cases} \\
Habitus
\begin{cases}
Operans: Effectus\ formales \\
Cooperans: Principium\ operationis^{64}
\end{cases}
\end{cases}
$$

The most striking feature of this scheme is that, while in the *De veritate* actual grace was only *gratia cooperans*, here it is both *operans* and *cooperans*. A clue to the possible origin of this development is given in the *corpus articuli* when St Thomas illustrates actual grace as operative by referring to conversion, *cum voluntas incipit bonum velle, quae prius malum volebat.*[65] Now if we examine St Thomas's successive treatments of the preparation for justification, we find the following development. In the commentary on the *Sentences*

63 *Summa theologiae*, 1-2, q. 111, a. 2. This article will be given more detailed study: see below, pp. 132–42. [See also below, pp. 245–50, 390–438.]
64 [Grace as an operative motion: internal act; as a cooperative motion: external act. Grace as an operative habit: formal effects; as a cooperative habit: the principle of operation.]
65 [when the will, which before was willing evil, begins to will the good]

this preparation is ascribed to providence working through such external causes as admonitions or loss of health.[66] In the *De veritate* the period of transition has begun: alternative to external causes there is mentioned a [*divinus instinctus*] *secundum quod Deus in mentibus hominum operatur*.[67] Finally, in the *Quodlibetum primum*, which belongs to the second Paris period, the beginning of conversion is attributed exclusively to such an internal operation, and any other view is branded as Pelagian.[68] Since this internal operation is prior to justification, it must be an actual grace. It is difficult to doubt that such is the origin of St Thomas's idea of actual grace as operative.

7   Conclusion

Since, however, further discussion of the interpretation of these passages would take us beyond the scope of the present chapter, we may now give our conclusions.

There is a clearly defined development in St Thomas's thought on *gratia operans et cooperans*. In the commentary on the *Sentences* actual grace is neither operative nor cooperative. In the *De veritate* it is said to be cooperative. In the *Summa theologiae* it is both operative and cooperative.

The deficiencies in St Thomas's earlier thought are matched by similar deficiencies in the thought of his immediate predecessors. We are dealing with the development, not of a single mind, but of the speculative theology of grace itself. The nature of this general movement was discussed in the first chapter. Here certain precise points have come to light: the great

---

66 *Super II Sententiarum*, d. 28, q. 1, a. 4. See Bonaventure, *In II Sententiarum*, d. 28, a. 2, q. 1 conc., cited above, note 16. According to Doms, St Albert does not appear to have treated the matter: *Die Gnadenlehre des sel. Albertus Magnus* 163–68.

67 [(a divine instinct) according as God operates in human minds] *De veritate*, q. 24, a. 15.

68 S. Thomae Aquinatis, *Quaestiones quodlibetales*, ed. P. Mandonnet (Paris: P. Lethielleux, 1926), q. 1, a. 7 [pp. 13–15; also in *S. Thomae Aquinatis Quaestiones quodlibetales*, ed. R. Spiazzi (Turin: Marietti, 1949) as q. 4, a. 2 of *Quodlibetum primum*; the latter is the text relied on here]. The passages just cited from the commentary on the *Sentences* and the *De veritate* do not mention the Pelagians. *Summa contra Gentiles*, 3, c. 152 mentions them yet attributes the *initium fidei* to habitual faith consequent to charity. In *Summa theologiae*, 1, q. 62, a. 2, ad 3m, there is an assertion of internal grace prior to justification and an implication of its necessity. Probably this passage is prior to the *Quodlibetum primum*; in any case the essential advance takes place in *Summa contra Gentiles*, 3, c. 149, which attributes all initiative to God on the ground that the creature is an instrument.

commentaries on the *Sentences* reveal a preoccupation with sanctifying grace; simultaneously the external graces of special providence, internal illuminations and inspirations, and many other things are lumped together under a general rubric of *gratia gratis data*. On the latter point there are noteworthy differences between St Albert, St Bonaventure, and St Thomas; still, the general statement remains true. Speculation on habitual grace is reaching its peak of perfection, but speculation on actual grace is hardly beyond its preliminary stages.

Though our inquiry is not as yet sufficiently advanced to outline St Thomas's elaboration of the idea of actual grace, we have found two points to be of special interest. The category of *gratia gratum faciens* is enlarged in the *De veritate* to make room for the divine gift of good thoughts and holy affections; this enlargement coincides with an advertence to the fact that St Augustine's *praeveniens* and *subsequens* must be two graces really distinct; there follows the affirmation of a divine guidance and aid that is distinct from habitual grace and is termed *gratia cooperans*. Further, the actual grace that is operative in the *Summa theologiae* is explicitly illustrated by conversion; now on this point St Thomas's thought had a long and nuanced history as is apparent from a comparison of *Super II Sententiarum*, d. 28, q. 1, a. 4; *De veritate*, q. 24, a. 15; *Summa contra Gentiles*, 3, cc. 149, 152; *Summa theologiae*, 1, q. 62, a. 2, ad 3m; *Quodlibetum primum*, a.7;[69] *De malo*, q. 6, a. 1, ad 1m, ad 21m; *Summa theologiae*, 1-2, q. 9, a. 6, ad 3m; ibid. 3, q. 85, a. 5.

69 [See above, note 68.]

I-3

Habitual Grace as *Operans et Cooperans*

> Si vero accipiatur gratia pro habituali dono, sic etiam duplex est
> gratiae effectus, sicut et cuiuslibet alterius formae: quorum primus
> est esse, secundus est operatio; sicut caloris operatio est facere cali-
> dum, et exterior calefactio. Sic igitur habitualis gratia, inquantum
> animam sanat vel iustificat, sive gratam Deo facit, dicitur gratia
> operans: inquantum vero est principium operis meritorii, quod
> etiam ex libero arbitrio procedit, dicitur cooperans.[1]

To sketch the content and the implications of the above passage is the
primary purpose of the present chapter. Incidentally, attention will be
drawn to the declining importance of habitual grace in St Thomas's successive works, and this will prepare for an inquiry into his concept of actual
grace as operative and cooperative.

Three main points are treated: (1) the general nature of the habit;
(2) habitual grace as a *gratia sanans*; (3) the infusion of habitual grace as a
premotion. Roughly, these three correspond to the position of St Thomas's
commentary on the *Sentences*, the development in the *De veritate*, and the

---

1 [But if grace is taken as a habitual gift, then too there is a twofold effect of
grace as there is of any other form whatever; of these the first is being, the
second is operation, as the operation of heat is to make (something) hot,
and (to give) external heating. In this way therefore habitual grace, in that
it heals the soul or justifies it or makes it pleasing to God, is called operative
grace; but in that it is the principle of a meritorious work, which proceeds
from free will too, it is called cooperative] *Summa theologiae*, 1-2, q. 111,
a. 2 c.

development which begins with the *Contra Gentiles* and is consummated in the *Summa theologiae*.

1   The General Nature of Habits

In estimating human nature St Thomas was a wholehearted pessimist. With conviction he would repeat, *numerus stultorum infinitus*.[2] And, as one might expect, for this low opinion of man he had at hand a very imposing metaphysical argument.

Agere sequitur esse: perfection in the dynamic field of operation is radically one with perfection in the static order of being. But perfection in the order of being is measured by the proportion of potency and act: the more refined the potency and the greater its actuation, the more perfect the resultant. Now, since God alone is *actus purus* with potentiality at zero and act at infinity, it follows that God alone operates with absolute perfection. Next stand the angels, existing beyond time and created in the full development of their natures; compounds of potency and act, for the most part they do what is right. But man is essentially a creature of time; at birth his higher powers are the spiritual counterpart of *materia prima*, and their indeterminate potentiality points at once in all directions; accordingly, since the good is ever unique and evil manifold, the odds always are that man will do what is wrong.[3]

With the human problem so clearly conceived, St Thomas has at once its solution: a greater actuation of human potency. However, as we should expect, this greater actuation is effected differently in the commentary on the *Sentences* and in later works. In the commentary on the *Sentences* habitual grace alone is *gratia operans et cooperans*.[4] But in the *De veritate*, the next systematic work, it is affirmed that no matter how perfect the habits one acquires or receives, there always remains the need of a divine operation which is a *gratia cooperans*.[5]

In the commentary on the *Sentences*, then, the problem of remedying human deficiency is met by considering the alternatives of external intervention and internal change. Either the rule of rectitude, divine wisdom,

---

2 [The number of stupid people is infinite: *Summa theologiae*, 1, q. 63, a. 9, ob. 2; 2-2, q. 60, a. 4, ob. 1; *Suppl.*, q. 97, a. 7, ob. 3. Thomas is quoting the Vulgate translation (not generally accepted today) of Ecclesiastes 1.15.]
3 See *Super I Sententiarum*, d. 39, q. 2, a. 2, ad 4m.
4 *Super II Sententiarum*, d. 26, q. 1, a. 6, ad 2m.
5 *De veritate*, q. 27, a. 5, ad 3m.

intervenes whenever man is about to act; or else that rule somehow becomes the inherent form of the potency to be regulated. But the former solution is unsatisfactory: interference is always a species of violence, and though, no doubt, divine interference would make man's operation proper, it would leave man himself just as bad as he had been. On the other hand, if one examines the nature of habits and dispositions, one finds that they constitute precisely the type of internal change required: they make the external rule of right action the internal form of the faculty's operation. A disposition is such a form in its incipient stages, when it is not well established and may easily be lost. A habit is such a form brought to perfection and, as it were, grafted on nature. For habits cling to us as does nature; they give operation the spontaneity and the delight characteristic of natural action; they make arts and skills as unimpeded and free as the use of one's own possessions. As Averroes said, *habitus ... est quo quis agit cum voluerit*; one has merely to want to, and the thing is done, if one has the habit.[6]

In the *De veritate* the basic ideas and the cosmic scheme remain the same, but the human problem has a far profounder solution. God alone is fully proportionate to Goodness and Truth, and so only God is absolutely impeccable.[7] Accordingly, impeccable operation is possible to man only when he is accorded the beatific vision, when God alone is the source and principle of his entire activity.[8] It follows that no habit or set of habits can make man's operation absolutely right,[9] for no habit or set of habits is equivalent to God himself, who alone has the property of absolutely right action. Finally, since the condition of this life normally excludes the beatific vision, it is necessary to combine the alternatives of internal change and external intervention, to add divine motions to infused grace.

Now this modification of the initial position naturally brings another in its train, for once it has been shown that external intervention has to be added to internal change, it becomes desirable to eliminate intervention's implication of violence. Perhaps it was with this end in view that St Thomas

---

6 *Super III Sententiarum*, d. 23, q. 1, a. 1.
7 *De veritate*, q. 24, a. 7 [ad fin.].
8 Ibid. a. 8; see a. 9.
9 *De veritate*, q. 27, a. 5, ad 3m; see *Summa theologiae*, 1-2, q. 109 [sic Lonergan; a. 9 of q. 109, suggested by J. Patout Burns, asks, 'Utrum ille qui iam consecutus est gratiam, per seipsum potest operari bonum et vitare peccatum, absque alio auxilio gratiae' (Whether the one who has already received grace can on his own do good and avoid sin, without any other help of grace)].

changed his theory of the gifts of the Holy Spirit;[10] at any rate the later theory presented in the *Summa theologiae* is a very adequate answer to the objection that external intervention is violent, or as we should say, unnatural. The moral virtues are of two kinds: those like prudence and justice which perfect the faculties in which they inhere; others like temperance and fortitude which render the lower faculties spontaneous in their subordination to higher faculties. Similarly, habits are of two kinds: the virtues perfect the individual that possesses them, but the gifts of the Holy Spirit make connatural to the creature the external guidance and aid of the Spirit of truth and love.[11] Nor is there any difficulty in meeting the other objection advanced in the commentary on the *Sentences*, that external intervention may improve human action but does not improve man himself. For the gifts of the Holy Spirit bring us into the region of pure supernaturality, a region that lies beyond the bounds of all created perfection. Just as beatitude is not human but divine and natural to God alone,[12] just as wisdom for us is not understanding but faith,[13] so the highest perfection of man cannot be immanent as are the virtues, but rather must link us dynamically with the sole source of absolute perfection.

Such appears to be the main line of development in the majestic sweep of St Thomas's thought on the problem of perfecting man. It begins with an insistence on the immanent perfection of the virtues; it ends with a nuanced theory in which the transcendent perfection of God is communicated to man through the double channel of immanent virtues and transient motions. Certain points call for particular attention.

First, the two aspects of habitual grace, *operans et cooperans*, result from the principle that *actus* is at once perfection and a source of further perfection,

10 See Joseph de Guibert, *Les doublets de saint Thomas d'Aquin: Leur étude méthodique. Quelques réflexions, quelques exemples* (Paris: Beauchesne, 1926) 100–25. For the views of earlier writers, see Odon Lottin, 'Les dons du Saint-Esprit chez les théologiens depuis P. Lombard jusqu'à s. Thomas d'Aquin,' *Recherches de théologie ancienne et médiévale* 1 (1929) 41–61. [This article is greatly expanded in 'Les dons du Saint-Esprit du xiie siècle à l'époque de saint Thomas d'Aquin,' in Lottin, *Psychologie et morale aux XIIe et XIIIe siècles*, vol. 3 (Gembloux, Belgium: J. Duculot, 1949) 33–433.]

11 *Summa theologiae*, 1-2, q. 68, a. 3; see ibid. a. 2.

12 See James E. O'Mahony, *The Desire of God in the Philosophy of St. Thomas Aquinas* (Cork: Cork University Press, and London: Longmans, Green, 1929).

13 St Thomas's development of this point has been presented by M.-D. Chenu, 'La théologie comme science au xiiie siècle,' *Archives d'histoire doctrinale et littéraire du moyen âge* 2 (1927) 31–71.

that *agere sequitur esse*. Because every habit is a perfection, the actuation and determination of an indeterminate potency,[14] it will have its immediate effects in the field of formal causality and its ulterior consequences in the field of efficient causality. The accident 'heat' is the ground both of the fire's being hot and of its heating other objects; in like manner grace or any other form is a principle of both *esse* and *operari*.[15]

Second, the term 'proportion' takes on an increasing significance as the *actus* basing the proportion increases. Thus, God, the angels, and men are all proportionate to the true and the good, for all are rational beings. But in God this proportion is such that divine operation cannot be defective; in the angels it implies only that for the most part operation will not fail; while in man it gives a mere possibility with no guarantee of success, so that for the most part men do what is wrong. Nevertheless, give man the virtues, and in place of the statistical law governing humanity one will have an approximation to the statistical law governing the angels. Man endowed with the virtues becomes an *agens perfectum* and, for the most part, does what is right; thus a will adorned with the virtue of justice performs just deeds with the spontaneity and the regularity with which fire moves upwards.[16]

Incidentally, one may note that this analogy of proportion resolves an apparent anomaly. In his later discussions of virtues in the will,[17] St Thomas asserts that they are necessary to man because justice exceeds the proportion of men taken individually and charity exceeds their proportion taken specifically. Yet at the same time he affirms that to love God above all things, so far from exceeding the proportion of man's powers, is natural to him and to every other creature.[18] The obvious solution seems to be the analogy of 'proportion': it is one thing to have an abstract admiration and approval for justice and the love of God; it is quite another uniformly to translate ideals and exalted principles into concrete living. The former results from

14 *Summa theologiae*, 1-2, q. 49, a. 4.
15 *Summa theologiae*, 1-2, q. 111, a. 2 c.: 'Si vero accipiatur gratia pro habituali dono, sic etiam duplex est gratiae effectus, sicut et cuiuslibet alterius formae: quorum primus est esse, secundus est operatio; sicut caloris operatio est facere calidum, et exterior calefactio' [translation in note 1, above]. See also our *Verbum: Word and Idea in Aquinas*, chapter 3 [CWL 2, pp. 106–51], for a fuller development of Aquinas's theory of operation.
16 *Super I Sententiarum*, d. 39, q. 2, a. 2, ad 4m; see *Summa theologiae*, 1, q. 49, a. 3, ad 5m [sic Lonergan, but the relevance is not clear; q. 49 of the *Prima secundae* is more to the point, but there is no 'ad 5m' in a. 3]; 1-2, q. 113, a. 7, ad 4m.
17 *De virtutibus in communi*, q. 1, a. 5; *Summa theologiae*, 1-2, q. 56, a. 6.
18 *Summa theologiae*, 1-2, q. 109, a. 3 c. and ad 2m.

rational nature as such; the latter presupposes the acquired and the infused virtues according as action is on the plane of the terrestrial or the celestial polity.[19]

Third, it would be a grave misinterpretation to ascribe to St Thomas the view that the supernatural virtues give merely the possibility of a type of action and do not make it spontaneous and connatural. His whole exposition is in terms of natural forms and natural inclinations: a virtue is a second nature, an actuation and determination of an indeterminate potency, and so *quasi quaedam forma per modum naturae tendens in unum.*[20] However, there does remain the objection from experience that the infused virtues do not appear always to make right action prompt, easy, and agreeable. To this St Thomas answered that neither acquired nor infused virtues totally eliminate the evil inclinations of passion; still, both operate against such inclinations, though in different ways. Acquired virtues make evil tendencies less sensible; the more rarefied infused virtues may not have this effect at all, but what they do accomplish is to break sin's dominion over us. Nor is the persisting sensible difficulty contrary to the nature of a virtue, for, as even Aristotle acknowledged, the pleasure proper to virtuous action may be, at times, no more than the absence of regret.[21] Perhaps the more radical answer to the objection would be that readiness, ease, and pleasure are the signs, the external consequences, of the virtues; such secondary effects may be covered over by other factors. Intrinsically a virtue is a determinate actuation: as such it is always analogous to natural spontaneity, for a nature is nothing but a determinate actuation.

2   Habitual Grace as *Gratia Sanans*

The general nature of the habit as a determination raises the question, Do habits in the will limit the will's freedom? No doubt Averroes was right in asserting, *habitus ... est quo quis agit cum voluerit.* No doubt St Thomas agreed with him, not only in the commentary on the *Sentences* but also in the *Summa theologiae.*[22] Nonetheless, a habit is the determination of an indeter-

---

19 This is the explanation St Thomas suggests in his *In Rom.*, c. 7, lect. 3.
20 [as if (it were) a certain form tending in the way of a nature to one thing] *De virtutibus in communi*, q. 1, a. 9 c.
21 Ibid. a. 10, ad 14m and ad 15m.
22 *Super III Sententiarum*, d. 23, q. 1, a. 1; *Summa theologiae*, 1-2, q. 50, a. 5 c. ['habitus est quo quis utitur cum voluerit' (a habit is that which one uses when one wants to)].

minate potency, and a habit in the will is a state of willingness, an incipient willing this and rejecting that.[23] Is there not something of a vicious circle in saying that we employ habits just as we will or please when our willingness and what pleases us is predetermined by our habits? Is there not something in the phrase, *qualis quisque est talis finis videtur ei?*[24]

This question in its theological form is in terms of *gratia sanans,* of the moral impotence of the sinner, of the liberation of human liberty by grace. In the early Augustinian tradition this aspect of grace received the greatest prominence, as we have seen, for the very good reason that the systematic elaboration of the idea of the supernatural had not as yet been attempted. It appears, however, that this excessive prominence was followed by a temporary eclipse when the idea of the supernatural was being worked out and applied. Thus one finds St Albert taking at its face value Peter Lombard's well-intentioned distinction beween *libertas a necessitate* and *libertas a peccato.* With the Lombard he affirms that man always enjoys *libertas a necessitate.* Unlike the Lombard he concludes that *non posse non peccare etiam damnabiliter* does not mean precisely what it says; for, he maintains, St Augustine's *peccata habendi dura necessitas* does not mean that the sinner cannot avoid future sins without grace; it only means that the sinner cannot have his past sins forgiven without grace.[25]

St Bonaventure had been of a contrary opinion,[26] but St Thomas in his commentary on the *Sentences* argues for his former master in the most downright fashion. There is no use saying that a sinner can avoid each separate sin but not all, for if he can avoid each, then he can avoid all. Nor is it any better to argue that he can avoid all for a time but not always, for resistance to sin makes one all the stronger against it. In short, freedom of choice pertains to human nature; sin does not destroy nature; therefore sin does not destroy freedom. The most that can be said is that because of sin it becomes difficult to avoid what once was avoided easily.[27]

23 *Summa theologiae,* 1-2, q. 49, a. 3.
24 [as anyone is, so will the end appear to him] The phrase occurs as an objection in Aristotle, *Nicomachean Ethics,* III, 5, 1114a 32. St Thomas's discussion is in *Sententia libri Ethicorum,* 3, lect. 13.
25 Albert, *Summa de creaturis,* 2, q. 70, a. 5 [*BA* 35: 588]; *In II Sententiarum,* d. 25, a. 6 [*BA* 27: 433–34]. Both works belong to the period 1240–50, according to Franz Pelster in Herder's *Lexikon für Theologie und Kirche* 1: 215 [Franz Pelster, 'Albertus Magnus,' *Lexikon für Theologie und Kirche,* ed. Michael Buchberger (Freiburg im Breisgau: Herder & Co., 1930) 214–16]. The position is corrected by Albert in his *Summa theologica,* 2, q. 100, mem. 2–4 [*BA* 33: 246–52], but this work is posterior to St Thomas's death.
26 Bonaventure, *In II Sententiarum,* d. 28, a. 2, q. 2 [*VB* 3: 296–300; *QB* 2: 684–87].
27 *Super II Sententiarum,* d. 28, q. 1, a. 2; ibid. d. 25, q. 1, a. 4.

In the *De veritate*, however, one finds a very pertinent quotation from St Augustine's *De gratia et libero arbitrio*. The Pelagians admitted that grace was necessary for the forgiveness of past sins; what they wanted to maintain was that grace was not necessary for the avoidance of future sins. It was on this score that St Augustine took them to task, citing the Our Father which asks not only *dimitte debita nostra*, but also *ne nos inferas in tentationem*. Accordingly, there is no use trying to make out that *non posse non peccare* merely means that grace is necessary for sins to be forgiven.[28]

To meet this datum, St Thomas refines his theory of the relations between the habits and freedom. The irrevocable fixity in evil proper to the demons[29] is not possible to man in this life.[30] For passion is momentary; bad habits of one kind can be overcome by good habits of another; and as by reasoning man falls into error, so by more reasoning can he be brought back to truth. Even when error exists in matters of principle, it can be corrected, not indeed by deduction, which presupposes true principles, but by collative thought and by the acquisition of the virtues, which effect a right attitude toward principles.[31]

Still, even in this life a relative fixity in evil results from sin. This is a necessary consequence of three truths: (A) explicit deliberation is not needed for an act to be free; (B) explicit deliberation is necessary for the sinner to avoid further sin; (C) it is impossible for a man to deliberate explicitly before every act, and so it is impossible for the sinner to avoid all sins. As the argument touches the very center of the relations between habits of will and human freedom, it will be well to make each point quite plain.

First (A), explicit deliberation is not needed for an act to be free. For instance, one does not weigh the pros and cons of eating before each meal, yet one eats freely. The same is true with regard to the whole routine of our lives, for in the main, human action is the outcome of habitual orientations of mind and will. Further, one finds the same domination of habits in sudden departures from routine, and for this reason Aristotle pointed out that a man's behavior in an emergency is the best indication of his virtue. On the other hand, this vast and almost palpable absence of explicit reflec-

---

28 *De veritate*, q. 24, a. 12, ob. 22 (1ae ser.).

29 St Thomas treats the fixity of the demons in evil many times: *Super IV Sententiarum*, d. 50, q. 1, a. 1; *De veritate*, q. 24, a. 10; *Summa contra Gentiles*, 4, c. 95 [ad fin.]; *Summa theologiae*, 1, q. 64, a. 2; *De malo*, q. 16, a. 5.

30 *De veritate*, q. 24, a. 11.

31 Ibid. c. and ad 4m. Such thought we associate with Newman; St Thomas gives Aristotle as his source.

tion and debate does not involve an equal absence of freedom in human living. Most actions of this type receive a real and full consent: for when there is antecedent willingness with respect to an end, means to the end have merely to present themselves and, unless some special consideration intervene, they will freely and, as it were, spontaneously be chosen. To cite the Latin:

> ... repentina sunt secundum habitum. Nec hoc est intelligendum quod operatio secundum habitum virtutis possit esse omnino absque deliberatione, cum virtus sit *habitus electivus*; sed quia habenti habitum *iam est in eius electione finis determinatus*; unde quandocumque aliquid occurrit ut conveniens illi fini, statim eligitur, nisi ex aliqua attentiori et maiori deliberatione impediatur.[32]

So much, then, for the first point: the antecedent willingness of the habit results in activity that is both spontaneous and free; the only brake on this spontaneity is explicit deliberation, a process of reasoning that constructs an alternative course of action.

It immediately follows (*B*) that anyone with a vicious habit will freely and, as it were, automatically sin as often as occasion arises unless, simultaneously with each occasion of sin, there also arises an explicit deliberation. But St Thomas goes further than this. Even if the sinner has committed but a single sin and so has not acquired a vice, still, from that one sin there remains in his will a spontaneous orientation, a *vis et inclinatio*, to the transitory good that he has made his end. In other words the difference between dispositions and habits is not that the latter are more efficacious than the former: both are spontaneous orientations, and while they last both are equally efficacious. The difference is that the habit is so rooted in one that its chances of survival are vastly greater; it is a disposition that has built itself a permanent home, that has reached out in all directions to eliminate all tendencies that would threaten its security. Accordingly, a mere disposition in the will is no less an antecedent willingness than the

---

32 [sudden (acts) are according to habit. Nor is this to be understood so that an operation in accord with a virtuous habit can be altogether without deliberation, since virtue is an *elective habit*; but because *there is already a determinate end in the choice* of the one possessing the habit; and therefore whenever something occurs as suitable to that end, at once it is chosen, unless it is prevented by some more attentive and more (intense) deliberation] Ibid. a. 12. [Emphasis is Lonergan's.]

established habit, and so even a single sin sets up an orientation that makes the sinner succumb to every further temptation unless he argues himself out of it.

But mortal sin, it may be objected, requires full advertence and full consent. That is true, but the point is this: a sinner can have both full advertence and full consent without having the measure of deliberation necessary to break down his spontaneous orientation. Full advertence is a realization that an act is sinful and against God; full consent is a real consent following full advertence. Certainly the sinner must have both of these if he is to commit another mortal sin. But suppose that he has both; does it follow that he has reflected sufficiently to argue himself out of sinning? Not at all. To know that an act is wrong and an offense against God is an efficacious motive to a will actuated by charity. But what moves the sinner is not an appeal to his pure love of God, for he does not love God. To touch his heart, the appeal must be directed to his self-love. To hold in check his appetites, considerations must be adduced that offer deterrents to egoism. Of course his heart always can be touched, for he has not the fixity in evil of the demons; deterrents can always be found, for what is against God is ultimately also against himself. But the present point is that the full advertence necessary for mortal sin neither touches his heart nor offers an efficacious deterrent, that a further and fuller advertence is required before the sinner can construct his resistance to further sin.

Third (C), habits are a human necessity. Man has to be spontaneously and antecedently in the right attitude, with the right orientation, for the excellent reason that it is quite impossible for man to be reasoning himself into the right attitude before each act. You may say that habits are needed merely to make action ready, easy, and agreeable. That is quite true. But it is also true that unless action is ready, easy, and agreeable, then for the most part it will not take place. Such was the statistical law established in the commentary on the *Sentences*. But now St Thomas advances from a mere statistical law to the limiting case in which sheer impossibility emerges. He had shown that the sinner stands in need of an extra measure of reflectiveness, a special advertence, if he is to avoid further sins. The question now is, Can a man endure the perpetual strain of such deliberateness? The answer is flatly negative. Deliberate vigilance can succeed for a time, but not for the whole time, nor even for a long time. If only he puts his mind to it, the sinner can resist every temptation. But he cannot constantly be putting his mind to it. Therefore, it is inevitable that he will give free course to the spontaneous orientation, to the *vis et inclinatio,* of his will; once he has done so, temptation has only to recur and again he will sin, freely.[33]

Thus the Lombard's *non posse non peccare* is reestablished; the vast sea of Augustinian thought, which flowed in the twelfth century but whose current was dammed while the speculative theorem of the supernatural was being elaborated and applied, now surges into the categories of the Thomist synthesis. Habitual grace, henceforth, is not only *elevans* but also *sanans.* Let us give a few illustrations.

An objection affirms, *Cogenti cupiditati voluntas resistere non potest.*[34] Nothing could summarize more effectively the kernel of St Thomas's account of moral impotence: self-love, *cupiditas,* makes sin connatural; it makes the avoidance of sin an impossible strain; it constitutes a servitude from which the only permanent liberation is the infusion of divine charity.[35] In similar fashion St Thomas accepts and interprets St Paul's *Non ... quod volo bonum,*

33 Ibid. Is he really free? At this period St Thomas conceives freedom as noncoercion and so has no difficulty; see *Super II Sententiarum,* d. 25, q. 1, a. 2; *De veritate,* q. 23, a. 4; *De potentia,* q. 10, a. 2, ad 5m [1ae ser.]; *De veritate,* q. 22, a. 5 c., ob. 4 and ad 4m (1ae ser.), ob. 3 and ad 3m (2ae ser.); q. 22, a. 8; q. 24, a. 1, ad 20m; q. 24, a. 10, ob. 5 and ad 5m; q. 24, a. 12, ad 10m (2ae ser.); *De potentia,* q. 3, a. 7, ad 14m. Later, in the *De malo,* when the determinist views of Parisian Averroists were being ventilated, St Thomas treats with extraordinary harshness the weak minds or frivolous wills that identify freedom with noncoercion. See *De malo,* q. 6, a. 1 c. init.; also Odon Lottin, 'Liberté humaine et motion divine,' *Recherches de théologie ancienne et médiévale* 7 (1935) 52–69, 156–73; and his earlier article, 'La date de la Question disputée "De Malo" de saint Thomas d'Aquin,' *Revue d'histoire ecclésiastique* 24 (1928) 373–88. [The latter article is found, slightly revised, in Lottin, *Psychologie et morale aux XIIe et XIIIe siècles,* vol. 6 (Gembloux, Belgium: J. Duculot, 1960) 353–72.]
      To return to our initial question, it would seem that noncoercion was simply a mode of speech in St Thomas's earlier works; it was common enough in his predecessors; and certainly it was not a true presupposition of his position, which rather is the law of psychological continuity formulated in *De malo,* q. 16, a. 5. On that interpretation the freedom of the sinner who cannot help sinning depends on the measure of his resistance to sin; if that resistance extends to the point where the physical strain reaches the peak of physical incapacity, then sin committed in that state is not formal but material; if the resistance does not produce physical incapacity, then it is the will that provides the ultimate determinant, and the culpability of the will in so doing would seem to be in some inverse proportion to the measure of physical debilitation. What more can be said? Certainly a glib distinction between *impotentia moralis* and *impotentia physica* throws no light on the issue.
34 [The will cannot resist a compelling cupidity] *De veritate,* q. 24, a. 12, ob. 12 (1ae ser.).
35 Ibid. a. 12 c. ad fin.

hoc ago,[36] St Augustine's comparison of the sinner's will to a crooked leg that cannot but limp along,[37] St Gregory's *Peccatum quod per paenitentiam non deletur, mox suo pondere ad aliud trahit*,[38] the old 'theologians' definition' of liberty as *quo bonum eligitur gratia assistente et malum gratia desistente*,[39] the *Glossa*'s description of the liberation of human liberty,[40] and, of course, Peter Lombard's account of the state of fallen man.[41]

But not only is there a revival of the psychological theories of grace so prominent in twelfth-century thought. There also is the coherent handling of what the twelfth century could and did assert but could not correlate with its other data. At the head of this list is the passage attributed to St Jerome, *homines semper peccare et non peccare posse*.[42] There follows a series of equivalent arguments from Holy Scripture, St Augustine, and human reason.[43] Finally, it is in this long discussion that St Thomas comes to grips with the twofold function of habitual grace to be described with schematic brilliance in the *Prima secundae*,[44] when he will hold in synthesis the distinction between the natural and the supernatural orders, the difference between Adam's state and our own, and the necessity of divine motions supplementing infused habits.[45]

So much for the development in speculative theology. Implicit in it there is discerned, easily enough, a philosophic doctrine that dispositions and habits of will constitute a very real limitation on human freedom. The human will does not swing back to a perfect equilibrium of indifference with every tick of the clock; its past operations determine its present orientation; and though this orientation has not the absolute fixity of angels and demons, still it is characterized by the relative fixity of psychological continuity. It can be changed, but such change always requires a cause.

The accurate formulation of this position, however much it is presup-

---

36 [I do not perform the good that I will (Romans 7)] Ibid. ob. 1 (1ae ser.).
37 Ibid. ob. 4 (1ae ser.); ob. 2 (2ae ser.).
38 [a sin that is not canceled by repentance soon by its weight drags (the sinner) to another] Ibid. ob. 5 (1ae ser.).
39 [(the faculty) by which the good, with the help of grace, is chosen, or evil (is chosen) when grace is lacking] Ibid. ob. 14 (1ae ser.).
40 Ibid. ob. 3 (1ae ser.).
41 Ibid. ob. 21 (1ae ser.).
42 [men are always able to sin and not to sin] Ibid. ob. 1 (2ae ser.); [see above, chapter 1, note 51, for Pelagian origin of this phrase].
43 Ibid. from ob. 2 to ob. 11 (2ae ser.).
44 *Summa theologiae*, 1-2, q. 109.
45 All these points are contained in *De veritate*, q. 27, a. 5, ad 3m.

posed in the *De veritate*,[46] I have not been able to find in any work earlier than the *De malo*. There one may read of three possible meanings of the expression 'volitional difference,' *velle diversa*. The third, which alone concerns us, is as follows.

Tertia autem diversitas in quam liberum arbitrium potest, attenditur secundum differentiam mutationis. Quae quidem non consistit in hoc quod aliquis diversa velit: nam et ipse Deus vult ut diversa fiant secundum quod convenit diversis temporibus et personis; sed mutatio liberi arbitrii consistit in hoc quod aliquis illud idem et pro eodem tempore non velit quod prius volebat, aut velit quod prius nolebat. Et haec diversitas non per se pertinet ad rationem liberi arbitrii, sed accidit ei secundum conditionem naturae mutabilis: sicut non est de ratione visivae potentiae quod diversimode videat; sed hoc contingit quandoque propter diversam dispositionem videntis, cuius oculus quandoque est purus, quandoque autem turbatus.

Et similiter etiam mutabilitas seu diversitas liberi arbitrii non est de ratione eius, sed accidit ei inquantum est in natura mutabili. Mutatur enim in nobis liberum arbitrium ex causa intrinseca, et ex causa extrinseca. Ex causa quidem intrinseca, vel propter rationem, puta cum quis aliquid prius nesciebat quod postea cognoscit; vel propter appetitum qui quandoque sic est dispositus per passionem vel habitum, ut tendat in aliquid sicut in sibi conveniens, quod cessante passione vel habitu sibi conveniens non est. Ex causa vero extrinseca, puta cum Deus immutat voluntatem hominis per gratiam de malo in bonum, secundum illud *Prov.* XXI, 1: *Cor regum in manu Dei, et quocumque voluerit vertet illud.*[47]

46 See the way St Thomas argues that the will of the demons cannot change and that man's can change, in *De veritate*, q. 24, aa. 10–11.
47 [But a third diversity in regard to which free will has power is considered according to difference in the change; that difference does not consist in this, that someone can will various things, for even God himself wills that various things be done according to what suits different times and persons; but the change of free will consists in this, that someone does not will the very same thing at the same time which earlier he did will, or that he wills what earlier he did not will. And this diversity does not belong per se to the nature of free will, but happens to it accidentally, according to the condition of a changeable nature: just as it does not belong to the nature of the visual potency that it sees in different ways, but this happens sometimes because of the different disposition of the one seeing, his eye being sometimes pure but sometimes disturbed.

The point is quite clear. Per se the will does not change, and so the angels decide their eternal destiny by a single act. *Per accidens* the will does change, not because it is a will, nor because it is a free will, but because it is *in natura mutabili* and either new knowledge, a modification of passion or of habit, or divine grace intervenes.

It is perhaps worth noting that in the *De veritate* St Thomas had discussed the change of the will effected by grace. *De veritate*, q. 22, a. 8, opens with two objections: the first is *cor regum in manu Dei*; the second is a snippet from the *glossa Augustini* to the effect that God operates in the hearts of men inclining their wills as he pleases.[48] The account of this operation is as follows.

> Cum igitur Deus voluntatem immutat, facit ut praecedenti inclinationi succedat alia inclinatio, et ita quod prima aufertur, et secunda manet. Unde illud ad quod inducit voluntatem, non est contrarium inclinationi iam existenti, sed inclinationi quae prius inerat ...[49]
>
> Immutat autem voluntatem dupliciter. Uno modo movendo tantum; quando scilicet voluntatem movet ad aliquid volendum, sine hoc quod aliquam formam imprimat voluntati; sicut sine appositione alicuius habitus, quandoque facit ut homo velit hoc quod prius non volebat. Alio vero modo imprimendo aliquam formam in ipsam voluntatem. Sicuti enim ex ipsa natura, quam Deus voluntati dedit, inclinatur voluntas in aliquid volendum ... ita ex aliquo superaddito,

---

And similarly too, changeableness or diversity of free will does not pertain to its nature, but is there accidentally inasmuch as it is in a changeable nature. For free will is changed in us both from an intrinsic cause and from an extrinsic cause. From an intrinsic cause, either on account of reason, as when a person did not know earlier something which he knows afterwards; or on account of desire, which is sometimes disposed in such a way by passion or by habit that it tends to something as to a thing suitable to it, which with the cessation of passion or habit is not suitable to it. And from an extrinsic cause, as when God changes a human will from evil to good through grace, according to that text of Proverbs 21.1: *The heart of kings is in the hand of God, and he will turn it wherever he will*] *De malo*, q. 16, a. 5 c.

48 *De veritate*, q. 22, a. 8. In *Summa theologiae*, 1-2, q. 79, a. 1, ad 1m, one is told that this *glossa* is from Augustine's *De gratia et libero arbitrio*.

49 [When, therefore, God changes the will, he brings it about that another inclination succeeds the previous one, and in such a way that the first is taken away and the second remains. And so, that to which the will is led is not contrary to a presently existing inclination, but to an inclination that was previously there] The passage continues on the theme of liberty as noncoercion; see above, note 33.

sicut est gratia vel virtus, inclinatur ulterius ad volendum aliquid aliud, ad quod prius non erat determinata naturali inclinatione.[50]

If one may presume a similar field of concepts in *De veritate*, q. 22, a. 8, and *De veritate*, q. 24, aa. 7–12, the function of the habit as a *gratia sanans* becomes quite plain. On the one hand, the sinner is confined by the law of psychological continuity to a perpetual repetition of his sins. On the other, the infusion of grace constitutes a permanent change in the inclination or spontaneous orientation of the will: it plucks out the heart of stone that made the sinner a slave to sin; it implants a heart of flesh to initiate a new continuity in justice. Finally, just as a vicious habit is not needed to set up slavery to sin, for a mere disposition suffices, so also the infusion of habitual grace is not the sole means God has for the liberation of liberty, for not only by imprinting a permanent form but also by a simple motion does God change the will of man. However, this last point calls for a separate inquiry.

3   The Infused Habit as a Premotion

In the *Summa theologiae* St Thomas employs an analogy from Aristotelian physics to correlate the three elements in the process of justification: the infusion of grace is *motio moventis*, the free acts of faith and repentance are *motus mobilis*, and the remission of sins is *perventio in finem* or *consummatio motus*.[51]

The same analogy had already been used in the discussion of the passions. Thus:

Agens autem naturale duplicem effectum inducit in patiens: nam primo quidem dat formam, secundo autem dat motum consequen-

---

50 [Now (God) changes the will in two ways. In one way, just by moving (it); namely, when he moves the will to will something, without imprinting some form on the will; as without the addition of some habit he sometimes brings it about that man wills what earlier he did not will. But (God moves it) in another way by imprinting some form on the will itself; for as the will is inclined to will something from the very nature which God gave it ... so through something added on, such as is grace or a virtue, the will is inclined further to willing something else, to which it was not earlier determined by a natural inclination] *De veritate*, q. 22, a. 8.
51 [the motion of the moving (force) ... the movement of the movable thing ... arrival at the end ... completion of the movement] *Summa theologiae*, 1-2, q. 113, a. 6.

tem formam; sicut generans dat corpori gravitatem, et motum con-
sequentem ipsam. Et ipsa gravitas, quae est principium motus ad
locum connaturalem propter gravitatem, potest quodammodo dici
amor naturalis ... Prima ergo immutatio appetitus ab appetibili
vocatur amor, qui nihil est aliud quam complacentia appetibilis; et
ex hac complacentia sequitur motus in appetibile, qui est desider-
ium; et ultimo quies quae est gaudium.[52]

Similarly:

Diversitas autem activi vel motivi quantum ad virtutem movendi,
potest accipi in passionibus animae secundum similitudinem
agentium naturalium. Omne enim movens trahit quodammodo ad
se patiens, vel a se repellit. Trahendo quidem ad se, tria facit in ipso.
Nam primo quidem, dat ei inclinationem vel aptitudinem ut in
ipsum tendat: sicut cum corpus leve, quod est sursum, dat levitatem
corpori generato, per quam habet inclinationem vel aptitudinem ad
hoc quod sit sursum. Secundo, si corpus generatum est extra locum
proprium, dat ei moveri ad locum. Tertio, dat ei quiescere, in locum
cum pervenerit: quia ex eadem causa aliquid quiescit in loco, per
quam movebatur ad locum. Et similiter intelligendum est de causa
repulsionis. In motibus autem appetitivae partis ...[53]

52 [A natural agent produces a twofold effect in the patient; for first of all it
gives a form, and secondly it gives the movement consequent on form; as
the generating (agent) gives a body gravity and the movement consequent
on that (form). And this gravity, which is the principle of movement towards the place that is connatural because of gravity, can in a certain way be
called natural love ... Therefore the first change of appetite by the desirable
is called love, which is nothing else than complacency in the desirable; and
from this complacency there follows movement toward the desirable, which
is desire; and finally the rest which is joy] Ibid. q. 26, a. 2.
53 [But the diversity of active or motive, insofar as it regards the power to
move, can be understood in the passions of the soul according to the likeness of natural agents. For every moving (power) in a certain way draws the
patient to itself or repels it. Now drawing it to itself, it operates three things
in the patient. For first it gives the patient an inclination or aptitude to tend
to it, as when a light body that is above gives lightness to the body affected,
through which it has an inclination or aptitude to be above. Secondly, if the
affected body is away from its proper place, it gives it motion towards its
place. Thirdly, it gives it rest when it has come to its place, because something rests in its place from the same cause through which it was moved to
its place. And we are to understand in the same way the case of repulsion.
But in motions of the appetitive faculty ...] Ibid. q. 23, a. 4.

The use of the same analogy in the discussion of justification is manifest, not merely from the terms *motio moventis, motus mobilis,* and *perventio in finem,* but also from a number of other indications. In the article on *gratia operans* one reads:

> Si vero accipiatur gratia pro habituali dono, sic etiam duplex est gratiae effectus, sicut et cuiuslibet alterius formae: quorum primus est esse, secundus est operatio; sicut caloris operatio est facere calidum, et exterior calefactio.[54]

Again in the definition of justification:

> ... iustificatio passive accepta importat motum ad iustitiam; sicut et calefactio motum ad calorem.[55]

And in describing the instantaneous character of the free act in justification:

> ... in eodem instanti in quo forma acquiritur, incipit res operari secundum formam: sicut ignis statim cum est generatus, movetur sursum; et si motus eius esset instantaneus, in eodem instanti compleretur. Motus autem liberi arbitrii, qui est velle, non est successivus, sed instantaneus. Et ideo non oportet quod iustificatio impii sit successiva.[56]

Now there is no difficulty in understanding why St Thomas should have turned to this analogy with physical theory when describing the transmutation effected at the instant of justification. As we have seen, there are two forms of psychological continuity in man: servitude to sin and the liberty of the sons of God. The instant of justification is the shift from one form to the

---

54 [translation in note 1, above] Ibid. q. 111, a. 2.
55 [justification, taken passively, means a movement to righteousness as does also heating mean a movement to heat] Ibid. q. 113, a. 1.
56 [in the same instant in which the form is acquired, the thing begins to operate according to the form; as fire moves upward as soon as it is generated; and if its movement were instantaneous, it would be completed in the same instant. But the movement of free will, which is to will, is not successive but instantaneous. And therefore it is not necessary that justification of the sinner be successive] Ibid. a. 7, ad 4m.

other; it puts an end to servitude; it is the beginning and the foundation of the liberty of grace. To make it perfectly plain that St Thomas did not fall into the error of so many minor theologians who deal in empty categories, let us transcribe a typical passage from the commentary on Romans.

> Alio modo dicitur aliquis esse sub lege, quasi a lege coactus; et sic dicitur esse sub lege, qui non voluntarie ex amore, sed timore cogitur legem observare. Talis autem caret gratia, quae si adesset, inclinaret voluntatem ad observantiam legis, ut ex amore moralia eius praecepta impleret. Sic igitur quamdiu aliquis sic est sub lege, ut non impleat voluntarie legem, peccatum in eo dominatur, ex quo voluntas hominis inclinatur ut velit id quod est contrarium legi ... Hanc autem gratiam facientem homines libere legem implere, non conferebant legalia sacramenta, sed conferunt eam sacramenta Christi.[57]

Thus St Thomas affirms that if an individual observes the law with regret and through fear then he is without grace, for grace inclines the will to love fulfilment of the law. Just as the sinner to avoid sin must be under a continuous and intolerable strain, so the justified enjoys the opposite spontaneity; if he is to sin, he must labor against his conscience.

Once this is understood, one readily grasps why the infusion of habitual grace is a premotion. It is a change from one spontaneity to another, a straightening out of man, placing his higher faculties in subordination to God and his lower faculties in subordination to reason.[58] When such a change is produced in adult consciousness,[59] it naturally gives rise to acts of free will, acts of faith and of repentance, that both acknowledge this change of attitude and result from it.

57 [Another way in which someone is said to be under the law is to be, as it were, coerced by the law; and one who is coerced by fear to observe the law, instead of (obeying it) voluntarily out of love, is said to be under the law in this way. But such a person lacks grace, which if it were present would incline the will to observance of the law, so that one would fulfil its moral precepts out of love. Thus then, as long as one is under the law in this way, so that he does not voluntarily fulfil the law, sin has dominion in him, from which a person's will is so inclined that he wills what is contrary to the law ... And the sacraments of the law did not confer this grace, which makes men fulfil the law freely, but the sacraments of Christ do confer it] *In Rom.*, c. 6, lect. 3 [§§ 497–98]; see *Summa theologiae*, 1-2, q. 108, a. 1, ad 2m.

58 *Summa theologiae*, 1-2, q. 113, a. 1.

59 St Thomas excepts the *pueri, furiosi*, and *amentes*: Ibid. a. 3 [ad 1m].

... Deus non sine nobis nos iustificat, quia per motum liberi arbitrii, dum iustificamur, Dei iustitiae consentimus. Ille tamen motus non est causa gratiae, sed effectus. Unde tota operatio pertinet ad gratiam.[60]

Just as the generation of fire results in immediate burning, so the infusion of the virtues results in immediate acts of virtue.[61] For habitual grace is like any other form: it gives not only *esse* but also *operari*.[62]

One must not suppose, however, that St Thomas always analyzed the instant of justification in the above manner. In the *De veritate*, for example, obstinacy in sin is defined as an incapacity to cooperate with grace.[63] Now

60 [God does not justify us without us, because we consent to the justice of God through a movement of free will while we are being justified. But that movement is the effect of grace, not its cause. And so the whole operation pertains to grace] Ibid. q. 111, a. 2, ad 2m.

61 Ibid. q. 113, a. 7, ad 4m.

62 Ibid. q. 111, a. 2 c. Fr del Prado in his *De gratia et libero arbitrio* expresses the opinion that St Thomas considered the will to be purely passive in the free acts elicited at the instant of justification. [Del Prado's position is treated by Lange, *De gratia* (see above, chapter 1, note 1) 472–74, § 598; Lange refers to pp. 192–239 of vol. 1 of del Prado's *De gratia et libero arbitrio* (see above, p. 3, note 1), where del Prado treats *Summa theologiae*, 1-2, q. 111, a. 2; see Lonergan's references below, pp. 135–36, notes 73, 74, and 76.] His argument seems to be that justification is an operative grace, which is not without foundation in *Summa theologiae*, 1-2, q. 111, a. 2, ob. 2 and ad 2m, and that when grace is operative then the will is *mota et non movens*, which is clearly stated in the corpus. I am inclined to disagree with this view, for St Thomas's definition of habitual grace as cooperative is that it is a principle of free acts ('inquantum vero est principium operis meritorii, quod etiam ex libero arbitrio procedit, dicitur cooperans' [insofar as it is the principle of a meritorious work, which proceeds from free will too, it is called cooperative]) while his definition of cooperative grace is *mens mota et movens* (ibid. c.). Further, that the grace of justification is purely and simply operative is not St Thomas's statement so much as that of the objicient, while St Thomas does say that 'gratia operans et cooperans est eadem gratia; sed distinguitur secundum diversos effectus' [operative grace and cooperative are the same grace; but (the grace) is distinguished according to (its) different effects] (ibid. ad 4m). Finally, St Thomas's eagerness to agree with Augustine, an eagerness that is palpable to anyone reviewing the development of his thought on grace, would hardly lead him to interpret St Augustine's *non iustificabit te sine te* [(God) will not justify you without you] by a passivity parallel to the passivity with which he interprets St Augustine's *quam Deus in nobis sine nobis operatur* [which God operates in us without us]. The basic problem of habitual grace as *operans et cooperans* was to find different meanings for these two texts. See below, n. 64.

63 *De veritate*, q. 24, a. 11; see ibid. a. 10.

this is meaningless when it is fully grasped that grace is what gives the capacity to cooperate, that it plucks out the heart of stone, however black, that will not cooperate, and gives the heart of flesh that leaps to cooperation. What, then, was the course of St Thomas's development on this point?

First, there exists a basic uniformity. At all times St Thomas distinguished between God's infusion of the virtues and our consent to that infusion. The former is always operative: *quam Deus in nobis sine nobis operatur.* The latter is always cooperative: *qui creavit te sine te, non iustificabit te sine te.*[64] Further, the act of consent is always causally dependent on the infusion of grace: for such acts are meritorious,[65] and without grace there is no merit. Finally, in the commentary on the *Sentences* and the *De veritate* the causal dependence of the act of consent appears to be solely with regard to the *forma meriti*; but in the *Summa theologiae* the dependence regards not only the *forma meriti* but also, as we have seen, the *motus liberi arbitrii* itself.

Thus, in the commentary on the *Sentences* there is the question, Do the free acts in justification precede the infusion of grace?[66] The answer is a series of distinctions. What is meant by precedence? If the reference is to a temporal order, the answer is negative, for the infusion of grace, the free acts, and the remission of sins are simultaneous. If the reference is to a causal order, then is it material or formal causality that is understood? For in material causality the free acts as dispositions precede; but in formal causality the free acts must follow.

64 [which God operates in us without us ... the one who created you without you, will not justify you without you] On these texts we have the following solutions. *Super II Sententiarum*, d. 27, q. 1, a. 2, ad 7m: '... Deus non iustificat nos sine nobis consentientibus ... Iustificat tamen nos sine nobis virtutem causantibus' [God does not justify us without us consenting ... But he justifies us without us causing a virtue].
  De veritate, q. 28, a. 3, ad 17: '... Deus virtutes in nobis operatur sine nobis virtutes causantibus, non tamen sine nobis consentientibus' [God effects virtues in us without us causing the virtues, but not without our consent].
  Summa theologiae, 1-2, q. 55, a. 4, ad 6m: '... virtus infusa causatur in nobis a Deo sine nobis agentibus, non tamen sine nobis consentientibus. Et sic est intelligendum quod dicitur, *quam Deus in nobis sine nobis operatur.* Quae vero per nos aguntur, Deus in nobis causat non sine nobis agentibus: ipse enim operatur in omni voluntate et natura' [infused virtue is caused in us by God without us acting, but not without us consenting. This is how we are to understand the words 'which God operates in us without us.' But those things that are done through us God causes in us not without our acting; for God operates in every will and nature].
65 *Summa theologiae*, 1-2, q. 112, a. 2, ad 1m, and loc. par.
66 *Super IV Sententiarum*, d. 17, q. 1, a. 4, qc. 2.

In the *De veritate* St Thomas explicitly rejects his later seriation that places the free acts after the infusion of grace but prior to the remission of sins. The infusion of grace and the remission of sins admit no intermediate.[67] Thus the free acts must either precede both or follow both. But they cannot simply precede, for they cannot be meritorious before grace is infused. Nor can they simply follow, for they are dispositions to the remission of sin.[68] It may be noted that this position in the *De veritate* is all the more surprising in view of the fact that St Thomas had already formulated his view that the infusion of grace involved a change in the inclination of the will.[69]

The root difficulty seems to have been the difficulty of systematizing Pelagian error, for only gradually does St Thomas appear to have acquired clear and distinct concepts of its many aspects. In the commentary on the *Sentences* Pelagianism seems to be simply the negation of the supernatural order.[70] In the *De veritate*, as we have seen, the moral impotence of the sinner adds a new aspect: it is Pelagian to say that without grace man can avoid further sin.[71] But the first mention of Pelagianism in connection with the *initium iustificationis* and the *initium fidei* is not in the treatment of the preparation for justification in the commentary on the *Sentences*[72] nor even in the *De veritate*[73] but, to my knowledge, in the *Contra Gentiles*.[74] Since there one finds the prevenience of divine grace formulated in terms of *motio moventis praecedit motum mobilis*,[75] one need look no further for the origin of the *Summa theologiae*'s series, in which the infusion of grace is *motio moventis*, the free acts are *motus mobilis*, and the remission of sin is *consummatio motus*.[76]

4   Conclusion

The foregoing study of St Thomas's thought on habitual grace as operative and cooperative has drawn attention to the following points. First, there is a

67 *De veritate*, q. 28, a. 8 c.
68 Ibid. and ad 1m to ad 7m (2ae ser.).
69 Ibid. q. 22, a. 8.
70 See *Super II Sententiarum*, d. 28, q. 1, aa. 1–3; see loc. par.
71 *De veritate*, q. 24, a. 12; see *Super II Sententiarum*, d. 28, q. 1, a. 2.
72 *Super II Sententiarum*, d. 28, q. 1, a. 4.
73 *De veritate*, q. 24, a. 15.
74 *Summa contra Gentiles*, 3, cc. 149 [ad fin.] and 152 [ad fin.].
75 [the motion of the moving (force) precedes the movement of the movable thing] Ibid. c. 149 [init.].
76 *Summa theologiae*, 1-2, q. 113, aa. 6–8.

development with regard to the role of the virtues in perfecting man: in the commentary on the *Sentences*, when habitual grace alone is operative and cooperative, the habits alone are considered as means of human perfection; in the *De veritate*, when an actual grace is recognized as cooperative, it is affirmed that a creature cannot get along without divine aid and guidance no matter how perfect his virtues; in the *Summa theologiae* actual grace is operative as well as cooperative, and the gifts of the Holy Spirit are defined in terms of connaturality to motion by an external principle. Second, there is development with regard to the necessity of virtues: in the commentary on the *Sentences* this necessity is merely in terms of statistical law; in the *De veritate* statistical law gives way to relative impossibility. Coincident with this development is a fuller grasp of the nature of Pelagianism and the transfusion of twelfth-century Augustinian thought into the Thomist synthesis. Third, there is development with regard to the prevenient action of grace on free will: in the commentary on the *Sentences* and the *De veritate* the free acts that take place in justification are informed by the infused grace; in the *Summa contra Gentiles* the prevenience of grace is expressed in terms of *motio moventis* and *motus mobilis*; in the *Summa theologiae* this terminology is developed on the analogy of Aristotelian physics, and the motion of free will as well as its information is attributed to the simultaneously infused habitual grace.

It would, perhaps, not be unreasonable to conclude that St Thomas's concept of actual grace underwent a concomitant variation.

I-4

St Thomas's Theory of Operation

In working out St Thomas's thought on habitual grace as operative and cooperative, it was possible to avoid speculative issues by appealing to parallel passages which sufficiently explained the analogies involved and the ideas employed. Unfortunately, now that we have to deal with actual grace, so simple a procedure can no longer be followed. St Thomas found the idea of the habit ready made, but he had to think out for himself the analogy of nature that corresponds to actual grace; and, if in this long labor he did not draw upon absolutely all the resources of the Arabic, Platonist, and Aristotelian philosophies at his disposal, at least his interpreters have shown a marked proclivity to exploit the potentialities which he neglected. Accordingly, to discover and follow him in his thought on actual grace, we must attain some familiarity with his historical and speculative background; in particular we must have precise ideas, and precisely his ideas, on the nature of operation, premotion, application, the certitude of providence, universal instrumentality, and the analogy of operation; we must also know the development of his thought on the idea of freedom, the various ways in which at different times he conceived God to move the will, the meaning of his central theorem of divine transcendence, and, to some extent, its relation to subsequent theories. Such questions naturally divide into two sections: those that deal with the theory of operation in a general way; those that refer specifically to the will and to divine control over the will. The former are the present concern; the latter will be discussed in chapter 5.

1   The Idea of Causation

Causation is the common feature of both operation and cooperation; its nature is of fundamental importance in this inquiry. But if St Thomas certainly disagreed with Hume, who held causation to be purely subjective, it is less clear what object he considered to constitute the objective reference of the proposition 'A causes B.' Was causation for him something in between A and B? Or was it simply the relation of dependence of B on A? Or was it some entity added to A as actually causing? Let us take each of these three views in turn.[1]

As to the first view, that causation is in between cause and effect, St Thomas constantly and explicitly denied it in the case of divine activity. Avicennist biology had distinguished between a *virtus motiva imperans* and a *virtus motiva efficiens*, and St Albert had drawn a parallel distinction between the *virtus divina increata* and a *virtus divina creata*.[2] But St Thomas, while he used the biological opinion at least in his commentary on the *Sentences*,[3] always asserted that God was his own virtue,[4] operated without any mediating virtue,[5] indeed operated *immediatione virtutis*.[6] The matter is less clear

1 On St Thomas's theory of operation, see also chapter 3 of our *Verbum* [see above, p. 48, note 15].
2 The *virtus motiva efficiens* was perhaps a gaseous substance; it was 'infusa in nervis et musculis contrahens chorda et ligamenta coniuncta membris, aut relaxans et extendens' [infused in the nerves and muscles, contracting the cords and ligaments joined to the members, or relaxing and extending (them)]. Albert, *Summa de creaturis*, 2, q. 68, a. 2 [*BA* 35: 560–61]. On the *virtus divina creata*, see Adam Sauer, *Die theologische Lehre der materiellen Welt beim heiligen Albert dem Grossen* (Würzburg: Richard Mayr, 1935) 133–36.
3 *Super II Sententiarum*, d. 18, q. 2, a. 3, ad 1m; see *Summa theologiae*, 1, q. 75, a. 3, ad 3m.
4 *Super librum De causis*, lect. 20, § 366; *Super I Sententiarum*, d. 37, q. 1, a. 1, ad 4m; *De potentia*, q. 3, a. 7 c. [ad fin.].
5 *Super II Sententiarum*, d. 15, q. 3, a. 1, ad 3m.
6 This idea, based on the parallel of the real and logical orders (*In II Metaphys.*, lect. 2, §§ 294–98), was derived from the *Posterior Analytics* (*Super I Sententiarum*, d. 37, q. 1, a. 1, ad 4m; *Summa contra Gentiles*, 3, c. 70 [§ 2464]), probably from Aristotle's discussion of many middle terms for one conclusion (*In II Post. anal.*, lect. 19, § 580). It is opposed to *immediatio suppositi* (*De potentia*, q. 3, a. 7 [ad fin.]); it applies to any principal cause (*Super I Sententiarum*, d. 12, q. 1, a. 3, ad 4m; d. 37, q. 1, a. 1, ad 4m; *In II Phys.*, lect. 6, § 196; it is closely related to the analogy of operation treated below. [Beginning with this footnote, references to *Summa contra Gentiles* at times give Marietti paragraph numbers (see bibliography), from either vol. 2 (Books 1 and 2) or vol. 3 (Books 3 and 4); but Latin quotations are from the Leonine edition.]

with regard to causation by creatures. Even in later works there is a variety of expressions which appear to imply something in between agent and recipient.[7] Still, it should seem that these are but modes of expression or of conception; for what is in between, if it is something, must be either substance or accident; but causation as such can hardly be another substance; and if it were an accident, it would have to be either the miracle of an accident without a subject, or else, what St Thomas denied,[8] an accident in transit from one subject to another.

On the second view, causation is simply the relation of dependence in the effect with respect to the cause. This is the Aristotelian position presented in the *Physics* and explained by St Thomas as follows. First of all, this analysis prescinded from the case of the mover being moved accidentally; for instance, a terrestrial body acts through contact and cannot touch without being touched; but this does not prove that the cause as cause undergoes change but only that the terrestrial body as cause does so.[9] In the second place, it was argued that the emergence of a motion or change involved the actuation of both the active potency of the cause and the passive potency of the effect.[10] In the third place, the thesis was stated: one and the same act actuates both potencies,[11] and this act is the motion produced in the object moved.[12] Fourthly, there came the ground of this position: if causation, *actio*, were an entity inherent in the cause, then, since it is a motion, it would follow either that 'omne movens movetur,' or else that motion inheres in a subject without the subject being moved; but the latter is contradictory, and the former would preclude the idea of an immovable mover; therefore, causation is not inherent in the cause but in the effect.[13] Finally, the objective difference between action and passion

---

7 For example, *Summa theologiae*, 1, q. 45, a. 3, ad 2m; *In III Phys.*, lect. 4, § 307; lect. 5, § 316.
8 *De potentia*, q. 3, a. 7 c. [init.].
9 *In III Phys.*, lect. 4, § 302.
10 Ibid. § 305. Definitions of active and passive potency: *In IX Metaphys.*, lect. 1, §§ 1768–85.
11 *In III Phys.*, lect. 4, § 306: '... oportet unum actum esse utriusque, scilicet moventis et moti: idem enim est quod est a movente ut a causa agente, et quod est in moto ut in patiente et recipiente' [therefore it is necessary that there be just one act of the two, namely, of the mover and of the moved; for it is the same thing that is from the mover as from agent cause, and is in the patient as receiver].
12 Ibid. §§ 303, 306.
13 Ibid. lect. 5, § 311. Just as motion in the cause as such implies an infinite series of movers with no first mover, so motion in the self-determining agent

was explained: both are really identical with the motion of the recipient; they differ notionally, for action is this motion as from the cause, *motus huius ut ab hoc,* while passion is the same motion as inhering in the effect, *motus huius ut in hoc.*[14]

It would seem that St Thomas accepted this Aristotelian analysis as true and did not merely study it as a detached and indifferent commentator. Not only did he repeat the same exposition in commenting the parallel passage in the *Metaphysics,*[15] while in the *De anima* he argued that sound and hearing, instances of action and passion, must be one and the same reality, else every mover would also be moved;[16] but in works that are entirely his own the same view at least occasionally turns up. In the *Summa theologiae* the definition of actual grace appeals to the third book of the *Physics* for the doctrine that 'actus ... moventis in moto est motus';[17] the analysis of the idea of creation was based upon the Aristotelian identification of action and passion with motion;[18] and the fact that this identification involved no confusion of action with passion was adduced to solve the objection against the Blessed Trinity, namely, that since the divine Persons were identical with the divine substance they must be identical with one another.[19] Still, this is not the whole story. In his commentary on the *Sentences* St Thomas brushed aside the notion that action and passion were

---

as agent involves an infinite regress of the self-determination. For a series of rediscoveries of this particular case of the Aristotelian argument, see Ludovicus de San, *Tractatus De Deo uno* (Louvain: C. Peeters, 1894), vol. 1, pp. 181–87; Wilhelm Hentrich, *Gregor von Valencia und der Molinismus* (Innsbruck: F. Rauch, 1928); Santo Santoro, 'Valenzianismo o Delfinismo?' *Estratto della Miscellanea Francescana* 38 (1938) 195–210; Agustino Trape, 'Il concorso divino nel pensiero di Egidio Romano,' unpublished thesis 615 (Rome: Gregorian University, 1938). For the difficulties of the opposite viewpoint when it comes to reconciling divine liberty with divine immutability, see Dominicus Bañez, *Scholastica commentaria in primam partem Summae theologicae S. Thomae Aquinatis,* 1, q. 19, a. 10 (Roma, 1584, p. 380 [Madrid: Editorial F.E.D.A., 1934, pp. 437–45; the Madrid edition has been used to check all of Lonergan's references to Bañez]); he had not thought of R.P. Garrigou-Lagrange's 'clair-obscur' but was in exactly the same fix [Reginald Garrigou-Lagrange, *Le sens du mystère et le clair-obscur intellectuel: Nature et surnaturel* (Paris: Desclée de Brouwer & Cie, 1934); see also below, p. 276].

14   *In III Phys.,* lect. 5, § 320.
15   *In XI Metaphys.,* lect. 9, §§ 2308–13.
16   *In III De anima,* lect. 2, § 592.
17   *Summa theologiae,* 1-2, q. 110, a. 2.
18   Ibid. 1, q. 45, a. 2 [ob. 2 and ad 2m].
19   Ibid. q. 28, a. 3, ad 1m.

one and the same reality,[20] while in the parallel passage in the *Summa theologiae* a solution is found that does not compromise the authority of Aristotle.[21] This difference involves a changed attitude, prior to the *Pars prima* and perhaps posterior to the *De potentia*,[22] raising the question of the initial Thomist view.

In earlier works, then, the theory of causation seems to have been worked out on the analogy of the familiar distinction between the *esse ad* and the *esse in* of the relation. In action one has to distinguish between a formal content described as *ut ab agente* or *ut ab agente in aliud procedens*, and, on the other hand, a reality, substantial or accidental, termed the *principium actionis* or the *causa actionis* or even loosely *actio*. This terminology is to be found no less in the commentary on the *Sentences* than in the *De potentia*,[23] but at least in the latter work it also is quite clear that the formal content is no more than a notional entity. In the two passages quoted below, the reader will be able to verify the following six propositions: (*A*) change from rest to activity is change in an improper and metaphorical sense; (*B*) the reverse change from activity to rest takes place without any real change in the agent; (*C*)

---

20 *Super II Sententiarum*, d. 40, q. 1, a. 4, ad 1m.
21 *Summa theologiae*, 1-2, q. 20, a. 6 c. and ad 2m.
22 Compare *De potentia*, q. 3, aa. 2–3, and q. 8, a. 2, ad 7m, with *Summa theologiae*, 1, q. 45, aa. 2–3, and q. 28, a. 3, ad 1m.
23 *Super I Sententiarum*, d. 32, q. 1, a. 1 [post med.]; *De potentia*, q. 7, a. 9, ad 7m. St Thomas used the term *actio* to denote: (*A*) the principle from which the action proceeds; (*B*) the effect which the action produces; (*C*) various aspects of the producing. In the sense (*A*), *actio* is the divine substance, the accidental act in the creature (*actio media intrinseca*), the accidental act in the medium (*actio media extrinseca*). In the sense (*B*), *actio* means perfection in general, *energeia*, or perfection produced in the agent (immanent action) or perfection produced in a subject distinct from the agent (transient action). In the sense (*C*), called by some later writers 'transient action,' we have the notional relation of the cause to the effect, the formal content of *ut ab agente*, the causal influxus of *actus ab agente in aliud*, and the Aristotelian real relation of the motion in the effect to the cause. While St Thomas always treats each issue with sufficient clarity for the matter in hand, the ambiguity of his terminology results in mystification for a reader who demands a complete explanation of everything in each isolated text. Particularly complex is the account of the distinction between immanent and transient action (*In IX Metaphys.*, lect. 8, §§ 1864–65; *Super I Sententiarum*, d. 40, q. 1, a. 1, ad 1m; *De veritate*, q. 8, a. 6; *Summa contra Gentiles*, 2, c. 1 [§§ 853, 855]; *Summa theologiae*, 1, q. 18, a. 3, ad 1m; q. 54, aa. 1–2). Other sources of difficulty are the *actio media* from the *Liber De causis* (see above, p. 67, notes 4–6 [*res media*], and *Summa theologiae*, 1, q. 54, a. 1, ad 3m, the tendency to use the term *operatio* to denote motion in the broad sense (see below, p. 84, note 84), and above all the issue treated in the text.

when the agent is acting there is no composition of agent and action; (*D*)
what remains unchanged is the *principium* or *causa actionis*; (*E*) what comes
and goes without changing the agent is the formal content, *ut ab agente*; (*F*)
the analysis holds even in the case of a created agent such as fire.

> Et ita relatio est aliquid inhaerens, licet non ex hoc ipso quod est
> relatio; sicut et actio ex hoc quod est actio, consideratur ut ab
> agente; inquantum vero est accidens, consideratur ut in subiecto
> agente. Et ideo nihil prohibet quod esse desinat huiusmodi accidens
> (*B*) sine mutatione eius in quo est, quia sua ratio non perficitur
> prout est in ipso subiecto, sed prout transit in aliud; quo sublato,
> ratio huius accidentis tollitur (*E*) quidem quantum ad actum, sed
> manet (*D*) quantum ad causam; sicut et subtracta materia, tollitur
> calefactio (*F*), licet maneat calefactionis causa.[24]

> Quod autem attribuitur alicui ut ab eo in aliud procedens non facit
> compositionem cum eo, sicut (*C*) nec actio cum agente ... sine ulla
> mutatione eius quod ad aliud refertur, potest relatio desinere ex sola
> mutatione alterius, sicut etiam de actione patet (*B*), quod non est
> motus secundum actionem nisi metaphorice et improprie; sicut (*A*)
> exiens de otio in actum mutari dicimus, quod non esset si relatio vel
> actio significaret aliquid in subiecto manens.[25]

24 [And so a relation is something inhering (in a subject), though that does
not result from the mere fact that it is a relation; as action, too, from the
fact that it is action, is considered as from an agent, but as an accident it is
considered as in the acting subject. And therefore, there is nothing to prevent an accident of this kind (*B*) from ceasing to be without (involving) a
change of that (subject) in which it is, because its being is not realized insofar as it is in that subject, but insofar as it passes on to another; with the
removal of that (passing on), the being of this accident is removed (*E*) in
what regards the act but remains (*D*) in what regards the cause; as is the
case also when, with the removal of the material (to be heated), the heating
(*F*) is removed, though the cause of heating remains] *De potentia*, q. 7, a. 9,
ad 7m.

25 [But that which is attributed to something as proceeding from it to something else does not enter into composition with it, as (*C*) neither does action (enter into composition) with the agent ... without any change in that
which is related to another, a relation can cease to be through the change
alone of the other; as also is clear about action (*B*), that there is no movement as regards action except metaphorically and improperly; as we say that
(*A*) one passing from leisure to act is changed; which would not be the case if
relation or action signified something remaining in the subject] Ibid. a. 8 c.

If our interpretation of these passages is correct, then at least in the *De potentia* St Thomas had arrived at a theory of action that was in essential agreement with Aristotle's. Evidently the two terminologies differ completely: on the Aristotelian view action is a relation of dependence in the effect; on the Thomist view action is a formal content attributed to the cause as causing. But these differences only serve to emphasize the fundamental identity of the two positions: both philosophers keenly realized that causation must not be thought to involve any real change in the cause as cause; Aristotle, because he conceived action as a motion, placed it in the effect; St Thomas, who conceived it simply as a formal content, was able to place it in the cause; but though they proceed by different routes, both arrive at the same goal, namely, that the objective difference between *posse agere* and *actu agere* is attained without any change emerging in the cause as such.[26]

This real agreement in terminological difference solves the problem of St Thomas's thought on causation. John of St Thomas listed the passages in which action is placed, now in the agent and now in the recipient; from this he drew the conclusion that action, according to St Thomas, was inchoatively in the agent and perfectively in the recipient.[27] But in point of fact St Thomas simply had two ways of saying that action involved no new entity in the agent; and so far was he from differing really from Aristotle that he seems to have been quite unaware of even his terminological departure from the Aristotelian position.[28] This latter fact not only solves Cajetan's

26 To later Scholastics this seemed impossible a priori: they held that 'Peter not acting' must be really different from 'Peter acting.' They refused to believe that St Thomas could disagree with them on this; in fact, St Thomas disagreed. See *In III Phys.*, lect. 5, §322, on the analogy of the predicaments; see *Super I Sententiarum*, d. 32, q. 1, a. 1; *De potentia*, q. 7, a. 8. For an apriorist attempt to eliminate this analogy, see F.-X. Maquart, 'Saint Thomas et l'action transitive,' *Revue de philosophie* 32 (1925) 142.

27 *Joannis a Sancto Thoma Naturalis Philosophia*, 1, q. 14, a. 4 (ed. Beato Reiser [Turin: Marietti, 1933], vol. 2, pp. 309–15).

28 The Aristotelian *actio* of *Physics*, III, 3 [202b 19–22] is identical with the Thomist *passio* of *In III Phys.*, lect. 5, §320. In *Summa theologiae*, 1, q. 45, a. 2 [ob. 2 and ad 2m], it is laid down that action and passion are identical with motion; also that in creation there is no motion. From this it follows that in creation there is neither action nor passion; but that is not the conclusion St Thomas draws. Why? Because after citing Aristotle, St Thomas immediately reverts to his own different terms: his action is a relation of the agent to the patient; his passion is a relation of the patient to the agent; these relations do not disappear when the motion is eliminated.

perplexity over the apparent divergence between the commentary on the *Physics* and regular Thomist usage but also provides the most conclusive evidence against such a position as Billuart's that a real distinction in the agent between *potentia agendi* and *ipsa actio* is one of the pillars of Thomist thought.[29]

2   Causation in Time

The previous section examined causation in the purely general case. It raised the question, What is the necessary and sufficient condition of the objective truth of the proposition '*A* causes *B*'? We have now to take a further step. A cause that acts in time acts at a given time, neither sooner nor later. We have to discover why it does not act sooner and what makes it act when it does.

This issue lies at the very foundation of the Aristotelian cosmic system in which the intermittent motions of terrestrial natures are caused by the perpetually and uniformly gyrating spheres, while this motion in its turn is caused by the immovable mover.[30] It was because Aristotle could not conceive the immovable mover as the immediate cause of the *quandoque moventia et mota* of this earth that he invented the mediatory role of the heavens and postulated a cosmic hierarchy.[31] But if Aristotle was so preoccupied with this problem, it cannot be supposed that St Thomas never gave it a thought or even that he treated it in some obscure or merely allusive manner. In fact, in his commentaries on Aristotle he was more explicit than Aristotle himself. His argument may be paraphrased as follows.

A motion taking place at a given time presupposes more than the existence of mover and moved, else why did the motion not take place sooner? Obviously there must have been some inability or impediment to account for the absence of motion. With equal evidence this inability or impediment must have been removed when the motion was about to take place. It is even more evident that such

29 Cajetan, *In Summam theologiae*, 1, q. 25, a. 1 [*LT* 4: 586]; F.C.R. Billuart, *Summa sancti Thomae*, vol. 3: *Tractatus De Gratia*, diss. 5, a. 2, §2 (Paris: Letouzey et Ané, 1880) 130.

30 See W.D. Ross, *Aristotle's Metaphysics*, vol. 1 (Oxford: At the Clarendon Press, 1924), Introduction, pp. cxxx–cliv ['Aristotle's Theology'].

31 Aristotle, *Physics*, VIII, 6 [260a 1–19]; *Metaphysics*, XII, 6 [1072a 9–18]; *De generatione et corruptione*, II, 10 [336a 23 – b 9].

removal must itself be another motion, prior to the motion in question; and though St Thomas did not use the term, we may refer to this prior motion as a premotion. Finally, the premotion necessarily involves a premover, and, if the problem of causation in time is to be solved, the premover must be distinct from the original mover and moved.[32]

This Aristotelian doctrine of premotion must be carefully distinguished from the later Bannezian doctrine. The latter postulates a premotion whenever a creature is a cause; but the Aristotelian doctrine postulates a premotion whenever a cause acts in time. Though practically the two universes of discourse coincide, for the human will is included explicitly among temporal agents,[33] it remains that there is a radical difference of approach. In the second place, the Bannezian premotion is *natura prius* and not *tempore prius*. But the Aristotelian premotion evidently is *tempore prius*: it led Aristotle to infer the eternity of the world on the ground that, since every change presupposed a prior change, there could be no first change;[34] and St Thomas refuted this conclusion, not by substituting a premotion that was *natura prius*, but by arguing that what came first was not in the category of change but creation, and that creation, so far from taking place in time, includes the production of time itself.[35] In the third place, the Bannezian premotion is constituted by a greater actuation of the agent; it gives the created agent a special participation of the pure act of being; and it tends to identify this special participation with an anti-Aristotelian and anti-Thomist *actio in agente*. On the other hand, the Aristotelian premotion as understood by St Thomas affects indifferently mover or moved, agent or patient; explicitly it is *vel ex parte motivi vel ex parte mobilis*;[36] and what it brings about is not some special participation of absolute being but, again explicitly, some relation, disposition, proximity that enables mover to act upon moved.[37] Finally, while the Bannezian premotion is a metaphysical mystery, the Aristotelian is as plain as a pikestaff. On the latter view an iceberg at the Pole will not be melted by the sun; to have the motion 'melting,' it is

32 *In VIII Phys.*, lect. 2, § 976.
33 Ibid. § 978.
34 Ibid. § 976.
35 Ibid. §§ 988–90; *Summa contra Gentiles*, 2, cc. 31–38.
36 [either on the side of the motive force or on that of the movable] *In VIII Phys.*, lect. 2, § 976; see § 978.
37 Ibid. § 978.

necessary to change the relative positons of the sun and the iceberg; and this may be done either by sending the iceberg towards the equator or moving the sun up above the Arctic Circle. Nothing could be simpler or more evident.

3   Aristotelian Premotion and Thomist Application

The question now arises: Did St Thomas have two theories of premotion, a theory derived from Aristotle in terms of time, and another metaphysical theory to correspond to the Bannezian concept of *praedeterminatio physica*? It has been thought that his theorem of God applying each agent to its activity[38] refers to such a metaphysical doctrine, and it is our immediate concern to examine this view. We beg to note that the issue here is not whether or not St Thomas taught physical predetermination but whether or not that was his meaning when he spoke of application.

In the first place, then, it is certain that St Thomas once used the term *applicare* to refer to an Aristotelian premotion. In the commentary on the *Metaphysics* he wrote, '... quando passivum appropinquat activo, in illa dispositione qua passivum potest pati et activum potest agere, necesse est quod unum patiatur et alterum agat; ut patet quando combustibile *applicatur* igni.'[39] Here we have the verb *applicare*; the context deals with Aristotelian premotion, as is clear both from its content and from the parallel passage in the commentary on the *Physics*.[40] Therefore, in at least one instance, application means Aristotelian premotion.

But this is not the sole coincidence of Thomist application and Aristotelian premotion. The latter is a condition of motion which is distinct from the existence of mover and moved; in similar fashion the former is distinct from the *collatio aut conservatio virtutis activae*.[41] Next, Aristotelian premotion holds for all agents in time, voluntary as well as natural; Thomist application proves that God operates in the operation no less of the will than of natural causes.[42] Again, Aristotelian premotion is prior in time; the exam-

---

38 *Summa contra Gentiles*, 3, c. 67 [§ 2418] and c. 70 [§ 2464]; *De potentia*, q. 3, a. 7; *Summa theologiae*, 1, q. 105, a. 5.
39 [when the passive (element) approaches the active in such a disposition that the passive can suffer and the active can act, it is necessary that one (of them) suffer and that the other act; as is clear when something combustible is *applied* to a fire] *In IX Metaphys.*, lect. 4, § 1818 [emphasis Lonergan's].
40 *In VIII Phys.*, lect. 2, § 978.
41 *De potentia*, q. 3, a. 7.
42 Ibid. [ad fin.].

ples of Thomist application lead to the same conclusion, for presumably the cook puts meat on the fire to apply the fire to cooking,[43] the woodsman swings his ax before the ax is applied to chopping,[44] the man moves his knife before the knife is applied to cutting.[45] Finally, like the Aristotelian premotion, the Thomist application seems to be *vel ex parte motivi vel ex parte mobilis*: in the examples of the knife and the ax, application is by moving the mover; in the example of cooking, application is by moving the moved.

In the third place, St Thomas does not merely assert but also proves that God applies all agents to their activity. In the *Contra Gentiles* this proof consists in referring the reader back to the Aristotelian demonstration of a first mover in *Contra Gentiles*, 1, c. 13. In the *De potentia* the proof is simply a description of the Aristotelian cosmic hierarchy: the terrestrial *alterantia alterata* are moved by the celestial *alterans non alteratum*,[46] and this successive dependence does not cease until one arrives ultimately at God; therefore, it necessarily follows that God moves and applies every agent.[47] I submit that this argument is valid only on the assumption that application is an Aristotelian premotion; nothing follows necessarily from the Aristotelian cosmic scheme except the intermittent motion that the cosmic scheme was erected to explain.

In the fourth place, Thomist application is effected by some motion.[48] But according to St Thomas, all motion is effected according to the divine plan, and this plan calls for a hierarchic universe in which the lowest things are moved by the middlemost and the middlemost by the highest.[49] Not only did St Thomas at all times clearly and explicitly affirm a mediated execution of divine providence, but he even argued that there would be no execution whatever of divine providence unless God controlled the free choices of men and of angels through whom the rest of creation was

43 *Summa contra Gentiles*, 3, c. 67 [§ 2418].
44 *Summa theologiae*, 1, q. 105, a. 5.
45 *De potentia*, q. 3, a. 7.
46 By definition, alteration is change in the *sensibilia per se* (*In VII Phys.*, lect. 4–5); it presupposes the local motion of its cause (*In VIII Phys.*, lect. 14, § 1088); hence the heavenly spheres, the highest cause undergoing local motion, are the *primum alterans*.
47 *De potentia*, q. 3, a. 7.
48 Ibid. and *Summa contra Gentiles*, 3, c. 67 [§ 2418].
49 *Super II Sententiarum*, d. 15, q. 1, a. 2; *De veritate*, q. 5, aa. 8–10; *Summa contra Gentiles*, 3, cc. 77–83; *De potentia*, q. 5, aa. 8–10; *Summa theologiae*, 1, q. 22, a. 3; q. 103, a. 6; q. 110, a. 1; q. 115, a. 3; and passim. [See the variations in these references in chapter II-3, below, p. 282, note 69.]

administered.[50] This position leaves no room for the theory that God gives each agent some ultimate actuation to constitute it as here and now acting.

In the fifth place, one must observe that the Thomist cosmic system does not admit the impertinence of crucial experiments. There exists an anomalous divergence between the general and the detailed affirmations of cosmic hierarchy. In general statements St Thomas always asserted a restricted hierarchy in the field of motion and change,[51] and this logically implies that every subordinate cause receives some actuation from the immediately higher cause. But when one gets down to details, one has to distinguish between the instances in which the fiction of celestial influence can be carried through plausibly and the instance in which it cannot and is not. Thus, the celestial spheres cause a secondary conservation of terrestrial beings,[52] a task that is as important as it is vague when one recalls that the mixture of humors that are health to a lion would be death to a man.[53] Similarly, the spheres effect the variation of the seasons and so have a large role in generation and corruption; moreover, the lower spheres each have their special influences, which have given rise to the epithets of saturnine, jovial, martial, mercurial, and the like.[54] Finally, they have a very clearly defined role to play in the speculative embryology[55] of the age, and this gives rise to the otherwise perplexing statement that 'homo generat hominem et sol.'

But take the instance of the substance 'fire,' with its accidental form 'heat' and its operation 'heating.' The law of cosmic hierarchy gives us the principle: '... quantumcumque ignis habeat perfectum calorem, non

---

50 *Summa contra Gentiles*, 3, c. 90 [§ 2654].
51 Brief description of hierarchy, *In VI Metaphys.*, lect. 3, §§ 1207–09; always affirmed, see note 49 above: but restricted inasmuch as God alone creates, *Super I Sententiarum*, d. 37, q. 1, a. 1; *Super II Sententiarum*, d. 1, q. 1, aa. 1–3; and alone can create, *Summa contra Gentiles*, 2, c. 21; 3, c. 66; *De potentia*, q. 3, a. 4; *Summa theologiae*, 1, q. 44, a. 2; *De substantiis separatis*, c. 10, § 103 bis; also restricted in the sense that God alone produces the soul or acts on the will interiorly, *Super II Sententiarum*, d. 15, q. 1, a. 3; *Summa contra Gentiles*, 3, cc. 84–89; *Summa theologiae*, 1, q. 115, a. 4; also restricted inasmuch as God could move corporeal things directly if he chose, *Summa theologiae*, 1, q. 105, aa. 1–2; and inasmuch as angels can and do intervene directly, *Summa theologiae*, 1, q. 110, a. 1, ad 2m.
52 *Summa theologiae*, 1, q. 104, a. 2.
53 *In VII Phys.*, lect. 5, § 918.
54 *In XII Metaphys.*, lect. 6, § 2511; lect. 9, § 2561.
55 *Summa theologiae*, 1, q. 118, a. 1, ad 3m.

alteraret nisi per motionem caelestis corporis.'[56] Now, what further perfection or actuation does the celestial body give to indefinitely perfect heat to enable it actually to warm something else? The matter is not left either to our fancy or to our logic, for St Thomas treated the issue in some detail; he maintained that fire is always *determinata ad calefaciendum* but this determination presupposes the activity of higher causes.[57] In other words, the influence of the spheres is necessary not because indefinitely perfect heat needs further actuation but because, according to the assumptions of cosmic hierarchy, a lower cause has to be a lower cause and, unless it is subordinate, then it cannot be a cause at all. To be contrasted with this position on the action of fire is the position on the instrumental action of the seed in generation: the latter besides its natural properties and the influence it receives from the generator also has *quidam calor ex virtute caelestium corporum.*[58] In this case the motion of the spheres produces something in the moved; but in the case of fire St Thomas had every opportunity to affirm such an effect but preferred simply to affirm the logic of the cosmic system without venturing to suggest that fire cannot burn unless the heat of the spheres is added to its own heat.[59]

Now, this anomaly of the cosmic hierarchy offers a very satisfactory explanation of the divergence among even the most studious interpreters of St Thomas. Follow the general principles, and the fact that a mover implies a motion in the moved will lead inevitably to a position resembling the Bannezian.[60] On the other hand, study the details, distinguish principles from evident fictions, reduce principles to a logical unity, and it is equally likely that one will attempt with Fr Stufler to make out that God moves all things merely because he conserves them.[61] Both procedures are

56 [no matter how perfect the degree in which fire has heat, it would not change anything without the motion of the heavenly body] *Summa theologiae,* 1-2, q. 109, a. 1.

57 *De potentia,* q. 5, a. 8, ad 1m; see *In II De caelo et mundo,* lect. 4, § 342; *Super IV Sententiarum,* d. 44, q. 3, a. 1, sol. 2 & 3.

58 [a certain heat from the power of the celestial bodies] *Summa theologiae,* 1, q. 118, a. 1, ad 3m.

59 Indeed, what is asserted with such confidence in the *De potentia* and the *Prima secundae* is only a probable opinion on the authority of Simplicius in the *In De caelo et mundo.* See the phrase 'cessante motu caeli' in *Super IV Sententiarum,* d. 44, q. 3, a. 1, sol. 2 & 3. See above, notes 56 and 57.

60 Bañez asserted only that a physical premotion was given for vital acts. Stufler extended the premotion to all action, making it a general theory of created causality, as his theory of conservation would imply.

61 See below, p. 83, note 83.

equally logical, and, for that very reason, both are mistaken. What St Thomas held is not a question of logic but a question of history. No doubt, logic and history would coincide were the Aristotelian cosmic hierarchy not a blunder. But it was a blunder, and the circumstances of his age forced St Thomas to take it over. Hence the very logical attempts of later interpreters could not escape the nemesis of giving the original blunder a new form; and by the very excellence of their logic they were bound to arrive at various different forms, for *ex falso sequitur quodlibet.*

4   The Essence of the Idea of Application

In the preceding section we argued that Aristotelian premotion and Thomist application coincide. Were, however, this coincidence perfect, one might expect the idea of application to make its appearance in the commentary on the *Sentences*; in fact, it does not appear before the *Contra Gentiles.* Accordingly, we have now to determine what the Thomist idea of application adds to Aristotelian premotion.

In this task the first step is to grasp the difference between the views of St Thomas and those of later theologians on the certitude of providence. To the latter, providence was certain in all cases because it was certain in each, because each and every action of the creature required some special divine intervention. But to St Thomas providence was certain in each case because it was the cause of all cases: the mover moves the moved if the pair are in the right mutual relation, disposition, proximity; the mover does not, if any other cause prevents the fulfilment of this condition; but both the combinations that result in motion and the interferences that prevent it must ultimately be reduced to God who is universal cause, and therefore divine providence cannot be frustrated.[62] The ground of this evident difference lies in the fact that, while later theologians were preoccupied with divine control of free will, St Thomas was preoccupied with the Aristotelian theorem that all terrestrial activity is contingent.

Aristotle had refuted determinism by appealing to the *per accidens*, that is, to the fortuitous combinations and interferences of causes and the fortuitous coincidences of unrelated predicates in the same subject.[63] He argued

---

62 *Summa theologiae*, 1, q. 103, a. 7; see *In VI Metaphys.*, lect. 3 [§§ 1215–16]; *Summa contra Gentiles*, 3, c. 94 [§ 2694]; *Summa theologiae*, 1, q. 115, a. 6; q. 116, a. 1.

63 Aristotle, *Metaphysics*, v, 6, 1015b 16–34; 7, 1017a 8–23; 30, 1025a 14–30.

that the *per accidens* upset both premises of the determinist position: it showed both that, granted the cause, the effect did not necessarily follow and, as well, that not every effect had a *causa per se*.[64] Moreover, not only did he deny the possibility of science with respect to the *per accidens*,[65] but he considered this objective lack of intelligibility to be absolute; the *per accidens* arose simply from the multipotentiality of prime matters[66] and not at all from the plans of divine providence, of which Aristotle knew nothing.[67]

Now, while Scotus looked upon Aristotle as a benighted pagan for his theory of terrestrial contingence, St Thomas adopted the more difficult policy of salvaging as much of Aristotle as was compatible with Christian doctrine. As one might expect, such a policy could not be executed at a single stroke. In the commentary on the *Sentences*, in which Avicenna was the great philosophic influence,[68] one finds clear and unequivocal affirmations of Christian providence; still, the speculative work gets little further than basic definitions,[69] and theoretical shortcomings are evident. Thus, both predestination and reprobation are in terms of divine foreknowledge with no apparent mention of divine causality.[70] Again, divine permission seems to be indifferent to opposite courses of creaturely ac-

64 Ibid. VI, 2, 1026a 33 – b 27; 3, 1027a 29 – b 17; XI, 8, 1064b 15 – 1065b 4; Thomas Aquinas, *In VI Metaphys.*, lect. 3, § 1203–14; *In I Peri herm.*, lect. 13–14, §§ 172–82; *Summa contra Gentiles*, 3, cc. 72, 86, 94, noting argument against Albumazar in c. 86 [§ 2622] and the inconstancy of terminology; for brief and clear account, see *Summa theologiae*, 1, q. 115, a. 6; q. 116, a. 1.
65 Aristotle, *Metaphysics*, VI, 2, 1027a 19–28; XI, 8, 1064b 15 – 1065b 1.
66 Ibid. VI, 2, 1027a 13; 3, 1027b 10–16; XI, 8, 1065a 25.
67 The activity of Aristotle's first mover is to contemplate himself (*Metaphysics*, XII, 7, 1072b 14–30) and be the object beloved by the animated heavens (ibid. 1072a 34 – b 14); his causality is efficient only in the sense of 'appetibile apprehensum movet appetitum' [the desirable thing when apprehended moves desire] (Ross, *Metaphysics*, I, Introduction, pp. cxxxiv–cxlv; *In III De anima*, lect. 15, § 830; hence Aristotle compares his universe to a Greek household in which the heavenly spheres, like sons of the family, have their course mapped out for them, while terrestrial bodies, like slaves and domestic animals, wander about at random (*In XII Metaphys.*, lect. 12, § 2633). See also above, p. 73, n. 31.
68 See M.-M. Gorce's contribution to 'Bibliographie critique,' *Bulletin thomiste* 7:6 (November 1930) 183.
69 *Super I Sententiarum*, d. 39, q. 2, aa. 1–2; d. 40, q. 1, aa. 1–2 [and qq. 2–3].
70 Predestination includes *propositum*, *praeparatio*, and *praescientia exitus* (ibid. d. 40, q. 1, a. 2); reprobation is *praescientia culpae et praeparatio poenae* (ibid. q. 4, a. 1 [*praeparatio poenae* not explicit]); see *De veritate*, q. 6, a. 3; *Summa theologiae*, 1, q. 23, aa. 3, 5.

tion;[71] and one can even read the words, '... multa fiunt quae Deus non operatur.'[72]

In the *De veritate* the question of the causal certitude of providence is raised.[73] In the case of necessary causes such as the celestial spheres, it is affirmed both with respect to general results and with respect to each particular effect. In the case of contingent causes such as terrestrial agents, it is affirmed with regard to general results but denied with regard to each particular case. However, there is an apparent exception to the latter rule, for dogmatic data require the affirmation of causal certitude with regard to the predestination of the elect. Still, this exception is only apparent. Not each act of the elect but only the general result of salvation is causally certain; just as God makes certain of the perpetuity of the species by the vast number of its members, so also he makes certain of the salvation of the elect by imparting so many graces that either the predestined does not sin at all or, if he does, then he repents and rises again.[74]

In the *Contra Gentiles*, this transitional position no longer appears. The theorem of divine transcendence was worked out, and Cicero's objection that causally certain providence and human freedom were incompatible was brushed aside as frivolous.[75] But this position will concern us in our next chapter; our immediate point is that simultaneously St Thomas had achieved the higher synthesis of Aristotelian contingence and Christian providence. In Aristotle, terrestrial contingence had its ultimate basis in his negation or neglect of providence: events happened contingently because there was no cause to which they could be reduced except prime matter, and prime matter was not a determinate cause. Antithetical to this position was the Christian affirmation of providence, for divine providence foresaw and planned and brought about every event. The Thomist higher synthesis was to place God above and beyond the created orders of necessity and contingence: because God is universal cause, his providence must be cer-

71 *Super I Sententiarum*, d. 47, q. 1, a. 2: '... permissio respicit potentiam causae ad utrumque oppositorum se habentem' [permission regards that power of a cause which can relate to each of (two) opposite (courses)]. See ibid. d. 40, q. 2, a. 1, ad 6m; *Super librum De causis*, lect. 24, §§ 398–99.
72 [many things are done which God does not operate] *Super I Sententiarum*, d. 47, q. 1, a. 2; yet see *Super II Sententiarum*, d. 37, q. 2, a. 2.
73 I use 'causal certitude' to translate 'certitudo ordinis' where the 'ordo' is 'ordo causae ad effectum' (*De veritate*, q. 6, a. 3 c.).
74 *De veritate*, q. 6, a. 3 c. [ad fin.].
75 *Summa contra Gentiles*, 3, c. 94 [§§ 2690, 2699].

tain; but because he is a transcendent cause, there can be no incompatibility between terrestrial contingence and the causal certitude of providence.[76]

It is now possible to answer the question raised at the beginning of this section, Why did not St Thomas affirm in the commentary on the *Sentences* that God applies all agents to their activity? Why did application in its technical sense make its first appearance in the *Contra Gentiles*?[77] The obvious answer is that before the latter work St Thomas had not solved the speculative problems incident to the conception of the causal certitude of providence. In the commentary on the *Sentences* and in the *De veritate* one can find affirmations both of Christian providence and of Aristotelian premotion; one can find them not only separately but also conjoined, as when the remote preparation for justification is explained by the loss of health or by a preacher's admonition or by anything of the sort that will stimulate the will, because all such things are due to divine providence.[78] It remains that in these works divine providence cannot be associated with Aristotelian premotion in any but a vague manner. Only when St Thomas settled down to the vast task of thinking out the Christian universe in the *Contra Gentiles* did he arrive at the truth that divine providence is an intrinsically certain cause of every combination or interference of terrestrial causes. By the same stroke would he arrive at the practically identical truth that God applies every agent to its activity. Accordingly, we are led to infer that the essence of the idea of application is the Aristotelian premotion as informed by the Thomist causal certitude of divine providence: 'Deus igitur per suum intellectum omnia movet ad proprios fines.'[79]

5   Universal Instrumentality

We now have to take another step forward towards our goal. We have examined the general case of the meaning of causation and the particular case of the cause in time. Before we can consider the analogy between the causation of the Creator and that of the creature, it is necessary to obtain a grasp of the Thomist concept of universal instrumentality.

First of all, then, this concept is a syncretist product. Not only did St Thomas accept the Aristotelian cosmic system of first mover, celestial

---

76 Ibid. c. 94. See above, p. xx, notes 62, 64.
77 It occurs in a perfectly general sense in *De veritate*, q. 17, a. 1.
78 *Super II Sententiarum*, d. 28, q. 1, a. 4; *De veritate*, q. 24, a. 15.
79 [God therefore moves all things to their proper ends through his intellect]
    De substantiis separatis, c. 14, § 129.

spheres, and terrestrial process, but he also accepted the Platonist idea of universal causes, that is, of causes that necessarily are the causes of any effect within a given category.[80] Among Thomist universal causes, two were most conspicuous: God, who alone was proportionate to the production of being, whether substantial or accidental; and the *corpus caeleste*, which had the official role of causing all terrestrial change.[81] Now, this Platonist-Aristotelian syncretism could not but have the corollary of universal instrumentality; for an instrument is a lower cause moved by a higher so as to produce an effect within the category proportionate to the higher;[82] but in the cosmic hierarchy all causes are moved except the highest, and every effect is at least in the category of being; therefore, all causes except the highest are instruments.[83]

So much for the fact of universal instrumentality. But, in the next place, if the instrument is to operate beyond its proper proportion and within the category of the higher cause, it must receive some participation of the

80 *Summa theologiae*, 1, q. 115, a. 1: '... si esset forma ignis separata, ut Platonici posuerunt, esset aliquo modo causa omnis ignitionis' [if there were a separate form of fire, as the Platonists maintained, it would be in some way the cause of all burning]. See text of *Liber De causis* to lect. 1, 4, 6, 18, of St Thomas's commentary [Marietti ed., pp. 3, 27, 44, 102].

81 *In VI Metaphys.*, lect. 3, § 1207–09; *De potentia*, q. 3, a. 7 c., on instrumentality [ad fin.]; *De substantiis separatis*, c.10, § 105, and c. 12, § 111; *Summa theologiae*, 1, q. 115, a. 3, ad 2m; *In II Phys.*, lect. 6, § 189; *De veritate*, q. 5, a. 9 [ad fin.].

82 Best definition of instrument, *De veritate*, q. 27, aa. 4 and 7. Origin of idea, Aristotle, *De generatione animalium*, II, 1, 734b 31 – 735a 26; cited in *Super IV Sententiarum*, d. 1, q. 1, a. 4, sol. 2, ad 4m. Idea presented in account of generation, *Super II Sententiarum*, d. 18, q. 2, a. 3; *De potentia*, q. 3, aa. 11–12; *In VII Metaphys.*, lect. 6–8; *Summa theologiae*, 1, q. 118, a. 1; in account of magic, *De operationibus occultis naturae* [*LT* 43: 183–86]; in account of instrumentality of spheres, *Super II Sententiarum*, d. 15, q. 1, a. 2; *Summa theologiae*, 1, q. 70, a. 3 [in the dissertation, Lonergan specifies 'ad 3m to ad 5m'; see below, p. 290, note 104]; and in treatment of Christ's mediation of prophecy, miracles, sacraments. On instrumentality of accidents, *Super II Sententiarum*, d. 1, q. 1, a. 4, ad 5m; *Summa theologiae*, 1, q. 115, a. 1, ad 5m; *In Aristotelis librum De sensu et sensato*, lect. 10, §§ 138–39. On limitations of instrument, *Summa theologiae*, 1, q. 45, a. 5; q. 118, a. 2.

83 This certainly is the meaning of *proprius effectus Dei*. Fr Stufler's attempt to reduce this idea to God's exclusive role in creation and conservation is based on a narrow selection of texts and overlooks the evident Platonist element in St Thomas's concept of the universal cause. See Johann Stufler, *Gott, der erste Beweger aller Dinge* (Innsbruck: Rauch, 1936) 67–83; also see the development in the premises of the analogy of operation, below pp. 88–90, notes 104–12.

latter's special productive capacity. Such a participation is variously termed by St Thomas an *intentio, virtus instrumentalis, vis artis, virtus artis, similitudo per modum cuiusdam defluxus, proportio per modum naturae incompletae, esse incompletum, esse spirituale*.[84] St Thomas explicitly affirmed the emergence of such a participation in every case of actual action by instruments of the universal principle of being;[85] but while to Fr Stufler this is most probably just a bit of imagery,[86] to the later Thomist school it is with unlimited certitude their physical predetermination. In this case one is confronted not only with the difficulty, already mentioned, of attempting to argue rigorously from the cosmic system; there is in addition an objective obscurity to the general Thomist theory of the instrument. St Thomas used the *virtus instrumentalis* not only to explain the universal mediation of our Lord's humanity, to explain miracles, prophecy, and the sacraments, but also to account for the occult operations of nature, the influence of magical pictures, and, with Aristotle, the generation of animals. The latter group clearly brings the element of myth into the theory of the instrument, and the presence of such myth precludes the possibility of determining what St Thomas must mean whenever he speaks of instrumentality.

But if we exclude the possibility of any apriorist solution, it remains that we do not consider the problem of the *virtus instrumentalis* insoluble in any given particular case; for in particular cases it may be possible to argue a

---

84 *Virtus artis* is the *forma apprehensa* of the artist on its way ('per modum cuiusdam defluxus,' *De veritate*, q. 27, a. 7) through the tools to the artifact. The *intentio* was the inverse process of the *forma coloris* through the medium to the eye. Both are analogous to the *esse incompletum* of corporeal motion. On light and color: best passage, *In II De anima*, lect. 14 [§§ 405–26]; also in *Super II Sententiarum*, d. 13, q. 1, a. 3; d. 19, q. 1, a. 3, ad 1m; *De potentia*, q. 5, a. 8 (singular position on light [ad fin.]); *Summa theologiae*, 1, q. 67 [in his dissertation Lonergan limits the reference here to a. 4; see below, p. 290, note 104]. Note that later works replace *intentio* by *esse spirituale*; see St Albert, *Summa de creaturis*, 2, q. 21, a. 5 (*BA* 35: 208); Scotus, *Oxon.*, 2, d. 13, q. 1 [*Commentaria oxoniensia ad IV libros magistri Sententiarum*, ed. Marianus Fernandez Garcia (Ad Claras Aquas prope Florentiam, 1914) 2: 527–30]. Next, on motion in broad sense, *In III De anima*, lect. 12; in strict sense, *In III Phys.*, lect. 2–3; *In XI Metaphys.*, lect. 9; the latter is found only in three categories, *In V Phys.*, lect. 2–4; *In VI Phys.*, lect. 5, § 796; lect. 12; *In XI Metaphys.*, lect. 12; on alteration, *In VII Phys.*, lect. 4–5; on augmentation, *In I De generatione et corruptione*, lect. 11–17; on relation of these to local motion, *In VIII Phys.*, lect. 14, § 1088. Finally, the analogy of *esse incompletum* is that as a motion is to its term, so the proportion of the instrumental cause is to that of the principal cause (*Summa theologiae*, 3, q. 62, a. 4).
85 *De potentia*, q. 3, a. 7, ad 7m.
86 Stufler, *Gott, der erste Beweger aller Dinge* 66–67; yet see p. 106.

posteriori from parallel passages, and fortunately there is a very convincing series of parallels to the instrumental virtue affirmed by *De potentia*, q. 3, a. 7, ad 7m. This series runs from the commentary on the *Sentences* to the *Summa theologiae*, and the parallel idea is the idea of fate.

The commentary on the *Sentences* points out that God is an intellectual agent and that his knowledge is causal, not because it is knowledge but only inasmuch as it resembles the plan or design or art in the mind of an artisan. Moreover, this divine plan has a twofold existence: primarily it exists in the mind of God, and there it is termed providence; secondarily it exists in the created universe and there it is termed fate.[87] The parallel seems manifest: if providence is the art of the divine artisan, then fate is the *virtus artis* in his tools. Next, in the *De veritate* one finds the following refinement: the divine ideas correspond to the essences of creatures, but providence corresponds to fate.[88] To this the *Contra Gentiles* adds that fate is impressed upon things, that it is unfolded in the course of events.[89] Hence, when in the *De potentia* St Thomas put to himself the crucial experiment of the cosmic system with respect to the operation of the first cause,[90] already he had in mind the concept of some real participation of the divine design that was distinct from the natural forms of things, that was impressed upon them as they entered into the dynamic order of events. Thus, the much disputed *De potentia*, q. 3, a. 7, ad 7m, really presents nothing new; it asserts that, besides the natural form permanent in any given natural object, actual activity postulates some *virtus artis, intentio, esse incompletum* from the universal principle of being. Further, if we wish to know what precisely this elusive entity is, we have only to go on to the *Summa theologiae*, where the idea of fate is expressed with a clarity and distinctness that defy equivocation.

The *Summa theologiae* repeats the distinction between the divine plan in the mind of God and fate which exists in the created order. It recalls the *quo actualiter agat* of the *De potentia* by adding that by fate things are ordained to produce given effects.[91] Again, as the *De potentia* explains that things cannot act without the *motus artis*, so the *Summa theologiae* explains in what sense they cannot but act because of fate.[92] Finally, the general theory of the *intentio* advanced that this entity was a cause, not in itself but only in

---

87 *Super I Sententiarum*, d. 39, q. 2, a. 1, ad 5m; d. 38, q. 1, a. 1.
88 *De veritate*, q. 5, a. 1, ad 1m (1ae ser.).
89 *Summa contra Gentiles*, 3, c. 93 [§ 2684].
90 *De potentia*, q. 3, a. 7, ob. 7.
91 *Summa theologiae*, 1, q. 116, a. 2 c.
92 Ibid. a. 3.

conjunction with other causes;[93] in the *Summa theologiae* one learns that fate is a cause, not in addition to, but in conjunction with, natural causes.[94] The parallel seems as complete as could reasonably be demanded. What, then, is fate? It is the order of secondary causes; it is their disposition, arrangement, seriation; it is not a quality, and much less is it a substance; it is in the category of relation. Together such relations give a single fate for the universe; taken singly, they give the many fates of Virgil's line, 'Te tua fata trahunt.'[95]

Thus the *intentio* of *De potentia*, q. 3, a. 7, ad 7m, emerges into the clear light of day and proves to be but another aspect of the application mentioned in the body of the same article. Application is the causal certitude of providence terminating in the right disposition, relation, proximity between mover and moved: without it motion cannot take place now; with it motion automatically results. But the *intentio* is fate, and fate is simply the dynamic pattern of such relations – the pattern through which the design of the divine artisan unfolds in natural and human history; again, without fate things cannot act, with it they do. Thus, fate and application and instrumental virtue all reduce to the divine plan, and the divergence between Aristotle and St Thomas is a divergence in the conception of God. Aristotle held that God moved all things by being the object of love for the intelligences or the animated spheres;[96] but to St Thomas God was more – a transcendental artisan planning history: 'Deus igitur per suum intellectum omnia movet ad proprios fines.'[97]

6   The Analogy of Operation

In the first section of this chapter we arrived at the conclusion that St Thomas conceived causation as a formal content in the cause and a real relation of dependence in the effect. The intervening sections have been preparing the way for the present question, How did St Thomas conceive the analogy between the causation of the Creator and that of the creature? The answer would seem to be that at all times St Thomas drew an implicit

93 *In II De anima*, lect. 14 [§§ 420–26]; *Super II Sententiarum*, d. 13, q. 1, a. 3; *De potentia*, q. 5, a. 8.
94 *Summa theologiae*, 1, q. 116, a. 2, ad 2m.
95 Ibid. ad 1m, ad 3m; see *Summa theologiae*, 3, q. 62, a. 4, ad 4m.
96 Aristotle, *Metaphysics*, XII, 7, 1072a 34 – b 14; see above p. 80, n. 67.
97 [God therefore moves all things to their proper ends through his intellect] *De substantiis separatis*, c. 14, § 129.

distinction between a basic and a proximate analogy. One reads in the commentary on the *Sentences*: 'Omnis ... virtus ab essentia procedit, et operatio a virtute; unde cuius essentia ab alio est, oportet quod virtus et operatio ab alio sit.'[98] The dependence, *esse ab alio*, of the virtue or principle of causation gives the basic analogy; the dependence of the operation itself gives the proximate analogy.

Both the basic and the proximate analogies were derived from the *Liber De causis*. The Arabic author of that very Platonist work had faced the Epicurean objection that the gods could not be supposed to 'mix' in the trifling affairs of this world. This argument for divine indifference was refuted by a distinction between divine and created activity. In lower causes there is to be found a *habitudo, res media, additio super esse*; this intermediate – whether intrinsic or extrinsic, whether an accidental form in the agent, as brightness in the sun, or an accidental form in the medium, as brightness in the atmosphere – gives rise to the impression that activity 'mixes' the agent with what he effects. But in the first cause there is no such *continuator, res media*, for God acts by his essence, the *prima bonitas* and *virtus virtutum*.[99] In this position it is easy to discern the origin of the Thomist analogy of the principle of operation. God is his own virtue; his essence, his potency, his action in the sense of principle of action – all are one.[100] On the other hand, in creatures one has to distinguish between the *ipsum agens* and the *virtus qua agit*.[101] Finally, in the *Pars prima* the principle of the limitation of act by potency is employed to demonstrate that in God substance and principle of action are one, while in creatures there must be the fourfold composition of essence and existence, accidental potency and accidental act.[102]

If the basic analogy is very easy to grasp, the proximate analogy involves the slightly difficult concept of 'causing causation.' Suppose Peter to stand

---

98 [every power proceeds from an essence, and operation (proceeds) from a power; and so the power and operation of a being that has its essence from another must (also) be from another] *Super II Sententiarum*, d. 37, q. 2, a. 2 c.

99 *Liber De causis*, the text to lect. 20–22 of St Thomas's commentary [Marietti ed., pp. 110, 115, 117]; see lect. 31 [Marietti ed., p. 144].

100 *Super I Sententiarum*, d. 37, q. 1, a. 1, ad 4m; *De potentia*, q. 3, aa. 3 and 7; *Summa theologiae*, 1, q. 25, a. 1; q. 54, a. 1.

101 [the agent itself ... the power by which it acts] *Summa contra Gentiles*, 3, c. 70 [§ 2464]; *Super I Sententiarum*, d. 37, q. 1, a. 1.

102 *Summa theologiae*, 1, q. 54, aa. 1–3. By the parallel with essence, 'virtus' here means limiting potency; it is not to be confused with the Aristotelian accidental forms 'heat,' 'cold,' etc., which are also termed 'virtutes' but are actually hot, cold, and in potency to their opposites.

sword in hand and then to lunge forward in such a way that the sword pierces Paul's heart. In this process there are only two products: the motion of the sword and the piercing of Paul's heart. But while the products are only two, the causations are three: Peter causes the motion of the sword; the sword pierces the heart of Paul; and, in the third place, Peter causes the causation of the sword, for he applies it to the act of piercing and he does so according to the precepts of the art of killing. The sword is strictly an instrument, and its very causation is caused. Now, if causation in general is a relation of dependence, a caused causation is a relation of dependent dependence. Again, if causation in general is a formal content, *ut ab agente in aliud procedens*, a procession, then to cause a causation is to make a procession proceed, to operate an operation, to operate within an operation. Such is the proximate analogy of operation.

This, too, St Thomas derived from the *Liber De causis*. In the first proposition of that work occurs the phrase: 'Et non fit igitur causatum causae secundae nisi per virtutem causae primae.'[103] In his commentary St Thomas called upon Proclus for elucidation.

> Proculus autem expressius hoc sic probat. Causa enim secunda cum sit effectus causae primae substantiam suam habet a causa prima. Sed a quo habet aliquid substantiam, ab eo habet potentiam sive virtutem operandi. Ergo causa secunda habet potentiam sive virtutem operandi a causa prima. Sed causa secunda per suam potentiam vel virtutem est causa effectus. Ergo, hoc ipsum quod causa secunda sit causa effectus habet a prima causa. Esse ergo causam effectus inest primo primae causae, secundo autem causae secundae.[104]

In this passage the idea of causing causation has its premise in creation-conservation: what causes the substance also causes the active potency; what

103 [Therefore the effect of the secondary cause occurs only through the power of the first cause].
104 [Now Proclus proves this more explicitly in this way. For a secondary cause, since it is the effect of a first cause, has its substance from the first cause. But that from which something has its substance is that from which it has its potency and power of operating. Therefore, a secondary cause has its potency or power of acting from the first cause. But the secondary cause, through its potency or power, is the cause of the effect. Therefore, this fact itself that the secondary cause is cause of the effect derives from the first cause. Therefore, to be cause of the effect belongs first to the first cause, and secondly to the secondary cause] *Super librum De causis*, lect. 1, § 24.

causes the active potency also causes what the latter causes – indeed, causes the causation itself; for 'hoc ipsum quod causa secunda sit causa effectus habet a causa prima.'

However, if we follow the development of St Thomas's thought on God operating the operation of the creature, we readily observe that, while in the commentary on the *Sentences* and in the *De veritate* St Thomas is ready to remain with the *Liber De causis* and appeal only to creation-conservation,[105] in the *Contra Gentiles* he lists six premises in proof of the proximate analogy,[106] in the *De potentia* he reduces these to four,[107] in the *Pars prima* he sets forth three categories of premises.[108] Evidently this variation is concomitant with the developed idea of providence that emerges in the *Contra Gentiles*: once St Thomas had grasped a theory of providence compatible with Aristotelian terrestrial contingence, he began at once to argue that the creature's causation was caused not merely because of creation and of conservation but also because of application, instrumentality, cosmic hierarchy, and universal finality. The *De potentia* prunes this exuberance and omits the last two grounds; the *Pars prima* restores the Aristotelian idea of God as cause according to the principle 'appetibile apprehensum movet appetitum.'

Besides this positive concept of the proximate analogy, there is a corresponding negative form: '... sicut habetur in libro de Causis, quando causa prima retrahit actionem suam a causato, oportet etiam quod causa secunda retrahat actionem suam ab eodem, eo quod causa secunda habet hoc ipsum quod agit per actionem causae primae.'[109] As is to be expected, this negative form undergoes the same variation in premises as the positive form. In the commentary on the *Sentences* and the *De veritate* we are told that

---

105 *De veritate*, q. 24, a. 14: 'Operationis enim naturalis Deus est causa, inquantum dat et conservat id quod est principium naturalis operationis in re ... sicut dum conservat gravitatem in terra, quae est principium motus deorsum' [For God is the cause of a natural operation, insofar as he gives and preserves that which is the principle of natural operation in the thing ... as when he preserves gravitation in the earth, which is the principle of downward motion]. See *Super I Sententiarum*, d. 37, q. 1, a. 1 c. and ad 4m; *Super II Sententiarum*, d. 1, q. 1, a. 4 c.; yet see ibid. d. 15, q. 1, a. 2 c.
106 *Summa contra Gentiles*, 3, c. 67; see cc. 66 and 70.
107 *De potentia*, q. 3, a. 7.
108 *Summa theologiae*, 1, q. 105, a. 5.
109 [as is stated in the book *On Causes*, when the first cause withdraws its action from the thing caused, it is necessary that the secondary cause withdraw its action from that same thing, because it is through the action of the first cause that the secondary cause has this fact itself that it acts] *De potentia*, q. 5, a. 8 c.

lower causes cannot act without God;[110] in later works we are told that they cannot act without the divine motion.[111]

This later affirmation of the proximate analogy in its inverse form is quite clear even from a purely logical approach. When St Thomas writes, 'quantumcumque ignis habeat perfectum calorem, non alteraret nisi per motionem caelestis corporis,'[112] one can hardly suppose him to mean that the heavenly spheres add some further perfection or actuation to what already is indefinitely perfect. When he immediately adds, 'quantumcumque natura aliqua corporalis vel spiritualis ponatur perfecta, non potest in suum actum procedere nisi moveatur a Deo,'[113] his meaning becomes manifest. If it is difficult to suppose that further perfection is added to what is as perfect as you please, it is absurd to fancy the substance 'fire' given every actuation conceivable and yet needing two further actuations, one from the spheres and still another from God.

In conclusion one may compare the Thomist with later positions. Both argue from the known motions of this world to the existence of a first mover; again, both argue from the perfection of the first mover to further conclusions about created motions. But while later speculators affirm the existence of other motions than those already known, after the fashion of the astronomers who argued from known planetary motions to the existence of other planets, the conclusion reached by St Thomas was simply a theorem – simply a profounder understanding of motions already known or supposed. As Newton affirmed a 'law' of gravitation, as Einstein affirmed a 'theory' of relativity, so too St Thomas affirmed the analogy of operation, namely, that the causation of the created cause is itself caused; that it is a procession which is made to proceed; that it is an operation in which another operates.

7   Conclusion

The fundamental point in the theory of operation is that operation involves no change in the cause as cause. On Thomist analysis it involves a formal

110 *Super II Sententiarum*, d. 1, q. 1, a. 4 c.; *De veritate*, q. 24, a. 14 c.
111 *Summa theologiae*, 1-2, q. 109, aa. 1 and 9.
112 [no matter how perfect the degree in which fire has heat, it would not change anything without the motion of the heavenly body] Ibid. a. 1.
113 [no matter how perfect the degree in which some corporeal or spiritual nature is constituted, it cannot proceed to its act unless it is moved by God] Ibid.

content between cause and effect; this is the procession, *ut ab agente in aliud procedens*. On Aristotelian analysis it involves a real relation of dependence in the effect. The two analyses are really identical though terminologically different. The consequent difficulty in terminology is heightened by the large variety of senses in which St Thomas employs the word *actio*.

Operation in time presupposes a premotion. But this premotion affects indifferently either the mover or the moved. Its function is simply to bring mover and moved in the right relation, mutual disposition, spatial proximity for motion naturally to ensue. When combined with the fact that God is the first mover in the cosmic hierarchy and that, as universal cause, God cannot be frustrated, this law of premotion yields the theorem that God applies all agents to their activity. This theorem occurred to St Thomas only in the *Contra Gentiles* when he had worked out his theory of providence. Though in its original form it is inseparably bound up with the Aristotelian cosmic scheme and the Aristotelian idea of terrestrial contingence, still it may readily be given an independent formulation.

Because the creature cannot act infinitely, it must have an object upon which or with respect to which it acts. Because the creature cannot create, it cannot provide itself with the objects of its own activity. Because God alone can create, God alone can provide such objects, and this provision is not by chance but in accordance with the divine plan. Therefore God applies all agents to their activity.

Again, the proportion of a cause is its nature; but God alone is being by nature, and so God is the sole proportionate cause of being; every other cause of being is an instrument. Further, the instrument, if it is to act, must have some participation of the proportion of the principal cause: unless the gramophone needle moves in the same dynamic pattern as did Caruso's vocal cords, the gramophone will not make you hear Caruso's voice. Similarly, without a participation of the art of the divine artisan, the creature cannot produce being, substantial or accidental. That participation is called fate; it is the dynamic pattern of world events, the totality of relations that constitute the combinations and interferences of created causes; it stands in the created order to the uncreated plan of the divine artisan as the vibrations of the ether stand to the inspiration of Beethoven.

Because St Thomas developed this idea by combining the Aristotelian cosmic hierarchy of motion with the Platonist idea of universal causes, all terrestrial agents are also instruments of the celestial spheres. However, this conventional position breaks down when submitted to crucial experiment. Though St Thomas was ready to credit the spheres with many marvelous influences, he was unwilling to affirm that fire cannot burn unless a celestial heat be added to the natural heat of that element; he simply asserted the logic of the cosmic scheme, that without the action of the *primum alterans* other causes of alteration could have no action.

This impossibility of having an action is but an instance of the general analogy of operation. Apart from the basic analogy which maintains that God acts by his substance while creatures act by an accidental form or act, there is also a proximate analogy. On Aristotelian analysis, the causation of the Creator is an unconditioned dependence while that of the creature is a dependent dependence. On Thomist analysis, the causation of the Creator is an unconditioned procession, an *ut ab agente* that presupposes no other action; but the causation of the creature is itself caused;[114] this 'causing causation' or making a procession proceed is regularly described by the formula of operating in the operation of another cause. In the commentary on the *Sentences* and the *De veritate* God operates the operation of creatures because he is creator and conserver; in later works other grounds are more prominently asserted, namely, application, instrumentality, finality. In parallel fashion earlier works state that the creatures cannot operate without

---

114 *De potentia*, q. 5, a. 8, ad 4m: 'Hoc autem est de ratione perfectionis supremi agentis, quod sua perfectio sibi sufficiat ad agendum alio agente remoto; unde hoc inferioribus agentibus attribui non potest' [Now this pertains to the nature of the supreme agent, that its perfection is sufficient for it to act when another agent is removed; and so this cannot be attributed to lower agents].

Ibid. ad 1m: '... virtus ignis semper est determinata ad calefaciendum, praesuppositis tamen causis prioribus quae ad actionem ignis requiruntur' [the power of fire is always determined (oriented) to heating, but with the causes presupposed which are required for the action of fire].

Ibid. ad 5m: '... ignis est proprium calefacere, supposito quod habeat aliquam actionem; sed eius actio dependet ab alio' [to heat is the property of fire, presupposed that it has some action; but its action depends on another].

De veritate, q. 22, a. 8: '... sicut omnis actio naturalis est a Deo, ita omnis actio voluntatis inquantum est actio, non solum est a voluntate ut immediate agente, sed a Deo ut primo agente' [as every natural action is from God, so every action of the will, insofar as it is action, is not only from the will as acting immediately, but from God as the first agent].

De potentia, q. 3, a. 7, Sed contra: 'Nec potest dici quod [Deus] aliud quam ipsa natura operatur, cum non appareat ibi nisi una operatio' [Nor can it be said that (God) operates something different from what nature operates, since nothing is found there except the one operation]. See *Summa contra Gentiles*, 3, c. 70 [§2465]. See the texts on *immediatio virtutis*, above p. 67, n. 6.

God, while later works state that they cannot operate without the divine motion.

The bearing of the foregoing on St Thomas's theory of *gratia operans et cooperans* is threefold. First, it enables one to get behind the sixteenth-century controversy to the intellectual field in which St Thomas did his thinking. Secondly, it stands to operative grace as general to particular. Thirdly, it is a necessary prerequisite to any attempt to understand the meaning and the development in Thomist texts on actual grace as operative and cooperative.

I-5

Divine Transcendence and Human Liberty

In the present chapter, we are concerned to determine what St Thomas held at different times on various points connected with the theory of *gratia operans*. His theory of operation has already been treated, and now we come closer to our subject to outline his concept of freedom, his ideas on divine action in the will, his explanations of the possibility of contingence and of sin.

1 The Freedom of the Will

Successively St Thomas transcended four influences in developing his theory of the will and its freedom. First of all, in his commentary on the *Sentences* he rejected St Albert's view that *liberum arbitrium* was a third faculty distinct from both intellect and will.[1] In the second place, this term, *liberum arbitrium*, loses its place of importance; it had its origin in the Stoic *autexousion* and it persisted until the *Pars prima* with distinct questions devoted to it and to the will;[2] but in the *Prima secundae* there are sixty-three articles in a row, and though all treat of the will, the term *liberum arbitrium* fails to appear in the title of a single one.[3]

More complex is the role played by the idea of freedom as noncoercion.

---

1 *Super II Sententiarum*, d. 24, q. 1, aa. 1–3; for St Albert, see Lottin, 'Le traité du libre arbitre depuis le chancelier Philippe jusqu'à saint Thomas d'Aquin' [see above, p. 19, note 84].
2 *De veritate*, qq. 22 and 24; *Summa theologiae*, 1, qq. 82–83.
3 *Summa theologiae*, 1-2, qq. 6–17.

This relic of the prephilosophic period of medieval thought appears in the commentary on the *Sentences*, but there any tendency to assert that the will is necessitated but not coerced and therefore free is rejected.[4] On the other hand, in the *De veritate*, the *De potentia*, and the *Pars prima* one does find incidental statements to the effect that noncoercion makes necessary acts free: of necessity yet freely God wills his own excellence,[5] the Holy Spirit proceeds,[6] the human will tends to beatitude,[7] the demonic will is fixed in evil,[8] and perhaps the sinner is impotent to avoid further sin.[9] This lapse in the teeth of contrary theory was repudiated with extreme vehemence in the later *De malo* as heretical, destructive of all merit and demerit, subversive of all morality, alien to all scientific and philosophic thought, and the product of either wantonness or incompetence.[10] The church agrees that it is a heretical view,[11] and the historian cannot but regard the relevant passages in the *De veritate*, the *De potentia*, and the *Pars Prima* as a momentary aberration.

The fourth influence St Thomas overcame was the Aristotelian doctrine that the will is a passive potency: 'appetibile apprehensum movet appetitum.'[12] It was in this way that Aristotle conceived his first mover as moving the animated heavens,[13] and it was on this ground that St Thomas affirmed God to operate in all operation as the *primum appetibile*.[14] Accordingly, in the *De veritate* and the *Pars prima* the act of appetition is passive,[15] and is described passively as *inclinari vel non inclinari*;[16] the will is a *mobile* with an act, *moveri*;[17] it has no parallel to the distinction between *intellectus agens et possibilis*.[18] Of course, this position is not rigidly maintained: the

---

4 *Super II Sententiarum*, d. 25, q. 1, a. 4; see ibid. d. 28, q. 1, a. 2.
5 *De veritate*, q. 23, a. 4.
6 *De potentia*, q. 10, a. 2, ad 5m [1ae ser.].
7 *De veritate*, q. 22, a. 5, ad 3m (2ae ser.); see ibid. c. and ad 4m (1ae ser.); *Summa theologiae*, 1, q. 82, a. 1, ad 1m.
8 *De veritate*, q. 24, a. 10, ob. 5 and ad 5m.
9 Ibid. a. 12, ad 10m (2ae ser.).
10 *De malo*, q. 6, a. 1 [init.]; compare *De veritate*, q. 22, a. 7.
11 *DB* 1094 [*DS* 2003].
12 *In III De anima*, lect. 15, §830 [sense, not words].
13 Aristotle, *Metaphysics*, XII, 7 [1072a 34 – b 14]; see Ross, *Aristotle's Metaphysics*, vol. 1, Introduction, p. cxxxiv.
14 *Summa contra Gentiles*, 3, c. 67 ['finem ultimum,' §2420]; see *Summa theologiae*, 1, q. 105, a. 5 ['summi boni'].
15 *De veritate*, q. 22, a. 3; *Summa theologiae*, 1, q. 80, a. 2.
16 *De veritate*, q. 22, a. 4.
17 *Summa theologiae*, 1, q. 82, a. 2, ad 2m, ad 3m; a. 3, ad 2m.
18 Ibid. q. 83, a. 4, ad 3m.

Pars prima attributes to the will a *moveri ex se*, and there are stronger expressions in the *De veritate*.[19] It remains that the active *se movet* is predicated not of the will but of man,[20] and this is what accords with the explicit theory; for the will moves the intellect and all the other potencies; but the motion of the will itself is attributed to the intellect;[21] and an infinite regress in the mutual causality exerted by intellect on will and by will on intellect is avoided by affirming the intellect to be the first mover.[22] These facts have been investigated by the brilliant Thomistic student, Dom Lottin, who has explained that the great development in the *De malo* and the *Prima secundae* was due to the challenge offered by the Parisian Averroists with their doctrine of determinism.[23] In these later works St Thomas conceived the distinction between the specification and the exercise of the act of will. The specification is caused by the intellect;[24] the exercise, by the self-motion of the will;[25] and this self-motion involves a first mover acting on the will itself.[26]

In the light of these developments it becomes a fairly simple matter to evaluate the relative importance of different elements in St Thomas's theory of freedom. A free act has four presuppositions: (*A*) a field of action in which more than one course of action is objectively possible; (*B*) an intellect that is able to work out more than one course of action; (*C*) a will that is not automatically determined by the first course of action that occurs to the intellect; and, since this condition is only a condition, securing indeterminacy without telling what in fact does determine, (*D*) a will that moves itself. All four are asserted by St Thomas but with varying degrees of emphasis at different times.

In the *De veritate* the first ground of the will's indeterminacy is the objective possibility of different courses of action: 'quia ad finem ultimum perveniri multis viis potest.'[27] From the commentary on the *Sentences* to the

---

19 Ibid. q. 105, a. 4, ad 2m; *De veritate*, q. 22, a. 6: '... potest ... exire in actum volendi respectu cuiuslibet, et non exire' [it is able to proceed to an act of willing in regard to any (object) whatever, and is able not to proceed]; ibid. a. 8: '... actio voluntatis inquantum est actio, non solum est a voluntate ...' [every action of the will, insofar as it is an action, is not only from the will].
20 *Summa theologiae*, 1, q. 83, a. 1, ad 3m.
21 *De veritate*, q. 22, a. 12; *Summa theologiae*, 1, q. 82, a. 4.
22 *De veritate*, q. 22, a. 12, ad 2m; *Summa theologiae*, 1, q. 82, a. 4, ad 3m.
23 Lottin, 'Liberté humaine et motion divine' [see above, p. 54, note 33].
24 *De malo*, q. 6, a. 1; *Summa theologiae*, 1-2, q. 9, a. 1.
25 *Summa theologiae*, 1-2, q. 9, a. 3.
26 Ibid. a. 4.
27 [because one can come in many ways to the ultimate end] *De veritate*, q. 22, a. 6.

Pars prima the center of the stage is held more and more by the capacity of intellect to think out different courses of action; and in the *Pars prima* this line of thought receives its crown in the observation that in working out a course of action, an *operabile*, the intellect does not move in the mold of the scientific syllogism but on the model of the dialectical syllogism or the rhetorical persuasion: 'Et pro tanto necesse est quod homo sit liberi arbitrii ex hoc ipso quod rationalis est.'[28] Finally, while it was always maintained that the will is not determined by the intellect,[29] it is only in the *De malo* and the *Prima secundae* that one finds an explicit answer to the question, What does determine the will? As we have seen, Aristotelian passivity of appetite is then transcended, and the freedom of man yields place to the freedom of the will; in consequence, attention is concentrated on the negative factor that the will is not determined by the intellect,[30] and on the positive factor that the will moves itself and in this self-motion is always free either to act or not act.[31]

Obviously, to select one of these four elements and to call it the essence of freedom, in the sense that freedom remains even though others are eliminated, is not the doctrine of St Thomas.[32] St Thomas asserted all four,

28 [And for this reason it is necessary that man have free will, from the very fact that he is rational] *Summa theologiae*, 1, q. 83, a. 1; *Super II Sententiarum*, d. 25, q. 1, a. 1; *De veritate*, q. 24, a. 1; *Summa contra Gentiles*, 2, c. 48. The advance in the *Pars prima* seems due to *In VI Eth.*, lect. 3–4; on connected notions see *In I Post. anal.*, lect. 42, §§ 374–76; *In II Phys.*, lect. 15; *In I Peri herm.*, lect. 14, §§ 183, 199; also *In II Metaphys.*, lect. 2, § 290; and *Summa contra Gentiles*, 2, cc. 28–30.

29 *Super II Sententiarum*, d. 25, q. 1, a. 2; *De veritate*, q. 22, a. 6; *Summa theologiae*, 1, q. 82, a. 2.

30 *Summa theologiae*, 1-2, q. 10, a. 2; q. 13, a. 6; *De malo*, q. 6, a. 1.

31 *Summa theologiae*, 1-2, q. 9, a. 3; q. 10, a. 2 [emphasis Lonergan's]: '… quantum ad exercitium actus … voluntas a *nullo* obiecto ex necessitate movetur' [in regard to the exercise of an act … the will is not moved of necessity by *any* object]; *De malo*, q. 6, a. 1: '… si consideretur motus voluntatis ex parte exercitii actus, non movetur ex necessitate' [if the movement of the will is considered from the side of the exercise of the act, it is not moved by necessity]; see above, p. 96, n. 19.

32 Yet such was the view of Bañez, *Scholastica commentaria in primam partem Summae theologicae S. Thomae Aquinatis*, 1, q. 19, a. 10 (Roma, 1584, pp. 381F, 382B [Madrid: Editorial F.E.D.A., 1934, pp. 443–44]): 'Habemus itaque necessarium esse ad libertatem actus voluntatis, quod indifferentia medii eligendi iudicetur per intellectum, et simul iudicetur tale medium determinandum ad finem … Quotiescumque actus voluntatis oritur ex praedicta radice iudicii, semper erit liber. Unde rursus colligo: Quidquid antecesserit vel comitabitur vel supervenerit ad actum voluntatis, si non tollat iudicium illud circa medium respectu finis, non destruet libertatem operationis. Haec consequentia evidens est, quia stante definitione actus liberi, necesse est

and he never excluded any one of the four. Moreover, the varying emphasis that is found in different writings is explained satisfactorily by the accidents of historical development. Finally, if one desires to know how the four are related, one has only to distinguish between proximate and prior causes in the ontological order. Why is the will free? Because it is not determined by the intellect and because it does determine itself. Why has man free will? Because man has an intellect that arrives contingently at different courses of action.[33] Finally, why are there free creatures? Because there is a universe in which different courses of action are objectively possible. Thus, the first cause is the objective possibility of different courses of action; the second cause is the intellect that knows this objective possibility; and the proximate cause is the will that selects, not because determined by the intellect, but through its own self-motion.

2   Divine Action on the Will

In virtue of the theorem of the analogy of operation St Thomas always held that God was more a cause of the will's act of choice than the will itself. This may be inferred from the commentary on the *Sentences*;[34] it is stated incidentally in the *De veritate*;[35] it is the subject of a special chapter in the *Contra*

---

actum esse liberum' [Accordingly, we have it as necessary for the freedom of the act of will that there be a judgment of intellect on the indifference of the means to be chosen, and at the same time that there be a judgment determining such and such a means to the end ... As often as the act of the will originates from the aforesaid root of judgment, it will always be free. And so I deduce a further step: No matter what has preceded or will accompany or has supervened on the act of the will, as long as it does not take away that judgment about the means in regard to the end, it will not destroy the freedom of the operation. This consequence is evident, because as long as the definition of a free act stands, it is necessary that the act be free].

33 The argument ran as follows: What is hot, heats; what is cold, cools; but the doctor may kill or cure, for knowledge is a *causa ad utrumque*. Still, the doctor cannot both kill and cure the same patient in the same illness. Hence knowledge as a cause implies the intervention of another factor that selects between alternatives. This other factor is the choice, *electio, proairesis* (*In IX Metaphys.*, lect. 2, §§ 1792–93; lect. 4, §§ 1819–20).

34 Combining *Super I Sententiarum*, d. 37, q. 1, a. 1, ad 4m, with the remark on God causing the act of choice in *Super II Sententiarum*, d. 28, q. 1, a. 4.

35 *De veritate*, q. 22, a. 8: '... actio voluntatis inquantum est actio, non solum est a voluntate ut immediate agente, sed a Deo ut a primo agente qui vehementius imprimit' [action of the will, insofar as it is action, is not only from the will as acting immediately, but from God as the first agent (and the one) who makes a more emphatic impression].

Gentiles;[36] it is taken for granted in the *Pars prima.*[37] This doctrine gives rise to special difficulties with regard to freedom and the possibility of sin, and these difficulties we shall consider presently;[38] but the doctrine itself is clear and indisputable, and so we need not be concerned with it here.

But besides the act of choice there is the will itself with its acquired orientation of natural and supernatural habits and dispositions,[39] and since the analogy of operation is a theorem, God cooperates in the production of the choice because he operates in the production, maintenance, or modification of the orientated will that chooses.[40] Now, we have already studied one instance of such divine operation, namely, the infused habit,[41] and it is our present purpose to inquire into the development of similar divine interventions within the will. This inquiry will prove to be a study of the influences exerted on St Thomas by Avicenna, St Augustine, Eudemus, and finally Aristotle.

For Avicenna the lowest of the emanating intelligences was the *intellectus agens* which produced and ruled the minds of men. Consistently St Thomas refused to ascribe any such role to a created intelligence; with equal consistency he transferred this very role to God.[42] Thus at all times St Thomas affirmed divine intervention in the will; and Avicenna had provided the speculative framework through which God entered.

However, if in the commentary on the *Sentences* this entry appears to consist solely in creation and the infusion of habitual grace, the influence of Holy Writ and of St Augustine made a wider breach in the *De veritate.* The objections to q. 22, a. 8, in the latter work begin with the citation of Proverbs 21.1: 'Cor regum in manu Dei est; quocumque voluerit, vertit illud.' This is followed up by a citation from St Augustine's *De gratia et libero arbitrio:* 'Manifestum est Deum operari in cordibus hominum ad inclinandas

---

36 *Summa contra Gentiles,* 3, c. 89.

37 *Summa theologiae,* 1, q. 23, a. 5: 'Non est autem distinctum quod est ex libero arbitrio, et ex praedestinatione; sicut nec est distinctum quod est ex causa secunda, et causa prima ... id quod est per liberum arbitrium, est ex praedestinatione' [But there is no distinction between what is from free will and what is from predestination, as there is no distinction between what is from a secondary cause and what is from the first cause ... what is from free will is from predestination]. See *Summa contra Gentiles,* 3, c. 70.

38 See below, pp. 104–16.

39 See above, pp. 49–58.

40 See above, pp. 86–90.

41 See above, pp. 58–64.

42 *Super II Sententiarum,* d. 25, q. 1, a. 2, ad 5m, ad 3m, ad 1m; *De veritate,* q. 22, aa. 8–9; *Summa contra Gentiles,* 3, cc. 87–89; *Summa theologiae,* 1, q. 115, a. 4; q. 105, a. 4; *Quaestiones quodlibetales,* 1, a. 7 [q. 4, a. 2]; *De malo,* q. 6, a. 1.

voluntates eorum in quodcumque voluerit.'[43] To such objections there was no riposte. St Thomas was content to explain that they meant that God could and did change the will of man.

His concept of such change is defined as follows: 'Cum igitur Deus voluntatem immutat, facit ut praecedenti inclinationi succedat alia inclinatio, et ita quod prima aufertur, et secunda manet.'[44] The question arises, Does *inclinatio* mean a choice, or an antecedent orientation? All that can be said with certainty is that it does not, in the context, mean a hypothetical or future choice, but either a past choice or orientation; for only the latter can be a *praecedens inclinatio*, only the latter can be taken away to have something else substituted in its stead.

Two modes of such change of will are distinguished: the infusion of a habit and the simple motion. The former has already been examined. The latter is described thus:

> Immutat autem voluntatem dupliciter.
> Uno modo movendo tantum; quando scilicet voluntatem movet ad aliquid volendum, sine hoc quod aliquam formam imprimat voluntati; sicut sine appositione alicuius habitus, quandoque facit ut homo velit hoc quod prius non volebat.[45]

Plainly, this states a change in the previous orientation of the will effected without the infusion of a habit. It may be understood by a consideration of the opposite case of the impotence of the sinner: as we have seen,[46] the sinner may be unable to avoid sin either because of a vicious habit or else because of a single mortal sin which leaves behind in the psychological continuity of the will a *vis et inclinatio* to evil; in like manner God may change what man cannot, either by infusing a new habit or by substituting one inclination for another.

43 [It is clear that God operates in human hearts to incline their wills to whatever he wishes] *De veritate*, q. 22, a. 8, ob. 1, ob. 2.
44 [When, therefore, God changes the will, he brings it about that another inclination succeeds the previous one, and in such a way that the first is taken away and the second remains] *De veritate*, q. 22, a. 8.
45 [Now (God) changes the will in two ways: in one way, just by moving (it); namely, when he moves the will to will something, without imprinting some form on the will; as without the addition of some habit he sometimes brings it about that man wills what earlier he did not will] Ibid.
46 Above, pp. 51–54, discussing *De veritate*, q. 24, a. 12.

After St Augustine came Eudemus posing as Aristotle. By juxtaposing Aristotle's theory of chance and fortune with Aristotle's theory of prudence, Eudemus had been faced with the difficulty that not only the imprudent sometimes make good out of sheer luck but also the prudent have to be lucky. For the prudent man in the concrete is prudent because he takes counsel; but even if he takes counsel about taking counsel, one cannot suppose an infinite regress. What accounts for the *initium consiliandi*? Eudemus answered by dividing men into three classes: the imprudent, the ordinarily prudent, and those favored few whose *initium consiliandi* comes from an *instinctus divinus*.[47] But St Thomas with his firmer grasp of wider principles saw that the need of some divine influence was universal; indeed, the problem of the *initium consiliandi* was but a particular case of the more general doctrine of Aristotelian premotion.[48] And thus it is that we find St Thomas attaining precision in his account of the *initium consiliandi* only in the measure that his theory of the will and of its premotion develops.[49]

This brings us to our fourth influence, Aristotle. It has been shown already that in the commentary on the *Sentences* St Thomas described the preparation for justification in terms of an Aristotelian premotion that was either an object for the will, such as an admonition, or else a new factor in the apprehension of the object, such as ill health, or finally anything else of the sort.[50] Let us term such premotions external. Now, we have already come across an entirely different type of premotion, namely, the infusion of habitual grace as it is described in the *Contra Gentiles* and the *Prima secundae*.[51] This premotion, which is within the will as such, may be termed internal.

Such premotion makes its first appearance in the *De veritate* in the form of

47 See Th. Deman, 'Le "Liber de bona fortuna" dans la théologie de S. Thomas d'Aquin,' *Revue des sciences philosophiques et théologiques* 17 (1928) 38–58.
48 See above, pp. 73–75.
49 Compare the texts: *Summa contra Gentiles*, 3, c. 89 [§ 2651]; *Summa theologiae*, 1, q. 82, a. 4, ad 3m; *Quaestiones quodlibetales*, 1, a. 7 [q. 4, a. 2]; *In Rom.*, c. 9, lect. 3, § 773; *In II Cor.*, c. 3, lect. 1, § 87; *In Phil.*, c. 1, lect. 1, § 12; all these are vague or intellectualist. But *De malo*, q. 6, a. 1, and *Summa theologiae*, 1-2, q. 9, a. 4, are explicitly a motion in the will. See also *De malo*, q. 3, a. 3, ob. 11; *Summa theologiae*, 1-2, q. 80, a. 1, ob. 3; q. 109, a. 2, ad 1m.
50 *Super II Sententiarum*, d. 28, q. 1, a. 4.
51 *Summa contra Gentiles*, 3, c. 149; *Summa theologiae*, 1-2, q. 113; see above, pp. 58–64. [Lonergan's offprint of the *Theological Studies* article, p. 539, has a marginal note in his hand referring to *Super IV Sententiarum*, d. 17, q. 1, a. 2, sol. 1, ad 1m, where St Thomas has 'vel etiam ex aliquo interiori instinctu quo cor hominis movetur a Deo' (or also from some internal impulse by which the human heart is moved by God].

an actual grace preparatory to justification. It is looked upon, not as absolutely necessary, but only as an alternative to the external premotion of the commentary on the *Sentences*. And one may be inclined to identify it with the change of will described above; for in this passage, as in the other, there is to be found an appeal to St Augustine's doctrine in the *De gratia et libero arbitrio* to the effect that God operates in many ways within the hearts of men.[52] The next text of importance seems to belong to the second Paris period when St Thomas denounced as Pelagian the view he formerly held, namely, that the preparation for justification could be explained in terms of admonitions, ill health, or anything of the sort. In this article of the *Quodlibetum primum*[53] it is stated that the preparation for justification can be accounted for only by a divine operation that is internal and of a type proved by Proverbs 21.1: 'Cor regis in manu Dei; quocumque voluerit vertet illud.' While this citation is again reminiscent of the article in the *De veritate* examined above, the theoretical explanation is not in terms of change of will but of the Eudemian *initium consiliandi*.

This position of the *Quodlibetum primum* finds a congruous speculative background when in the *De malo* a distinction is drawn between the two lines of causation that converge in effecting the act of choice in the will: there is the line of causation *quoad specificationem actus*; there is another line *quoad exercitium actus*. Thus we have two first causes: the object that is apprehended by the intellect as the end, and the agent that moves the will to this end. The consequent process is that the will moves the intellect to take counsel on means to the end, and then the object apprehended as means, together with the will of the end, moves the will to a choice of the means.[54] Thus the rejection of the Aristotelian passivity of the will eliminates the old position that the intellect is first mover; now there are two first movers, the intellect *quoad specificationem actus*, and God *quoad exercitium actus*. Both are required for the emergence of an act of choice; on the other hand, the lack of either will explain the absence of the subsequent process of taking counsel and choosing.

How perfectly this position synthesizes the various elements and influences hitherto considered appears in the *Prima secundae*. There we find the proof of an external first mover of the will of the type postulated by Eudemus derived from the fact of change of will.

---

52 *De veritate*, q. 24, a. 14 c.
53 *Quaestiones quodlibetales*, 1, a. 7 [q. 4, a. 2].
54 *De malo*, q. 6, a. 1.

Manifestum est autem quod voluntas incipit velle aliquid, *cum hoc prius non vellet.* Necesse est ergo quod ab aliquo moveatur ad volendum. Et quidem ... ipsa movet seipsam, inquantum per hoc quod vult finem, reducit seipsam ad volendum ea quae sunt ad finem ... Et si quidem ipsa moveret seipsam ad volendum [finem], oportuisset quod mediante consilio hoc ageret ex aliqua voluntate praesupposita. Hoc autem non est procedere in infinitum. Unde necesse est ponere quod in primum motum voluntatis voluntas prodeat ex instinctu alicuius exterioris moventis, ut Aristoteles concludit in quodam capitulo *Ethicae Eudemicae.*[55]

The same position takes a more general form almost immediately: because God creates the soul, he alone can operate within the will; again, because the will tends to the *bonum universale,* this tendency cannot be the effect of any particular cause but only of the universal cause, God.[56] Hence

... Deus movet voluntatem hominis, sicut universalis motor, ad universale obiectum voluntatis, quod est bonum. Et sine hac universali motione homo non potest aliquid velle ... Sed tamen interdum specialiter Deus movet aliquos ad aliquid determinate volendum, quod est bonum: sicut in his quos movet per gratiam.[57]

Now, this special motion, which is a grace, may indeed be habitual grace, a

55 [Now it is clear that the will begins to will something when it had not previously willed it. It is necessary, therefore, that it be moved to willing by something else. And indeed ... it moves itself insofar as through willing the end it reduces itself to willing the means to the end ... And if it were to move itself to willing the end, it would have to do this, through a mediating deliberation, on the basis of some presupposed willing. But one cannot proceed (this way) without limit. And so it is necessary to hold that the will proceeds to the first movement of willing from the stimulus of some external mover, as Aristotle concludes in a certain chapter of the *Eudemian Ethics*] *Summa theologiae,* 1-2, q. 9, a. 4.
56 Ibid. a. 6. [Lonergan's text in *Theological Studies* as well as *Grace and Freedom* add a reference to *Summa theologiae,* 1, q. 54, a. 2. But this does not seem correct.]
57 [God moves the human will, as universal mover, to the universal object of the will, which is the good. And without this universal motion man cannot will anything ... But nevertheless God sometimes moves some people in a special way to will something determinately, which is a good; for example, in those whom he moves by grace] *Summa theologiae,* 1-2, q. 9, a. 6, ad 3m.

point we have studied already;[58] but it may also be an actual grace that is a change of will. Parallel to *De veritate*, q. 22, a. 8, and to *Quodlibetum primum*, a. 7, there is the following sentence in the *De malo* in the account of psychological continuity.

> Ex causa vero extrinseca, puta cum Deus immutat voluntatem hominis per gratiam de malo in bonum, secundum illud *Prov.* XXI, 1: *Cor regum in manu Dei, et quocumque voluerit vertet illud.*[59]

And – what is still more pertinent – there is the *actus interior* which is an actual grace that is *operans*, 'praesertim cum voluntas incipit bonum velle, quae prius malum volebat.'[60]

3   The Possibility of Contingence

This problem has already been presented. On the one hand, St Thomas maintained not only free acts but also all terrestrial activity to be contingent;[61] on the other hand, he affirmed God's eternal knowledge to be infallible, his eternal will to be irresistible, and his action through intellect and will to be absolutely efficacious.[62] Now, if God knows every event infallibly, if he wills it irresistibly, if he effects it with absolute efficacy, then every event must be necessary and none can be contingent. Such is the problem. An account of the solution offered by St Thomas falls into three sections: first, certain fallacies must be seen through; secondly, the basic solution has to be presented; thirdly, variations on the basic theme have to be noticed.

58 See above, pp. 58–64.
59 [And from an extrinsic cause, as when God changes a human will from evil to good through grace, according to that text of Proverbs 21.1: *The heart of kings is in the hand of God, and he will turn it wherever he will*] *De malo*, q. 16, a. 5; see above, pp. 56–57.
60 *Summa theologiae*, 1-2, q. 111, a. 2.
61 *De veritate*, q. 6, a. 3; *Summa contra Gentiles*, 3, cc. 72, 86, 94; *In VI Metaphys.*, lect. 3; *Summa theologiae*, 1, q. 116, aa. 1 and 3; q. 115, a. 6; *In I Peri herm.*, lect. 14, §§ 186–90.
62 *In I Peri herm.*, lect. 14, § 191: '... ut, scilicet, ex hoc ipso quod aliquid est cognoscibile cadat sub eius cognitione, et ex hoc ipso quod est bonum cadat sub eius voluntate: sicut ex hoc ipso quod est ens, aliquid cadit sub eius virtute activa ...' [by this very fact that something is knowable it falls under his knowledge, and by this very fact that it is good it falls under his will, just as by this very fact that it is a being it falls under his active power]. More explicit statements in references given below, pp. 106–10, nn. 69–80.

The first fallacy lies in a misconception of time. To a temporal being our four-dimensional universe has three sections: past, present, and future. To an eternal 'now' this division is meaningless. On this point St Thomas never had the slightest doubt: he was always above the pre-Einsteinian illusions that still are maintained by our cosmology manuals;[63] strenuously and consistently he maintained that all events are present to God.[64]

The second fallacy lies in supposing God's knowledge of the creature, or his creative will and operation, to be some reality in God that would not be there if he had not created. God is immutable. He is entitatively identical whether he creates or does not create. His knowledge or will or production of the created universe adds only a *relatio rationis* to the *actus purus*.[65] They are predications by extrinsic denomination.[66] Further, it is to be observed that a fallacy on this point is closely connected with fallacious ideas of time. For there can be no predication by extrinsic denomination without the actuality of the extrinsic denominator: else the *adaequatio veritatis* is not satisfied. Accordingly, to assert that God knows this creature or event, that

---

63 The *nunc* of a temporal being changes inasmuch as the being itself changes; the *nunc* of an immutable being is timeless, eternal (*In IV Phys.*, lect. 18, §§ 585–86). There would be as many times as motions, and so no simultaneity, were not all motions caused by the temporal motion of the celestial spheres (ibid. lect. 17, §§ 573–74). Different worlds have no common time (*Super I Sententiarum*, d. 37, q. 4, a. 3, post med.; *Super II Sententiarum*, d. 2, q. 1, a. 2). Without motion and a measure for it, such as space, there could be no time (*In IV Phys.*, lect. 17, §§ 577, 580). 'Before time' is an illusory figment of the imagination (*Super II Sententiarum*, d. 1, q. 1, a. 5, ad 13m; *In XII Metaphys.*, lect. 5, § 2498). God produces time just as any other creature (*In VIII Phys.*, lect. 2, § 989; *Summa contra Gentiles*, 2, cc. 31–38). Neither God nor even an angel knows or wills either at a time or during a time; both stand outside the network of temporal relations just as much as outside the network of spatial relations (*In I Peri herm.*, lect. 14, §§ 195, 197).

64 *Super I Sententiarum*, d. 38, q. 1, a. 5 c. and ad 4m; *Summa contra Gentiles*, 1, cc. 66–67 [§§ 547–48, 557, 564]; *Summa theologiae*, 1, q. 14, a. 13; *In I Peri herm.*, lect. 14, § 195; *Quaestiones quodlibetales*, 11, a. 3 [q. 3, a. 1]; ibid. 12, a. 3 [q. 3, a. 1], ad 1m. [Lonergan adds by hand in an offprint of *Theological Studies* a reference to *De veritate*, q. 2, a. 12.] Ingenuously, Bañez attempted to explain why St Thomas was resting his case on the idea of time; he said St Thomas wished to give all sorts of solutions (*Scholastica commentaria in primam partem Summae theologicae S. Thomae Aquinatis*, 1, q. 14, a. 13 [Roma, 1584, p. 314B; Madrid: Editorial F.E.D.A., 1934, p. 352]). St Thomas does not seem to offer more than one solution for foreknowledge, and that is in terms of time.

65 *Summa theologiae*, 1, q. 13, a. 7.

66 See above, p. 72, n. 26.

he wills it, that he effects it, is also *ipso facto* to assert that the creature or event actually is.[67]

The third fallacy is a confusion of hypothetical with absolute necessity. If *A*, then *A*: granted the protasis, the apodosis follows necessarily. But this necessity is not absolute, standing in its own right, but hypothetical, resulting only from the protasis. Moreover, what hypothetically is necessary, absolutely may be either necessary or contingent. On this point St Thomas is so insistent that no more need be said.[68]

A fourth fallacy is post-Thomist. It fails to grasp that God is not some datum to be explained, that he is absolute explanation, pure intelligibility in himself, and the first cause and last end of everything else. Accordingly, attempts are made to explain God, to explain the attributes that are identical with God, to reconcile the predicates that have their ontological ground in the absolute simplicity of God. The result is a pseudo profundity ending in insoluble problems, such as, How can God know the contingent? How can his *concursus* make him omnipotent without destroying human liberty? and so forth.

So much for the fallacies that befog the issue and lead down blind alleys. Our next point is to observe an identical line of thought running from the commentary on the *Sentences* to the *Pars tertia*. In the *Commentary on the Sentences*:

> Praescientia [Dei] etiam non imponit necessitatem rebus ... ratione adaequationis ad rem scitam quae [adaequatio] ad rationem veritatis et certitudinis scientiae exigitur, quia adaequatio ista attenditur scientiae Dei ad rem non secundum quod [res] est in causis suis, in quibus est ut possibile futurum tantum, sed ad ipsam rem, secundum quod habet esse determinatum, prout est praesens, et non futurum.[69]

---

67 'Actually is' where the present tense of the 'is' is not my present nor yours but God's; compare the Augustinian eternity of truth.

68 *Summa theologiae*, 1, q. 14, a. 13, ad 2m; *Super I Sententiarum*, d. 38, q. 1, a. 5, ad 4m; *In I Peri herm.*, lect. 14, § 196.

69 [(God's) foreknowledge ... does not impose necessity on things ... by reason of the correspondence with the thing known which is required for the concept of the truth and of the certitude of knowledge, because that correspondence of God's knowledge with the thing is relevant, not as it (the thing) exists in its causes, in which it exists as a possible future only, but (in relation) to the thing itself inasmuch as it has determinate being as present and not as future] *Super I Sententiarum*, d. 40, q. 3, a. 1.

This passage defines briefly and exactly the issue with which St Thomas deals. The equation of intellect and reality in certain knowledge might be thought to impose necessity on the known. St Thomas admits that it would, if the known *qua* known were future, for certain knowledge must be verified. If the future is known with certainty, then necessarily it must come to be; and what necessarily must come to be, is not contingent but necessary. But St Thomas denies that God knows events as future. He is not in time but an eternal 'now' to which everything is present. Hence when you say, 'If God knows this, this must be,' the 'this' of the apodosis must be taken in the same sense as the 'this' of the protasis. But the 'this' of the protasis is present; therefore, the 'this' of the apodosis is present; it follows that 'this must be' is not absolute but hypothetical necessity: 'necesse ... est Socratem currere dum currit.'[70]

It may be worth while pointing out that the same solution is to be had if one argues in terms of the second fallacy given above. 'God knows this' is true by an extrinsic denomination. There is no extrinsic denomination without the actuality of the extrinsic denominator. Therefore, the actuality of the 'this' is included in the protasis, and its reappearance in the apodosis is not absolute but hypothetical necessity: if *A*, then *A*.

Moreover – and now we come to grips with the issue – the solution not only is not a mere function of time but not even an exclusive function of knowledge. Exactly the same solution holds if the objection takes the form: If God wills this, this must be.

> ... quamvis voluntas Dei sit immutabilis et invincibilis, non tamen sequitur quod omnis effectus eius sit necessarius necessitate absoluta quam habet res a causa sua proxima, sed solum necessitate conditionata, sicut et de praescientia dictum est.[71]

Take the tip, and you will find that the solution given for knowledge is equally valid for divine will. Nor is there any use objecting that there is no parity, that knowledge as such is not causal, while will is; for, according to St

70 [it is necessary that Socrates be running when he is running] Ibid. d. 38, q. 1, a. 5, ad 4m.
71 [although the will of God is unchangeable and invincible, still it does not follow that every effect of his is necessary with the absolute necessity which the thing has from its proximate cause, but only (necessary) with a conditioned necessity, as was said also of foreknowledge] Ibid. d. 47, q. 1, a. 1, ad 2m.

Thomas, God does not know passively, by being acted upon by the object after the fashion of our senses. He knows actively: 'scientia Dei est causa rerum' – part of the production of the object and not its subsequent effect.[72]

What holds both for divine knowledge and divine will also holds for divine operation, which is by intellect and will. Nor is this position peculiar to the commentary on the *Sentences*. In the *Pars prima* fate, the *virtus instrumentalis* of divine government,[73] is said to be contingent in one sense but necessary, hypothetically, in another:

> ... fatum, secundum considerationem secundarum causarum, mobile est: sed secundum quod subest divinae providentiae, immobilitatem sortitur, non quidem absolutae necessitatis, sed conditionatae; secundum quod dicimus hanc conditionalem esse veram vel necessariam, *Si Deus praescivit hoc futurum, erit.*[74]

And so far from weakening in the course of time, this solution is again affirmed in the *Pars tertia*, where an explicit generalization is made.

> ... aliquid potest dici possibile vel impossibile dupliciter: uno modo, simpliciter et absolute; alio modo, ex suppositione. Simpliciter igitur et absolute loquendo, possibile fuit Deo alio modo hominem liberare quam per passionem Christi ... Sed ex aliqua suppositione facta, fuit impossibile. Quia enim impossibile est Dei praescientiam falli et eius voluntatem seu dispositionem cassari, supposita praescientia et praeordinatione Dei de passione Christi, non erat simul possibile Christum non pati ... Et est eadem ratio de omnibus his quae sunt praescita et praeordinata a Deo: ut in prima parte habitum est.[75]

---

72 [God's knowledge is the cause of things] Ibid. d. 38, q. 1, a. 1; *Summa contra Gentiles*, 1, c. 67 [§ 560]; *Summa theologiae*, 1, q. 14, a. 8.
73 See above, pp. 82–86.
74 [fate, from the viewpoint of secondary causes, is changeable; but as subject to divine providence, it shares in unchangeableness, not indeed that of absolute but of conditioned necessity; in the way in which we say that this conditional is true or necessary, 'If God knows this will be, it will be'] *Summa theologiae*, 1, q. 116, a. 3.
75 [something can be called possible or impossible in two ways: in one way, simply and absolutely; in another way, on a supposition. Speaking then simply and absolutely, it was possible for God to set man free in another

So much for the existence of a basic solution of the problem of contingence to be found not only in the first book of the commentary on the *Sentences* but also in the third part of the *Summa theologiae*.

Once this basic solution is grasped, it is an easy step to the doctrine of divine transcendence. The solution as such is negative. It does not affirm a property of divine knowledge, will, and action; as such, it only solves an objection. But because the objection can always be solved by distinguishing between hypothetical and absolute necessity, it is not difficult to discern therein a property, to state positively what the objection and its solution state in a negative form.

Such a positive statement is the affirmation that God knows with equal infallibility, he wills with equal irresistibility, he effects with equal efficacy, both the necessary and the contingent. For however infallible the knowledge, however irresistible the will, however efficacious the action, what is known, willed, effected is no more than hypothetically necessary. And what hypothetically is necessary, absolutely may be necessary or contingent.

This brings us to our third point, namely, the accidental variations on the basic theme. It has already been shown that in the commentary on the *Sentences* and the *De veritate* St Thomas did not hold the causal certitude of providence, and that he affirmed it in the *Contra Gentiles* through a qualification of the Aristotelian refutation of determinism by means of the *per accidens*.[76] Thus it is in the *Contra Gentiles* that the positive doctrine of divine transcendence makes its first appearance, and it does so in the form of a retort: You object that providence is necessarily efficacious; I retort that therefore what providence intends to be contingent will inevitably be contingent.[77] In the *Pars prima* the same position is expressed more positively in terms of the efficacy of the divine will: God produces not only reality but also the modes of its emergence; among these are necessity and contingence.[78] In the commentary on Aristotle's *Peri hermeneias* we are told to

---

way than through the passion of Christ ... But if we make a certain presupposition, it was impossible. For, since it is impossible for the foreknowledge of God to be fallible, and for his will or disposition to fail, (then) supposing the foreknowledge and preordination of God on the passion of Christ, it was not simultaneously possible that Christ not suffer ... And the same reasoning holds for all these things that are foreknown and foreordained by God, as was concluded in the first part] *Summa theologiae*, 3, q. 46, a. 2.

76 See above, pp. 79–82.

77 *Summa contra Gentiles*, 3, c. 94 [§ 2695c].

78 *Summa theologiae*, 1, q. 19, a. 8.

conceive the divine will as standing outside the order of contingence and necessity.[79] In the *De substantiis separatis* there is a useful analogy from the geometer who not only makes triangles but also makes them equilateral or isosceles at his pleasure.[80]

However, these variations on a basic theme must not be taken to imply that divine transcendence is a property that can be attributed to any creature, even to the Bannezian *praemotio*.

> Hoc autem non potest dici de voluntate humana, nec de aliqua alia causa: quia omnis alia causa cadit iam sub ordine necessitatis vel contingentiae; et ideo oportet quod vel ipsa causa possit deficere, vel effectus eius non sit contingens, sed necessarius.[81]

If, then, a *gratia operans* were to produce a contingent effect with irresistible efficacy, it could not be a creature; it would have to be God.

Again, though the geometer can make triangles either equilateral or

79 *In I Peri herm.*, lect. 14, § 197.
80 *De substantiis separatis*, c. 15, § 137. This is not the whole story; the variations are more nuanced and more complex. We think of any creature as a contingent being; but Aristotle thought of the heavens as necessary beings; hence the apparent anomaly of the *via tertia* (*Summa theologiae*, 1, q. 2, a. 3); regularly St Thomas uses the terms *contingens* and *possibile* in three senses: a corruptible creature; the *per accidens*; the free act of the will. In the commentary on the *Sentences* contingence is regularly ascribed to the proximate cause (*Super I Sententiarum*, d. 38, q. 1, a. 5; d. 39, q. 2, a. 2, ad 2m; d. 40, q. 3, a. 1; d. 47, q. 1, a. 1, ad 2m); but it is seen in *De veritate*, q. 23, a. 5, that this implies that God could not create a contingent (corruptible) being such as a cow. Henceforth we find it stated that God not only gives being, but also the mode of being. This does not seem to have anything to do with *ad modum liberi* [in the way of a free (agent)], which has its counterpart in the *ad modum naturae* [in the way of a nature] of the virtues; its reference is to the analogy of operation (*De veritate*, q. 24, a. 1, ad 3m; *De malo*, q. 6, a. 1, ad 3m; see above, pp. 86–90). Another and different point is that from *Summa theologiae*, 1, q. 14, a. 13, ad 2m. It might be argued that St Thomas did not consider temporal objects to be really and ontologically present to God but only cognitionally; in fact that seems to be the meaning of that text, but not of other texts; and so I fancy it might better be argued that in the *Pars prima*, St Thomas was following what he thought to be the line of least resistance for the understanding of his readers.
81 [But this cannot be said about the human will nor about any other cause, because every other cause falls under the order of necessity or contingence; and therefore it is necessary either that the cause itself can fail, or that its effect is not contingent but necessary] *In I Peri herm.*, lect. 14, § 197; see *In VI Metaphys.*, lect. 3, § 1222.

isosceles at his pleasure, still his pleasure does not extend to the possibility of making equilateral triangles with only two sides equal. Similarly, when God irresistibly produces a contingent effect, he does so, not through a necessitated, but through a contingent cause.[82] So much for the possibility of contingence.

4   The Possibility of Sin

One has only to read St Thomas to realize that this question did not worry him a great deal,[83] and our present purpose is to discover the root of this strange insouciance; for the problem has worried others. Bañez offered to solve it by means of a two-lane highway: along one lane there is what God effects, and that must be; along the other lane is what God does not effect, and that cannot be. This solution does not appear to be perfect, inasmuch as it gives the impression that, though God does not cause the sinner's sinning, he does make it impossible for him to do what is right.[84] Molina also offered to solve the problem, with a four-lane highway: two lanes are in the hypothetical order of the *futuribilia*, in which God knows what Peter would or would not do under given circumstances; two more lanes are in the real order in which God provides or does not provide the situations in which Peter sins or does not sin. And this solution is thought to lack perfection inasmuch as in the hypothetical order God does not appear to be God; as R.P. Garrigou-Lagrange asked R.P. d'Alès, 'Is God determining or determined?'[85]

A first observation is that St Thomas appears to have thought neither in a two-lane nor in a four-lane but in a three-lane highway. Thus he distin-

82 *Summa theologiae*, 1, q. 19, a. 8; *In I Peri herm.*, lect. 14, § 197; etc.
83 *Super II Sententiarum*, d. 37, q. 2; *Summa contra Gentiles*, 3, c. 162; *Summa theologiae*, 1, q. 49, aa. 1–3; *De malo*, q. 3, aa. 1–2; *Summa theologiae*, 1-2, q. 79, aa. 1–3. Contrast on the angels *Summa theologiae*, 1, q. 63, aa. 5–6, with the probably later *De malo*, q. 16, a. 4.
84 Bañez, *Scholastica commentaria in primam partem Summae theologicae S. Thomae Aquinatis*, 1, q. 14, a. 13 (Roma, 1584, p. 314D [Madrid: Editorial F.E.D.A., 1934, p. 353]): '... alia futura contingentia cognoscit Deus in suis causis, prout sunt determinatae a prima causa: malum vero culpae futurum cognoscit in sua causa, quatenus non est determinata a prima causa ad bene operandum' [God knows other future contingents in their causes, as they are determined by the first cause: but he knows the future evil of guilt in its cause, as not determined by the first cause to operate properly].
85 [Reginald Garrigou–Lagrange, 'Le dilemme: "Dieu déterminant ou déterminé,"' *Revue thomiste* (nouvelle série) 11 (1928) 193–210].

guishes between what God wills to happen, what he wills not to happen, and
what he permits to happen.

> Deus igitur neque vult mala fieri, neque vult mala non fieri: sed vult
> permittere mala fieri. Et hoc est bonum.[86]

This strange trichotomy is also implicit in a distinction between the way
God wills moral evil and the way he wills physical evil:

> Unde malum culpae, quod privat ordinem ad bonum divinum, Deus
> *nullo modo* vult. Sed malum naturalis defectus, vel malum poenae
> vult, volendo aliquod bonum, cui coniungitur tale malum.[87]

There is what God wills in no way whatever, and what he wills by willing
something else; the second of these implies a third way of God's willing,
namely, God's direct willing of the something else. Further, this trichotomy
is found not only in the voluntary order but also in the order of the realities
willed.

> ... sicut creatura decideret in nihilum nisi per divinam potentiam
> contineretur, ita etiam deficeret in *non bonum*, si non contineretur a
> Deo. Non tamen sequitur, quod nisi contineretur a Deo per gratiam,
> rueret in *peccatum*; nisi solum de natura corrupta, quae de se habet
> inclinationem ad malum.[88]

If, then, we prescind from the case of moral impotence in corrupt nature,
we have a distinction between *non bonum* and *peccatum*; and if we add to

---

86 [Therefore God neither wills that evils occur, nor wills that evils not occur,
but he wills to permit evils to occur. And this is good] *Summa theologiae*, 1, q.
19, a. 9, ad 3m; on why it is good to permit evil, see ibid. q. 23, a. 5, ad 3m.
87 [And therefore God does not in any way will the evil of guilt, which withdraws the order to the divine good. But he wills the evil of natural defect or
the evil of punishment, in willing something good to which such an evil is
joined] Ibid. q. 19, a. 9 c.; see ibid. q. 49, a. 2; 1-2, q. 79, a. 1.
88 [as a creature would fall into nothing unless it were held fast by the divine
power, so also it would fall into non-good if it were not held fast by God. But
it does not follow that, unless it were held fast by God through grace, it
would fall into sin; unless (this be true) only of fallen nature, which of itself
has an inclination to evil] *De malo*, q. 16, a. 4, ad 22m.

these two the obvious third, *bonum*, we have our trichotomy with regard to the terms of activity.

Nor is St Thomas content with a trichotomy of the will and of the objects willed; he also suggests a trichotomy in the intellectual field. Objective truth is commensurability of the object to the intellect; it is the inverse of subjective truth, in which the intellect conforms to the object; and it is of two kinds, absolute and relative. Relative objective truth is commensurability to a created intellect. Absolute objective truth is commensurability to the intellect of God. Now, falsity is the negation of truth and has all its divisions. Interestingly enough, in the *Pars prima* St Thomas asks if there is absolute objective falsity. He answers:

> ... in rebus dependentibus a Deo, falsitas inveniri non potest per comparationem ad intellectum divinum, cum quidquid in rebus accidit, ex ordinatione divini intellectus procedat: nisi forte in voluntariis agentibus tantum, in quorum potestate est subducere se ab ordinatione divini intellectus; in quo malum culpae consistit, secundum quod ipsa peccata falsitates et mendacia dicuntur in Scripturis, secundum illud Psalmi IV: *ut quid diligitis vanitatem et quaeritis mendacium?* Sicut per oppositum operatio virtuosa veritas vitae nominatur, inquantum subditur ordini divini intellectus; sicut dicitur Ioan. III: *qui facit veritatem, venit ad lucem.*[89]

In this passage an assertion of absolute objective falsity appears as an afterthought; it begins hesitantly with a *nisi forte*; but it gains momentum as it proceeds, and it ends on the level of the Johannine antithesis of Light and Darkness.

In this doubtful passage what appears decisive is the argument offered: *malum culpae* must be an absolute objective falsity if it consists in *subducere se*

---

89 [in things that depend on God, falsity cannot be found by comparison with the divine intellect, since whatever happens in things proceeds by decree of the divine intellect: except perhaps in voluntary agents only, who have it in their power to withdraw themselves from the decree of the divine intellect; it is in this that the evil of guilt consists, as in the scriptures sins themselves are called falsities and lies, according to that text of Psalm 4: why do you love vanity and seek a lie? Just as on the other side, virtuous operation is called the truth of life, inasmuch as it is subjected to the decree of divine intellect, as is said in John, chapter 3: the one who does the truth comes to the light] *Summa theologiae*, 1, q. 17, a. 1 c.

ab ordinatione divini intellectus – that is a definition. But does the sinner really withdraw from the ordinance of divine intellect? It is not too difficult to find passages in which St Thomas states or implies as much. Thus, after maintaining in *Pars prima*, q. 103, a. 7, that nothing can occur *praeter ordinem divinae gubernationis*, St Thomas at once proceeds to ask whether anything can revolt *contra ordinem divinae gubernationis*. The answer to this is a distinction between general and specific ends, between universal governance and its execution by particular causes. In the response St Thomas is content to deny revolt in the former sense. His idea is from Boethius: 'non est aliquid quod summo huic bono vel velit vel possit obsistere.' His argument is that the sinner does not withdraw totally from divine governance, for the sinner intends some good; and the implication is that in some partial manner the sinner does withdraw and therefore is rightly punished.[90]

Again, St Thomas does not seem to represent God planning both merits and sins on the sixteenth-century model. His idea of the divine plan and divine providence is intimately connected with the idea of law, the law which the sinner violates.[91] Both are defined as *ratio ordinandorum in finem*.[92] And it is in this context that St Thomas's brief yet downright solutions of the question whether God is responsible for sin have their full validity.[93] Thus we are brought to the conclusion that *malum culpae* really is a *subducere se ab ordinatione divini intellectus*, and that therefore it is absolute objective falsity.

This means that the trichotomy found in willing and in the objects willed is also found in the more fundamental order of truth: besides the positive objective truth of being and the negative objective truth of not-being, there is also the objective falsity of moral lapse. To develop the argument further, it is necessary to translate this objective falsity into terms of subjective truth. When, then, it is said that moral lapse is objective falsity, it is not implied that moral lapse is not objective. Obviously it is objective, and so it admits

---

90 [Boethius: there is nothing that wills or is able to resist this supreme good – Aquinas quotes the text in the Sed contra to the article here referred to] Ibid. q. 103, a. 8, ad 1m.
91 Read *Summa contra Gentiles*, 3, cc. 111–14.
92 Compare *Summa theologiae*, 1, q. 22, a. 1, with 1-2, q. 91, aa. 1–6. Still, there is a real difference inasmuch as reprobation is a part of providence (1, q. 23, a. 3); but that does not settle the issue until it is shown just how reprobation forms part of providence. Is it part of a mechanistic blueprint, as the modern mind is prone to assume? Or is it a toleration of failure in a universe of finalistic spontaneity?
93 See references given above, p. 111, note 83.

the subjective truth to be found in empirical affirmations of its existence and empirical classifications of its kinds. What objective falsity excludes is understanding, the explanatory science that follows an empirical science when the object of the empirical knowledge is objective truth. For, obviously, the possibility of our understanding anything is ultimately due to the object's commensurability to the divine intellect; and in absolute objective falsity it is precisely this commensurability that is lacking. We can know sin as a fact; we cannot place it in intelligible correlation with other things except *per accidens*; that is, one sin can be correlated with another, for deficient antecedents have defective consequents; but the metaphysical surd of sin cannot be related explanatorily or causally with the integers that are objective truth; for sin is really irrational, a departure at once from the ordinance of the divine mind and from the dictate of right reason. The rational and the irrational cannot mix, except in fallacious speculation. And this precept is not merely relative to man; it is absolute. The mysteries of faith are mysteries only to us because of their excess of intelligibility; but the *mysterium iniquitatis* is mysterious in itself and objectively, because of a defect of intelligibility.

If such a view appears very strange to modern theologians who tend to affirm a universal intelligibility that embraces even sin, still it could not fail to fit spontaneously and harmoniously into the categories of Thomist thought. Aristotle's universe had only a limited intelligibility; it included the *per accidens*,[94] which could never be an object of science, and which radically refuted even natural determinism. Now, St Thomas departed from this position by his affirmations of divine providence and divine transcendence, and such a departure leaves terrestrial contingence intact. Moreover, it gives the *per accidens* intelligibility, not absolutely, but only inasmuch as coincidences, concurrences, interferences are reducible to the divine design. Accordingly, if sin is a withdrawal from the ordinance of divine intellect, if it is something that God wills neither to be nor not be, if in a word it is a third member of the trichotomy we have been examining, then sin is a *per accidens* that does not reduce to divine design. Thus, however much the unintelligibility of sin may sound strange to the modern theologian, for St Thomas it was no intruder into the Aristotelian framework, but, on the contrary, a partial acceptance of Aristotelian views.

It will serve both to clarify the foregoing and to verify the hypothesis that we have been developing, if we turn to the manner in which St Thomas

94 See above, pp. 79–81.

contrasts predestination and reprobation. Both predestination and reprobation are eternal. But while predestination gives the elect both their merits
and their consequent reward, the reprobate have their sins from themselves
alone, and thus sin is a cause of punishment in a way in which merit is not a
cause of glory.[95] Now this position is not explained by the Bannezian two-
lane system, for on that system God's policy of inactivity makes the defect of
sin inevitable, so that the sinner has not his sins merely from himself, nor
really is there any difference between right action's relation to glory and
sin's to punishment. Again, the Molinist four-lane theory has perhaps never
claimed to be more than the solution of a problem St Thomas is presumed
not to have noticed. In any case, I fail to see how it could be considered as
an interpretation of the data in St Thomas on contingence and sin.

But the trichotomy we have been examining leads precisely to the position on reprobation that has been outlined. Because sin is a surd, an
irrational, an objective falsity, it cannot have as antecedent either cause or
non-cause, where by non-cause is meant a policy of inaction that makes sin
inevitable; for both cause and non-cause are instances of intelligible correlation, and the irrational cannot be so correlated. Thus, while reprobation
precedes in virtue of divine omnipotence and omniscience, still this precedence is a mere empirical, and in no way an intelligible, antecedence. It
does not cause, or lead to, or result in, the sin. And so it leaves sin to be a
first in its own order, to be due to the sinner alone, and to be a ground for
punishment in a way in which merit is not a ground for glory.

5   Conclusion

This chapter brings to a close our survey of the materials St Thomas had at
hand for the evolution of his concept of actual grace as operative and
cooperative. As is apparent, the theory of liberty we have outlined had the
singular merit of making possible a theory of operative grace; for on this
theory, as opposed to that of Scotus,[96] the free act emerges from, and is
conditioned by, created antecedents over which freedom has no direct
control. It follows that it is possible for God to manipulate these anteced-

---

95 *In Rom.*, c. 9, lect. 2, §§ 763–64; see *Summa theologiae*, 1, q. 23, a. 3 c. and ad
2m; *Summa contra Gentiles*, 3, c. 163 [§ 3333].

96 See the comparisons in Johannes Auer, *Die menschliche Willensfreiheit im
Lehrsystem des Thomas von Aquin und Johannes Duns Scotus* (Munich: Max
Hueber, 1938) [285–303].

ents and through such manipulation to exercise a control over free acts themselves:

> ... creatura rationalis gubernat seipsam per intellectum et volun-
> tatem, quorum utrumque indiget regi et perfici ab intellectu et
> voluntate Dei. Et ideo supra gubernationem qua creatura rationalis
> gubernat seipsam tamquam domina sui actus, indiget gubernari a
> Deo.[97]

Indeed, both above and below, both right and left, the free choice has determinants over which it exercises no control. God directly controls the orientation of the will to ends; indirectly he controls the situations which intellect apprehends and in which will has to choose; indirectly he also controls both the higher determinants of intellectual attitude or mental pattern and the lower determinants of mood and temperament;[98] finally, each free choice is free only *hic et nunc*, for no man can decide today what he is to will tomorrow.[99] There is no end of room for God to work on the free choice without violating it, to govern above its self-governance, to set the stage and guide the reactions and give each character its personal role in the drama of life.

Still, none of these created antecedents can be rigorous determinants of the free choice: God alone has the property of transcendence. It is only in the logico-metaphysical simultaneity of the atemporal present that God's knowledge is infallible, his will irresistible, his action efficacious. He exercises control through the created antecedents – true enough; but that is not the infallible, the irresistible, the efficacious, which has its ground not in

97 [a rational creature governs itself by intellect and will, both of which need to be ruled and completed by the intellect and will of God. And therefore, besides the government by which a rational creature governs itself, as having dominion over its act, it needs to be governed by God] *Summa theologiae,* 1, q. 103, a. 5, ad 3m; see *Summa contra Gentiles,* 3, c. 113 [§ 2873]: 'Participat igitur rationalis creatura divinam providentiam non solum secundum gubernari, sed etiam secundum gubernare: gubernat enim se in suis actibus propriis et etiam alia' [A rational creature participates therefore in divine providence, not only as governed but also as governing, for it governs itself in its own proper acts and governs other things too]. Also, ibid. 3, c. 90 [§§ 2654 and 2658].
98 *Summa contra Gentiles,* 3, c. 91 [§ 2662].
99 Ibid. c. 155 [§ 3282].

the creature but in the uncreated, which has its moment not in time but in the cooperation of eternal uncreated action with created and temporal action. Again, the antecedents per se always incline to the right and good.[100] But the consequent act may be good or it may be sinful: if it is good, all the credit is God's, and the creature is only his instrument; but if it is evil, then inasmuch as it is sin as such, it is a surd (preceded, indeed, by a divine permission which is infallible without being a cause or non-cause), and so in the causal order a first for which the sinner alone is responsible.

100 For the detailed account of the hardening of Pharaoh's heart, see *In Rom.*, c. 9, lect. 3, §§ 780–82; also the correction of St Augustine, *De veritate*, q. 22, a. 8, ad ob.; and *Summa theologiae*, 1-2, q. 79, a. 1, ad 1m.

I-6

Actual Grace as *Operans et Cooperans*

The earlier chapters have been bracketing the present inquiry. First, the whole field was reviewed, and so actual grace was studied from above. Next, we took up the parallel and complementary question of habitual grace. Thereafter, the materials for a concept of actual grace were assembled. If now we have to deal directly with actual grace as operative and cooperative, our method remains unchanged, inasmuch as now we bracket the principal text, *Prima secundae*, q. 111, a. 2. Thus our first concern is *gratia cooperans* in the *De veritate*; next, *gratia praeveniens* in the *Contra Gentiles*; in the third place, the idea of conversion from the commentary on the *Sentences* to the *Pars tertia*; then, the definition of *gratia operans*; and finally, after we have seen how St Thomas applies his analysis of the will and his theorem of universal instrumentality to the doctrine of grace, the content of the *auxilium* that is *operans et cooperans* in the *Prima secundae*.

1   *Gratia Cooperans* in the *De Veritate*

In his commentary on the *Sentences* St Thomas had acknowledged only a single grace in each individual.[1] Distinctions between *praeveniens* and *subsequens* as between *operans* and *cooperans* were not real but notional.[2] But when the same issue recurs in the *De veritate* the authority of St Augustine forces the recognition of an actual grace that is *cooperans*.[3]

---

1 *Super II Sententiarum*, d. 26, q. 1, a. 6; see above, pp. 22–23.
2 Ibid. ad 2m.
3 *De veritate*, q. 27, a. 5, ad 3m; see above, pp. 35–37.

> ... gratia cooperans dicetur secundum quod [gratuita Dei voluntas]
> in libero arbitrio operatur, motum eius causando, et exterioris actus
> executionem expediendo, et perseverantiam praebendo, in quibus
> omnibus aliquid agit liberum arbitrium.[4]

These few lines are not very informative, nor will much more be learnt by detailed study.

There is an objective obscurity in the phrase *motum eius causando*, for one cannot expect St Thomas to conceive the motion of the will more clearly and distinctly than he conceives the will itself.[5] In the *De veritate* it is not taken for granted that the will of the end is a distinct act from the choice of means; on the contrary, willing the end is to the will what the sense of touch is in the organ of sight;[6] and though the desire of happiness is the principle and foundation of all willing,[7] still the question whether the will intends end and means in one act or in two is met with the response that sometimes it is one act and sometimes two.[8] Under these circumstances it is not surprising that a single phrase from St Augustine's *De gratia et libero arbitrio* is interpreted in terms of general cooperation in *De veritate*, q. 24, a. 1, ad 3m, of change of will in q. 22, a. 8, of internal premotion of the will in q. 24, a. 14.[9] Thus, while *motum eius causando* means God's cooperation in the choice, perhaps it does not exclude change of will or premotion of will, though certainly it does include some activity on the part of the will itself: 'aliquid agit liberum arbitrium.'

With regard to the second effect of *gratia cooperans*, namely, *exterioris actus executionem expediendo*, there is an interesting series of responses on the text from Jeremiah, 'Non est in homine via eius, nec viri est dirigere gressus suos.' On three different occasions this is proposed as an objection against free will. In the *De veritate* a possible interpretation in terms of man's natural

---

4 [grace will be called cooperative according as it operates in free will, causing its movement, and expediting the execution of an external act, and granting perseverance, in all of which free will does something] Ibid. ad 1m; see above, pp. 37–40.
5 See above, pp. 94–104.
6 *De veritate*, q. 22, a. 5.
7 Ibid.
8 Ibid. a. 14.
9 [The 'single phrase' from Augustine is 'Manifestum est Deum operari in mentibus hominum ad convertendas voluntates eorum in quodcumque voluerit' (It is clear that God operates in the minds of men in order to turn their wills to whatever he wishes). Lonergan had written 'q. 24, a. 15' for the last reference, but the relevant passage is in q. 24, a. 14.]

incapacity for meritorious action is set aside on the authority of a reputed St Gregory of Nyssa, who interpreted the text in terms of external providence; man proposes but God disposes.[10] In the *Pars prima* external providence is still the main interpretation, and man has full autonomy in his choices, *supposito tamen divino auxilio.*[11] In the *De malo* two interpretations are put forward on an equal footing: the first is that the execution of choices remains in the hands of God; the second recalls that 'non volentis neque currentis sed miserentis est Dei' and explains this in terms of the Eudemian first mover that accounts for the *initium consiliandi.*[12] The interest of this series of responses is that it links the *gratia cooperans* of the *De veritate* with that of the *Prima secundae*; for the latter seems to combine the two ideas of the *De malo* inasmuch as 'ad hunc actum [exteriorem] Deus nos adiuvat, et interius confirmando voluntatem ut ad actum perveniat, et exterius facultatem operandi praebendo.'[13]

The third effect, perseverance, needs no comment. It stands between impeccability, which excludes the possibility of sin, and habitual grace, which eliminates antecedent tendency to sin.[14] It results from the combination of good choices and good performance and so, in the abstract, does not add to the ideas examined above. In closing this section we may note that the *gratia cooperans* of the commentary on 2 Corinthians, c. 6, lect. 1, appears to be the same as that of the *De veritate.*

2   Gratia Praeveniens in the Contra Gentiles

Already we have had occasion to draw attention to a development in the concept of habitual grace as prevenient. In the commentary on the *Sentences* and the *De veritate* the free acts in the instant of justification are informed by the infused grace yet are said to precede the latter from the viewpoint of material causality. In the *Summa theologiae* this distinction is dropped, and

---

10 Ibid. q. 24, a. 1, ad 1m. [The Vulgate text of Jeremiah 10.23 is 'non est hominis via eius, nec viri est ut ambulet et dirigat gressus suos'; the quotation in ob. 1 is close to this, as also in ob. 4 of the next reference; it is exact in ob. 1 of the text in note 12.]

11 [with the supposition, however, of divine help] *Summa theologiae,* 1, q. 83, a. 1, ad 4m.

12 *De malo,* q. 6, a. 1, ad 1m.

13 [for this act too God helps us, both strengthening the will internally that it may come to act, and providing externally the faculty of operating] *Summa theologiae,* 1-2, q. 111, a. 2.

14 *De veritate,* q. 24, a. 13.

the infusion of grace is characterized as *motio moventis,* while the consequent free acts are the *motus mobilis* on the analogy of Aristotelian physics.[15] The later analysis seems much more in accord with the truth of divine prevenience, and its origin is, perhaps, a chapter in the *Contra Gentiles* in which there occurs the phrase 'motio ... moventis praecedit motum mobilis.'[16] The main argument there is drawn from a series of aspects of man's instrumentality with respect to his supernatural end, but there is also a confirmatory argument from scripture. The history of one of the texts involved, Romans 9.16, throws no little light on St Thomas's correlation of divine prevenience with instrumental theory.

In the comment of the *Glossa ordinaria*[17] on the text 'Igitur non volentis neque currentis sed miserentis est Dei,'[18] one learns that the text is not satisfied by a mere assertion of the necessity of divine mercy. Free will also is necessary, yet one cannot say, 'Non miserentis est Dei sed volentis est hominis.'[19] Entire credit, then, must be given to God; for God 'hominis

15 See above, pp. 58–64.
16 [the motion of the moving (force) precedes the movement of the movable thing] *Summa contra Gentiles,* 3, c. 149 [§ 3217]. The phrase 'motio ... moventis praecedit motum mobilis ratione et causa' [the motion of the moving (force) precedes the movement of the movable thing in concept and causality] is not free from all appearance of ambiguity. Franciscus de Sylvestris Ferrariensis in his commentary on the passage tried to take *motio moventis* as the Aristotelian *actio in passo,* which really is identical with the *passio,* the *motus mobilis* [*LT* 14: 439–40]. One might be inclined to interpret the phrase on the analogy of *Summa theologiae,* 1-2, q. 113, a. 6, and this would make the *motio moventis,* the infused grace, really distinct from the *motus mobilis,* the free act. In the third place, one might take the *motio moventis* as the notional relation that is the *actio in agente,* and perhaps this is the most obvious meaning of the final words, 'ratione et causa.' As a fourth interpretation there is the confident Bannezian view that St Thomas evidently is thinking of their *praemotio physica.*
17 *PL* 114: 502, § 16. This passage is to be found in St Augustine, *Enchiridion, PL* 40, 248, § 32. [Actually, the passage in the *Glossa* is different from that in the *Enchiridion.* The *Glossa* is as Lonergan quotes it in the text, but the *Enchiridion* passage is as follows: '... hominis voluntatem bonam et praeparat adiuvandam, et adiuvat praeparatam ... Nolentem praevenit, ut velit, volentem subsequitur, ne frustra velit' (see translation below, note 20). Moreover, in *Theological Studies* 3 (1942) 557, Lonergan added the following to the footnote: 'The *Glossa* makes no acknowledgment but does cite another passage from St Augustine which, according to an editor of St Thomas (Vivès, 8, 339 n.), is also from the *Enchiridion,* c. 98, *PL* 40, 277; but while this passage does contain the *incipit,* I have not been able to find the closing words there.']
18 [It depends not on human will or exertion but on God who shows mercy]
19 [It depends not on God who shows mercy, but on human will]

voluntatem bonam et praeparat adiuvandam et adiuvat praeparatam; volentem praevenit ut velit; volentem subsequitur ne frustra velit.'[20]

If the author of the *Glossa* was content to repeat the Augustinian formulae, St Thomas in his commentary on the *Sentences* makes a first, very brief, speculative effort to interpret the text in terms of change of will.[21] But in his commentary on Romans he argues out the issue to conclude to instrumentality.

> Sed si hoc solum ... intellexisset Apostolus [scilicet, sine me nihil potestis facere], cum etiam gratia sine libero arbitrio hominis non velit neque currat, potuisset e converso dicere: Non est miserentis Dei, sed volentis et currentis, quod aures piae non ferunt.
>
> Unde plus aliquid est ex his verbis intelligendum, ut scilicet principalitas gratiae Dei attribuatur.
>
> Semper enim actio magis attribuitur principali agenti, quam secundario, puta si dicamus quod securis non facit arcam, sed artifex per securim. Voluntas autem hominis movetur a Deo ad bonum. Unde supra VIII, v. 14 dictum est: *Qui spiritu Dei aguntur, hi sunt filii Dei*. Et ideo hominis operatio interior non est homini principaliter, sed Deo attribuenda. – Phil. II, 13: *Deus est qui operatur in nobis velle et perficere pro bona voluntate.*[22]

20 [God both prepares the assisted good will of man, and assists the prepared good will; he goes before the (unwilling) will that it may will; and he follows the willing will lest it will in vain (translation follows the correct 'nolentem,' not the incorrect 'volentem'; see the next note).]

21 *Super II Sententiarum*, d. 25, q. 1, a. 2, ad 1m. [The difference between the *Glossa* and Thomas might be a function of Thomas's using Augustine's own text. In fact, the *Glossa* did not simply repeat the Augustinian formulae, as Lonergan says; it changed Augustine's 'nolentem' to 'volentem.']

22 [But if the Apostle had meant only this (that is, without me you can do nothing), since even grace does not 'will' or 'run' without man's free will, he could have made the contrary statement: 'It does not depend on God who shows mercy but on (human) will and exertion,' which is intolerable to pious ears.

And so something more is to be understood by these words, namely, that the principal role be attributed to the grace of God.

For an action is always attributed more to the chief agent than to the secondary; for example, if we say that the axe does not make the box, but the craftsman makes it with an axe. But human will is moved by God to the good. And so it was said above: '... all who are led by the Spirit of God are children of God' (8.14). And therefore a man's internal operation is not to be attributed principally to man but to God. – Philippians 2.13: '... for it is God who is at work in you, enabling you both to will and to work for his good pleasure'] *In Rom.*, c. 9, lect. 3, §777.

In this passage the argument proceeds from scripture to the instrumentality of man. The inverse procedure was followed in the chapter of the *Contra Gentiles* where arguments for prevenience from instrumentality were followed by an explanation of scripture.

> Hinc est quod dicitur ...: *Non ex operibus iustitiae quae fecimus nos, sed secundum suam misericordiam salvos nos fecit.* Et ...: *Non volentis,* scilicet velle, *neque currentis,* scilicet currere, *sed miserentis Dei*: quia scilicet oportet quod ad bene volendum et operandum homo divino praeveniatur auxilio; sicut consuetum est quod effectus aliquis non attribuitur proximo operanti, sed primo moventi; attribuitur enim victoria duci, quae labore militum perpetratur ...[23]

In the context of this passage, as also to a less extent in that of the preceding, the reader will notice the absence of the later, fully developed, theory of the will. However, as Romans 9.16 has given us the connection between grace and instrumentality, so will the theory of conversion give the connection between grace and the developed theory of the will.

3   Conversion

Though the *Contra Gentiles* correlated prevenience and instrumentality, it still explained the *initium fidei* by a gift of faith resulting from charity.[24] The *Pars prima* in its turn explains conversion by instrumentality: just as heat cannot generate flesh unless it act as the instrument of a nutritive soul, so too the powers of an angel cannot be directed to a supernatural end

---

23 [That is why it is said (Titus 3.5): *He saved us, not because of any works of right-eousness that we had done, but according to his mercy.* And (Romans 9.16): *It depends not on human will,* that is, to will, *or exertion,* that is, to run, *but on God who shows mercy* – because, namely, it is necessary for right willing and acting that man receive divine prevenient help; as in general usage an effect is attributed, not to the proximate agent but to the first mover; for victory, which was achieved by the labor of the soldiers, is attributed to the general] *Summa contra Gentiles,* 3, c. 149 [§ 3222].

24 *Summa contra Gentiles,* 3, c. 152 [§§ 3242 and 3248]. According to Landgraf, 'Grundlagen für ein Verständnis der Busslehre des Früh- und Hochscholastik' [see above, p. 18, note 77], the term *prima gratia* invariably denoted justifying faith until the middle of the thirteenth century. In fact, *prima gratia* still has that connotation, though, of course, no one now connects it with the *initium fidei.*

without the aid of grace.[25] But now there is this notable difference, that three types of conversion are distinguished: the perfect conversion of the beatific vision, the meritorious conversion of habitual grace, and the preparatory conversion that does not involve the infusion of a habit but simply the *operatio Dei ad se animam convertentis*.[26] Such preparatory conversion had been variously conceived: in the second book of the commentary on the *Sentences* it was an external Aristotelian premotion or else God's cooperation in the free choice;[27] in the fourth book and in the *De veritate* the alternatives were an external premotion or an *instinctus divinus* within the will.[28] But in the *Quodlibetum primum* of the second Paris period the alternative of an external premotion was eliminated on dogmatic grounds while the internal motion of the will was explained in terms of the Eudemian first mover.[29] To complete the movement there was needed only the developed theory of the will. But though this was had in the *De malo*,[30] and though the text, 'Igitur non volentis neque currentis, etc.,' turns up immediately,[31] it is only through the context that one can gather that grace effects the will of the end. Thus, while there is in the *De malo* some difference from the vague appeal of the *Contra Gentiles* to customary speech,[32] this difference is mainly potential.

Such potentiality seems reduced to act in the *Prima secundae*. God as external principle moves the will to the end, and in special cases he moves it by grace to a special end.[33] Conspicuous among the latter is conversion, which is expressed entirely in terms of willing the end.

25 *Summa theologiae*, 1, q. 62, a. 2 c.
26 [the operation of God converting the soul to himself] Ibid. ad 3m; see the words of *Summa theologiae*, 1-2, q. 111, a. 2, in the description of *gratia operans*: 'praesertim cum voluntas incipit bonum velle, quae prius malum volebat' [especially when the will, which before was willing evil, begins to will the good].
27 *Super II Sententiarum*, d. 28, q. 1, a. 4.
28 *Super IV Sententiarum*, d. 17, q. 1, a. 2, sol. 1, ad 1m; *De veritate*, q. 24, a. 15.
29 *Quaestiones quodlibetales*, 1, a. 7 [q. 4, a. 2]; on the Eudemian first mover, see above, p. 101.
30 *De malo*, q. 6, a. 1.
31 Ibid. ob. 2 and ad 1m.
32 *Summa contra Gentiles*, 3, c. 149 [§ 3222]: '... consuetum est quod effectus aliquis non attribuitur proximo operanti, sed primo moventi ...' [in general usage an effect is attributed, not to the proximate agent but to the first mover].
33 *Summa theologiae*, 1-2, q. 9, a. 4; a. 6, ad 3m. In the latter passage, 'ad aliquid determinate volendum' [to will something determinately] might be thought incompatible with 'Sub bono autem communi multa particularia bona

Necesse est enim, cum omne agens agat propter finem, quod omnis causa convertat suos effectus ad suum finem. Et ideo ... necesse est quod ad ultimum finem convertatur homo per motionem primi moventis ... Sic igitur, cum Deus sit primum movens simpliciter, ex eius motione est quod omnia in ipsum convertantur secundum communem intentionem boni ... Sed homines iustos convertit [Deus] ad seipsum sicut ad specialem finem, quem intendunt, et cui cupiunt adhaerere sicut bono proprio ...[34]

This passage has a special bearing on *gratia operans*, which finds its illustration, 'praesertim cum voluntas incipit bonum velle, quae prius malum volebat.'[35] But not only does *gratia operans* effect the will of the end in the case of conversion; it would seem to do so in all instances of divinely inspired action for, once the end is willed, grace becomes cooperative.

... cooperari alicui videtur pertinere ad inferius agens, non autem ad principalius. Sed gratia principalius operatur in nobis quam liberum arbitrium; secundum illud Rom. ix: *Non est volentis neque currentis, sed miserentis Dei.* Ergo gratia non debet dici cooperans ...

Ad tertium dicendum quod cooperari dicitur aliquis alicui non solum sicut secundarium agens principali agenti, sed sicut adiuvans ad praesuppositum finem. Homo autem per gratiam operantem

---

continentur, ad quorum nullum voluntas determinatur' [But many particular goods are contained under the common good, and the will is not determined to any of these] of q. 10, a. 1, ad 3m. Strictly, there is not the slightest incompatibility: grace moves the will to God, who is determinate indeed but also the *universale bonum* (q. 9, a. 6) beyond all limitation or classification; further, grace moves the will to God not by adding 'potency' in the sense of limitation and contraction, but by being a further actuation, and so giving expansion and enlargement. The really free are those who enjoy the freedom of the sons of God; perfect love of God is perfect detachment from created excellence and perfect liberty in choice.

34 [For it is necessary, since every agent acts for the sake of an end, that every cause convert its effects to its end. And therefore it is necessary that man be converted to his ultimate end by the motion of the first mover ... In this way, therefore, since God is the first mover simply, it is as a result of his motion that all things are converted to him according to the common intention of good ... But God converts righteous men to himself as to a special end that they intend and to which they desire to adhere as to a proper good] *Summa theologiae*, 1-2, q. 109, a. 6.

35 [especially when the will, which before was willing evil, begins to will the good] Ibid. q. 111, a. 2.

adiuvatur a Deo ut bonum velit. Et ideo, praesupposito iam fine, consequens est ut gratia nobis cooperetur.[36]

Here the metaphysical category of instrumentality is given a psychological content. The objection from Romans 9.16 states the metaphysical minimum that grace is a principal cause. The answer is in terms of the dependence, psychological as well as metaphysical, of the choice of means on the will of the end. For a more detailed account of this dependence, we turn to the *Pars tertia.*

> ... de paenitentia loqui possumus dupliciter. Uno modo, quantum ad habitum ... Alio modo possumus loqui de paenitentia quantum ad actus quibus Deo operanti in paenitentia cooperamur.[37] Quorum actuum primum principium est Dei operatio convertentis cor: secundum illud *Thren.* ult.: *Converte nos, Domine, ad te, et convertemur.* – Secundus actus est motus fidei. – Tertius actus est motus timoris servilis, quo quis timore suppliciorum a peccatis retrahitur. – Quartus actus est motus spei, quo quis, sub spe veniae consequendae, assumit propositum emendandi. – Quintus actus est motus caritatis, quo alicui peccatum displicet secundum seipsum, et non iam propter supplicia. –Sextus actus est motus timoris filialis, quo, propter reverentiam Dei, aliquis emendam Deo voluntarius offert.[38]

---

36 [to cooperate with someone seems to pertain to a lower agent, not to the principal one. But grace operates in us in a more important way than free will, according to that text of Romans 9.16, 'it depends not on human will or exertion, but on God who shows mercy.' Therefore grace should not be called cooperative ...
   To the third argument it must be said that someone is said to cooperate with someone, not only as a secondary agent with the principal agent, but as one assisting to a presupposed end. But man through operative grace is assisted by God to will the good. And therefore, with the end now presupposed, the consequence is that grace cooperates with us] Ibid. ob. 3 and ad 3m.

37 In the very next article we are told that the acts of faith, servile fear, and hope may precede justification (*Summa theologiae*, 3, q. 85, a. 6). Hence the divine operation here in question ('Dei operatio convertentis cor' [the operation of God converting the heart]) may be an actual grace. See *Summa theologiae*, 1-2, q. 112, a. 2, ad 2m.

38 [we can talk about repentance in two ways. In one way, as regards the habit ... In another way we can talk of repentance as regards the acts by which in repentance we cooperate with God in his operation. The first principle of these acts is the operation of God converting the heart, according to that

This instance of divine operation and our cooperation may be due in its first four acts to actual grace.[39] Nor is it difficult to distinguish the operation from the cooperation. The first act does not presuppose any object apprehended by the intellect; God acts directly on the radical orientation of the will. On the other hand, the acts of faith, of servile fear, and of hope obviously presuppose an intellectual apprehension. Further, conversion is the cause of the other acts; it is their *primum principium* in the passage quoted, and in the *ad tertium* from it proceeds the act of fear. But what is this causality? 'Homo ... per gratiam operantem adiuvatur a Deo ut bonum velit. Et ideo, praesupposito iam fine, consequens est ut gratia nobis cooperetur.'[40] Thus there appears a notable parallel between habitual grace and actual as operative and cooperative: in both cases operative grace changes the radical orientation of the will, *motio moventis*, and then the changed will responds in a new way to the apprehensions of intellect, *motus mobilis*.[41] Thus instrumental theory and psychological theory work into synthesis with the Augustinian *in nobis sine nobis* and, no less, the *nobiscum*.

4   The Definition of *Gratia Operans*

The early medieval theologians tended to multiply terms with respect to grace not so much to denote differences of meaning as to keep pace with the facility of St Augustine's rhetoric. After Peter Lombard, however, the couplet *operans et cooperans* became the dominant formula, with the result that in the early thirteenth century we find Peter of Capua and Philip the Chancellor explaining *praeveniens et subsequens* to have the same meaning as *operans et cooperans*.[42] In his commentary on the *Sentences* St Thomas held to

---

text of Lamentations, 'Restore us to yourself, O Lord, that we may be restored.' – The second act is the movement of faith. – The third act is the movement of servile fear, by which one is withdrawn from sins by the fear of punishments. – The fourth act is the movement of hope, by which one in hope of gaining pardon adds the purpose of amending. – The fifth act is the movement of charity by which sin is displeasing to someone in itself and not now because of punishments. – The sixth act is the movement of filial fear, by which because of reverence for God one voluntarily offers amends to God] *Summa theologiae*, 3, q. 85, a. 5.

39 See above, n. 37.

40 [Man through operative grace is assisted by God to will the good. And therefore, with the end now presupposed, the consequence is that grace cooperates with us] *Summa theologiae*, 1-2, q. 111, a. 2, ad 3m.

41 See above, pp. 58–64.

42 See Landgraf, 'Die Erkenntnis des helfenden Gnade in der Frühscholastik' [see above, p. 5, note 5] 181.

this identification, except in the case of the beatific vision, which was a *gratia subsequens* but not a *gratia cooperans.*[43] On the other hand, the *De veritate* and the *Summa theologiae* reveal a marked tendency to differentiate the two pairs of terms. Thus, *praeveniens et subsequens* suggests a sequence, and so we find both *De veritate*, q. 27, a. 5, ad 6m, and *Prima secundae*, q. 111, a. 3, drawing up lists of graces or of effects of grace. The *Summa theologiae* gives the sequence: (1) a spiritual cure; (2) good will; (3) good performance; (4) perseverance; (5) glory. Any item is said to be *praeveniens* with respect to those that follow, *subsequens* with respect to those that precede; so that the same thing may be, from different viewpoints, both prevenient and subsequent.

On the other hand, *operans et cooperans* tends to be used to denote diversity of causal function. If our suggested reading is correct,[44] the definition of the *De veritate* is

> Operans enim dicitur gratia respectu illius effectus quem sola efficit; cooperans vero dicitur respectu illius effectus quem sola non efficit, sed cum libero arbitrio cooperante.[45]

In any case, this certainly is the definition of the *Summa theologiae*, where we find

> Operatio enim alicuius effectus non attribuitur mobili, sed moventi.[46] In illo ergo effectu in quo mens nostra est mota et non

43 See above, pp. 30, 31.
44 See above, p. 37–38, note 54.
45 [For grace is called operative in regard to that effect which it operates alone, but cooperative with regard to that effect which it does not operate alone but with the cooperation of free will] *De veritate*, q. 27, a. 5, ad 1m. [Lonergan's wording is left in the text; again, see above, p. 38, note 54.]
46 *Operatio effectus* is attributed, not to the *mobile* but to the *movens*; on the other hand, *operatio immanens* is attributed not to the *movens* (the object seen, understood, willed) but to the *mobile*; I see the color though the color causes my seeing; see *In III De anima*, lect. 12, §766: '... iste motus simpliciter est alter a motu physico. Et huiusmodi motus dicitur proprie operatio, ut sentire et intelligere et velle. Et secundum hunc motum anima movet seipsam secundum Platonem, inquantum cognoscit et amat seipsam' [that movement is simply different from physical movement. And a movement like this, such as sensing and understanding and willing, is properly called an operation. And according to this movement Plato held that the soul moves itself, insofar as it knows and loves itself]. The essential difference of the motion that is properly *operatio* is that it is *actus existentis in actu* [the act of something existing in act] while the motion of the *Physics* is *actus existentis in potentia* [the act of something existing in potency].

movens, solus autem Deus movens, operatio Deo attribuitur: et
secundum hoc dicitur gratia operans. In illo autem effectu in quo
mens nostra et movet et movetur, operatio non solum attribuitur
Deo, sed etiam animae: et secundum hoc dicitur gratia cooperans.[47]

Such a definition implies that one and the same grace produces some
effects by itself and others in conjunction with free will. This entitative
identity of *gratia operans* with *gratia cooperans* was affirmed in principle in the
De veritate.

> ... relatio non multiplicat essentiam rei. Sed cooperans supra
> operantem nonnisi relationem addit. Ergo eadem est gratia per
> essentiam operans et cooperans.[48]   .

However, the undeveloped state of the theory of the will prevented the *De
veritate* from making the same actual grace both *operans* and *cooperans*.[49] In
the *Summa theologiae* this difficulty disappears, and there is no reason for
supposing that the following represents a statement of principle that is not
also a statement of fact.

> ... divisio debet dari per opposita. Sed operari et cooperari non sunt
> opposita: idem enim potest operari et cooperari. Ergo inconveni-
> enter dividitur gratia per operantem et cooperantem ...
>   Ad quartum dicendum quod gratia operans et cooperans est
> eadem gratia; sed distinguitur secundum diversos effectus, ut ex
> dictis patet [in corp. art.].[50]

---

47 [For the operating of some effect is not attributed to the movable thing but
    to the (actively) moving thing. In that effect, therefore, in which our mind
    is moved but not (actively) moving, and God alone is the mover, the opera-
    tion is attributed to God: and this is accordingly called operative grace. But
    in that effect in which our mind is both moved and (actively) moving, the
    operation is attributed not to God alone but also to the soul: and this is
    accordingly called cooperative grace] *Summa theologiae,* 1-2, q. 111, a. 2.
48 [a relation does not make the essence of a thing multiple in number. But
    cooperative grace does not add anything except a relation to operative
    grace. Therefore, operative and cooperative are essentially the same grace]
    De veritate, q. 27, a. 5, Sed contra.
49 See above, pp. 119–21 and 40.
50 [a division should be given through opposites. But to operate and to coop-
    erate are not opposites: for the same thing can operate and cooperate.

Thus, one and the same grace is both operative and cooperative; it is operative when God alone acts; it is cooperative when both God and the will combine to produce an effect.

There is a slight anomaly to the definition inasmuch as it is not grace but God that is conceived as operating and cooperating. However, this is fully in accordance with the ideas of St Augustine, who spoke perhaps exclusively of divine operation and cooperation, to leave the coinage of the terms *gratia operans et cooperans* to early medieval theology. To quote only the passages St Thomas quoted in the *Summa theologiae*:

> Cooperando Deus in nobis perficit quod operando incipit: quia ipse ut velimus operatur incipiens, qui volentibus cooperatur perficiens[51] ... Ut autem velimus, operatur: cum autem volumus, ut perficiamus nobis cooperatur.[52]

But not only did St Augustine speak of God operating and cooperating; it is also true that this viewpoint fits in very nicely with St Thomas's instrumental theory. Man is not the instrument of grace, but man is the instrument of God. Moreover, man is not an instrument in the same sense as irrational creatures, 'quae tantum aguntur, et non agunt';[53] on the contrary, he participates in divine governance not only by a *gubernari* but also by a *gubernare*,[54] being governed by God on a level above that of his own self-governance.[55] Thus the two effects of the one grace, *mens mota et non movens*

    Therefore grace is not suitably divided by operative and cooperative ...

      To the fourth argument it has to be said that operative and cooperative grace are the same grace; but (the grace) is distinguished according to (its) different effects, as is clear from what has been said] *Summa theologiae*, 1-2, q. 111, a. 2, ob. 4 and ad 4m.

51 [in cooperating God brings to completion in us what in operating he begins; because the One who begins by operating so that we may will brings (the work) to completion by cooperating with those who will] Ibid. Sed contra.

52 [that we will (God) operates; but when we will he cooperates with us that we may perform] Ibid. c.; but the reading of the passage in Migne is, 'Ut ergo velimus *sine nobis* operatur; cum autem volumus, *et sic volumus ut faciamus*, nobiscum cooperatur' [Therefore he operates without us that we may will; but when we will, and so will that we perform, he cooperates with us] *PL* 44, 901.

53 [which are only subjected to action, and do not act] *Summa theologiae*, 1, q. 103, a. 5, ad 2m.

54 [to be governed ... to govern] *Summa contra Gentiles*, 3, c. 113 [§ 2873].

55 *Summa theologiae*, 1, q. 103, a. 5, ad 3m.

and *mens mota et movens*, stand in splendid harmony with the theories of providence, instrumentality, and the nature of the will.

However, this differentiation of *operans et cooperans* from *praeveniens et subsequens* was not without its price. St Augustine no more identified *gratia operans* with *cooperans* than *praeveniens* with *subsequens*. For him divine operation was at the beginning of the spiritual life; it was illustrated by the good will of Peter offering to die for our Lord and then denying him. On the other hand, divine cooperation was a later and more perfect grace, illustrated by the good will of Peter when he confessed Christ publicly and died a martyr. 'Ipse ut velimus operatur incipiens qui volentibus cooperatur perficiens.'[56] Presently we shall have to return to this divergence between the definitions St Thomas proposes and the Augustinian texts to which he appeals.

5   *Actus Interior et Exterior*

In his commentary on the *Sentences* St Thomas had attempted, not very successfully,[57] to correlate St Augustine's good will and good performance with the technical terms *actus interior et exterior*. In the *De veritate*, this attempt was given up.[58] In the *Summa theologiae* it reappeared, for in the response to *Prima secundae*, q. 111, a. 2, grace is divided into actual and habitual; each of these is subdivided into *operans et cooperans*; the latter terms are defined; and the definitions are applied first to actual and then to habitual grace. The application of the definitions to actual grace reintroduces the *actus interior et exterior*.

> Est autem in nobis duplex actus. Primus quidem interior voluntatis.
> Et quantum ad istum actum, voluntas se habet ut mota, Deus autem
> ut movens: et praesertim cum voluntas incipit bonum velle, quae
> prius malum volebat. Et ideo secundum quod Deus movet humanam
> mentem ad hunc actum, dicitur gratia operans. – Alius autem actus
> est exterior; qui cum a voluntate imperetur, ut supra habitum est,
> consequens est ut ad hunc actum operatio attribuatur voluntati. Et
> quia etiam ad hunc actum Deus nos adiuvat, et interius confirmando

---

56 [The One who begins by operating so that we may will brings (the work) to completion by cooperating with those who will] See above, p. 5.
57 See above, pp. 33–35.
58 See above, p. 40.

voluntatem ut ad actum perveniat, et exterius facultatem operandi praebendo; respectu huius actus dicitur gratia cooperans. Unde post praemissa verba[59] subdit Augustinus: *Ut autem velimus operatur: cum autem volumus, ut perficiamus nobis cooperatur.* – Sic igitur, si gratia accipiatur pro gratuita Dei motione qua movet nos ad bonum meritorium, convenienter dividitur gratia per operantem et cooperantem.[60]

Since this passage has received a notable variety of interpretations, it may be well to begin by passing some of them in review.

Cajetan simultaneously offered two interpretations. One of them may be excluded at once, namely, that St Thomas prescinded from the underlying acts of will and spoke only of the *forma meriti.*[61] Such a view cannot be had from the text: *motione gratuita* is not *motione gratuita qua gratuita; bonum meritorium* is not *bonum meritorium qua meritorium.* True, St Thomas did speak of the *forma meriti* in his commentary on the *Sentences,*[62] but there is abundant evidence that his thought on grace developed notably in the interval.[63] Finally, if *actus interior voluntatis* does not mean an act of will, then what would?

The systematic Bannezian interpretation of the passage is that *gratia operans* is the *praemotio physica,* the *applicatio potentiae ad actum,* while *gratia*

---

59 That is, in the Sed contra.
60 [But there is a twofold act in us. The first is an internal act of the will; and in regard to that act the will has the role of being moved, and God the role of mover; and this is the case especially when the will, which before was willing evil, begins to will the good. And therefore, in that God moves the human mind to this act, grace is called operative. – But the other act is external, and since this is commanded by the will, as was determined above, the consequence is that for this act the operation is attributed to the will. And because for this act too God helps us, both strengthening the will internally that it may come to act and providing externally the faculty of operating, (therefore) in regard to this act, grace is called cooperative. And therefore after the words quoted above (Sed contra) Augustine subjoins: But that we will, (God) operates; but when we will, he cooperates with us that we may perform. – So it is therefore that if grace is taken for the gratuitous movement of God, with which he moves us to a meritorious good, grace is suitably divided by operative and cooperative] *Summa theologiae,* 1–2, q. 111, a. 2.
61 Cajetan, *In Summam theologiae,* 1-2, q. 111, a. 2, § III [*LT* 7: 319].
62 *Super II Sententiarum,* d. 26, q. 1, a. 5, ad 4m ['forma per quam (actus) meritorius est' (the form by which an act is meritorious)]; see above, pp. 31, 32.
63 See above, pp. 35–42.

cooperans is the consequent act. Against this, other followers of Bañez object that such an interpretation does not fit the data;[64] it gives a *gratia operans et cooperans* for the internal act, and then another *gratia operans et cooperans* for the external act. A more radical objection has already been proposed, namely, that St Thomas defined and affirmed the Aristotelian premotion, while the Bannezian system runs counter to an imposing number of Thomist doctrines and texts.[65]

Franciscus Zigon has maintained[66] that *mota et non movens, solus autem Deus movens* does not mean what it says; it is to be taken in the sense of *voluntas mota et se movens sed non movens membra corporis*. Now, it is perfectly true that before St Thomas had his developed theory of will, he was content to be rather vague in speaking of divine operation. Examples of this have been given already.[67] But St Thomas also taught that the mind progresses from the general and confused to the particular and precise; and it would be hard to be more precise than *mens mota et non movens, solus autem Deus movens*.

Cajetan's other interpretation was that the *actus interior* might be identified with the act produced by the Eudemian first mover of *Prima secundae*, q. 9, a. 4; and this act is to be considered free both because the will can dissent and because God moves the will sweetly according to its condition.[68] The reasons given for asserting freedom do not seem convincing. The will cannot dissent in the same act, for then it would be both willing and not willing the same object, not merely at the same time but by one and the same act. No doubt it can dissent in another act; but how does that freedom make the other act free? Again, it is true that God moves the will according to its condition; but the Thomist texts which affirm that the condition of the will is to be free when *mota et non movens* were repudiated in the *De malo*;[69] and even when St Thomas held the Aristotelian theory of the will as a passive faculty, he wrote: 'si voluntas ita moveretur ab alio quod ex se nullatenus moveretur, opera voluntatis non imputarentur ad meritum vel

64 For references, see del Prado, *De gratia et libero arbitrio* [see above, p. 3, note 1], vol. 1, pp. 236–38, in note.
65 Above, pp. 73–75, 78–79, 83, 84–85, 86, 97–98, 111, 116, ...
66 Franciscus Zigon, *Divus Thomas arbiter controversiae de concursu divino. Dissertatio critica* (Gorizia: Narodna Tiskarna, 1923). [The bibliographical information was found in *Ephemerides theologicae lovanienses* 1 (1924) 283.]
67 *Summa contra Gentiles*, 3, c. 149; *In Rom.*, c. 9, lect. 3, §§773, 777. [See notes 22, 23, 32 above.]
68 Cajetan, *In Summam theologiae*, 1-2, q. 111, a. 2, §11 [*LT* 7: 319].
69 See above, p. 95.

demeritum.'[70] Later, when he had corrected the Aristotelian position by distinguishing between specification and exercise of the act of choice, he argued, '... voluntas domina est sui actus, et in ipsa est velle et non velle. Quod non esset, si non haberet in potestate movere seipsam ad volendum; ergo ipsa movet seipsam.'[71] Now if freedom, *domina sui actus*, proves self-motion, then necessarily the absence of self-motion, *mota et non movens*, proves the absence of freedom. That is the *modus tollens* of the hypothetical argument: deny the consequent and you must deny the antecedent.

John of St Thomas advanced that the *actus interior* was the will of the end, an indeliberate act, and a free act.[72] If it is the will of the end, it must be an indeliberate act; for to deliberate is to take counsel about the means; and to do that presupposes the will of the end. However, the freedom of this indeliberate act is open to the same objections as Cajetan's second opinion.

Fr Norbert del Prado has attempted to buttress this position. Bañez had

70 [if the will were moved by another in such a way that it was not in any degree moved by itself, the works of the will would not be imputed for merit or demerit] *Summa theologiae*, 1, q. 105, a. 4, ad 3m.

71 [the will is master of its own act, and to will and not will is in (its power), which would not be the case if it did not have it in its power to move itself to willing; therefore it moves itself] Ibid. 1-2, q. 9, a. 3, Sed contra.

72 This is somewhat simplified. John of St Thomas considers *gratia operans* to be the *qualitas per modum transeuntis* (that is, the Bannezian *praemotio*) which is prior to both deliberate and indeliberate acts [*per modum qualitatis transeuntis*, Joannes a Sancto Thoma, *Cursus theologicus: In Summam theologiae D. Thomae*, vol. 6: *In Primam secundae Divi Thomae, Quaestiones CIX–CXIV, De gratia* (Paris: Vivès, 1885, reprinted Quebec: Les Presses Universitaires Laval, 1951) 1-2, q. 111, a. 2, diss. 23, a. 1, VIII, p. 804]. The basis of this view is the assumption that if we elicit an act we produce it (ibid. IX, p. 805), which is to confuse *operatio effectus* with *operatio immanens* (see above, p. 129, note 46). However, he goes on to assert that the effect of *gratia operans* is the act which we elicit without deliberation (ibid. X, p. 805), while the effect of *gratia cooperans* is the act consequent to taking counsel (ibid. XI, p. 806). Later, in meeting an objection, he advances that the indeliberate act effected by *gratia operans* is free (ibid. XVII, p. 808). His ground for this is to be discovered in *Summa theologiae*, 1, q. 63, a. 5 c. and ad 3m, where we learn that the good angels merited in the first instant of their creation but the bad angels could not sin in the first instant because that operation is from the cause of their being. But in the later *De malo*, q. 16, a. 4, St Thomas rejects this reason as invalid and gives an entirely new solution, to the effect that in the first instant the angels acted in the natural order, and so neither merited by a perfect conversion to God nor sinned by aversion from him. Perhaps the view of the *Pars prima* might lead to the conclusion John of St Thomas drew from it; but in point of fact St Thomas came to a different conclusion, and perhaps this was from fear of arriving at his disciple's view.

said: 'Nullus effectus, cuius Deus solus sit causa, potest esse contingens.'[73] Perhaps with this in mind, del Prado attempted to distinguish between mere passivity and *mota et non movens*. In the latter case there is an *actus voluntatis* and so a *voluntas agit*.[74] But this appears to involve a confusion of *operatio immanens* and *operatio effectus*. Every *operatio effectus* involves an *agere* in the sense of activity, but, as is clear from the *corpus*, God alone operates an effect.[75] On the other hand, an *operatio immanens* may be purely passive yet attributed to the patient: seeing, understanding, willing the end are passive; yet I see, understand, will the end. But because in these instances *operatio attribuitur mobili*, one has no reason for asserting that the *mobile* is active.

Fr del Prado has another argument: justification is a *gratia operans*; but, 'dum iustificamur, Dei iustitiae consentimus';[76] therefore, the effect of a *gratia operans* is a free act. The major premise does not seem free from flaws. It is not St Thomas but the hypothetical second objicient who implies that the grace of justification is from every point of view a *gratia operans*. According to St Thomas, justification basically is the infusion of habitual grace; again, according to St Thomas habitual grace is *operans* in its formal effects and *cooperans* in producing the meritorious acts of free will.[77] Hence inasmuch as 'per motum liberi arbitrii, dum iustificamur, Dei iustitiae consentimus,'[78] habitual grace is not operative but cooperative; on the

---

73 [No effect of which God alone is the cause can be contingent] Bañez, *Scholastica commentaria in primam partem Summae theologicae S. Thomae Aquinatis*, 1, q. 19, a. 8, conc. 6 (Roma, 1584, p. 370E [Madrid, 1934, p. 431]).

74 del Prado, *De gratia et libero arbitrio*, vol 1, pp. 237–38, note on Gonet.

75 *Summa theologiae*, 1-2, q. 111, a. 2: 'Operatio ... alicuius effectus non attribuitur mobili, sed moventi. In illo ergo effectu in quo mens nostra est mota et non movens, solus autem Deus movens ...' [the operating of some effect is not attributed to the movable thing but to the (actively) moving thing. In that effect, therefore, in which our mind is moved but not (actively) moving, and God alone is the mover] See above, p. 129, n. 46.

76 [we consent to the justice of God while we are being justified] del Prado, *De gratia et libero arbitrio*, vol. 1, p. 234.

77 *Summa theologiae*, 1-2, q. 111, a. 2: '... habitualis gratia, inquantum animam sanat vel iustificat, sive gratam Deo facit, dicitur gratia operans; inquantum vero est principium operis meritorii, quod etiam ex libero arbitrio procedit, dicitur cooperans' [habitual grace, insofar as it heals the soul or justifies it or makes it pleasing to God, is called operative grace; but insofar as it is the principle of a meritorious deed, which proceeds from free will too, it is called cooperative].

78 [we consent to the justice of God through a movement of free will while we are being justified] Ibid. ad 2m.

other hand, since this motion of free will is effected by the habitual grace, the total operation is due to grace: 'Ille tamen motus non est causa gratiae, sed effectus. Unde tota operatio pertinet ad gratiam.'[79] The significance of these final words is that they repudiate the earlier view of the commentary on the *Sentences* and of the *De veritate* which made the free acts in justification prior to the infused grace from the viewpoint of material causality.[80]

So much for interpretations of *actus interior et exterior* which appear unsatisfactory. The difficulty of the passage would seem to be this: it gives a *duplex actus*, one internal to the will and one external; but the theory of the will gives a *triplex actus*: will of the end, choice of means, and bodily execution. If we denote the pair by *A* and *B*, and the trio by *X*, *Y*, and *Z*, respectively, then the possible interpretations may be listed as follows: (1) *A* is *X*, and *B* is *Y*; (2) *A* is *X*, and *B* is *Z*; (3) *A* is *X*, and *B* includes both *Y* and *Z*; (4) *A* includes both *X* and *Y*, and *B* is *Z*; (5) *A* is *Y*, and *B* is *Z*. Something can be said for each of these possibilities.

There is strong external evidence for the last on the list, namely, that the internal act is the election and the external act the bodily execution. Time and again, even in his later works, St Thomas indisputably uses the terms in that sense: in the *De malo* in treating internal and external sins,[81] in the *Prima secundae* in the general theory of morality,[82] in contrasting the aims of divine and of civil law,[83] and in comparing the Old Law and the New;[84] and in the *Secunda secundae* in treating the virtues.[85] This widespread and contemporary uniformity is imposing. On the other hand, it is not a law of nature nor can it do more than establish a strong antecedent probability with regard to a different text and context. Indeed, when St Thomas was treating morality, law, virtue, and sin, the only part of the *actus voluntarius* that could concern him was the election and its execution. Grace moves in a broader context, nor is there a complete lack of external evidence that the *actus interior voluntatis* has a special reference to the end. Thus, in the *Prima secundae*:

79 [But that movement is the effect of grace, not its cause. And so the whole operation pertains to grace] Ibid.
80 See above, pp. 63, 64.
81 *De malo*, q. 2, a. 2 c. and ad 1m, ad 5m–6m, ad 8m, ad 11m–13m; a. 3; etc.
82 *Summa theologiae*, 1-2, qq. 18–20.
83 Ibid. q. 98, a. 1.
84 Ibid. q. 108, aa. 1–3.
85 Ibid. 2-2, qq. 2–3, 24–43, in the division of questions; in the text, especially q. 3, a. 1; q. 31, a. 1, ad 2m.

In actu autem voluntario invenitur duplex actus, scilicet actus interior voluntatis, et actus exterior: et uterque horum actuum habet
suum obiectum. Finis autem proprie est obiectum interioris actus
voluntarii: id autem circa quod est actio exterior, est obiectum eius.
Sicut igitur actus exterior accipit speciem ab obiecto circa quod est;
ita actus interior voluntatis accipit speciem a fine, sicut a proprio
obiecto.[86]

This quotation is the more convincing because it is truncated. There seems
to me little doubt that the *actus exterior* is the merely corporeal act, and it
might be argued rather soundly that the proper object of the election is the
end, because in choosing the means what the will really wills is the end.[87]
Still, it must be conceded that in another context *actus interior* might mean
simply the will of the end, especially since the act of will, properly so called,
is with respect to the end.[88]

If one turns from general usage to the text itself of *Prima secundae*, q. 111,
a. 2, the second or third of our list of possibilities seems to attain overwhelming evidence. For four cogent reasons the *actus interior* should be
identified with willing the end. The first reason is the *solutio ad tertium*:
operative grace effects good will, and so, with the will of the end attained,
grace becomes cooperative.[89] The second reason is that the principal
instance of the *actus interior* is conversion, 'praesertim cum voluntas incipit
bonum velle'; but just a few questions previously,[90] St Thomas had explained conversion in terms of the first mover directing created wills to his

86 [But in the (category of) voluntary act there is found a twofold act, namely,
    the internal act of the will and the external act; and each of these acts has
    its object. But the end is properly the object of the internal act of the will,
    and that about which the external act is concerned is the object of that act.
    Therefore, just as the external act gets its species from the object about
    which it is concerned, so the internal act of the will gets its species from the
    end as from its proper object] Ibid. 1-2, q. 18, a. 6.
87 Ibid. q. 8, a. 2 c.: 'Ea vero quae sunt ad finem, non sunt bona vel volita
    propter seipsa sed ex ordine ad finem ... unde hoc ipsum quod [voluntas]
    in eis [mediis] vult est finis' [But those things which are means to an end
    are not good or willed for their own sake but from their being ordered to
    an end ... and so the very thing which the will wills in them is the end].
88 Ibid.: 'Si autem loquamur de voluntate secundum quod nominat proprie
    actum, sic, proprie loquendo, est finis tantum' [But if we speak of the will,
    according as properly it names an act, then strictly speaking it is of the end
    only].
89 Ibid. q. 111, a. 2, ad 3m.
90 Ibid. q. 109, a. 6.

end. The third reason is that in conversion there are free acts resulting from the divine motion;[91] and in the article on repentance in the *Pars tertia*,[92] in which both divine operation and our cooperation are said to be illustrated, we have a *primum principium* which is *Dei operatio convertentis cor* to correspond to *voluntas mota et non movens*, and then a series of acts to correspond to man's free cooperation. The fourth reason is from the developed theory of the will: because the will is *domina sui actus* it moves itself, it is *se movens*;[93] but this self-motion presupposes the activity of an external principle, moving the will to the end in virtue of which it moves itself to the means;[94] thus only in the will of the end is the *voluntas mota et non movens*. The nature of the *actus interior* seems demonstrably to be the will of the end effected by the Eudemian first mover.

At first sight the *actus exterior* seems to be the purely corporeal execution: 'qui cum a voluntate imperetur.' But a few lines later we have: 'interius confirmando voluntatem ut ad actum perveniat et exterius facultatem operandi praebendo'; and these words seem to make it clear that the external act includes an internal act of will. One might endeavor to evade this by saying that the act at which the will arrives, 'ut ad actum perveniat,' is the causal *influxus*, the production of the bodily execution. But this is not satisfactory, for the need of grace in good performance is not to aid efficacious will in effecting its *imperium* but to change mere good desires into efficacious willing. Once the will really wills, the bodily act follows: indeed, 'tanta est facilitas, ut vix a servitio discernatur imperium.'[95] On the other hand, to will yet fail to perform means that really the will fails.

> ... animus, quando perfecte imperat sibi ut velit, tunc iam vult: sed quod aliquando imperet et non velit, hoc contingit ex hoc quod non perfecte imperat. Imperfectum autem imperium contingit ex hoc,

---

91 Ibid. ad 4m: '... hominis est praeparare animam, quia hoc facit per liberum arbitrium; sed tamen hoc non facit sine auxilio Dei moventis et ad se attrahentis, ut dictum est (in corp. art.)' [it pertains to man to prepare the soul, because he does this by free will; but nevertheless he does not do it without the help of God moving him and drawing him to himself, as was said (in the body of the article)].

92 Ibid. 3, q. 85, a. 5.

93 Ibid. 1-2, q. 9, a. 3, Sed contra.

94 Ibid. a. 4.

95 [so great is the facility that command is hardly distinguished from servitude] Ibid. q. 17, a. 9, Sed contra.

quod ratio ex diversis partibus movetur ad imperandum vel non imperandum: unde fluctuat inter duo, et non perfecte imperat.[96]

In this passage the *imperium* is taken strictly as an act elicited in the intellect, and the question treated is the ordering of an act of will. However, though the *imperium* is elicited in the intellect, this is done under the influence of the will.[97] Accordingly, the responsibility for failure to act devolves ultimately upon the inefficacy of the will of the end, or, more generally, upon the failure or inability of rational appetite to dominate the situation.[98] It would seem that the obvious meaning of *interius confirmando voluntatem ut ad actum perveniat* is also the right interpretation; *actus exterior* includes the act of will that orders the bodily execution.

For these reasons we are led to consider as alone probable the third of the hypotheses listed above: the internal act of will is with respect to the end; the external act is not merely the bodily execution but also the act of will commanding this execution. It is true that there is a lack of symmetry to this conclusion, but not a lack of symmetry that is unexplained. For the radical anomaly of the passage is that St Thomas is illustrating his metaphysically conceived definitions of *gratia operans et cooperans* by St Augustine's temporal sequence of *operando incipit* and *cooperando perficit*. St Thomas's definitions are in terms of a single grace that is both *operans* and *cooperans*, while St Augustine's phrases refer to two graces separated by a notable interval of time.[99]

Thus, fully to understand *Prima secundae*, q. 111, a. 2, one must grasp that the new wine of speculative theology is bursting the old bottles of Pelagian controversy. The Pelagians took their distinction between good will and good performance from the Stoics. The exigences of controversy made St Augustine model his divine operation and cooperation into a point-for-

---

96 [when the soul perfectly commands itself to will, then already it does will; but the fact that sometimes it commands and does not will is due to this, that it does not perfectly command. And this imperfect command is due to this, that reason is moved from different sides to command and not to command; and so (the soul) fluctuates between two things and does not command perfectly] Ibid. a. 5, ad 1m.

97 Ibid. a. 1.

98 See the commentary on the text, 'Non enim quod volo bonum, hoc ago: sed quod odi malum, hoc facio,' *In Rom.*, c. 7, lect. 3, §§ 562–66. In the case of the sinner the *volo* is inefficacious, the *ago* a complete act; in the case of the justified the *volo* is efficacious, but the *ago* is a *motus primo-primus*.

99 See above, p. 132.

point refutation of Pelagian error. But St Thomas was engaged in the far vaster task of working out the intelligible unity of all dogmatic data. He had to take into account not merely the text, 'Nemo potest venire ad me nisi Pater, qui misit me, traxerit eum,'[100] but also such a general text as 'qui spiritu Dei aguntur, ii sunt filii Dei.'[101] Hence, while St Augustine is content to affirm his *operatur incipiens*, St Thomas has to take a broader view to consider the beginnings of the spiritual life not as unique but as a single instance of a more general law; accordingly he does not say, 'cum voluntas incipit bonum velle,' but 'praesertim cum voluntas incipit bonum velle.' The general law is that man is always an instrument; that his volitional activity deploys in two phases; that in the first phase he is governed, *mota et non movens*, while in the second he governs, *et mota et movens*; that the first phase is always a divine operation while in the second the theorem of cooperation necessarily follows;[102] and finally that, inasmuch as motions to the *bonum meritorium* and its supernatural goal are graces,[103] the general law of instrumentality then becomes the special gift of *gratia operans et cooperans*. Now this adaptation of the speculative materials of instrumental and voluntary theory into a doctrine of grace not only implies that conversion is but a

---

100 [No one can come to me unless drawn by the Father who sent me] In the commentary on John, c. 6, lect. 5, § 935, St Thomas distinguishes three ways in which the Father draws us: first, through the intellect, whether this be by the objective evidence of miracles or by the internal revelation of the type granted Peter, to whom flesh and blood did not reveal Christ's divinity; secondly, through the action of the intellect on the will, for 'trahit sua quemque voluptas' [everyone's pleasure draws him], and in Christ there shines forth the majesty of the Father and the beauty of the Son who is Truth; thirdly, through direct action on the will, the *instinctus interior*, 'cor regis in manu Domini.' This exposition does not go much beyond *Summa contra Gentiles*, 3, cc. 89–91.

101 [all who are led by the Spirit of God are children of God] On this text the commentary on Romans, c. 8, lect. 3, § 635, also appeals to the *instinctus interior*, to the fact that man is not the principal cause of his free acts. The position is indistinct as in the *Contra Gentiles*.

102 The phrase 'consequens est ut … cooperetur' [the consequence is that (grace) cooperates (with us)] (*Summa theologiae*, 1-2, q. 111, a. 2, ad 3m) reveals the theorem that underlies the proximate analogy of operation. Unless cooperation were a theorem, it could not be a conclusion to the fact *praesupposito iam fine*. On the theorem, see above, pp. 89–90.

103 *Summa theologiae*, 1-2, q. 111, a. 2, Sed contra: '… operationes Dei quibus movet nos ad bonum, ad gratiam pertinent' [the operations of God by which he moves us to good pertain to grace]. More explicitly in the corpus actual grace is the gratuitous motion by which we are moved to meritorious good.

single instance of *gratia operans*, but also involves that good performance is but one instance of *gratia cooperans*. As is plain from the *Pars tertia*, the *gratia cooperans* need not refer to an external act; for in the *actus quibus Deo operanti in paenitentia cooperamus*,[104] the divine operation is *Dei operatio convertentis cor*, while our cooperation consists in the internal acts of faith, servile fear, and hope. Thus the logic of speculative theology reaches far beyond the exigences of controversy, nor can incidental anomaly or lack of symmetry be surprising when, to the interpretation of Augustinian texts, St Thomas brings a technique of metaphysical analysis that is adapted and evolved to embrace the whole range of scriptural teaching and Catholic doctrine.

104 [the acts by which in repentance we cooperate with God in his operation]
   Summa theologiae, 3, q. 85, a. 5.

Concluding Summary

The thought of Aquinas on *gratia operans* was but an incident in the execution of a far vaster program. If on the surface that program was to employ the Aristotelian scientific technique against the diehard traditionalism of the current Christian Platonists and, at the same time, to inaugurate historical research by appealing to the real Aristotle against the Parisian Averroists, in point of fact no less than in essence it was to lay under tribute Greek and Arab, Jew and Christian, in an ever renewed effort to obtain for Catholic culture that *aliquam intelligentiam eamque fructuosissimam*[1] which is the goal of theological speculation.[2] Within the frame of so universal an undertaking the treatment of any particular issue could not but be incidental. The works of St Thomas do not include a *De gratia et libero arbitrio*. They are made up of the two great strategic campaigns – the *Contra Gentiles* and the *Summa theologiae* – to think out the Catholic position in philosophy and to put new order into the sprawling theology dominated by the Lombard's *Sentences*. Supporting these vast movements were the successive drives of the *Quaestiones disputatae*, the forays of the *Quodlibetales*, the emergencies met in the *Opuscula*; finally, the base of all these operations lay in the commentaries on Holy Writ and on

---

1 *DB* 1796 [*DS* 3016].
2 If it is true that the acceptance of Christianity led to the withering of Icelandic culture, then the human importance of the Scholastic effort of *fides quaerens intellectum* may be measured by the contrasting intellectual vitality of Western Europe. [This note, found in *Theological Studies*, was omitted from *Grace and Freedom*.]

Aristotle where, I think more than elsewhere, the wealth of the theologian and the stature of the philosopher stand revealed.

It is not to be regretted that St Thomas did not adopt a specialist viewpoint, for it is the nemesis of all specialization to fail to see the woods for the trees, to evolve ad hoc solutions that are indeed specious yet profoundly miss the mark for the very reason that they aim too intently at a limited goal. There is a disinterestedness and an objectivity that comes only from aiming excessively high and far, that leaves one free to take each issue on its merits, to proceed by intrinsic analysis instead of piling up a debater's arguments, to seek no greater achievement than the inspiration of the moment warrants, to await with serenity for the coherence of truth itself to bring to light the underlying harmony of the manifold whose parts successively engage one's attention. Spontaneously such thought moves towards synthesis, not so much by any single master stroke as by an unnumbered succession of the adaptations that spring continuously from intellectual vitality. Inevitably such a thinker founds a school, for what he builds is built securely, and what the span of mortal life or the limitations of his era force him to leave undone, that nonetheless already stands potentially within the framework of his thinking and the suggestiveness of his approach. Finally, the greater such a genius is, perhaps the more varied will be the schools that appeal to him; for it is not to be taken for granted that the ever lesser followers of genius will be capable of ascending more than halfway up the mountain of his achievement or even, at times, of recognizing that one mountain has many sides.

Such was the stamp of Aquinas, and in the particular and limited field that has been the object of this study it was his lot to work out to its term a prolonged effort in theological speculation. Peter Lombard had divided grace itself into operative and cooperative, and, insofar as he attempted any systematic explanation of its nature and its necessity, he tended to conceive it psychologically.[3] When St Thomas began to write, the theory of the supernatural habit had been explored, yet the distance that remained to be traversed before grace could be divided into habitual and actual, to be then subdivided into *operans* and *cooperans*, may be measured roughly from the ambiguities of St Albert's *gratia gratis data*,[4] from his opinion that *liberum arbitrium* was a third faculty distinct from intellect and will,[5] from his

3 See above, pp. 11–14.
4 See above, pp. 24–26.
5 See above, p. 94.

curious distinction between *virtus divina increata* and *virtus divina creata* with its origin in Avicennist biological lore.[6]

In his commentary on the *Sentences* St Thomas did not advance beyond St Albert, inasmuch as the latter conceived only habitual grace as *operans et cooperans*.[7] Yet already the master of speculation is at work. The *virtus divina creata* was rejected.[8] The analogy of operation was affirmed, though as yet the premise of the proximate analogy was but creation and conservation.[9] *Liberum arbitrium* was identified with intellect and will.[10] Perfection in operation was correlated with the degree of actuation in being, and the role of habits was seen on a cosmic scale.[11] Divine knowledge of the contingent future was explained by inverting the Aristotelian position: Aristotle had denied that the contingent future was true; St Thomas affirmed its truth, to deny that it was future to God.[12] Finally, a parallel solution was indicated for the problem of divine will and contingence, and this gave at once a negative statement of divine transcendence.[13]

In the *De veritate* wider reading forced the acknowledgment that the sinner cannot avoid future sins without grace,[14] and that the justified need other graces besides the supernatural habit.[15] Thus the theory of habits was retouched,[16] and actual grace emerged as *cooperans*,[17] but whether actual grace was divine cooperation, or a change in the orientation of the will, or any internal premotion, was not clearly conceived.[18] At the same time, providence as predestination was granted a statistically certain causality,[19] and the positive conception of divine transcendence made its first very incomplete appearance in the affirmation that God himself produces the mode of contingence in creating corruptible beings.[20]

The *Contra Gentiles*, that vast undertaking to think out the Catholic posi-

6 See above, p. 67.
7 See above, pp. 26–35.
8 See above, pp. 67, 68.
9 See above, p. 88–89.
10 See above, p. 94.
11 See above, pp. 45–47.
12 See above, pp. 106, 107.
13 See above, pp. 107–109.
14 See above, pp. 51–54.
15 See above, pp. 35–37.
16 See above, pp. 46, 47.
17 See above, pp. 37–40.
18 See above, p. 120.
19 See above, p. 78.
20 See above, p. 110, note 80.

tion in Aristotelian terms, insisted on the prevenience of divine grace and expressed this dogmatic fact in the metaphysical category of instrumentality.[21] Concomitantly, the premises of the proximate analogy of operation shifted from their earlier exclusive attention to creation and conservation to embrace application and instrumentality;[22] again concomitantly, the causal certitude of providence was affirmed generally by denying the absoluteness of the Aristotelian *per accidens*;[23] and in the same context the theorem of divine transcendence moved to positive statement with respect to the contingence not merely of the corruptible but also of the *per accidens* and the free choice.[24] Already the main lines of the Thomist position had been laid down, though the problem of the *initium fidei* was solved by the prevenience of habitual grace;[25] and there was no precise statement of the manner in which divine activity makes the human will its instrument.

Such questions gradually found their solution in the *Pars prima*, the *Quodlibetum primum*, and the *De malo*. On dogmatic grounds, the preparation for justification became exclusively the effect of an internal grace;[26] and later the way was opened for a definition of this grace when a distinction was drawn between the specification and the exercise of the act of will,[27] and analysis advanced from the liberty of man as a rational creature to the liberty of the will as a self-moving faculty.[28] Seen in this perspective, the *Prima secundae* naturally possesses its long series of questions on the will, on habits, and on grace, and it is upon the answers there given that converge the multitudinous developments of the previous fifteen years. Still, as if to insist upon meaning and to contemn terminological primness – the solitary achievement of lesser minds – St Thomas employed different analogies for *motio moventis* and *motus mobilis* in treating actual and habitual grace. In actual grace the two are identified: 'actus moventis in moto est motus,'[29] according to Aristotle's *actio in passo*;[30] in habitual grace the *motio moventis* is the infused habit while the *motus mobilis* is the entitatively distinct and causally dependent free act with its analogy in Aristotle's physical

---

21 See above, pp. 121–22.
22 See above, pp. 89–90.
23 See above, pp. 81–82.
24 *Summa contra Gentiles*, 3, c. 94 [§§ 2695c, 2696].
25 See above, p. 124, note 24.
26 See above, p. 125.
27 See above, p. 96.
28 See above, pp. 96, 97.
29 *Summa theologiae*, 1-2, q. 110, a. 2 c.
30 See above, pp. 68, 69.

theory of natural motion proceeding from form.[31] Nonetheless, in both cases the same theory of instrumentality and of freedom is in evidence: the will has its strip of autonomy, yet beyond this there is the ground from which free acts spring; and that ground God holds and moves as a fencer moves his whole rapier by grasping only the hilt. When the will is *mota et non movens, solus autem Deus movens, dicitur gratia operans*. On the other hand, when the will is *et mota et movens, dicitur gratia cooperans*. In habitual grace divine operation infuses the habit, to become cooperation when the habit leads to free acts;[32] in actual grace divine operation effects the will of the end to become cooperation when this will of the end leads to an efficacious choice of means; and though the expression of this is perturbed by a divergence between St Augustine's controversial concerns and St Thomas's speculative interests,[33] still this superposition of different viewpoints fails to hide the fact that metaphysics and psychology, divine providence and human instrumentality, grace and nature at last have meshed their intricacies in synthesis.

This fact of synthesis cannot perhaps be expressed, for synthesis in a field of data is like the soul in the body, everywhere at once, totally in each part and yet distinct from every part. But to be certain of the fact of synthesis is as easy as to be certain of the fact of soul. One has only to remove this or that vital organ and watch the whole structure tumble into ruin; the old unity and harmony will disappear, and in its place will arise the irreconcilable opposition of a multiplicity. Thus, to St Thomas cooperation was a theorem, something known by understanding the data already apprehended and not something known by adding a new datum to the apprehension, something like the principle of work and not something like another lever, something like the discovery of gravitation and not something like the discovery of America.

Remove this key position and it becomes impossible to reconcile human instrumentality with human freedom: one can posit a *praedeterminatio physica* to save instrumentality, or one can posit a *concursus indifferens* to save self-determination; one cannot have a bit of both the antecedents and the whole of both the consequents. There is a material resemblance between the Molinist *gratia excitans* and the Thomist *gratia operans*, but the resemblance is only material, for the Molinist lacks the speculative acumen to

31 See above, pp. 58–64.
32 *Summa theologiae*, 1-2, q. 111, a. 2 c.
33 See above, pp. 127–28.

make his grace leave the will instrumentally subordinate to divine activity. But the Bannezian has exactly the same speculative blind spot: because he cannot grasp that the will is truly an instrument by the mere fact that God causes the will of the end, he goes on to assert that God also brings in a *praemotio* to predetermine the choice of means.

To take another instance of this breakup of synthesis into irreconcilable alternatives, we have seen that St Thomas did not entirely give up the Aristotelian position of the unintelligibility of the *per accidens*; in the case of sin it remained a surd to thought. And this Aristotelian survival accounts perfectly for the triple category – the positive truth of what is, the negative truth of what is not, and the objective falsity of *malum culpae* – in which the Thomist *artifex divinus* operates. But remove this key position and you will find yourself confronted with a choice between divine governance and divine sanctity. The Bannezian position with its double category leaves no doubt about divine governance, but it has been thought very open to the objection that God by his inactivity is as responsible for sin as by his activity he is responsible for merit. At the opposite pole, the Molinist rightly attempts to obtain more than two categories, but by his *scientia media* he arrives at four, and, as these are ambiguous, generates further differences on the issue of *ante et post praevisa merita*, with divine governance slightly more prominent on one view and with divine sanctity more clearly in evidence on the other.

To take a third instance of the bipolarity of disintegrating synthesis,[34] St Thomas affirmed divine transcendence: with equal infallibility, efficacy, irresistibility, God knows, wills, effects both the necessary and the contingent; nor does it make the slightest difference whether the contingent in question be present, past, or future relatively to us, for the question is of God, who is not in time. Now, such a transcendence the Bannezian more than admits in God; he transfers it to the *praedeterminatio physica*, a creature, in the hope of saving the freedom of the will; and by that very transference he reveals the thoroughness of his transposition of Thomist thought, which explicitly affirmed the exclusiveness of this divine attribute.[35] On the other hand, the Molinist equally fails to understand divine transcendence, but instead of conferring it on a creature he takes the opposite route to find

34 On bipolar disintegration in the general historical field, see Arnold J. Toynbee, *A Study of History* (Oxford: Oxford University Press, 1939), vol. 5, p. 376 to vol. 6, p. 132. [This note in *Theological Studies* was omitted from *Grace and Freedom*.]

35 See above, p. 110, note 81.

refuge in divine knowledge of the *futuribilia*. And as the Bannezian failure
to understand transcendence was employed to defend the *praedeterminatio
physica*, so the Molinist failure was employed to generate through the
scientia media an excess of categories for handling the surd of sin.

At this point our study may end. Our purpose throughout has been to
determine the thought by following through the thinking of St Thomas on
gratia operans. We have examined the situation when he began to write; we
have seen in itself and in its various ramifications the historical development of his own position; we have found grounds for suggesting that his
position stands as a higher synthesis to the opposition of later theories.
Many other questions might have been introduced, as the reader familiar
with this field will be aware; but they have not seemed to belong to this
investigation. May it be found by those who, like St Thomas, are drawn
'admirabili delectatione et amore veritatis quae est ipse Filius Dei,'[36] to
have thrown some light on the principles, the method, and the doctrine of
the *Communis Doctor*.

36 [(drawn) by the admirable delight and love of the truth which is the very
    Son of God] *Super Ioannem*, c. 6, lect. 5, §935.

PART TWO

Gratia Operans:
A Study of the Speculative
Development in the Writings
of St Thomas Aquinas

Being a Thesis undertaken under the direction of the Reverend
Charles Boyer, S.J., and submitted at the Pontifical Gregorian
University, Rome, towards partial satisfaction of the conditions for
the Doctorate in Sacred Theology

... trahuntur etiam a Filio, admirabili delectatione et amore
veritatis, quae est ipse Filius Dei.   St Thomas of Aquin

Preface

Theologians have perhaps always been aware of the existence of a development in the theory of grace to be found in the writing of St Thomas
Aquinas. But to determine its precise character and significance was hardly
possible until a number of related investigations had been undertaken.
Among these, most notable are, in the field of grace, Dr Artur Landgraf's
researches in the whole earlier period, Dr Johann Schupp's detailed study
of Peter Lombard, Dr Herbert Doms's presentation of the thought of St
Albert the Great. The theory of free will has been most patiently examined
from St Anselm to St Thomas, and an important discovery in the order of St
Thomas's works has been made, by Dom Odon Lottin. Finally, though from
a negative viewpoint, an almost exhaustive study of St Thomas's theory of
motion has been conducted by Fr Johann Stufler.

By an analysis of the idea of speculative development, the present work
systematizes the movement in the theory of grace from St Augustine to St
Thomas, and with the aid of subsidiary investigations arrives at the conclusion that the problem of the relations of grace and liberty occupied St
Thomas's attention from the *De veritate* to the *Prima secundae*, that his
thought underwent a more or less continuous development, and that his
ultimate position is a synthesis in which the Augustinian or psychological
theory of the need of grace has an extremely significant role.

I wish to acknowledge my indebtedness to R.P. Suermondt, o.p., President of the Commission for the Leonine Edition of St Thomas, who gave
me exceptional information on the MSS authority for a conjecture in the

De veritate, to Fr Heinrich Lennerz, s.j., and Fr Franz Pelster, s.j., both ever ready to answer questions and give aid, and especially to Fr Charles Boyer, s.j., who suggested the inquiry, directed me in it, and despite the pressure of many duties found time to read the manuscript.

Introduction

A study of St Thomas's thought on *gratia operans* offers a threefold interest. It reveals him working into synthesis the speculative theorems discovered by his predecessors. It brings to light the development of his own mind. It suggests an attitude and direction of thought distinct from the one resulting in the impasse of the controversy *de auxiliis.*

It is necessary that the study move on the level of this interest, not merely incidentally, but systematically, not merely by way of a footnote expressing a judgment with which the reader may be expected to agree in view of the evidence adduced, but by way of a scientific conclusion in which the inductive process of the whole inquiry terminates. The grounds for this assertion are, perhaps, evident. Without the integral unity so postulated, an inquiry would presuppose that the unimportant issues can be settled scientifically while the important ones are merely matters of personal opinion. The effect of such a presupposition is only too well known. In the question treated in these passages it is notorious that for over three centuries theologians have been studying St Thomas's thought on grace, with Molinists uniformly concluding that the medieval doctor would have been a Molinist and Bannezians with equal conviction arriving at the conclusion that he was a Bannezian. Unless a writer can assign a method that of itself tends to greater objectivity than those hitherto employed, his undertaking may well be regarded as superfluous.

It remains that, though a method which solves the problem is possible, its use makes extreme demands on a reader. It involves the exposition and use of a theory of the history of theological speculation. It rules out the arts of presentation which by emphasis and selection make reading easy and fallacy still easier. It postulates a capacity to see in several hundred pages which discuss a great variety of points a single argument with a major premise in the theory of development and a minor in a number of facts.

While apologizing most sincerely for the use of so complicated a procedure, we would point out that we have no alternative. A study of St Thomas's thought on *gratia operans* cannot but be historical. A historical study cannot but be inductive. An inductive conclusion, though it may be certain when negative, can for the most part be no more than probable when positive. If that probability is to be, not an opinion, but a scientific conclusion, no other method than the one we have adopted appears available.

Because the inquiry is historical, it does not open with the a priori scheme of current systematic theology with its point of view, its definitions, its interests, and its problems. That would be simply to ask St Thomas a series of questions which he did not explicitly consider – had he done so, there would be no need to ask them today – and then work out the answers from a consideration of St Thomas's answer to questions which we do not explicitly consider. Patently such a procedure would be fallacious: it would be deducing an extrapolation from the thought of St Thomas before taking the trouble to find out what St Thomas was really thinking about.

On the other hand, though the inquiry is historical, there is no acceptance of the principles of positivism. To refute such principles lies outside the scope of this introduction. Suffice to say that even historians have intelligence and perform acts of understanding; performing them, they necessarily approach questions from a given point of view; and with equal necessity the limitations of that point of view predetermine the conclusions they reach. From this difficulty positivism offers no escape, for as long as men have intelligence, the problem remains, and were they deprived of intelligence and became mere observers of fact like jellyfish, then they would be truly positivists but their positivism would not be of any service to them.

It remains that history can follow a middle course, neither projecting into the past the categories of the present nor pretending that historical inquiry is conducted without a use of human intelligence. That middle course consists in constructing an a priori scheme that is capable of synthesizing any possible set of historical data irrespective of their place and time, just as the science of mathematics constructs a generic scheme capable of synthesizing any possible set of quantitative phenomena. In the present work this generic scheme is attained by an analysis of the idea of a development in speculative theology.

The procedure provides a true middle course. On the one hand, it does not deny, as does positivism, the exigence of the human mind for some scheme or matrix within which data are assembled and given their initial correlation. On the other hand, it does not provide a scheme or matrix that prejudices the objectivity of the inquiry. The quantitative sciences are objective simply because they are given by mathematics an a priori scheme of such generality that there can be no tendency to do violence to the data for the sake of maintaining the scheme. But the same benefit is obtained for the history of speculative theology by an analysis of the idea of its development, for the analysis does yield a general scheme but it does so, not from a consideration of particular historical facts, but solely from a consideration of the nature of human speculation on a given subject.

To express more concretely the nature of this benefit, it will suffice to say that the argument will be able to proceed, not from the twentieth century through the sixteenth to the thirteenth but from the fourth century through the twelfth to St Thomas. So far from allowing the haunting figures of Dominicus Bañez and Ludovicus Molina to dominate our investigation of St Thomas's thought, we hope to make it continuously evident that these great theologians wrote three centuries after St Thomas had ended his brilliant career.

Because the inquiry is historical, it cannot but be inductive. It is possible to construct a priori a general scheme of the historical process because the human mind is always the human mind. But there is no more a possibility of filling in the details of that scheme a priori than there is of predicting the future. Concretely, when commentators tell us that St Thomas *must* mean this or that, either they are misusing the word 'must' – which connotes necessity – or else they are claiming to demonstrate in a science that does not proceed by demonstration. It is possible to exclude any given interpretation with certitude, for then one merely has to produce evidence that St Thomas contradicts it. But the only possible way to demonstrate an interpretation is to enumerate the entire list of speculative possibilities, demonstrate that the enumeration is complete (that is the difficult point), and then exclude all views except one.

For this reason we aim at certitude only in negative conclusions; in positive ones we are content with probability.

The degree of probability attained will appear from the structure of the induction to be made.

In the first place, all guessing is excluded by the method. The argument does not consist in proposing and then verifying hypotheses. Instead of hypotheses there is used the a priori scheme of speculative development, which is not a hypothesis but a demonstrable conclusion. Consequently, instead of assembling the data and guessing at their significance, the argument employs what strategists term a 'pincer' movement. It does so in five distinct stages.

First, it determines the general form of the speculative movement on the nature of grace from St Augustine to St Thomas. The analysis of such a movement has revealed that there are seven phases in the normal evolution of an explanation by a compound theorem. It happens that the explanation of the necessity of grace in the *Prima secundae* is a compound theorem and that each of the six earlier phases can easily be verified in earlier works. The procedure is essentially the same as when a mathematician works out an equation from general considerations and then a physicist evaluates the unknown coefficients by objective measurements. Just as the physicist obtains the formula for a natural law, so also by this means do we obtain the basic form of the development that extends from the fifth century to the thirteenth. Thus, without making any hypotheses on the nature of grace, we are able to correlate statements made by different people at different times merely in virtue of the assumption that the people in question were all men, all thinking, and historically interdependent in their thought.

Such is the first inductive movement. The second proceeds inversely from the particular to the general; it consists in assembling the explicit statements on the nature of *gratia operans* to be found in the writings of St Augustine, St Anselm, Peter Lombard, St Albert the Great, and St Thomas.

The third and fourth movements are incidental. In simpler sciences than the history of speculative theology, the 'pincer' process from both general to particular and particular to general would suffice to yield the conclusion. But it happens that speculative theology is a very peculiar science. Its problems have to do with the relations between the natural and the supernatural orders. Inasmuch, then, as speculative theology conceives the supernatural on the analogy of the natural, it is necessary to make a special inquiry into St Thomas's idea of operation. Inasmuch as there is a natural element within the field of the theological problem, it is necessary to make another special inquiry into St Thomas's theory of the human will, its liberty, the limitations of its liberty, and the general way in which God operates upon it. Both of these inquiries are subsidiary, undertaken not for their own sakes but principally to eliminate misinterpretations of St Thomas's position and to reveal that his mind is far more resourceful than is commonly supposed.

With this work accomplished, it is possible to return to the main problem: the idea of operative grace. As it is only in the *Prima secundae* that St Thomas posits an operative grace that is not habitual but actual, and as none of his predecessors had thought things out with such finesse and precision as to be able to entertain, explicitly and formally, that very complex idea, we are content briefly to treat his position in the *Sentences* and the *De veritate* – where operative grace is habitual grace – and concentrate our attention on the well-known 1-2, q. 111, a. 2.

Throughout the study of St Thomas, strict attention is paid to the chronological order of his work, and our conclusions are drawn mainly from the works whose sequence is known, namely, the commentary on the *Sentences*, the *De veritate*, the *Contra Gentiles*, the *De potentia*, the *Pars prima*, the *Quodlibetum primum*, the *De malo*, and the *Prima secundae*. The commentary on the Epistle to the Romans and the commentaries on Aristotle's *Physics*, *Metaphysics*, and *Peri hermeneias* form an extremely useful subsidiary source; I do not make use of them in establishing the line of development of thought on particular questions, but as far as their content goes, they appear to be contemporary with the *Pars prima*. As is plain, the degree of importance to be attached to the chronological sequence varies in almost every question that is raised. It is paramount with respect to the theory of grace, which is well known to have developed.[1] The same is true with respect to the theory of free will. On the other hand, St Thomas's theory of divine foreknowledge is always the same, and his theory of premotion is always the same in itself, though naturally it varies with the variation in the theory of the will. Finally, with regard to opinions which St Thomas never held, there is no need to bother at all about the sequence of his writings.

So much, then, for the nature of the inquiry before us. It may be well to add a statement of what we do not propose to do.

We are not engaged in proposing a theory in speculative theology. We are giving an account of someone else's theories. And in that task we are not concerned with the implications of his position, the ulterior develop-

---

1 The existence of a development in St Thomas's thought on grace is explicitly affirmed by Capreolus (*In II Sententiarum*, d. 28, q. 1, a. 3, §4 ad fin.), Didacus Deza Hispalensis (*In II Sententiarum*, d. 28, q. 1, a. 3, not. 1, ad fin.), Cajetan (*In Summam theologiae*, 1-2, q. 109, a. 6 [*LT* 7: 300–301]), Dominicus Soto (*De natura et gratia*, lib. 2, c. 3). The pertinent remarks they make are quoted by Hermann Lange, *De gratia* [see above, p. 3, note 1] 91 note 2, and 146 note 1.

ment of his position, or even the defense of his position. We ask what he said, why he said it, and what he meant in saying it.

Confined to the history of theological speculation, per se the inquiry is confined to the thought of a single writer. Discussion of anyone else's views or opinions is purely incidental. Thus, earlier writers are considered because of the influence they would exert on St Thomas whether directly or indirectly. Later writers are considered inasmuch as their views provide a clear formulation either of what St Thomas meant or of what he certainly did not mean. As the earlier writers are helpful because of their influence on St Thomas, so the later writers must be considered because of their influence on the reader. For this reason it has seemed unnecessary to attempt any exposition of later opinions: for if the reader has been influenced by them, he is already acquainted with them; if he has not been influenced by them, then he will find it simpler to grasp St Thomas's thought by direct study.

Concerned solely with an account of the thought of a single writer, we are concerned solely with that thought as speculative. Dogmatic truths are one thing; their speculative correlation and unification is quite another. A perfect expression of dogmatic truth, as when a child repeats his catechism or an eleventh-century theologian recites the creed, is no evidence of a speculative position. On the other hand, speculative deficiency is no proof of heterodoxy. The two are really distinct, and this work presupposes that distinction. Moreover, the two are disparate, so that no specialized inquiry can possibly deal with both at the same time. Hence when we speak of speculative development, we do not mean the development of dogma: as far as our argument goes there need be no dogmatic development whatever from St Paul to the Council of Trent; and the reason why there is no such need is that speculative development and dogmatic development are quite different; for instance, there can be speculative decline, as in the fourteenth and fifteenth centuries; but I do not believe one can speak of dogmatic decline within the church.

This distinction is, of course, of primary importance. The reason why certain writers are able to 'demonstrate' that St Thomas in all his work held exactly their views on actual grace, when in point of fact St Thomas himself did not hold the same view in all his works, is that they argue from a dogmatic to a speculative continuity. *Ex falso sequitur quodlibet.*

Finally, confined to the history of the speculation of a single writer with other writers and other questions all excluded, we are not aiming at writing a manual *De gratia* or even *De gratia operante.* We do not propose to offer any systematic treatise or to show how a treatise might be developed from St Thomas's thought. Thus, we are able to omit entirely the question of the entitative perfection of gratuitous dispositions prior to justification. In a systematic inquiry on operative grace, that question could not be omitted. But in a historical inquiry one has to limit oneself to what appears to be, not in the forefront of modern speculation, but in the forefront of St Thomas's thought.

II-1

The Form of the Development

The fundamental problem of the present inquiry is to determine scientifically the unity and coherence of a vast body of historical data. Evidently, a study of St Thomas's thought in its historical expansion and significance cannot be objective if undertaken from the viewpoint of later ideas, problems, and theories. What is required is a point of vantage outside the temporal dialectic, a matrix or system of thought that at once is as pertinent and as indifferent to historical events as is the science of mathematics to quantitative phenomena. For unless such a viewpoint is attained and maintained, then of necessity the inquiry will reduce to a sterile compilation of uninterpreted facts or else a fallacious projection of current categories into a period in which they did not exist.

With the aim of solving this problem, the present chapter treats four points: the content of speculative theology; the four elements in speculative theology; the manner in which these elements combine to give the successive phases of a speculative development; and finally, the seven phases in the speculative development extending from St Augustine to St Thomas.

This 'form' of the development automatically provides a scientific viewpoint for the rest of the investigation. It eliminates a host of impertinent questions which otherwise would spontaneously be introduced into the inquiry to give it a false bias and encourage a search – too often successful – to find in an author what the author never dreamt of. Apart from this essential negative benefit, it enables one who lives in a later age to understand those whose thought belongs to almost a different world, and it does so, not by the slow and incommunicable apprehension that comes to the specialist after years of study, but logically through ideas that are defined, arguments that can be tested, and conclusions that need only be verified. Thus, the finer fruits of historical study are taken out of the realm of personal opinion and made part of the common heritage of science.

1   The Content of Speculative Theology

Speculative theology does not exist in the pure state. The ordinary textbook, for instance, contains a variety of very different things. There are series of passages from scripture with here a longer and there a shorter exegesis. There are extracts from the Fathers and, beside them, bibliographical notices and summaries of the results of patristic study. There are references to and quotations from councils and pontifical pronouncements. Lists and discussions of the opinions of theologians combine with a ubiquitous maze of technical terms and with sets of proofs of quite different natures. Finally, dominating and uniting all else is the formidable array of theses, each with its theological censure and its place of importance anywhere between the summit of *de fide definita* and the minimum of *probabilior*. Still, this multiplicity and variety is anything but confusion. The whole has a unity and cohesion more remarkable and less trivial than that of the multiplication table. And it is theological speculation, which is not confined to some part but penetrates the whole structure, that has brought to light and formulated this organicity in revealed truth.

It is necessary to insist that speculation is not confined to what are termed 'proofs from reason' or *argumenta convenientiae*. The unity of the treatise, the very idea of a treatise, the attempt to prove, to correlate, the array of theses, the technical terms that are to be found in the enunciation of the thesis and still more in its definition and explanation, the distinction of theological censures and of different kinds of argument, all is a fruit of speculation. But though speculation enters everywhere, it is also true that everywhere its role is very subordinate. It provides the technical terms with their definitions; it does not provide the objects that are defined. It gives the arrangement and order of the subject; it does not give what is arranged and put into order. It reveals the unity and cohesion; but it neither creates nor discovers what has the unity and is shown to hang together. It is the work of the human intellect; but what it works upon is the Word of God.

Thus the content of speculative theology is the content of a pure form. It is not something by itself but the intelligible arrangement of something else. It is not systematic theology but the system in systematic theology. For the human mind to grasp truth and make it at once an effective spring and a higher form of action, there must be the process of assimilation: a process of distinguishing and correlating and organizing; of drawing out implications, of discovering their mutual coherence, and of constructing instances into groups and groups into species and species under genera till finally an ultimate unity is attained. The labor of this process is with difficulty repeated in the four years the seminarian has at his disposal. But that labor is negligible when compared with the vast effort that was needed in the first instance, when the men of Europe emerged from the chaos of a broken empire and the distress of barbaric invasion, and gave their leisure to the construction not only of cathedrals of stone but also of the more enduring cathedrals of the mind.[1]

2   Elements in Speculative Theology

To define speculative theology with greater exactitude, its four elements are now considered: theorems, terms, dialectical positions, and technique.

2.1   Theorems

The 'theorem' may be defined as the difference between a common notion and a scientific concept.

For example, the common notion of 'going faster' and the scientific concept of 'acceleration' partly coincide and partly differ. They coincide inasmuch as both apprehend one and the same objective fact. They differ inasmuch as the common notion apprehends no more than the fact, while the scientific concept elaborates it by understanding it. First, 'acceleration' generalizes 'going faster' to include 'going more slowly.' Second, it submits it to the subtle analysis of the calculus and enriches it with the endless implications of d^2s/dt^2. Third, it gives it a significant, indeed a fundamental, place in the general theory of natural phenomena.

Thus the 'theorem' is the scientific elaboration of a common notion. It denotes, not the notion as elaborated, but simply the elaboration: not 'going faster' nor even 'going more slowly,' but solely the generalization,

---

1 On the manner in which speculative theology was conceived in England in the first half of the thirteenth century and the unmitigated distrust of Books of Sentences some fifty years earlier, see Franz Pelster, 'Die Bedeutung der Sentenzenvorlesung für die theologische Spekulation des Mittelalters' [see above, p. 11, note 38].

the analysis, the enrichment with implications and with significance for a system of thought.

To turn to an example from theology, the term 'supernatural' in the writings of St Thomas is clearly a scientific concept. It is a technical term, and it is used profusely; it has an exact philosophic definition; the implications of that definition are worked out and consistently faced; finally, it has a significance for a system of thought, for in St Thomas the 'supernatural' is fundamental to his whole treatment of the order of grace.

Still, theology did not always possess this scientific concept.[2] In Peter Lombard, the 'supernatural' is simply a common notion. He does not use the term, though he has about twenty more or less equivalent expressions.[3] He fails to note the disproportion between the order of nature and the order of grace, though he does state some related propositions.[4] And that this implies a defect in speculative development would seem to be proved from his unsatisfactory solution of an elementary difficulty in connection with the nature of merit.[5]

2.2 Terms

Terms are an obvious product of speculation.

Words denote aspects of reality that are significant from a given point of view. The analytic processes of speculative thought necessarily result in a complex transition from the latent to the evident, from the vague to the definite, from the implicit to the explicit, from the naked fact to its scientific elaboration. Parallel to this process and its necessary consequent, there is another process in which old words received more precise meanings and new words are introduced.

To give two examples: 'sacrament' is an old word that received a precise definition; 'actual grace' is a new term which does not occur even in St Thomas; he speaks of the *auxilium divinum*.

The consequent problem for dogmatic thought is well known: the theologian must ever bear in mind the distinction between the language of

---

2 See Artur Landgraf, 'Studien zur Erkenntnis des Übernatürlichen in der Frühscholastik' [see above, p. 15, note 62]; August Deneffe, 'Geschichte des Wortes "supernaturalis,"' *Zeitschrift für katholische Theologie* 46 (1922) 337–60.
3 See Johann Schupp, *Die Gnadenlehre des Petrus Lombardus* [see above, p. 15, note 61] 20–22.
4 Ibid. 23.
5 Ibid. 65.

dogmatic sources and the language of scientific thought. But it is less clear that historians have attended sufficiently to a similar problem of their own: not only must they distinguish between the language of the sources and the scientific language of their own day; they must also take into account the scientific language of the period they are treating.

2.3   The Dialectical Position

Scientists have what may be called a 'methodological position.' They will maintain incompatible theories simultaneously: because of general phenomena, light has to be an undulation; because of special problems, it is an emission of particles. The basis of this position is that at present the scientist is ignorant of the truth but in the future, as far removed as you please, he will possess the complete explanation of all phenomena.

The 'dialectical position' of the theologian is at once more radical and more coherent.

On the one hand, it maintains that different truths of faith – or doctrines of faith and certain conclusions of the human reason – cannot be contradictory. Truth is one, and God is truth. Hence, no matter how great the opposition may appear to be, it is always possible to attain the negative coherence of noncontradiction.

On the other hand, it maintains that at no point of time will the human understanding enjoy a full explanation of all doctrines of faith. For ultimately theology deals with mystery, with God in his transcendence. Speculation may construct the terms and theorems apt to correlate and unify dogmatic data; but the unification it attains cannot be explanatory in its entirety; the mind attains a symmetry, but its apex, the ultimate moment and the basis of its intelligibility, stands beyond the human intellect.

Thus the 'dialectical position' is the assertion of the negative coherence of noncontradiction but the simultaneous denial of the positive coherence of complete understanding.

2.4   Technique

The necessity of a speculative 'technique' is threefold. The whole field of data must be envisaged, or thought is unbalanced. The natural element in problems must be accurately analyzed, or thought is vague. Questions must be taken in their proper order, or the conclusion will be no more than the reemergence of the initial problem in a more acute form.

Philosophia ancilla theologiae: it supplies the necessary breadth of view; it is the accurate analysis of the natural element in theological problems; its method is also a method for the systematic treatment of the question of theology.[6]

It is to be observed that technique not only gives the form but also influences the content of speculative thought.

First of all, the philosophic analysis of the natural element in a theological problem (for instance, the analysis of free will in the problem of grace and liberty) obviously determines part of the solution of that problem. In the second place, there is influence by analogy. Nature is a theophany. So also, on a higher mode, is revelation and the economy of the supernatural order. It follows that an analogy exists between the field of philosophy and that of theology, and that philosophic analysis reveals distinctions and relations which may be transposed in some fashion into theological theorems.

This influence does a great deal to explain certain problems in the history of theology. But it will be preferable to consider here, not any actual instance, but a purely fictitious one; for we wish simply to make an abstract point and so had best avoid the complexity of concrete instance. Let us suppose some speculator at a period prior to the elaboration of the scientific definition and divisions of grace; let us also suppose that he derived his technique from Platonic thought, in particular from the *Liber De causis*, which may be by Alfarabi. For him, then, motion would be caused by Life, and life by the Absolute Life; further, he would have some vague distinction between *substantia* and *actio*, but this would still be awaiting development into a distinction between substance and accident. Now not only is it most probable that our hypothetical thinker would be likely to conceive grace in terms of life or perhaps intelligence on the analogy of his system of philosophy. What is much more important is that it would not occur to him to ask

---

6 It is not infrequently implied that theological speculation is a particularly odious vice peculiar to Catholics. What must be meant is not that Catholics speculate while non-Catholics refrain, but that Catholic speculation is systematic work and the result of centuries of collaboration, while the non-Catholic, as he is his own prophet and pope, thinks it a slight matter to be his own theologian as well. Anyone who reflects on religious doctrine enters the field of theological speculation: the question of the child, the difficulties of the adult, the flood of books and articles on the 'religious problem' – all are essentially speculative. Reflection and speculation are irrepressible in man. Non-Catholics, so far from attempting to repress these natural tendencies, allow them the free play of tropical vegetation.

whether or not grace is an accident in the soul, and if an accident, whether there are graces entitatively distinct, and if that is so, whether some of these are habitual gifts and others transient. The whole range of such questions lies entirely outside his field of vision. Not aware of such distinctions in the natural order, he will not make his first discovery of them in the supernatural. He does not deny them, certainly not. The point is that he simply fails to think of them. A person who has never heard of De Moivre's theorem cannot be accused of the error of rejecting that theorem; and no matter how exact and familiar his knowledge of Euclid, that is no proof that he would refuse to consider the employment of complex numbers. His position on the point is a pure 'futurable': what would take place under circumstances that do not exist. Similarly with regard to the hypothetical disciple of Alfarabi: his speculation is defective, but the theological defect, provided it involves no rejection of what is explicit in the dogmatic sources, is the defect not of error but of ignorance or even of nescience.[7]

3   Phases in the Development of Theological Speculation

The next point is the correlation of the elements: 'theorems,' 'terms,' 'dialectical positions,' 'technique.' As these may be combined in different ways, and as some combinations are naturally prior to others, the result of this correlation is a succession of different phases.

The term 'phases' is used in an analogous sense. Phases in development are not functions of the variable 'time,' like the phases of the moon, but complex functions of two principal variables, 'theorems' and 'technique.' Accordingly, what we hope to establish is not any a priori form of history but mere sets of abstract categories that have a special reference to the historical process.

It will be well at once to summarize what follows.

First is outlined the *preliminary phase.* It is collection and classification of dogmatic data relative to speculative problems. Such collection and classification is found, relative to particular questions in the controversial writings of the Fathers, relative to all questions in a Book of Sentences.

Second are contrasted the *initial and final dialectical positions.* Theological speculation never explains mysteries, but it does advance *from an initial position* in which the mystery is not distinguished from adjacent merely philosophic problems and the connection between the different mysteries

7 On the distinction, see Thomas Aquinas, *De malo*, q. 3, a. 7.

is not defined, *towards a final position* in which the pure element of mystery stands in isolation from all else.

Third are studied the *intermediate phases.* These are of two kinds: either the speculative development arises from external influences or it arises from the attainment of internal coherence.

If development arises from external influences, it sets up *intermediate phases from developing technique.* Such developments are of three kinds: first, developments in philosophy itself, such as the substitution of Aristotelian thought for Platonic; second, philosophic clarification of the natural element in the dialectical positions, for instance, coherently maintaining a philosophic definition of human liberty and not defining liberty as the capacity to do good when one has grace; third, the introduction of philosophic analogies into the theological field, for instance, affirming the grace of justification to be habitual.

If, on the other hand, development arises from the speculative attainment of internal coherence, it sets up *intermediate phases from developing theorems.* Thus, in the simplest case of any complexity, namely, the correlation of two theorems related as species and genus, there are no less than seven phases.

3.1   The Preliminary Phase

Since speculative theology is the systematic element in the presentation of dogmatic truths, its preliminary phase will consist in the first movements towards an explanatory unification of the data to be found in the dogmatic sources.

Thus, a commentary on holy scripture is, of its nature, a pre-speculative work. Such were the commentaries written by the Fathers, the medieval *Glossa,*[8] St Thomas's *Catena aurea.* The same is true of St Thomas's commentaries on St Paul, which rather make use of speculative knowledge than raise speculative questions.

On the other hand, the controversial works of the Fathers and the medieval books of Sentences evidently constitute an initial phase in speculative thought. The Fathers collect numerous passages from scripture to bear on a single point: for instance, St Augustine weaves together an array of texts on grace in vigorous polemic against the Pelagians. Similarly a book

---

8 On the composition of the *Glossa* see Beryl Smalley, 'Gilbertus Universalis, Bishop of London (1128–34), and the Problem of the "Glossa Ordinaria"' [see above, p. 11, note 37].

of Sentences collects and classifies dogmatic data in their relation to series of speculative questions. In neither case is an explanatory unification of the data the deliberate object of the work. In both cases there is a manifest preparation for the pure speculative effort: for one cannot speculate without having something to speculate about.

This would seem to be the reason why innumerable speculative theologians wrote commentaries on the *Sentences* of Peter Lombard.

In the first place, his work was eminently suited to be the basis of speculative thought. He belonged to the reaction against the excesses of Peter Abelard. He wrote to refute the heretical tendencies of his day. But his refutation was not by argument but by appeal to authority: he proposed to present the teachings of the Fathers adding but little of his own, to oppose the heretical *placitum*, the satisfaction of the understanding, with the *verum* of dogmatic truth. And to this avowed positive tendency he adds the advantage of a classified collection of data.[9]

In an article already mentioned, Fr Pelster has drawn attention to this significance of books of Sentences. So far from putting an end to the *placita* of speculation, Peter Lombard seems simply to have provided speculation with a solid basis: the scandalized Prior at Worcester attributes the evil spirit of his day to the similar *Sentences* of Peter of Poitiers; later Richard Fishacre tells his pupils at Oxford that modern masters teach only moral theology directly from scripture; the discussion of dogmatic questions is based on a book of Sentences.[10]

9 On the general character of Peter Lombard's work, see Schupp, *Die Gnadenlehre des Petrus Lombardus* 289–98. On the purpose of his *Sentences*, see Peter's Prologue. Noteworthy are the remarks [*QL* 1: 3], 'Sicubi ... parum vox nostra insonuit, non a paternis discessit limitibus' and '"Non ... debet ... labor ... videri superfluus, cum multis ... sit necessarius," brevi volumine complicans Patrum sententias, appositis eorum testimoniis, ut non sit necesse quaerenti librorum numerositatem evolvere, cui brevitas collecta quod quaeritur offert sine labore' [If our voice has not resounded sufficiently anywhere, (still) it has not departed from the limits established by the Fathers; '(this) labor should not seem superfluous, since it is needed by many,' (as it) gathers into a small space the opinions of the Fathers, setting forth their testimonies, so that it is not necessary for the researcher to peruse a multitude of books, (since) without labor on his part a compact collection offers him what is sought. – The quotation within the quotation, according to Peter's editors, is from Augustine.]
10 See Pelster, 'Die Bedeutung der Sentenzenvorlesung ...' 250–54. Note that Peter of Poitiers's *Sentences* are based on the Lombard's (ibid. 251). The passage from Richard Fishacre reads, 'Verumptamen tantum altera pars sc. de moribus instruendis a magistris modernis, cum leguntur sancti libri, docetur; alia tamquam difficilior disputacioni reservatur. Hec autem pars

A final point in this connection is the loose relation between the book of Sentences and its later commentaries. Fr Pelster generalizes: 'Je weiter man sich von der Zeit des Lombarden entfernte, um so löser würde die Verbindung zwischen seinem Text und der behandelten Frage. Immer aber bis zum 16. Jahrhundert blieb diese materielle Verbindung zwischen Sentenzenvorlesung und theologischer Spekulation bestehen.'[11] The point that concerns us is the fact of development which imposes this ever looser connection between Sentences and commentary. To take the example of operative grace, Peter Lombard makes it the fundamental and practically the sole topic of the twenty-sixth distinction of his second book; St Thomas has six articles on this distinction, but operative grace does not enter into consideration until the fifth article; the development between Peter and St Thomas had raised four prior questions that had to be settled before the operative character of grace could be considered.

3.2   Initial and Final Dialectical Positions

Theorems develop, terms change, technique increases, but the dialectical position always remains. Thus it is this position that is the constant element and, as it were, constitutes the identity of any particular development in speculative theology. Nonetheless, there is a difference between the initial and the final dialectical position.

Initially there is simply the affirmation of two apparently opposed truths. Grace is necessary; but the will is also free. Scripture asserts both; scripture is the Word of God; therefore, both are true.

On the other hand, the final dialectical position by the use of technique and the development of theorems has eliminated all but the essence of the mystery. It leaves to faith not human problems, nor the human element in religious problems, but the pure formulation of the point that cannot be encompassed by the human understanding. Before appealing to the dialectical position, it settles the prior questions. Grace is necessary: but what is

---

difficilior de canone sanctarum scripturarum excerpta in isto libro, qui sentenciarum dicitur, ponitur' (ibid. 255) [However, when the holy books are read, only the second part is taught, namely, on instruction in morals by teachers of our time; the other part, as being more difficult, is reserved for disputation. But this more difficult part, consisting of excerpts from the canon of the holy scriptures, is located in that book which is called (a book) of sentences].

11 Pelster, 'Die Bedeutung der Sentenzenvorlesung ...' 252.

grace, what are its divisions, what is the mode of its action, what is its efficacy, what is the difference between this efficacy and the certitude of divine providence, the infallibility of divine foreknowledge, the irresistibility of divine will? And the will of man is free: but what is the will, what is its act, what are the conditions and the causes of that act, what precisely is freedom, what are the limitations of freedom, what is the connection between the limitations of human freedom and the necessity of grace? If the problem is a mystery in the strictest sense of the term, as is the mystery of the Blessed Trinity, then, even after all these questions have been satisfactorily settled, it will still be necessary to frame the conclusion in the dialectical position. But there is a manifest difference between this final dialectical position and the initial position that simply asserts the compatibility of grace and free will.

3.3 Intermediate Phases from Developing Technique

One cause of the transition from the initial to the final dialectical position is philosophic development. It will have this influence partly because it provides the analogous basis for theorems and partly because it defines the natural element in the initial dialectical position. But before treating these two points, it will be well to say something on philosophic development itself.

3.3.1 The Development of Philosophy

A distinction has to be drawn between the endless variety of philosophic schools that succeed one another in ever growing confusion and, on the other hand, the development of the philosophy that is the *philosophia perennis*.

Philosophy as *philosophia perennis* is man's apprehension of the eternal and immutable. Like all limited being, it is potentiality and achievement, *dynamis* and *energeia*, potency and act. Its potency is the love of wisdom: it is detachment, orientation, inspiration. Its act is the triumph of the reason systematically revealing the light of the eternal in the light of common day. For all time the potency is represented by Plato, the act by Aristotle. And so from the nature of the case the development of the *philosophia perennis* is rectilinear; it can embrace differences as wide as those that exist between the pagan from Stagira and the Christian saint of Aquino; yet, however great such differences may appear outwardly, it remains that they emerge only to make more systematically certain and secure a position that is unique because it is central.

The existence of a *philosophia perennis* is not refuted but confirmed by the flux of the philosophies. For it is only too apparent that if philosophy's goal is the eternal, still philosophers are forever succumbing to the spirit of their age, becoming part of its limited culture, turning their thoughts to its crises and problems. This influence of the Platonic 'unreal' is the supreme obstacle both to philosophic achievement and to the conservation of what has been achieved; nor does the emergence of the perfect thinker suffice; the environment also must ring true, and the time must be propitious. It needed an Athens that could boast in the tone of the Funeral Oration, if Socrates was to discuss instead of simply teaching as did Gautama, if Plato was to perpetuate a vision of an ideal polity instead of crystallizing a code of manners as did Confucius. On the other hand the shadow of infelicity hung too heavily over the Empire for thinkers to be balanced; they were too much of the world and Epicureans, or too much against it and Stoics, or too eager to escape it and neo-Platonists. As for the febrile modern mind demanding perpetual change yet horrified by the monsters it begets, let Touchstone ask, 'Shepherd, hast thou any philosophy?'

3.3.2 Developing Technique and the Dialectical Position

The essential moment in the transition from the initial to the final dialectical position is the emergence of a systematic distinction between reason and faith. It is to be observed, however, that this distinction must not only be enunciated in general but also applied to each particular problem. The only way to make clear the difficulty of such an application is to give an example. We consider the definition of human liberty.

The condemnation of Peter Abelard's proposition, *Quod liberum arbitrium per se sufficit ad aliquod bonum*,[12] quite possibly led to the peculiar definition of liberty to be found in Peter Lombard:[13] 'Liberum vero arbitrium est

12 [That free will is enough by itself for (doing) some good] *DB* 373 [*DS* 725].
13 Dom Odon Lottin has shown that this definition appeared for the first time after the Council of Sens (1140) in the *Sententiae divinitatis*; see his article, 'Le "Summa Sententiarum" est-elle postérieure aux sentences de Pierre Lombard?' *Revue néo-scolastique de philosophie* 28 (1926) 284–302. See Schupp, *Die Gnadenlehre des Petrus Lombardus* 107, note 6. [Lottin's first section, pp. 286–93, treats the definition of free will; see p. 290 for Lonergan's precise point.]

facultas rationis et voluntatis, qua bonum, gratia assistente, eligitur, vel malum, eadem desistente.'[14] Plainly this is to assert the dialectical position on the relation between grace and liberty at the very moment one defines liberty: it makes it impossible to find any opposition between grace and liberty as defined,[15] though it leaves it very doubtful that the definition is correct.[16] In fact, when the Lombard wished to make clear the nature of liberty, he turned to the definition of Boethius[17] and wrote: (Liberum arbitrium) 'philosophi definientes dixerunt liberum de voluntate iudicium, quia potestas ipsa et habilitas voluntatis et rationis ... libera est ad utrumlibet, quia libere potest moveri ad hoc vel ad illud.'[18] The speculative defect of the position in the *Sentences* is that this definition cannot be consistently and coherently maintained.

On the other hand, speculative development will consist precisely in making possible the coherent use of a philosophic definition of liberty. The problem is not that we do not know what liberty is, or that we do not know what grace is; what we do not know is how to reconcile the two. But this third question is not to be confused with the others.

14 [But free will is the faculty of reason and will by which the good, with the help of grace, is chosen, or evil (is chosen) when grace is lacking] Peter Lombard, *Sententiae*, 2, d. 24, c. 3 [*QL* 1: 421].

15 This device is the essence of the argument in St Anselm's and St Bernard's treatment of the problem. See *PL* 158, 491–98, and 182, 1001–1004. Their dialectical definitions of liberty are at the root of the complexity, variation, and unsatisfactoriness described by Dom Lottin, *La théorie du libre arbitre depuis s. Anselme jusqu'à s. Thomas d'Aquin* [see above, p. 13, note 47]. The reader will find the complementary complexity, variation, and unsatisfactoriness recounted by Professor Landgraf, 'Die Erkenntnis der helfenden Gnade in der Frühscholastik' [see above, p. 5, note 5].

16 It does not occur to Peter Lombard to exploit the possibilities of such a definition. His interests are not speculative enough for that. He affirms 'non potest non peccare' [is not able not to sin] (*Sententiae*, 2, d. 25, c. 6 [*QL* 1: 431]) and also 'et peccare et non peccare posse' [able to sin and not to sin] (Ibid. d. 28, c. 4 ad fin. [*QL* 1: 456; on the origins of this phrase, see above, p. 13, note 51]). His distinction between *libertas a necessitate* and *libertas a peccato* (Ibid. d. 25, cc. 7–8 [*QL* 1: 432–35]) is wholesome but purely dialectical. See Schupp, *Die Gnadenlehre des Petrus Lombardus* 105–15.

17 Boethius, *In librum Aristotelis De interpretatione*, Editio secunda, lib. 3 (*PL* 64, 492).

18 [The philosophers, in defining (free will) said that the free will of the willing faculty, because it is the very power and aptitude of will and reason ... is free to (choose) either of two options, because it can be freely moved to this or to that] *Sententiae*, 2, d. 25, c. 1 [*QL* 1: 428]. The definition is developed by St Thomas, *De veritate*, q. 24, a. 1.

To put the same point in different terms: science and truth are not formally identical. Science is knowledge of a thing in its causes: formal, material, efficient, final. Truth is simply the equation of judgment and the objective field. It follows that all truth is not science, that not any truth can be laid down as a first principle, and that least of all can a theological dialectical position be made the initial premise of a speculative elaboration.

It is in these intricacies of the distinction between faith and reason, and not merely in the general enunciation of the distinction, that theology prior to St Thomas was involved.[19]

3.3.3 The Theorem and Developing Technique

Not only does speculative theology derive from philosophy the clarification of the natural or human element in its problem. It also finds in the natural order, as philosophically analyzed, the analogies necessary for the scientific conception of purely theological data.[20]

We have already given an abstract and hypothetical illustration of the influence philosophy may exercise in this fashion.[21] It will be well to consider here a concrete example. For the use of such analogies seems an extremely simple matter. In point of fact there is nothing more complicated and difficult than their first emergence. The great discoveries of men are not too numerous, and the greater they are, the more incredibly simple they appear. We are apt to be surprised, not that Columbus thought of sailing west to the Indies, but that no one else did it before him; not that Newton, according to the legend, associated the falling apple with the falling moon, but that there could have been intelligent men before him who did not. It will serve, then, both to enforce a true historical perspective and to introduce the subject of operative grace, if we outline the history of the view that grace is a *donum habituale*.

There is prima facie a difficulty to this position. Scripture attributes the forgiveness of sin and justification to conversion, faith, and charity. These seem to be not habits. But infant baptism is immemorial and its reason recognized to be that it opens the gates of heaven. No great reflection or profound thought should seem necessary to arrive at the following conclu-

---

19 A detailed discussion of the point cannot be undertaken here. But I believe the reader will find ample and convincing evidence in the works of Dom Lottin and Professor Landgraf cited in note 15.

20 See [the First] Vatican Council, session 3, c. 4, *DB* 1796 [*DS* 3016].

21 See above §2.4.

sion: the baptized infant is heir to the kingdom of heaven; the heir to the kingdom is justified; and accordingly justification, in its essence, lies not in acts but in the habitual order. But in point of fact, the effect of infant baptism could not be satisfactorily determined by the early Scholastics. Though hardly a canonist or a speculative writer failed to raise the question, it remained unsolved until the first half of the thirteenth century.[22]

It would be a gross oversimplification to fancy that the whole difficulty was unfamiliarity with the Aristotelian concept of the habit. It is true that this is part of the difficulty. But there were two different and far profounder difficulties.

In the first place, a thoroughgoing scientific attitude was a prerequisite. Many authors were content simply to quote St Augustine's remark: the baptized infant does not make an act of faith but it does receive the sacrament of faith.[23] That, of course, is perfectly true. But *redit quaestio*, What precisely is it to receive the sacrament of faith?[24]

In the second place, there was the distortion of the speculative field by what we later shall term the 'third phase.'[25] The idea of the supernatural became a scientifically elaborated concept with Philip the Chancellor. Speculators prior to this development, the key position to the whole theory of grace, were like men at sea without a compass. Lacking a metaphysical framework in terms of *natura*, they naturally tended to understand grace psychologically. Thus sin and especially original sin was conceived as a darkening of the understanding and a weakening of the will.[26] Similarly, grace and justification were in the main conceived as the opposite states, the enlightened intelligence of faith and the comforted will of charity.[27]

St Anselm pushed this psychological interpretation of grace to the extreme limit by defining justice as *rectitudo voluntatis propter se servata*.[28] More

---

22 Landgraf, 'Grundlagen für ein Verständnis der Busslehre der Früh- und Hochscholastik' [see above, p. 18, note 77] 170.
23 *DB* 410, 483 [*DS* 780, 904].
24 Landgraf, 'Die Erkenntnis der heiligmachenden Gnade in der Frühscholastik' [see above, p. 16, note 68] 40 [*DFG* 206–207].
25 See below, §4.5.
26 Landgraf, 'Die Erkenntnis der heiligmachenden Gnade ...' 30 [*DFG* 203].
27 Ibid. 31–39 [*DFG* 203–205].
28 [rectitude of the will maintained for its own sake] See St Anselm's *De veritate*, c. 12 (*PL* 158, 480–84 [Schmitt 1: 191–96]); *De conceptu virginali*, c. 4 (*PL* 158, 436–38 [Schmitt 2: 143–45]). It is worth noting the parallel definition of free will (*De libero arbitrio*, c. 3, *PL* 158, 494 [Schmitt 1: 212]): 'liberum arbitrium non esse aliud, quam arbitrium potens servare rectitudinem voluntatis propter ipsam rectitudinem' [free will is nothing else than a will that is able to preserve rectitude of will for the sake of that rectitude itself].

than this, he also gave the problem of infant baptism a solution which, if brilliant and containing an essential element of the truth, nonetheless tended to postpone indefinitely the true solution. Briefly, his position was this: the infant cannot have justice, for it elicits no act of will; but this incapacity is sinful before baptism because of Adam's sin; on the other hand, because baptism removes the *culpa*, the infant's incapacity becomes excusable.[29]

Combining with this false orientation of the issue was the lack of agreement on the nature of a virtue. Peter Lombard gives the two opinions: first, that the virtue is a habit and not an act; second, that the virtue is not a habit but an internal as opposed to an external act.[30] Though he obviously inclines to the former view, he does not venture to decide the question.[31] In fact, there seem to have been a good number of theologians who assumed or maintained that a virtue which is not an act is inconceivable;[32] and this perhaps led to the explicit distinction between the remission of sins and the infusion of grace.[33]

Finally, it is to be observed that when obscurity was ended by the influence of the manifestly heretical demand of the Waldenses and Cathari for the rebaptism of adults baptized in infancy and, as well, by the Aristotelian concept of the habitual state,[34] even then the solution did not consist in an

---

29 *De conceptu virginali*, c. 29 (*PL* 158, 462–64 [Schmitt 2: 172–73]). See for a fuller presentation together with an account of the influence of this position, Landgraf, 'Der Gerechtigkeitsbegriff des hl. Anselm v. Canterbury und seine Bedeutung für die Theologie der Frühscholastik' [see above, p. 10, note 36].

30 Peter Lombard, *Sententiae*, 2, d. 27 [*QL* 1: 444–52].

31 Ibid. c. 12 [*QL* 1: 451–52].

32 Instances are Abelard and Peter of Capua. See Landgraf, 'Der Gerechtigkeitsbegriff des hl. Anselm ...' 169 [*DFG* 44–45]; 'Grundlagen für ein Verständnis der Busslehre ...' 186.

33 Thus, Magister Martinus: '... Spiritus sanctus dicitur dari dupliciter, aut quantum ad peccati remissionem, prout datur parvulis, aut quantum ad virtutum collationem, prout datur adultis' [The Holy Spirit is said to be given in two ways, either in regard to the remission of sin, as is the case with little ones, or with regard to the bestowal of the virtues, as is the case with adults]. Cited from Landgraf, 'Die Erkenntnis der heiligmachenden Gnade ...' 46 [see *DFG* 209]. See the following pages.

It is to be noted that in the letter *Maiores Ecclesiae causas*, written at the end of 1201, Pope Innocent III in citing the solutions of the theologians to the problem of infant baptism gives in first place the view that distinguishes between grace and the remission of sin. The view that the virtues are infused *quoad habitum non quoad usum* appears in second place and is introduced with 'nonnullis vero dicentibus.' See *DB* 410 [*DS* 780].

34 Landgraf, 'Die Erkenntnis der heiligmachenden Gnade ...' 42, 64 [*DFG* 207, 219].

immediate identification of grace with justification. Philip the Chancellor distinguished four elements in our participation of the life of Christ: *vivificari*, which is grace and regards the soul itself; *illuminari*, which is faith and regards the intellect; *uniri*, which is charity and regards the will; *rectificari*, which is justice and regards the whole man.[35] This influence of the psychological analysis of the nature of sin and grace is clearly to be found in St Thomas's analysis of the process of justification.[36]

To conclude, we may cite the decision given in connection with the errors of Petrus Ioannis Olivi:

> Verum quia quantum ad effectum baptismi in parvulis reperiuntur doctores quidam theologi opiniones contrarias habuisse, quibusdam ex ipsis dicentibus, per virtutem baptismi parvulis quidem culpam remitti, sed gratiam non conferri, aliis econtra asserentibus, quod et culpa iisdem in baptismo remittitur, et virtutes ac informans gratia infunduntur quoad habitum, etsi non pro illo tempore quoad usum: Nos autem attendentes generalem efficaciam mortis Christi, quae per baptisma applicatur pariter omnibus baptizatis, opinionem secundam, quae dicit, tam parvulis quam adultis conferri in baptismo informantem gratiam et virtutes, tamquam probabiliorem, et dictis Sanctorum et doctorum modernorum theologiae magis consonam et concordem, sacro approbante Concilio duximus eligendam.[37]

3.4 Intermediate Phases from Developing Theorems

In the last section we considered the relations between philosophy and

35   Ibid. 61 [*DFG* 217–18]. See 56–62 [*DFG* 212–18].
36   For example, *Summa theologiae*, 1-2, q. 113.
37   [But because certain learned theologians are found to have had contrary opinions on the effect of baptism on little ones, with some of them saying that through the power of baptism guilt is indeed remitted in little ones, but grace is not given, and others asserting on the contrary that guilt is remitted to them in baptism, and as well the virtues and informing grace are infused as to the habit, though not for the time being as to exercise (of the habit), we on our part, attending to the general efficacy of the death of Christ, which through baptism is applied equally to all the baptized, have judged, and the sacred Council agrees (with us), that the second opinion, which says that informing grace and the virtues are conferred on little ones as much as on adults, is the more probable one, and the one more in harmony and concord with the utterances of the saints and of modern doctors of theology, and the one to be chosen] *DB* 483; see 410 [*DS* 904, 780].

theological speculation. Here are to be considered the interrelations of different theorems within the theological field itself. We begin with a few distinctions and then enumerate typical phases of a speculative development. With this the analysis of a speculative development will be complete.

3.4.1 The Set of Cognate Theorems

One scientific concept is not a science. The analysis of motion, for instance, calls for the following: distance, time, velocity, acceleration, mass, momentum, energy. Together they may be said to constitute a set of cognate theorems. Similarly, any object of scientific thought will require more than one theorem for a full account of it. And, to give an example that we propose to use throughout the next section, the theory of the necessity of grace is based on two theorems: first, the theorem of the supernatural; second, the theorem of the different states of man. One must have grace both because eternal life is a supernatural state and because fallen man cannot avoid sin without grace: no small part of the difficulties occasioned by Pelagianism arises from the fact that it is not one error but two; it denies outright the necessity of grace and so denies both the supernatural character of eternal life and the effects of original sin.

3.4.2 The Relation of Cognate Theorems

In the mathematical sciences the relation of different theorems is simply the difference of their elements: if distance is s and time t and mass m, then velocity is ds/dt, acceleration d^2s/dt^2, momentum is $m.ds/dt$, and energy $m.v.dv$, where v is ds/dt.

In a purely rational science there is only the combination of genus and species. In the instance of the necessity of grace, the necessity from the supernatural end is generic, for it regards man simply as a creature; on the other hand, the various states of man are specifically different initial positions with regard to the attainment of eternal life.

3.4.3 The Order of the Development of the Theorems

The general law is perfectly simple. The mind begins from the particular and works to what is most general; it then returns from the most general through the specific differences to the particular.

But that is just the general law. For what we are dealing with is not the discovery of some one theorem but the discovery of a set of cognate theorems.

Now each theorem in the set has four distinct elements: first, analysis; second, generalization; third, unfolding of implications; fourth, systematic significance.

On the other hand, while analysis and generalization regard the single theorems, systematic significance regards not each single theorem in itself but each one in its relations to all the others. Further, while the unfolding of implications logically follows from the analysis, in point of fact it is extremely difficult for the implications to be explicitly grasped before the systematic significance has been determined. The reason may be that implications are endless and only the systematic significance of the theorem will reveal which implications deserve attention.

So much for preliminaries. Let us now ask in what order theorems are discovered and what are the implications of that order.

From the general principle that the mind moves from the particular to the general, it follows that the specific theorem is discovered before the generic.

The implications of this order are as follows.

First, the specific theorem is adverted to and analyzed: it is seen to explain something.

Second, the specific theorem is generalized: all parallel differences are considered and coordinated.

Third, its implications are worked out, and there will be a tendency to give it the systematic significance of alone constituting the solution to the whole problem.

Fourth, the insufficiency of the specific theorem to account for the whole problem leads to the discovery of the generic theorem.

Fifth, the generic theorem is analyzed, generalized, has its implications worked out.

Sixth, there is a tendency to make the generic theorem serve as the full solution of the problem. The reason for this is complex: on the one hand, the 'third phase' resulted in a distortion of the speculative field by attempting to explain everything in terms of the specific theorems; on the other, the discovery of the generic theorem leads not only to its generalization and to the unfolding of its implications but also to the development of cognate theorems that had been obscured in the third phase.

Seventh, the insufficiency of the generic theorems is adverted to, and there follows the rediscovery of the specific theorem in a new setting. This gives the synthesis of generic and specific theorems.

If it happens that there is one or more intermediate species, the course of the development is vastly complicated. The principles remain the same.

To illustrate the seven phases is too large a task to be carried on in a corner, and so the reader will find it in the next section. There it will be seen that the speculative movement from St Augustine's *De correptione et gratia* to the *Prima secundae* of St Thomas is fundamentally a function of the generic and specific theorems on the necessity of grace.

4   General Antecedents of the Development in St Thomas's Doctrine on Operative Grace

At first sight it appears to the investigator of the thought of St Thomas's predecessors that operative grace is just a name floating aimlessly on the current of early medieval speculation and now given one meaning, now another entirely different. Closer scrutiny reveals that this would be a very superficial interpretation of the facts, for operative grace is not merely a name floating on the surface but also the very shape and inclination of the riverbed hidden beneath. The fundamental data of the necessity of grace and of the liberty of the will, so unequivocally asserted by St Augustine, are also the fundamental data of early speculation on the nature of grace, and it is the unresolved problem of their reconciliation that deeply and obscurely yet ever effectively sets the stage and drives forward the movement of thought.

To establish the point, we ask and then answer seven questions suggested by the analysis of a speculative development. St Thomas explains the need of grace, generically by the theorem of the supernatural, specifically by fallen nature. How, precisely, was this explanation discovered?

First, then, is the discovery of the specific theorem. Who first explained some aspect of the necessity of grace by distinguishing between the need of our first parents before the fall and, on the other hand, our need subsequent to the fall?

Second, there is the generalization of the specific theorem. Who formulated the doctrine of the different states of man, omitting consideration of *natura pura?*

Third, there is the *tendency* to use the specific theorem as the sole explanation of the need of grace. What historical evidence is there for the existence of such a tendency? Note that the question does not apply to thinkers such as Baius and Jansenius who explicitly rejected the theorem of the supernatural. It applies to thinkers who *tended* to positions *resembling* those of Jansenius, not because they rejected the idea of the supernatural but because they did not grasp its significance in a theory of grace.

Fourth, there is the discovery of the generic theorem. Who first formulated the theorem of the supernatural and for what reason?

Fifth, there is the generalization of the generic theorem. What are some instances of this generalization?

Sixth, there is the *tendency* to use the generic theorem alone in solving the whole problem. Who *tended* to deny a difference between the different states of man, to overlook the fact of moral impotence?

Seventh, there is the synthesis of generic and specific theorems. Who made that synthesis for the first time?

Such is our a priori scheme. It may be mistaken, but at least it is something tangible that can be refuted. It is not an intuition, analyzed, unproved, asserted. It is not merely a habit of mind prejudicing the issue, but something above the issue that will lead to its solution. We now turn to the facts, beginning with the *primum quoad nos* and working backwards.

4.1   The Seventh Phase

The synthesis of the generic and specific theorems on the necessity of grace is to be found in the *Prima secundae* of St Thomas.

> Sic igitur virtute gratuita superaddita virtuti naturae indiget homo in statu naturae integrae *quantum ad unum,* scilicet ad operandum et volendum bonum supernaturale. Sed in statu naturae corruptae, *quantum ad duo:* scilicet ut sanetur; et ulterius ut bonum supernaturalis virtutis operetur, quod est meritorium. Ulterius autem in utroque statu indiget homo auxilio divino ut ab ipso moveatur ad bene agendum.[38]

The synthesis could not be clearer or more explicit. But what is the point of mentioning the need of divine providence?

38 [Thus, then, there is one respect in which man in the state of integral nature needs a gratuitous power superadded to the power of nature, namely, (the power) to do and will a supernatural good. But in the state of fallen nature, there are two respects (in which he needs something gratuitous added): namely, for healing, and further to perform a good work of supernatural power, which is meritorious. Further still, in both states man needs divine help in order to be moved by that help to act righteously] *Summa theologiae,* 1-2, q. 109, a. 2 [emphasis added by Lonergan].

4.2   The Sixth Phase

Prior to the ultimate synthesis there is a tendency to make the generic theorem alone suffice. An article in the *De veritate*, parallel to the article just cited, explains why St Thomas in the *Prima secundae* sharply distinguishes between the need for grace and the need for providential assistance. For in the earlier article his thought clearly turns on two points alone: the supernatural and providential assistance. It is too long to cite in its entirety but the essential moment is the following.

> Ad hoc ergo bonum quod est supra naturam humanam, constat liberum arbitrium non posse sine gratia; quia, cum per huiusmodi bonum homo vitam aeternam meretur, constat quod sine gratia homo mereri non potest.
>   Illud autem bonum quod est naturae humanae proportionatum, potest homo per liberum arbitrium explere ...
>   Quamvis autem huiusmodi bona homo possit facere sine gratia gratum faciente, non tamen potest ea facere sine Deo ...[39]

A clearer case of the tendencies to an excessive use of the generic theorem is to be found in the treatment of the problem of moral impotence. This

---

39 [It is clear therefore that free will cannot without grace (do) a good work which is above human nature; because, since through this kind of good man merits eternal life, it is clear that man cannot have merit without grace.
      But man is able to fulfil through free will that good which is proportionate to human nature ...
      But although man can perform good works of this kind without the grace that makes him pleasing (to God), still he cannot perform them without God] *De veritate*, q. 24, a. 14. It is to be noted that the problem of synthesizing the generic and specific theorems is here complicated by the absence of a clearly formulated category of actual grace. The formulation of the idea of habitual grace has already been described: the discovery that the definition of a habit meant a grace that did not completely satisfy requirements was not immediate; further, to find the complement to the habit was not easy, for, as we shall see later, St Thomas had to transform Aristotle's physical theory of motion into a metaphysical theory. Passages that clearly show an absence of the distinction between actual grace and general providence are: *De veritate*, q. 24, a. 15; *Super II Sententiarum*, d. 28, q. 1, aa. 1–4. In St Albert: *Summa de creaturis*, 2, q. 70, a. 5 [*BA* 35: 589]; also his *In II Sententiarum*, d. 25, a. 6 [*BA* 27: 433–34]. For St Bonaventure, see Franz Mitzka, 'Die Lehre des hl. Bonaventura von der Vorbereitung auf die heiligmachende Gnade' [see above, p. 25, note 16].

problem has its definitive solution already in the *De veritate*[40] but an earlier stage of thought is to be found in St Thomas's and in St Albert's commentaries on the Lombard. Both attempt to reduce the *non posse non peccare* to the sinner's inability to obtain the remission of his sins without grace.[41]

4.3 The Fifth Phase

This phase, the systematic generalization of the generic theorem, lay in working out the application of the idea of the supernatural. Thus, Alexander of Hales used the idea to solve the otherwise insoluble problem of merit in our first parents.[42] St Albert the Great's development of the theory of sanctifying grace is known,[43] and the systematic elaboration of St Thomas is familiar.[44]

4.4 The Fourth Phase

The discovery of the generic theorem is the emergence of the scientific concept of the supernatural.

40 *De veritate*, q. 24, a. 12; see *Summa theologiae*, 1-2, q. 109, a. 8.
41 For St Thomas, see *Super II Sententiarum*, d. 28, q. 1, a. 2. St Albert is similarly in difficulty in *In II Sententiarum*, d. 25, a. 6 [*BA* 27: 433–34], and in *Summa de creaturis*, 2, q. 70, a. 5 [*BA* 35: 588]. Where before the difficulty was complicated by the lack of a clear distinction between general providence and actual grace, here the difficulty is obviously the reconciliation of *non posse non peccare* with liberty. In his early *Summa* (the later corrects this – see *Summa theologiae*, 2, q. 100, mem. 2-4 [*BA* 33: 246–52]) St Albert insists that the Lombard did not mean to deny *libertas de necessitate*. He derives his solution from an appeal to St Augustine, who had said *peccatum habendi dura necessitas*; this he rightly interprets as regarding the remission of sin, but falsely supposes to cover the whole issue. St Thomas simply repeats this position in his earliest work: taking it over from his master, he is at first much more downright about it; more brilliant, he solves the point definitively in his next work. In this connection it has been pointed out to me by R. P. Henri Bouillard, who is investigating the matter, that the medieval theologians do not seem to cite the Second Council of Orange. This makes the speculative defect less surprising than it appears at first sight. See also on the question, Lange, *De gratia* [see above, p. 3, note 1] 140–51.
    [Bouillard's point has now been made in print; see his *Conversion et grâce chez s. Thomas d'Aquin* (Paris: Aubier, 1944) 94–95, 97, 98–102, 114–21 (references as in the book's index, *see* Orange).]
42 Landgraf, 'Studien zur Erkenntnis des Übernatürlichen ...' 385–86 [*DFG* 200].
43 See, for instance, Herbert Doms, *Die Gnadenlahre des sel. Albertus Magnus* [see above, p. 18, note 80].
44 *Summa contra Gentiles*, 3, cc. 52, 147–63.

Professor Landgraf has shown that the discovery was the work of Philip the Chancellor and that it arose not from studying the idea of grace, nor from distinguishing the natural and the infused virtues, but from the distinction between natural and meritorious love of God. The existence of the problem had been denied by St Bernard of Clairvaux and Hugh of St Victor[45] but was reestablished by William of Auxerre, who affirmed a natural *amor amicitiae erga Deum*.[46] Philip distinguished natural and rational appetite; asserted the former to be self-regarding, the latter to tend absolutely to the *honestum*; and then subdistinguished two rational appetites, one following reason, another following faith; the former of these is *dilectio naturalis*, the latter is charity.[47]

Forerunners were Praepositinus, who had argued that the *naturalia* were in a different category from the *gratuita* because reason was the highest thing in nature and faith was above reason,[48] and Stephen Langton, who had seen the connection between *gratuitum*, *gratum faciens*, and *meritum*.[49] Still, neither attained to Philip's idea of an entitative disproportion between nature and grace.[50]

4.5   The Third Phase

The third phase was the inadequacy of the specific theorem alone: the modern theologian can well understand that speculation on grace without the basic theorem of the supernatural was in hopeless difficulties. A few of the manifestations of the unsatisfactoriness of the third phase are:

First, the doctrine of merit hangs in midair without any speculative support. This, of course, in no way interferes with the enunciation and affirmation of the doctrine; but it does make the solution of difficulties impossible.[51] It is of importance to remember always that the origin of the

45   Landgraf, 'Studien zur Erkenntnis des Übernatürlichen ...' 374 [*DFG* 194].
46   Ibid. 377 [*DFG* 197].
47   Ibid. 381–84 [*DFG* 197-99].
48   Ibid. 214 [*DFG* 180].
49   Ibid. 214–15 [*DFG* 181].
50   Ibid. 219 [*DFG* 182].
51   Thus, the Lombard accurately describes the need of grace in our first parents (*Sententiae*, 2, d. 24, c. 1 [*QL* 1: 419]): creation was enough to enable man to avoid sin, but not enough to merit eternal life; for that another grace besides creation was needed. But he goes wrong when he tries to explain why the avoidance of sin by our first parents in the period prior to the infusion of grace would not be meritorious: he admits we merit when we merely avoid sin, but always [maintains?] that that is because we have difficulty; in the state of original innocence there was no difficulty and so no

scientific concept of the supernatural was the problem of merit: this fact explains points in St Thomas that might otherwise be obscure.[52]

Second, there could be no satisfactory distinction between the *naturalia* and the *gratuita*: Radulfus Ardens is simply yielding to the logic of the third phase when he states that originally all the virtues were natural but that now they are gratuitous because they were lost by original sin.[53] The effect of this speculative tendency was not to deny the *gratuita* but to deny the *naturalia*: as late as the early thirteenth century one can find a writer to maintain that without divine charity there are no virtues.[54] In the same category falls Peter Abelard's disjunction of charity and cupidity and St Bernard of Clairvaux's assertion that nature in itself is crooked.[55]

Third, it was impossible to have a satisfactory definition of grace. Here again this involved no obscuration of the dogmatic fact: universally it is asserted that grace is what is due to God's free gift and not due to man's desert.[56] The difficulty was to find something that was not grace in the strict sense of the term.[57]

Fourth, we may recall the tendency to a purely psychological interpretation of the nature of grace that we illustrated above when treating the emergence of the idea of habitual grace.[58]

Fifth, a further consequent of the purely psychological interpretation of the nature of grace was the difficulty in holding a clear theory on human liberty. This point has already been illustrated from Peter Lombard.[59] But

---

merit. In commenting this passage St Albert cannot understand the Lombard's position; he was not aware of the intervening development (see his *In II Sententiarum*, d. 25, a. 6 [*BA* 27: 433–34]). This provides a perfect illustration of misinterpretation due to ignorance of development. For a rich collection of twelfth-century positions regarding our first parents, see Landgraf, 'Die Erkenntnis der helfenden Gnade ...' 403–22 [*DFG* 82–99].

52 See, for example, his *Summa theologiae*, 1-2, q. 112, a. 2, ad 1m.
53 Landgraf, 'Studien zur Erkenntnis des Übernatürlichen ...' 212 [*DFG* 180].
54 Ibid. 191 [*DFG* 163–64].
55 Ibid. 195, 374; see whole section, 352–89 [*DFG* 164–65, 194, whole section, 183–201].
56 Ibid. 9–13 [*DFG* 148–50].
57 Ibid. 14–29 [*DFG* 150–64]. Cardinal Laborans defined grace in the strict sense (*veri nominis*) as everything one has at birth or receives afterwards; he admits then two narrower senses, first, everything the elect have at birth or receive afterwards, and second, the virtues of the elect. The example should provide a realization of the difficulty of defining grace in the third phase. It is to be found in Landgraf, ibid. 20–21 [*DFG* 159–60].
58 See above, pp. 175–78.
59 See above, pp. 173–74.

immediately a further point may be made; because the lack of the scientific concept of the supernatural made a scientific concept of liberty impossible, the emergence of the former concept would release speculation on liberty. Thus we find speculation on the nature of liberty beginning with Philip the Chancellor.[60] When it is grasped that the nature of liberty was for the first time undergoing systematic development simultaneously with the first extension of the scientific concept of the supernatural, it is not at all surprising that St Albert and St Thomas in their early writing find the doctrine of moral impotence too anomalous for assimilation.[61] But the full explanation is had only when the formulation of the specific theorem in the second phase is taken into consideration.

4.6   The Second Phase

The second phase is the systematic generalization of the specific theorem: in the example under consideration, it is the systematic generalization of the difference between our first parents and ourselves in the need for grace. According to Professor Landgraf,[62] Peter Lombard gives the final formulation of the distinction between the four states of human liberty.[63]

---

60 See Lottin, *La théorie du libre arbitre depuis s. Anselme jusqu'à s. Thomas d'Aquin.* A few citations will emphasize the point: 'Le chancelier Philippe a le mérite *d'avoir-introduit les questions relatives à la nature du libre arbitre* ... Toutefois l'ordonnancè de ces trois questions est voilée dans l'exposé du chancelier. Mais Alexandre de Halès a su les distinguer soigneusement. Et ces mêmes questions seront reprises, avec quelques variantes, par Albert le Grand, Odon Rigaud et saint Bonaventure ...' [pp. 125–26]. 'Alexandre de Halès ... Odon Rigaud ... s'efforcèrent de scruter la raison foncière du libre arbitre, posant ainsi *les premiers fondements de la doctrine philosophique de la liberté*' [p. 126].
　　In other words, speculation on the nature of liberty has its obscure beginning in Philip. The philosophic basis of liberty is worked out by Alexander of Hales and Odon Rigaldi. After early attempts to harmonize the definitions of Boethius, St Anselm, St Bernard, and the one attributed to St Augustine by the Lombard, 'saint Bonaventure trouvait, à juste titre, pareil travail assez stérile' [p. 126]. The citations are from Lottin, 'Le traité du libre arbitre depuis le chancelier Philippe jusqu'à saint Thomas d'Aquin' [see above, p. 19, note 84] 266, 266–67, 267 [*La théorie du libre arbitre depuis* ... 125–26]. The italics are our own.
61 See above, §4.2, p. 184, note 41.
62 Landgraf, 'Die Erkenntnis der helfenden Gnade ...' 425 [*DFG* 102]; see pp. 422–37, 562–75 [*DFG* 99–112, 114–28]. [Landgraf's reference on p. 425 is to Hugh of St Victor rather than to Peter Lombard. Peter's debt to Hugh can be judged from Lonergan's next note.]
63 *Sententiae*, 2, d. 25, c. 6 [*QL* 1: 431]: '"Et possunt notari in homine quatuor status *liberi arbitrii*.

That the need for grace is expressed in terms of human liberty is easily understood in a period prior to the theorem of the supernatural.

4.7 The First Phase

Alone the first phase remains to be illustrated. It is the emergence of the specific theorem, the first apprehension of the significance of a difference, with regard to the need of grace, between Adam and ourselves. Clearly this should be attributed to St Augustine. It is easy to select a series of phrases from his speculative *De correptione et gratia* that not only bear on the point but also foreshadow future development.[64] To suppose that this first essay

---

"*Ante peccatum enim* ad bonum nil impediebat, ad malum nil impellebat ... tunc sine errore ratio iudicare, et voluntas sine difficultate bonum appetere poterat.

"*Post peccatum vero,* ante reparationem gratiae, premitur a concupiscentia et vincitur ... potest peccare et non potest non peccare, etiam damnabiliter.

"*Post reparationem vero* ... premitur a concupiscentia, sed non vincitur ... ut possit peccare propter libertatem et infirmitatem, et possit non peccare ad mortem propter libertatem et gratiam adiuvantem ...

"*Post confirmationem vero* ... nec vinci nec premi poterit, et tunc habebit non posse peccare."'

[And four states of free will can be noted in man.

For before sin there was nothing to impede the good, and nothing to impel to evil ... then reason was able to judge without error, and will able without difficulty to desire the good.

But after sin, before the reparation of grace, (man) is oppressed by concupiscence and conquered ... he is able to sin and unable not to sin, even to the incurring of damnation.

But after reparation ... (man) is oppressed by concupiscence, but is not conquered ... so that because of liberty and weakness he is able to sin, and because of liberty and helping grace he is able not to sin ...

But after confirmation (in grace) ... he will be unable either to be oppressed or conquered, and then he will have the inability to sin].

Two points are to be observed: first, the tendency to conceive grace psychologically, the illumination of the intellect and the strengthening of the will; second, the fact that the need for grace was so explicitly conceived in terms of moral impotence naturally tended to eclipse the idea of moral impotence when the need for grace was seen to lie in the supernatural character of eternal life. [The quotations within the quotation from the Lombard are attributed by his editor to Hugh of St Victor; the emphasis is Lonergan's.]

64 Augustine, *De correptione et gratia,* c. 12, § 33, *PL* 44, 936: 'Quapropter, bina ista quid inter se differant, diligenter et vigilanter intuendum est; posse non peccare, et non posse peccare' [On this account, we must diligently and

in speculation constitutes 'all you know and all you need to know' on the nature of grace, perseverance, predestination, and human liberty has been the source of not a few 'vertical invasions' of the barbarian. The monumental work of Cornelius Jansen[65] is but the full flower of a far more universal tendency: to seek a speculative system, complete in all its parts and details, where no such system exists or, at most, exists only in embryonic form. To know and unequivocally to state the doctrine of grace is one thing; it is

attentively grasp the difference in that pair of terms: able not to sin, and not able to sin]. Ibid. §34, 937: 'Primo itaque homini, qui in eo bono quo factus fuerat rectus acceperat posse non peccare ...' [To the first man, who had been righteous in that good in which he was created, had been given the ability not to sin]. Ibid.: '... praedestinatis non tale adiutorium perseverantiae datur, sed tale ut eis perseverantia ipsa donetur; non solum ut sine isto dono perseverantes esse non possint, verum etiam ut per hoc donum non nisi perseverantes sint' [such a help to perseverance is not given to the predestined, but such that perseverance itself is given; not only so that without that gift they are unable to persevere, but also so that by means of this gift they are actually persevering and not failing to do so]. Ibid. §35, 937–38: 'Maior quippe libertas est necessaria adversus tot et tantas tentationes, quae in paradiso non fuerunt ... Illi (Adae) ergo sine peccato ullo data est, cum qua conditus est, voluntas libera, et eam fecit (Ada) servire peccato: horum vero (praedestinatorum) cum fuisset voluntas serva peccati, liberata est per illum qui dixit, *Si vos Filius liberaverit, tunc vere liberi eritis* (Ioan. VIII, 36) ... Huic peccato (impaenitentiae finalis) ultra non serviunt, non prima conditione, sicut ille, liberi; sed per secundum Adam Dei gratia liberati, et ista liberatione habentes liberum arbitrium quo serviant Deo, non quo captiventur a diabolo. Liberati enim a peccato servi facti sunt iustitiae (*Rom.* VI, 18), in qua stabunt usque in finem' [A greater liberty is needed against so many and such strong temptations, which did not exist in paradise ... To him (Adam) therefore was given without any sin the free will with which he was created, and he (Adam) made it a slave to sin; but of these (who are predestined), when (their) will had been the slave of sin, it was liberated by him who said, *If the Son has set you free, then you will be truly free* (John 8.36) ... To this sin (of final impenitence) they are no longer slaves, not free in that first state as he was, but by the grace of God set free through the second Adam, and in that liberation having the free will by which they are slaves to God, not that by which they are taken captive by the devil. For set free from sin they are made slaves to justice (Romans 6.18), in which they will stand to the very end].

65 For a close analysis of *De correptione et gratia*, see Charles Boyer, 'Le système de saint Augustin sur la grâce. Paraphrase du "De Correptione et Gratia,"' *Recherches de science religieuse* 20 (1930) 481–505. On Jansenism, see the article by Jean Carreyre in *Dictionnaire de théologie catholique*, vol. 8:1 (Paris: Letouzey et Ané, 1924) columns 318–529. A summary of the *Augustinus* [of Jansenius] is to be had in English; see Nigel Abercrombie, *The Origins of Jansenism* (Ox-

quite another to ask what precisely is grace, whether it is one or many, if many, what are its parts and their correlation, what is its reconciliation with liberty, what is the nature of its necessity. These speculative issues St Augustine did not offer to treat, and it is a question without meaning to ask his position on them. To illustrate the point with the hardy perennial, the supernatural, it is easy to show that St Augustine flatly denied grace to be nature. It is easy to understand that, when writing to the monks of Hadrumetum, he thought of comparing the elect in Christ with Adam but did not think of comparing both with the philosophic abstraction termed *natura pura*. But to ask whether or not the scientific concept of the supernatural is according to the mind of St Augustine is like studying Euclid's elements to find out the truth about multidimensional geometries: in both you find the data that lead to the later conclusion; in neither is the later theorem explicitly formulated.

4.8 Conclusion

How, then, does this sketch show that *gratia operans* is the fundamental problem in the whole movement from St Augustine to St Thomas?

To answer this, one need only observe that the problem of *gratia operans* is the problem of good will: grace operates the goodness of good will.

Now in the period of the specific theorem, there is no explicit distinction between the two senses of this goodness: the goodness of moral action, and the goodness of supernatural elevation. There follows a twofold consequence. First, since the aspect of moral goodness is the one explicitly understood, the theory of grace tends to a psychological form. Second, since the aspect of supernatural elevation is not explicitly grasped by theory, the whole weight of the doctrine of the necessity of grace presses down on liberty: this forces the dialectical position into the concept of liberty itself.

Next in the period of the generic theorem – about twenty years elapsed between the death of Philip the Chancellor and the *De veritate* of St Thomas – there is intense speculative activity. The psychological concept of grace combines with the supernatural aspect to give the infused virtue: but the

---

ford: At the Clarendon Press, 1936) 126–53. It is worth noting that in their third phase the medieval thinkers moved uneasily in the limited orbit of Baius's and Jansenius's thought, but, as soon as they could, escaped from it.

distinction between general divine assistance and actual grace is not immediately grasped.[66] Similarly the supernatural seems to express the total reason for the necessity of grace.[67]

But this defect has its compensation, for the idea of liberty is released and receives a purely speculative development. After some hesitation between the opposed views that liberty is a habit and liberty is a potency, the former view, which results from placing the dialectical position in the definition of liberty, is eliminated, and a purely philosophic concept is accepted.

This indeed sets the problem of the necessity of grace despite the existence of liberty in all its acuteness. How St Thomas meets this issue is the topic of the four chapters to follow.

5   The Methodological Conclusion

It has been shown that speculative theology consists in four elements: theorems, technique, terms, and a dialectical position. Of these the essential speculative element is the theorem.

Now it is plain from the distinction between the common notion and the theorem that a common notion cannot be used to prove the existence of a theorem. The latter is a reflective addition to the former, and it takes place only in conscious and deliberate reflection.

This fact has a most important methodological implication, namely, that the so-called 'implicit speculative position' is an impossibility. Either a speculative position exists explicitly or else one merely has common notions. Such notions have no doubt an exigence for speculative elabora-

66 Thus, St Albert, *In II Sententiarum*, d. 25, a. 6 [ad ob. 1, *BA* 27: 434]: 'auctoritates non probant nec dicunt, quod *sine gratia* non possit aliquis resistere [tentationi], sed quod non potest *sine Deo*: et hoc plane verum est: quia in Deo vivimus, et movemur, et sumus: et nisi ipse continue contineat, et salvet, et moveat, nihil possumus esse et operari: *sed hoc non ponit gratiam specialem*' [the authorities do not prove, nor do they say, that *without grace* one cannot resist (temptation) but they say that *without God* one cannot (do so); and this is plainly true, because in God we live and move and are; and unless he continually contains, and saves, and moves, we can be nothing and do nothing; *but this does not affirm a special grace*]. [The emphasis is Lonergan's.]
67 Ibid. Solutio: 'Si tamen ponatur (homo) habere solum liberum arbitrium, videtur mihi quod adhuc potest resistere tentationi' [If, however, (man) is affirmed to have only free will, it seems to me that he can still resist temptation].

tions, but that exigence does not prove that any given thinker met the exigence.

Hence, throughout the argument to follow, 'implicit speculative positions' have to be disregarded. They can be nothing but a fiction, the projecting of the categories of later thought into the writings of an earlier period.

II-2

The Data of the Inquiry

The first inductive movement gave the form of the development extending from St Augustine to St Thomas. It lets us know what to expect. The second movement consists in assembling the data on *gratia operans* and *cooperans*: the explicit statements of St Augustine, St Anselm, Peter Lombard, St Albert, and St Thomas are in turn presented. The inquiry is here purely factual, and no attempt is made to reach ultimate conclusions. Instead, attention is concentrated on grasping what exactly each author actually said, under what circumstances, and, in the case of St Thomas, who treats the issue differently on three occasions, with what reasons.

1   St Augustine's *De Gratia et Libero Arbitrio*

Four points are considered: the occasion and character of the work; the outline of its content; the denotation of the term 'grace'; and the division of grace into operative and cooperative.

Immediately, however, two prior questions may be raised: Why begin from St Augustine? Why select one of his works for special study instead of giving a summary of his whole position?

As to the first question, there is no doubt that an examination of the whole of St Thomas's thought on grace would have to begin from the Greek Fathers. But our concern is not with grace as the elevation and divinization of the soul; it is with the relations between grace and liberty. Speculative thought on this issue begins with the emergence of the Pelagian heresy and the writings of St Augustine.

Next, a summary of St Augustine's thought is precisely what is not wanted, for a summary is always a presentation in terms of modern ways of thinking and conceiving. But the whole point in considering the historical antecedents to St Thomas's position is to learn to conceive issues in the manner in which they were conceived before St Thomas wrote. To achieve this end, nothing but an accurate account of what was explicitly advanced by St Thomas's predecessors is of any use. Since we cannot examine all of St Augustine's writings, we examine the one most pertinent to our inquiry.

The choice of the other three writers is on an obvious principle; each is an outstanding thinker in a well-defined phase of early Scholasticism; in addition, Peter Lombard and St Albert certainly exerted a direct influence on St Thomas.

1.1 The Occasion and Character of the Work

The *De gratia et libero arbitrio*, presumably written about the year 426 or 427, was addressed *Ad Valentinum et cum illo monachos*. Apparently it was accompanied by the two letters *Ad Valentinum*.[1] Of these the first defines the occasion.

> Venerunt ad nos duo iuvenes, Cresconius et Felix, de vestra congregatione se esse dicentes, qui nobis retulerunt, monasterium vestrum nonnulla dissensione turbatum, eo quod quidam in vobis sic gratiam praedicent, ut negent hominis esse liberum arbitrium; et, quod est gravius, dicant, quod in die iudicii non sit redditurus Deus unicuique secundum opera eius.[2]

It further appears that St Augustine was concerned over this trouble in the monastery of Hadrumetum. On discovering that the young men had very inadequate ideas on Pelagianism, he delayed their return until after the feast of Easter.[3] In particular he feared that this imperfect grasp of the issue

1 Letters 214, 215. *PL* 44, 875–80. [The title is editorial in *PL*; Augustine wrote, 'to my brother Valentine and the brothers who are with him.']
2 [Two young men, Cresconius and Felix by name, have come to us, stating that they are from your community. They have reported to us that your monastery is disturbed by a certain discord by reason of the fact that some among you so extol grace as to deny that man has free will, and, what is worse, they say that on the day of judgment God is not going to render to each according to his works] Letter 214, §1, 875–76.
3 See letter 215, §§ 1–3, 877–80.

was at the root of all the trouble, and he asked to have the source of discord sent to him.[4]

Thus the *De gratia et libero arbitrio* not only aims to show the necessity of grace, the freedom of the will, and the remotely gratuitous but proximately meritorious character of eternal life. There is also, throughout, a visible effort to profit by the occasion and explain, at least in part, the general nature of Pelagianism.

In its character the work clearly belongs to the preliminary phase. The effort of the human mind consists in a clear grasp of issues and a forceful presentation of scriptural argument. The greatness of St Augustine does not lie in any mastery of speculative technique, in the exactitude of explicit distinctions, the elaboration of theorems, the synthetic apprehension of multiple correlations. On the contrary, his genius is precisely that, unaided by these devices of conscious reflection, he nonetheless is able to maintain a profoundly coherent position, not intermittently but through thousands of pages, not by oversimplification but by an intense and vital grasp of hundreds of passages from scripture, not by abstract formulation but by relentlessly tracking down, confronting, and confuting each assertion and each evasion of Pelagian thought.

To understand the *De gratia et libero arbitrio* one has to live fifteen hundred years ago. The questions raised are not the logical series of issues that would emerge from the application of a philosophic technique. They are the questions of Cresconius and Felix, and only incidentally the questions of all time. The concepts used are the common notions with which they would be familiar. The arguments are simply passages from Holy Writ. The solution of difficulties is scripture again. And distinctions are not formulated but only indicated by the juxtaposition of apparently opposed texts.

The work has a manifest presupposition: the Christian faith. It is not the opinion of St Augustine but the doctrine of the church that is at stake. It is not his thought but the testimony of scripture that is to be accepted.[5] And the one acceptance that is of real moment is the acceptance of faith. What the monks believe, they also do well to pray to understand; for understanding depends on free will, and grace, here as elsewhere, is needed. But if

---

4 Letter 214, §6, 877–78.
5 *De gratia et libero arbitrio*, c. 20, §41, *PL* 44, 905–906: 'Satis me disputasse arbitror ... et sic disputasse ut non magis ego quam divina ipsa Scriptura vobiscum locuta sit evidentissimis testimoniis veritatis' [I believe I have argued enough ... and have so argued that not I but rather divine scripture itself has spoken to you in the utterly clear testimonies of truth].

they do not understand: 'ubi sentitis vos non intelligere, interim credite divinis eloquiis.'[6]

This presupposition of faith is of the greatest methodological importance. When a writer addresses himself to the assent of faith and tells his readers that if they pray they may understand, then manifestly an interpreter who offers a synthetic summary of the doctrine exposed presupposes the grace of understanding in himself and his readers. A scientific inquiry can make no such presupposition, and so must limit itself to an account of the doctrines to be accepted on faith. Principally for this reason have we avoided all explanatory summaries of St Augustine's thought.

1.2   Outline of the Work

If the work has not exactly a plan, at least attention successively focuses on different points. There is free will (cc. 2–3, §§ 2–5). Grace is necessary (cc. 4–19, §§ 6–40). God controls all wills (cc. 20–21, §§ 41–43). The judgments of God are just but inscrutable (cc. 22–23, §§ 44, 45).

1.2.1   Free Will

First, free will exists. 'Revelavit autem nobis per Scripturas suas sanctas, esse in homine liberum voluntatis arbitrium.'[7] That is the point to be proved, that free will is a truth to be received on faith. The argument that follows is a mosaic of texts from the Old Testament and the New. There is no definition of freedom and no philosophic proof of freedom. What is a rigorous consequence, though not so obvious, is that there are no philosophic difficulties about freedom. Such difficulties as do arise are solved not by distinctions but by a juxtaposition of the compensating and mutually limiting texts of scripture which form the basis of theological distinctions and are the proof of their existence and legitimacy. 'Watch and pray,' because you have free will. 'Pray,' because you need grace.[8] In this antithetical presentation Augustine is a master. 'Gratia Dei sum id quod sum'

---

6   [where you realize that you do not understand, believe meanwhile the divine utterances] Letter 214, § 7, 877–78. See *De gratia et libero arbitrio*, c. 1, § 1, 881; ibid. c. 24, § 46, 911–12.
7   [(God) has revealed to us through his holy scriptures that there is free choice of will in man] Ibid. c. 2, § 2, 882.
8   Ibid. c. 4, § 9, 887.

calls for 'gratia eius in me vacua non fuit, sed plus omnibus illis laboravi.'[9] 'Fili, noli deficere a disciplina Domini' is met with 'Ego rogavi pro te, Petre, ne deficiat fides tua.'[10]

The ambiguity that in early medieval thought resides in the distinction between *libertas a necessitate* and *libertas a peccato* has its origin in this procedure of St Augustine's. From the liberty of free will to the liberation from sin, he passes with an ease that does not betray the slightest sense of inconsequence.[11] But this is no explicit dialectical position, even though it does contain the whole mystery. Neither is it a theory of liberty, unless you take the liberty to develop his thought for him and then attribute your creation to his mind. But it is much more a dialectical position than a theory of liberty. For the method and procedure of setting one text of scripture against another to justify an acceptance of all is simply without meaning unless the faith is presupposed, and unless the acceptance of revealed truth without any scientific understanding is regarded as a matter of course. Such a preponderance of the dialectical position over vague and even over explicit theoretical tendencies is what constitutes the essential continuity of Catholic thought.

1.2.2 Grace and the Pelagians

As free will is a dogmatic truth, so also is the necessity of grace. What St Augustine means by grace will be considered in the next section. Here the aim is simply to make clear the ideas that direct and govern his exposition.

He is writing to monks, and so he draws his first argument from passages in scripture that prove the necessity of a special grace for the life of the

---

9   [By the grace of God I am what I am (1 Corinthians 15.10) ... grace toward me has not been in vain. On the contrary, I worked harder than any of them (ibid.)] Ibid. c. 5, § 12, 888.
10 [My child, do not despise the Lord's discipline (Proverbs 3.11) ... Peter, I have prayed for you that your own faith may not fail' (Luke 22.32)] Ibid. c. 4, § 9, 887.
11 An instance occurs, c. 15, § 31, 899: 'Semper est autem in nobis voluntas libera, sed non semper est bona. Aut enim a iustitia libera est, quando servit peccato, et tunc est mala: aut a peccato libera est, quando servit iustitiae, et tunc est bona' [But will is always free in us, though it is not always good. For either it is free from righteousness when it serves sin, and then it is evil; or it is free from sin when it serves righteousness, and then it is good]. Such a passage simply puts in words of ordinary speech his familiar use of such texts as John 8.36, Romans 6.18, etc.

celibate. At the same time, opportunities are not lost to cite parallel texts that show free will to exist.[12]

For reasons already indicated,[13] he suspects that the monks need to be taught something about the exact nature of Pelagian error; the next thirty-one paragraphs are devoted largely to this end.

First is refuted the Pelagian view that grace is given according to our merits,[14] and incidentally it is explained that though eternal life is a grace given according to our merits, still our merits exist only in virtue of graces, so that eternal life is absolutely a grace and only relatively a reward.[15]

Second, the Pelagian evasions that grace is the law, knowledge of the law, nature, free will, or exclusively the remission of sins, are refuted.[16]

Third, the more subtle evasion that grace is due to our initial good will is attacked. The Pelagian thesis is cited.

> 'Etsi non datur [gratia] secundum merita bonorum operum, quia
> per ipsam bene operamur; tamen secundum merita bonae voluntatis
> datur: quia bona voluntas,' inquiunt, 'praecedit orantis, quam
> praecessit voluntas credentis, ut secundum haec merita gratia
> sequatur exaudientis Dei.'[17]

St Augustine's answer is to show that the good will involved in faith and prayer is as much due to grace as the good will of actual performance. It is in this section of the work that the distinction between operative and cooperative grace arises.[18] What is to be grasped is that it arises in answer to a Pelagian distinction.

1.2.3 Divine Mastery

After the existence of both grace and free will is established, the argument turns to a point speculatively related to grace as the cause of good will.

12 Ibid. c. 4, §§ 6–9, 885–87.
13 See above, note 3.
14 *De gratia et libero arbitrio*, cc. 5–10, §§ 10–22, 887–95.
15 Cc. 8–9, §§ 19–21, 892–94.
16 Ibid. cc. 11–13, §§ 23–26, 895–97.
17 [Although (grace) is not given according to the merits of our good works, for it is through grace that we are able to do good works, nevertheless it is given according to the merits of good will, because, they say, the good will of a person praying precedes (grace), and is itself preceded by the will of a person believing, so that according to these merits the grace of the God who hears follows] Ibid. c. 14, § 27, 897.
18 The section runs from c. 14 to c. 19, §§ 27–40, 897–905.

... Scriptura divina si diligenter inspiciatur, ostendit non solum bonas hominum voluntates quas ipse facit ex malis, et a se factas bonas in actus bonos et in aeternam dirigit vitam, verum etiam illas quae conservant saeculi creaturam, ita esse in Dei potestate, ut eas quo voluerit, quando voluerit, faciat inclinari, vel ad beneficia quibusdam praestanda, vel ad poenas quibusdam ingerendas, sicut ipse iudicat, occultissimo quidem iudicio, sed sine ulla dubitatione iustissimo.[19]

Such are the hardening of the heart of Pharaoh, the flight of Israel from the men of Hai, the resistance in Palestine to Joshua, the cursing of David by the son of Gemini, the treason of Judas, and the hatred of the Jews in crucifying Christ.[20]

1.2.4 The Mystery

Finally, St Augustine exposes his explicit dialectical position. 'O altitudo divitiarum sapientiae et scientiae Dei! quam inscrutabilia sunt iudicia eius, et investigabiles viae eius.'[21] The trouble is that men suppose human good to precede divine favor. Let them consider the baptism of infants. They wail and struggle when receiving the sacrament; what a crime if they were free in their actions. And what merit of theirs precedes, if, now and then, pagan children are baptized while those born in the faith die before christening? The Lord has concluded all in infirmity that he might have mercy on all. But this is not 'Do evil that good may come.' Rather it is 'We have done evil, and good has come.' Do not attribute folly or injustice to the fount of all wisdom and justice. Grasp that the judgments of the Lord are inscrutable, that if the Lord hardened the heart of Pharaoh, this does not exclude nor

---

19 [divine scripture, if it is carefully studied, shows that not only the good wills of men, which he made out of bad wills, and having made them good directs them to good works and to eternal life, but also those wills which maintain the creature of the world are so subject to the power of God that he makes them incline where he wills, when he wills, either to granting benefits to some, or to inflicting punishments on some, as he himself judges by a judgment most hidden indeed but without any doubt most just] Ibid. c. 20, §41, 906.

20 The argument runs from §41 to §43, 905–909.

21 [O the depth of the riches of the wisdom and knowledge of God! How unsearchable are his judgments and how inscrutable his ways! (Romans 11.33)] Ibid. c. 22, §44, 910.

prevent Pharaoh from hardening his own heart.[22] Be assured that the labor of your life is not in vain, and that if grace is not given according to your merits, eternal life is according to your works.[23]

1.3 The Meaning of the Term 'Grace'

The connotation of the term is known: the gratuitous, what is not due. What is important is the denotation. For St Augustine uses any text that suits his point, nor does he confine his attention to those that refer exclusively to what we would term actual grace.

Grace, then, is the gift of God. But 'Omne datum optimum, et omne donum perfectum desursum est, descendens a Patre luminum.'[24] Thus it is the gift of a vocation to the monastic life[25] or the most efficacious vocation of St Paul.[26] It is salvation given 'per lavacrum regenerationis et renovationis Spiritus sancti, quem ditissime effudit super nos, per Iesum Christum Salvatorem nostrum, ut iustificati ipsius gratia, haeredes efficiamur secundum spem vitae aeternae.'[27] It is the justification of the unjust.[28] It is faith working through charity.[29] It is being a child of God and moved by the Spirit of God.[30] It is creation in Christ Jesus in whom all things are made new.[31] It is his aid without whom nothing can be done.[32] It is not the law, nor knowledge of the law, nor nature.[33] It is not simply the remission of sins but also power to avoid them in the future.[34] It is preceded neither by the

---

22 Ibid. c. 23, § 45, 911: '... et Deus induravit per iustum iudicium, et ipse Pharao per liberum arbitrium' [and God hardened (the heart of Pharaoh) by a just judgment, and Pharaoh himself by free will].
23 This section embraces cc. 22–23, §§ 44–45, 909–11.
24 [Every good gift and every perfect gift is from above, coming down from the Father of lights (James 1.17)] Ibid. c. 6, §15, 890.
25 Ibid. c. 4, §7, 886.
26 Ibid. c. 5, §12, 888–89.
27 [through the water of rebirth and renewal by the Holy Spirit. This Spirit he poured out on us richly through Jesus Christ our Savior, so that, having been justified by his grace, we might become heirs according to the hope of eternal life (Titus 3.5–7)] Ibid. c. 5, §12, 889.
28 Ibid. c. 6, §13, 889–90; §14, 890; c. 12, §24, 895–96.
29 Ibid. c. 7, §18, 892.
30 Ibid. c. 11, §23, 895.
31 Ibid. c. 8, §20, 892–93.
32 Ibid. c. 5, §10, 888; c. 6, §13, 890.
33 Ibid. cc. 11–13, §§23–25, 895–96.
34 Ibid. c. 13, §26, 896–97.

desert of our good works nor by the welcome of our good will. What precede are evil deserts and bad will.[35] Above all, grace is charity.[36]

Such is the global apprehension of grace in the *De gratia et libero arbitrio.* Distinctions between sanctifying grace and the infused virtues, between habitual grace and actual, are, of course, in no way denied. Neither are they affirmed.

1.4 Operative and Cooperative Grace

The origin of the distinction is St Augustine's rejection of the Pelagian assertion that, though grace may be needed for good works, it is given according to the merit of the good will that believes and prays. His refutation is on the following lines.

Faith is itself the fruit of grace. *Misericordiam consecutus sum, ut fidelis essem.*[37]

As evil deserts precede the grace that leads to meritorious action,[38] so evil will precedes the good will which God by his grace produces.

> Et dabo eis, inquit, cor aliud, et spiritum novum dabo eis; et evellam cor lapideum de carne eorum, et dabo eis cor carneum, ut in praeceptis meis ambulent, et iustificationes meas observent, et faciant eas: et erunt mihi in populum, et ego ero eis in Deum, dicit Dominus.[39]

What could be more absurd than to speak of good will preceding grace when the effect of grace is to remove a heart of stone and give a heart of

---

35 Ibid. c. 5, §12, 888–89; c. 14, §29, 898.

36 Ibid. c. 18, §37, 903: '... unde est in hominibus caritas Dei et proximi, nisi ex ipso Deo? Nam si non ex Deo, sed ex hominibus, vicerunt Pelagiani: si autem ex Deo, vicimus Pelagianos' [whence is there in men love of God and of neighbor, unless from God himself? For if (it is) not from God but from men, the Pelagians have conquered; but if (it is) from God, we have conquered the Pelagians]. Considerable space is devoted to charity, cc. 17–19, §§34–40, 902–905.

37 [I received mercy that I might be faithful (1 Corinthians 7.25)] Ibid. c. 14, §28, 897.

38 See ibid. c. 5, §12, 888–89.

39 [I will give them a new heart, and put a new spirit within them; I will remove the heart of stone from their flesh and give them a heart of flesh, so that they may follow my statutes and keep my ordinances and obey them. Then they shall be my people, and I will be their God (Ezekiel 11.19–20)] Ibid. c. 14, §29, 898.

flesh? But let us not argue. In the same passage the prophet tells why God produces this change. Not because of deserts, but because of his Holy Name, the Name that Israel's sin has dishonored.[40] Yet even in the divine victory over obduracy of heart, it is not to be supposed that free will does nothing. Else why the command, *Nolite obdurare corda vestra?* Why does even Ezekiel say:

> Proicite a vobis omnes impietates vestras ... facite vobis cor novum et
> spiritum novum, et facite omnia mandata mea. Utquid moriemini
> domus Israel, dicit Dominus? quia nolo mortem morientis, dicit
> Adonai Dominus, [sed] convertimini et vivetis [vivite].[41]

But how is it that he who says *Facite vobis* also says *Dabo vobis?* Why does he command, if he is the giver? Why does he give, if man is the doer? Our will is always free, but it is not always good; for it is either free from justice, and then it is evil; or it is liberated from sin, and then it is good. But grace is always good, and it both makes an evil will into a good will, and advances incipient good will to perfection.[42]

The Pelagians thought they had a good point when they argued, God does not command what man cannot perform. Who does not know that? But still, God does command some things we cannot perform, that we may know what graces to pray for and so perform. The Psalmist commands, *Cohibe linguam tuam a malo.* But he also prays, *Pone, Domine, custodiam ori meo.*[43]

After establishing separately that grace is responsible both for good will and for good performance, he now repeats both points simultaneously. This gives the basic passages on operative and cooperative grace. There is no need of commentary: we copy them out indicating in the margin 'op(erans)' and 'coop(erans).'[44]

---

40 Ibid. § 30, 898–99 (Ezekiel 36.22–27).
41 [Cast away from you all the transgressions that you have committed against me, and get yourselves a new heart and a new spirit! Why will you die, O house of Israel? For I have no pleasure in the death of anyone, says the Lord God. Turn, then, and live (Ezekiel 18.31–32)] Ibid. c. 15, § 31, 899. [Augustine's Latin differs slightly from the Vulgate; note Lonergan's 'Proicite,' as in Lewis and Short, contrasted with Augustine's 'Projicite'; also he chooses the variant 'sed' where Migne puts 'et' in first place; and he adds the variant 'vivite' not given in Migne.]
42 Ibid. c. 15, § 31, 899–900.
43 [Keep your tongue from evil ... O Lord, set a watch before my mouth (Psalm 34.13; 141.3)] Ibid. c. 16, § 32, 900.
44 [See below, note 54, for Lonergan's general footnote reference for all of these quotations.]

coop.   Certum est enim nos mandata servare, si volumus: sed quia praeparatur voluntas a Domino, ab illo petendum est ut tantum velimus, quantum sufficit ut volendo faciamus.[45]

op.   Certum est nos velle, cum volumus: sed ille facit ut velimus bonum, de quo dictum est, quod paulo ante posui, *Praeparatur voluntas a Domino*; de quo dictum est, *A Domino gressus hominis dirigentur, et viam eius volet*; de quo dictum est, *Deus est qui operatur in vobis et velle.*[46]

coop.   Certum est nos facere, cum facimus: sed ille facit ut faciamus, praebendo vires efficacissimas voluntati, qui dixit, *Faciam ut in iustificationibus meis ambuletis, et iudicia mea observetis et faciatis.*[47]

op.   Cum dicit, *faciam ut faciatis*: quid aliud dicit, nisi, *auferam a vobis cor lapideum*, unde non faciebatis; *et dabo vobis cor carneum*, unde faciatis? Et hoc quid est, nisi, *Auferam cor durum*, unde non faciebatis; et dabo cor obediens, unde faciatis.[48]

coop.   Ille facit ut faciamus, cui dicit homo, *Pone, Domine, custodiam ori meo.* Hoc est enim dicere, Fac ut ponam custodiam ori meo: quod beneficium Dei iam fuerat consecutus, qui dixit, *Posui ori meo custodiam.*[49]

op.   Qui ergo vult facere Dei mandatum et non potest, iam quidem habet voluntatem bonam, sed adhuc parvam et invalidam ...[50]

coop.   poterit autem, cum magnam habuerit et robustam. Quando enim

45   [For it is certain that we keep the commandments if we will (to do so); but because the will is prepared by the Lord, we must ask from him that we may will as much as is needed for us to do what we will.]

46   [It is certain that we will when we will; but that we will the good, he brings it about of whom that is said which I stated a little earlier, *The will is prepared by God*, he of whom it is said, *Our steps are made firm by the Lord, when he delights in our way* (Psalm 37.23), of whom it is said, *It is God who is at work in you both to will* (and to work for his good pleasure; Philippians 2.13). – 'Praeparatur voluntas a Domino' is based on the erroneous LXX reading; see *DS* 374.]

47   [It is certain that we act when we act, but it is he who makes us act by providing most efficacious powers to the will, he who said, *I will make you follow my statutes and be careful to observe my ordinances* (Ezekiel 36.27).]

48   [When he says, *I will make you act*, what else is he saying if not, *I will remove from you the heart of stone* which was the source of your failure to act, *and I will give you a heart of flesh* which will cause you to act? And what else is this if not, *I will remove the hard heart*, which was the cause of your not acting, and I will give an obedient heart which will cause you to act.]

49   [He it is who makes us act to whom man says, *Set a guard over my mouth, O Lord.* For this is to say, Make me set a guard over my mouth. And this gift of God he had already received who said, *I placed a guard on my mouth* (Psalm 39.2). – Augustine has the perfect tense, *posui ... custodiam*, where the future tense is the common reading.]

50   [The one who wants to keep God's commandments and cannot, already indeed has good will, but a will that is still small and weak ...]

martyres magna illa mandata fecerunt, magna utique voluntate, hoc est, magna caritate fecerunt: de qua caritate ipse Dominus ait, *Maiorem hac caritatem nemo habet, quam ut animam suam ponat pro amicis suis ...*

Ipsam caritatem apostolus Petrus nondum habuit, quando timore Dominum ter negavit ...[51]

op.   Et tamen quamvis parva et imperfecta, non deerat, quando dicebat Domino, *Animam meam pro te ponam* ...: putabat enim se posse, quod se velle sentiebat. Et quis istam etsi parvam dare coeperat caritatem, nisi ille qui praeparat voluntatem[52]

both   et cooperando perficit, quod operando incipit? Quoniam ipse ut velimus operatur incipiens, qui volentibus cooperatur perficiens. Propter quod ait Apostolus, *Certus sum quoniam qui operatur in vobis opus bonum, perficiet usque in diem Christi Iesu ...* Ut ergo velimus, sine nobis operatur; cum autem volumus, et sic volumus ut faciamus, nobiscum cooperatur: tamen sine illo vel operante ut velimus, vel cooperante cum volumus, ad bona pietatis opera nihil valemus. De operante illo ut velimus, dictum est, *Deus est enim qui operatur in vobis et velle.* De cooperante autem cum iam volumus et volendo facimus: *Scimus,* inquit, *quoniam diligentibus Deum omnia cooperantur in bonum.*[53]

coop.   Quid est, *omnia,* nisi et ipsas terribiles saevasque passiones? Sarcina quippe illa Christi, quae infirmitati gravis est, levis efficitur caritati.

---

51   [he will be able, however (to keep God's commandments), when he has a great and robust (will). For when the martyrs kept those great commandments, they did so with a great will, that is, with a great charity; of this charity the Lord himself says, *No one has greater love than this, to lay down one's life for one's friends* (John 15.31) ...
    This charity the apostle Peter did not yet have, when through fear he three times denied the Lord ...]

52   [And nevertheless charity was not lacking to him, though it was small and imperfect, when he said to the Lord, *I will lay down my life for you* (John 13.37). For he thought he could do what he felt himself wanting to do. And who began to give that charity, small though it was, except the one who prepares the will]

53   [and completes by cooperating what he began by operating? For beginning he operates to make us will who completing cooperates with those willing. For this reason the Apostle says, *I am confident of this, that the one who began a good work among you will bring it to completion by the day of Jesus Christ* (Philippians 1.6). That we will, therefore, he operates without us; but when we will, and so will that we do, he cooperates with us; but without him, either operating that we will or cooperating when we will, we are unable to do any good works of piety. Of him who operates that we will, it is said, *It is God who is at work in you both to will.* But of him who cooperates when we already will and willing (go on to) perform, *We know,* he says, *that all things work together for good* (Romans 8.28).]

> Talibus enim Dominus dixit esse suam sarcinam levem ..., qualis
> Petrus fuit quando passus est pro Christo, non qualis fuit quando
> negavit Christum.[54]

To conclude: St Augustine does not distinguish between operative and
cooperative grace, but between God operating on an evil will to make it
incipiently good, and cooperating with a good but weak will to make it strong.
Even in the former case the will acts freely, as we have seen.[55] And the distinction consists in an appeal to scripture in answer to an evasion attempted
by the Pelagians.

2   St Anselm

Two points are briefly treated: the character of his thought, and his position
on prevenient and subsequent grace.[56]

2.1   The Character of His Thought

St Augustine's problem was to confront a living heresy and define the
content of Holy Writ on a complex issue, not by a technique of abstract
thought, but by a masterly series of juxtaposed texts. When St Anselm
wrote, the faith was accepted and secure, but the problems of the mind
appeared insoluble.[57] His task was the highly speculative work of establishing the abstract possibility of solutions.

---

54 [What is *all things* if not those terrible and cruel sufferings? The burden, of
    course, is that of Christ, which is heavy for weakness but is made light by
    charity. For the Lord said his burden was light to such as Peter was when he
    suffered for Christ, not to such as he was when he denied Christ.] Ibid. cc.
    16–17, §§ 32–33, 900–901. There follow the four columns in praise of char-
    ity, which *si non ex Deo, sed ex hominibus, vicerunt Pelagiani* [if (it is) not from
    God but from men, the Pelagians have conquered].
55 See above, p. 202.
56 A distinction between *operans-cooperans* and *praeveniens-subsequens* does not
    appear before the *Prima secundae* of St Thomas, q. 111, aa. 2–3.
57 He expresses this difference in *Tractatus de concordia praescientiae et
    praedestinationis nec non gratiae cum libero arbitrio*, c. 11, *PL* 158, 522 (Schmitt
    2: 264): '... fuerunt quidam superbi, qui totam virtutum efficaciam in sola
    libertate arbitrii consistere sunt arbitrati: et sunt nostro tempore multi, qui
    liberum arbitrium esse aliquid penitus desperant' [there have been certain
    proud people who thought the whole efficacy of the virtues consisted in the
    liberty alone of judgment; and there are many in our time who completely
    despair about the existence of free will (see Lonergan's translation, pp. 7–8
    above)].

He grasped the need of philosophic thought and composed treatises on the will, free choice, truth. But writing in the form of the dialogue he naturally failed to separate philosophy and theology. Both suffer. As we have seen, he has no distinction between habitual and actual grace.[58] His idea of liberty is simply a deduction from the problem of the relations between grace and liberty.[59] Accordingly, his theory of liberty is nothing but the unconscious formulation of a dialectical position.[60]

Within the limitations of his time, St Anselm is a genius. His thought on the reconciliation of grace and liberty blocks out in bold but exact lines the only course of a possible solution. In the *Tractatus de concordia praescientiae et praedestinationis nec non gratiae Dei cum libero arbitrio*, seven chapters are devoted to divine foreknowledge,[61] three to predestination,[62] fourteen to grace.[63] The way he puts the questions reveals at once a master in speculative thought. He does not ask, How does one explain God's foreknowledge of a free act? He asks, Is foreknowledge of a free act a contradiction? He shows that it is not, and having shown that, he leaves to future thinkers nothing more to do than fill in the details. As we shall see, St Thomas prolongs his thought to almost the ultimate stage of refinement.[64]

His thought on grace proceeds from his definition of liberty: *libertas arbitrii est potestas servandi rectitudinem voluntatis propter ipsam rectitudinem*. The fundamental theorem is that a right act of willing presupposes the rightness of the will. Granted this rightness, the will can keep it by acting rightly. If the rightness is lost by wrong action, the will cannot act rightly (*servitus peccati*) since right action presupposes rightness of will. But though it cannot act rightly, it retains liberty, which, by definition, is the capacity to retain rightness.[65]

---

58 See above, pp. 176–77, §3.3.3.
59 See *De libero arbitrio, PL* 158, 489–506 [Schmitt 1: 207–26].
60 This statement follows immediately from the preceding.
61 *PL* 158, 507–19 [Schmitt 2: 245–60].
62 Ibid. 519–21 [Schmitt 2: 260–62].
63 Ibid. 521–40 [Schmitt 2: 263–87].
64 I do not say absolutely but almost the ultimate stage of refinement, for St Thomas did not make his position unmistakable to every reader.
65 *De libero arbitrio, PL* 158, 492–95, 503 (cc. 3 and 11 especially) [Schmitt 1: 210–13, 222–23]. This may seem elaborate trifling. I cannot here digress to show that it is not. But despite its technical deficiencies, it would seem to grasp in global fashion the ultimate issue.

2.2 His Position on Prevenient and Subsequent Grace

The connection between grace and liberty appears as soon as St Anselm identifies the rightness of the will with justice.

> Quicumque autem ex his salvantur, per iustitiam salvari dubium non est. Iustis enim promittitur vita aeterna: quia *iusti in perpetuum vivent, et apud Dominum est merces eorum.*[66] Quod autem iustitia sit rectitudo voluntatis, sacra saepe monstrat auctoritas.[67]

His next step is to demonstrate that this rightness or justice can be had only through grace. The argument runs:

> Consideremus nunc utrum aliquis hanc rectitudinem non habens, eam aliquo modo a se habere possit. Utique a se illam habere nequit, nisi aut volendo aut non volendo. Volendo quidem nullus valet eam per se adipisci; quia nequit eam velle, nisi illam habeat.[68] Quod autem aliquis non habens rectitudinem voluntatis, illam valeat per se non volendo assequi, mens nullius accipit. Nullo igitur modo potest eam creatura habere a se. Sed neque creatura valet eam habere ab alia creatura. Sicut namque creatura nequit creaturam salvare; ita non potest illi dare per quod debeat salvari. Sequitur itaque quia nulla creatura rectitudinem habet, quam dixi voluntatis, nisi per gratiam.[69]

66 Wisdom 5.16.
67 [But whoever from among these are saved, there is no doubt that they are saved by righteousness. For eternal life is promised to the righteous, because *the righteous live forever, and their reward is with the Lord.* But that righteousness is rectitude of will, the sacred authority often shows] *Tractatus de concordia,* c. 12, *PL* 158, 522 [Schmitt 2: 264].
68 Because 'voluntas non est recta quia vult recte; sed recte vult quoniam est recta' [the will is not right because it wills rightly; rather does it will rightly because it is right] *Tractatus de concordia,* c. 13, 523 [Schmitt 2: 265–66].
69 [Let us now consider whether someone who lacks this rectitude is able to have it in some way from his own resources. Certainly he cannot have it of himself except by either willing or not willing. No one indeed is able to obtain it through himself by willing, because he is not able to will it unless he has it. But that someone who lacks rectitude of will is able to obtain it through himself by not willing, the mind of no one accepts that. In no way therefore can a creature have it from himself. But neither can a creature have it from another creature. For as creature is unable to save creature, so (one creature) cannot give another (that) through which it must be saved.

From this position St Anselm has no difficulty in solving all points connected with grace and freedom. There can be no merit before the gift of rectitude; free will can merit afterwards by retaining its rectitude, but this merit is due to the rectitude given.

Accordingly, the grace that gives the will rightness and enables it to will rightly is termed *praeveniens*; what appears to be the same grace, inasmuch as it maintains this rightness of will, is termed *subsequens*:

> Quibus autem modis, post eandem rectitudinem acceptam, liberum arbitrium gratia adiuvet ut servet quod accepit: quamvis non omnes valeam enumerare, multifariam enim hoc facit; tamen non erit inutile aliquid inde dicere. Nemo certe servat rectitudinem hanc acceptam, nisi volendo; velle autem illam aliquis nequit, nisi habendo: habere vero illam nullatenus valet, nisi per gratiam. Sicut ergo illam nullus accipit, nisi gratia praeveniente; ita nullus eam servat, nisi *eadem gratia subsequente*. Nempe, quamvis illa servetur per liberum arbitrium, non tamen est tantum imputandum libero arbitrio, quantum gratiae, cum haec rectitudo servatur; quoniam illam liberum arbitrium nonnisi per gratiam praevenientem et subsequentem habet et servat.[70]

As it stands, the passage leaves a good deal open to question. It would be well to know exactly whether and to what extent *praeveniens* and *subsequens* are technical terms, whether the *eadem gratia* is simply literary or, to some extent, metaphysical. But on these points we cannot pause, and, did we, it probably would only be to attempt to determine what in itself is undetermined.

And thus it follows that no creature has the rectitude of will of which I speak except through grace] Ibid. 523–24 [Schmitt 2: 266].

70 [I cannot enumerate all the ways in which, after the same rectitude has been received, grace aids free will to preserve what it received, for it does this in a great diversity of ways; still, it will not be useless to say something under that heading. Certainly no one preserves this rectitude that has been received except by willing; but no one is able to will it except by having it; but there is no way one is able to have it except through grace. Therefore, just as no one receives it except by prevenient grace, so no one preserves it except *by the same grace* (acting) *subsequently*. Namely, although it is preserved through free will, nevertheless it is not to be imputed so much to free will as to grace, when this rectitude is preserved; because free will does not have and retain it except through prevenient and subsequent grace] *Tractatus de concordia*, c. 14, 524–25 [Schmitt 2: 267].

Grace, for St Anselm in his speculation, is what gives and maintains the rectitude of the will. That rectitude as willed is the justice which wins eternal life.

Grace is prevenient in giving the will its rectitude; it is subsequent in maintaining – more than the will itself – the same rectitude.

3   Peter Lombard

Three points are treated: the period; the context of *gratia operans*; the doctrine on the subject.

3.1   The Period

First we must draw on the mine of information: Professor Landgraf. Discussing the terminology of early Scholasticism he has written:

> In the whole of early Scholasticism the term *gratia actualis* does not occur. This need cause no surprise to anyone who reflects that at that time the psychological interpretation of grace was dominant, and that a grace before justification was mentioned only tentatively and with distinctions. The root of this was the origin of speculation in the Pauline epistles, which, almost exclusively, speak of grace and its necessity only in connection with justification. Thus early thought envisaged, for the most part, only the grace of justification, which because of its connection with faith presented at the same time the permanence of a virtue and the causation of activity.
>
> The dominance of Augustinian thought in the early period makes perfectly natural the frequency of such terms as *gratia operans*,[71] *cooperans, gratia adiutrix, gratia adiuvans, gratia auxiliatrix, gratia praeveniens, gratia praeveniens* and *subsequens, gratia praeventrix, gratia aspirans, gratia suscitans*. There are such combinations as *gratia praeveniens, comitans, cooperans;* or *benedictio praeveniens, adiuvans, consummans;*[72] *gratia conservatrix, operans, cooperans;* or *gratia incipiens, et perseverans et salvans;* also *gratia praeveniens et cooperans*. There are

---

71 The elenchus of his references I cannot copy out. See the reference below, note 73.

72 See Schupp on the Lombard's use of the term *misericordia* instead of *gratia, Die Gnadenlehre des Petrus Lombardus* 26.

expressions such as *gratia excitat, gratia operans compungit mentem et excitat; gratia praevenit, adiuvat, suscipit.* After Peter Lombard the dominant terms are *gratia operans* and *cooperans.* Still, Peter of Capua, for instance, explains, when speaking of *gratia operans* and *cooperans: Hoc idem est quod alibi dicitur preveniens subsequens.* A similar remark is to be found in Philip the Chancellor's *Summa de bono.*

In the twelfth century all these expressions referred exclusively to the grace of justification. In the beginning of the thirteenth century Guerricus de S. Quintino uses the term *gratia praeparans* – with an antithetical *cooperans* – to refer to a grace prior to justification. Also denoting a grace distinct from justification is the *gratia excitans* – as opposed to *informans* – to be found in Langton, in his pupil Gaufrid of Poitiers, in the clearly dependent William of Auxerre and John of Treviso, and finally in the unidentified Collection of Questions, Cod. British Museum Harley 325.[73]

The foregoing provides a clear picture of the situation. The language of St Augustine gradually crystallizes into a terminology. The later eminence of *gratia operans* and *cooperans* is due to Peter Lombard. And what first attracts attention in the field of grace is the grace of justification.

3.2 The Context of Sententiae, *2, d. 26, on Prevenient and Subsequent Grace*

To carry on the brilliant speculation of St Anselm was an impossible task. There was needed a broader dogmatic basis to clarify theological thought, a closer philosophic analysis to define nature and provide the analogies for the supernatural, and above all an explicit and systematic distinction between philosophic and theological speculation. The notable confusions of Gilbert de la Porrée and Peter Abelard on the latter point provoked a reaction that turned interest to a study of the dogmatic sources. Such, we have already indicated, is the general definition of the Lombard's position.[74]

The twenty-sixth distinction of his second book begins with a demonstrative pronoun: *Haec est gratia operans et cooperans.* Accordingly, we must turn back to distinction twenty-five. The last paragraphs read:

73 Landgraf, 'Die Erkenntnis der helfenden Gnade in der Frühscholastik' [see above, p. 3, note 5] 179–81.
74 See above p. 170.

Libertas ergo a peccato et a miseria per gratiam est, libertas vero a necessitate per naturam.

Utramque libertatem, scilicet naturae et gratiae, notat Apostolus, cum ex persona hominis non redempti ait: *Velle adiacet mihi, perficere autem non invenio* [Romans 7.18]; ac si diceret: Habeo libertatem naturae, sed non habeo libertatem gratiae; ideo non est apud me perfectio boni. Nam voluntas hominis, quam naturaliter habet, non valet erigi ad bonum efficaciter volendum vel opere implendum, nisi per gratiam liberetur et adiuvetur: liberetur quidem ut velit; et adiuvetur ut perficiat; quia, ut ait Apostolus [Romans 9.16], *non est volentis* velle*, neque currentis* currere, id est operari, *sed miserentis Dei; qui operatur in nobis velle* et operari bonum [Philippians 2.13], cuius (Dei) gratiam non advocat hominis voluntas vel operatio, sed ipsa gratia voluntatem praevenit praeparando, ut velit bonum, et praeparatam adiuvat, ut perficiat.[75]

This is the end of the twenty-fifth distinction, on which immediately follows: *Haec est gratia operans et cooperans.*

In the foregoing citation we may note an advance over St Anselm inasmuch as the Lombard has, in this passage, moral impotence reduced to an incapacity of efficacious willing,[76] and explicitly asserts that nature has freedom from necessity. Also to be observed is the tendency to conceive grace psychologically.

75 [Freedom from sin and misery is therefore had through grace; but freedom from necessity through nature.
     The Apostle refers to each (form of) liberty, namely, that of nature and that of grace, when, speaking in the person of one who is not redeemed, he says, *I can will what is right, but I cannot do it* (Romans 7.18), as if he were saying: I have freedom of nature, but I have not freedom of grace; therefore the perfection of the good is lacking in me. For the will that a man has by nature is not able to be lifted up to will a good efficaciously or to carry it out in action unless it is liberated and helped by grace: liberated, that is, that he may will, and lifted up that he may perform; because, as the Apostle says (Romans 9.16), *it depends not on human will or exertion, but on God who shows mercy, who is at work in you, enabling you both to will and to perform* the good (Philippians 2.13). And it is not man's will or exertion that summons his (God's) grace, but rather grace leads the way for will, preparing it to will the good, and aids the will thus prepared, to bring to completion] Peter Lombard, *Sententiae,* 2, d. 25 [c. 9, *QL* 1: 435–36].
76 St Anselm's liberty – a capacity to retain rectitude – is, in the absence of rectitude, similar to the capacity to see an object that is absent when you are in the dark and blindfold (Anselm, *De libero arbitrio,* c. 4, *PL* 158, 495 [Schmitt 1: 214]).

3.3 *The Doctrine of* Sententiae, *2, d. 26, on* Gratia Operans

The twenty-sixth distinction of the second book is a long series of citations from St Augustine. Omitting them, we may give the Lombard's position in his own words.

> Haec est gratia operans et cooperans; operans enim gratia praeparat hominis voluntatem, ut velit bonum; gratia cooperans adiuvat, ne frustra velit.
>
> Unde Augustinus ...[77]
>
> ... operans enim est quae praevenit voluntatem bonam, ea enim liberatur et praeparatur hominis voluntas ut sit bona, bonumque efficaciter velit; cooperans vero gratia voluntatem iam bonam sequitur adiuvando.
>
> Unde Augustinus ...[78]
>
> His testimoniis aperte insinuatur, quia voluntas hominis gratia Dei praevenitur atque praeparatur ut fiat bona, non ut fiat voluntas, quia et ante gratiam voluntas erat, sed non erat bona et recta voluntas.[79]
>
> Ecce hic expresse habes, quia gratia praevenit bonae voluntatis meritum, et ipsa voluntas bona pedissequa est gratiae, non praevia.[80]
>
> Et si diligenter intendas, nihilominus tibi monstratur, quae sit ipsa gratia voluntatem praeveniens et praeparans, scilicet fides cum dilectione.
>
> Ideoque Augustinus ...[81]

77 [This is operative and cooperative grace; for when operative, grace prepares the will of man that he may will the good; and cooperative grace helps that he may not will in vain. And therefore Augustine ...] *Sententiae*, 2, d. 26, c. 1 [*QL* 1: 436].

78 [For operative grace is that which prepares a good will; for by means of this grace the will of man is liberated and prepared that it may be good and that it may efficaciously will the good. But cooperative grace follows assisting a will that is now good. And therefore Augustine ...] Ibid. [*QL* 1: 436–37].

79 [In these testimonies the (position) is clearly introduced that the will of man is led and prepared by the grace of God that it may become good, not that it may become will. Because it was will before grace, but it was not a good and upright will] Ibid. [*QL* 1: 437].

80 [See, you have it clearly stated here that grace is prior to the merit of a good will, and that this good will is a follower of grace, not the leader] Ibid. c. 2 [*QL* 1: 438].

81 [And, nevertheless, if you attend diligently, it will be shown you what this grace is that is prior to and prepares the will, namely, faith with love. And therefore Augustine ...] Ibid. c. 3 [*QL* 1: 439].

Hic aperte ostenditur, quod fides est causa iustificationis, et ipsa est gratia et beneficium, quo hominis praevenitur voluntas et praeparatur.

Unde Augustinus ...[82]

Such is the thesis. *Gratia operans* prevents and prepares the will; it makes it will the good; it liberates it from sin and the *non posse non peccare* of the unregenerate. It is *fides quae per dilectionem operatur*. Next come the difficulties.

(1) Non est tamen ignorandum, quod alibi Augustinus significare videtur, quod ex voluntate sit fides ...

Ad quae respondentes dicimus ... haec ideo dicta ita sunt, quia non est fides nisi in eo qui vult credere, cuius bonam voluntatem fides praevenit, non tempore, sed causa et natura.

(2) Caeterum hanc quaestionem magis acuunt et urgent verba Augustini ... Hic videtur insinuare, quod cogitatio bona praecedat fidem, et ita bona voluntas praeveniat fidem, non praeveniatur; quod praedictis adversari videtur.

Ad hoc autem dicimus, quod aliquando cogitatio bona sive voluntas praevenit fidem, sed non est illa bona voluntas vel cogitatio qua recte vivitur: illa enim sine fide et caritate non est. Nam ut ait Augustinus ...

Qui verba Augustini praemissa secundum hanc distinctionem considerat, nullam ibi repugnantiam fore animadvertit, non ignorans, etiam ante gratiam praevenientem et operantem, qua voluntas bona praeparatur in homine, praecedere quaedam bona ex Dei gratia et libero arbitrio, quaedam etiam ex solo libero arbitrio, quibus tamen vitam non meretur, nec gratiam qua iustificatur.[83]

82 [Here it is clearly shown that faith is the cause of justification, and it is the grace and benefit by which the will of man is given a lead and is prepared. And therefore Augustine ...] Ibid. [*QL* 1: 439].

83 [(1) But we should not ignore the fact that in another place Augustine seems to mean that faith is from the will ...

In reply to this we say ... the reason for such statements is that there is no faith except in one who wishes to believe, and in such a person faith is prior to good will, not in time, but in cause and nature.

(2) Besides, the words of Augustine put this question more sharply and urgently ... Here he seems to imply that a good thought precedes faith, and so good will is prior to faith rather than the converse; and this seems to contradict what was said previously.

But to this we say that sometimes a good thought or (good) will is prior to

The second difficulty shows that the psychological concept of grace is no more than a tendency which is deserted the moment a real difficulty arises. In that passage the Lombard is obviously feeling for something more adequate: he places graces previous to prevenient grace. One may note that the good deeds that precede faith and charity are the familiar *agros colere et domos aedificare.*

The first point in the twenty-seventh distinction is the relation between *gratia operans* and *cooperans.*

> Hic considerandum est cum praedictum sit, per gratiam operantem et praevenientem voluntatem hominis liberari ac praeparari, ut bonum velit, et per gratiam cooperantem et subsequentem adiuvari, ne frustra velit, utrum una et eadem sit gratia, id est unum munus gratis datum, quod operetur et cooperetur; an diversa, alterum operans, et alterum cooperans.
>
> Quibusdam non irrationabiliter videtur, quod una et eadem sit gratia, idem donum, eadem virtus, quae operatur et cooperatur, sed propter diversos eius effectus dicitur operans et cooperans. Operans enim dicitur, inquantum liberat et praeparat voluntatem hominis, ut bonum velit; cooperans, inquantum eandem adiuvat, ne frustra velit, scilicet ut opus faciat bonum. Ipsa enim gratia non est otiosa, sed meretur augeri, ut aucta mereatur et perfici.[84]

---

faith; but this is not that good will or thought by which one lives rightly. For this latter does not exist without faith and charity. For as Augustine says ...

One who considers the aforesaid words of Augustine according to this distinction observes that there will be no contradiction; (for) he knows that even before prevenient and operative grace, by which good will is prepared in man, there are benefits that precede, some from the grace of God and free will, some even from free will alone, but one does not merit life nor is one justified by these] Ibid. cc. 4, 7 [*QL* 1: 440–43].

84 [Here, having said that man's will is liberated and prepared by operative and prevenient grace that it may will the good, and (having said also that man's will) is helped by cooperative and subsequent grace so that it does not will in vain, (a question arises) which we must consider, (namely,) whether it is one and the same grace, that is, one benefit freely given, that operates and cooperates; or whether there are distinct things, one operating, the other cooperating.

To some it seems, reasonably enough, that they are one and the same grace, the same gift, the same virtue which operates and cooperates. It is called operative inasmuch as it liberates and prepares man's will to will the good; it is called cooperative inasmuch as it helps that same will not to will in vain, that is, (helps it) that it may perform a good work. For this grace is not idle but merits to be increased, that being increased it may merit also to be completed] Ibid. d. 27, c. 1 [*QL* 1: 444].

This identification of *gratia operans* and *cooperans* is quite to be expected when the grace in question is, in its content, *fides quae per dilectionem operatur.* As we have already pointed out, the Lombard does not attempt to decide whether a virtue is a habit as opposed to an act, or an internal act as opposed to an external act. But he manifestly inclines to the former view, and in a later chapter metaphorically describes a virtue in this fashion.

> Propterea quidam non inerudite tradunt, virtutem esse bonam mentis qualitatem sive formam, quae animam informat; et ipsa non est motus vel affectus animi, sed ea liberum arbitrium iuvatur, ut ad bonum moveatur et erigatur; et ita ex virtute et libero arbitrio nascitur bonus motus vel affectus animi, et exinde bonum opus procedit exterius. Sicut pluvia rigatur terra, ut germinet et fructum faciat; nec pluvia est terra nec germen nec fructus; nec terra germen vel fructus; nec germen fructus; ita gratis terrae mentis nostrae, id est libero arbitrio voluntatis, infunditur pluvia divinae benedictionis, id est, inspiratur gratia – quod solus Deus facit, non homo cum eo – qua rigatur voluntas hominis, ut germinet et fructificet; id est, sanatur et praeparatur, ut bonum velit, secundum quod dicitur operans; et iuvatur ut bonum faciat, secundum quod dicitur cooperans. Et illa gratia virtus non incongrue nominatur, quia voluntatem hominis infirmam sanat et adiuvat.[85]

These passages, I think, will suffice to provide, not indeed a detailed knowledge of the Lombard's thought, but a sufficient introduction to St Thomas. For though the former's influence on the latter is notable, still it is

85 [On that account some (authors) hold not without learning, that virtue is a good quality or form of mind that informs the soul, and it is not a movement or affection of the soul, but free will is helped by it to be moved or elevated to the good; and thus from virtue and free will is born a good movement or affection of the soul, and on that basis a good work proceeds externally. As the earth is watered by rain to sprout and bring forth fruit, and rain is not earth nor sprout nor fruit, and earth is not sprout nor fruit, and sprout is not fruit, so the rain of divine blessing is freely poured upon the earth of our mind, that is, upon the free faculty of the will; that is, grace is infused – something God alone does, not man with him – by which the will of man is watered, that it may sprout and bring forth fruit; that is, it is healed and prepared that it may will the good, on the basis of which it is called operative; and is helped that it may do the good, on the basis of which it is called cooperative. And that grace is fittingly called virtue, because it heals and helps the weak will of man] *Sententiae*, 2, d. 27, c. 6 [*QL* 1: 447–48].

due to such explicit thought as has been cited and not to the details that modern research can collect and classify. It will be well, then, to conclude with a summary.

First, the Lombard admits the existence of graces prior to justification, but he does not term them prevenient or operative.

Second, he affirms good acts without any grace, such as the building of houses and the cultivation of the land.

Third, he inclines to the view that *gratia operans* and *cooperans* are one and the same grace; that they receive different names because of their different effects.

Fourth, the effect of *gratia operans* is the liberation of the will from moral impotence, *non posse non peccare*; positively it is an efficacious will of the good, *ut bonum velit, ut efficaciter velit.*

Fifth, though this psychological conception of grace is the most common form of expression, still when the Lombard is faced with the difficulty of the *bona cogitatio* that precedes faith, he immediately asserts that such good thoughts or good will do not merit eternal life.

Sixth, *gratia operans* is *fides quae per dilectionem operatur*; it is a virtue and more probably a habit.

Seventh, *gratia cooperans* has for its effect the performance of good deeds corresponding to good will.

4   St Albert the Great

Three points are treated: his historical position, his terminology on grace, his doctrine on *gratia operans*.

4.1 The Historical Position

Like Alexander of Hales, St Albert takes over the theory of the supernatural from Philip the Chancellor.[86] Like him, he also devotes a great deal of thought to the elaboration of a theory of liberty.[87] This twofold labor results in a speculative tendency that is antithetical to the tendency of Peter Lombard. The point is illustrated by two examples.

---

86 See above p. 184. See Doms, *Die Gnadenlehre des sel. Albertus Magnus,* chapters 1–9 [8–162].
87 See Lottin, *La théorie du libre arbitre depuis s. Anselme jusqu'à s. Thomas d'Aquin* [108–15].

Peter Lombard posited an intermediate stage of original innocence between the creation of Adam and the infusion of grace. In this period he rightly held that Adam neither suffered from moral impotence when confronted with temptation, nor, on the other hand, could merit, for merit presupposes grace. But, not having a firm grasp of the idea of the supernatural, he was at a loss to explain why Adam could not merit when he resisted temptation, and this led to his assertion that resistance was not meritorious unless it was difficult.[88]

Commenting on this passage, St Albert finds it unintelligible. The idea of the supernatural is so familiar to him that he fancies the Lombard must be distinguishing between grace and virtue, for virtue presupposes difficulty, or again, that the resistance which is not meritorious is resistance to a sin which one does not even consider.[89]

On the other hand, Peter Lombard places the idea of moral impotence in the foreground of his thought on grace. Without grace, man suffers *non posse non peccare etiam damnabiliter*. By grace, man is liberated from this onus of evil and enabled efficaciously to will the good.[90] But St Albert, because of his effort to work out a coherent theory of human liberty, at first tries to evade *non posse non peccare*[91] and in his later *Summa theologica* admits it without offering more than a metaphorical explanation.[92]

4.2 Terminology with Regard to Grace

The Lombard distinguished between *gratia gratis dans*, which is God himself, and *gratis data*, which is the infused virtue, faith operating through charity, *gratia operans*.[93]

St Albert's fundamental distinction is between *gratia gratum faciens*, which gives the *forma meriti*, and *gratia gratis data*, which does not. The former is a highly elaborate concept backed by a whole philosophy. The latter is little more than a vague gesture. Dr Herbert Doms lists seven distinct meanings: (1) *natura rationalis cum potentiis suis*; (2) the natural moral goodness of the

---

88 *Sententiae*, 2, d. 24, c. 1 [*QL* 1: 419–21].
89 *In II Sententiarum*, d. 24, a. 4 [*BA* 27: 400].
90 *Sententiae*, 2, dd. 25–26 [*QL* 1: 428–43].
91 *Summa de creaturis*, 2, q. 70, a. 5 [*BA* 35: 588]; *In II Sententiarum*, d. 25, a. 6 [*BA* 27: 433–34].
92 *Summa theologica*, 2, q. 100, mem. 2–4 [*BA* 33: 246–52].
93 *Sententiae*, 2, d. 27, c. 7 [*QL* 1: 448].

will; (3) such preternatural gifts as Adam possessed before the fall; (4) such supernatural aids as the unformed habits of faith and hope, servile fear, imperfect movements to salvation; (5) inspiration, miracles, and the like; (6) the assistance of the angels; (7) the indelible character. Combining with each of these, and differing according to their differences, is in the eighth place the divine activity, which not merely conserves in being and moves to action, but conserves in goodness and moves to good action.[94]

In this connection it is well to note the conspicuous absence in St Albert's writings of an account of the preparation for grace. There is no lack of possible explanations of this defect, for St Albert's interest in all fields of knowledge, the long years he spent on Aristotle, his special attention to the ideas of merit and liberty, can readily combine to account for his neglect of a contemporary development. Nonetheless, the contemporary development does exist, especially in William of Auvergne, Alexander of Hales, St Bonaventure,[95] and St Thomas. Perhaps a comparative study of these authors, from the viewpoint of their main lines of thought and especially their interest in Aristotelianism, might throw further light upon the issue.

4.3 St Albert on Gratia Operans

By *gratia operans* St Albert understands the *forma supernaturalitatis* in the will; by *gratia cooperans* the *forma meriti* in the good act. Such is his explicit doctrine. But he also has an implication of the habit as a virtue controlling good action. Thus, with the usual identification of *praeveniens* and *operans* he writes:

> ... gratia praeveniens est quae omne nostrum meritum praevenit, et haec est quae operatur esse bonum in voluntate per informationem voluntatis: oportet enim voluntatem habitualem informatam esse gratia, antequam bonus actus meritorius eliciatur ex illa. Subsequens autem invenitur primo in ea [voluntate?] quae meretur: quia habitum immediate sequitur actus: et ideo dicitur cooperans, quia

94 Doms, *Die Gnadenlehre des sel. Albertus Magnus* 167–68.
95 See Doms, *Die Gnadenlehre des sel. Albertus Magnus* 163–66. [A note in Lonergan's hand refers us, on this point of the preparation for grace, to p. 65 of his thesis (pp. 209–10 above) where there is a summary statement of points made by Landgraf in 'Die Erkenntnis der helfenden Gnade ...', to p. 37 of his thesis (pp. 183–84 above), and to Landgraf's 'Die Vorbereitung auf die Rechtfertigung ...']

libero arbitrio [liberum arbitrium?] in merito ministrat materiam actus: sed formam per quam est efficacia meriti, dat gratia quae est in anima et libero arbitrio: et ideo dicit Magister in sequenti distinctione, quod usus virtutis et gratiae partim est a libero arbitrio sicut a causa.⁹⁶

That St Albert here thinks of grace exclusively as a formal cause is confirmed by the manner in which he meets the following difficulty in the next article:

(a) Cum enim dicitur gratia operans: aut intelligitur operari se, aut voluntatem, aut se in voluntate. Si se: hoc non potest esse: quia nihil operatur se vel facit. Si autem voluntatem intelligitur facere: hoc iterum nihil est: quia voluntas ante hoc fuit. Si autem se in voluntate: hoc iterum nihil est: quia nihil facit seipsum nec in se, nec in alio: ergo male intelligitur gratia operans.

(b) Si dicas, quod facit bonam voluntatem: quaeritur, quid supponit ly *bonam*? Constat autem, quod non voluntatem secundum se, sed [secundum quod est] gratia informatam: ergo idem est facere bonam voluntatem, quod se facere in voluntate: et sic redit primum.⁹⁷

96 [prevenient grace is that which is prior to all our merit, and this it is which operates good in the will by informing the will; for habitual will has to be informed by grace before a good and meritorious act is elicited from it. But subsequent (grace) is found first in that (will?) which merits, because act follows habit immediately; and it is called cooperative on this account that in merit free will provides the matter of the act, but the form by which merit has efficacy is given by grace, which is in the soul and free will; and therefore the Master says in the following distinction that the exercise of virtue and grace is partly from free will as from a cause] *In II Sententiarum*, d. 26, a. 6 [*BA* 27: 453].

97 [(a) For when it is called operative grace, it is understood to operate either itself, or the will, or itself in the will. If itself: this cannot be, because nothing operates or makes itself. If it is understood (to operate) the will: again this is nothing, because the will existed before this. But if itself in the will: once again this is nothing, because nothing makes itself, either in the self or in another; therefore, grace is badly understood (to be) operative.

(b) If you say that it makes good will, the question is, what is the supposit of that word 'good'? But it is clearly not the will as such but as informed by grace. Therefore, to make good will is the same as to make oneself in the will. And so the first option returns.]

He answers:

> Dicendum ad primum, quod operans dicitur, quia operatur esse
> bonum in voluntate: et dicitur operari sicut forma facit esse, non
> sicut efficiens. Hoc autem facere quod est formae, non est nisi
> diffusio sui in formato. Et ideo bene concedo, quod forma absolute
> accepta actu formae non efficientis facit se in formato: sed nihil facit
> se secundum eamdem considerationem acceptum: et efficiens non
> facit se etiam in diversis considerationibus acceptum: sed quia forma
> non proprie facit, sed dat, et suum dare est diffusio sui et informatio,
> ideo forma dat esse quod est actus illius formae, et operatur, et hoc
> [quod operatur] est esse suum in formato.   Primae autem obiec-
> tiones procedebant quasi gratia esset operans per modum efficientis,
> et non formae.[98]

However, though the solution of these two objections consists in affirming
that grace operates as a formal cause and not as an efficient cause, it
remains that, when St Albert comes to explaining how grace is the principal
and free will the subordinate cause, he makes use of the idea of the habit or
virtue as effecting the free act.

> Si dicas, quod gratia movet et excitat liberum arbitrium ad agendum:
> et ideo est principalior. Tunc quaeritur, Utrum moveat naturaliter
> vel violenter? ...
>   Ad aliud quod quaeritur, Utrum moveat violenter vel naturaliter?
> Dicendum, quod nulla est divisio: quia voluntarius motus, nec

---

98 [To the first point it has to be said that it is called operative because it operates good in the will, and it is said to operate in the way form makes being,
not in the way an efficient (cause) does. But this making which belongs to
form is nothing but a diffusion of itself in what is formed. And therefore I
readily concede that form taken absolutely, by the act of a form and not the
act of an efficient (cause), makes itself in what is formed: but nothing
makes itself when we take (the self) under the same aspect: and an efficient
(cause) does not make itself even when we take (the self) under different
aspects: but because a form does not properly make, but gives, and its giving
is a diffusion of itself and an information, therefore form gives the being
which is the act of that form, and operates, and this (operating) is its being
in what is formed. But the earlier objections were proceeding as if grace was
operative in the way of an efficient (cause) and not in the way of a form] *In
II Sententiarum*, d. 26, a. 7 [*BA* 27: 455]. Compare Thomas Aquinas, *Summa
theologiae*, 1-2, q. 111, a. 2, ad 1m.

naturalis, nec violentus est:[99] et ipsa [gratia] movet ut perfectio voluntatis. Sed verum est, quia movet in modum naturae, sicut dicit etiam Tullius de virtute. Tamen est habitus voluntarius: et ideo in talibus innati sumus suscipere [perfectionem?], et perfectio est ab assuetudine in virtute civili: sed in gratia perfectio est ab infusore gratiae: et ideo illae quaestiones ridiculosae sunt.[100]

This comparison of the habit to a natural form – to what we should term a natural spontaneity – appears still more clearly in the following.

... et bene concedo, quod liberum arbitrium est secundarium in opere illo tribus de causis: quarum una est, quia gratia est primum movens, sicut habitus movet in modum inclinantis naturae ad impetum actus alicuius, ut grave inclinat deorsum. Secunda est: quia ipsa non dat proprietatem sive accidentalem formam, sed formam substantialem meriti, a qua est tota meriti efficacia: ita ut actus sine forma illa, non est meritorius, nec valeret vitam aeternam. Tertia causa est quam tangit Augustinus, quia regit liberum arbitrium: et liberum arbitrium est ut iumentum obediens.[101]

99 See Scotus's idea of free action.
100 [If you say that grace moves and inspires free will to act, and is therefore the more important (factor): then the question is, Does it move naturally or violently? ...
     To the other question, Does it move violently or naturally? It has to be said that there is no division there, because a voluntary motion is neither natural nor violent, and it (grace) moves as a perfection of the will. But it is true that it moves after the manner of nature, as even Tullius says of virtue. Still, it is a voluntary habit; and therefore in such matters it is natural for us to receive (a perfection?); and in civil virtue the perfection comes from habituation; but in grace the perfection comes from the one who infuses grace: and therefore those questions are ridiculous] *In II Sententiarum*, d. 26, a. 7 [*BA* 27: 454–55].
101 [and for three reasons I readily concede that free will is secondary in that operation. One of these is that grace is a first mover, as habit moves after the manner of nature inclining towards the impetus of some act, as a heavy object turns downward. The second is that it (grace) does not give a property or accidental form, but the substantial form of merit, from which comes the entire efficacy of merit, so that an act without that form is not meritorious, nor would it have any value for eternal life. The third cause is one that Augustine touches on, that (grace) governs free will, and free will is like an obedient beast of burden] *In II Sententiarum*, d. 26, a. 7 [*BA* 27: 455].

The meaning seems to be that there is double causality of grace with regard to the free act. First, there is the formal causality that regards the *modum actus*: this supplies the second reason for the superiority of grace to the will, for this *modus* is what makes the difference between an act that is meritorious and one that is not. Second, there is the causality of the *habitus*, which is *in modum naturae* and gives the will a spontaneity in right action such as that of a stone in gravitation. In two ways this gives rise to a priority of grace in causation; first, such a perfection of nature is a first mover; second, such a perfection confines the will to right action, *regit liberum arbitrium, et liberum arbitrium est ut iumentum obediens.*

So great has been the influence of Scotus that it is hard for us to conceive the habit as a principle of limitation of free acts. Scotus, because of his antithesis between natural and free activity, cannot admit the habit to exercise any such influence on the will.[102] Accordingly, when he treats St Augustine's *caritas se habet ad liberum arbitrium sicut sessor ad equum*, he distinguishes between the *substantia actus* and the *ratio meriti* (*modus actus*), and asserts that with regard to the latter, charity is the principal cause and the faculty is the subordinate cause, but with regard to the *substantia actus*, the potency is the principal cause eliciting the act and using the habit, while the habit is the subordinate cause inclining the potency to the act.[103]

All that we would observe is that this is in no way the position of St Albert, who made grace the principal cause from both points of view.

5   St Thomas's Commentary on the *Sentences*

In his first work St Thomas follows and slightly develops the position of his master, St Albert.

102 Thus he writes: '... habitus est causa naturalis; igitur si ipsa sit causa principalis movens potentiam, moveret eam per modum naturae; et per consequens, cum potentia agat eo modo quo movetur, ageret per modum naturae ... et ita omnis actio potentiae habitualis esset naturalis, et nulla libera: quod est inconveniens' [habit is a natural cause; therefore if it is the principal cause moving a potency, it would move the potency after the manner of a nature; and, as a consequence, since a potency acts in the way in which it is moved, it would act after the manner of a nature ... and so every act of a habituated potency would be natural, and none would be free; which is objectionable] *Oxon.*, 1, d. 17, q. 2, n. 8, § 793 [*Commentaria oxoniensia ad IV libros magistri Sententiarum*, ed. Marianus Fernandez Garcia (Ad Claras Aquas prope Florentiam, 1912) 1: 792]; see q. 3, n. 6, § 802 [799–800]. In q. 3, n. 8, he points out that the opposite view is equally if not more probable, but his theory of operative grace follows the other position.

103 See *Oxon.*, 1, d. 17, q. 3, nn. 24–27, § 818 [817–18].

In commenting on the twenty-sixth distinction of the second book – a distinction which the Lombard devoted entirely to his doctrine of operative grace – St Thomas first asks four prior questions: (1) *Utrum gratia sit aliquid creatum in anima*; (2) *Utrum gratia sit accidens*; (3) *Utrum gratia sit in potentia vel anima sicut in subiecto*; (4) *Utrum gratia sit virtus.* His answers are well known. Grace is a creature, an accident, in the essence of the soul, and not a virtue but the ontological basis of the virtues. Accordingly, we turn at once to the fifth question, *Utrum gratia dividatur convenienter in gratiam operantem et cooperantem.*

In the response he begins by considering prevenient and subsequent grace. First, he draws up a scheme of abstract sequences. Second, he turns to St Augustine to verify his sequences.

He draws up a scheme of abstract sequences:

> Respondeo dicendum, quod gratia habet in nobis diversos effectus ordinatos. Primum enim quod facit est hoc quod dat esse quoddam divinum. Secundus autem effectus est opus meritorium quod sine gratia esse non potest. Tertius effectus est praemium meriti, scilicet ipsa vita beata, ad quam per gratiam pervenitur. In actibus etiam est quidam ordo: primum est opus interius voluntatis; secundum est opus exterius quo voluntas completur.[104]

These give three pairs of terms: merit and eternal life; the internal act and the external; grace and merit. All are found in St Augustine:

> ... et secundum hoc quandoque Augustinus diversimode videtur accipere gratiam praevenientem et subsequentem: quia, considerato ordine meriti ad praemium quod sequitur, nominat gratiam praevenientem, quae principium est merendi; gratiam vero subsequentem, ipsum habitum gloriae, qui in nobis beatam vitam efficit, ut patet in auctoritate.[105] Secundum vero ordinem actus

---

104 [I reply that it has to be said that grace has various ordered effects in us. For the first thing it does is this, that it gives a certain divine being. The second effect is meritorious work, which cannot be without grace. The third effect is the reward of merit, namely, the blessed life itself, to which one comes through grace. There is also a certain order in (these) acts: first comes the internal work of the will; second comes the external work by which the will is completed] *Super II Sententiarum*, d. 26, q. 1, a. 5 c.

105 The 'auctoritas,' presumably, is 'gratia praevenit ut pie vivamus et subsequitur ut semper cum illo vivamus; et nunc praevenit ut vocemur et tunc

interioris ad exteriorem, ponit gratiam praevenientem, quae causat
motum bonae voluntatis, gratiam vero subsequentem quae opus
exterius complet; unde dicit quod *praevenit voluntatem ut velit bonum,*
subsequitur ut compleat sive perficiat; et sic in *Littera* quasi per totum
videtur accipere praevenientem et subsequentem.[106] Secundum vero
ordinem esse quod dat ad actum qui est operatio, sic ponit gratiam
praevenientem quae animae quoddam esse salubre confert, et
gratiam subsequentem quae opus meritorium causat; unde dicit,
quod *praevenit ut sanemur, et subsequitur ut sanati negotiemur.*[107]

He now turns to consider operative and cooperative grace, and observing
that in this sense grace has no reference to the state of the blessed in
heaven, infers that in the other two senses prevenient and subsequent grace
may also be operative and cooperative. He writes:

Sed distinctio gratiae operantis et cooperantis proprie accipitur
tantum prout pertinet ad statum vitae praesentis; unde dupliciter

---

subsequitur ut glorificemur' [grace precedes that we may live piously and
follows that we may live always with him; and precedes now that we may be
called and follows then that we may be glorified]. See *Super II Sententiarum,*
d. 26, q. 1, a. 5, ob. 5 and ad 5m.

106 St Thomas has obviously made a careful study of the citations from St Augustine in Peter Lombard, and has noticed the tendency to a psychological
concept of grace.

107 [and accordingly Augustine seems sometimes to understand prevenient and
subsequent grace in different ways; because, considering the order of merit
to the reward which follows, he calls (that) grace prevenient which is the
principle of meriting, and (calls) subsequent grace the habit itself of glory,
which (habit) causes the blessed life in us, as is clear in the (quoted) authority. But considering the order of internal act to external, he makes that
grace prevenient which causes the movement of good will, but (makes) that
grace subsequent which completes the external deed. And so he says that *it*
precedes the will that it may will the good, follows that it may complete or perfect
(the act). And it is in this way in practically the whole text that he seems to
understand prevenient and subsequent. But considering the order of the
being it gives to the act which is the operation, from this viewpoint he
makes that grace prevenient which confers on the soul a certain healthful
being, and (makes) subsequent that which causes a meritorious deed; and
so he says that *it precedes that we may be healed, and follows that being healed we*
may carry on life] *Super II Sententiarum,* d. 26, q. 1, a. 5 c. Contrast the *esse*
divinum of his own schematic sequence with the *esse salubre* that he finds in
St Augustine. Above all, note his method: first, a general analysis determining the abstract possibilities of *preceding* and *subsequent* graces, and then the
empirical examination of what St Augustine actually says.

distingui potest. Uno modo ut per gratiam operantem significetur
ipsa gratia, prout esse divinum in anima operatur, secundum quod
gratum facit habentem; et per gratiam cooperantem significetur ipsa
gratia secundum quod opus meritorium causat, prout opus hominis
gratum reddit. Alio modo secundum quod gratia operans dicitur,
prout causat voluntatis actum; et cooperans secundum quod causat
exteriorem actum in quo voluntas completur, vel [Parma: per]
perseverantiam in illo. Et utroque modo cooperans et operans dicit
idem quod praeveniens et subsequens.[108]

Now while the meaning is reasonably clear, it will be well to exclude all
possibility of doubt by considering the objections.

The first objection is that grace is radicated in the soul and not in the
potency, and so has no bearing on action.

Ad primum ergo dicendum, quod quamvis non immediate gratia ad
opus referatur, tamen est per se causa operis meritorii, licet mediante virtute; et ideo non est inconveniens si per operantem et
cooperantem distinguatur.[109]

The second objection is the one already met in St Albert: if grace is
operative, it causes either itself or something else; neither position is ten-
able.

Ad secundum dicendum, quod gratia operans secundum unam
acceptionem dicitur operari in anima, non effective, sed formaliter,

108 [But the distinction of operative and cooperative grace is properly understood only as it pertains to the state of the present life; so it can be distinguished in two ways. In one way so that by operative grace there is signified
grace as it operates divine being in the soul, according as it makes pleasing
the one who has it; and by cooperative grace there is signified grace according as it causes a meritorious deed, as making a human deed pleasing. Another way (of making the distinction) is to understand operative grace as it
causes an act of will; and to understand cooperative grace according as it
causes the external act in which the will is completed, or causes perseverance in that (act). And in both cases cooperative and operative say the same
thing as prevenient and subsequent] Ibid.
109 [To the first objection it has to be said that, although grace is not ordered
immediately to a work, still it is the cause per se of a meritorious work, even
if a virtue is mediator; and therefore it is not unsuitable if (grace) is distinguished by operative and cooperative] Ibid. ad 1m.

secundum quod quaelibet forma facit esse aliquod in subiecto, sicut albedo facit esse album; unde per hunc modum gratia dicitur operans, quia formaliter hominem Deo gratum facit.[110] Secundum vero aliam acceptionem dicitur operans effective, secundum quod habitus effective causat opus; ita enim gratia motum meritorium voluntatis operatur eliciendo ipsum, licet mediante virtute, propter quod operans dicitur.[111]

The third objection is that no deed is so much the work of grace that it is not also the work of free will. Accordingly, if grace is cooperative because it cooperates with will, then all grace is cooperative.

Ad tertium dicendum, quod si accipiatur gratia operans secundum primam acceptionem, tunc planum est quod effectus quos operatur formaliter, ipsa sola operatur; sicut enim sola albedo formaliter facit album parietem, ita sola gratia formaliter gratum facit. Sed secundum aliam acceptionem verum est quod ipse motus voluntatis non est a gratia sine libero arbitrio; et tamen quia se habet gratia ut principale, quia inclinat in talem actum per modum cuiusdam naturae, ideo ipsa sola talem actum dicitur operari, non quod sine libero arbitrio operetur, sed quia est principalior causa, sicut gravitas dicitur operari motum deorsum.[112]

110 This is certainly sanctifying grace.
111 [To the second objection it has to be said that operative grace, according to one understanding, is said to operate in the soul, not effectively but formally, in the way that any form at all gives a certain being in the subject, as whiteness makes white being; and so in this way grace is called operative, because it formally makes man pleasing to God. But according to another understanding it is called operative effectively, in the way a habit causes a work effectively; for in this way grace operates a meritorious movement of the will, eliciting the movement, even if a virtue is mediator, and on this account it is called operative] Ibid. ad 2m.
112 [To the third objection it has to be said that, if grace is considered operative according to the first understanding, then it is plain that it alone operates the effects which it operates formally; for as whiteness alone formally makes a wall white, so grace alone formally makes one pleasing. But according to the other understanding it is true that this movement of the will is not from grace without free will; and nevertheless, because grace has the principal role, because it inclines to such an act in the way of a certain nature, therefore it alone is said to operate such an act, not that it operates without free will, but because it is the principal cause, as gravity is said to operate a downward movement] Ibid. ad 3m. In both these cases [ad 2m and ad 3m] what is dealt with is grace operating the internal act. From 'ad 2m' we have that it

To cooperate, according to the fourth objection, is to be a subordinate agent. But grace is always the principal agent. Therefore grace is not cooperative.

> Ad quartum dicendum, quod si dicatur gratia cooperans secundum quod causat quemcumque motum vel extrinsecum vel intrinsecum,[113] sic dicitur cooperans non quia non sit principalis causa in agendo, sed quia liberum arbitrium ministrat substantiam actus, et a gratia est forma per quam meritorius est;[114] unde illud quod gratia ministrat est sicut ultimum complementum: et propter hoc dicitur cooperans, quasi complens illud quod per liberum arbitrium ut praeiacens exhibetur. Si autem accipiatur cooperans prout respicit actum exteriorem tantum, sic dicitur cooperans non propter principalitatem liberi arbitrii ad gratiam, sed propter principalitatem actus ad actum; actus enim interiores in moralibus potiores sunt exterioribus, ut in x *Ethic.*, cap. xii, Philosophus dicit; unde convenienter gratia secundum quod causat principalem actum, dicitur operans; et secundum quod causat secundarium, dicitur cooperans.[115]

The fifth objection is against the identification of prevenient with operative, subsequent with cooperative grace. St Thomas admits that eternal life cannot be termed a cooperative grace, but maintains that otherwise the two

---

is *mediante virtute*, and that the operation is not formal but efficient. From 'ad 3m' we have that free will acts as a subordinate cause, that grace acts after the fashion of the *forma gravitatis*. It follows that in the second sense, *gratia operans* is the influence of the infused virtue on the internal act of will.

113 From the context this refers to sanctifying grace.

114 Sanctifying grace is the formal cause of the meritoriousness of both the internal and external acts: in both cases the *substantia actus* is from the free will, but the *forma meriti* is from sanctifying grace. See *Super II Sententiarum*, d. 26, q. 1, a. 5, ad 4m. [Lonergan also referred to *De veritate*, q. 27, a. 5, ad 4m, but that reference does not seem correct.]

115 [To the fourth objection it has to be said that, if grace is called cooperative according as it causes any movement whatever, either extrinsic or intrinsic, then it is called cooperative, not because it is not the principal cause in acting, but because free will provides the substance of the act, and from grace comes the form through which it is meritorious; and so that which grace provides is like an ultimate complement, and on this account it is called cooperative, as if completing that which is presented through free will as antecedent. But if cooperative is understood as it regards the external act only, then it is called cooperative not because of the principal role of

distinctions are objectively identical. This position is apparently deserted in the *Summa theologiae*.[116]

It will be well to conclude by drawing up a scheme of the division.

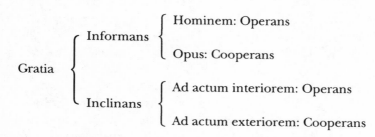

In confirmation of the distinct interpretation just given, namely, that the four distinctions all refer to different aspects of habitual grace, we may cite the answer to the second objection in the following article.[117]

> Ad secundum dicendum, quod quocumque modo distinguatur (gratia), maxime quantum ad duas distinctiones, operans et cooperans, praeveniens et subsequens, non differunt essentia sed *ratione* tantum; una enim forma est quae dat esse, et quae est principium operis; unus etiam habitus est qui elicit actum extrinsecum et intrinsecum; unde eadem gratia est operans et cooperans. Nec dicitur praeveniens et subsequens propter ordinem gratiae ad gratiam, sed propter ordinem effectus ad effectum.[118]

---

free will with regard to grace, but because of the principal role of one act with regard to another; for in moral matters internal acts prevail over external, as the Philosopher says in *Ethics* x, c. 12; and so grace is suitably called operative according as it causes the principal act, and is called cooperative according as it causes the secondary act] Ibid. ad 4m. In the second sense, operative and cooperative do not mean a difference in the way grace acts, for in both cases grace cooperates with free will; see ad 3m. They signify a different type of act with which grace, *mediante virtute*, cooperates. In other words, the cooperation of grace in the internal act is termed *gratia operans*, but in the external act *gratia cooperans*, because the internal act is cause of the external: *propter principalitatem actus ad actum*. To this excess of subtlety St Thomas does not return.

116 *Summa theologiae*, 1-2, q. 111, aa. 2–3.
117 'Utrum gratia sit multiplex in anima.' The answer is negative. *Super II Sententiarum*, d. 26, q. 1, a. 6, sol. and ad 2m.
118 [To the second objection it has to be said that, whatever way (grace) is distinguished, most especially in regard to the two distinctions, operative

6   St Thomas in the *De Veritate*

In his next work St Thomas modifies his view that there is only one grace in each individual and consequently modifies his division of grace into operative and cooperative.

The matter is treated under four headings: antecedents; the change; the cause of the change; the effect of the change on *gratia operans et cooperans*.

6.1 Antecedents

In Peter Lombard *gratia gratis data* denoted the grace of justification, faith operating through charity.[119] Perhaps it was Stephen Langton that gave currency to the term *gratia gratum faciens*.[120] In St Albert *gratia gratum faciens* denotes habitual grace, while *gratia gratis data* tends to be used to cover all the gifts of God.[121] With regard to St Thomas we may omit consideration of his commentary on the *Sentences*, where his position is clearly the same as St Albert's,[122] and turn immediately to the *De veritate*.

In the *De veritate*, q. 24, a. 14, the question is, *Utrum liberum arbitrium possit in bonum sine gratia*. It will be well to begin from the final remark in the response, which seems to define current terminology: 'Sed communiter loquentes utuntur nomine gratiae pro aliquo dono habituali iustificante' – ordinary usage restricts the term 'grace' to denoting a habitual gift that constitutes justification. From this meaning of the term 'grace' it would

---

and cooperative, prevenient and subsequent, there is no real distinction but only a *mental* one; for it is one form which gives being and which is the principle of the work; also it is one habit which elicits the extrinsic (act) and the intrinsic; and therefore the same grace is both operative and cooperative. Nor is it called prevenient and subsequent because of the order of grace to grace, but because of the order of effect to effect] Ibid. ad 2m.

119 Peter Lombard, *Sententiae*, 2, d. 27, c. 7 [*QL* 1: 448]. On the twelfth-century difficulty in defining grace see above, pp. 209–10; also Landgraf, 'Studien zur Erkenntnis des Übernatürlichen in der Frühscholastik' 9–37.

120 See above, p. 185; Landgraf, 'Studien zur Erkenntnis des Übernatürlichen in der Frühscholastik' 214–15 [*DFG* 181].

121 See above, pp. 217–18; '... aut est gratia gratis data, aut gratia gratum faciens. Si gratia gratis data, de hoc non quaeritur: quia et potentiae animae et virtutes et caetera omnia quae a Deo habentur, sunt gratiae gratis datae' [either it is grace given free or it is grace making one pleasing. If it is grace given free, that is not the question here; because both the potencies of the soul and the virtues and everything else which is had from God are graces given free] Albert, *In II Sententiarum*, d. 26, a. 11, Sed contra [*BA* 27: 465].

122 See, for example, *Super II Sententiarum*, d. 28, q. 1, aa. 1–4.

follow that man can do good without grace. But such a conclusion, without qualification, would be unacceptable. Accordingly, St Thomas expresses himself as follows.

> Ad hoc ergo bonum quod est supra naturam humanam, constat liberum arbitrium non posse sine gratia ... Illud autem bonum quod est naturae humanae proportionatum, potest homo per liberum arbitrium explere ... potest agros colere, domos aedificare, et alia plura bona facere sine gratia operante. Quamvis autem huiusmodi bona homo possit facere sine *gratia gratum faciente* non tamen potest ea facere *sine Deo*, cum nulla res possit in *naturalem* operationem exire nisi virtute divina, quia causa secunda non agit nisi per virtutem causae primae, ut dicitur in lib. *de Causis* ... Unde, si gratiam Dei velimus dicere non aliquod habituale donum, sed ipsam misericordiam Dei, per quam interius motum mentis operatur, et exteriora ordinat ad hominis salutem; sic nec *ullum* bonum homo potest facere sine gratia Dei. Sed communiter loquentes utuntur nomine gratiae pro aliquo dono habituali iustificante.[123]

Two points call for observation. First, what is needed to do good seems to be simply *concursus generalis*: it is needed for any good deed whatever, even digging and building; it is needed for *operatio naturalis*; to dispense with it would be to act *sine Deo*. Second, this divine assistance appears to be contrasted with *gratia gratum faciens*, which regards acting above the proportion of nature: on the one hand there is *sine gratia gratum faciente*, on the other *sine Deo*.

---

123   [It is clear then that for this good which is above human nature, free will can do nothing without grace ... But man can execute through free will that good which is proportionate to human nature ... he can cultivate fields, build houses, and do many other good things without operative grace. But although he can do good things of this kind without *the grace that makes him pleasing*, still he cannot do them *without God*, since nothing can proceed to its *natural* operation except by divine power, because a secondary cause does not act except through the power of the first cause, as is said in the book *On causes* ... And therefore if we wish to designate as grace of God, not some habitual gift, but the mercy itself of God, through which he operates internally a movement of the mind and orders external things to man's salvation, in this sense man can do *no* good without the grace of God. But in common parlance they use the name of grace for some habitual justifying gift] *De veritate*, q. 24, a. 14 c.

6.2 The Change

If now we turn to *De veritate*, q. 27, a. 5, we find *gratia gratum faciens* extending its denotation and limiting the field of *sine Deo*.

The question is, *Utrum in uno homine sit una tantum gratia gratum faciens*. The same question, in a far less precise form,[124] had already been put in the commentary on the *Sentences*. Now it is answered in a different manner.

The first step is to set aside *gratia gratis data*, giving it the precise signification, however, of prophecy and the working of miracles.[125]

The second is to distinguish two senses of *gratia gratum faciens*:

> Gratia ... gratum faciens ... dupliciter accipitur: *uno modo* pro ipsa divina acceptatione, quae est gratuita Dei voluntas; *alio modo* pro dono quodam creato, quod formaliter perficit hominem, et facit eum dignum vita aeterna.[126]

The third step is to demonstrate that in the second sense – grace as a gift that makes an individual formally acceptable to God and worthy of eternal life – there is only one grace in each man.

The fourth step is to make a distinction with regard to the *gratuita voluntas divina*, the first sense of *gratia gratum faciens*. For the divine will may be considered either in itself or in its effects: in the former case grace again is one; but in the latter it is many. The former does not interest us, the latter does.

> ... ex parte autem effectuum divinorum potest esse multiplex; ut dicamus omnem effectum quem Deus facit in nobis ex gratuita sua voluntate, qua nos in suum regnum acceptat, pertinere ad *gratiam gratum facientem*; sicut quod immittat nobis bonas cogitationes et sanctas affectiones.[127]

---

124 *Utrum gratia sit multiplex in anima* [Whether grace is multiple in the soul], *Super II Sententiarum*, d. 26, q. 1, a. 6.

125 See *De veritate*, q. 27, a. 1. This, I think, is the first time in St Thomas that *gratia gratis data* is given so precise a meaning.

126 [The grace that makes one pleasing is understood in two ways: in one way for the divine acceptance itself, which is a gratuitous will of God; in another way for a certain created gift, which formally perfects man and makes him worthy of eternal life] *De veritate*, q. 27, a. 5 c.

127 [but it can be multiple on the side of the divine effects; as when we might say that every effect that God works in us from his gratuitous will, by which

Thus, any effect of the divine acceptation unto eternal life is termed a *gratia gratum faciens*, and the example is good thoughts and holy desires.

There is, it seems to me, a marked difference between this and q. 24, a. 14, which was examined in the preceding section. Points of contact do exist. In the earlier article divine mercy providentially arranging external events and internally cooperating with the soul unto its salvation is termed a grace, but not *gratia gratum faciens*. In the present article, it is not divine mercy but the gratuitous will of God accepting unto his kingdom, nor is it the general expression – *interius motum mentis operatur* – but something more specific – *immittat bonas cogitationes et sanctas affectiones*.

6.3 The Cause of the Change

What was most striking in *De veritate*, q. 24, a. 14, was the absence of the specific theorem on the necessity of grace. It was flatly asserted that grace, in the broad sense of that article, was necessary for any good deed, even for digging and building. But in the parallel article, 1-2, q. 109, a. 2, we are explicitly told that even fallen nature can of itself do some good acts, such as digging and building.

There is, then, an antecedent probability that the reason why St Thomas enlarged his concept of *gratia gratum faciens* was that he adverted to the specific theorem on the necessity of grace.

Now it happens that the specific theorem does come to light in *De veritate*, q. 27, a. 5, ad 3m. The third objection to the view that there is only one *gratia gratum faciens* in each individual is as follows.

> Praeterea, nullus habet necesse petere id quod iam habet. Sed habens gratiam praevenientem necesse habet petere subsequentem, secundum Augustinum. Ergo non est una gratia praeveniens et subsequens.[128]

In the answer, the position of the commentary on the *Sentences*, that *gratia*

---

he accepts us into his kingdom, pertains to *the grace that makes one pleasing*, for example, that he sends us good thoughts and holy desires] Ibid. [Lonergan's emphasis].

128 [Besides, no one needs to ask for what he already has. But one who has prevenient grace needs to ask for subsequent, according to Augustine. Therefore prevenient and subsequent grace are not one grace] *De veritate*, q. 27, a. 5, ob. 3.

praeveniens and *subsequens* differ only notionally,[129] is no longer maintained. Instead we hear the specific theorem, not applied to different states of liberty as in Peter Lombard, but to different needs of divine grace.

> Ad tertium dicendum, quod quantumcumque homo habeat habitum gratiae, semper tamen indiget divina operatione, qua in nobis operatur modis praedictis; et hoc propter infirmitatem nostrae naturae, et multitudinem impedimentorum, quae quidem non erant in statu naturae conditae:[130] unde magis tunc poterat homo stare per se ipsum quam nunc possint habentes gratiam, non quidem propter defectum gratiae, sed propter infirmitatem naturae; quamvis etiam tunc indigerent divina providentia eos dirigente et adiuvante. Et ideo habens gratiam necesse habet petere divinum auxilium, quod ad gratiam cooperantem pertinet.[131]

The position is not altogether clear in its details: what is certain is that a fundamental idea has come to light to be worked out with greater precision and clarity in the *Prima secundae*. What concerns us immediately is that the habitual gift is no longer considered alone sufficient; a *divinum auxilium* is also needed, not because of a defect in the habit, but because of the infirmity of our fallen nature and the great number of obstacles to a good and holy life.

6.4 Grace as Operative and Cooperative

The first objection to the thesis of *De veritate*, q. 27, a. 5, is to the effect that *gratia gratum faciens* is divided into operative and cooperative. But nothing by itself is both operative and cooperative. Therefore, there is not merely one *gratia gratum faciens* in each individual.

129 *Super II Sententiarum*, d. 26, q. 1, a. 6, ad 2m.
130 See Augustine, *De correptione et gratia*, c. 12, §35, *PL* 44, 937–38.
131 [To the third objection it has to be said that no matter to what extent one has the habit of grace, still one always needs the divine operation, by which (God) works in us in the ways aforesaid, and this on account of the weakness of our nature and the multitude of impediments which did not exist in the original state of nature. And therefore man was better able then to stand by himself than those are now who have grace, not indeed because of a deficiency in grace but because of the weakness of nature; although even then they would need divine providence directing and guiding them. And therefore one who has grace needs to ask the divine help, which pertains to cooperative grace] *De veritate*, q. 27, a. 5, ad 3m.

The second paragraph of the *Sed contra* rejects the principle of this objection.

> ... relatio non multiplicat essentiam rei. Sed gratia cooperans supra operantem nonnisi relationem addit. Ergo eadem est gratia per essentiam operans et cooperans.[132]

However, the answer to the first objection treats the issue not merely in principle but also in detail. It distinguishes between the *donum habituale* and the *effectus gratuitae divinae voluntatis*. In the former case the same grace is both operative and cooperative. In the latter, operative grace is the grace of justification; cooperative includes the other effects of divine favor; hence, in this respect, the two are really different. The answer reads:

> Ad primum ... dicendum quod gratia operans et cooperans potest distingui et ex parte ipsius gratuitae Dei voluntatis, et ex parte doni nobis collati.
>
> Operans enim dicitur gratia respectu (illius effectus quem sola efficit; cooperans autem dicitur respectu) illius effectus quem sola non efficit, sed cum libero arbitrio cooperante.[133] Ex parte vero gratuitae Dei voluntatis, gratia operans dicetur ipsa iustificatio impii, quae fit ipsius doni gratuiti infusione. Hoc enim donum *sola gratuita divina voluntas* causat in nobis, nec aliquo modo eius causa est liberum arbitrium,[134] nisi per modum dispositionis sufficientis.
>
> Ex parte vero eiusdem [gratuitae Dei voluntatis] gratia cooperans dicetur secundum quod in libero arbitrio operatur, motum eius causando, et exterioris actus executionem expediendo, et perseverantiam praebendo, in quibus omnibus aliquid agit liberum

---

132 [a relation does not make the essence of a thing multiple in number. But cooperative grace does not add anything except a relation to operative grace. Therefore operative and cooperative are essentially the same grace] *De veritate*, q. 27, a. 5, Sed contra.

133 From the context I conjectured the line in brackets. R.P. Suermondt, President of the Commission for the Leonine Edition, very kindly informed me that this is to be found, with slight variations, in *Cod. Vat. Ottob.*, 204, 208, 214, 187; *Urb.*, 134; it is missing in *Cod. Vat. Lat.*, 781, 785, 786; *Reg.*, 1883. It is to be noted that the exceptional critical value of *Cod. Vat. Lat.*, 781, ends with *De veritate*, q. 22, a. 11. [See above, p. 37, note 54. The Leonine edition of the *De veritate* was not available at the time of editing.]

134 Because free will does not operate, grace is operative.

arbitrium.[135] Et sic constat quod aliud est gratia operans et
cooperans.

Ex parte vero doni gratuiti eadem gratia per essentiam dicetur
operans et cooperans: *operans quidem,* secundum quod informat
animam: ut operans formaliter intelligatur per modum loquendi
quo dicimus quod albedo facit album parietem; hoc enim nullo
modo est actus liberi arbitrii;[136] *cooperans vero* dicetur secundum
quod inclinat ad actum intrinsecum et extrinsecum, et secundum
quod praestat facultatem perseverandi usque in finem.[137]

The general scheme of the division is clear. The effects of divine favor are
manifold: operative grace is the grace of justification, the infusion of habitual grace; cooperative grace is the *divinum auxilium* that supplements
habitual grace because of the infirmity of fallen human nature.[138] But
habitual grace is essentially one thing: inasmuch then as it acts formally, it is
operative grace; but inasmuch as it acts efficiently, it is cooperative.[139]

135 Because free will does operate, grace is cooperative.
136 Because free will does not operate, grace is operative.
137 [To the first objection it must be said that operative and cooperative grace
    can be distinguished both from the side of the gratuitous will of God him-
    self, and from the side of the gift bestowed on us.
       For grace is called operative in regard to that effect which it operates
    alone, but cooperative with regard to that effect which it does not operate
    alone but with the cooperation of free will.
       But from the side of the gratuitous will of God, operative grace will be
    called the justification itself of the wicked, which is effected by the infusion
    of this gratuitous gift; for *the gratuitous will alone of God* causes this gift in us,
    nor is free will in any way its cause unless by way of a sufficient disposition.
       But from the side of the same (gratuitous will of God) grace will be called
    cooperative according as it operates in free will, causing its movement, and
    expediting the execution of an external act, and granting perseverance, in
    all of which free will does something. And so it is clear that operative grace
    is other than cooperative.
       But from the side of the gratuitous gift essentially the same grace will be
    called operative and cooperative. It is operative as informing the soul – the
    way operative is formally understood in the manner of speaking in which we
    say that whiteness makes a wall white – for in no way is this the act of free
    will. But it will be called cooperative as inclining to an intrinsic or extrinsic
    act, and as furnishing the power of persevering to the end] *De veritate,* q. 27,
    a. 5, ad 1m.
138 '... divinum auxilium, quod ad gratiam cooperantem pertinet' [divine help,
    which pertains to cooperative grace] Ibid. ad 3m.
139 To be noted is the difference between *praestat facultatem perseverandi,* attrib-
    uted to habitual grace, and *perseverantiam praebendo,* attributed to the

As a whole, the division is clearly unbalanced. The grace of justification appears in both members. It is operative grace in the first member. It is both operative and cooperative in the second member.

To be noted is that the second member here corresponds to the basic division in the commentary on the *Sentences*. The change has obvious advantages. First, it eliminates the excessive subtlety of grace cooperating as a formal cause by causing the meritoriousness (*forma meriti, modus actus*) of the free act. Second, it eliminates the unsatisfactory oddity of grace being termed operative when it cooperates with free will in the internal act, cooperative when it cooperates with free will in the external act. But these eliminations also eliminate a really important point made in the *Sentences*. There it was observed that *quasi per totum in Littera* St Augustine had made the distinction between operative and cooperative correspond to the distinction between the internal and external act, between good will and good performance. But in the *De veritate* both members of the division have cooperative grace referring to both internal and external acts.

This unsatisfactoriness will lead to a new treatment of the subject in the *Prima secundae*.

7   From the *De Veritate* to the *Prima Secundae*

Though *gratia operans* is not explicitly treated during this interval, there occurs a very relevant development in St Thomas's thought. Five points are treated: the definition of Pelagianism; the *prima gratia*; the preparation for habitual grace; the *Quodlibetum primum*; and the significance of Romans 9.16.

7.1   The Definition of Pelagianism

It is a simple matter to define Pelagianism after studying St Thomas's articles in question 109 of the *Prima secundae*. But St Thomas could not employ this simple method before writing the *Prima secundae*. To orientate the reader, we give specimens of his successive statements with regard to Pelagianism.

---

divinum auxilium. This would seem to correspond to the distinction between the possibility of perseverance and actual perseverance, which is made in *De veritate*, q. 24, a. 13.

Super II Sententiarum, d. 28, q. 1, a. 1: *Utrum homo possit facere aliquod bonum sine gratia* ... Pelagiani, facultatem liberi arbitrii ampliantes, dicunt ... quod ... homo per liberum arbitrium in quodlibet bonum opus potest sine aliqua gratia superaddita, etiam in opus meritorium.[140]

Ibid. a. 2: *Utrum homo sine gratia possit vitare peccatum* ... in hoc errabat Pelagius, aestimans hominem propriis operibus sine gratia posse se a peccatis praeteritis absolvere satisfaciendo.[141]

Ibid. a. 3: *Utrum homo possit implere praecepta Dei sine gratia* ... et ideo Pelagius erravit, qui simpliciter[142] impleri praecepta legis posse sine gratia posuit.[143]

Ibid. a. 4: *Utrum homo possit se praeparare ad gratiam sine aliqua gratia*.[144] Pelagius does not seem to be mentioned.

De veritate, q. 24, a. 12: *Utrum liberum arbitrium sine gratia in statu peccati mortalis possit vitare peccatum mortale...* Pelagius ... dicens, absque Dei gratia hominem peccatum evitare.[145]

De veritate, q. 24, a. 14: *Utrum liberum arbitrium possit in bonum sine gratia*.[146] Pelagius does not seem to be mentioned.

140 [*Whether man is able to do a good work without grace* ... The Pelagians, expanding the faculty of free will, say ... that ... man by free will has the capacity, without some grace being added, for any good work, even for a meritorious work] *Super II Sententiarum*, d. 28, q. 1, a. 1.
141 [*Whether man can without grace avoid sin* ... in this Pelagius erred, judging that man can by his own works, without grace, by making satisfaction, absolve himself from his past sins] Ibid. a. 2.
142 '... simpliciter implere' [simply to fulfil] in the context means '... cum caritate' [with charity].
143 [*Whether man can without grace fulfil the precepts of God* ... and therefore Pelagius, who held that the precepts of God could be simply fulfilled without grace, was in error] Ibid. a. 3.
144 [*Whether man can without grace prepare himself for grace*] Ibid. a. 4.
145 [*Whether free will in a state of mortal sin can without grace avoid mortal sin* ... Pelagius ... saying that without the grace of God man avoids sin] *De veritate*, q. 24, a. 12. See *Super II Sententiarum*, d. 28, q. 1, a. 2; *Summa contra Gentiles*, 3, c. 160; *Summa theologiae*, 1-2, q. 109, a. 8.
146 [*Whether free will is capable of a good (deed) without grace*] *De veritate*, q. 24, a. 14. See *Super II Sententiarum*, d. 28, q. 1, a. 1; *Summa theologiae*, 1-2, q. 109, a. 2.

De veritate, q. 24, a. 15: *Utrum homo sine gratia se possit praeparare ad habendum gratiam.*[147] Pelagius does not seem to be mentioned.

Summa contra Gentiles, 3, c. 147: *Quod homo indiget divino auxilio ad beatitudinem consequendam* ... Pelagianorum, qui dixerunt quod per solum liberum arbitrium homo poterat Dei gloriam promereri.[148]

Summa contra Gentiles, 3, c. 149: *Quod divinum auxilium homo promereri non potest* ... Pelagianorum, qui dicebant huiusmodi auxilium propter merita nobis dari; et quod iustificationis nostrae initium ex nobis sit, consummatio autem a Deo.[149]

Summa contra Gentiles, 3, c. 152: *Quod divina gratia causat in nobis fidem* ... Pelagianorum, qui dicebant quod initium fidei in nobis non erat a Deo sed a nobis.[150]

From the foregoing it appears that in the *Sentences* the explicit concept of Pelagianism is that it denies the supernatural character of merit. In the *De veritate* the assertion that one in the state of mortal sin can avoid further mortal sins is affirmed to be Pelagian. In the *Contra Gentiles* it is argued that to attribute justification to merits or the beginning of faith to man is also Pelagian.[151]

---

147 [*Whether man can, without grace, prepare himself for having grace*] *De veritate*, q. 24, a. 15. See *Super II Sententiarum*, d. 28, q. 1, a. 4; *Quaestiones quodlibetales*, 1, a. 7 [q. 4, a. 2]; *Summa theologiae*, 1-2, q. 109, a. 6.
148 [*That man needs divine help for obtaining beatitude* ... of the Pelagians, who said that by free will alone man could merit the glory of God] *Summa contra Gentiles*, 3, c. 147.
149 [*That man cannot merit divine help* ... of the Pelagians, who were saying that this kind of help is given us on account of merits, and that the beginning of our justification is from us, but its consummation is from God] *Summa contra Gentiles*, 3, c. 149.
150 [*That divine grace causes faith in us* ... of the Pelagians, who were saying that the beginning of faith in us was not from God but from us] *Summa contra Gentiles*, 3, c. 152.
151 The development of St Thomas's thought in the field of grace has been common knowledge at least since the sixteenth century. See Cajetan, *In Summam theologiae*, 1-2, q. 109, a. 6; Dominicus Soto, *De natura et gratia*, lib. 2, c. 3; Lange, *De gratia* 141–47. [Lonergan gave the Lange pp. as 140–52, but only 141–47 are directly concerned with Aquinas. See also above, p. 20, note 94; p. 159, note 1.]

7.2   *The* Prima Gratia *in the* De Veritate *and the* Contra Gentiles

In his 'Grundlagen für ein Verständnis der Busslehre der Früh- und Hochscholastik,' Professor Artur Landgraf, investigating medieval thought on faith as the *prima gratia,* asserted that until the middle of the thirteenth century the term *prima gratia* without exception denoted the grace of justification.[152] In the two works here under consideration it would seem that St Thomas did not immediately improve on his predecessors.[153]

In the *De veritate*, in answering an objection on prevenient and subsequent grace, he wrote:

> Ad sextum dicendum, quod gratia praeveniens et subsequens dicitur secundum ordinem eorum quae in esse gratuito inveniuntur: quorum quidem *primum* est subiecti informatio, sive impii iustificatio, quod idem est ...[154]

It is to be noted that this occurs in the very article in which we have already observed the introduction of a *divinum auxilium* subsequent to justification and distinct from it.[155]

The treatment of grace in the *Contra Gentiles* is highly speculative. First, it is established that the beatific vision lies beyond the natural capacity of any creature.[156] Then in turn are deduced the necessity of grace,[157] the necessity of habits,[158] and that grace causes in us charity,[159] faith,[160] and hope.[161] In its principles, the whole of St Thomas's theory of grace is complete. It remains that all the details do not seem as yet established.

---

152 See Landgraf, 'Grundlagen für ein Verständnis der Busslehre der Früh- und Hochscholastik' [see above, p. 18, note 77] 181. Note that the statement refers to the term *prima gratia.*

153 The statement refers to an explicit speculative development.

154 [To the sixth objection it has to be said that prevenient and subsequent grace are named according to the order of those things which are found in gratuitous being, of which *the first* is the bestowal of form on the subject, or the justification of the wicked, which is the same thing] *De veritate*, q. 27, a. 5, ad 6m.

155 See above, p. 233.

156 *Summa contra Gentiles*, 3, c. 52.

157 Ibid. 3, c. 147.

158 Ibid. 3, c. 150.

159 Ibid. 3, c. 151.

160 Ibid. 3, c. 152.

161 Ibid. 3, c. 153.

Thus the recognition that it is Pelagian to attribute justification to our merits[162] or the beginning of faith to our good will[163] does not immediately lead to the affirmation of a *divinum auxilium* prior to the grace of justification. There is nothing to show that the faith, hope, and charity that are caused by grace[164] are not the infused virtues that accompany justification. It is true that St Thomas speaks of a movement, but the movement in question is the movement from the state of nature to the beatific vision, not explicitly a movement of intellect and will prior to justification. There is a scheme into which such movements could be fitted, but the possibility of a later idea is not proof of its prior existence.

Indeed, so far from adding a *divinum auxilium* prior to justification, the *Contra Gentiles* attributes the *divinum auxilium* that is subsequent to justification to the external action of divine providence.[165]

7.3   The Preparation for Grace in the Commentary on the Sentences *and the* De Veritate

It has already been noted that in these works St Thomas does not seem to speak of the Pelagians in connection with the *initium fidei*.

In the commentary on the *Sentences* a distinction is drawn between divine providence and habitual grace. To prepare for the latter, providential assistance is needed. But this divine aid may take any form. Thus:

> ... gratia dupliciter potest accipi: vel ipsa divina providentia ... vel aliquod donum habituale ... Si ergo primo modo accipitur gratia, nulli dubium est quod homo sine gratia Dei non potest se praeparare ad habendum gratiam gratum facientem ... omne enim motum necesse est ab alio moveri. Nec differt quidquid sit illud quod huius- modi variationis occasionem praebeat, quasi voluntatem excitando, sive sit admonitio hominis, vel aegritudo corporis, vel aliquid huius- modi: quae omnia constat divinae providentiae subiecta esse ...[166]

---

162 Ibid. 3, c. 149.
163 Ibid. 3, c. 152.
164 Ibid. 3, cc. 151–53.
165 Ibid. 3, c. 155. There is no allusion to fallen nature as in *De veritate*, q. 27, a. 5, ad 3m. See *De veritate*, q. 24, a. 13, and *Summa theologiae*, 1-2, q. 109, a. 9: the former lacks, the latter has the 'specific theorem.'
166 [grace can be taken in two ways: either as divine providence itself ... or as some habitual gift ... If therefore grace is taken in the first way, no one doubts that man without grace cannot prepare himself for having the grace that makes one pleasing ... for everything that is moved has to be moved by

In the *De veritate* the position is not essentially changed. Divine mercy is spoken of as well as divine providence. An internal movement is offered as an alternative to external influence, or else in combination with it. But there is not an affirmation of the necessity of internal change of heart produced by God.

> Si autem per gratiam gratis datam intelligant divinam providentiam, qua misericorditer homo ad bonum dirigitur; sic verum est quod sine gratia homo non potest se praeparare ... oportet quod ad hoc inducatur aliquibus exterioribus actionibus, aut corporali aegritudine, aut aliquo huiusmodi; *vel* aliquo interiori instinctu ... *vel* etiam utroque modo.[167]

It is to be observed that in both cases the theory of motion underlying these explanations of the preparation for grace is derived from the eighth book of Aristotle's *Physics*.

7.4 Quaestiones Quodlibetales, *q. 1, a. 7 [q. 4, a. 2]*

In this article there appears an explicit recognition of the necessity of an internal change of heart prior to justification. This position is derived from a further consideration of Pelagian thought; it resolves the problem of the *prima gratia* and the preparation for grace; and, what concerns us, it will supply a *divinum auxilium* that is a *gratia operans*.

The question reads, *Utrum homo absque gratia per solam naturalem arbitrii libertatem possit se ad gratiam praeparare.*[168]

---

another. Nor does it matter what it is that offers the occasion for this kind of variation, arousing the will, so to speak, whether it be a human admonition, or sickness of body, or something of this sort, all of which are clearly subject to divine providence] *Super II Sententiarum*, d. 28, q. 1, a. 4.

167 [But if by the grace that makes one pleasing they understand divine providence, by which man is mercifully directed to the good, then it is true that without grace man cannot prepare himself ... it is necessary that he be brought to this by some external actions, either corporeal sickness, or something of this sort, *or* by some internal impulse ... *or* also in both ways] *De veritate*, q. 24, a. 15.

168 [Whether man, without grace by the natural liberty alone of will, can prepare himself for grace] The chronological sequence: *Sentences, De veritate, Contra Gentiles, Pars prima, Quodlibetum primum, De malo, Prima secundae*, seems securely established by Dom Lottin. See 'La date de la Question disputée "De Malo" de saint Thomas d'Aquin' and 'Liberté humaine et motion divine' [for both articles, see above, p. 54, note 33].

The response begins with an account of Pelagian thought.

> Respondeo dicendum, quod in hac quaestione cavendus est error
> Pelagii, qui posuit quod per liberum arbitrium homo poterat
> adimplere legem, et vitam aeternam mereri; nec indigebat auxilio
> divino nisi quantum ad hoc quod sciret quid facere deberet, secun-
> dum illud Psalm. CXLII, 10: *Doce me facere voluntatem tuam.*[169]

It will be recalled that the foregoing was the idea of Pelagianism that St
Thomas had in the commentary on the *Sentences*. He continues:

> Sed quia hoc nimis parum videbatur, ut solam scientiam haberemus
> a Deo, caritatem autem, qua praecepta legis implentur, haberemus a
> nobis, ideo postmodum Pelagiani posuerunt, quod initium boni
> operis est homini ex se ipso, dum consentit fidei per liberum arbi-
> trium; sed consummatio est homini a Deo.[170]

This aspect of Pelagianism is the central issue in St Augustine's *De gratia et
libero arbitrio*. It was recognized to be Pelagian by St Thomas in the *Contra
Gentiles*. But though one can find there an abstract scheme for a fully
developed theory of conversion, one does not find an explicit application
of the point to the preparation for grace.[171] Such an explicit application is
here made immediately.

> Praeparatio autem ad initium boni operis pertinet. Unde ad errorem
> Pelagianum pertinet dicere, quod homo possit se ad gratiam prae-
> parare absque auxilio divinae gratiae: et est contra Apostolum, qui
> dicit ad Phil. I, 6: *Qui coepit in vobis opus bonum, ipse perficiet.* Dicen-

---

169 [I reply that it has to be said that in this question the error of Pelagius, who
held that by free will man was able to fulfil the law and merit eternal life,
must be avoided; nor (according to him) did man need divine help except
in this regard that he might know what he had to do, according to that text
of Psalm 142.10: *Teach me to do your will*] *Quaestiones quodlibetales*, q. 1, a. 7
[q. 4, a. 2].

170 [But because this seemed too little, (namely,) that we should have knowledge alone from God but the charity by which the precepts of the law are
fulfilled we should have from ourselves, afterwards the Pelagians affirmed
that the beginning of a good work is (possible) to man from himself when
he consents to faith by free will, but that the consummation comes to man
from God] Ibid.

171 Read *Summa contra Gentiles*, 3, cc. 149, 158.

dum est ergo, quod homo indiget auxilio gratiae non solum ad
merendum, sed etiam ad hoc quod se ad gratiam praeparet; aliter
tamen et aliter. Nam meretur homo per actum virtutis, cum non
solum bonum agit, sed bene, ad quod requiritur habitus, ut dicitur
in II *Ethic.*, et ideo ad merendum requiritur habitualiter gratia.[172]

There follows an explicit rejection of the sufficiency of external influences,
that is, of the position of the commentary on the *Sentences* and the *De veritate*.

Sed ad hoc quod homo praeparet se ad habitum consequendum,
non indiget alio habitu, quia sic esset procedere ad infinitum.
Indiget autem auxilio divino non solum quantum ad exteriora
moventia, prout scilicet ex divina providentia procurantur homini
occasiones salutis, puta praedicationes, exempla, et interdum
aegritudines et flagella; sed etiam quantum ad interiorem motum,
prout Deus cor hominis interius movet ad bonum secundum illud
Prov. XXI, 1, *Cor regis in manu Dei; quocumque voluerit, vertet illud.* Et
quod hoc necessarium sit, probat Philosophus in quodam cap. *de
Bono fortunae.*[173]

On the excerpt from the *Magna moralia* and the *Eudemian Ethics*, that, in the
Middle Ages, went under the title *Liber De bono fortunae*, more will be said

172 [But preparation pertains to the beginning of a good work. And so it pertains to the error of the Pelagians to say that man can, without the help of
divine grace, prepare himself for grace; it is also against the Apostle who
says in Philippians 1.6: *the one who began a good work among you will bring it to
completion.* It has to be said therefore that man needs the help of grace not
only for meriting but also for this that he prepare himself for grace. But the
need differs in the two cases. For man merits by an act of virtue, when he
not only does the good, but does it properly; for this a habit is required, as
is said in *Ethics*, II, and therefore for meriting, grace is habitually required]
Quaestiones quodlibetales, q. 1, a. 7 [q. 4, a. 2].
173 [But man, to prepare himself to acquire a habit, does not need another
habit, because that would be a process to infinity. But he needs the divine
help not only in what regards external movers, as for example by divine
providence there are procured for man occasions of salvation – think of
sermons, examples, and sometimes sicknesses and scourgings – but also in
what regards internal movement, as God moves the heart of man internally
according to that text of Proverbs 21.1, *The king's heart is (a stream of water) in
the hand of the Lord; he will turn it wherever he will.* And that this is necessary
the Philosopher proves in some chapter of the book *On the Good of Fortune*]
Ibid.

later. All that need be noted for the present is that the preparation for grace is no longer conceived in terms of the eighth book of Aristotle's *Physics*.[174]

7.5 *The Significance of Romans 9.16*

The text *Igitur non volentis neque currentis sed miserentis est Dei* is an important clue to the thought of St Thomas on operative grace. It is cited by Peter Lombard at the end of *Sententiae*, 2, d. 25 with the comment

> ... cuius gratiam non advocat hominis voluntas vel operatio, sed ipsa gratia voluntatem praevenit praeparando, ut velit bonum; et praeparatam adiuvat, ut perficiat.[175]

It is also cited by St Thomas in the third objection to 1-2, q. 111, a. 2, where the Lombard's answer is put in terms of St Thomas's distinction between the will of the end and the will of the means.

Since one cannot will the means without first willing the end, the similarity of that distinction to St Anselm's affirmation that only the *recta voluntas* can will *rectitudo* is apparent. But what is most interesting is that in *Contra Gentiles*, 3, c. 149, the text is interpreted in terms of St Thomas's theorem of universal instrumentality: the same idea appears in *Summa theologiae*, 1, q. 83, a. 1, ad 2m. In the *De malo*, q. 6, a. 1, ad 1m, the text is again interpreted: here to the idea of instrumentality is added the fact that God is the first principle of the act of will. Thus, we apparently have to deal with a synthesis of the metaphysical theorem of universal instrumentality, the psychological analysis of the will and of the process of the free act, and the view that God is the first mover of the self-moving will.

The commentary on Romans connects such a synthesis with dogmatic truth by the following argument: if grace is simply a cause or condition of good action, then, since the same is true of free will, it would be possible to

---

174 The first reference to the *Liber De bono fortunae* occurs in *Summa contra Gentiles*, 3, c. 89. The verse, 2 Corinthians 3.5, which is here cited in the *Sed contra*, is explained in St Thomas's commentary on St Paul on the same principle (*In II Cor.*, c. 3, lect. 1 [§§ 86–87]). The commentary on Romans (c. 9, lect. 3 [§ 773]) has the same idea, though there subordinated to a point from Aristotle's *Metaphysics*.

175 [it is not the will or operation of man that summons his (God's) grace, but grace itself precedes the will, preparing it to will the good, and helps bring the prepared will to completion] Peter Lombard, *Sententiae*, 2, d. 25 [c. 9, *QL* 1: 436].

invert St Paul's affirmation and say, *Non est miserentis Dei sed volentis et currentis.* Such an inversion is preposterous. Therefore, grace must be the principal cause and free will the instrumental cause.

The texts here referred to will be quoted in the fifth chapter [II-5]. The third and fourth chapters are devoted to clearing up obscurities in St Thomas's theory of instrumentality, of the will, of its motion, and of its liberty.

8   *Summa Theologiae,* 1-2, q. 111, a. 2

The treatment of operative grace is here, as in the commentary on the *Sentences,* explicit; the title reads, *Utrum gratia convenienter dividatur per operantem et cooperantem.*[176]

The central thought in St Augustine's *De gratia et libero arbitrio* is presented in the *Sed contra* and again in the response. It is interesting to note in the former a syllogism.

> Sed contra est quod Augustinus dicit, in libro *de Grat. et Lib. Arb.* [cap. 17]: *Cooperando Deus in nobis perficit quod operando incipit: quia ipse ut velimus operatur incipiens, qui volentibus cooperatur perficiens.* Sed operationes Dei quibus movet nos ad bonum, ad gratiam pertinent. Ergo convenienter gratia dividitur per operantem et cooperantem.[177]

The response begins by recalling the more fundamental division of grace into actual and habitual: a step that has seemed more and more superfluous to successive generations of Thomists yet, I think, would have appeared as notable to St Augustine, St Anselm, Peter Lombard, and St Albert as the law of inverse squares to Aristotle.

> Respondeo dicendum quod, sicut supra dictum est [q. 110, a. 2], gratia dupliciter potest intelligi: uno modo, divinum auxilium, quo

176 [Whether grace is suitably distinguished by operative and cooperative] *Summa theologiae,* 1-2, q. 111, a. 2.

177 [But on the other side there is what Augustine says in the book *On Grace and Free Will* (chapter 17): in cooperating God brings to completion in us what in operating he begins; because the One who begins by operating so that we may will brings (the work) to completion by cooperating with those who will. But the operations of God by which he moves us to the good pertain to grace. Therefore grace is suitably distinguished by operative and cooperative] Ibid. Sed contra.

nos movet ad bene volendum et agendum; alio modo, habituale donum nobis divinitus inditum.[178]

This passage raises three questions. Two of these are to be investigated later. One is to be dismissed immediately.

The first question is this: if we dutifully turn back to q. 110, a. 2, we find a reference to the theory of motion in Aristotle's *Physics*. But this is not, as in the commentary on the *Sentences* and the *De veritate*, to the eighth book but to the third book. Why the change?

The second question arises from the words *quo nos movet ad bene volendum et agendum*. The reader will recall the citation already made from the *Quodlibetum primum* in which the distinction between *bene agere* and *bonum agere* was made. Does, then, the use of *bene* here imply that St Thomas is confining operative grace to justification and the period subsequent to justification? Cajetan thinks this the more probable view[179] and on this basis constructs a far-fetched interpretation. Fr de San, in his polemic against Didacus Alvarez, enthusiastically follows him.[180] Are they right?

The third question is connected with the second, though hardly with St Thomas. Subsequent to Fr Stufler's earnest study of St Thomas there has arisen a learned debate: Does St Thomas consider grace prior to justification to be *entitative supernaturale?* The difficulty with this debate is that the question is badly put. Modern theologians divide grace into *entitative supernaturale*, such as sanctifying grace, and *supernaturale quoad modum*, such as a miracle or a prophecy. The student of St Thomas, if he would ask intelligent questions about St Thomas's thought, must base his divisions of the supernatural in St Thomas's thought. It is not sufficient to have some sort of an approximation. Now it seems to me that St Thomas's thought calls for a distinction within the later category of the *entitative supernaturale*. However, to prove this point would call for another thesis, and so, in the present work, we propose to doubt the legitimacy of this recent debate and so to prescind from it entirely.

St Thomas proceeds to argue that both habitual and actual grace are divided into operative and cooperative.

---

178 [I reply that it has to be said that, as was said above (q. 110, a. 2), grace can be understood in two ways: in one way (as) the divine help by which he moves us to willing and acting properly; in another way (as) a habitual gift divinely conferred on us] Ibid. c.

179 See Cajetan, *In Summam theologiae*, 1-2, q. 111, a. 2, §§ III, V [*LT* 7: 319].

180 de San, *Tractatus De Deo uno* [see above, p. 69, note 13], vol. 1, pp. 701–10.

Utroque autem modo gratia dicta convenienter dividitur per operantem et cooperantem. Operatio enim alicuius effectus non attribuitur mobili, sed moventi. In illo ergo effectu in quo mens nostra est mota et non movens, solus autem Deus movens, operatio Deo attribuitur: et secundum hoc dicitur *gratia operans*. In illo autem effectu in quo mens nostra et movet et movetur, operatio non solum attribuitur Deo, sed etiam animae: et secundum hoc dicitur *gratia cooperans*.[181]

This would seem to define the difference between operative and cooperative grace. First, it is pointed out that what counts is the number of agents. If there is only one cause, then there is operation. If there are two or more causes, there is cooperation. Second, the application is made. An effect in the order of grace that is produced by God alone is attributed to operative grace. An effect that is produced both by God and by man is attributed to cooperative grace. It may be noted that the term *mens* is simply the Augustinian equivalent, common enough in early Scholasticism, for the more philosophic *anima*: in the passage cited, the two are evidently interchangeable.

The next step is the application of the definition to the two cases of *gratia operans et cooperans*.

Est autem in nobis duplex actus. Primus quidem interior voluntatis. Et quantum ad istum actum, voluntas se habet ut mota, Deus autem ut movens: et praesertim cum voluntas incipit bonum velle, quae prius malum volebat. Et ideo secundum quod Deus movet humanam mentem ad hunc actum, dicitur *gratia operans*. – Alius autem actus est exterior; qui cum a voluntate imperetur, ut supra habitum est [q. 17, a. 9], consequens est ut ad hunc actum operatio attribuatur voluntati. Et quia etiam ad hunc actum Deus nos adiuvat, et interius confirmando voluntatem ut ad actum perveniat, et exterius facultatem

---

181   [But in both ways the grace we speak of is suitably divided by operative and cooperative. For the operating of some effect is not attributed to the movable thing but to the (actively) moving thing. In that effect, therefore, in which our mind is moved but not (actively) moving, and God alone is the mover, the operation is attributed to God: and accordingly it is called *operative grace*. But in that effect in which our mind is both moved and is (actively) moving, the operation is attributed not to God alone but also to the soul: and this is accordingly called *cooperative grace*] *Summa theologiae*, 1-2, q. 111, a. 2 c.

operandi praebendo; respectu huius actus dicitur *gratia cooperans.*
Unde post praemissa verba subdit Augustinus [ibid.]: *Ut autem
velimus, operatur: cum autem volumus, ut perficiamus nobis cooperatur.* –
Sic igitur si gratia accipiatur pro gratuita Dei motione qua movet nos
ad bonum meritorium, convenienter dividitur gratia per operantem
et cooperantem.[182]

This passage raises a number of interesting questions.

The most obvious question is, What is the *actus interior?* Is it simply the
initium consiliandi, as perhaps the context suggests? Or is it the election,
according to the usual meaning of *actus interior?* For that matter, what is the
actus exterior? Does it regard the merely corporeal movement? Or does it
refer to the *actus humanus,* and so include the election?

Again, according to the ad 4m, *gratia operans et cooperans est eadem gratia;
sed distinguitur secundum diversos effectus, ut ex dictis patet* [in corp. art.].[183]

Are we to restrict the reference of this response, which is as general as the
objection it answers, to the sole case of habitual grace? If so, on what
grounds? If not, then the whole point of St Augustine's distinction between
an initial grace giving good will and a further grace giving good performance disappears. How is that to be accounted for?

In addition to the above questions, which arise from the text itself, there
are the questions that arise from later controversy. Does *voluntas mota et non
movens* mean *praemota?* Is this passive movement of the will free? Is such
freedom intelligible?

182 [But there is a twofold act in us. The first is an internal act of the will; and
in regard to that act the will has the role of being moved, and God the role
of mover; and this is the case especially when the will, which before was
willing evil, begins to will the good. And therefore, in that God moves the
human mind to this act, grace is called operative. – But the other act is
external, and since this is commanded by the will, as was determined above
(q. 17, a. 9), the consequence is that for this act the operation is attributed
to the will. And because for this act too God helps us, both strengthening
the will internally that it may come to act and providing externally the faculty of operating, (therefore) in regard to this act, grace is called cooperative. And therefore after the words quoted above (Sed contra) Augustine
subjoins: But that we will, (God) operates; but when we will, he cooperates
with us that we may perform. – So it is therefore that if grace is taken for the
gratuitous movement of God, by which he moves us to a meritorious good,
grace is suitably divided by operative and cooperative] Ibid.
183 [operative and cooperative are the same grace; but (the grace) is distinguished according to (its) different effects, as is clear from what has been
said (in the body of the article)] Ibid. ad 4m.

Finally, due to the differences between St Thomas and later thought, which is lost in metaphysical theories of motion and *concursus*, there arises the question, What precisely is the psychological mechanism of *ut bonum velit*? Is it more closely related to the thought of the sixteenth century or to the thought of Peter Lombard?

Having indicated the questions to be answered, not always with certitude, we pass on to the division of habitual grace.

> Si vero accipiatur gratia pro habituali dono, sic etiam duplex est gratiae effectus, sicut et cuiuslibet alterius formae: quorum primus est esse, secundus est operatio; sicut caloris operatio est facere calidum, et exterior calefactio. Sic igitur habitualis gratia, inquantum animam sanat vel iustificat, sive gratam Deo facit, dicitur *gratia operans*: inquantum vero est principium operis meritorii, quod etiam ex libero arbitrio procedit, dicitur *cooperans*.[184]

This, by now, is relatively familiar ground. It is the thought of St Albert, and of St Thomas in the commentary on the *Sentences* and, more proximately, in the *De veritate*. Nonetheless, a few questions arise.

Here, as before, the habit is conceived not merely as the possibility of supernatural action but also as the cause of good acts. This is particularly evident from parallel passages in q. 113 on justification. Does this function of the habit throw any light on the *ut bonum velit* of the other operative grace?

Second, the parallel passages in q. 113 give great attention to the axiom *motio moventis praecedit motum mobilis*. But the reference to Aristotle's *Physics* in q. 110, a. 2, presents us with another axiom, *motio moventis est motus mobilis*. How did St Thomas manage to hold both of these views at the same time?

Such are some of the questions presented by the notoriously obscure[185]

---

184 [But if grace is taken as a habitual gift, then too there is a twofold effect of grace as there is of any other form whatever; of these the first is being, the second is operation, as the operation of heat is to make (something) hot, and (to give) external heating. In this way therefore habitual grace, insofar as it heals the soul or justifies it or makes it pleasing to God, is called *operative grace*; but insofar as it is the principle of a meritorious deed, which proceeds from free will too, it is called *cooperative*] Ibid. c.

185 Fr N. del Prado has observed that not even all strict Thomists are agreed on the interpretation. See his *De gratia et libero arbitrio*, vol. 1, pp. 194, 236 note. [On p. 194 del Prado is speaking more of the differences between Augustine and Thomas, between Molina and Suarez, and between Thomists and Molinists.]

article of the *Summa theologiae* on operative grace. Summary answers are easy but are not helpful. The purpose of the following chapters will be to investigate changes in St Thomas's thought parallel and related to the changes in his conception of operative grace. This procedure may help eliminate a few mistaken interpretations.

9   Summary

It will be well to pass in review the whole movement that has been studied.

First, there is the semi-Pelagian admission that grace is necessary for good deeds though not always necessary for initial good will.

St Augustine asserts that grace is needed for initial good will, though even here the will is free, and a still greater grace is needed for actual performance.

St Anselm, aiming at giving some account of free will, defined justice as *rectitudo voluntatis propter se servata.* Since this justice leads to salvation, it can come only from God. Since the will cannot act rightly unless it is in itself right, it is argued that the will is always free but it can be good only when grace is given.

Peter Lombard conceives *gratia operans* as the grace of justification, *gratia cooperans* as the same grace in its vital productivity.

St Albert explicitly conceives *gratia operans* as the *forma supernaturalitatis* in the will, *gratia cooperans* as the *forma meriti* in good deeds. Implicitly there is present in his thought the idea that the infused virtue has all the influence and power of natural spontaneity. This is illustrated by the gravitation of bodies.

In his commentary on the *Sentences* St Thomas, under the influence of the citations from St Augustine in Peter Lombard, articulates both elements in St Albert's thought. As a formal cause, grace is operative in sanctifying man, cooperative in making his works meritorious. As an efficient cause, grace is operative in cooperating with free will for the production of the internal act, cooperative in cooperating with free will for the production of the external act. The grace referred to is one, and all the distinctions are notional; it consists in sanctifying grace and the infused virtues.

In the *De veritate* the fundamental cause of differences appears to be St Augustine's real distinction between prevenient and subsequent grace: after receiving prevenient, one has still to pray for subsequent grace. This clearly accounts for the enlargement of the concept of *gratia gratum faciens* to include a *divinum auxilium* that is a *gratia cooperans* subsequent to justification. It would also account for the extrinsic theory of the grace of perseverance to be found in the *Contra Gentiles*: the incorporation of Augustine's point would not lead immediately to a grasp of the insufficiency of the theory of motion in the eighth book of Aristotle's *Physics*. Other changes are incidental. The anomaly in the commentary on the *Sentences* – operative grace as an efficient cause cooperates with free will – is eliminated. The excessive subtlety of cooperative grace producing the *forma meriti* in the free act is also omitted. And these changes are at the expense of the real gain in the *Sentences*: there operative grace referred to the internal act, cooperative grace to the external act; now cooperative grace refers equally to both.

In the *Quodlibetum primum* there emerges the synthesis of a number of previous tendencies: the increasing clarity and fulness of the idea of Pelagianism; the significance of the *Liber De bono fortunae* as contrasted with the eighth book of the *Physics*; the problem of preparation for grace. The resultant is a *divinum auxilium* producing a change of heart prior to justification.

In the *Prima secundae* the distinction between *donum habituale* and *divinum auxilium* is clearly established, but the theory of motion on which the latter is based is not, it would seem, from the *Liber De bono fortunae* nor from the eighth but from the third book of Aristotle's *Physics*. The division of habitual grace into operative and cooperative is the same as in the *De veritate*. The *divinum auxilium* is operative when the will is moved but not moving, and this is in the internal act; it is cooperative when the will both moves and is moved, and this is in the external act. The meaning of these statements is not too clear.

II-3

The First Subsidiary Investigation: The Idea of Operation in St Thomas

The necessity of this subsidiary inquiry arises from the nature of speculative theology: it constructs its theorems with respect to the supernatural order by appealing to the analogy of nature.

Alone that fact does not account for the length of the present chapter. Conspiring to impose such a need are a number of factors. There is the speculative difficulty connected with the precise nature of causality or operation, to which must be added the difficulty of convincing others that St Thomas solved this problem in a definite manner. There is the historical difficulty, for the theory of operation appears in connection with the theory of grace in quite different forms: plainly the most exact knowledge of the general idea is necessary if we are to understand the significance of St Thomas's successive appeals to the eighth book of Aristotle's *Physics*, then to the *Eudemian Ethics*, and finally to the third book of the *Physics*. Further, though we believe that in its ultimate form St Thomas's *gratia operans* is an extremely simple idea, it remains that the simple idea derives a great deal of its significance from its metaphysical and cosmic background in such theorems as the affirmation of universal instrumentality and the efficacy of divine will; in any case, it will be necessary to determine just what is the relation between the general world view of *Deus operans* and the particular theory of *gratia operans*. Finally, there are the well-known controversies which have brought issues to a very fine point indeed: to ignore them in a treatment of operative grace is not altogether possible.

The chapter treats in turn six points: the distinction between *posse agere* and *actu agere*; the idea of premotion, of application, of instrumental participation, and of *immediatio virtutis*; it concludes with a study of the idea of cooperation.

Throughout, a purely historical viewpoint is maintained. What precisely did St Thomas say, and what did he mean?

1   Posse Agere, Actu Agere

The question, though familiar, is not too easy to define.[1] *Posse agere* means that a given agent is able to act yet not actually acting. *Actu agere* means that the agent is not merely able to act but actually acting.

Now it is evident that the two propositions, *potest agere, actu agit*, cannot both be true with respect to the same agent and the same activity at the same time. The two, as defined, are contradictory: the first means that he is not acting; the second that he is acting.

It is also evident that there must be a real difference between the real situation in which *potest agere* is verified and, on the other hand, the real situation in which *actu agit* is verified. For contradictory propositions cannot be verified in identical situations.

But, while everyone must admit the necessity of a real difference in the objective situations, the point in dispute is whether or not there is per se and necessarily a real difference in the agent qua agent. For when the agent is actually acting, the real difference in the objective situation is supplied very obviously by the effect of his activity; and it makes no difference whether this effect be immanent or transient.

But not only is there no a priori reason for asserting a real difference in the agent qua agent; there is no possibility of such an a priori reason existing. For if there were, then the conclusion would be universal. If it

---

1 If the terminology of *actus primus, actus secundus* is used, then great care must be taken in interpreting St Thomas. He has three senses for this pair of terms. First, the substance is *actus primus*, the accident is *actus secundus* (for example, *Summa theologiae*, 1, q. 76, a. 5, Sed contra [erroneous reference, it seems]). Second, the habit is *actus primus* and the operation is *actus secundus*. Third, in metaphysical potencies such as the intellect of the angel, the potency as such is really distinct from its act (*Summa theologiae*, 1, q. 54, a. 3). Note that this distinction is never applied to the *virtutes elementares*, which are accidental forms and always in act (fire is always hot, water is always wet, hence, *forma quaedam habens esse firmum et ratum in natura*). Obviously, the distinction between *posse agere* and *actu agere* is identical with none of these: neither created substance, nor angelic potency (*potentia passiva*), nor habit are a full *posse agere*. Hence, a fourth sense must be ascribed to *actus primus et secundus*. Some writers appear confused on this point.

were universal, then *omne movens movetur*. If *omne movens movetur*, there can be no *motor immobilis*. If no *motor immobilis*, there can be no motion. If no motion, then no action.

Still, though not universal and not following from the nature of the agent as such, it might be that in the creature there is a real difference between *posse agere* and *actu agere*. That defines the question of this section. Does St Thomas make any distinction between creator and creature in this respect? It is known that he does hold that the creator acts in virtue of a substantial act while the creature acts in virtue of an accidental act, and that is certainly where he places the essential difference (see *Summa theologiae*, 1, q. 54, aa. 1–3, which demonstrate the proposition). But the question is whether in addition to this he also places in the creature a real distinction between a *posse agere* and *actu agere*.

No evidence has ever been produced that he holds such a view, and the purpose of this section is simply to relate the vicissitudes of St Thomas's thought on *actio*. In an early period he disagreed with Aristotle (§1.1); in a later period he agreed with Aristotle but retained his own earlier terminology (§1.2); and at all times there are a variety of meanings which he attributes to the term *actio* (§1.3). The one very clear point is that, if he made a real distinction between *posse agere* and *actu agere*, then he did so only in his mind and never in his writing.[2]

1.1 Actio *in the Early Period*

It will be well to begin with an explicit rejection of Aristotle's doctrine.

> Videtur quod possit esse eadem actio bona et mala. Quia, ut in III *Physic.*, text. 22, dicitur, idem est motus qui in agente est actio et in patiente passio, secundum substantiam, ratione differens; sicut eadem est via ab Athenis ad Thebas, et de Thebis ad Athenas. Sed contingit actionem esse malam, et passionem bonam; unde dicitur: 'Actio displicuit,' scilicet Iudaeorum; 'Passio grata fuit,' scilicet Christi. Ergo contingit eundum actum esse bonum et malum.[3]

---

2 On later opinions, see below, §1.3.5.
3 [It seems that the same action can be both good and evil. For, as is said in the *Physics* III, text. 22, it is the same movement substantially, with a mental difference, which is action in the agent and passion in the patient; as it is the same road from Athens to Thebes and from Thebes to Athens. But it

The objection is a valid argument. According to Aristotle *actio* and *passio* are one and the same reality. According to common doctrine the action of the Jews was wicked, the passion of our Lord was good. Therefore one and the same reality can be both good and bad.

The answer is a flat rejection of Aristotle's position. This rejection is supported by an appeal to Avicenna.

> Ad primum ergo dicendum, quod cum actio sit in agente et passio in patiente, non potest esse idem numero accidens quod est actio et quod est passio, cum unum accidens non possit esse in diversis subiectis; unde etiam Avicenna dicit quod non est eadem numero aequalitas in duobus aequalibus, sed specie tantum.[4] Sed quia eorum differentia non est nisi penes terminos, scilicet agens et patiens, et motus abstrahit ab utroque termino: ideo motus significatur ut sine ista differentia, et propter hoc dicitur quod motus est unus ...[5]

Here, then, *actio* and *passio* are two different accidents in two different subjects; it is simply impossible for the two to be one and the same thing. Avicenna is the man to follow.

But to show at once that there are two periods in St Thomas's thought, the treatment of the same objection in the *Prima secundae* may be cited; here the answer is that what physically is one may morally be manifold. In the response the distinction is drawn.

---

can happen that the action is bad and the passion good; and therefore it is said, *The action was displeasing*, namely that of the Jews, *The passion was pleasing*, namely, that of Christ. Therefore it can happen that the same act is good and evil] *Super II Sententiarum*, d. 40, q. 1, a. 4, ob. 1.

4 If *A* and *B* are equal, the equality of *A* to *B* is a different entity from the equality of *B* to *A*.

5 [To the first objection it has to be said that, since action is in the agent and passion in the patient, the accident cannot be numerically the same which is an action and which is a passion, since one accident cannot be in different subjects; and therefore Avicenna too says that the equality is not numerically the same in two equal things, but only specifically (the same). But because their difference is found only in the terms, namely, the agent and the patient, and movement abstracts from both terms, therefore the movement is understood as (being) without that difference, and on this account it is said that the movement is one] Ibid. ad 1m. The latter part of the answer refers to Aristotle's argument [as found in ob. 1]. See *In III Phys.*, lect. 5.

Si ergo accipiatur unus actus prout est in genere moris, impossibile est quod sit bonus et malus bonitate et malitia morali. Si tamen sit unus unitate naturae, et non unitate moris, potest esse bonus et malus.[6]

And so to the same objection as that cited above:

Ad secundum dicendum quod actio et passio pertinent ad genus moris, inquantum habent rationem voluntarii. Et ideo secundum quod diversa voluntate dicuntur voluntaria, secundum hoc sunt duo moraliter, et potest ex una parte inesse bonum, et ex alia malum.[7]

The difference between the two answers is manifest. In the commentary on the *Sentences* Aristotle is rejected and Avicenna cited. In the *Summa* an answer is found that leaves Aristotle's position untouched.

It has been shown that in the commentary on the *Sentences actio* is in the agent. The next question is, What precisely is the *actio* that is in the agent?

The answer to this is a distinction.

Some of the predicaments denote an inherent reality, such as quality and quantity. Others involve a relativity, in which one must distinguish between their principle, which is some inherent form, and their *ratio formalis*, which is not. The obvious example of this is *actio*.

... secundum diversam naturam generis diversus est modus deno-minationis. Quaedam enim genera secundum rationem suam signifi-cant *ut inhaerens*, sicut qualitas et quantitas, et huiusmodi; et in talibus not fit denominatio nisi per formam inhaerentem, quae est principium secundum aliquod esse substantiale vel accidentale.[8]

---

6 [If therefore one act is taken as it is in the genus of morality, it is impossible that it be good and evil with a moral goodness and a moral wickedness; but if it is one with the unity of a nature, and not with the unity of morals, it can be good and evil] *Summa theologiae*, 1-2, q. 20, a. 6.

7 [To the second objection it has to be said that action and passion pertain to the genus of morality insofar as they have the character of being voluntary; and therefore insofar as (actions) are called voluntary with reference to a different will, in this respect they are morally two, and on one side good can inhere (in a subject) and on another evil] Ibid. ad 2m.

8 The truth of the assertion, 'The goose is white and weighs ten pounds,' posits in the goose two entitative determinations: a quality, whiteness; and a quantity, ten pounds weight.

Quaedam autem significant secundum rationem suam, *ut ab alio ens*, et non *inhaerens* sicut praecipue patet in actione. Actio enim, secundum quod est actio, significatur *ut ab agente*; et quod sit ab agente, hoc accidit sibi inquantum est accidens.[9] Unde in genere actionis denominatur accidens per id quod ab eo est, et non per id quod principium eius est, sicut dicitur actione agens; nec tamen actio est principium agentis, sed e converso.[10] Et si per impossibile poneretur esse aliquam actionem quae non esset accidens non esset inhaerens, et tamen denominaret agentem; et tunc agens denominaretur per id quod ab eo est, et in eo non est ut inhaerens. Sed quia cuiuslibet actionis principium est aliqua forma inhaerens, ideo aliquid potest dici *agens* duobus modis: vel ipsa actione, quae denominat agentem, et non est principium eius; vel forma, quae est principium actionis in agente ...[11]

The foregoing is not extremely clear. Still, certain points are certain: action is not predicated in the same way as quality and quantity. There is the

9   One might have expected *quod sit in agente hoc accidit ei inquantum est accidens*. Then there would be the parallel to *esse in* and *esse ad*. The question treated pertains to the theory of the Blessed Trinity. [In fact the Mandonnet edition has *in agente*, but the edition Lonergan used had *ab agente*.]

10   In other words, the predication 'Peter acts' denominates Peter as acting. But the denomination is based not on the principle of Peter's action but on what comes from that principle.

11   [there is a different mode of denomination according to the different nature of the genus. For some genera according to their proper character are understood *as inhering*, for example, quality and quantity and such; and in such beings there is no denomination except by the inherent form, which is a principle according to some being, substantial or accidental. But some genera according to their proper character are understood *as being from another* and not *inherent*, as is especially clear in action. For action, as action, is understood *as from an agent*, and that it is from (see note 9) the agent just happens to it insofar as it is an accident. And so in the genus of action an accident is denominated by that from which it is, and not by that which is its principle, as 'agent' is named from 'action'; and nevertheless action is not the principle of the agent, but the contrary is the case. And if by an impossible (hypothesis) it were supposed that there is some action which was not an accident it would not be inherent, and nevertheless it would denominate the agent, and then the agent would be denominated by that which is from it and is not in it as inhering. But because the principle of any action whatever is some form that is inherent, therefore something can be called *agent* in two ways: either by the action which denominates the agent and is not its principle, or by the form which is the principle of action in the agent] *Super I Sententiarum*, d. 32, q. 1, a. 1.

principle of action, which is a form inhering in the agent. There is also a *ratio formalis* that is termed *ut ab agente* and that seems to be asserted in virtue of the effect resulting from the principle. In brief, though the passage is not conclusively against the real distinction between *posse agere* and *actu agere*, nonetheless it would embarrass anyone who maintained that distinction.

However, the same point comes up in the *De potentia*, and here the parallel between action and the *esse in* and *esse ad* of relations is quite manifest. Further, the point at issue is settled quite definitely: *actio* ceases to be without any change in its subject. It would be a little difficult to maintain that something real ceases to be without any change being involved. After the nature of relation is exposed, the argument turns to *actio*.

> Et ita relatio est aliquid inhaerens, licet non ex hoc ipso quod sit relatio; sicut et actio ex hoc quod est actio, consideratur *ut ab agente*; in quantum vero est accidens, consideratur ut in subiecto agente. Et ideo nihil prohibet quod esse desinat huiusmodi accidens sine mutatione eius in quo est, quia sua ratio non perficitur prout est in ipso subiecto, sed prout transit in aliud; quo sublato, ratio huius accidentis tollitur quidem quantum ad actum, sed manet quantum ad causam; sicut et subtracta materia, tollitur calefactio, licet maneat calefactionis causa.[12]

This would seem to be clear. *Calefactio* is *actu agere*; *calefactionis causa* is *posse agere*. Still, the transition from the one to the other is an illustration of the removal of *actio* without any change occurring in its subject. Yet note that *actio* is in the subject.

It might be too much to expect that St Thomas should also very conveniently assert that the converse transition from *posse agere* to *actu agere* is

12 [And so a relation is something inhering (in a subject), though that does not result from the mere fact that it is a relation; as action, too, from the fact that it is action, is considered *as from an agent*, but as an accident it is considered as in the acting subject. And therefore there is nothing to prevent an accident of this kind from ceasing to be without (involving) a change of that (subject) in which it is, because its being is not completed insofar as it is in that subject, but insofar as it passes on to another; with the removal of that (passing on), the being of this accident is removed in what regards the act but remains in what regards the cause; as is the case also when, with the removal of the material (to be heated), the heating is removed, though the cause of heating remains] *De potentia*, q. 7, a. 9, ad 7m [Lonergan's emphasis].

without any real change in its subject; yet the following is sufficiently clear to be really convincing.

> ... relatio in hoc differt a quantitate et qualitate: quia quantitas et qualitas sunt quaedam accidentia in subiecto remanentia; relatio autem non significat, ut Boethius dicit, *ut in subiecto manens*, sed *ut in transitu quodam ad aliud*; unde et Porretani dixerunt, relationes non esse inhaerentes, sed assistentes, quod aliqualiter verum est, ut posterius ostendetur. Quod autem attribuitur alicui *ut ab eo in aliud procedens* non facit compositionem cum eo, sicut nec actio cum agente. Et propter hoc etiam probat Philosophus in v *Phys.*, quod in *ad aliquid* non potest esse motus: quia, sine ulla mutatione eius quod ad aliud refertur, potest relatio desinere ex sola mutatione alterius, sicut etiam de actione patet, quod non est motus secundum actionem nisi metaphorice et improprie; sicut exiens de otio in actum mutari dicimus, quod non esset si relatio vel actio significaret aliquid in subiecto manens.[13]

Here, apparently out of deference to Boethius, *manens* is used where previously there has been *inhaerens*. Here again, unlike quantity and quality, relation and action cease to exist without any change in their subjects. But in addition there is the negation of a real distinction between agent and action: *quod autem attribuitur alicui 'ut ab eo in aliud procedens' non facit compositionem cum eo.* Finally, metaphors apart, there is no *motus secundum actionem*, no real difference involved in the transition from the *otium* of *posse agere* to the *actus* of *actu agere*.

13 [a relation differs from quantity and quality in this, that quantity and quality are accidents of some kind that remain in the subject; but, as Boethius says, 'relatio' does not mean *as remaining in the subject*, but *as in a certain transit to another*; and therefore the Porretan school too said that relations are not inherent but assisting, which is true in a way, as will be shown later. But that which is attributed to something *as proceeding from it to something else* does not enter into composition with it, as neither does action (enter into composition) with the agent. And on this account the Philosopher too proves in the *Physics*, book 5, that there cannot be motion in (*the being related*) *to something*, because without any change in that which is related to another, a relation can cease to be through the change alone of the other; as also is clear about action, that there is no movement as regards action except metaphorically and improperly; as we say that one passing from leisure to act is changed; which would not be the case if relation or action signified something remaining in the subject] Ibid. q. 7, a. 8.

Briefly, one might in three different ways assert a real difference between *posse agere* and *actu agere*. First, one might say that the emergence of the predicament *actio* involved a real change. Second, one might say that the presence of the predicament *actio* involved a composition. Third, one might say that the disappearance of the predicament *actio* involved a real change. Again, the same view might be denied in three ways. One might deny that the emergence of the predicament *actio* involved a real change: such a denial St Thomas makes when he asserts that there is no *motus secundum actionem* except metaphorically and improperly. Again, one might deny that the presence of the predicament *actio* involved a real composition: such a denial is to be found in St Thomas's assertion *non facit compositionem cum eo*. In the third place, one might deny that the disappearance of the predicament *actio* involved a real change: and such a denial is explicit in the repeated *sine mutatione eius in quo est*.

Since, then, St Thomas makes use of all possible means to deny a real distinction between *posse agere* and *actu agere*, one cannot but conclude that perhaps he means what he says.

However, to preclude the more facile type of tergiversation, it will be well to add a few observations.

First, the statements quoted are perfectly general. They are of the utmost generality possible. They are made with regard to the predicament *actio* as such. Such statements admit no exceptions.

Second, the statements quoted are from passages that deal with the theory of the Blessed Trinity and the theory of divine immutability. It might be suggested that, though St Thomas speaks generally, really he is envisaging a very special case. To put the objection bluntly, St Thomas says one thing and means another.

This position is untenable for three reasons. First, the assumption that St Thomas says one thing and means another necessarily eliminates St Thomas entirely: for if what St Thomas says is not the sole criterion of what he means, then the sole criterion is what any Tom, Dick, or Harry fancies him to mean. That is absurd.

The second reason is that St Thomas is a coherent thinker. He will not hold a view simply to solve difficulties in speculating about the divine Persons or the divine attributes, and then turn around to adopt another theory when he comes to an analysis of the facts of experience.

The third reason is that, as a matter of fact, St Thomas is not exclusively envisaging a very special case. He explicitly applies his theoretical position to one of the four elements, fire; he distinguishes between *calefactio* and *calefactionis causa*; and the distinction between the two is such that the *calefactio* can cease *sine mutatione eius in quo est.*

1.2 The Aristotelian Position

It has been shown that up to the *De potentia* St Thomas considered *actio* to be in the agent, that he explicitly rejected Aristotle's view which identifies *actio* with *passio*, that in the *Prima secundae* he solves the difficulty of the *Sentences* without rejecting Aristotle. In his commentaries on the *Metaphysics*, the *Physics*, and the *De anima*, the Aristotelian position is exposed, accepted, and defended.

The fundamental exposition is in the third book in the *Physics*,[14] in which Aristotle works out the nature of motion.

Seven terms are used: *motivum, movens, mobile, motum, motus, actio, passio.* Their definitions are as follows.

> *Motivum est id quod potest movere.*
> *Movens est id quod movet.*
> *Mobile est id quod potest moveri.*
> *Motum est id quod movetur.*
> *Motus est actus existentis in potentia in quantum huiusmodi.*
> *Actio est motus ut ab hoc, ut ab agente.*
> *Passio est motus ut in hoc, ut in patiente.*

The doctrine is concerned with the objective content of these terms. It may summarily be expressed as follows.

First, there is no real distinction between *motivum* and *movens*.

Second, there is an adequate real distinction between *movens* and *motus*, between *movens* and *mobile*, between *mobile* and *motus*.

Third, there is a real but inadequate distinction between *mobile* and *motum*, *motus* and *motum*.

Fourth, the reality of *motus* is common to both *actio* and *passio*. In other words, there is one entity, *motus*, which from its relation to its origin is termed *actio*, which from its relation to its subject is termed *passio*.

Fifth, both the active potency of the *motivum* and the passive potency of the *mobile* have a transition from potency to act. But the two transitions do not involve two acts. There is only one act for both potencies. This one act

14 *In III Phys.*, lect. 4–5.

pertaining to both is the *motus*. The *motus* is in the *mobile* but from the *movens*. And, inasmuch as it is in the *mobile*, it is *passio*; inasmuch as it is from the *movens*, it is *actio*.

Sixth, the foregoing does not involve a denial of the distinction between *actio* and *passio*. Going from Thebes to Athens is not going from Athens to Thebes. But the road from Thebes to Athens is the same as the road from Athens to Thebes. Similarly, though the reality of *actio* and *passio* is basically the single entity *motus*, still this one reality in the relativity of its dynamism has two terms, an origin and a subject; inasmuch as it is from the origin it is *actio*; inasmuch as it is in the subject it is *passio*.

So much for an exposition of the doctrine; St Thomas's commentary may now be considered. This falls into two parts. In the first he simply presents Aristotle's position. In the second he raises the general question of the nature of predication. With regard to the former it might be maintained that St Thomas was merely telling what Aristotle meant without taking any responsibility for it. But such an interpretation cannot be placed on the second part where he deals with a large issue that goes quite beyond the text of Aristotle.

First, with regard to the mover, one has to distinguish between its being moved as a mover and its happening to be moved when moving.

> ... quamvis movens moveatur, motus tamen non est actus moventis, sed mobilis secundum quod est mobile. Et hoc consequenter manifestat (Aristoteles) per hoc quod moveri *accidit* moventi, et non per se ei competit ...[15]

Second, the question arises whether motion is in the mover or in the moved.

> Solet enim esse dubium apud quosdam, utrum motus sit in movente aut in mobili. Sed hoc dubium declaratur ex praemissis.[16] Manifestum est enim quod actus cuiuslibet est in eo cuius est actus; et sic manifestum est quod actus motus est in mobili, cum sit actus mobilis, causatus tamen in eo a movente.[17]

15 [although the thing moving is moved, still movement is not the act of the thing moving but of the movable thing insofar as it is movable. And this he (Aristotle) shows afterwards, reasoning that being moved *just happens to* the thing moving, and does not belong to it per se] Ibid. lect. 4, § 302.
16 That is, the definition of motion.
17 [It is usual for doubt to arise among some as to whether movement is in the mover or in the movable thing. But this doubt is resolved from what has

Third, it is shown that the *motivum* must have some act.

> Quidquid enim dicitur secundum potentiam et actum, habet
> aliquem actum sibi competentem: sed sicut in eo quod movetur
> dicitur mobile secundum potentiam inquantum potest moveri,
> motum autem secundum actum inquantum actu movetur; ita ex
> parte moventis motivum dicitur secundum potentiam, inquantum
> scilicet potest movere, motus autem in ipso agere, id est, inquantum
> agit actu. Oportet igitur utrique, scilicet moventi et mobili,
> competere quemdam actum.[18]

Here, then, the distinction between *posse agere* and *actu agere* is clearly drawn,
and the question is put, What constitutes the reality of *actu agit*? One need
only read the next paragraph to see what St Thomas considers Aristotle's
view on the matter.

> ... ostendit (Aristoteles) quod idem sit actus moventis et moti.
> Movens enim dicitur inquantum aliquid agit, motum autem in-
> quantum patitur; sed idem est quod movens agendo causat, et quod
> motum patiendo recipit. Et hoc est quod dicit, quod movens est
> *activum mobilis*, id est, actum mobilis causat. Quare oportet unum
> actum esse utriusque, scilicet moventis et moti: idem enim est quod
> est a movente ut a causa agente, et quod est in moto ut in patiente et
> recipiente.[19]

---

been said. For it is clear that the act of anything at all is in that to whom the
act belongs; and thus it is clear that the act of movement is in the movable
thing, since it is the act of the movable thing, but caused in it by the mover]
Ibid. § 303.

18 [Whatever is said as regards potency and act has some act pertaining to it.
But just as, in the thing that is moved, 'movable' is said as regards potency
insofar as it can be moved, but 'moved' (is said) as regards act insofar as it is
actually moved, so from the side of the mover, 'moving power' is said as
regards potency insofar, namely, as it can move, but movement (is) in the
agent itself, that is insofar as it actually moves. It is therefore necessary that
some act pertain to each, that is, to mover and to movable] Ibid. § 305.

19 [He (Aristotle) shows that the same act is act of the mover and the moved.
For 'mover' is said insofar as something acts, but 'moved' insofar as it is
changed; but it is the same thing which as mover causes by acting and which
as moved is changed by receiving. And this is what he says (in stating) that
the mover is the 'active force of the movable thing,' that is, it causes the act
of the movable thing. And therefore it is necessary that there be just one act
of the two, namely, of the mover and of the moved; for it is the same thing
that is from the mover as from agent cause, and is in the patient as receiver]
Ibid. § 306.

There is, then, one and the same *actus* actuating both the active potency of the mover and the passive potency of the moved; and this one and the same *actus* is not in the mover but from the mover and in the moved.

Aristotle has a full realization of the paradox of his position, and accordingly proceeds to draw a list of the objections that may be raised against it by considering the terms *actio* and *passio*. He begins by taking it for granted that *actio* is a motion and *passio* a motion; he then asks whether there are one or two motions. On the supposition that there are two, it would follow that either the motion *actio* is in the agent and the motion *passio* is in the recipient, or that both motions are in the agent, or that both are in the recipient. He excludes the view that any motion is in the agent on the following grounds.

> Si enim aliquis dicat quod actio est in agente et passio in patiente; actio autem est motus quidam, ut dictum est; sequitur quod motus sit in movente ... In quocumque autem est motus, illud movetur; quare sequitur vel quod omne movens moveatur, vel quod aliquid habeat motum et non moveatur; quorum utrumque videtur inconveniens.[20]

In the present passage St Thomas leaves it to the intelligence of his reader to see the inconvenience. To put *motus* in the mover without the mover being moved is a contradiction. On the other hand, to assert that *omne movens movetur* is to eliminate the possibility of a *motor immobilis*; and as a *motor immobilis* is required if there is any motion at all, *omne movens movetur* eliminates all motion. Parmenides would have won.

But while the whole argument of the *Physics* cannot be anticipated in the third book, in the commentary on the *De anima* St Thomas explicitly notes that *omne movens movetur* is not a necessary truth because *actio est in passo*. His occasion is Aristotle's assertion that sound and hearing are one and the same objective reality.

> Manifestum est autem, quod auditus patitur a sono; unde necesse est, quod tam sonus secundum actum, qui dicitur sonatio, quam

---

20 [For if someone says that action is in the agent and passion in the patient, but action is a certain movement, as has been said, it follows that movement is in the mover ... But wherever there is movement in a thing, that thing is moved; and therefore it follows, either that every mover is moved, or that something has movement and is not moved. And both of these (conclusions) seem unacceptable] Ibid. lect. 5, § 311.

auditus secundum actum, qui dicitur auditio, sit in eo quod est
secundum potentiam, scilicet in organo auditus. Et hoc ideo, quia
actus activi et motivi fit in patiente, et non in agente et movente.
Et ista est ratio, quare non est necessarium, quod omne movens
moveatur. In quocumque enim est motus, illud movetur. Unde, si
motus et actio, quae est quidam motus, esset in movente, sequeretur
quod movens moveretur.[21]

The following remark reveals St Thomas's personal view. To posit a real
distinction between *posse agere* and *actu agere* in the agent implies *omne
movens movetur*. That clearly denies any *motor immobilis* and so the possibility
of any motion. So far, then, from this distinction being the very stuff and
fiber of St Thomas's thought, it is considered by him to be a fundamental
error, an error of the type he characterizes exactly and truly in the the *De
malo*, q. 6, a. 1 c.

It has been shown that Aristotle, St Thomas independently of Aristotle,
and St Thomas commenting Aristotle all agree in denying that there is in
the cause qua cause any real difference between *posse agere* and *actu agere*.
But as soon as St Thomas finishes his exposition of Aristotle in *In III Phys.*,
lect. 5, he raises the general question of the nature of the predicaments and
of predication. A few quotations will be well worth the space.

... sciendum est quod ens dividitur in decem praedicamenta non
univoce, sicut genus in species, sed secundum diversum modum
essendi. Modi autem essendi proportionales sunt modis praedicandi.
Praedicando enim aliquid de aliquo altero, dicimus hoc esse illud:
unde et decem genera entis dicuntur decem praedicamenta.[22]

21 [But it is clear that hearing (faculty or organ) receives from the sound; and
so it is necessary that both the sound as regards (its) act which is called
sounding, and hearing as regards its act which is called hearing, be in that
which is according to potency, namely, in the organ of hearing. And this (is
necessary) because the act of the active and moving thing is realized in the
recipient and not in the agent and mover. And that is the reason why it is
not necessary that every mover be moved. For wherever there is movement
in a thing, that thing is moved. And so if movement and action, which is a
certain movement, were in the mover, it would follow that the mover would
be moved] *In III De anima*, lect. 2, § 592.
22 [one must realize that being is divided into ten predicaments, not
univocally as a genus (is divided) into species, but according to the variety
in (their) mode of being. But the modes of being are proportional to the
modes of predicating. For in predicating something of something else, we
say that this is that; and so also the ten genera of being are called the ten
predicaments] *In III Phys.*, lect. 5, § 322.

In other words, there is the logico-metaphysical parallel, but all predication is not of the same nature. The ten predicaments are not univocally but analogically *entia*. To continue:

> Tripliciter autem fit omnis praedicatio.
>
>   Unus quidem modus est, quando de aliquo subiecto praedicatur id quod pertinet ad essentiam eius, ut cum dico *Socrates est homo*, vel *homo est animal*; et secundum hoc accipitur praedicamentum substantiae.
>
>   Alius autem modus est quo praedicatur de aliquo id quod non est de essentia eius, tamen inhaeret ei. Quod quidem vel se habet ex parte materiae subiecti, et secundum hoc est praedicamentum quantitatis ... aut consequitur formam, et sic est praedicamentum qualitatis ... aut se habet per respectum ad alterum, et sic est praedicamentum relationis ...
>
>   Tertius autem modus praedicandi est, quando aliquid extrinsecum de aliquo praedicatur per modum alicuius denominationis ... Sic igitur secundum quod aliquid denominatur a causa agente, est praedicamentum passionis, nam pati nihil est aliud quam suscipere aliquid ab agente: secundum autem quod e converso denominatur causa agens ab effectu, est praedicamentum actionis, nam actio est actus ab agente in aliud, ut supra dictum est.[23]

The foregoing is extremely pertinent, for it attacks the very root of the error we are combatting. Why is a real distinction between *posse agere* and *actu*

---

23 [But all predication occurs in (one of) three ways.
    There is one way when there is predicated of some subject that which pertains to its essence, as when I say 'Socrates is a man,' or 'a man is an animal'; and according to this way is understood the predicament of substance.
    But another way is that in which there is predicated of a thing something which is not of its essence but still inheres in it. And this may be from the side of the matter of the subject, and accordingly there is the predicament of quantity ... or it follows the form, and so there is the predicament of quality ... or its being is that of reference to another, and so there is the predicament of relation.
    But there is a third way of predicating when something extrinsic is predicated of something by way of some denomination ... In this way therefore according as something is denominated from the agent cause, there is the predicament of passion, for to suffer is nothing else than to receive something from the agent. But according as on the contrary the agent cause is denominated from the effect, there is the predicament of action, for action is an act (going) from the agent to another, as was said above] Ibid.

agere so easily foisted on St Thomas? Because *Peter can act but is not acting and Peter is actually acting* are contradictory propositions. Therefore, there must be an objective real difference involved by the transition from the truth of one proposition to the truth of the other. That is perfectly true. What is overlooked is that the emergence of the effect does supply such a real difference in the objective field. And the reason why it is overlooked is that it is assumed that all predication is of exactly the same nature, that *ens* divides univocally into the ten predicaments the way a genus divides into its species. Such a blunder cannot be attributed to St Thomas.

There is no need to give the data from the commentary on the *Metaphysics*. The doctrine is identical. The exposition of the doctrine is identical. Notably enough, there is the same spontaneous introduction of an explanation of the analogy of predication. The one difference is that the treatment is much briefer.[24]

1.3 Terminology

Objections that may be raised against the foregoing are of two kinds. It may be said that the argument applies only to transient action: suppose that it does, that does not show that St Thomas ever affirmed the contradictory with respect to immanent action; but in point of fact the argument is perfectly general, it appeals to general principles, and, particularly in the *De potentia*, what is treated is the idea of *actio* as such.

More serious difficulty may arise from innumerable passages in St Thomas, for he uses the term *actio* in a variety of senses. To forestall such objections, the present section is devoted to an account of the use of the term *actio*. Four points are treated. First, the acceptance of Aristotle's theorem involves no change in terminology. Second, the term *actio* is frequently equivalent to the Greek *energeia* (*actus*): in this sense *actio* is immanent or transient. Third, confusions arise from the superposition of the above complications on those of the terms *operatio, motus*. Fourth, the meaning of *actio media* is examined. This is not a complete list of all the difficulties but merely an indication of the principal causes of confusion.

1.3.1 *Actio qua Actio*

By *actio qua actio* is meant the predicament as such, the pure difference between *posse agere* and *actu agere*.

24 *In XI Metaphys.*, lect. 9, §§ 2308–13.

In this respect St Thomas's terminology is almost always the same. One might have thought there would be a radical change after his firsthand contact with Aristotle. In fact, he accepts Aristotle's position but keeps his own terminology.

A striking illustration can be had in the commentary on the *Physics*. In *In III Phys.*, lect 5, §320, he is exposing Aristotle's thought and has *motus ut ab hoc* as *actio*, and *motus ut in hoc* as *passio*. But in §322, in his discussion of predication, *actio* is *actus ab agente in aliud*, while *passio*, so far from being *motus ut in hoc*, is an extrinsic denomination from the agent.

The *actus ab agente in aliud* recalls the *ut ab eo in aliud procedens* of *De potentia*, q. 7, a. 8, and that seems little more than an expansion of *ut ab agente* of *Super I Sententiarum*, d. 32, q. 1, a. 1.

Hence it is not surprising to find in the *Pars prima*, after a reference to Aristotle's *Physics*, book 3:

> ... licet actio sit idem motui, similiter et passio, non tamen sequitur, quod actio et passio sint idem; quia in actione importatur respectus *ut a quo est motus in mobili*, in passione vero *ut qui est ab alio*.[25]

This is simply Aristotle's theorem but St Thomas's terminology.

A more striking example is to be found in the theory of creation. In the *Pars prima* St Thomas argues that, since *actio* is *motus ut ab hoc* and in creation there is no motion, it follows that *creatio* is simply the relation. But though Aristotle's theorem is the basis of the whole argument here, Aristotle's terminology is no more used than in the earlier treatment in the *De potentia*.[26]

A study of the passages referred to will, I think, convince the reader that in the *De potentia* St Thomas has not yet accepted Aristotle's theorem, while in the *Pars prima* he has. On the other hand, he refuses to alter the

25 [although action is the same as movement, and similarly passion, still it does not follow that action and passion are the same; because in action there is implied a reference 'as that from which there is movement in the movable thing,' but in passion (the reference is) 'as that which is from another'] *Summa theologiae*, 1, q. 28, a. 3, ad 1m. Note that Aristotle's *Physics* [is] here applied to the immanent processions of the Blessed Trinity. See the somewhat parallel *De potentia*, q. 8, a. 2, ad 7m. The point made is fully explained in *In III Phys.*, lect. 5, §320.

26 *Subtracto autem motu ab actione et passione, nihil remanet nisi relatio* [With the removal of movement from action and passion, nothing remains except a relation] *Summa theologiae*, 1, q. 45, a. 3 c. See ibid. ad 1m, and a. 2, ad 2m. Turn then to *De potentia*, q. 3, aa. 2–3.

terminology previously worked out in his theory of the divine processions and of creation.[27]

1.3.2 *Actio, Energeia*

In Aristotle the predicaments of action and passion are *poiêsis* and *pathêsis*. On the other hand, potency and act are *dunamis* and *energeia*; further, act as perfection, attainment, is *entelekheia*.

In the ninth book of the *Metaphysics*[28] he is proving that act is prior to potency: this is the equivalent of the theorem *unumquodque agit secundum quod est actu*. Incidentally, he distinguishes between two kinds of *energeia*: one immanent, such as seeing; the other transient, such as building.

Now, if *energeia* is translated not by *actus* but by *actio*, there will follow a distinction between immanent and transient action instead of immanent and transient act. If, at the same time, it is assumed that *actio* is in the agent and *passio* in the recipient,[29] the result will be a marvelously confused terminology.

But in the commentary on the *Sentences* St Thomas held *actio* to be in the agent, *passio* in the recipient, and he apparently had a text that translated *energeia* by *actio*. The result is the following.

> Ad primum ergo dicendum, quod, ut Philosophus tradit in IX *Metaphys.*, text. 16, actionum quaedam transeunt in exteriorem materiam circa quam aliquem effectum operantur, ut patet in actionibus naturalibus, sicut ignis calefacit lignum, et in artificialibus, sicut aedificator facit domum ex materia; et in talibus actio [i.e., *energeia*] est recepta in eo quod fit per modum passionis, secundum quod motus est in moto ut in subiecto: et ideo in talibus est invenire actionem [i.e., St Thomas's predicament] in re agente, et passionem in re patiente.[30]

27 Whether this is [done] inadvertently or deliberately I cannot say.
28 Aristotle, *Metaphysics*, IX, 8; see Thomas Aquinas, *In IX Metaphys.*, lect. 7–9. [This note is the work of the editors.]
29 Recall that Aristotle identifies *actio* and *passio* with the *motus*.
30 [To the first objection it has to be said that, as the Philosopher teaches in *Metaphysics*, IX, text. 16, some actions pass into external matter, in regard to which they operate some effect, as is clear in actions of nature, as fire heats wood, and in actions on artifacts, as a builder makes a house out of his materials. And in such actions, the action (that is, *energeia*) is received in that which is affected as a type of movement, according to the principle that

It would seem that *actio* has two different meanings here, for it is both *recepta in eo quod fit per modum passionis* and at the same time it is *in re agente.*[31]

Unless *actio* is taken as a translation of *energeia*, such a passage as the following is unintelligible.

> ... quando praeter actum [A] ipsum potentiae, qui est actio [A'], sit aliquod operatum, actio [B''] talium potentiarum est in facto, et actus facti, ut aedificatio in aedificato ... Et hoc ideo, quia quando praeter actionem [A'] potentiae constituitur aliquod operatum, illa actio [B''] perficit operatum, et non operantem. Unde est in operato sicut actio [B''] et perfectio eius, non autem in operante.
>
> Sed quando non est aliquod opus operatum praeter actionem [A] potentiae, tunc actio [B''] existit in agente et ut perfectio eius, et non transit in aliquid exterius perficiendum; sicut visio est in vidente ...[32]

Here *actio* regularly means *energeia*. The one exception is in the incidental phrase *cui est actio*. Even there, the reference is not to the *ratio formalis* of the predicament, for that is at least notionally distinct from *actum ipsum potentiae*, but to its *esse in*, which is identical with *actum ipsum potentiae*.

For another instance in which it is particularly evident that *actio* is *energeia*,

---

movement is in the thing moved as in a subject; and therefore in such actions one can find action (that is, Thomas's predicament) in the agent thing and passion in the patient thing] *Super I Sententiarum*, d. 40, q. 1, a. 1, ad 1m.

31 Is this the origin of the extremely obscure distinction, *actio divina est formaliter immanens et virtualiter transiens* [divine action is formally immanent and virtually transient]?

32 [when besides the act (A) of the potency, which is an action (A'), there is something produced, the action (B'') of such potencies is in the thing made, and (is) the act of the thing made, as the (act of) building (is) in the (completed) building ... And this (is so) because when besides the action (A') of the potency some product is constituted, that action (B'') completes the product and not the thing operating. And therefore it (the action) is in the product as its action (B'') and (as) its completion, but not in the thing operating.

But when there is not some work produced besides the action (A) of the potency, then the action (B'') exists in the agent and (is there) as its perfection and does not pass over into something external to be completed; as vision (does) in the one seeing] *In IX Metaphys.*, lect. 8, §§ 1864–65. A means causal *actus*, B the *actus* that is effected. A' is the causal *actus* as *actus*, A'' is the causal *actus* as causal. B' is the immanent effect, B'' is the transient effect.

see *Summa theologiae*, 1, q. 54, a. 1, where *actio, actus,* and *actualitas* appear to be interchangeable terms.

1.3.3 *Actio, Operatio, Motus*

Though St Thomas does make sporadic efforts to stabilize a terminology, he seems to have been too occupied with real issues to be successful in fixing the meaning of all the words he uses. Thus, while *operatio* tends to denote the immanent act, it does so in two different senses: it is both the production of the immanent act, and the immanent act that is produced. Thus:

> ... duplex est actio. Una quae procedit ab agente in rem exteriorem, quam transmutat; et haec est sicut illuminare, quae etiam proprie *actio nominatur*. Alia vero actio est, quae non procedit in rem exteriorem, sed stat in ipso agente ut perfectio ipsius; et haec proprie dicitur operatio.[33]

Here the ambiguity of *actio* as the predicament and *actio* as the *energeia* effected by the activity is evident. In the first sentence *actio transmutat rem exteriorem*: it is the predicament. In the second sentence the *actio* is the *perfectio* that is immanently produced: it is the *energeia* that is effected.

One may not infer from the foregoing that *actio* will be restricted to transient activity, for in the *Contra Gentiles* we have in an introductory explanation:

> Prima igitur dictarum operationum, tamquam simplex operantis perfectio, *operationis* vindicat sibi nomen, vel etiam *actionis*: secunda vero, eo quod sit perfectio facti, *factionis* nomen assumit.[34]

Here it might seem that *operatio* and *actio* are used to translate the general term *energeia*, while *factio* is derived from Aristotle's predicament. As in the

---

33 [action is twofold. There is one that proceeds from the agent (and passes) into the external thing that it changes; and this is like (the action) 'to illuminate,' which also is properly *called action*. But there is another action which does not pass into an external thing, but stays in the agent itself as its perfection; and this is properly called operation] *De veritate*, q. 8, a. 6.

34 [Therefore the first of the aforesaid operations, as a simple perfection of the operator, claims for itself the name of *operation* or also of *action*; but the second, since it is a perfection of the thing made, assumes the name of *making*] *Summa contra Gentiles*, 2, c. 1.

De veritate cited above, *operatio* does not mean producing an immanent act but having one: for the reference is to God, whose immanent acts are not produced.

At this point the different senses of *actio* superpose on the different senses of *motus*. *Motus* is any of three or perhaps four things:

First, St Thomas's metaphysical idea of *transitus de potentia in actum*.

Second, Aristotle's physical idea, *actus existentis in potentia in quantum huiusmodi*: this can occur only in divisible and corporeal beings, as is demonstrated in *In VI Phys.*, lect. 5.

Third, Aristotle's loose sense of motion: seeing, understanding, loving; it is to be remembered that these are not immanent transitions from potency to act but immanent acts, *actus existentis in actu*. This is identical with the Platonic sense of motion, according to which God moves.[35]

Fourth, St Thomas's references to Aristotle's loose sense as a *titulus coloratus* for his metaphysical idea, for example, *Summa theologiae*, 1-2, q. 109, a. 1.

It is to be observed that the ambiguity of this last is identical with the ambiguity noted above on *operatio*. There results such a passage as the following.

> ... duplex est actio: una, quae transit in exteriorem materiam, ut calefacere et secare; alia, quae manet in agente, ut intelligere, sentire et velle. Quarum haec est differentia: quia prima actio non est perfectio agentis quod movet, sed ipsius moti; secunda autem actio est perfectio agentis. Unde, quia motus est actus mobilis, secunda actio, inquantum est actus operantis, dicitur motus eius; ex hac similitudine, quod, sicut motus est actus mobilis, ita huiusmodi actio est actus agentis; licet motus sit actus imperfecti, scilicet existentis in potentia, huiusmodi autem actio est actus perfecti, id est existentis in actu, ut dicitur in III *de Anima* [text. 28] ... Et per hunc modum etiam Plato posuit quod Deus movet se ipsum ...[36]

35 *In III De anima*, text. 28; *Summa contra Gentiles*, 1, c. 13; etc.
36 [action is twofold. There is one act that passes into external matter, like heating and cutting. There is another which remains in the agent, like (the action) to understand, to sense, and to will. And the difference of these (acts) is this, that the first action is not the perfection of the agent which does the moving but of the thing moved, but the second action is a perfection of the agent. And so, since movement is the act of the movable thing, the second action, insofar as it is the act of the operator, is called its movement, a name based on this likeness that, as movement is the act of

1.3.4 *Actio Media*

The fourth cause of obscure terminology is the *actio media* of Avicenna and the *Liber De causis.*

It is either intrinsic, an accidental form inhering in the agent as the *additio super esse* of the *De causis*; or extrinsic, as Avicenna's *virtus motiva efficiens*, St Albert's *virtus divina creata*, and more obviously the radiation of light or heat.[37]

Neither *actio media* is to be attributed to God.

> ... Deus ... non agit aliqua operatione media vel intrinseca, vel extrin-
> seca, quae non sit sua essentia: quia suum velle est suum facere, et
> suum velle est suum esse.[38]

But in the created will there is an *actio media* which is not the essence of the will.

> Aliud est agens per voluntatem, et in hoc distinguendum est: quod
> quoddam agit actione media quae non est essentia ipsius operantis;
> et in talibus non potest sequi effectus novus sine nova actione ...
> Quoddam vero sine actione media vel instrumento, et tale agens est
> Deus ...[39]

Here, the *actio media* appears to refer simply to the accidental act produced in the will when it makes its election. It is the *actio media intrinseca.* On the other hand, when an *actio media* is denied to the intellect the context

---

a movable thing, so an action of this kind is an act of the agent, though movement is an act of an imperfect thing, namely, of what exists in potency, whereas an action of this type is an act of a completed thing, that is, of something existing in act, as is said in *De anima*, III (text. 28) ... And in this way Plato too held that God moves himself] *Summa theologiae*, 1, q. 18, a. 3, ad 1m.

37 See below, § 5.3.

38 [God ... does not act by some mediate operation, be it either intrinsic or extrinsic, which is not his essence; because his willing is his doing, and his willing is his being] *Super II Sententiarum*, d. 15, q. 3, a. 1, ad 3m.

39 [Another (type of agent) is an agent through willing, and in this we must distinguish: there is an agent that acts by (means of) a mediate action which is not the essence of the operator itself, and in such cases a new effect cannot follow without a new action ... But there is (an agent that acts) without a mediate action or an instrument, and God is that kind of agent] *Super II Sententiarum*, d. 1, q. 1, a. 5, ad 11m (1ae ser.).

requires reference to the *actio media extrinseca.* What is denied is that knowledge is a transient activity of the knower on the known.[40]

The reader may be inclined to suspect that the image of light proceeding from the sun to the earth, or warmth proceeding from the fire through the room, may lie at the root of St Thomas's clinging to his old formula for predicamental action, namely, *ut ab agente in aliud transiens,* instead of taking over Aristotle's far simpler terminology. Such a view would, however, be a gross simplification of a very complex issue.

In the first place, St Thomas, irrespective of his own desires in the matter, has to write so as to be understood by his contemporaries; he has to answer their objections as they would formulate them; finally, he would only discredit his position if, by an excess of zeal, he seemed to reject what was true in cruder views.

In the second place, the Aristotelian terminology overlooks what to St Thomas was an essential point in the analysis of action, namely, that it sets up a twofold relation. He does not use Aristotle's *motus ut ab hoc* and *motus ut in hoc* because the theory of the divine processions requires an *ut a quo* and a *qui ab alio.*

In the third place, though he denies *actio media* in the intellectual act, he quite emphatically affirms the double relativity of the dynamism in intellection.[41]

In the fourth place, though he denies both intrinsic and extrinsic *actio media* in the case of God, still he is quite willing to say *ideo etiam creatio significatur ut media inter Creatorem et creaturam.*[42]

Thus, though the *actio media* may have been both a useful image and a useful mode of speech, it in no way clouds thought.

It is on that point that this account of St Thomas's use of the term *actio* must end. Though the confusions of interpreters of St Thomas on this matter are numerous, grave, and distressing, there is no confusion of any moment in the thought of St Thomas. He is above words.

1.3.5 Historical Note

The subsequent history of the term *actio* is rather rich in anomalies. The following may be mentioned.

40 See *De veritate,* q. 8, a. 6, ad 11m, and *Summa theologiae,* 1, q. 54, a. 1, ad 3m.
41 For example, *Summa theologiae,* 1, q. 28, a. 1, ad 4m.
42 [therefore creation too is understood as mediating between Creator and creature] *Summa theologiae,* 1, q. 45, a. 3, ad 2m.

(a) The Platonist view that *actio* is a relation in the cause,[43] which was developed and followed by St Thomas, is subsequently regarded as an opinion peculiar to the Scotist school. On the other hand, the Aristotelian analysis which St Thomas simply presents in commenting the *Physics* and the *Metaphysics* is commonly considered Thomist.[44]

(b) Probably owing to the difficulty of grasping that in immanent action there is a cause and an effect – a difficulty possibly increased by the anomalies in St Thomas's terminology – only a relatively small number of writers raise the question of the analysis of *actio* when the effect is immanent.[45] Though they employ the same argument as did Aristotle – namely, that *omne movens movetur* results in an infinite series – there does not seem to be any recognition that Aristotle had faced and solved the problem in precisely their fashion.

(c) Cajetan observing that St Thomas normally considered *actio* to be in the agent[46] seems to have been the first to desert what had previously and has since been termed the Thomist view.

(d) He is followed by John of St Thomas, who attempts a reconciliation of the two positions by the compromise of putting the *actio* half in the cause and half in the effect.[47] In this manner he succeeds in contradicting Aristotle, St Thomas's independent discovery, and St Thomas's agreement with Aristotle. He also derives an excellent argument in favor of the

---

43 See *Super librum De causis*, the text to lect. 20 and 31.

44 Suarez affirms this and naturally follows what he considers the Thomist view. See Francisco Suarez, *Disputationes metaphysicae*, ed. C. Berton (Hildesheim: Georg Olms Verlagsbuchhandlung, 1965), disp. 48, sect. 4 [vol. 2, p. 890, §6], where references are given to Hervaeus (Quodlib. 4), Capreolus (in 2, distinct. 1, q. 2, art. 3; in 4, d. 49, q. 1, art. 3), Soto (*3 Phys.*, q. 1, conc. 5), Ferrariensis (*In Summam contra Gentiles*, 2, c. 1; 2, c. 9; 3, c. 149), Soncinas (5 Met., q. 37). [References to Hervaeus, Capreolus, and Soncinas are given just as they appear in the Berton edition; the Ferrariensis reference is slightly expanded; '3 Phys.' is mentioned in Berton, but not Soto; nor is there reference there to *Contra Gentiles* 3, c. 149.]

45 See Agustino Trape, 'Il concorso divino nel pensiero di Egidio Romano,' unpublished thesis 615 (Rome: Gregorian University, 1938); Santo Santoro, 'Valenzianismo o Delfinismo?' *Estratto della Miscellanea Francescana* 38 (1938) 195–210; Wilhelm Hentrich, *Gregor von Valencia und der Molinismus* (Innsbruck: F. Rauch, 1928); Ludovicus de San, *Tractatus De Deo uno* (Louvain: C. Peeters, 1894), vol. 1, pp. 181–87.

46 Cajetan, *In Summam theologiae*, 1, q. 25, a. 1 [*LT* 4: 586].

47 *Joannis a Sancto Thoma Naturalis Philosophiae*, 1, q. 14, a. 4 (ed. Beato Reiser [Turin: Marietti, 1933], vol. 2, pp. 309–15).

Bannezian theory of physical premotion,[48] and his singular view seems to be implied by Fr N. del Prado.[49]

(e) The common expression *actio divina ad extra est formaliter immanens et virtualiter transiens* would be a use of the Platonist-St Thomas-Scotist manner of speech. On the other hand, the view that makes divine action formally transient would be Aristotelian.

(f) The common difficulty of reconciling divine immutability with divine liberty would seem to have a triple source: confused ideas on the nature of *actio*; a failure to grasp that premotion is required only in the *agens in tempore*; a curious analysis of free will which places freedom in the immanent effect and not in the immanent cause. The first two imply that God could not cause without changing. The third implies that God could not cause freely without producing in himself a contingent effect. Adding the three confusions together divine liberty becomes what is sometimes termed a metaphysical *clarum-obscurum*.

(g) Dominicus Bañez, unable to solve the problem of divine liberty,[50] concludes that human liberty cannot be more perfect than the divine.[51] As the only liberty he can ascribe to God is a judgment on an objectively indifferent object of choice, he thinks the same is quite enough to make man free. Accordingly, he profits by the occasion to point out that no matter what God foreknows, intends, or does with respect to the will, the act of will cannot but be free provided divine activity does not interfere with the judgment on the object of choice.[52]

(h) The Bannezian theory of physical premotion (not to be confused with that of St Thomas and of Aristotle, which is briefly presented in the next section) does not seem to arise from any explicit theory of *actio* but rather from a neglect of such theory. Thus Didacus Alvarez, when discussing sufficient grace, appeals to Cajetan, Medina, and the Ferrariensis as favoring his distinction between *posse agere* and *actu agere*. Not only is the

---

48 Ibid. q. 25, a. 2; Reiser, vol. 2, pp. 493–503.
49 Norbert del Prado, *De gratia et libero arbitrio* [see above, p. 3, note 1], vol. 2, p. 252.
50 Dominicus Bañez, *Scholastica commentaria in primam partem Summae theologicae S. Thomae Aquinatis*, 1, q. 19, a. 10 (Roma, 1584, p. 380 [Madrid: Editorial F.E.D.A., 1934, p. 442]).
51 Ibid. Rome (1584) 381 F, 382 B [Madrid (1934) 443–44; see above, p. 97, note 32].
52 Ibid. In the next chapter, § 1, it will be necessary to determine whether this is an instance of St Thomas's intellectualism or an instance of the logical dictum *ex falso sequitur quodlibet*.

appeal worthless, for the authors in question are discussing perseverance and so may mean no more than that there is a real difference between the possibility of an effect and the effect itself, but had Fr Alvarez taken the trouble to consult the Ferrariensis just six chapters earlier he would have found a very forceful refutation of his opinion.[53] Billuart goes so far as to affirm that a real distinction between *actio* and *potentia agendi* is one of the pillars of St Thomas's thought.[54]

2   Physical Premotion

Though St Thomas does not posit a real difference between *posse agere* and *actu agere*, nonetheless he always maintains the well-known Aristotelian doctrine of physical premotion. In the present section the nature of that doctrine is presented.

In proving the eternity of the world, Aristotle points out that the existence of mover and moved is not sufficient to account for the actuality of a motion. If mover and moved exist, motion is merely possible. For actual motion it is further necessary that they be in such a situation, mutual relation, or disposition, that the one can act on the other. Thus, let the heat of the equator be the mover and the cold of an iceberg be the moved: does the existence of the heat and of the cold suffice to account for the melting of the iceberg? The answer is that the existence accounts merely for the possibility of that motion or change. For actual motion the two must be brought together. Bringing them together is the premotion. And the premotion may consist either in a change of the mover (shifting the equator up to the pole) or in a change of the moved (the southward drift of the iceberg).

From the nature and necessity of premotion it follows that no motion can be the first in time, that is, that motion is eternal. For any motion that is not eternal was at some time nonexistent; therefore, there was a premotion to make it actual; and there was a premotion to that premotion; and so on to infinity. St Thomas presents the argument as follows.

---

53 Didacus Alvarez, *De auxiliis divinae gratiae*, 8n disp. 79 [reference as given by Lonergan; his bibliography has: 'D. Alvarez, *De Auxiliis Divinae Gratiae*, Lugduni 1620]. The relevant passages in the Ferrariensis are *In Summam contra Gentiles*, 3, cc. 155 and 149 [*LT* 14].

54 F.C.R. Billuart, *Summa s. Thomae*, vol. 3: *Tractatus De gratia*, diss. 5, a. 2, § 2 (Paris: Letouzey et Ané, 1880) 130.

... oportebit dicere quod sit alia mutatio prius facta in movente vel mobili ... quod sic patet. Quies enim est privatio motus: privatio autem non inest susceptivo habitus et formae nisi propter aliquam causam: erat ergo aliqua causa vel ex parte motivi vel ex parte mobilis, quare quies erat: ergo ea durante, semper quies remanebat. Si ergo aliquando movens incipiat movere, oportet quod illa causa quietis removeatur. Sed non potest removeri nisi per aliquem motum vel mutationem: ergo sequitur quod ante illam mutationem, quae dicebatur esse prima, sit alia mutatio prior, qua removetur causa quietis.[55]

The point to be observed is that it makes no difference whether the premotion changes the mover or the moved: this squares with Fr Stufler's discovery of the distinction between essential and accidental potency; if premotion is required in the mover, then it is in essential potency; if it is required in the moved, then the mover is in accidental potency.[56] But it also squares with the metaphorical transition from potency to act of *De potentia*, q. 7, a. 8; for if the mover changes from potency to act simply in virtue of a change in the moved, then the change in the mover is *metaphorice et improprie.*

Next, observe that the doctrine of physical premotion is universal. It will be well to copy out St Thomas at length on this point, for he has suffered from neglect.

Dicit ergo (Aristoteles) quod ex quo ita est, quod simili modo se habet in iis quae agunt secundum naturam et secundum intellectum, possumus universaliter de omnibus loquentes dicere, quod

55 [it will be necessary to say that there is another change made previously in the moving (power) or the movable ... which is seen as follows. For a state of rest is the privation of movement; but a privation is not had in what is susceptible of a habit or form except by reason of some cause; there was therefore some cause, either on the side of the motive force or on that of the movable, which was the reason for the state of rest; therefore, while that lasted, the state of rest always remained. If therefore at some time a moving force begins to move, it is necessary that that cause of rest be removed. But it cannot be removed except through some movement or change. It follows therefore that before that change which was said to be first, there be another prior change by which the cause of rest is taken away] *In VIII Phys.*, lect. 2, §976.

56 See *In VIII Phys.*, lect. 8 [§§1029 and 1036]; *De veritate*, q. 11, a. 1, ad 12m; Stufler, *Gott, Der erste Beweger aller Dinge* (see above, p. 83, note 83) 5–8.

quaecumque sunt possibilia facere aut pati aut movere vel moveri, non penitus possibilia sunt, idest non possunt movere aut moveri in quacumque dispositione se habeant; sed prout se habent in aliqua determinata habitudine et propinquitate ad invicem.[57]

Et hoc concludit ex praemissis: quia iam dictum est quod tam in agentibus secundum naturam, quam in agentibus secundum voluntatem, non est aliquid causa diversorum, nisi in aliqua alia habitudine se habens.[58] Et sic oportet quod quando appropinquant ad invicem movens et motum convenienti propinquitate, et similiter cum sunt in quacumque dispositione quae requiritur ad hoc quod unum moveat et aliud moveatur, necesse sit hoc moveri, et aliud movere.[59]

Si ergo non semper erat motus, manifestum est quod non se habebant in ista habitudine ut tunc unum moveret et aliud moveretur: sed se habebant sicut non possibilia tunc movere et moveri; postmodum autem se habent in ista habitudine ut unum moveat et aliud moveatur. Ergo necesse est quod alterum eorum mutetur.

Hoc autem videmus accidere in omnibus quae dicuntur ad aliquid, quod numquam advenit nova habitudo, nisi mutationem utriusque vel alterius; sicut si aliquid, cum prius non esset duplum, nunc factum est duplum, etsi non mutetur utrumque extremorum, saltem oportet quod alterum mutetur. Et sic si de novo adveniat habitudo per quam aliud moveat et aliud moveatur, oportet vel utrumque vel alterum moveri prius.[60]

57 On such a *dispositio* in the will, see *Summa theologiae*, 1-2, q. 10, a. 1, ad 2m; contrast the essential potency of the will, ibid. q. 9, a. 3, ad 2m; a. 4. On the cosmic aspect of such a *dispositio* see the treatment of fate, *Summa theologiae*, 1, q. 116, a. 2. See below, §4.3.

58 St Thomas makes an exception in the case of God; the reason is obvious, for God is not in time, and so the argument, which presupposes time, does not apply. See *In VIII Phys.*, lect. 2, §975.

59 On the necessity of motion once the *habitudo* is attained, see the parallel passage in *In IX Metaphys.*, lect. 4, §§1818–22.

60 [He (Aristotle) therefore says that from the fact that the situation is similar in those (agents) which act according to nature and (those which act) according to understanding, we can say, speaking universally about everything, that all things which it is possible to make or suffer, or to move (actively) or be moved, are not simply possible (patients); that is, they cannot move or be moved in any disposition whatever in which they exist, but (only) insofar as they exist in some determinate relationship and propinquity to one another.
And this he concludes from what had been said earlier; because it was

Clearly, there is no opposition between the theory of *actio* held by Aristotle or that held by St Thomas and, on the other hand, the theory of physical premotion which both of them hold. But perhaps St Thomas also held another and more metaphysical theory of physical premotion such as that of Bañez. Perhaps he did. But the *onus probandi* is on those who make the assertion. So far they have never attempted to show that there are two distinct theories of physical premotion in St Thomas.

3   Application

St Thomas affirms a number of times[61] that *Deus omnia applicat*. His meaning is the same as when he affirms that God moves all things to their appointed ends by his intellect.[62] This is proved as follows. First, application can mean physical premotion, for in the parallel passage in the *Metaphysics* it is so used. Second, application does mean physical premotion, for the assertion that God applies all things is deduced from the fact that God is an Aristotelian first mover. Third, the significance of the affirmation of universal divine application is to be found in the divergence between Aristotle and St Thomas: St Thomas's first mover is an intellectual agent, while Aristotle's is merely a final cause.

---

already stated that, as much in agents acting according to nature as in those which act according to will, there is nothing which is the cause of diversity unless it is something existing in some other relationship. And thus it is necessary that, when the mover and the moved approach one another in suitable propinquity, and likewise when they are in any disposition at all which is required for this that one move actively and the other be moved, it is then necessary that one be moved and the other move.

If therefore there was not always movement, it is clear that they did not exist in such a relationship that one should move and the other be moved; but they were like those things that cannot, (as they) then (exist), move and be moved. But afterwards they are in such a relationship that one (of them) moves and the other is moved. Therefore it is necessary that one of the two be changed.

But we see this to be the case in everything that is characterized as (related) to another, (namely) that a new relationship never occurs except by a change of both or of one (of them); as when something which before was not double is now made double, although it may not be the case that each of the extremes is changed, it is necessary that at least one (of them) be changed. And thus if there occur again a relationship by means of which one (of them) moves and the other is moved, it is necessary that either both or one (of them) be moved first] *In VIII Phys.*, lect 2, §978.

61 *Summa contra Gentiles*, 3, cc. 67 [§2418] and 70 [§2464]; *De potentia*, q. 3, a. 7; *Summa theologiae*, 1, q. 105, a. 5.

62 *De substantiis separatis*, c. 14, §129.

3.1 Application May Mean Physical Premotion

From the parallel passage in the *Metaphysics* it is evident that application can mean physical premotion. The two passages are as follows:

> *In IX Metaphys.*, lect. 4, § 1818: '... quando passivum appropinquat activo, in illa dispositione qua passivum potest pati et activum potest agere, necesse est quod unum patiatur et alterum agat; ut patet quando combustibile *applicatur* igni.'[63]

> *In VIII Phys.*, lect. 2, § 978: '... oportet quod quando appropinquant ad invicem movens et motum convenienti propinquitate, et similiter cum sunt in quacumque dispositione quae requiritur ad hoc quod unum moveat et aliud moveatur, necesse sit hoc moveri, et aliud movere.'[64]

Since in the *Metaphysics* the physical premotion of a *combustibile* to sufficient proximity to a fire is termed an application, it follows that application can mean an Aristotelian physical premotion.

3.2 Application Does Mean Physical Premotion

Since God is said to apply all things because he is first mover (in the Aristotelian sense), therefore application cannot be anything but physical premotion (in the Aristotelian sense).

The major is evident. The Aristotelian first mover is posited to account for the existence of the infinite series of terrestrial motions, in which each prior motion is a physical premotion to each subsequent motion.[65] There-

63   [when the passive (element) approaches the active in such a disposition that the passive can suffer and the active can act, it is necessary that one (of them) suffer and that the other act; as is clear when something combustible is *applied* to a fire.]

64   [it is necessary that, when the moving force and the thing moved approach one another with a suitable propinquity, and likewise when they are in any disposition at all which is required for this that one move actively and the other be moved, it is then necessary that one be moved and the other move.]

65   The eighth book of Aristotle's *Physics* demonstrates a cosmic scheme: there is an immovable first mover; there is an eternal and uninterrupted first motion (that of the heavenly spheres); there is the eternal series of *generabilia* and *corruptibilia* which sometimes move and sometimes do not. The argument is as follows; lect. 1, motion has to be accounted for; lect. 2–4, motion is eternal; lect. 5 and 6, some things sometimes move and

fore, the first mover (in the Aristotelian sense) is the cause of all motion and premotion (in the Aristotelian sense).

The minor is proved, first from St Thomas's general acceptance of the Aristotelian cosmic scheme, second from the manner in which he proves that God moves and applies all natural and voluntary agents.

(a) St Thomas accepts the Aristotelian cosmic scheme. Though there are differences, these are not pertinent to the issue before us. Thus, there are a number of Avicenna's Platonist tendencies in St Thomas,[66] and there is the denial that the intermediate beings create.[67] But though God is the sole cause of *esse*, creatures are the cause of *fieri*.[68] Hence the execution of providence is mediated:[69] to be observed is the fact that the execution of providence is a motion[70] and that there are no motions except those intended by providence;[71] hence did God not control the wills of angels and of men, there could be no execution whatever of providence in either the spiritual or material world.[72] In particular, the essential feature of the

---

sometimes do not move; lect. 7–13, there must be a *primum se movens*, one part moving and the other moved, to account for the continuity and perpetuity of the terrestrial series as a series (see especially lect. 12); lect. 14–20, the first motion must be perpetual and uniform circular local motion; lect. 21–23, the first mover must be spiritual.

Aristotle's fundamental idea is that the first mover cannot be the cause of the terrestrial *quandoque moventia*, because then he would have to act differently at different times and so himself need physical premotion; on the other hand, the *primum mobile* or *corpus caeleste* is constantly changing and so can cause the *quandoque moventia*. See *In VIII Phys.*, lect. 13, §§ 1084–85; *In XII Metaphys.*, lect. 6, §§ 2510–13; *In II De generatione et corruptione*, text. 56. Hence the *corpus caeleste* is the *primum alterans* or the *alterans non alteratum*: because it is moved locally it can cause alteration (*In VIII Phys.*, lect. 14, § 1088).

66 Avicenna deduces the Aristotelian hierarchy beginning from the first principle and proceeding along the lines of Plotinian emanations: this gives the cosmic structure a great measure of rigidity not to be found in Aristotle. Contrast *De potentia*, q. 5, a. 8, with *In II De caelo et mundo*, lect. 4, § 342 [see above, p. 78, note 57, where the *De potentia* passage is specified further as q. 5, a. 8, ad 1m].

67 *Summa theologiae*, 1, q. 45, a. 5, and passim.

68 *Super I Sententiarum*, d. 37, q. 1, a. 1; *Summa theologiae*, 1, q. 104, a. 1.

69 *Super II Sententiarum*, d. 15, q. 1, a. 2; *De veritate*, q. 5, aa. 8–9; *Summa contra Gentiles*, 3, cc. 77–79, 82, 91, 92; *Summa theologiae*, 1, q. 22, a. 3; q. 103, a. 6; q. 110, a. 1; q. 115, a. 3; and passim.

70 *Summa theologiae*, 1, q. 103, a. 5, ad 2m.

71 Ibid. 1-2, q. 109, a. 1; *Summa contra Gentiles*, 3, c. 94; *Summa theologiae*, 1, q. 19, a. 6; q. 103, a. 7.

72 *Summa contra Gentiles*, 3, c. 90 [§ 2654].

Aristotelian scheme, the function of the heavenly spheres, is repeatedly affirmed.[73]

(b) Not only does St Thomas accept the Aristotelian cosmic scheme, but in *De potentia*, q. 3, a. 7, he deduces from that scheme his conclusion that God moves and applies all things. His argument is as follows.

> Et quia natura inferior agens non agit nisi mota,[74] eo quod huiusmodi corpora inferiora sunt alterantia alterata;[75] caelum autem est alterans non alteratum,[76] et tamen non est movens nisi motum,[77] et hoc non cessat quousque perveniatur ad Deum:[78] *sequitur de necessitate* quod Deus sit causa actionis cuiuslibet rei naturalis ut movens et applicans virtutem ad agendum.[79]

73 *Super II Sententiarum*, d. 15, q. 1, a. 3 [ad 3m & ad 4m]; *De veritate*, q. 5, a. 9; *De potentia*, q. 5, aa. 7–10; q. 3, a. 7; *Summa contra Gentiles*, 3, cc. 82, 86; *Summa theologiae*, 1, q. 115, a. 3; and passim.

74 The terrestrial agent is *quandoque movens* (*In VIII Phys.*, lect. 5–6) and so needs premotion (ibid. lect. 2, §§ 976–78).

75 Motion is necessarily change either of place, of sensible quality, or of corporeal magnitude (*In V Phys.*, lect. 2–4; *In XI Metaphys.*, lect. 12). Alteration is change in sensible quality (*In VII Phys.*, lect. 4–5). There must be a *causa per se* for the series of terrestrial motions, and that cause must be outside the terrestrial series (*In VIII Phys.*, lect. 12). According to Aristotle, it cannot be the first mover and must be the *primum mobile* (*In VIII Phys.*, lect. 13, §§ 1084–85; ibid. lect. 14–20 [Lonergan wrote, '*In XII Metaphys.*, lect. 14–20,' but there are only twelve *lectiones* in that book; the change to *In VIII Phys.* is an editorial suggestion. See above, note 65.] St Thomas expresses the same need for the *primum mobile*, *Summa theologiae*, 1, q. 115, a. 3; *Summa contra Gentiles*, 3, c. 91.

76 The heavenly spheres are *non alteratum*, because change of place is not entitative (*In III Phys.*, lect. 5, § 322). But they cause alteration, for they change their position: that the cause change its locus is necessary if it alters (*In VIII Phys.*, lect. 14, § 1088). See *In XII Metaphys.*, lect. 6; *In VIII Phys.*, lect. 13, §§ 1084–85; *In II De generatione et corruptione*, text. 56.

77 On the *motor caeli*, see *Summa theologiae*, 1, q. 70, a. 3.

78 On angelic administration, see *De veritate*, q. 5, a. 8; *Summa contra Gentiles*, 3, c. 78; *Summa theologiae*, 1, q. 110, a. 1.

79 [And because an agent lower nature does not act unless it is moved – because of the fact that lower bodies of this kind are changed in (the act of) changing (others), while the heavens change (others) without being (themselves) changed – and nevertheless there is no mover unless it is moved, and this does not end till we come to God, *it follows of necessity* that God is the cause of the action of any natural thing whatever, as moving and applying a power to its action] *De potentia*, q. 3, a. 7. The *virtus rei naturalis* is not to be confused with the *virtus vel potentia operativa* of the angel in *Summa theologiae*, 1, q. 54, a. 3. The latter is a metaphysical potency limiting act. The former is

Has anyone tried to show that the Bannezian theory of physical premotion follows with necessity from the Aristotelian hierarchy? When anyone begins to make the attempt, it will be time to think of refuting the view. Meanwhile, *quod gratis asseritur gratis negatur.*

(c) The proof in *Contra Gentiles*, 3, c. 67, that God applies all things offers no ground for reasonable doubt that St Thomas understands by application a physical premotion in the Aristotelian sense.

> Quidquid applicat virtutem activam[80] ad agendum, dicitur esse causa illius actionis: artifex enim applicans virtutem rei naturalis ad aliquam actionem, dicitur esse causa illius actionis, sicut coquus decoctionis, quae est per ignem.[81] Sed omnis applicatio virtutis ad operationem est principaliter et primo[82] a Deo. Applicantur enim virtutes operativae[83] ad proprias operationes per aliquem motum vel corporis, vel animae.[84] Primum autem principium utriusque motus est Deus. Est enim primum movens omnino immobile, ut supra [1, c.13] ostensum est.[85] Similiter etiam omnis motus voluntatis quo applicantur aliquae virtutes ad operandum, reducitur in Deum sicut in primum appetibile[86] et in primum volentem.[87]

---

an Aristotelian accidental form, *forma quaedam habens esse firmum et ratum in natura.* Water is always wet, fire is always hot, nor is there any question of a transition from potency to act, as is evident from *De potentia*, q. 5, a. 8, ad omnia.

80 On the *virtutes activae, Summa theologiae*, 1, q. 115, a. 3, ad 2m.

81 The fire cooks because it is hot; the cook cooks because he sets the meat on the fire.

82 That is, as head of the hierarchy of movers: the first mover moves more than any lower mover. [Lonergan here referred to *In VIII Phys.*, lect. 11, §11; there does not seem to be any such number in any edition.]

83 The *virtus operativa* may be active, as is the heat of fire; or it may be passive, as the angelic intellect of *Summa theologiae*, 1, q. 54, a. 3.

84 The promotion or application of the *virtus* is effected by some corporeal or spiritual movement, not by a transition of the *virtus* from *posse agere* to *actu agere.*

85 It is not possible, and there has never been any attempt, to deduce the Bannezian theory from *Summa contra Gentiles*, 1, c. 13.

86 God uses the will to apply *virtutes operativae* because he is the *final* cause of the will's activity. This is incompatible with the Bannezian theory.

87 [Anything that applies an active power to (its) action is said to be the cause of that action; for an artisan, applying the power of a natural thing to some action, is said to be the cause of that action, as a cook in regard to cooking, which is (done) by fire. But all application of a power to its operation is principally and foremost by God. For operative powers are applied to their

It is clear that the cook applies the meat to the fire by a physical premotion in the Aristotelian sense. St Thomas says that God is the first cause of this and every other application, for God is the *motor immobilis*.

(d) In *Summa contra Gentiles*, 3, c. 70, God is again said to be the cause of all application, and the proof is the hierarchy of *virtutes*. In *Summa theologiae*, 1, q. 105, a. 5, one reads that God not merely applies but also conserves in being all forms.

(e) To conclude, if the followers of the Bannezian view [wish] to argue from St Thomas's *applicatio* to their *praemotio physica*, they have first of all to explain how St Thomas can deduce the *applicatio* in their sense from the cosmic hierarchy. Until they do so, they have no claim to pose as interpreters of St Thomas. Meanwhile, there is a convincing cumulation of evidence in favor of the view that by application St Thomas means physical premotion in his sense and Aristotle's sense, namely, that the transition of a situation from a state of rest to a state of activity presupposes a previous motion of some kind or other.

3.3 Application and Providence

The significance of the affirmation of universal divine application lies in the fundamental divergence between Aristotle and St Thomas.

Aristotle's problem of motion was to find a sufficient cause for the perpetuity and continuity of the terrestrial process as a process. Motion A presupposes motion B, motion B presupposes motion C, and so to infinity. But none of the movers within the process accounts for the process as a whole; nor do all of them together, for they are not together. Therefore there has to be a mover outside the process to account for the process as such.[88]

Now while Aristotle's wheeling heavens do necessitate continuous change on earth,[89] it remains that they do not account for anything more than the continuity of that change. They make it necessary that something keeps

---

proper operations by some movement of body or soul. But the first principle of both these motions is God. For he is the first and altogether immovable mover, as was shown above (book 1, chapter 13). Similarly too, every motion of the will by which certain powers are applied to (their) operation is reduced to God as to the first thing desired and the first thing willing] *Summa contra Gentiles*, 3, c. 67. On this [*et in primum volentem*] see the next section [3.3].

88 *In VIII Phys.*, lect. 12; *In XII Metaphys.*, lect. 5.
89 *In VIII Phys.*, lect. 13, §§1084–85; *In XII Metaphys.*, lect. 6.

happening; they do not determine precisely what is to happen.[90] And much less does the first mover do so, for he acts simply as final cause.[91] Thus the idea of divine design and controlling providence is simply absent from Aristotle's cosmic scheme; he compares the world to a household: the heavenly bodies, like the sons of the family, have their conduct mapped out for them; the terrestrial agents, like slaves and domestic animals, move a good deal at random.[92] Nor could Aristotle have conceived things differently, once he had made the radical mistake of thinking that the first mover could not cause anything but one perpetual and unvarying motion.[93]

Now St Thomas's solution to Aristotle's fundamental error is the affirmation that God acts by his intellect.[94] The inference from the affirmation of the intellectual character of divine action is that God is the *causa per se* of every coincidence of mover and moved, every conjunction of causes, every combination of effects.[95]

Hence when St Thomas affirms that God applies all agents to their activities, he is indeed thinking of God as the cause of all motion. But the significance of his affirmation goes far beyond that. God is the cause of each particular motion inasmuch as his mind plans and his will intends the endless premotions that make up the dynamic pattern of the universe and provide the real guarantee against entropy. It is not enough that things be

90 *Summa contra Gentiles*, 3, c. 86; *Summa theologiae*, 1, q. 115, a. 6; *In VI Metaphys.*, lect. 3; *In I Peri herm.*, lect. 14, §§185–91.
91 *In XII Metaphys.*, lect. 7.
92 *In XII Metaphys.*, lect. 12, § 2633.
93 See *In VIII Phys.*, lect. 13, §§1084–85.
94 The *Summa contra Gentiles* is to a great extent simply the philosophy of the Gentiles made into a Christian philosophy by means of the principle, *Deus agit per intellectum.* Book 1, cc. 44–96, deal with divine intellect and will; book 2, cc. 1–45, treat of the emergence of creatures; book 3, cc. 64–97, deal with providence; book 3, cc. 111–46, deal with divine government by law. The central issue is the possibility of the world not being eternal (2, cc. 31–38); this contradicts Aristotle on a fundamental point (*In VIII Phys.*, lect. 2–4); and what precedes is the preparation, and what follows is but a consequence of this closely reasoned affirmation of the intellectual character of divine activity.
95 *De veritate*, q. 6, a. 3, is somewhat Aristotelian. This is corrected in *Summa contra Gentiles*, 3, c. 94; *Summa theologiae*, 1, q. 19, a. 6; q. 103, a. 7. Here the starting point of the line of thought is the objection from Aristotle in *Summa contra Gentiles*, 3, c. 94: hence *In VI Metaphys.*, lect. 3; *Summa theologiae*, 1, q. 116, a. 1; *In I Peri herm.*, lect. 14, §§185–91, are also parallel. For the Aristotelian idea of the *per accidens* see, in addition, *In V Metaphys.*, lect. 9; *In VI Metaphys.*, lect. 2; *In XI Metaphys.*, lect. 8. All coincidence, conjunction, combination simply reduces to the general category of the *per accidens*.

kept moving by the moving heavens; the order of the universe has to be maintained, and that is due not to the heavens but to divine providence.[96] Thus the basic significance of *Deus omnia applicat* is this:

> Non est autem alicuius causa Deus, nisi sicut intelligens, cum sua substantia sit suum intelligere ... Unumquodque autem agit per modum suae substantiae. Deus igitur per suum *intellectum* omnia *movet* ad proprios fines. Hoc autem providere est.[97]

and so this:

> ... praeter ordinem particularis causae nihil provenit nisi ex aliqua alia causa impediente,[98] quam quidem causam necesse est reducere in primam causam universalem ... Cum igitur Deus sit prima causa universalis non unius generis tantum, sed universaliter totius entis; impossibile est quod aliquid contingat praeter ordinem divinae gubernationis.[99]

Because God is an intellectual agent, he is not merely the first cause of all physical premotions; he is the cause of the premotions as intended premotions. An intended premotion is an application.

4   *Virtus Instrumentalis*

There remains the mysterious *intentio* of *De potentia*, q. 3, a. 7, ad 7m. Since for centuries this has provided Bannezians with their most formidable

---

96 *De veritate*, q. 5, a. 2; *Summa contra Gentiles*, 3, c. 64; *Summa theologiae*, 1, q. 22, a. 2.

97 [But God is not the cause of something except as he is intelligent, for his substance is his understanding ... And everything acts through the mode of its substance. God therefore *moves* all things to their proper ends through his *intellect*. But this is to be provident] *De substantiis separatis*, c. 14, § 129.

98 On the *causa impediens* see *Summa contra Gentiles*, 3, c. 94; *In VI Metaphys.*, lect. 3 [§ 1193]; *Summa theologiae*, 1, q. 115, a. 6; *In I Peri herm.*, lect. 14, §§ 185–91.

99 [nothing occurs outside the order of a particular cause, unless some other cause impedes (its action), which (other) cause has to be reduced to the first universal cause ... Since God therefore is the first universal cause, not just of one genus, but universally of the totality of being, it is impossible for anything to happen outside the order of divine governance] *Summa theologiae*, 1, q. 103, a. 7. See ibid. q. 19, a. 6; q. 22, a. 2, ad 1m; and the passages cited in note 98.

argument in favor of *praemotio physica*, it is necessary to investigate St Thomas's meaning.

Three points are to be settled: the nature of instrumental causality; the ground for the assertion of universal instrumentality; the nature of the *intentio* in *De potentia*, q. 3, a. 7, ad 7m.

4.1   The Nature of the Instrument

There are two aspects to the cause as a cause. First, it must be something in act: *omne ens agit quatenus est actu*. Second, the something that it is must be proportionate to the effect intended: *omne agens agit sibi simile*.

Next, there are four ways in which a cause may possess proportion to an effect. First, in virtue of a natural form: thus, fire has the form or *virtus* of heat, and it causes heat in other things. Second, in virtue of a more eminent form: thus, the *corpus caeleste* is neither hot nor cold, wet nor dry, yet as *primum alterans* it is the principal cause of all emergence of heat, cold, humidity, and dryness; it does all this in virtue of a more eminent form. Third, in virtue of an idea in the mind: thus, a master builder is not a cathedral, nor something more eminent than a cathedral, and yet he is proportionate to the production of cathedrals because he has an idea of a cathedral in his head. Fourth, in virtue of an idea that is on its way from the mind to the effect: thus, the idea of the master builder guides the masons and carpenters, and these guide the motions of their bodies and of their tools; because the idea is somehow immanent in the motions, it is eventually realized in the effect. Such is the presentation in *De veritate*, q. 27, a. 7.

However, St Thomas expresses the idea of different kinds of proportion in another manner. In defining motion Aristotle explained that it is not 'something' but a process 'towards something.' It is not included in any of the ten *genera entis*, but it is the process towards three of them; it is 'towards being in a place,' 'towards being of a certain kind,' 'towards being of a certain size.'[100] This intermediate between not being and being, the process towards being something, a motion, is termed an *esse incompletum*.

Reverting now to the examples just given from *De veritate*, q. 27, a. 7, one can say that the fire is proportionate to its effect *per modum naturae completae*, that the sun is proportionate to its multiple effects, for it is a *causa aequivoca*,[101]

---

100   *In III Phys.*, lect. 3, §296; *Super IV Sententiarum*, d. 1, q. 1, a. 4, qc. 2, ad 1m;
      De veritate, q. 27, a. 4, ad 5m; *Summa theologiae*, 3, q. 62, a. 4, ad 2m.
101   The *causa univoca* directly follows the rule *omne agens agit sibi simile*; the
      causa aequivoca is proportionate *eminentiori modo*.

per modum naturae completae et eminentioris; that the master builder is proportionate to his effect, not indeed *per modum naturae* for he is not a cathedral, but *per formam apprehensam* for he is an intellectual agent; finally, that the instrument is proportionate to its effect not *per modum naturae completae*, nor *per formam apprehensam*, but *per modum naturae incompletae, per quoddam esse incompletum.* The theory is that just as a motion is the *esse incompletum* of its term – for instance, 'becoming white' is an incomplete 'being white' – so also the proportion of the instrument is an incomplete realization of the proportion of the principal cause.[102]

It is now possible to define the instrument: an instrument in the broad sense is any *movens motum*;[103] an instrument in the strict sense is a cause that is proportionate to its effect *per modum naturae incompletae.* Thus, the moon illuminates the earth in virtue of the light it receives from the sun: it is a *movens motum* but it is not an instrument in the strict sense, for the moon is bright *per modum formae completae.* On the other hand, in the generation of animals the seed is an instrument in the strict sense, for it is not an animal nor something more eminent than an animal and yet it is the cause of an animal.[104]

102 *Super IV Sententiarum*, d. 1, q. 1, a. 4, qc. 2, ad 1m: '... entia incompleta, per se loquendo, non sunt in aliquo genere nisi per reductionem: sicut motus quantum ad suam substantiam reducitur ad illud genus in quo sunt termini motus ... Unde et virtus haec quae est in sacramentis reducitur ad idem genus in quo est virtus completa principalis agentis' [incomplete beings, considered per se, are not in any genus except by reduction, just as motion, as regards its substance, is reduced to that genus in which the terms of the motion are found ... And therefore this power too which is in the sacraments is reduced to the same genus in which is found the complete power of the principal agent].

103 See *In VIII Phys.*, lect. 9, §1041, for an example of this usage.

104 This is the doctrine of *De veritate*, q. 27, a. 4. The generation of animals appears to be the source for the theory of instrumental causality. See Aristotle, *De generatione animalium*, II, 1, 734b 31 – 735a 26; St Albert, *Summa de creaturis*, 2, q. 17, a. 3 (*BA* 35: 154–55); Thomas Aquinas, *Super II Sententiarum*, d. 18, q. 2, a. 3; *De potentia*, q. 3, aa. 11–12; *In VII Metaphys.*, lect. 6–8; *Summa theologiae*, 1, q. 118, a. 1. The instrument in the *Summa* is far more Aristotelian than that in the commentary on the *Sentences.*

The fundamental idea of the whole analysis would seem to be the Aristotelian parallel between nature and art in *In VII Metaphys.*, lect. 6–8.

From that parallel comes St Thomas's analogy: *sicut artifex est ad artificiata, ita Deus ad naturalia.* This does not seem to occur in the *Summa contra Gentiles.* It is fundamental and synthetic in the *Summa theologiae*: see 1, q. 16, a. 1 (objective truth); q. 17, a. 1 (objective falsity); q. 14, a. 8 (*scientia Dei causa rerum*); q. 21, a. 2 (truth and justice); q. 22, a. 2 (providence); 1-2, q. 93, a. 1 (*lex aeterna*; see ibid. aa. 3–4).

4.2   The Hierarchic Ground for Universal Instrumentality

St Thomas systematizes the Aristotelian hierarchy on somewhat Platonist lines. God as *primum movens,* and the *corpus caeleste* as *primum alterans,* are affirmed to be universal causes. Just as the Platonic Idea cannot but be the cause of every participation of the Idea,[105] so there cannot be an *ens* that is

---

But besides this equivalence between ideas and essences or forms, there is also the theory of cognition based on the view that knowledge arises from the immateriality of a form (*Summa theologiae,* 1, q. 14, a. 1): now just as the idea, *species intentionalis,* in the mind of the artisan is his proportion to his work of art, so also the *esse incompletum* of the *species,* the pattern of instrumental movements, is the proportion of the instrument. [Lonergan adds by hand here, '1a, q. 87, a. 1, ad 3m: *intellectus in actu est intellectum in actu,* etc.]

Now the favorite illustration of the *esse incompletum* of a form or an idea appears to be *color in aere.* Heat is not merely in the fire and in the object heated: it is also in the intervening space *per modum naturae completae;* the air is really heated. But a color is in the object, and it is in the eye or sense of vision, but the intervening air is not colored; hence the *species coloris in aere* is *per modum naturae incompletae,* it is *sola intentio,* that is, the specification of knowledge but not an act of knowing; it is an *esse spirituale* but it is not an *esse completum* like the soul or a spiritual faculty or a spiritual act; it has merely *esse spirituale incompletum.*

Hence on the nature of light and color, see St Albert, *Summa de creaturis,* 2, q. 21, a. 5 (*BA* 35: 205–10); Thomas Aquinas, *Super II Sententiarum,* d. 13, q. 1, a. 3; d. 19, q. 1, a. 3, ad 1m; *De potentia,* q. 5, a. 8 [ad fin.]; *Summa theologiae,* 1, q. 67, a. 4; *In II De anima,* lect. 14. Note that the *intentio* by itself cannot cause anything but a sensation, a perception; to produce a physical effect it must be immanent in a motion; compare the gramophone record which has the *intentio,* the *virtus artis,* permanently, but renders the work of art only inasmuch as it is moved. Further observe that in later works the term *intentio* is replaced by *esse spirituale:* in *Summa theologiae,* 3, q. 64, a. 8, ad 1m, as H.D. Simonin has noted (['La notion d'"intentio" dans l'oeuvre de S. Thomas d'Aquin'] *Revue des sciences philosophiques et théologiques* 19 [1930] 445–63), it is denied that there is an *intentio* in the [inanimate] instrument.

On the limitations of instrumental causality, see *Summa theologiae,* 1, q. 45, a. 5; q. 118, a. 2. On the theory of the sacraments, see Cajetan, *In Summam theologiae,* 3, q. 62, a. 4 [*LT* 12: 25–26]; q. 78, a. 4 [*LT* 12: 211–12]. On the instrumentality of the heavenly spheres, *Super II Sententiarum,* d. 15, q. 1, a. 2; *Summa theologiae,* 1, q. 70, a. 3, ad 3m to ad 5m; *De operationibus occultis naturae; De potentia,* q. 5, aa. 7–10. On the instrumentality of accidents, *Summa theologiae,* 1, q. 115, a. 1, ad 5m; see q. 118, a. 1.

105 *Summa theologiae,* 1, q. 115, a. 1 c.: '... si esset forma ignis separata, ut Platonici posuerunt, esset aliquo modo causa omnis ignitionis' [if there were a separate form of fire, as the Platonists maintained, it would be in some way the cause of all burning].

not produced by *ipsum esse* nor a *res naturalis* that is not produced by the *causa speciei.*[106]

4.3   The Intentio of De Potentia, q. 3, a. 7, ad 7m

Ad septimum dicendum, quod virtus naturalis quae est rebus naturalibus in sua institutione collata, inest eis ut quaedam forma habens esse ratum et firmum in natura.[107] Sed id quod a Deo fit in re naturali, quo actualiter agat,[108] est ut intentio sola,[109] habens esse quoddam incompletum,[110] per modum quo colores sunt in aere, et virtus artis in instrumento artificis.[111] Sicut ergo securi per artem dari potuit acumen, ut esset forma in ea permanens, non autem dari ei potuit quod vis artis esset in ea quasi quaedam forma permanens,

---

106 For a statement of the hierarchy as such, see *In VI Metaphys.*, lect. 3, §§ 1207–09. For the *causa speciei* and the Platonist tinge in this conception, see *De substantiis separatis*, c. 10, § 105; *Summa theologiae*, 1, q. 115, a. 3, ad 2m; see ibid. q. 104, aa. 1-2. The basic principle of the systematization, *quanto virtus alicuius causae est perfectior, tanto ad plura se extendit*, is attributed to Proclus in the commentary on the *Liber De causis*, lect. 1, § 29; it is repeated in *De potentia*, q. 3, a. 7; *In II Phys.*, lect. 6, § 188–89; *De substantiis separatis*, c. 10, § 104. For Platonism in the concept of God, *ipsum esse separatum, ipsum intelligere separatum*, see *De substantiis separatis*, c. 14, § 120.

    That God is universal cause of being can, of course, be proved without appeal to the Platonist analogy: the proportion of a cause is determined by its nature; only the divine nature or essence is being; therefore, God alone is the proportionate cause of being. It follows immediately that any creature causes being only instrumentally.

    Though St Thomas in the commentary on the *Sentences* and the *De substantiis separatis* uses the principle that God is the universal cause of being to prove that God alone can create, it does not follow, as Fr Stufler seems to assume (*Gott, der erste Beweger aller Dinge* 67–83), that the principle has no further implications.

    Finally, note that Aristotle implies the *primum mobile* to be a universal cause: 'first' means 'presupposed' by all other motion.

107 Fire is always hot, water is always wet, etc.

108 Compare *In VIII Phys.*, lect. 2, § 978. The existence of mover and moved does not suffice for more than the possibility of motion; for actual motion they must be in the right situation, disposition, relation. See above, § 2.

109 *Sola*, presumably not an act of knowledge but merely its specification.

110 Were the *intentio* an act of knowledge, it would have *esse completum*.

111 Heat heats the intermediate air, color does not color the intermediate air (hence, *natura incompleta*). Art is an idea in the mind; an instrument qua instrument has not a mind, nor fully realized ideas, but some participation of an idea, namely, the pattern of instrumental movements. The gramophone record preserves such a pattern permanently.

nisi haberet intellectum;[112] ita rei naturali potuit conferri virtus
propria, ut forma in ipsa permanens, non autem vis qua agit ad esse
ut instrumentum primae causae; nisi daretur ei quod esset universale
essendi principium: nec iterum virtuti naturali conferri potuit ut
moveret se ipsam,[113] nec ut conservaret se in esse: unde sicut patet
quod instrumento artificis conferri non oportuit quod operaretur
absque motu artis; ita rei naturali conferri non potuit quod operaretur absque operatione divina.[114]

The question is, What is the *intentio, esse incompletum, virtus artis, vis artis,*
motus artis, which God as universal cause of all being confers on creatures to
enable them actually to produce being?

One has only to examine the parallel passages. God is the divine artist,
artisan, architect. The design of providence, *ratio gubernationis divinae,* works
through creatures towards the achievement of the *gloria Dei externa.* Obviously, just as there is a participation, a *virtus,* in the tools of the artisan, so
also there is a participation, a *virtus artis divinae,* in the whole created
universe. This view is not peculiar to the *De potentia;* it gradually develops
from the commentary on the *Sentences* to the *Pars prima.*

---

112 *Vis* has apparently no muscular connotation: the *vis artis* cannot exist per-
     manently in the instrument because the instrument has no intellect. Appar-
     ently, St Thomas did not foresee the gramophone.
113 *Quidquid movetur, ab alio movetur* [Whatever is moved is moved by another].
114 [To the seventh argument it has to be said that the natural power which is
     given to natural things at their institution is in them as a certain form hav-
     ing its being solidly based in nature. But that which is done by God in a
     natural thing, enabling it to act in actuality, is (there) as intention alone,
     having a certain incomplete being, in the manner in which colors are in the
     atmosphere and the efficacy of art is in the instrument of the artisan. As
     then sharpness can be given artificially to the axe, so that it would be a
     permanent form in it, but it could not be given to it that the efficacy of the
     art should be in it as a certain permanent form unless it had intelligence, so
     too its proper efficacy could be given to a natural thing as a permanent
     form in it, but not the force by which it acts as an instrument of the first
     cause to (produce) being, unless it were given to it that it be a universal
     principle of being. Nor again could it be conferred on a natural power that
     it should move itself, or that it should maintain itself in being. And there-
     fore as it is clear that it was not necessary to confer on the artisan's instru-
     ment that it should operate without the motion of art, so it could not be
     conferred on a natural thing that it should operate without divine opera-
     tion] *De potentia,* q. 3, a. 7, ad 7m. This conclusion corresponds to the con-
     clusion of the objection.

Thus, in the commentary on the *Sentences* divine knowledge is a cause just as the knowledge of an artist is a cause.

> ... scientia secundum rationem scientiae non dicit aliquam causa-
> litatem, alias omnis scientia causa esset: sed inquantum est scientia
> artificis operantis res, sic habet rationem causae respectu rei oper-
> atae per artem. Unde sicut est causalitas artificis per artem suam, ita
> consideranda est causalitas divinae scientiae.[115]

Further, the conception, plan, design of the divine artist has a twofold existence: first and essentially in the mind of God; second and derivatively in creatures. In the former case it is termed providence, in the latter, fate.

> ... providentia et fatum differunt per essentiam: sicut enim forma
> domus est aliud per essentiam, secundum quod est in mente artificis
> ubi nomen artis habet, et secundum quod est in lapidibus et lignis
> ubi artificiatum dicitur; ita etiam ratio gubernationis rerum aliud
> esse habet in mente divina, ubi providentia dicitur, et aliud in causis
> secundis, quarum officio gubernatio divina expletur: ex quibus
> fatum dicitur ...[116]

Here, plainly, providence is affirmed to be really different from fate; further, fate is something for it has *aliud esse*; again, it is in secondary causes, and, indeed, inasmuch as these causes execute divine government. It can hardly be denied that the fundamental elements of *De potentia*, q. 3, a. 7, ad 7m, are to be found in the very first book of the commentary on the *Sentences*.

115 [knowledge in its character as knowledge does not imply any causality, otherwise all knowledge would be a cause; but insofar as it is the knowledge of the artisan using things, in this way it has the character of a cause with respect to the thing used by art. And therefore as there is causality in the artisan through his art, so must be considered the causality of divine knowledge] *Super I Sententiarum*, d. 38, q. 1, a. 1.

116 [providence and fate differ essentially; for as the form of a house is essentially different as it exists in the mind of the artisan, where it has the name of art, and as it exists in stones and pieces of wood, where it is called an artifact, so also the nature of the government of things has one kind of being in the divine mind, where it is called providence, and another in secondary causes, by means of which divine government is executed; from these it is called fate] *Super I Sententiarum*, d. 39, q. 2, a. 1, ad 5m. [Thomas goes on to provide an etymology for *fatum*, and the 'ex quibus' refers as much ahead to the etymology as behind to what is included in the quotation.]

In the *De veritate* a distinction is drawn between the forms of creatures, which are participations of divine ideas, and on the other hand, fate, which is a participation of divine providence.

> ... sicut se habet idea ad speciem rei, ita se habet providentia ad fatum.[117]

The fundamental distinction between providence and fate reappears in the *Contra Gentiles.*

> ... ipsa ordinatio secundum quod in mente divina est, nondum rebus impressa, providentia est; secundum vero quod iam est explicata in rebus, fatum nominatur.[118]

At this point the passage in the *De potentia* was written; if the reader will refer back to it, he will observe how natural it is for St Thomas to appeal to the *virtus artis divinae* which is fate when the operation of God in secondary causes is denied.

This connection of fate with the activity of secondary causes is clearly expressed in the *Pars prima.*

> ... divina providentia per causas medias suos effectus exequitur. Potest ergo ipsa ordinatio effectuum dupliciter considerari. Uno modo, secundum quod est in ipso Deo: et sic ipsa ordinatio effectuum vocatur providentia. – Secundum vero quod praedicta ordinatio consideratur in mediis causis a Deo ordinatis ad aliquos effectus producendos, sic habet rationem fati.[119]

No closer parallel to the passage in the *De potentia* could be desired than

---

117 [as the idea is to the species of the thing, so is providence in relation to fate] *De veritate*, q. 5, a. 1, ad 1m.

118 [that ordination, as it exists in the divine mind, (and is) not yet imposed on things, is providence; but as (it exists) once it is executed in things, it is named fate] *Summa contra Gentiles*, 3, c. 93.

119 [divine providence executes its effects through mediate causes. That ordination of effects can therefore be considered in two ways. In one way, as it exists in God himself, and then this ordination of effects is called providence. – But according as the aforesaid ordination is considered in mediate causes ordained for the production of some effects, in this way it has the character of fate] *Summa theologiae*, 1, q. 116, a. 2 c.

... fatum est in ipsis causis creatis, inquantum sunt ordinatae a Deo ad effectus producendos.[120]

For, in the first place, divine providence is like the conception of an artist, while fate is the same conception according to another mode of existence; in the second place, fate is in the secondary causes; in the third place, fate is in these causes qua ordained by God to produce given effects. As nothing can act without the participation of the divine art, so with this participation nothing can fail to act. This is stated explicitly.

Et ideo dicendum est quod fatum, secundum considerationem secundarum causarum, mobile est: sed secundum quod subest divinae providentiae, immobilitatem sortitur, non quidem absolutae necessitatis, sed conditionatae; secundum quod dicimus hanc conditionalem esse veram vel necessariam, *Si Deus praescivit hoc futurum, erit.*[121]

Thus, St Thomas connects his idea of fate with his brilliant theorem on divine transcendence and the efficacy of divine will.[122]

Further, this affirmation of a fate is in no way opposed to the repeated assertion that the *sola intentio* by itself cannot produce any effect except a perception. For

... intantum fatum habet rationem causae, inquantum et ipsae causae secundae, quarum ordinatio fatum vocatur.[123]

Nor is it opposed to his repeated assertion that the execution of divine providence is not immediate but mediated: whether one uses one instrument or one million instruments, they are all instruments, and the *virtus*

120 [fate exists in these created causes, insofar as they are ordained by God for the production of effects] Ibid.
121 [And therefore it has to be said that fate, from the viewpoint of secondary causes, is changeable; but as subject to divine providence, it shares in unchangeableness, not indeed that of absolute necessity but of conditioned; in the way in which we say that this conditional is true or necessary, 'If God knows this will be, it will be'] Ibid. a. 3 c.
122 On divine transcendence, see §2 in the next chapter.
123 [fate has the attribute of cause in the degree in which secondary causes themselves (are causes), the ordering of which is called fate] *Summa theologiae,* q. 116, a. 2, ad 2m.

artis is automatically transmitted through the series, for it is simply the seriation, the arrangement, the pattern of the instruments in their movements.

> ... causaliter Dei potestas vel voluntas potest dici fatum. Essentialiter vero fatum est ipsa dispositio seu series, idest ordo, causarum secundarum.
>
> ... fatum dicitur dispositio, non quae est in genere qualitatis; sed secundum quod dispositio designat ordinem, qui non est substantia, sed relatio. Qui quidem ordo, si consideretur per comparationem ad suum principium, est unus: et sic dicitur unum fatum. Si autem consideretur per comparationem ad effectus, vel ad ipsas causas medias, sic multiplicatur: per quem modum Poeta dixit, *Te tua fata trahunt.*[124]

This *dispositio* may very naturally be identified in single instances with the *dispositio* or *habitudo* that must exist between mover and moved if the one is to move the other: thus, we have the idea of physical premotion which is necessary *quo actualiter agat.* Next, if this *dispositio* is considered in its relations to all other secondary causes, then there is the *intentio*, the participation of divine art in the secondary cause. Again, if the *dispositio* is taken in conjunction with the divine will, it is the term of the *applicatio*, for, as has been shown, application is premotion as intended. Finally, all of these *dispositiones* taken together give fate.

Admittedly St Thomas's thought on the issue is rather complex. But if he ever dreamt of a Bannezian *praemotio physica*, he simply could not have asserted that fate is merely the arrangement of secondary causes. For the *praemotio physica* is far too obviously fatal not to be mentioned by its originator when fate itself is under discussion.

124 [causally the power or will of God can be called fate. But essentially fate is the disposition itself or series, that is, the order of secondary causes.
... fate is called a disposition, not that which is had in the genus of quality, but according as disposition designates an order, which is not a substance but a relation. And that order, considered in comparison to its principle, is one; and in this way fate is called one. But if it is considered in comparison to (its) effects or to those mediate causes, then it is multiplied, in the way in which the poet said, 'Your fates draw you'] Ibid. ad 1m, ad 3m. Compare: 'vis principalis agentis instrumentaliter invenitur in omnibus instrumentis ordinatis ad effectum, prout sunt *quodam ordine* unum' [the efficacy of the principal agent is found instrumentally in all the instruments ordered to the effect, as being one *in a certain order*] *Summa theologiae*, 3, q. 62, a. 4, ad 4m.

5   The Degrees of Causality

It has been shown that the theory of application and of instrumental participation are nothing but speculative elaborations of the Aristotelian cosmic system. Three theorems on the degrees of causality represent speculative elaborations from a different viewpoint, namely, the relative importance of the different hierarchic movers. They are considered in turn.

5.1 Magis Movet

In proving that metaphysic is the truest of the sciences Aristotle enunciated his theorem on degrees of being.

> Unumquodque inter alia maxime dicitur, ex quo causatur in aliis aliquid univoce praedicatum de eis; sicut ignis est causa caloris in elementatis. Unde, cum calor univoce dicatur de igne et de elementatis corporibus, sequitur quod ignis sit calidissimus.[125]

Accordingly, since metaphysic deals with first principles which are the basis and presupposition of all other truth, it follows that metaphysic is the truest of the sciences. Again, if A by moving B causes B to move C, then, because A is the cause of B's moving C, it follows that C is more moved by A than by B.

> Omne enim quod movetur, magis movetur a superiore movente quam ab inferiori, et per consequens multo magis a primo movente.[126]

This theorem is perfectly simple and straightforward.

125 [In every case that is said to be highest among others from which there is caused in others something predicated univocally of them, as fire is the cause of heat in the things formed of elements. And therefore, since heat is said univocally of fire and of bodies formed from elements, it follows that fire is hot in the highest degree] *In II Metaphys.*, lect. 2, § 292.
126 [For everything that is moved is moved more by the higher mover than by the lower, and consequently much more by the first mover] *In VIII Phys.*, lect. 9, § 1047. The principle is used by Aristotle to show that the first mover cannot be moved in any of the species of motion in which the lower *mobilia* are moved. Since the first is the ultimate cause of all these motions and more a cause than the intermediate movers, it follows that they cannot be effected in him.

5.2 Vehementius Imprimit

This is from the first proposition of the *Liber De causis*. Its basic principle St Thomas enunciates in these terms:

> ... si albedo esset separata, ipsa albedo simplex esset causa omnium alborum inquantum sunt alba, non autem aliquid albedine participans. Secundum hoc ergo Platonici ponebant quod id quod est ipsum esse est causa existendi omnibus; id autem quod est ipsa vita est causa vivendi omnibus; id autem quod est ipsa intelligentia est causa intelligendi omnibus.[127]

Now in the first proposition an effect, *esse vivum humanum*, is examined. On the ground that the cause of *humanum* can cease acting without destroying the *vivum*; that the cause of the *vivum* can cease acting without destroying the *esse*; that, on the other hand, were the cause of *vivum* to cease acting, then the *humanum* is eliminated; and that, were the cause of *esse* to cease acting, then both *vivum* and *humanum* are eliminated: it is argued that the higher cause *prius intrat, vehementius imprimit, et tardius recedit*.[128]

Since St Thomas conceives his hierarchy as a hierarchy of universal causes with God as the *universale principium essendi* and the heavenly spheres as *causa speciei*, he is quite justified in using this theorem to express the degrees of causality in his own hierarchy.

All that is to be observed is that the conclusion means no more than the premises justify. One is not to interpret *vehementius imprimit* with the imagination. Like *prius intrat* and *tardius recedit*, these expressions mean nothing more than this: the activity of the higher cause is a presupposition of the activity of the lower.

---

127 [if whiteness were separate, simple whiteness itself, and not something participating in whiteness, would be the cause of all white things insofar as they are white. Accordingly, the Platonists held that that which is being itself is the cause of being for all things; and that which is life itself is the cause of living for all things; and that which is intelligence itself is the cause of understanding for all things] *Super librum De causis*, lect. 3, § 80. Compare *De veritate*, q. 5, a. 9, ad 7m.

128 [enters first, makes a stronger impression, and leaves later] See *Super librum De causis*, lect. 1, §§ 13 [prius advenit], 14 [plus influit ... tardius recedit ... prius ei advenit], and 26 [vehementius imprimit ... tardius recedit].

5.3 Immediatio Virtutis

While the foregoing theorems are very simple, the present one is notably complex. It is a reaction against Avicenna, a use of the *Liber De causis*, and an appeal to Aristotle.

Avicenna in his analysis of animal motion distinguished between *virtus motiva imperans* and *virtus motiva efficiens*. The former is immanent in the *pars irascibilis* and *concupiscibilis*. The latter is the principle of their transient action. It is described by St Albert, who follows Avicenna in this matter, as

> ... infusa in nervis et musculis contrahens chorda et ligamenta coniuncta membris, aut relaxans et extendens.[129]

Not content to follow Avicenna, St Albert uses this doctrine as the analogy for his explanation of divine activity. Accordingly, he distinguishes in God between an immanent *virtus divina increata* and a transient *virtus divina creata*.[130]

On the other hand, the twentieth proposition of the *Liber De causis* meets the Epicurean view that the gods cannot be distracted from Elysian pleasures and mixed up in the affairs of this world. The solution is the assertion that God acts by his essence. Other agents have between them and their effects a *habitudo, continuator, res aliqua media, additio super esse, actio*:[131] for instance, perhaps, the light of the sun as in the sun and in the medium, the heat of the fire as in the fire and in the atmosphere between the fire and the object heated. It follows that such agents are 'mixed up' in the things they effect. But God acts by his essence; one and the same thing is the *prima bonitas*, the *primum esse*, and the *virtus virtutum*.[132]

Now in St Thomas we find a trace of Avicenna, a good deal of the *Liber De causis*, and a new idea out of Aristotle's *Posterior Analytics*. This last must now be explained.

129 [infused in the nerves and muscles, contracting the cords and ligaments joined to the members, or relaxing and extending (them)] Albert, *Summa de creaturis*, 2, q. 68, a. 2 [*BA* 35: 560–61].
130 See Adam Sauer, *Die theologische Lehre der materiellen Welt beim heiligen Albert dem Grossen* [see above, p. 67, note 2] 133–36.
131 See *Super librum De causis*, lect. 20, § 366, and lect. 31, §§456–57.
132 See ibid. lect. 20.

For Aristotle the explanatory syllogism with the middle term the cause of the predicate[133] is the ideal and the goal of science. Naturally he raises the question occasioned by the plurality of middle terms, asking whether inquiry is to begin from the most general of these or from the lowest. His answer is that one should begin from the nearest and least general – for confusion lurks in generalities – and then by successive steps advance to the most general, which will be the immediate cause of the predicate. Here 'immediate' has its etymological sense of 'nonmediated,' 'logical first.' Thus, Socrates is mortal, because he is a man; a man is mortal, because he is an animal; an animal is mortal, because its material cause is composed of contraries. The three middle terms are 'man,' 'animal,' 'with material cause composed of contraries.' The first of these is the least general. The last is the real cause of mortality: not only does it make 'animal,' 'man,' and 'Socrates' mortal; it also is the cause of 'animal' making 'man' mortal, and of 'man' making 'Socrates' mortal. The gist of the thought is presented by St Thomas as follows.

> ... oportet semper media accipere quae sunt propinquiora subiecto, in quo quaeritur causa illius communis causati; et sic oportet procedere quousque perveniatur ad id quod est immediatum communi causato. Et huius rationem assignat, quia illud quod est ex parte eius quod continetur sub aliquo communi, est ei causa quod sit sub illo communi:[134] sicut si *D* est sub *B*, et si *C* sit causa *D* quod *B* insit ei. Et ex hoc sequitur ulterius quod *C* sit causa quod *A* insit *D*; et quod *A* insit *C*, *B* est causa. Ipsi autem *B* inest *A* per se ipsum et immediate.[135]

133 To be observed is the assumption of the parallel between the logical and real orders. It is fundamental to both St Thomas and Aristotle. Compare: 'Sicut ... est dispositio rerum in esse, ita et in veritate' [As things are disposed in being, so also are they disposed in truth] *Summa contra Gentiles*, 1, c. 62. The *locus classicus* is *In II Metaphys.*, lect. 2 [§§ 294–98].

134 That is, the middle term is the cause of the predicate in the subject; this is the idea of the explanatory syllogism. See *In I Post. anal.*, lect. 4, § 40; H.W.B. Joseph, *An Introduction to Logic*, 2nd ed. (Oxford: At the Clarendon Press, 1916), is very good on the subject.

135 [we must always take the media which are nearer the subject in which we seek the cause of that common effect; and we must proceed in this way until we come to that which is immediate to the common effect. And he assigns the reason for this, namely, that that which is from the side of what is contained under something common is the cause for its being under that common (predication): for example, if *D* is under *B*, and if *C* is the cause for *D* that *B* is in it. And from this it follows further that *C* is the cause that *A* is in *D*; and *B* is the cause that *A* is in *C*. But *A* is in *B* itself per se and immedi-

Here we are clearly in the pure regions of the logico-metaphysical parallel. We have now to observe the way these extremely diverse elements influence St Thomas, combine in his thought, and there are purified. This observation will help to eliminate misinterpretation.

First, though he uses Avicenna's distinction of *virtus motiva imperans* and *virtus motiva efficiens* at least once in the commentary on the *Sentences*,[136] he refuses to follow St Albert in applying it to God.[137]

Second, he makes common use of the concept of the *res media*:

> Operatio reducitur sicut in principium in duo; in ipsum agentem, et in virtutem agentis, qua mediante exit operatio ab agente.[138]

> In quolibet enim agente est duo considerare, scilicet rem ipsam quae agit, et virtutem qua agit: sicut ignis calefacit per calorem.[139]

Third, since God does not act by a *res media* but by his essence,[140] and since an agent must be present in the respect in which it acts, it is inferred that the divine essence is present where it acts.[141]

Fourth, coupled with the theorem on divine presence in the commentary on the *Sentences* and in the *De potentia*, though not in the *Contra Gentiles*,[142] is

ately] *In II Post. anal.*, lect. 19, §580. The meaning of the symbols may be had by any four terms of descending generality: *A*, material; *B*, animal; *C*, man; *D*, Socrates. Thus, if Socrates is an animal, and if this is because Socrates is a man; if, further, Socrates is material because he is a man; and if man is material because he is an animal; then *per se et immediate* an animal is material.

136 *Super II Sententiarum*, d. 18, q. 2, a. 3, ad 1m [while Thomas does not here use the words 'virtus motiva efficiens,' the idea is present].

137 '... Deus ... non agit aliqua operatione media vel intrinseca vel extrinseca quae non sit sua essentia: quia suum velle est suum facere, et suum velle est suum esse' [God ... does not act by means of some mediate operation, either intrinsic or extrinsic, which is not his essence: because his willing is his doing, and his willing is his being] *Super II Sententiarum*, d. 15, q. 3, a. 1, ad 3m. This is not merely the position but also the reason to be found in the *Liber De causis*.

138 [An operation is reduced as to a principle to two (factors): to the agent itself and to the agent's power by means of which the operation proceeds from the agent] *Super I Sententiarum*, d. 37, q. 1, a. 1, ad 4m.

139 [For in any agent whatever there are two (factors) to consider, namely, the agent itself and the power by which it acts, as fire heats by heat] *Summa contra Gentiles*, 3, c. 70 [§2464].

140 See above, note 137.

141 *De potentia*, q. 3, a. 7.

142 See above, notes 138, 139, 141.

Aristotle's theorem on the immediacy of first principles. The universal causes of the hierarchy permit this transposition just as much as the use of the Platonist *vehementius imprimit*. The argument is as follows.

> Sint *A*, *B*, *C* tres causae ordinatae, ita quod *C* sit ultima, quae exercet operationem; constat tunc quod *C* exercet operationem per virtutem suam; et quod per virtutem suam hoc possit, hoc est per virtutem *B* et ulterius per virtutem *A*. Unde si quaeritur quare *C* operatur, respondetur per virtutem suam; et quare per virtutem suam: propter virtutem *B*; et sic quousque reducatur in virtutem causae primae in quam docet Philosophus quaestiones resolvere in *Posterior. analyt.*, lib. II, text. 22, et in II *Physic.*, text. 38. Et ita patet quod cum Deus sit prima causa omnium, sua virtus est immediatissima omnibus.[143]

Plainly, this theorem is simply an exploitation of the parallel between the logical and the real orders.

There is, finally, another aspect of the same point. Just as the higher middle term is the cause of the lower causing the predicate in the subject, so, inversely, one may say that the higher middle term conjoins the lower to the predicate. Mediation and conjunction are equivalent. 'Animal' makes 'man' make Socrates material. What makes 'Socrates' material? 'Man.' What makes 'man' make Socrates material? 'Animal.' Similarly in the order of efficient causes, the provost can do things because he does them in the name of the king; the *virtus* of royal authority mediates between the provost and what he would effect, it conjoins the *virtus* of the provost to the effect.[144]

---

143 [Let *A*, *B*, *C* be three causes in an ordered series so that *C* is the ultimate one performing the action. It is clear that *C* performs the action by its own power; and the fact that it is able through its own power to (do) this, this is through the power of *B* and further through the power of *A*. And therefore if it is asked, Why does *C* act? the reply is, Through its own power. And why through its own power? Through the power of *B*. And so on till (the series) is reduced to the power of the first cause, to which the Philosopher, in book II of the *Posterior Analytics*, text. 22, and book II of the *Physics*, text. 38, teaches (us) to resolve questions. And thus it is clear that, since God is the first cause of all things, his power is most immediate to all things] *Super I Sententiarum*, d. 37, q. 1, a. 1, ad 4m. The reference to 'text. 22' in book II of the *Posterior Analytics* is to a connected subject, but there the question is definition and not immediate first principles. In *In II Phys.*, lect. 6, §196, there is the same idea, though without any elaboration, as in *In II Post. anal.*, lect. 19, §580.

144 *Super I Sententiarum*, d. 12, q. 1, a. 3, ad 4m. Compare *De potentia*, q. 3, a. 7. [For further elaboration on the references, see above, p. 67, note 6.]

Perhaps these theorems belong to the exuberance of St Thomas's youth.[145] In any case they in no way justify a Bannezian interpretation.

6   The Theory of Cooperation

One of the most startling features of the celebrated dispute on *concursus divinus* is the somewhat ingenuous assumption that everyone knows precisely what it is to 'cause,' 'operate,' 'cooperate.' Our long investigation of St Thomas's thought on *actio*, supported as it is by the study of premotion, application, instrumental participation, and the degrees of causality, provides a safe starting point for the present inquiry; it also suggests that past discussion may have suffered from a neglect of more fundamental ideas.

6.1   The Issue Defined

Cooperation in general means that two or more causes combine for the production of a single effect. Each cause has its own *actio*, and the question is, What are the relations between the different *actiones*? Presumably, it makes no difference whether one uses the Aristotelian idea of action, namely, the relation of the effect to the cause, or the Thomist *ratio formalis*, namely, *ut ab agente, in aliud procedens.*

Different instances of cooperation must be distinguished.

First, there is coordinate cooperation: two men pull a boat. Each cause exerts its *actio*. The two *actiones* are distinct, and their combination is according to vectorial addition. Such cooperation would seem to presuppose space as an intrinsic condition. With it we are not concerned.

Second, there is accidental cooperation: Abraham begat Isaac, Isaac begat Jacob. Here again there are two *actiones*, and the two are distinct. With this we are not concerned.

Third, there is serial cooperation: Peter kills Paul with a sword. This is the object of our discussion.

The essential feature of serial cooperation is that it involves not two but three *actiones*. Peter moves his sword according to the precepts of the art of killing; the sword so moved kills Paul; and, in the third place, Peter kills Paul.

145 The theorem of 'immediatio virtutis' is not used to prove divine presence in *Summa contra Gentiles*, 3, c. 70; it is not mentioned even in the article on divine presence in *Summa theologiae*, 1, q. 8, a. 1, nor in the article on God's operation in the operation of creatures, *Summa theologiae*, 1, q. 105, a. 5.

The assertion that there are three *actiones*[146] does not mean that there are three products: if there were three products, then there would be no cooperation. The third *actio* is the cooperation; it is the operation of the higher cause in the operation of the lower.

Hence, a twofold error is to be avoided.

First, one must not deny the third *actio*. That would eliminate the difference between accidental and serial cooperation. Peter kills Paul but Abraham does not beget Jacob. Isaac could beget Jacob, even though Abraham were dead; but the sword cannot kill Paul unless it is moved by Peter.

Second, one must not assert a third product. It is true that Peter not merely moves the sword but also kills Paul. But this truth in no way implies [a third product. Only if] Peter not merely runs through with the sword but also strangled Paul, would there be a third product. There is a third *actio*, even when he does not strangle Paul.

Now these two errors correspond to the two positions between which St Thomas steers a middle course. He does not deny a third *actio*, and so differs from Durandus, who is reputed to have held that God merely creates and conserves. He does not affirm a third product, and so he differs from Bañez, who posits a *praemotio physica*, and from Molina, who posits a *concursus simultaneus*.

The point to be grasped is that to deny the position of Bañez or of Molina is not to affirm the position of Durandus.

6.2 Deus Operatur in Omni Operante

St Thomas does not merely affirm that God alone creates, that he conserves all things in being, that he is the first mover and so the cause of all physical premotion,[147] that he acts by his intellect and so all premotions are intended by him and therefore applications, that the design of providence is the dynamic pattern of an instrumental universe just as the idea of the artist is the pattern of the movements of his tools. That is just so much scaffolding. It is no more than a list of reasons for affirming the central theorem, namely, *Deus operatur in omni operante*.

146 There are three *actiones* according to Aristotle's terminology. St Thomas normally speaks as though there were two *actiones*, of which the second is in virtue of the first. His idea seems to be derived from the *Liber De causis*. See *De veritate*, q. 24, a. 14 c. ['q. 29, a. 14' in the autograph has to be an error; 'q. 24, a. 14' seems correct].
147 The reader will recall that the continued existence of mover and moved is not sufficient for actual motion; there is such a thing as entropy.

The created cause cannot have an operation, unless in that operation is the operation of God. The created agent cannot have an *actio* without there being an attribution of the same *actio* to God. From the created principle there cannot proceed an *ut ab agente in aliud* without this procession proceeding still more from God *qui vehementius imprimit, qui immediatius agit.*

Further, since this affirmation of divine operation in all other operation is the affirmation of a theorem, of a conclusion, and since there cannot be a conclusion without a premise, the argument can be reversed. One may not only say that if God moves all things, then he operates in all operation. One may also say that unless God moves, then the creature cannot operate.

Thus, there are two points to be established: first, God operates in all operation; second, unless God moves, then the creature cannot operate.

6.2.1 The Direct Statement: God Operates in All Operation

The point may be illustrated from the *De veritate*, the *Summa contra Gentiles*, the *De potentia*, and the *Summa theologiae*.

In the *De veritate* one reads that God operates in the will as he operates in nature.

> Potest autem Deus voluntatem immutare ex hoc quod ipse in voluntate operatur sicut in natura: unde, sicut omnis actio naturalis est a Deo, ita omnis actio voluntatis inquantum est actio, non solum est a voluntate ut immediate agente, sed a Deo ut primo agente, qui vehementius imprimit.[148]

The meaning is not obscure: the *actio voluntatis inquantum est actio* would seem to be the *ut ab agente in aliud procedens*, the *ratio formalis* of *actio*. This is asserted to be not merely a procession from the will but much more a procession from God. The Platonist theorem of the degrees of causality is mentioned. And one also learns that God's operation in nature is the same as this operation in the operation of the will.

In the *Contra Gentiles* there is a chapter entitled *Quod Deus est causa operandi omnibus operantibus*. The title is immediately repeated in the first paragraph: *Deus est causa omnibus operantibus ut operentur*. This paragraph

148 [But God can change the will through this, that he operates in the will as in nature: and therefore, as every natural action is from God, so every action of the will, insofar as it is an action, is not only from the will as acting immediately, but from God as the first agent (and the one) who makes a stronger impression] *De veritate*, q. 22, a. 8.

shows that the creature is a cause of being inasmuch as it acts *virtute divina*: in other words, the *virtus divina* is required for its *actio*. The second paragraph argues that since God is the cause of the *virtus* from which proceeds the creature's *operatio*, therefore he is the cause of the *operatio*. The third paragraph argues that since God's conservation of the *virtus* is necessary if the *virtus* is to have an *actio*, therefore God is the cause of the *actio*; the idea is not that attributed to Durandus, namely, that God conserves and the *virtus* acts on its own; a comparison is made with the appearance of colors: just as colors cannot show themselves unless the sun maintains its light, so a created *virtus* cannot have an *operatio* unless God maintains his influence. The fourth paragraph argues that since God *primo et principaliter* applies all agents, therefore God is the cause of their *actio*. The fifth paragraph argues that all lower agents act in virtue of the higher agents; since, then, *causa actionis magis est id cuius virtute agitur quam etiam illud quod agit*, God is more the cause of any *actio* than any subordinate agent. The sixth paragraph[149] argues that since God ordains all things to their ends, therefore every agent acts *virtute divina*, and so God is the cause of all *actio*.[150]

For six different reasons St Thomas affirms God to be the cause of the *actio* of the creature. We conclude that divine operation in the operation of the creature is St Thomas's central theorem and that the manner in which he arrives at this theorem is of minor importance.

Three chapters later the same question is treated from a different viewpoint. It would seem that one *actio* cannot proceed from two causes; if it proceeds from one, then it does not proceed from the other; if one is sufficient, the other is superfluous; if one produces the effect, then there is nothing for the other to produce. Omitting the subordinate arguments, the objection is

> Quibusdam autem difficile videtur ad intelligendum quod effectus naturales et Deo attribuantur et naturali agenti.
>
> Nam una actio a duobus agentibus non videtur progredi posse. Si igitur actio per quam effectus naturalis producitur, procedit a corpore naturali, non procedit a Deo.[151]

---

149 In this paragraph the term *operatio* is used in the Aristotelian sense and so denotes the effect.

150 *Summa contra Gentiles*, 3, c. 67.

151 [But to some people it seems difficult to understand that natural effects may be attributed both to God and to a natural agent.

For it does not seem possible that one action should proceed from two agents. If then an action by which a natural effect is produced proceeds from a natural body, it does not proceed from God] Ibid. 3, c. 70.

The *actio* in question is the *ut ab agente in aliud*: it proceeds from the cause, and it produces the effect. The difficulty is the obvious one: How can two causes do one 'producing'?

The solution is that the lower agent acts, has an *actio*, in virtue of the higher agents.

> Oportet ergo quod actio inferioris agentis non solum sit ab eo
> per virtutem propriam, sed per virtutem omnium superiorum
> agentium.[152]

The theorem on the degree of causality, derived from the *Posterior Analytics*, is introduced.[153] Finally, it is affirmed that the effect is not partly from one cause and partly from the other, but the whole is from each cause though in different manners.[154]

In *De potentia*, q. 3, a. 7, the thought is manifestly identical. The title is, *Utrum Deus operetur in operatione naturae*. The sedulously neglected *Sed contra* introduces four considerations, namely,

> ... sicut ars praesupponit naturam, ita natura praesupponit Deum.
> Sed in operatione artis operatur natura ... Ergo et Deus in oper-
> atione naturae operatur.
>
> ... secundum Philosophum, homo generat hominem et sol. Sed
> sicut operatio hominis in generatione dependet ab actione solis, ita
> et multo amplius actio naturae dependet ab actione Dei. Ergo
> quidquid operatur natura etiam Deus operatur.
>
> ... nihil potest operari nisi sit ens. Sed natura non potest esse nisi
> Deo operante ... Ergo natura non potest agere nisi Deo agente.
>
> ... virtus Dei est in qualibet re naturali, quia Deus in omnibus
> rebus esse dicitur per essentiam et potentiam et praesentiam. Sed

152 [It has to be, then, that the action of a lower agent is from it not only through its own power, but through the power of all the higher agents] Ibid.

153 Ibid.: '... virtus supremi agentis invenitur ex se productiva effectus, quasi causa immediata; sicut patet in principiis demonstrationum, quorum primum est immediatum' [the power of the highest agent is found to be productive of an effect of itself, as the immediate cause, as is clear in the principles of demonstrations, of which the first (principle) is immediate].

154 The difference between St Thomas's *concursus* and that of Molina is not great: St Thomas would be willing to identify the *actio* with the effect as does Aristotle. Thus the main difference is that Molina has the effect partly from the first cause, partly from the secondary cause. There is, of course, a notable difference in the way each proves his conclusions.

non est dicendum quod virtus divina secundum quod est in rebus sit otiosa. Ergo secundum quod est in natura operatur. Nec potest dici quod aliud quam ipsa natura operatur, cum non appareat ibi nisi una operatio. Ergo in qualibet naturae operatione Deus operatur.[155]

The last remark, *non appareat ibi nisi una operatio*, seems significant: it is equivalent to a denial of a third product. After proving the existence of the first mover from the movements of experience, St Thomas does not infer the existence of unexperienced motions from the existence of the first mover. Such a procedure would be illegitimate. What he does is establish theorems with respect to the movement of experience.[156]

The corpus of *De potentia*, q. 3, a. 7, has already received sufficient attention; it is a selection from the arguments of *Contra Gentiles*, 3, c. 67; the conclusion is the same as before.[157]

155 [as art presupposes nature, so nature presupposes God. But nature operates in the operation of art ... Therefore God too operates in the operation of nature.
   ... according to the Philosopher man and the sun generate a man. But as the operation of man in generating depends on the action of the sun, so also and much more fully does the action of nature depend on the action of God. Therefore God operates whatever nature operates.
   ... nothing can operate unless it exists. But nature cannot exist except by the action of God ... Therefore nature cannot act except by the agency of God.
   ... the power of God is in any natural thing whatever, because God is said to be in all things by his essence, by his power, and by his presence. But it must not be said that the divine power as it is in things is otiose. Therefore as found in nature it operates. Nor can it be said that (God) operates something different from what nature operates, since nothing is found there except the one operation. Therefore God operates in any operation whatever of nature] *De potentia*, q. 3, a. 7, Sed contra.
156 An argument may prove either an existence or a theorem: for instance, one may prove the existence of another continent, or another planet, or another element; but one may also prove simply a theorem, the law of falling bodies, the principle of work, the circulation of the blood. In the former case one knows a new thing; in the latter one understands better a thing already known. The followers of Bañez suppose St Thomas to be proving a new existence when plainly he is simply establishing in a variety of ways a new theorem.
157 *De potentia*, q. 3, a. 7 ad fin.: 'Sic ergo Deus est causa *actionis* cuiuslibet inquantum dat virtutem agendi, et inquantum conservat eam, et inquantum applicat actioni, et inquantum eius virtute omnis alia virtus agit' [In this way then God is the cause of any *action* whatever insofar as he gives the power of acting, and insofar as he preserves it, and insofar as he applies it to action, and insofar as through his power every other power acts]. The fourth rea-

In the *Pars prima*[158] the argument undergoes a notable simplification. There are three forms of active causality: final, efficient, formal. In each respect it is to be affirmed that *Deus operatur in omni operante*. The first is most interesting: the final cause is really a cause, for it is the cause of the activity of the efficient cause; therefore any effect is causally related to the final cause; but any causal relation is an *actio* of some sort, and so, even on the ground of finality, God operates in all operation.

So much for the direct statement of the theorem.

6.2.2 The Indirect Statement: Unless God Moves, the Creature Cannot Act

The Platonist systematization of the Aristotelian hierarchy[159] results in a notable rigidity. It is extremely doubtful that Aristotle would maintain that a stack of dry hay enveloped by fire would not burn without the help of the *corpus caeleste*. St Thomas does so, most emphatically in the *De potentia*, but with less assurance in the *De caelo*.[160]

The difficulties against the necessity of the *corpus caeleste* in such a case are manifest: there is nothing for it to do. The fire is hot and determined to act;[161] the material is to hand;[162] the two are in contact.[163] Then, why will the hay not burn? Because fire can have an *actio* only in virtue of the action of the *corpus caeleste*. Unless one supposes that the situation has been produced by the *corpus caeleste*, and so that the fire is its instrument, action is impossible.[164]

---

son, as stated, may appear identical with the conclusion; really it is distinct, for inasmuch as it is a premise, it refers to the instrumentality of the creature's operation.

Note that here, as in *Super I Sententiarum*, d. 37, q. 1, a. 1, ad 4m, *immediatio virtutis* is used to prove divine presence in the operation. God is the principle of causality.

158 *Summa theologiae*, 1, q. 105, a. 5.
159 See above, §4.2.
160 *De potentia*, q. 5, a. 8; *In II De caelo et mundo*, lect. 4, §342.
161 *De potentia*, q. 5, a. 8, ad 1m.
162 Ibid. ad 2m.
163 Ibid. ad 6m.
164 '... ignis est proprium calefacere, supposito quod habeat aliquam actionem; sed eius actio dependet ab alio, ut dictum est' [to heat is the property of fire, presupposed that it has some action; but its action depends on another, as has been said] Ibid. ad 5m. This is the point that recurs throughout the corpus and the solutions to objections. It is not a matter of a new motion being required, but a necessity of dependence, of instrumentality.

A better known instance of the indirect statement is in *Summa theologiae*, 1-2, q. 109, a.1.

> Usus autem quilibet quemdam motum importat ... Videmus autem in corporalibus quod ad motum non solum requiritur ipsa forma quae est principium motus vel actionis; sed etiam requiritur motio primi moventis. Primum autem movens in ordine corporalium est corpus caeleste. Unde quantumcumque ignis habeat perfectum calorem, non alteraret nisi per motionem caelestis corporis. Manifestum est autem quod, sicut omnes motus corporales reducuntur in motum caelestis corporis sicut in primum movens corporale; ita omnes motus tam corporales quam spirituales reducuntur in primum movens simpliciter, quod est Deus. Et ideo quantumcumque natura aliqua corporalis vel spiritualis ponatur perfecta, non potest in suum actum procedere nisi moveatur a Deo. Quae quidem motio est secundum suae providentiae rationem; non secundum necessitatem naturae, sicut motio corporis caelestis.[165]

The Bannezian theory of *praemotio physica* cannot be considered an interpretation of this passage: if the perfect agent needs to be reduced from *posse agere* to *actu agere*, then is it God or is it the *corpus caeleste* that causes this transition in the perfectly hot fire? If God effects this change, then what is it that the *corpus caeleste* does? If the *corpus caeleste* effects the *actu agere*, then what does God do?

It should seem that the passage is parallel to *De potentia*, q. 5, a. 8. The fundamental idea is the Aristotelian theorem of physical premotion, namely, the existence of the agent is insufficient for *actio* unless the agent acts

---

165 [Now any use whatever implies some motion ... But we see in corporeal things that there is required for motion not only the form which is the principle of motion and of action, but there is required also the motion of the first mover. But the first mover in the order of corporeal things is a heavenly body, and therefore, no matter how perfect the degree in which fire has heat, it would not change anything without the motion of the heavenly body. Now it is clear that, as all corporeal motions are reduced to the motion of a heavenly body as to a first corporeal mover, so all motions, corporeal as well as spiritual, are reduced to the mover who is simply first, who is God. And therefore no matter how perfect the degree in which some corporeal or spiritual nature is constituted, it cannot proceed to its act unless it is moved by God. And this motion is according to his providence, and not according to the necessity of nature like the motion of a heavenly body] *Summa theologiae* 1-2, q. 109, a. 1.

eternally. But this basic idea is placed in the context of a cosmic scheme in which God and the *corpus caeleste* are universal causes. Because the latter is the *primum alterans*, there can be no alteration except by its instruments. Because the former is the *primum movens*, there can be no motion except in its instruments. If *motio* is an *actio* in St Thomas's sense, then the passage simply asserts the dependence of the lower *actio* on the higher. If the *motio* is an *actio* in Aristotle's sense, *motio moventis est motus mobilis*, this is not to make the already perfect agent still more perfect, but a prerequisite of its being in a situation in which it can act.

The precise nature of St Thomas's thought may best be seen by comparing *De veritate*, q. 24, a. 14, with *Summa theologiae*, 1-2, q. 109, a. 9.

In the former passage divine operation in the operation of the creature is based on creation and conservation.

> ... nulla res possit in naturalem operationem exire nisi virtute divina, quia causa secunda non agit nisi per virtutem causae primae, ut dicitur in libro *de Causis* [propos. 1] ... Operationis enim naturalis Deus est causa, inquantum dat et conservat id quod est principium naturalis operationis in re, ex quo de necessitate determinata operatio sequitur; sicut dum conservat gravitatem in terra, quae est principium motus deorsum.[166]

Now in the *Prima secundae* it is still true that God operates in the operation of the creature because he conserves, but a new factor has entered into consideration. The created cause cannot act merely because it is conserved; it is an *agens in tempore* and needs premotion before it can begin actually to act; and as God is the first mover, moving all things by his intellect, the cause of all the coincidences and combinations that constitute premotions, it follows that no matter how perfect a thing is and how much it is conserved, still without premotion or application it cannot act. Accordingly, though it is true that things do act *virtute conservationis*, it is necessary, as well, that they act *virtute motionis divinae*. Hence

166 [nothing can proceed to its natural operation except by the divine power, because a secondary cause does not act except through the power of the first cause, as is said in the book *De causis* ... For God is the cause of a natural operation, insofar as he gives and preserves that which is the principle of natural operation in the thing, from which by necessity a determinate operation follows; as when he preserves gravitation in the earth, which is the principle of downward motion] *De veritate*, q. 24, a. 14.

Indiget tamen auxilio gratiae secundum alium modum, ut scilicet a Deo moveatur ad recte agendum. Et hoc propter duo. Primo quidem, ratione generali: propter hoc quod, sicut supra dictum est [art.1, huius q.], nulla res creata potest in quemcumque actum prodire nisi virtute motionis divinae.[167]

The motion here is clearly the premotion in the Aristotelian sense.

6.2.3 Conclusion

St Thomas's theory of *concursus*, of divine cooperation in all other operation, is a theorem.

The theorem is proved from a variety of principles: in the commentary on the *Sentences* one reason is given;[168] in *Contra Gentiles*, 3, c. 67, there are six reasons; in *Contra Gentiles*, 3, c. 70, there are three reasons; in *De potentia*, q. 3, a. 7, there are four reasons; in *Summa theologiae*, 1, q. 105, a. 5, it would seem that St Thomas tired of enumerating reasons and simply gave categories of reasons, namely, final causality, efficient causality, formal causality.

The theorem is distinct from the affirmation of divine presence: in the *Sed contra* of the article in *De potentia* divine presence is a premise and the theorem is a conclusion; in the *corpus* of the same article the theorem is a premise and divine presence is a conclusion.

The theorem is simply a theorem. As our examination of the ideas of physical premotion, application, and *virtus instrumentalis* established, there is no evidence for the Bannezian view that St Thomas is proving the existence of additional motions. He proves the existence of the first mover and then a theorem with respect to the operation of creatures. On the other hand, the negation of additional motions is not equivalent to the position attributed to Durandus: on that position God is no more a cause of the operation of a creature than Abraham is the father of Jacob.[169] The three positions are well illustrated by the example, Peter runs Paul through with his sword: according to St Thomas, Peter kills Paul; according to

---

167 [But he needs the help of grace in another way, namely, to be moved by God to acting rightly. And this on two acccounts. First, by a general reason, on this account that, as was said above (article 1 of this question), no created thing can proceed to any act whatever except through the power of a divine motion] *Summa theologiae*, 1-2, q. 109, a. 9.

168 *Super I Sententiarum*, d. 37, q. 1, a. 1, ad 4m.

169 Note that Abraham is not the father of Jacob. Isaac is the father of Jacob.

Durandus, Peter merely moves a sword; according to the later theory of concursus, Peter not merely moves his sword but also with his own hands strangles Paul.

6.3 Grace as Cooperative

The purpose here is to treat the idea of cooperation in the context of grace.

Since an operation is a notional relation in what operates, it follows that cooperation is simply an additional notional relation.

> ... relatio non multiplicat essentiam rei. Sed cooperans supra operantem nonnisi relationem addit. Ergo eadem est gratia per essentiam operans et cooperans.[170]

Again, since the relations which are denoted by operation and cooperation are notional relations, it follows that the distinction between operative and cooperative grace derives from the effects produced.

> ... divisio debet dari per opposita. Sed operari et cooperari non sunt opposita: idem enim potest operari et cooperari. Ergo inconvenienter dividitur gratia per operantem et cooperantem ...
>
> Ad quartum dicendum quod gratia operans et cooperans est eadem gratia; sed distinguitur secundum diversos effectus.[171]

Finally, as the higher cause operates the operation of the lower, there can be no distinction between what is produced by the one and what is produced by the other.

> ... isti videntur distinxisse inter id quod est ex gratia, et id quod est ex libero arbitrio, quasi non possit esse idem ex utroque ... Non est

170 [a relation does not make the essence of a thing multiple in number. But cooperative grace does not add anything except a relation to operative grace. Therefore, operative and cooperative are essentially the same grace] *De veritate*, q. 27, a. 5, Sed contra.

171 [a division should be given through opposites. But to operate and to cooperate are not opposites: for the same thing can operate and cooperate. Therefore, grace is not suitably divided by operative and cooperative ...

To the fourth argument it has to be said that operative and cooperative grace are the same grace; but (the grace) is distinguished according to (its) different effects] *Summa theologiae*, 1-2, q. 111, a. 2, ob. 4 and ad 4m.

autem distinctum quod est ex libero arbitrio, et ex praedestinatione; sicut nec est distinctum quod est ex causa secunda, et causa prima: divina enim providentia producit effectus per operationes causarum secundarum ... Unde et id quod est per liberum arbitrium, est ex praedestinatione.[172]

7   Summary and Conclusions

(a) The analogy of creator and creature in the field of action is not that in the latter there is, while in the former there is not, a real difference in the agent qua agent between *posse agere* and *actu agere*.

(b) The analogy is that the creator acts in virtue of his substance, eternally, without presupposition or conditions, while the creature acts in virtue of an accidental perfection (*Summa theologiae*, 1, q. 54, aa. 1–3), presupposes an object with respect to which it acts (ibid. q. 45, a. 5), and requires a premotion or application to act with respect to that object (*In VIII Phys.*, lect. 2, §§ 976, 978); since there is no such thing as chance (*In VI Metaphys.*, lect. 3; *In I Peri herm.*, lect. 14, §§ 190–91; *Summa theologiae*, 1, q. 116, a. 1), God cannot but control all created activity (*Summa contra Gentiles*, 3, c. 94; *Summa theologiae*, 1, q. 103, a. 7), a control that is exercised according to the designs of divine providence (*Summa theologiae*, 1-2, q. 109, a. 1) and that is immanent in the dynamic cosmos as a fate (*Summa theologiae*, 1, q. 116, aa. 2–3) and as the art of a craftsman in his tools (*De potentia*, q. 3, a. 7, ad 7m); it follows that the operation of the creature is in virtue of the operation of the creator, and that, were it not, the creature could not act, for God alone is proportionate to the production of being.

(c) The general theory of motion is a theory of providence and a subtle elaboration of the idea and conditions of cosmic order. It provides a background and a context for a theory of *gratia operans*, for it shows God to be operating in all things and it reveals all creatures, as agents, to be instrumental. But it is not itself a theory of grace, for grace is a divine intervention over and above the nature of things and not a purely specula-

---

172 [these people seem to have made a distinction between what is from grace and what is from free will, as if there could not be the same from each ... But there is no distinction between what is from free will and what is from predestination, as there is no distinction between what is from a secondary cause and what is from the first cause. For divine providence produces effects through the operations of secondary causes ... And so too what is from free will is from predestination] *Summa theologiae*, 1, q. 23, a. 5 c. Compare *Summa contra Gentiles*, 3, c. 70.

tive conclusion following with metaphysical necessity from the conditions of nature.

(d) The theory of the preparation for grace in *Super II Sententiarum*, d. 28, q. 1, a. 4, would seem to be an attempt to make general providence serve as a grace; on the other hand the appeal to the *Eudemian Ethics* appears as an indication of the way in which a divine intervention might be introduced; finally, the use of the pure analysis of action from *In III Phys.*, lect. 5, that is to be found in *Summa theologiae*, 1-2, q. 110, a. 2, would seem to be a systematization of this special divine intervention. The study of the exact nature of this intervention will occur in the next chapter.

(e) While our conclusions do not exactly coincide with those of other interpreters, they may derive confirmation from all. Thus, we agree with the Bannezian synthesis of premotion, application, instrumental participation, and fate, but we think the explanation of the transition from rest to activity found in *In VIII Phys.*, lect. 2, to be more germane to St Thomas than their distinction between *posse agere* and *actu agere*. In general we have no difficulty in accepting the conclusions of Fr Stufler, though on a number of points there is a measure of disagreement. Finally, we are inclined to believe that did Fr Sertillanges, O.P., work out in detail the general position he has indicated, he would be in entire agreement with the views here advanced.[173]

173 [Lonergan gives no reference, but his bibliography lists A.-D. Sertillanges, 'Note sur la nature du movement d'après S. Thomas d'Aquin,' *Revue des sciences philosophiques et théologiques* 17 (1928) 235–40.]

II-4

The Second Subsidiary Investigation: Divine Operation in the Will

A number of parallel movements, which may be united under the heading 'Divine Operation in the Will,' accompanied the development of St Thomas's thought on *gratia operans*.

Most notable among these is the acceptance of the Augustinian or psychological theory of the necessity of grace. This adds to the general affirmation of the need of habits a law of psychological continuity to account for the impotence of the sinner. On combining this law with the other limitations of human liberty (there is free choice neither with respect to the end nor with respect to the series of free choices), one sees that the instrumental character of human freedom[1] is verified not merely by a metaphysical position but also by a psychological analysis.

Solidary with this main movement, which is treated in §§3–5, there is a gradual development from the Aristotelian *appetibile apprehensum movet appetitum* to the affirmation of both general and special premotion internal to the will (§6). Most significant is the remark that the special premotion is a grace.

The first two sections of this chapter (§§1, 2), though far from unconnected with the subject of our inquiry, nonetheless regard more particularly the questions raised by later speculation. In the first St Thomas's theory of liberty is examined. In the second an attempt is made to determine his position on divine foreknowledge, on the efficacy of divine will, and on the reconciliation of human instrumentality with divine sanctity.

---

1 Recall (chapter II-2, §7.5) that human instrumentality is inferred from Romans 9.16.

1   The Idea of Liberty

Though in his earlier works St Thomas speaks of liberty as the negation of coercion, and does so not merely incidentally but systematically,[2] he is not to be thought a Jansenist. In the *De malo* this opinion is rejected with all possible vehemence[3] and, to my knowledge, does not recur.[4] But not even are St Thomas's earlier works to be considered infected with error: though the denunciation in the *De malo* necessitates a modification of earlier forms of expression, no position need be changed.[5]

2   There is an incidental identification of liberty with noncoercion in *Super II Sententiarum*, d. 25, q. 1, a. 2. This becomes systematic especially in the *De veritate*. Five distinct acts are said to be necessary yet free: (a) God's will of his own goodness (*De veritate*, q. 23, a. 4); (b) the procession of the Holy Ghost (*De potentia*, q. 10, a. 2, ad 5m [1ae ser.]); (c) the natural appetite for happiness (*De veritate*, q. 22, a. 5 c., ob. 4, and ad 4m [1ae ser.] and ob. 3 and ad 3m [2ae ser.]; ibid. q. 24, a. 1, ad 20m; *Summa theologiae*, 1, q. 82, a. 1, ad 1m); (d) the immutable will of the demons (*De veritate*, q. 24, a. 10, ob. 5 and ad 5m); (e) the impotent will of the sinner (*De veritate*, q. 24, a. 12, ad 10m [2ae ser.]). The use of 'non est cogens' in *De potentia*, q. 3, a. 7, ad 14m [sense but not words] is incidental.
3   Five charges constitute the attack on the identification of liberty with the absence of coercion. First, it is heretical. Second, it destroys the concept of merit and demerit. Third, it is subversive of the very principles of morality. Fourth, it is alien to all philosophic and scientific thought. Fifth, it is the sort of opinion that is proposed either through impishness or because the incompetent are confronted with fallacies they cannot see through. *De malo*, q. 6, a. 1 c. init.
4   Use of St Augustine's remark in *De civitate Dei*, book 5, chapter 10, recurs in the *Sed contra* of *Summa theologiae*, 1-2, q. 6, a. 4. However, the passage is there used to deny the coercion of the will, not to justify a compatibility between freedom and necessity.
5   The point may be proved by enumeration. First, God's will of his own goodness, the procession of the Holy Spirit, and man's natural appetite for beatitude are henceforth said to be necessary and free: this change has no ulterior implications. Second, the immutable will of the demons is absolutely free *in causa*, for they freely chose to rebel; it is now free in the choice of this or that evil act, but necessitated in the choice of some evil. That is the position of *De malo*, q. 16, a. 5. No more than that was asserted, really, in *De veritate*, q. 24, a. 10 [ad 5m]. Third, the impotent will of the sinner is absolutely free *in causa*; it is free to sin or not in any particular act; it will necessarily commit some mortal sin. That is the position of *Summa theologiae*, 1-2, q. 109, a. 8; that is precisely what is asserted in *Summa contra Gentiles*, 3, c. 160 ad fin.; and no more is asserted in *De veritate*, q. 24, a. 12 [ad 10m (2ae ser.)].
    The genesis of the idea in St Thomas would seem to be as follows. In the commentary on the *Sentences* he took over the current and popular notion that freedom was the absence of coercion: *Super II Sententiarum*, d. 25, q. 1, a. 2, proves that the will is not forced with the same reason [by which]

A similar historical process seems to have provided Dominicus Bañez with some ground for asserting that the freedom of the will arises exclusively from the indifference of the object presented by the intellect.[6] The refutation of this view is best attained by following the development of St Thomas's thought.

The initial achievement was the rejection of St Albert's view that the *liberum arbitrium* was a third potency distinct from intellect and will.[7]

But, though the *liberum arbitrium* is no longer a distinct entity, St Thomas continues to write about it and the will in separate questions.[8] Not only does he write about the two in separate questions, but he treats freedom principally when he treats *liberum arbitrium*, and then he speaks not of the liberty of the will but of the liberty of man. It is worth following this evolution of thought.

The fundamental thesis from the commentary on the *Sentences* to the *Pars prima* inclusively is that the free agent is the cause of its own determination. The determination in question is not the determination of the will but the determination of action generally. Such determination comes from the intellect, and intellectual beings are free, not because they move from an intrinsic [principle] (as the *gravia* and *levia*), not because they move themselves (as do plants and animals), not because they judge (for the lamb judges the wolf dangerous), but because they are the masters and makers of their judgment, they construct the form of their own activity.[9]

Summa theologiae, 1-2, q. 10, a. 2, proves that the will is not determined by its object. In the *De veritate*, as we shall see (below, § 5.2.3), he took over the psychological theory of the necessity of grace, that is, the Augustinian tradition on *libertas a coactione, a peccato, a miseria*. In this enormous movement of thought, the idea of liberty as noncoercion slipped into his thought, was used systematically, but in no way falsified his position. When, in writing the *De malo*, he adverted to the use to which this idea could be put, he rejected it with the utmost vigor.

6 See Dominicus Bañez, *Scholastica commentaria in primam partem Summae theologicae S. Thomae Aquinatis*, q. 19, a. 10 (Roma, 1584, pp. 381E-382D [Madrid: Editorial F.E.D.A., 1934, pp. 443–44]).

7 *Super II Sententiarum*, d. 24, q. 1, a. 3. For St Albert, see Lottin, *La théorie du libre arbitre depuis S. Anselme jusqu'à S. Thomas D'Aquin* [see above, p. 13, note 47; on p. 94, note 1, Lonergan refers more precisely to the article 'Le traité du libre arbitre depuis le chancelier Philippe jusqu'à saint Thomas d'Aquin' (see also above, p. 19, note 84)].

8 *De veritate*, q. 22, is on the will; q. 24 is on *liberum arbitrium*. *Summa theologiae*, 1, q. 82, is on the will; q. 83 is on *liberum arbitrium*. But in the *Prima secundae*, qq. 6–17 are on the will, yet the *liberum arbitrium* does not figure in the title of any article.

9 This position is already implicit in *Super II Sententiarum*, d. 25, q. 1, a. 1. It is elaborately presented in *De veritate*, q. 24, a. 1, an elaboration prepared with

But does the judgment necessitate the act of will? Must the *bonum appre-hensum* move the appetite? This is consistently denied, but in the commentary on the *Sentences* in the treatment of the *liberum arbitrium*,[10] in the *De veritate* and the *Pars prima* in the treatment of the will,[11] in the *Peri hermeneias* and the *De malo* incidentally.[12]

How is it that the will need not be determined, need not be moved and yet, on the other hand, can be determined and moved by the object on which reason decides? That is a question that is not explained in the earlier works. It took the great controversy in Paris over the passivity of the will[13] to break down the inertia of the distinction of will and *liberum arbitrium* in the mind of St Thomas, and bring him to explain how the will is active and how precisely the will can act or not act no matter what the object presented may be.[14] With that explanation all are familiar: the will is in act with respect to an end, so moves itself from potency to act with respect to the means to the end. Nor is this contrary to the principle

---

the greatest skill in *De veritate*, q. 22, aa. 1–5. It is repeated summarily, but in a variety of ways in *Summa contra Gentiles*, 2, c. 48. It makes its final appearance in *Summa theologiae*, 1, q. 83, a. 1.

In the last passage cited, an important change may be noted. In the *De veritate* and the *Contra Gentiles* the question of *liberum arbitrium* is considered settled by *liber est qui est causa sui*: it was enough to show that man himself caused the form of his activity; his judgment is reflective and not mere instinct. But in *Summa theologiae*, 1, q. 83, a. 1, the issue is examined more profoundly, and it is shown that there is no necessity in man's making the judgment that he does make. Not only does man judge his judgment, but the judgment he makes is contingent.

For the idea of contingence as nonsyllogistic inference, see the general theorem of the parallel of the logical and the real in *In II Metaphys.*, lect. 2, and its application to necessity in *In II Phys.*, lect. 15; *In I Post anal.*, lect. 42; see *Summa contra Gentiles*, 2, cc. 28–30. [For more precision in some of these references, see above, chapter I-5, p. 97, note 28.]

10 *Super II Sententiarum*, d. 25, q. 1, a. 2.

11 *De veritate*, q. 22, a. 6; *Summa theologiae*, 1, q. 82, a. 2.

12 *In I Peri herm.*, lect. 14; *De malo*, q. 3, a. 3.

13 See Lottin, 'Liberté humaine et motion divine' [see above, p. 54, note 33]. It would be inexact to think that St Thomas held a purely passive or a determinist theory of the will at any time. I think the accurate statement is that in the earlier works he does not attempt to explain how it is that the will causes and determines its own acts.

14 Observe that both in the *De malo* and in the *Prima secundae* St Thomas distinguishes between the exercise of the act of will and its determination or specification. In the latter respect, liberty is limited: reason cannot but select the infinite good. In the former respect, liberty is unlimited: the will may act or it may refuse to think of the object proposed. See *De malo*, q. 6, a. 1; *Summa theologiae*, 1-2, q. 10, a. 2 c. init.

quidquid movetur ab alio movetur, for the will is not both in act and in potency in the same respect.[15]

Thus, there are four reasons why the will is said to be free. First, because the means to the end is not a necessary but an optional means. Second, because the practical judgment is contingent. Third, because the *bonum apprehensum* does not efficaciously move the will. Fourth, because the will may or may not move itself to its free act. Because a historical accident prevented St Thomas from attending to these four points at once is not a reason for saying that he means what he says when he asserts this one but not when he asserts that one: he asserts all four. Much less is an interpreter entitled to reject St Thomas's assertion that the will is a *causa ad utrumque* that determines itself by its own intellect,[16] assert that it is a *causa ad utrumque* determined by a non-Aristotelian and non-Thomist *praemotio physica,* and then claim it is nevertheless free because St Thomas places the basis of freedom in the indifference of the practical judgment or of the object of choice. Yet that is what Dominicus Bañez has done.[17]

---

15 See *In IX Metaphys.*, lect. 1, § 1776. For Scotus's position see his *In IX Metaphys.*, q. 15 [*Opera omnia* (Paris: Vivès, 1891–), vol. 7, pp. 606–20]. For a comparison, see Johannes Auer, *Die menschliche Willensfreiheit im Lehrsystem des Thomas von Aquin und Johannes Duns Scotus* [see above, p. 116, note 96] 285–303. The divergence is not, of course, that one affirms and the other denies self-motion to the will; both admit that. But while Scotus holds that the faculty of the will is an *actus virtualis* (that is, a causal act, not formally similar to the effect, but proportionate *modo eminentiori*) capable of producing the act of will with respect to the good in general, St Thomas denies such a possibility. His reason is that the will as a potency is an *inclinatio universalis* which can be caused by no participation of the absolute but only by the *bonum universale,* just as *materia prima* can be caused by God alone; next, that since the will can be caused by God alone, so its operation can be caused by God alone, for only the cause of a nature can produce a natural motion in that nature; any other motion must be violent. Thus, the only *actus virtualis* that can cause the motion of the will to the end is the *actus purus* (*Summa theologiae,* 1-2, q. 9, a. 6 ['universale bonum' for 'actus purus'; Lonergan refers also to *Summa theologiae,* 1, q. 54, a. 2, but this does not seem correct]). This position spontaneously integrates with the argument from the impossibility of a prior infinite series of motions in the will *quoad exercitium actus* (1-2, q. 9, a. 4 [*quantum ad exercitium actus*]), and so clarifies what had been the hitherto obscure *instinctus divinus* derived from the *Liber De bona fortuna.* On this see below, §6.5.

16 *Super II Sententiarum,* d. 25, q. 1, a. 1. See *De veritate,* q. 24, a. 1; *Summa contra Gentiles,* 2, c. 48; *Summa theologiae,* 1, q. 83, a. 1; *De malo,* q. 3, a. 3, ad 5m. See above, note 9.

17 Bañez, *Scholastica commentaria in primam partem Summae theologicae S. Thomae Aquinatis,* 1, q. 19, a. 10 (Roma, 1584, pp. 381F–382B [Madrid: Editorial F.E.D.A., 1934, pp. 443–44]): 'Habemus itaque necessarium esse ad libertatem actus voluntatis, quod indifferentia medii eligendi iudicetur per

If, however, one should ask which of the four reasons for freedom is the essential reason, it should seem that the last is at once necessary and sufficient. The first three are *causae cognoscendi*, and they may be present as in the case of the demons with respect to the choice between good and evil without the will being, here and now, free.[18] But the last, the will's ability to move or not move itself, is the *causa essendi*: it is the *primum quoad se* from which the other three can be deduced as conditions;[19] it solves the ultimate problem in the *via inventionis*[20] and so is the first proposition in the *via doctrinae*; it defines, not the *liberum arbitrium*, which is the global difference between rational and irrational creatures, but free will, which is the central faculty in the process of free self-determination.

Since, then, the *dominium sui actus*, the ability to produce or not produce this act, is the essence of freedom, it follows that a pure passivity cannot be free.[21]

intellectum, et simul iudicetur tale medium determinandum ad finem ... Quotiescumque actus voluntatis oritur ex praedicta radice iudicii, semper erit liber. Unde rursus colligo: Quidquid antecesserit vel comitabitur vel supervenerit ad actum voluntatis, si non tollat iudicium illud circa medium respectu finis, non destruet libertatem operationis. Haec consequentia evidens est, quia stante definitione actus liberi, necesse est actum esse liberum' [Accordingly, we have it as necessary for the freedom of the act of will that there be a judgment of intellect on the indifference of the means to be chosen, and at the same time that there be a judgment determining such and such a means to the end ... As often as the act of the will originates from the aforesaid root of judgment, it will always be free. And so I deduce a further step: No matter what has preceded or will accompany or has supervened on the act of the will, as long as it does not take away that judgment about the means in regard to the end, it will not destroy the freedom of the operation. This consequence is evident, because as long as the definition of a free act stands, it is necessary that the act be free].

18 *De malo*, q. 16, a. 5, ad 11m, compares the responsibility of the demons to that of a drunkard.

19 Unless, of course, one so interprets *Summa theologiae*, 1-2, q. 10, a. 2, as to assert that the will is free *quoad exercitium actus* even with respect to the infinite good. If such an interpretation – it is the literal interpretation of the passage – is preferred, then there is no debate on the question. Ability to act or not act is the sole criterion of liberty.

20 It explains how it is that the will does accept or not accept a given object; without an explanation of that point, there is no complete theory of even *liberum arbitrium*.

21 Observe that the *dominium sui actus* pertains not to the act that is dominated, namely, the act freely produced in the will with respect to the means, but to the act that dominates, that causes, that freely produces the will of the means. Thus, freedom is a quality in an *actio*, and an *actio* is a *ratio formalis* or notional relation. This point eliminates considerable confusion that exists in the reconciliation of divine liberty with divine immutability.

2   The Possibility of Liberty

If St Thomas held that the essence of freedom lay in the will's capacity either to act or not act, it would seem that he must have a solution to the trite objection: The will cannot act without God, therefore liberty cannot be the will's capacity either to act or not act.

Indeed, in St Thomas God infallibly knows what the will is to do, he efficaciously decrees what the will is to do, he irresistibly brings it about that the will do what he foreknows and decrees. Under such circumstances, to say that the will does this or that according to its good pleasure is, it may seem, preposterous.

But this is not all. Granted the will freely chooses and executes what God infallibly foreknows, decrees, and effects, it remains that God is principal cause, universal cause, eternal cause, while the will is instrumental, particular, temporal. If, then, God is for these reasons more a cause of the good that the will does than is the will itself, it would seem that he is also more a cause of the evil. And if the will is sinful because its works are evil, then how evade the conclusion that God is still more sinful?

These are the sixteenth-century problems that block the view and obstruct the passage from our minds to St Thomas's thought on operative grace. It is necessary to eliminate them, for otherwise no matter how numerous the texts we adduce and how cogent their evidence, the intellect of the reader will necessarily remain in doubt.

The section falls into two parts: divine foreknowledge and human liberty is treated in the first place; next, the idea of divine transcendence is studied.

2.1 Divine Foreknowledge and Human Liberty

The fundamental difficulty in the problem is, according to St Thomas, the imagination.[22] First, then, this difficulty is surmounted; second, St Thomas's solution is given; third, the sixteenth-century question is raised in its most general form, Is there any difference between God's knowledge of good and his knowledge of evil acts of will?

---

22 He explicitly affirms an eternal vision to counteract the anthropomorphic image: see *Super I Sententiarum*, d. 38, q. 1, a. 5 [c. and ad 4m]; *Summa contra Gentiles*, 1, cc. 66–67 [§§ 547–48, 557, 564]; *Summa theologiae*, 1, q. 14, a. 13; *In I Peri herm.*, lect. 14, § 195.

2.1.1 The Elimination of Anthropomorphism

The first anthropomorphic difficulty arises from fancying that God knows what the will does before the will does it. God does not know any event before or simultaneously or afterwards. To know in such a manner, one must know in time; God knows eternally.[23]

Hence, the object of God's knowledge cannot be 'what was' or 'what will be,' for relative to God's knowledge there is neither past nor future. No more can the object be 'What is,' if the 'is' retains its temporal connotation and is opposed to either 'was' or 'will be,' for God's knowledge is not simultaneous with anything else. God knows 'what is' where the 'is' has the timelessness of the logician's copula.

But how, then, does God know time? He knows time because he knows all that is; among all the things that are, there are motion and the measure of motion and the motion as measured: knowing motions as measured is knowing time.[24]

The second anthropomorphic difficulty is to fancy that because one can add to the finite, therefore one can add to the infinite. To the infinite no addition can be made. God is entitatively the same whether he creates or does not create; his knowledge is the same; his will is the same; his activity is

---

23 Einstein's position would not have been surprising to St Thomas; he held that if there were more than one world, there would not be a common simultaneity (*Super I Sententiarum*, d. 37, q. 4, a. 3 [post med.]); that if all motions were not caused by the *primum mobile* (and they are not), then there would be as many times as motions (*In IV Phys.*, lect. 17, §§ 573–74). Time is a measure of motion: without motion and a measure for it such as space, there could be no time (*In IV Phys.*, lect. 17, §§ 577, 580). 'Before time' is a figment of the imagination (*Super II Sententiarum*, d. 1, q. 1, a. 5, ad 13m; *In XII Metaphys.*, lect. 5, § 2498), and so the question, Why did God not create sooner? is meaningless. God created time, acts eternally (*Summa contra Gentiles*, 2, cc. 31–38; see *In VIII Phys.*, lect. 2, § 989). The *nunc* of a temporal being changes inasmuch as the being changes; the *nunc* of an immutable being cannot change; such a *nunc* is eternity (*In IV Phys.*, lect. 18, §§ 585–86).

24 If I see a man crossing the street, I see the space he traverses but not the time. The time of his motion in crossing equates with the time of my motion in seeing. Consequently, I do not see time as an object like space but experience it as I experience an emotion. But an angel or God not merely apprehends the space as an object but also the time as an object. For in neither case is the apprehension a sensible perception, with space in the percept and time in the perceiving, but the intuition of a four-dimensional object that cannot be imagined though it may be expressed by algebraic symbols.

the same. For all of these are infinite and really identical with each other and with the infinity of substance that is *ipsum esse.*

But while this is as certain as is the simplicity and immutability of God, it does contain a problem. For if God creates, then he knows, wills, and does something that otherwise he does not know, will, or do. What constitutes the objective difference?

The objective difference is constituted by three *actiones,* an *actio* of knowing, an *actio* of willing, an *actio* of performing. But an *actio* according to its *ratio formalis* is a notional relation, [and] according to its principle or foundation is some reality. Therefore, to say that God knows, wills, does adds three notional relations; but it adds only one additional reality, namely, what is known, willed, done. It cannot put a new 'knowing' in God nor a new 'willing' in God nor a new 'doing' in God, for God already is infinite, *ipsum esse, ipsum intelligere, ipsum amare,* and *actus purus.* Finally, to bring this analysis to an ultimate degree of refinement, note that the notional relation of the knowing or willing is predicated eternally, while the notional relation of the doing is predicated *ex tempore.*[25]

25 *Summa theologiae,* 1, q. 13, a. 7, ad 3m: '... operatio intellectus et voluntatis est in operante: et ideo nomina quae significant relationes consequentes actionem intellectus et voluntatis, dicuntur de Deo ab aeterno. Quae vero consequuntur actiones procedentes, secundum modum intelligendi, ad exteriores effectus, dicuntur de Deo ex tempore, ut Salvator, Creator, et huiusmodi' [the operation of intellect and will is in the one operating, and therefore the names which signify the relations consequent on the action of intellect and will are said about God from eternity. But those (relations) which are consequent on actions proceeding according to the mode of understanding to external effects, (these) are said about God from time, for example savior, creator, and the like].
      The passage is not without the complications of the different senses of the term *actio.* God neither knows nor acts in time: from that point of view both predications are eternal. On the other hand, the *energeia* of knowing is eternal, but the *energeia* of the creature is temporal: from that point of view the former predication is timeless, the latter temporal. In the article, the different viewpoints seem to superpose; compare *Summa contra Gentiles,* 2, cc. 31–38, on creation *ab aeterno.*
      Observe that the passage stands well beyond the level of the common difficulty that supposes a 'time' when there are no temporal objects. St Thomas does not argue that creation cannot be predicated *ab aeterno* because there is a 'time' when there are no creatures: such a view he explicitly rejects as sheer imagination (*Super II Sententiarum,* d. 1, q. 1, a. 5, ad 13m; *In XII Metaphys.,* lect. 5, § 2498; *In VIII Phys.,* lect. 2, § 989; *Summa contra Gentiles,* 2, cc. 31–38).

2.1.2 The Reconciliation of Divine Foreknowledge and
Human Liberty

From the foregoing it will be apparent that any consideration of the issue
that is not strictly logical cannot but be both illusory and futile. It is not
surprising, then, that St Thomas conceives the issue in an abstract and
dialectical fashion. Treating predestination in the commentary on the
Sentences he refers back to his earlier treatment of providence in the following terms.

> Praedestinatio enim includit in suo intellectu praescientiam et
> providentiam ... Praescientia ... non imponit necessitatem rebus nec
> inquantum est causa ... nec ratione adaequationis ad rem scitam
> quae ad rationem veritatis et certitudinis scientiae exigitur, quia
> adaequatio ista attenditur scientiae Dei ad rem non secundum quod
> [res] est in causis suis, in quibus est ut possibile futurum tantum, sed
> ad ipsam rem, secundum quod habet esse determinatum, prout est
> praesens, et non futurum ...[26]

The passage is worth detailed study.

Two manners in which foreknowledge might necessitate events are distinguished: inasmuch as the knowledge is a cause of the event, and that
does not here concern us; inasmuch as the truth or the knowledge makes
the actuality of the event necessary, and that is the present question.

Next, with regard to the truth of the knowledge, two *adaequationes veritatis*,
equations between knowledge and reality, are distinguished. There is the
adaequatio of divine knowledge to the event as something future and now
existing only *in causa*. There is the *adaequatio* of divine knowledge to the
event as something present and so existing *in se ipso.*

---

26 [For predestination includes in its concept foreknowledge and providence ... Foreknowledge ... does not impose necessity on things, neither
insofar as it is a cause ... nor by reason of the correspondence with the thing
known which is required for the concept of the truth and of the certitude
of knowledge, because that correspondence of God's knowledge with the
thing is relevant, not as it (the thing) exists in its causes, in which it exists as
a possible future only, but (in relation) to the thing itself inasmuch as it has
determinate being as present and not as future] *Super I Sententiarum*, d. 40,
q. 3, a. 1.

The third, and last, element in the statement is that the *adaequatio* to be considered is not that between the knowledge and the event as future, but that between the knowledge and the event as present. In the latter case the event is not necessitated *ratione adaequationis*.

But two questions arise.

First, why should one consider the *adaequatio* of divine knowledge not to the event as future but to the event as present? Because the former is false and the latter is true. All things are eternally present to God. Hence St Thomas insists on this point in each successive treatment of the issue: see *Super I Sententiarum*, d. 38, q. 1, a. 5; *Summa contra Gentiles*, 1, cc. 66–67; *Summa theologiae*, 1, q. 14, a. 13; *In I Peri herm.*, lect. 14, § 195.

Second, why does this *adaequatio*, which relates and equates divine knowledge not to the event *in causis* but to the event *in se ipso*, eliminate the problem of necessity from divine foreknowledge? Because once the event is, it can no longer be necessitated; any necessity then is necessarily hypothetical necessity; and that is compatible with contingence. *Omne enim quod est dum est necesse est esse.* And this is the other essential and constantly repeated point in St Thomas's solution. See the same passages as those listed above.

Turning now to the objection from which this discussion began, let us ask St Thomas for his solution. It was said that the essence of freedom cannot lie in the will's capacity either to act or not act; for God knows precisely what it will do; therefore it is impossible for it to do otherwise.

After considering a number of solutions to objections of this type, St Thomas gives his own as follows.

> Et ideo aliter dicendum est, quod antecedens [God's knowledge] est necessarium absolute, tum ex immobilitate actus [God's immutability] tum etiam ex ordine ad scitum [the *relatio rationis* is *ex aeterno*]; quia ista res non ponitur subiacere scientiae divinae nisi dum est in actu secundum quod determinationem et certitudinem habet. Ipsum enim necesse est esse dum est; et ideo similis necessitas est inserenda in consequente, ut scilicet accipiatur ipsum quod est Socratem currere, secundum quod est in actu; et sic terminationem et necessitatem habet. Unde patet quod si sumatur Socratem currere secundum hoc quod ex antecedente sequitur, necessitatem habet; non enim sequitur ex antecedente nisi secundum quod substat divinae scientiae, cui subiicitur prout consideratur praesentialiter in suo esse actuali; unde etiam sic sumendum est consequens, quo-

modo patet quod consequens necessarium est: necesse est enim
Socratem currere dum currit.[27]

First, this solution may be summarized. Second, an application may be
made to the definition of liberty.

If God knows this, this must be. If the antecedent is absolutely necessary,
then the consequent is necessary. The antecedent is absolutely necessary.
Therefore the consequent is necessary.

St Thomas concedes the minor but distinguishes major and conclusion.
For though the antecedent is absolutely necessary, the consequent may be
necessary either absolutely or hypothetically. If the necessity of the consequent is hypothetical, then the consequent may still be contingent: for
hypothetical necessity is compatible with contingence.

Next, to show that the necessity of the consequent is not absolute but
hypothetical, he argues as follows.

If God knows this, this must be. The 'this' of the consequent must be in
all respects identical with the 'this' of the antecedent. But the 'this' of the
antecedent is actually existing, for God's knowledge is eternal. Therefore
the 'this' of the consequent is actually existing.

But the necessity of existence in what actually exists is hypothetical.
Therefore the necessity of the consequent, 'this must be,' is hypothetical.

Take, now, the objection against the definition of liberty: If God knows
the act of will, then the act of will must be and so cannot either be or not be.
Plainly the answer is that the conclusion follows if God's knowledge bears
on the act of will *in causis suis* but not if it bears on the act *in se ipso*. But the

---

27 [And therefore another response has to be given, namely, that the antecedent is necessary absolutely, first by reason of the immutability of the act
(God), then too by reason of its relation to the thing known, for that thing
is not posited as falling under divine knowledge except while it is in act
according to the determination and certitude it has; for while it is, it is
necessary that it be. And therefore a similar necessity is to be inserted into
the consequent, namely that this (fact) that Socrates is running be taken as
it is in act; and in this way it has determinateness and necessity. And therefore it is clear that if (the fact that) Socrates is running is taken according to
the way it follows from its antecedent, it has necessity; for it does not follow
from its antecedent except according to the way it falls under divine knowledge, to which it is subjected as it is considered according to its presence in
its actual being; and therefore the consequent too is to be taken in this way,
and in this way it is clear that the consequent is necessary: for it is necessary
that Socrates be running while he is running] *Super I Sententiarum*, d. 38, q.
1, a. 5, ad 4m.

latter is true and the former false. Therefore the objection against the definition of liberty is a fallacy.

2.1.3 The Difference between Divine Foreknowledge of Good and of Evil[28]

Under the influence of the Scotist tradition,[29] both Bañez and Molina attempt to explain how God foreknows, and accordingly posit their *decreta praedeterminantia* and *scientia media*. Both positions palpably differ from the pure metaphysics of St Thomas,[30] but the question[31]

Such an exigence for development must arise either from the foreknowledge as knowledge or from the foreknowledge as knowledge of such an event.

On the former account there neither is nor can be any such exigence. God is self-explanatory and not to be explained in terms of anything different; God is his knowledge; therefore divine knowledge neither is to be explained nor can be explained.

If, however, divine foreknowledge is considered from the viewpoint of

---

28 [Under this section title Lonergan wrote, 'Quod[libetales] 5 q 1 a 2 scientia Dei ut ars cognoscitiva B & M [boni et mali] causativa boni tt [tantum].'

29 See the passages collected from Scotus by Fr H. de Montefortino relative to *Summa theologiae*, 1, q. 14, a. 13 [*Summa theologica Ex operibus eius concinnata ... per Hieronymum de Montefortino* (Rome: Ex typographia Sallustiana), vol. 1 (1900), pp. 374–83]: it is precisely in the Scotist field of a mistaken concept of eternity and of prior and posterior *signa*, that the whole of both Bannezian and Molinist thought moves.

30 Bañez implicitly admits the difference when in his commentary on *Summa theologiae*, 1, q. 14, a. 13, after giving his own conclusions in terms of predetermination, he asks why St Thomas is so preoccupied with time and hypothetical necessity, points which in no way figure in his explanation. His quite unsatisfactory answer is that St Thomas is anxious to give all possible solutions to the problem (St Thomas gives only one); that St Thomas wishes to give God intuitive knowledge of future contingent events (St Thomas does not mean that God knows by looking at things: what then is this intuitive knowledge?). See Bañez, *Scholastica commentaria in primam partem Summae theologicae S. Thomae Aquinatis*, 1, q. 14, a. 13 (Roma, 1584, p. 314B [Madrid: Editorial F.E.D.A., 1934, p. 352]).

The Molinist *scientia media* can explain the contingence of only future acts of free will, but St Thomas's explanation covers the *contingentia in maiori et minori parte* as well. According to Molina, God's foreknowledge makes the falling of a stone necessary; according to St Thomas God's foreknowledge leaves the falling of a stone contingent. See *In I Peri herm.*, lect. 14, §§ 189–95.

31 [The paragraph ends in mid-sentence, but see above, note 28.]

the object known, then a need of future explanation is evident. *Scientia Dei est causa rerum.*[32] God is not the cause of sin.

Bañez's solution to this problem is well known.[33] God knows what is by causing it; God knows what is not by not causing it; sin is not a reality; therefore God knows sin inasmuch as he is not the cause of the opposite good.

But, while according to Bañez there are only two categories, namely, what God causes and what God does not cause, there are according to St Thomas three distinct categories, namely, positive truth, negative truth, and objective falsity. Positive truth corresponds to what God causes; negative truth corresponds to what God does not cause; objective falsity is a third category that contains one element, *malum culpae.*[34]

32 [God's knowledge is the cause of things] The phrase simply means that other knowledge arises from the action of the object on the knower; in God the action is the other way about. It is not an explanation of knowledge in God. St Thomas clearly affirms the absolute character of God's knowledge when treating the *futura contingentia* in the *Peri hermeneias*: 'ex hoc ipso quod aliquid est cognoscibile cadat sub eius cognitione, et ex hoc ipso quod est bonum cadat sub eius voluntate: sicut ex hoc ipso quod est ens, aliquid cadit sub eius virtute activa' [by this very fact that something is knowable it falls under his knowledge, and by this very fact that it is good it falls under his will, just as by this very fact that it is a being it falls under his active power] *In I Peri hermeneias*, lect. 14, §191. It is only because God necessarily has infallible knowledge with respect to everything knowable that foreknowledge constitutes a problem.

33 Bañez, *Scholastica commentaria in primam partem Summae theologicae S. Thomae Aquinatis*, 1, q. 14, a. 13 (Roma, 1584, p. 314D [Madrid: Editorial F.E.D.A., 1934, p. 353]): '... alia futura contingentia cognoscit Deus in suis causis, prout sunt determinatae a prima causa: malum vero culpae futurum cognoscit in sua causa, quatenus non est determinata a prima causa ad bene operandum' [God knows other future contingents in their causes, as they are determined by the first cause: but he knows the future evil of guilt in its cause, as not determined by the first cause to operate properly].

34 This would seem to be the proper inference from *Summa theologiae*, 1, q. 17, a. 1, *Utrum falsitas sit in rebus.* St Thomas conceives *veritas simpliciter* as conformity to the divine intellect, *falsitas* as nonconformity. He writes (*Summa theologiae*, 1, q. 17, a. 1): 'in rebus dependentibus a Deo, falsitas inveniri non potest per comparationem ad intellectum divinum, cum quidquid in rebus accidit, ex ordinatione divini intellectus procedat: nisi forte in voluntariis agentibus tantum, in quorum potestate est subducere se ab ordinatione divini intellectus; in quo malum culpae consistit, secundum quod ipsa peccata falsitates et mendacia dicuntur in Scripturis, secundum illud Psalmi iv: *ut quid diligitis vanitatem et quaeritis mendacium?* Sicut per oppositum operatio virtuosa veritas vitae nominatur, inquantum subditur ordini divini intellectus; sicut dicitur Ioan. iii: *qui facit veritatem, venit ad lucem'* [in things that depend on God, falsity cannot be found by comparison with the divine

Similarly, there are three categories with regard to the divine will; there is what God wills to take place; there is what God wills not to take place; and, in the third place, there is what God permits to take place.[35]

Finally, with regard to execution there are three categories: first, there is the good that God effects; second, there is the good that God does not effect; and third, there is the sin for which the sinner is alone responsible.[36]

---

intellect, since whatever happens in things proceeds by decree of the divine intellect: except perhaps in voluntary agents only, who have it in their power to withdraw themselves from the decree of the divine intellect; it is in this that the evil of guilt consists, as in the scriptures sins themselves are called falsities and lies, according to that text of Psalm 4: *why do you love vanity and seek a lie?* Just as on the other side, virtuous operation is called the truth of life, inasmuch as it is subjected to the decree of divine intellect, as is said in John, chapter 3: *the one who does the truth comes to the light*].

The positive truth that the sun shines is something that is positively and conforms to the divine design. The negative truth that the sun does not shine on us is something that is not positively and yet conforms to the divine design. But the objective falsity of *malum culpae* is something that is not positively and further does not conform to the *ordinatio divini intellectus*.

It is obviously impossible for Bañez to speak of anything as withdrawing itself from the ordination of the divine intellect. St Thomas not only speaks of it but cites scripture as his ground for doing so.

35 *Summa theologiae*, 1, q. 19, a. 9: 'Unde malum culpae, quod privat ordinem ad bonum divinum, Deus nullo modo vult. Sed malum naturalis defectus, vel malum poenae vult, volendo aliquod bonum, cui coniungitur tale malum: sicut, volendo iustitiam, vult poenam; et volendo ordinem naturae servari, vult quaedam naturaliter corrumpi' [And therefore God does not in any way will the evil of guilt, which withdraws the order to the divine good. But he wills the evil of natural defect or the evil of punishment, in willing something good to which such an evil is joined. As in willing justice he wills punishment, and willing that the order of nature be kept he wills that some things be naturally dissolved]. See the argument in 1-2, q. 79, a. 1. *Summa theologiae*, 1, q. 19, a. 9, ad 3m: 'Deus igitur neque vult mala fieri, neque vult mala non fieri: sed vult permittere mala fieri. Et hoc est bonum' [Therefore God neither wills that evils occur, nor wills that evils not occur, but he wills to permit evils to occur. And this is good]. For the reason why it is good in God to permit sin, see ibid. 1, q. 23, a. 5, ad 3m.

36 *Summa theologiae*, 1, q. 17, a. 1: '... in quorum potestate est subducere se ab ordinatione divini intellectus' [who have it in their power to withdraw themselves from the decree of the divine intellect]. *Summa theologiae*, 1, q. 103, a. 8, ad 1m: '... dicuntur aliqui vel cogitare vel loqui vel agere contra Deum, non quia *totaliter* renitantur ordini divinae gubernationis, quia etiam peccantes intendunt aliquod bonum: sed quia contranituntur cuidam determinato bono, quod est eis conveniens secundum suam naturam aut statum' [some are said to think or speak or act against God, not because they *totally* resist the order of divine government – because even those sinning intend some good – but because they struggle against some deter-

Thus, St. Thomas's divine *artifex* is not at all anthropomorphic. He is not restricted to two categories: what he conceives and what he does not conceive; what he wills and what he does not will; what he effects and what he does not effect. That is Bannezian doctrine. In St Thomas, though there is in this as in so many other respects no fully developed theory, still there are sufficient indications of three categories: there is objectively positive truth and negative truth and absolute falsity; there is what God wills to take place, what God wills not to take place, and what God permits; there is what God effects, and there is not what God does not effect, but there is also what God neither effects nor does not effect.

A few deductions with respect to the nature of St Thomas's transcendent *artifex* may not be out of place. It will be simplest to proceed from the idea of *falsitas obiectiva*.

First, then, *falsitas obiectiva* is not false in the sense that it is false to say that the sinner sins. That the sinner sins, is true. This truth is what constitutes the objectivity of objective falsity.

Second, the falsity of objective falsity is nonconformity to the divine intellect, nonparticipation of divine intelligibility, just as the truth of objective truth is conformity to the divine intellect and participation of divine intelligibility (see *Summa theologiae*, 1, q. 16, a. 1; q. 17, a. 1).

Third, just as objective truth is the object of intelligence and understanding, just as the presence of objective truth is the possibility of understanding and explanation, so also objective falsity is the negation of an object of intelligence and understanding, and the presence of objective falsity is the negation of the possibility of understanding or explanation. This is self-evident to anyone who has reflected on the critical problem: the possibility

---

mined good which is suitable to them according to their nature or state].
Summa theologiae, 1-2, q. 79, a. 2, ad 2m: '... Deus sic est causa actus [peccati], quod *nullo modo* est causa defectus concomitantis actum. Et ideo non est causa peccati' [God is in such a way the cause of the act (of sin) that he is *in no way* the cause of the defect that accompanies the act. And therefore he is not the cause of sin] (see a. 1, ad 3m). *De malo*, q. 16, a. 4, ad 22m: '... sicut creatura decideret in nihilum nisi per divinam potentiam contineretur, ita etiam deficeret in *non bonum*, si non contineretur a Deo. Non tamen sequitur, quod nisi contineretur a Deo per gratiam, rueret in *peccatum*; nisi solum de natura corrupta, quae de se habet inclinationem ad malum' [as a creature would fall into nothing unless it were held fast by the divine power, so also it would fall into *non-good* if it were not held fast by God. But it does not follow that, unless it were held fast by God through grace, it would fall into *sin*; unless (this be true) only of fallen nature, which of itself has an inclination to evil].

of our understanding objects is their objective intelligibility, their participation of the absolute intelligibility of God. Note that understanding, explaining, is not the same as knowing: one can know without understanding or explaining; for instance, one can know the facts to be understood or explained. Thus, the difference between the fact of sin and other facts is that the latter are not merely to be known as facts but also are to be understood and explained (positivism to the contrary), while the fact of sin is simply to be known and cannot be understood or explained. Again, though other facts may happen not to be explained or understood, still they could be, for they participate divine intelligibility; but the fact of sin, the objectivity of objective falsity, not merely happens not to be understood or explained from a subjective defect on our part, but cannot be understood or explained from its own objective defect. This may be summed up by saying that sin is a fact but not a problem: it is a fact, for it is objective; it is not a problem, for there is no objective intelligibility to be known.

Fourth, just as the mathematician can treat simultaneously both ordinary numbers and complex numbers (such as root minus one) on condition that he equates ordinary numbers to ordinary numbers and complex numbers to complex numbers but does not equate ordinary numbers to complex numbers, so also the philosopher or theologian can think and reason about God and man and sin, predestination, reprobation, efficacious and sufficient grace, only on condition that he relates what is intelligible to what is intelligible, but does not explanatorily relate the unintelligible to the intelligible.

The grounds for this canon are as follows.

First, the intelligible can be related to the intelligible: that is the nature of all understanding and explanation as it exists in a finite mind; whenever we understand, we understand something; only God's understanding is absolute, *ipsum intelligere*, and so simple, absolute, one, and without relation.

Second, the unintelligible cannot be related to the intelligible: this is self-evident for the relation in question is explanatory relation, so that to relate the unintelligible to the intelligible would be to explain the unintelligible. But the unintelligible is what cannot be explained.

Third, the unintelligible can be related to the unintelligible: there is a certain explanation of sin in terms of other prior sin, but the reason for this is not any intelligibility in sin; it is simply due to the fact that sin is also evil, a privation of the good; one privation leads to another, not because a privation does anything but because a deficient cause produces a defective effect.

Now to apply this analysis of *falsitas obiectiva* to the three problems of the controversy *De auxiliis*: first, what is God's knowledge of sin? second, what is the difference between efficacious and sufficient grace? third, why does not divine reprobation make God responsible for the sinner's damnation?

With regard to divine foreknowledge of sin, first, it is plain that God knows eternally and *in particulari* all sins. The fact of sin is objective and knowable: *ex hoc ipso quod aliquid est cognoscibile cadit sub eius cognitione*. But God does not understand sin, for sin has no intelligibility to be understood: *unumquodque cognoscitur secundum quod est*, for any other knowledge would be error. And therefore sin is not part of God's *ordo divini intellectus*, *ordinatio divinae gubernationis* (*Summa theologiae*, 1, q. 17, a. 1; q. 103, a. 8, ad 1m): for that *ordo* and *ordinatio* is intelligible.

With regard to the difference between efficacious and sufficient grace, there is no difference entitatively. Both *ab intrinseco* are proportionate causes of changes of will: but in the one case the changed will because changed consents to the change, and this follows from the nature of the case; in the other case the changed will though changed does not consent to the change but reverts to evil, and, like all other sin, this is unintelligible, a fact but not a problem.

With regard to God's innocence of the fate of the reprobate, observe that reprobation is both antecedent and infallible (*Summa theologiae*, 1, q. 23, a. 3; *In Rom.*, c. 9, lect. 2 [§ 764]) as also is predestination. But the latter is a cause of merits and of glory. The former is a permission to sin but not a cause of sin (*Perditio tua ex te Israel*). Now why can the one be a cause yet not the other? Because there are not two categories but three. How can reprobation be antecedent and not a cause? It is antecedent because it is a divine act. It is not a cause because sin has no cause, but is unintelligible, inexplicable, and not to be related explanatorily to the intelligible. But if it is antecedent yet not a cause, and if there are three categories and not two, then how can it be infallible? The answer to that lies in the theory of divine transcendence: God's knowledge is infallible.

The reader may now expect a synthesis, a presentation of the successive *signa rationis*, so that he can take in at a glance the whole theory. Such a synthesis is impossible: the unintelligible cannot be worked into a synthesis, for then it would be related to the intelligible. But it would seem that the blessed in heaven who participate the intellect of the transcendent *artifex* are most enthralled with the vision of divine sanctity, and so they exclaim perpetually, Holy! Holy! Holy!

2.2 *Divine Transcendence and Human Liberty*

The argument has followed out the implications of St Thomas's position because that position has to be placed in the environment of the *De auxiliis* if that controversy is to be set aside and the study of St Thomas himself be made possible. Now we return from the implications of St Thomas's position to that position in itself. Three points have yet to be considered: his theory of divine transcendence, his meaning in the phrase *ad modum liberi*, and his solution to the objection *Deus causa peccati*.

2.2.1 Divine Transcendence

The basic point in the theory of divine transcendence is the generalization of the solution to the problem of foreknowledge and liberty. It has been shown that in the proposition, *If God knows this, this must be*, the consequent *this must be* is not absolutely but hypothetically necessary. Now divine knowledge, divine will, and divine operation are really identical. Therefore, what holds with regard to divine knowledge necessarily holds with regard to divine will and divine operation. Accordingly, to the proposition, *If God wills this, this must be*, or to the proposition, *If God does this, this must be*, the same answer is available: this must be with hypothetical necessity, I grant; with absolute necessity, I deny.

This generalization can be found in any of St Thomas's works. Thus, in the commentary on the *Sentences*:

> ... quamvis voluntas Dei sit immutabilis et invincibilis, non tamen sequitur quod omnis effectus eius sit necessarius necessitate absoluta quam habet res a causa sua proxima, sed solum necessitate conditionata, sicut et de praescientia dictum est.[37]

In the *Pars prima*:

> ... fatum, secundum considerationem secundarum causarum, mobile est: sed secundum quod subest divinae providentiae, immobilitatem

---

37 [although the will of God is unchangeable and invincible, still it does not follow that every effect of his is necessary with the absolute necessity which the thing has from its proximate cause, but only (necessary) with a conditioned necessity, as was said also of foreknowledge] *Super I Sententiarum*, d. 47, q. 1, a. 1, ad 2m.

sortitur, non quidem absolutae necessitatis, sed conditionatae; secundum quod dicimus hanc conditionalem esse veram vel necessariam, *Si Deus praescivit hoc futurum, erit.*[38]

And in the *Pars tertia*:

> ... aliquid potest dici possibile vel impossibile dupliciter: uno modo,
> simpliciter et absolute; alio modo, ex suppositione. Simpliciter igitur
> et absolute loquendo, possibile fuit Deo alio modo hominem liber-
> are quam per passionem Christi: *quia non est impossibile apud Deum
> omne verbum*, ut dicitur Luc. 1. Sed ex aliqua suppositione facta, fuit
> impossibile. Quia enim impossibile est Dei praescientiam falli et eius
> voluntatem seu dispositionem cassari, supposita praescientia et
> praeordinatione Dei de passione Christi, non erat simul possibile
> Christum non pati, et hominem alio modo quam per eius passionem
> liberari. Et est eadem ratio de omnibus his quae sunt praescita et
> praeordinata a Deo: ut in prima parte habitum est.[39]

Plainly, divine will and divine operation are assimilated to divine foreknowledge. The same solution of hypothetical and absolute necessity *is valid in
each case and in all three together.*[40]

38 [fate, from the viewpoint of secondary causes, is changeable; but as subject
   to divine providence, it shares in unchangeableness, not indeed that of
   absolute but of conditioned necessity; in the way in which we say that this
   conditional is true or necessary, 'If God knows this will be, it will be'] *Summa
   theologiae*, 1, q. 116, a. 3.
39 [something can be called possible or impossible in two ways: in one way,
   simply and absolutely; in another way, on a supposition. Speaking then
   simply and absolutely, it was possible for God to set man free in another way
   than through the passion of Christ: *for nothing will be impossible with God*, as is
   said in Luke 1. But if we make a certain presupposition, it was impossible.
   For, since it is impossible for the foreknowledge of God to be fallible, and
   for his will or disposition to fail, (then) supposing the foreknowledge and
   preordination of God on the passion of Christ, it was not simultaneously
   possible that Christ not suffer, and that man be set free in another way than
   by his passion. And the same reasoning holds for all these things that are
   foreknown and foreordained by God, as was concluded in the first part]
   Summa theologiae, 3, q. 46, a. 2.
40 Two reasons may be assigned for the generalization. First, what is true of
   foreknowledge must also be true of will and operation, for the three are
   really the same. Second, the predication, *God wills this* or *God does this*, is of
   the same nature as the predication, *God knows this*. In each case is added a
   relatio rationis to the *actus purus* and the term of the relation is not a possibil-

Because this is so, there arises a special prerogative of God as agent: he stands outside the [order] of all other causes, and his effects are necessary or contingent at his choice, yet the contingent effects emerge with all the infallibility, efficacity, and irresistibility that are to be found in necessary effects.

The idea may readily be deduced from the fundamental proposition, If God knows, wills, does this, then this must be. On the one hand, the 'this' of the consequent is necessary, and so God's knowledge is infallibile, his will irresistible, his action efficacious. On the other hand, the necessity of the 'this' may be either absolute or hypothetical; which it is depends on 'what' is known, willed, done by God. If God intends to produce the necessary, then the effect cannot but be necesary. If he intends to produce the contingent, then the effect cannot but be contingent.

Since everything depends on the divine intention, and since an intention is an act of will, St Thomas commonly refers to this property of divine transcendence as the efficacy of divine will.[41]

---

ity (God might will this, God might do this) but an actuality (God wills this, does this). Finally, there is the same basic difficulty in all three cases, namely, the idea of time: just as God does not know in time, neither does he will in time, nor act in time. On the eternity of divine action, see *Summa contra Gentiles*, 2, cc. 31–38; on God's will of what is not yet, ibid. 1, c. 79. In the latter passage St Thomas does not endeavor to raise the reader to the level of the concept of eternity.

41 See *Summa theologiae*, 1, q. 19, a. 8; *In VI Metaphys.*, lect. 3 [§§1218–22]; *De substantiis separatis*, c. 14 [§§120–25]; *In I Peri herm.*, lect. 14, §197. The connection of these passages with the generalized theorem on divine foreknowledge appears clearly from *Summa theologiae*, 1, q. 19, a. 8, ad 3m: '... ea quae fiunt a voluntate divina, talem necessitatem habent, qualem Deus vult ea habere, scilicet, vel absolutam, vel conditionalem tantum' [those things which are done by divine will have that necessity which God wishes them to have, namely, either absolute or only conditional].

Confusion in the interpretation of St Thomas's thought partly arises from the four senses in which he uses the term 'contingent,' namely, a creature, a corruptible creature (for example, *Summa theologiae*, 1, q. 2, a. 3, *tertia via* [*possibilia esse et non esse*]), the 'per accidens' (for example, *Summa theologiae*, 1, q. 115, a. 6; q. 116, a. 1), and a free act of will.

Two points merit particular attention.

In the commentary on the *Sentences* contingence is regularly attributed to the contingent action of the proximate cause (*In I Sententiarum*, d. 38, q. 1, a. 5; d. 39, q. 2, a. 2, ad 2m; d. 40, q. 3, a. 1; d. 47, q. 1, a. 1, ad 2m). In *De veritate* (q. 23, a. 5) it is seen that this implies that God could not create a corruptible creature, a cow or a turnip; the position is accordingly corrected. God can give the mode of contingence even without the help of the *corpus caeleste*. This of course refers to the production of the *prima individua*

2.2.2 Ad Modum Liberi

Evidently St Thomas would [not] dream of attributing the property of divine transcendence to any created cause: such a view he explicitly excludes on two distinct occasions.[42] So there is no need to argue the point. It remains that we explain what St Thomas does mean by *ad modum liberi*.

The fundamental point arises from his theorem *Deus operatur in omni operante*. Because this theorem is a theorem and not the gratuitous supposition of another motion, because the discovery of it is like the discovery of the principle of work and not like the discovery of a new continent or planet, it is quite manifest that God's operation in the operation of nature must be *ad modum naturae*. On the other hand, were the divine operation like St Albert's *virtus divina creata* or Bañez's *praemotio physica*, it necessarily would be an addition to nature and not *ad modum naturae*. Thus:

> ... Deus operatur in unoquoque agente etiam secundum modum illius agentis; sicut causa prima operatur in operatione causae secundae, cum secunda causa non possit in actum procedere nisi per virtutem causae primae. Unde per hoc quod Deus est causa operans in cordibus hominum, non excluditur quin ipsae humanae

---

arborum et brutorum animalium. It does not mean that God is a *causa impedibilis* and so can directly give the mode of the *per accidens*; nor does it mean that God can create a free act without the action of a free will (see *De veritate*, q. 24, a. 1, ad 3m). The fact that St Thomas speaks generally of contingence proves nothing: see the idea of contingence implicit in *Summa contra Gentiles*, 3, c. 72; contrast with this the argument against Albumazar in ibid, 3, c. 86 [§ 2622].

Again, observe that the *certitudo ordinis* of divine providence (see *De veritate*, q. 6, a. 3; the correction of this in *Summa contra Gentiles*, 3, c. 94; the repetition in *Summa theologiae*, 1, q. 19, a. 6; q. 103, a. 7) is not a distinct certitude from that of divine transcendence and efficacy. Such an opinion is explicitly excluded by *Summa theologiae*, 1, q. 116 a. 3, and it contradicts the whole of St Thomas's theory of foreknowledge.

42 *In I Peri herm.*, lect. 14, § 197: '...omnis alia causa cadit iam sub ordine necessitatis vel contingentiae; et ideo oportet quod vel ipsa causa possit deficere, vel effectus eius non sit contingens, sed necessarius' [every other cause already falls under the order of necessity or of contingence; and therefore it is necessary either that the cause itself can fail or that its effect is not contingent but necessary]; see *In VI Metaphys.*, lect. 3, § 1222. Accordingly the Bannezian *praemotio physica* cannot be foisted off on St Thomas: he makes efficacy an exclusive property of God, and rejects in anticipation the suggestion that a created cause could infallibly and irresistibly produce a contingent effect.

mentes sint causae suorum motuum; unde non tollitur ratio
libertatis.[43]

Now this divine operation in the operation of the free will has all the
properties of divine transcendence: it is the *actio* of God. Therefore, God
will infallibly and irresistibly produce the effect he intends, and the effect
will be contingent or necessary according to the nature of the cause God
uses as an instrument in the production of the effect. Thus:

> ... Deus movet quidem voluntatem immutabiliter propter efficaciam
> virtutis moventis, quae deficere non potest; sed propter naturam
> voluntatis motae, quae indifferenter se habet ad diversa, non
> inducitur necessitas, sed manet libertas; sicut etiam in omnibus
> providentia divina infallibiliter operatur; et tamen a causis con-
> tingentibus proveniunt effectus contingenter, inquantum Deus
> omnia movet proportionabiliter, unumquodque secundum suum
> modum.[44]

In this passage, besides the theorem of divine transcendence and that of
Deus operatur in operatione creaturae, there is at least the supposition of a
third, namely, fate.

Fate is the *virtus artis divinae in universo instrumentali.* In itself it is simply
the dynamic pattern of the four-dimensional universe, the order and arrangement of all secondary causes. So considered, that is, *in sensu diviso*, it is
a cause inasmuch as the secondary causes are causes, and it produces
necessary or contingent effects necessarily or contingently according to the
nature of the secondary causes. But this is not the whole story, but a mere

43 [God operates in every agent also according to the way of that agent; as the
first cause operates in the operation of a secondary cause, since a secondary
cause cannot proceed to its act except through the power of the first cause.
And therefore the fact that God is a cause operating in the hearts of men
does not prevent human minds themselves from being causes of their movements; and therefore the character of freedom is not taken away] *De veritate*,
q. 24, a. 1, ad 3m.

44 [God does immutably move the will because of the efficacy of the moving
power, which cannot fail; but because of the nature of the will that is
moved, which is indifferent to various things, there is no imposition of
necessity but freedom remains; as also in everything divine providence
operates infallibly; and nevertheless effects proceed contingently from
contingent causes, inasmuch as God moves all things according to proportion, everything according to its mode] *De malo*, q. 6, a. 1, ad 3m.

abstraction: it is prescinding from God who creates, conserves, moves, applies, and so orders and arranges; further, it is prescinding from God who operates efficaciously in the operation of every creature. Fate, then, taken really, that is, in conjunction with God, *in sensu composito*, is immobile, infallible, irresistible, efficacious: the effects are still necessary or contingent according to the nature of their causes; but the contingent effects do not emerge contingently but infallibly, irresistibly, efficaciously.[45] As is plain, this theorem is simply the summation of all instances of efficacious divine operation in the operations of creatures.

Thus, when God moves the will to the end, then this motion to the end contingently implies the will's self-motion to the means *in sensu diviso*; it infallibly implies the will's self-motion to the means *in sensu composito*.

2.2.3 *Deus Causa Peccati*

While the theorem of divine transcendence shows that there is no incompatibility between the divine artist and the contingency of the corruptible creature, of the *per accidens*, or of the free act of will, it is not in itself an explanation of the problem of sin.

Because God knows, wills, and causes Peter to do this, therefore Peter does this. His doing it is hypothetically necessary. God is the principal cause of his doing it, and Peter simply an instrument.[46] Further, God is universal cause, and so responsible for all the circumstances, conditions, motives, and dispositions of mood and temperament that led to Peter doing it.

But it happens that the 'this' which Peter did is a sin. Because Peter is the free cause of the act, he is responsible and a sinner. But God is still more a cause than Peter and still freer than Peter. Therefore God is more a sinner than Peter.

That, I think, is the obvious difficulty. It will be well to analyze it.

---

45 *Summa theologiae*, 1, q. 116, a. 3: '... fatum, secundum considerationem secundarum causarum, mobile est: sed secundum quod subest divinae providentiae, immobilitatem sortitur, non quidem absolutae necessitatis, sed conditionatae' [fate, from the viewpoint of secondary causes, is changeable; but as subject to divine providence, it shares in unchangeableness, not indeed that of absolute but of conditioned necessity]. On the nature of fate, see above pp. 293–96.
   Note that the use of *in sensu composito* and *in sensu diviso* above is not that of the Bannezians, who apply it to *praemotio physica*, but simply a consequence of St Thomas's theorem of divine transcendence.
46 That is, *quoad productionem entis*.

First is the *actus peccati*. It is an immanent act effected in Peter's will, the *voluntas qua reducta de potentia in actum*. It is also, perhaps, some *actus imperatus* consequent to the act effected in the will.

Second, there is the *defectus* or *deformitas peccati*. This pertains to the *actus peccati*, not as an entity but as a privation; it is the absence of conformity to the rule of rectitude.

Third, there is the *causa actus peccati*; there is the proximate cause, namely, the will in act with respect to the end; there is the first cause, God *operans in omni operante*.

Fourth, there is the *causa defectus* or *causa deformitatis*. This is the *ratio culpae*. The whole problem is solved if it can be shown that while both Peter and God are *causae actus peccati*, Peter alone is *causa defectus* or *deformitatis*.

St Thomas attends to this problem principally in the *De malo* and the *Prima secundae*.[47] The essential element in his thought is that one can be the *causa actus deformis* without being the *causa deformitatis*. The former has its criterion in the laws of cause and effect. The latter has its criterion in the laws of morality.

Peter is not merely the *causa actus deformis* but also the *causa deformitatis*.

---

47 *De malo*, q. 3, aa. 1-2; *Summa theologiae*, 1-2, q. 79, aa. 1-2. In the commentary on the *Sentences* the question was not acute. Then reprobation was conceived as *praescientia culpae et praeparatio poenae* (*Super I Sententiarum*, d. 40, q. 4, a. 1 [sense not words]) which is not the same as *permissio culpae et praeparatio poenae* (*Summa theologiae*, 1, q. 23, a. 3 [sense not words]); for in the commentary on the *Sentences* grace is not prepared equally for all because, though God is equally towards all, all are not equally towards him (*Super I Sententiarum*, d. 40, q. 2, a. 1, ad 6m); moreover, *multa fiunt quae Deus non operatur*, and with regard to permission of evils by divine consequent will it is said (*Super I Sententiarum*, d. 47, q. 1, a. 2), 'potest fieri oppositum eius quod permissum est: quod tamen fit secundum permissionem, quia permissio respicit potentiam causae ad utrumque oppositorum se habentem' [the opposite of what is permitted can be done; this, however, is done according to permission, because permission regards that power of a cause which can relate to each of (two) opposite (courses)]. In the *Pars prima* reprobation is not merely foreknowledge of sin but also permission, which is an act of divine will and antecedent to the sinner's sinful will; but though antecedent, it is not, like predestination, a cause (q. 23, a. 3 [ad 2m]). In the parallel commentary on Romans we are told that reprobation is eternal and not temporal, presumably antecedent and not consequent; that as predestination prepares glory, so reprobation prepares damnation; but while predestination prepares merits, reprobation does not prepare sins; so that while the foreknowledge of merits cannot be the cause of predestination, still foreknowledge of sin is the cause of reprobation inasmuch as the latter is the preparation of damnation (*In Rom.*, c. 9, lect. 2 ad fin. [§§ 763–64]).

He is the former because he produced a given act. He is the latter because in producing it, he did what he ought not have done.

God is the *causa actus deformis* but not the *causa deformitatis*. He is the former because he produced the act as principal and universal cause. He is not the latter because in doing so he did not do what he ought not have done.

Thus:

> ... deformitas peccati non consequitur speciem actus secundum quod est in genere naturae, sic autem a Deo causatur; sed consequitur speciem actus secundum quod est moralis, prout causatur ex libero arbitrio.[48]

> ... homo qui peccat, licet per se non velit deformitatem peccati, tamen deformitas peccati, aliquo modo cadit sub voluntate peccantis, dum, scilicet, magis eligit deformitatem peccati incurrere quam ab actu cessare. Sed deformitas peccati nullo modo cadit sub voluntate divina, sed consequitur ex hoc quod liberum arbitrium recedit ab ordine voluntatis divinae.[49]

The question, then, is simply this: Is God morally bound to refrain from operating Peter's operation when Peter sins?[50]

48 [the deformity of sin does not follow the species of the act as it exists in the genus of nature, in that way it is caused by God; but it follows the species of the act as being moral, the way it is caused by free will] *De malo*, q. 3, a. 2, ad 2m.

49 [the one who sins, though he does not per se will the deformity of sin, still the deformity of sin falls in some way under the will of the one sinning, namely, while he chooses rather to incur the deformity of sin than to cease from his act. But the deformity of sin in no way falls under the divine will, but follows from this that free will withdraws from the order of the divine will] Ibid. ad 1m. With regard to God not in any way willing sin, consider *Summa theologiae*, 1, q. 19, a. 9, ad 3m: 'Deus ... neque vult mala fieri, neque vult mala non fieri: sed vult permittere mala fieri. Et hoc est bonum' [God neither wills that evils occur, nor wills that evils not occur, but he wills to permit evils to occur. And this is good]. This presupposes the category of *falsitas obiectiva*; see *Summa theologiae*, 1, q. 17, a. 1: '... in voluntariis agentibus ... in quorum potestate est subducere se ab ordinatione divini intellectus; in quo malum culpae consistit' [in voluntary agents ... who have it in their power to withdraw themselves from the decree of the divine intellect; it is in this that the evil of guilt consists]. See ibid. 1-2, q. 79, a. 1, ad 3m; a. 2, ad 2m.

50 Such is the assumption of ibid. q. 79, a. 1 c.

Per se it is certain that God is not: for God is impeccable and yet he operates the operation of all sinners.

It remains that there is a *per accidens* in the matter, namely, a mistaken theory about God's operation which would imply God to be morally bound to refrain from operating the operation of the sinner. Such a theory is one that posits simply two categories, that asserts that unless God makes it infallibly certain that Peter does not sin, then God makes it infallibly certain that Peter does sin. For, though in such a case it would remain that the sinner sinned freely, it nonetheless would also be true that God is more a sinner than man. Evidently so, for morality prohibits making others sin.

But, as we have already indicated, St Thomas does not hold any theory of two and only two categories such as that of Bañez. He does not develop his three categories into an explicit system, but he scatters through his pages fairly frequent assumptions of them. On the point in hand, there is

> ... sicut creatura decideret in nihilum nisi per divinam potentiam contineretur, ita etiam deficeret in non bonum, si non contineretur a Deo. Non tamen sequitur, quod nisi contineretur a Deo per gratiam, rueret in peccatum; nisi solum de natura corrupta, quae de se habet inclinationem ad malum.[51]

Here three categories are evident: *bonum, non bonum, peccatum*. Unless God makes the creature good, then it is not good; but it does not follow that unless God makes the creature gratuitously good, then the creature sins; that holds only in the case of fallen nature.

So much for the fundamental solution. But further objections may be considered to clarify the issue. These are four: first, from the fact that God is principal cause; second, from the fact that God moves the will to the end; third, from the fact of the *massa damnata*; fourth, in the case of a first sin, as that of the angels.

First, then, God does not merely operate the operation of the creature; he operates it more than the creature does; he operates *immediatione virtutis*; and his operation *prius intrat, vehementius imprimit, tardius recedit*.

---

51 [as a creature would fall into nothing unless it were held fast by the divine power, so also it would fall into non-good if it were not held fast by God. But it does not follow that, unless it were held fast by God through grace, it would fall into sin; unless (this be true) only of fallen nature, which of itself has an inclination to evil] *De malo*, q. 16, a. 4, ad 22m. On the special case of fallen nature, see below §5.2.

On the exact meaning of these theorems on the degrees of causality, see above in chapter 3. If one allows one's imagination to hypostatize theorems into motions, then the objection is valid. Further, if one substitutes for St Thomas's theorem on instrumentality (which makes the creature an instrument *quoad productionem entis*) a predetermining *praemotio* which regards not simply the *ratio entis* but also its determination, then, again and separately, the objection is valid. But the objection in neither of those senses is valid against St Thomas.[52]

Second, when God moves the will to the end, it is as certain as fate in *sensu composito* that the means chosen by the sinner will be sinful.

This sounds imposing. But the certitude of fate *in sensu composito* coincides with the certitude that the sinner is sinning when he is sinning. In point of fact, when God moves the will to the end, this movement of itself tends to the good; the divine intention is that the sinner do what is right. St Thomas presents this situation as follows.

> ... instinctu quodam interiori moventur homines a Deo ad bonum et ad malum. Unde Augustinus dicit in libro *De Gratia et libero arbitrio* [cap. 22], quod Deus operatur in cordibus hominum ad inclinandas eorum voluntates quocumque voluerit, sive ad bona pro sua misericordia, sive ad mala pro meritis eorum. Unde et Deus dicitur saepius suscitare aliquos ad bonum ... Dicitur etiam suscitare aliquos ad malum faciendum ... Aliter tamen ad bonum, aliter ad mala: nam ad bona inclinat hominum voluntates directe et per se, tamquam actor bonorum; ad malum autem dicitur inclinare vel suscitare homines occasionaliter, inquantum scilicet Deus homini aliquid proponit vel interius, vel exterius, quod, quantum est de se, est inductivum ad bonum; sed homo propter suam malitiam perverse utitur ad malum ... Et similiter Deus quantum est de se, interius instigat hominem ad bonum, puta regem ad defendendum iura regni sui vel ad puniendum rebelles. Sed hoc instinctu bono malus homo abutitur secundum malitiam cordis sui ... Et hoc modo circa Pharaonem accidit,

52 *De veritate*, q. 24, a. 1, ad 4m: '... causa prima dicitur esse principalis simpliciter loquendo, propter hoc quod magis influit in effectum; sed causa secunda secundum quid principalis est, inquantum effectus ei magis conformatur' [the first cause is said, speaking without qualification, to be principal, on this account that it has a greater influence on the effect; but a secondary cause is principal in a certain respect, insofar as the effect is more conformed to it].

qui cum a Deo excitaretur ad regni sui tutelam, abusus est hac excitatione in crudelitatem.[53]

It would seem that there is no fault to be found with the movement of the will to the end.

Still, this leads to a third objection. Though the movement of the will is good and to the good, nonetheless it leads to sin *occasionaliter*. When the heart of man is infected with malice, then a good movement to the good is not enough; what is wanted is an operative grace that will transform an evil heart into a good heart, a heart of stone into a heart of flesh. This is true: the sins of the morally impotent reduce to their first sin, and moral impotence reduces to the fall of man.[54] But the point to be grasped is that neither the sins of the sinner nor the sin of our first parents constitute a claim in justice against God. There is, indeed, a claim to mercy, but God is free to choose his own manner of being merciful.

This finally brings us to the possibility of the first sin. St Thomas treats it in some detail in the *Pars prima* and then again and somewhat differently in the *De malo*.[55] But the ultimate solution to this problem can be had only by an explicit theory of *falsitas obiectiva*. Why did the angels sin? There is no 'why.' Later sins can be reduced to earlier sins and to the general corruption of fallen nature. But the first sin is first in the order of unintelligibility. There is no prior unintelligible to be alleged in mitigation of it. It is the

---

53 [men are moved by God to good and to evil by a certain internal impulse; and therefore Augustine says in his book *On Grace and Free Will*, chapter 22, that God operates in the hearts of men in order to incline their wills wherever he wishes, whether because of his mercy to good things, or because of . their deserts to evil things. And therefore God is often said to stimulate some to do good ... He is also said to stimulate some to do evil ... In one way, however, to good, in another way to evil: for he inclines human wills directly and per se to good things, as the agent of good things; but he is said to incline or stimulate men to evil as giving occasion (for it), insofar, that is, as God proposes to man something, internal or external, that in itself is inducement to good; but man because of his malice uses (this) for evil ... And likewise God, for his part, instigates man to good, for example, a king to defend the rights of his kingdom or to punish rebels; but an evil man abuses this good impulse according to the malice of his heart ... And it happened in this way with regard to Pharaoh, who when he was roused by God to the protection of his kingdom abused this stimulus to exercise cruelty] *In Rom.*, c. 9, lect.3 ad fin. [§ 781].
54 See *De malo*, q. 3, a. 1, ad 9m, ad 16m.
55 *De malo*, q. 16, a. 4. Compare *Summa theologiae*, 1, q. 62, a. 3, [ob. 2 and] ad 2m; q. 63, aa. 5–6.

mysterium iniquitatis in its pure form, and that mystery cannot be understood: the divine mysteries are understood by God, and that we do not understand them is because of their excess of intelligibility; but the mystery of iniquity is not an excess but a complete absence of intelligibility and an absolute impossibility of understanding. Still, if one understands that there is nothing to be understood, no cause of sin to be sought, no explanation to be made, then one knows all that there is to be known. That is the point of the third category.

2.3 Logical Summary

The various elements in the argument are here collected for the convenience of the reader.

(1) The Timeless Copula. If you choose to imagine time as a finite line, then eternity is not to be imagined as an infinite line but as a point outside the finite line. Eternity is the negation of time. Duration is merely an image of eternity as though eternity were time, or else it is the same as time.

It is true to say of any creature whatever: This is actually existing. It is not true to say of anything whatever: This is actually existing *now*, if the *now* is temporal. It is true to say of anything whatever: This is actually existing *now*, if the *now* is eternal. God's *now* is eternal.

(2) The Analogy of Predication. It is true that John is a man (substantial predication), learned (accidental predication), and a teacher (extrinsic denomination from the learning John causes). All three predications are true, objective, real, and equally so.

Note that by a teacher is here meant not a person who is learned, who speaks most of the time in a school, who knows all the tricks of pedagogy, and so on. A teacher is one who causes learning in others.

(3) Divine Attributes. There is no accidental predication with respect to God, for God is simple and immutable.

There is substantial predication with respect to God. All substantial predications are necessarily true whether or not God creates.

All other predication with respect to God involves extrinsic denomination and presupposes its term as actually existing *sub specie aeternitatis*.

To this there are three objections.

First, it cannot be really and objectively true that God causes this when there is no change in God. Solution: there cannot be any change in God, and it is really and objectively true that God causes everything yet need cause nothing.

Second, it cannot be really and objectively true that God knows this when there is no change in God. Solution: God's knowledge is infinite, and so there is no possibility of adding to his knowledge by changing him; further, it is really and objectively true that God knows this as actually existing and would not know it as actually existing unless he created it.

Third, it cannot be really and objectively true that God makes a free choice when there is no change in God. Solution: a free choice is not the contingent effect but the cause of a contingent effect; freedom lies in the *dominium sui actus*; the *dominium* does not lie in the act that is dominated but in the act which dominates; but the act which dominates is not the will of the means (which is effected) but the will of the end (which is necessary in itself, but free as a cause of something else). Hence there is no possibility of adding to God's freedom by putting in him a contingent effect, for it is not the contingent effect which is free but its cause. And in any case God is immutable.

(4) Divine Transcendence. Since any predication with respect to God *ad extra* presupposes the actual existence (*sub specie aeternitatis*) of the term, it follows *both* that if God knows or wills or does this, this must be *and* that the necessity of the 'this' is not absolute but hypothetical.

(5) The Grounds of Necessity and Contingence. *Necessarium et possibile sunt divisiones entis.*

Hence the ground of necessity and contingence is the divine intellect, the measure of all reality.

The ground of this being necessary or of this being contingent is *causally* the divine will deciding upon the realization of the necessary or contingent thing but *formally* the passive realization of the divine idea of necessity or contingence by the divine will.

(6) Divine Antecedence. Antecedence may be pure, relative, compound.

Pure antecedence is that of God with respect to any limited being or to any summation of limited beings. That God knows the fall of Peter is pure antecedence with respect to a single event. That God predestines Peter is pure antecedence with respect to a series of events.

Relative antecedence is the antecedence of one term to another in the series that God knows, wills, causes.

Compound antecedence is the conjunction of pure and relative antecedence. Thus, if *A* and *B* are two terms in a series, then the antecedence of *A* to *B* is relative, but the antecedence of *A* to *B* through the infinity of divine knowledge, will, and causality is compound.

The nexus of pure antecedence is hypothetical necessity: this is compatible both with absolute necessity and with contingence.

The nexus of relative antecedence is either necessary or contingent; it cannot be both, and it must be either one or the other.

The nexus of compound antecedence is either absolutely necessary or else contingent and hypothetically necessary; which it is follows from the nexus of relative antecedence.

(7) Predetermination. Since God is not determined but exactly the same whether he creates or does not create, the only possible prior determination is that in the finite series of events. If the prior determination is a necessary cause, the event is necessary. If it is a contingent cause, the event is contingent.

(8) The Conditionally Antecedent Will of God. The antecedence treated above is absolute. By the conditionally antecedent will of God may be meant: the *actus purus* with respect to a hypothetical situation; the per se effect of divine activity, as in the case of Pharaoh treated in the commentary on Romans; or the utility of prayer treated in *Contra Gentiles*, 3, c. 95; or what God wills *in universali*, as in the commentary on 1 Timothy, c. 2, lect. 1 [§62]. On universal salvific will, see *Super Ioannem*, c. 6, lect. 5 [§§937–38] .

(9) The Divine Architect. The divine architect is not to be conceived anthropomorphically as though he disposed of only two categories. He disposes of three categories.

There is what he plans, wills, executes, and this is actually existing *sub specie aeternitatis*.

There is what he does not plan, does not will, and does not execute, and this is either nothing or else it is *malum culpae*. If the latter, then God knows it, permits it, and cooperates with its perpetrator. He knows it because it is objective, but does not plan it because it is not intelligible. He permits it, and this permission is good and to the manifestation of the divine attributes, but he does not will it to be, just as he does not will it not to be.

(10) *Deus Causa Peccati*. Divine knowledge and permission of sin is just as much antecedent as divine planning and divine will of what is good.

But divine planning and divine will are causes: because God willed and planned this, therefore this is.

On the other hand, divine knowledge and permission are not causes: God knows and permits and, then but not therefore, sin takes place.

The ultimate ground of the difference is that sin as such is unintelligible and not to be explained. To make the nexus a *therefore* is to explain. To make the nexus a *then* is simply to state a sequence.

It would be easier to find an explanatory relation between the number of bald heads in Siam and the number of Aztec monuments in Peru than to find an explanatory relation between divine permission and sin, for in the latter case there is certainly none at all: sin is unintelligible and cannot be explained. Note that causality is a species of explanation.

Nonetheless, divine knowledge and permission of sin is *in particulari*, antecedent, infallible, efficacious: for God is not limited even by the possibility of sin.

To the objection, *Deus causa peccati*, God causes the sinful act: the entity of this act is related to God by a causal relation, but God causes the sin neither by compound nor by pure antecedence; not by compound antecedence, for God moves to the good; not by pure *antecedence*, for in operating the operation of the sinner he does not do what he ought not to do.[56]

(11) *Scientia Media.* It may be asked whether divine knowledge of sin is prior to divine permission of sin or divine permission of sin is prior to divine knowledge of sin.

The Molinist system would require the former to be true. The Bannezian system would require the latter to be true.

Since the distinction between divine intellect and divine will has no foundation except in our limited natures, and since both divine knowledge and divine will are self-explanatory because identical with the divine substance, it would seem most probable that the question is meaningless.

(12) Essence of St Thomas's Position. We have not infinite minds and so cannot comprehend predestination and reprobation. We know certain truths from philosophy and revelation. We can develop a technique to solve difficulties against these truths. Most of such difficulties arise from an anthropomorphic concept of God.

3   Transition from the Modern Viewpoint

The bearing of the preceding discussion on St Thomas's theory of operative grace is largely extrinsic. The points made pertain to the sixteenth-century field of speculation on the issue, and they have been treated because to a modern reader they constitute the essential questions. But if, for the sake of the reader, attention has been paid to these points, now for the sake of a historical knowledge of St Thomas it is necessary to direct attention to quite different channels.

56 [The editors have made some changes in this paragraph. In the autograph it reads: 'To the objection, *Deus causa peccati*, God causes the sinful act; the entity of this act is related to God by a causal relation: God causes the sin neither by compound nor by pure antecedence; not by compound antecedence, for God moves to the good; not by pure *antecedence*, for in operating the operation of the sinner he does not do what he ought to do.']

It was shown in the first chapter that St Thomas eventually effected the synthesis of the generic and the specific theorems on the necessity of grace, that he worked into a single theory both the doctrine of the supernatural, which was first formulated explicitly by Philip the Chancellor, and, on the other hand, the more primitive psychological theory on the liberation by grace of free will.

Now it is primarily to the latter field of thought that pertains the idea of operative grace. Historically the point is evident.[57] But its intrinsic evidence is no less convincing: for if there are no limitations from which liberty is to be liberated, then to operate on liberty is as paradoxical as to mold a statue out of water; on the other hand, if there are limitations on human liberty, then operation beyond the limits cannot possibly conflict with freedom.

Accordingly, one may distinguish three aspects in the effect of divine operation: the free act is, first, a reality, second, a right act, and third, a supernatural or meritorious act. Now, from the viewpoint of a theory of operative grace, it is plain that to explain how God effects the free act as a reality may be useful knowledge inasmuch as it answers prior questions, but to treat this point alone is to leave untouched the problem peculiar to operative grace. Similarly, an explanation of the supernatural character of the meritoriousness of free acts, however interesting in itself, is not really to the point. The issue that concerns us is this: How does God operate man's operation of a right act inasmuch as that act is right? It is here that there is an apparent conflict between divine activity and human liberty, whether one conceives the rightness as that of moral rectitude, or that distinctive of acts leading to justification, or in the instant of justification, or consequently making for spiritual advancement and final perseverance. For the whole moral aspect of freedom, as opposed to its metaphysical or psychological aspects, lies in the fact that man is responsible for his choice between right and wrong. But if man is responsible for the wrong he does, then he must be able to do what is right. If he is able to do what is right, then where does grace come in?

Observe that this problem, though parallel to that of the preceding section, is not identical. Just now we confronted the problem that man can either act or not act, yet cannot act without God and cannot choose except what God intends. But the new problem is that man can choose either right or wrong, yet needs grace to choose what is right. The former problem is an apparent conflict between God and *libertas exercitii*, and its solution lies in

---

57   Contrast the theories of Peter Lombard (above, chapter II-2, §3) and St Albert (above, chapter II-2, §4).

divine transcendence. The new problem is an apparent conflict between the necessity of grace and *libertas specificationis*, and here the solution must be different: for grace is a finite entity which does not participate in the divine prerogative of transcendence.[58]

The aim of the two sections is to give an account of St Thomas's thought on the limitations of human liberty, or what is equivalent, on the need of operative grace.

4   The General Theory of the Need of Operative Grace

The problem in this and the following section has already been defined. Man is free to do right or wrong and yet needs grace to do what is right.

The more specific elements in St Thomas's complex and highly nuanced solution are treated in the next section (§5). Here the general foundation of his thought is explained.

The basic idea is a distinction between different senses of the term 'proportion.' With one sense, we are all familiar: a cause is proportionate to an effect when it can produce it. To this, three other senses must be added.

There is the proportion of impeccability, of the cause that cannot fail to operate properly.

There is the proportion of the *agens perfectum*, that is, of the cause that will, as a matter of fact, operate properly most of the time.

There is the proportion of the *agens imperfectum*, that is, of the cause that can act properly not merely in any instance but in all instances, yet, as a matter of fact, does operate properly only *in minori parte*.

The above conception may be illustrated from a consideration of the theory of impeccability, of the need of habits, and of the general need of grace.

4.1   The Theory of Impeccability

Because man is not impeccable, he can be in need of grace to will the good.

Not only is man not impeccable, but absolute impeccability is possible to him only by the grace of the beatific vision.[59] The reasons for this statement are as follows.

---

58 Bannezian thought seems to suffer gravely from a confusion on this point. St Thomas is explicit in affirming that only God can infallibly produce a contingent effect. See *In VI Metaphys.*, lect. 3, §1222; *In I Peri herm.*, lect. 14, §197.

59 *De veritate*, q. 24, aa. 7–9.

Only a cause fully proportionate to its effect and not subject to extrinsic interference is naturally incapable of defective operation, of sin. But the finality of man is the true and the good, and God alone is fully proportionate to truth and goodness. Therefore God alone is naturally impeccable.[60]

But if man is so closely united to God that God becomes the principle of all man's action, then the possibility of sin is excluded. Thus, the beatific vision realizes all knowledge, concrete as well as abstract; it transforms the body and so excludes the interference of the lower man with intellectual operation; it unites the will with God in perfect charity.[61]

Without the beatific vision, there cannot be absolute impeccability in a creature. A relative impeccability is, however, possible. Graces can do for the soul what special privilege did for Adam's body before the fall. For Adam's body was not intrinsically immortal, such as was Adam's soul. It was rendered immortal by a combination of internal perfections and external protection. In similar fashion man can be made relatively impeccable in this life.[62]

4.2 The Need of Habits of Operation

In point of fact, though capable of a grace of impeccability, man is naturally the most imperfect of all creatures. Every other grade of being, in virtue of its nature, operates properly at least *ut in maiori parte*. In man evil predominates. This follows from his nature. The reason may be seen in a comparison of the material and spiritual orders.

The heavenly bodies are full realizations of their potency and cannot become anything else; they always operate properly. The *generabilia* are also *corruptibilia*: in them nature succeeds for the most part. But *materia prima* is pure deficiency.

Again, in the spiritual order, God is pure act and absolutely impeccable; the angels are *in genere intelligibilium ut actus*, and they do right in the main; but man is the spiritual counterpart of *materia prima*; his intellect is, at birth, like a *tabula rasa*; since, then, evil is multiform and the good unique, man for the most part does what is wrong.[63]

---

60 *De veritate*, q. 24, a. 7 [ad fin.]. Though the categories of the human intellect and will are universal, still only God is absolute truth and goodness. The human categories give the possibility of willing the good for its own sake, knowing the truth for its own sake. But they are not the absolute realizations of truth and goodness and so do not exclude the possibility of sin.

61 *De veritate*, q. 24, a. 8.

62 Ibid. a. 9.

63 *Super I Sententiarum*, d. 39, q. 2, a. 2, ad 4m. Note that fallen human nature and nature as such coincide.

The problem is, then, How make man right? How perfect him? How bring him and his operation into conformity with the rule and measure of rectitude, the divine wisdom and goodness?

There are two possible solutions. First, *per modum passionis*: let the potency to be regulated be moved by the rule of rectitude. Second, *per modum qualitatis inhaerentis*: let the rectitude of the rule become the form of the potency to be regulated.

The first solution is open to difficulties. If man's rectitude is simply imposed upon him extrinsically, then this is a species of violence: man's operation is made good, but man himself is not. Thus, one is left with the second solution.

What about the inherent quality?

Distinguish, in the first place, the degrees of its perfection. Incipiently it is simply a disposition. When it is consummated and, as it were, grafted on nature, then it is termed a habit. On this account a disposition is said to be *facile mobilis* and a habit *difficile mobilis*: for what has become a part of nature is not easily lost.

For the same reason the presence of a habit is indicated by ease and delight in operation: what is natural is easy and agreeable.

Finally, for the same reason, Averroes says that a habit is *quo quis agit cum voluerit*. For a habit makes operation one's property, and use of a habit is as unimpeded as use of one's own possessions.

So much for the signs and consequences of the habit. Essentially it is a form determining and perfecting an indeterminate potency.[64]

To conclude, as a man without habits does what is right only *in minori parte*, so with them he becomes an *agens perfectum*. The will perfected with the virtue of justice performs acts of justice with the spontaneity and regularity with which fire moves upwards.[65]

4.3   The Need of Grace

Just as the theory of the need of habits is based on the theory of the nature of impeccability,[66] so the theory of the need of grace for good action[67] is based on the theory of the need of habits.

---

64   *Super III Sententiarum*, d. 23, q. 1, a. 1. See *Summa theologiae*, 1-2, q. 49, a. 4.

65   *Super I Sententiarum*, d. 39, q. 2. a. 2, ad 4m. See *Summa theologiae*, 1, q. 49, a. 3, ad 5m [thus Lonergan, but the relevance is not clear; q. 49 of the *Prima secundae* is more to the point (see previous note), but there is no 'ad 5m' in a. 3].

66   Impeccability follows from perfect actuation; the need of habits follows from the need of actuation, determination, in indeterminate potencies.

67   We still prescind from the need of grace for meritorious action.

The doctrine of the commentary on the *Sentences* that has just been outlined later becomes more precise and specific. In the *Contra Gentiles* there is substituted for the normative theory, which makes divine goodness and wisdom the rule and measure of right action, a dynamic theory in terms of God's bringing man to his last end. The two aspects of good action and meritorious action superpose, but there is no neglect of the former and concentration on the latter such as is to be found in more recent speculation.[68] In the *De virtutibus in communi* and the *Prima secundae* the need of virtues in the will is discussed. Two reasons are assigned: the will needs the virtue of charity to be inclined towards the good that is beyond the proportion of the species; it also needs the virtue of justice to be inclined to the good that is beyond the proportion of the individual. Charity transcends human nature; justice transcends egoism.[69]

The latter point calls for some explanation. In what sense is egoism so natural to man that justice transcends his natural proportion? In the *Pars prima* one is assured that the natural inclination of the will, as that of every spontaneity, is to love God more than self.[70] It should seem that, since God is absolute goodness, and justice a participation of this absolute, therefore the natural love of God more than self implies a natural love of justice more than self.

The answer would seem to lie in the distinction between the proportion that gives capacity for perfection and the proportion that makes imperfection impossible or exceptional. Thus, the will as a potency (a) naturally tends to the absolute good, (b) is naturally capable of eliciting acts with respect to absolute goodness, but without the added perfection of virtues does so rarely, (c) with the second nature of the virtues spontaneously and so regularly does the right thing, and (d) with the grace of impeccability always does what it should.

This solution, which merely summarizes the points already made in this section, enables one to interpret such a passage as the following.

> Diligere autem Deum super omnia est quiddam connaturale homini; et etiam cuilibet creaturae non solum rationali, sed irrationali et etiam inanimatae, secundum modum amoris qui unicuique creaturae competere potest ... Unde homo in statu naturae integrae dilectionem sui ipsius referebat ad amorem Dei sicut ad finem, et

68 *Summa contra Gentiles*, 3, cc. 148 and 150–53.
69 *De virtutibus in communi*, q. 1, a. 5; *Summa theologiae*, 1-2, q. 56, a. 6.
70 *Summa theologiae*, 1, q. 60, a. 5.

similiter dilectionem omnium aliarum rerum. Et ita Deum diligebat
plus quam seipsum, et super omnia. Sed in statu naturae corruptae
homo ab hoc deficit secundum appetitum voluntatis rationalis, quae
propter corruptionem naturae sequitur bonum privatum, nisi
sanetur per gratiam Dei.[71]

Now, St Thomas holds that sin does not deprive man of what is natural:
therefore, even after the fall, man naturally loves God more than himself.
The difference between the two states is that before the fall man not merely
tends to the good absolutely but also acts accordingly, while afterwards he
does the evil he would not do and omits the good that he would do. In any
case, such is St Thomas's interpretation of the passage in the seventh
chapter of Romans.[72]

71 [But to love God above all things is something connatural to man and even
to any creature, not only the rational but the irrational and even the inani-
mate, according to the way of love which is fitting to each creature ... And
therefore man in the state of integral nature referred love of himself to love
of God as to an end, and similarly love of all other things. And in this way he
loved God more than himself, and above all things. But in the state of fallen
nature man falls short of this as regards the desire of rational will, which,
because of the corruption of nature, follows a private good, unless it is
healed by the grace of God] *Summa theologiae*, 1-2, q. 109, a. 3.

72 *In Rom.*, c.7, lect. 3, §565: 'Dicit ergo primum quantum ad omissionem boni
non enim ago hoc bonum quod volo agere. Quod quidem uno modo potest
intelligi de homine sub peccato constituto: et sic hoc quod dicit *ago* est
accipiendum secundum actionem completam, quae exterius opere exer-
cetur per rationis consensum. Quod autem dicit *volo* est intelligendum non
quidem de voluntate completa, quae est operis praeceptiva, sed de voluntate quadam incompleta, qua homines in universali bonum volunt, sicut et
in universali habent rectum iudicium de bono, tamen per habitum vel
passionem perversam pervertitur hoc iudicium et depravatur talis voluntas
in particulari, ut non agat quod in universali intelligit agendum et agere
vellet' [Therefore he speaks first about the omission of good: 'For I do not
do this good which I wish to do.' This can be understood of man as constituted under sin; and thus the fact that he says 'do' is to be taken according
to complete action, which is exercised in a deed externally through the
consent of reason. But the fact that he says 'wish' is to be understood, not of
the complete will which issues a precept to act, but of a certain incomplete
will, by which men will the good in the universal, just as they also have a
right judgment on the good in regard to the universal, still through habit or
perverse passion this judgment is perverted and this will is corrupted in
regard to the particular, so that he does not do what in the universal he
understands should be done and he would wish to do].
In other words, the natural tendency to the good in general becomes,
practically, a velleity. Thus, there is room for a grace to make the will tend
effectually to the good. Such would seem to be the sense of *ut bonum velit* in
Summa theologiae, 1-2, q. 111, a. 2 c. [sense not words].

To conclude, the general theory of the need of grace for good action is that human nature after the fall can desire to do what is right but, in the main, will fail to do so effectually. The general theory does not affirm any impossibility of effectual good action either in single cases or in all cases. It states a fact: man does not in the main do what is right. It accounts for the fact: man has a need of habits of operation if he is to do what is right as a general rule. But it is only the special theory of the need of grace that establishes an impossibility of good action without grace. To that we turn in the next section.

5   Special Theory of the Need of Operative Grace

On this background of a general improportion of man to good perform-ance St Thomas constructs his theory of the need of grace. As in the previous section, so here the argument prescinds from the well-known theory of the supernatural and of merit to treat in turn the need of grace *quoad substantiam actus* first in the sinner, second in preparation for justifi-cation, third after justification.

As this need of grace corresponds to the function of operative grace and, as it were, defines the latter's effect, it will be well to begin with an account of the relation of this need to human liberty. Thus, there are four points: psychological continuity, the need of grace in the sinner, the need in preparation for justification, the need after justification.

5.1 The Law of Psychological Continuity

St Thomas never affirms that the freedom of the will implies a perfection of equilibrium and indifference that is born afresh with every tick of the clock. A change of will is a motion in the will; that motion must have its propor-tionate cause; and the ticking of the clock is not a proportionate cause. Since a large number, if not all, of the difficulties against God's operation in the will arise from the assumption that the will perpetually and automati-cally springs back to perfect poise and equilibrium, it is necessary to copy out a flat denial of so preposterous an opinion.

> Tertia autem diversitas in quam liberum arbitrium potest, attenditur secundum differentiam mutationis. Quae quidem non consistit in hoc quod aliquis diversa velit: nam et ipse Deus vult ut diversa fiant secundum quod convenit diversis temporibus et personis; sed mutatio liberi arbitrii consistit in hoc quod aliquis illud idem et pro

eodem tempore non velit quod prius volebat, aut velit quod prius
nolebat. Et haec diversitas non per se pertinet ad rationem liberi
arbitrii, sed accidit ei secundum conditionem naturae mutabilis:
sicut non est de ratione visivae potentiae quod diversimode videat;
sed hoc contingit quandoque propter diversam dispositionem
videntis, cuius oculus quandoque est purus, quandoque autem
turbatus.

Et similiter etiam mutabilitas seu diversitas liberi arbitrii non est
de ratione eius, sed accidit ei inquantum est in natura mutabili.
Mutatur enim in nobis liberum arbitrium ex causa intrinseca, et ex
causa extrinseca. Ex causa quidem intrinseca, *vel* propter rationem,
puta cum quis aliquid prius nesciebat quod postea cognoscit; *vel*
propter appetitum qui quandoque sic est dispositus per passionem
vel habitum, ut tendat in aliquid sicut in sibi conveniens, quod
cessante passione vel habitu sibi conveniens non est. Ex causa vero
extrinseca, puta cum Deus immutat voluntatem hominis per gratiam
de malo in bonum, secundum illud *Prov.* XXI, 1: *Cor regum in manu
Dei, et quocumque voluerit vertet illud.*[73]

73 [But a third diversity in regard to which free will has power is considered
according to difference in the change; that difference does not consist in
this, that someone can will various things, for even God himself wills that
various things be done according to what suits different times and persons;
but the change of free will consists in this, that someone does not will the
very same thing at the same time which earlier he did will, or that he wills
what earlier he did not will. And this diversity does not belong per se to the
nature of free will, but pertains to it accidentally, according to the condition
of a changeable nature: just as it does not belong to the nature of the visual
potency that it sees in different ways, but this happens sometimes because of
the different disposition of the one seeing, his eye being sometimes pure
but sometimes disturbed.

And similarly too, changeableness or diversity of free will does not pertain
to its nature, but is there accidentally inasmuch as it is in a changeable
nature. For free will is changed in us both from an intrinsic cause and from
an extrinsic cause. From an intrinsic cause, *either* on account of reason, as
when a person did not know earlier something which he knows afterwards;
or on account of desire, which is sometimes disposed in such a way by passion *or* by habit that it tends to something as to a thing suitable to it, which
with the cessation of passion or habit is not suitable to it. And from an extrinsic cause, as when God changes a human will from evil to good through
grace, according to that text of Proverbs 21.1: *The heart of kings is in the hand
of God, and he will turn it wherever he will*] *De malo*, q. 16, a. 5. St Thomas does
not enounce this principle of psychological continuity elsewhere. He certainly presupposes it in the *De veritate* (see q. 24, aa. 8–10, where immutability of will is established by an elimination of the possible causes of change,

The point is clear and emphatically made. Per se the will does not change: thus, the angels decide their eternal destiny by a single choice. *Per accidens* it may be changed. But this *per accidens* is not a vague gesture of the voice; it is accurately defined. It is conditioned: the free agent must be *in natura mutabili.* Its causes are assigned: they are either intrinsic or extrinsic; if they are intrinsic then they are either a change in one's knowledge, or a change in one's passions, or a change in one's habits; if the cause is extrinsic, then it is God operating in the will.

5.2 The Impotence of the Sinner

While in the commentary on the *Sentences* St Thomas does not consider the sinner's need for grace to be absolute (§5.2.1), this position is changed in the *De veritate* (§5.2.2). The change involves the acceptance of the Augustinian or psychological theory of the need of grace (§5.2.3), and this acceptance is later maintained in synthesis with the theory of the supernatural (§5.2.4).

5.2.1 The Position in the Commentary on the *Sentences*

Previously to the formulation of the theory of the supernatural by Philip the Chancellor[74] the traditional position on the need of grace was expressed by a distinction between *libertas a coactione, libertas a peccato,* and *libertas a miseria.* The first liberty was from nature, the second was the effect of operative grace, the third was the prerogative of the blessed in heaven.[75] As has already been indicated,[76] it took some time for the theorem on the supernatural to be correlated accurately with earlier thought.

Accordingly, in the commentary on the *Sentences* St Thomas flatly denies that the sinner cannot avoid mortal sin without the help of grace.

> Cum igitur libera electio vel fuga boni seu mali ad naturam liberi arbitrii pertineat, non potest esse ut per peccatum subtrahatur

---

namely, the reason, passion, habit, divine operation in the will). Perhaps the use of the idea of liberty as noncoercion in the *De veritate* and its rejection in the *De malo* (see above, §1) have something to do with this clear and explicit statement on psychological continuity.

74 See above, chapter II-1, §4.4.

75 See Peter Lombard, *Sententiae,* 2, d. 25 [c. 8: 'libertas triplex, scilicet a necessitate, a peccato, a miseria,' *QL* 1: 432].

76 See above, chapter II-1, §4.2.

homini facultas fugiendi peccatum, sed solum quod minuatur, ita scilicet quod illud peccatum quod homo ante vitare de facili poterat, postmodum difficulter vitet ... peccatum mortale requirit consensum determinatum; unde si (homo) potest vitare hoc et illud, potest eadem ratione vitare omnia. Nec iterum potest dici quod ad tempus vitet, et non diu: quia liberum arbitrium resistens malo, non efficitur infirmum ad malum vitandum, sed multo fortius; unde multo magis postea potest vitare peccatum quam ante.[77]

Coherently with this position St Thomas considers *libertas a peccato* and *a miseria* to be merely a matter of the degree of perfection of liberty and in no way to affect its essence.[78]

5.2.2 *De Veritate*, q. 24, aa. 11–12

In his next work St Thomas denies that such fixity in evil as characterizes the demons[79] is possible in this life.[80] Passion is ephemeral. A bad habit does not totally corrupt the soul.[81] As it is by reasoning that man falls into error, so by more reasoning he can be brought back to truth;[82] even when error exists in matters of principle, they can be corrected, not indeed by deduction, but by collative thought and by the acquisition of the virtues which effect a right attitude to principles.[83] The avoidance of sin may be difficult, but it is not absolutely impossible.

77 [Therefore since free choice or flight from good or evil pertains to the nature of free will, it cannot be that there should be withdrawn from man the faculty of fleeing sin, but only that it should be diminished, that is, in such a way that that sin which before a person could avoid with ease he afterwards avoids with difficulty ... mortal sin requires determinate consent, and therefore if (a man) can avoid this and that (sin), he can by the same token avoid them all. Nor again can it be said that he avoids for a time and not for long: because free will in resisting evil is not made weak for avoiding evil but much stronger; and therefore much more can he avoid sin afterwards than before] *Super II Sententiarum*, d. 28, q. 1, a. 2.

78 Ibid. d. 25, q. 1, a. 4; see a. 2.

79 *De veritate*, q. 24, a. 10; see *Super IV Sententiarum*, d. 50, q. 1, a. 1; *Summa theologiae*, 1, q. 64, a. 2; *Summa contra Gentiles*, 4, c. 95 [ad fin.]; *De malo*, q. 16, a. 5.

80 *De veritate*, q. 24, a. 11.

81 That is, one bad habit can be corrected by exploiting another good habit, for example, excessive concupiscence by acts of fortitude. See ibid. a. 10.

82 Contrast the naturally immutable intelligence of the angel: ibid. a. 10.

83 The thought would seem to be much the same as in Newman's *Grammar of Assent* [John Henry Newman, *An Essay in Aid of a Grammar of Assent* (London, New York, Toronto: Longmans, Green and Co., 1930: original publica-

Just what St. Thomas understands by 'difficulty' in avoiding sin appears in the next article.[84] The sinner can avoid any mortal sin but cannot avoid all mortal sins. The paradox is explained by an extremely subtle psychological analysis, and the conclusion is reached by the combination of three factors.

The first factor is that an explicit deliberation is not necessary for a free act. The second is that an explicit deliberation is necessary if the sinner is not to sin again. The third is that it is impossible for a man to deliberate explicitly in all his actions. It follows that the sinner who does not need explicit deliberation to act freely, but does need it to avoid further sin, and yet cannot always have it, will inevitably yet freely sin, even mortally, unless aided by grace. Each factor is considered in turn.

Explicit deliberation is not needed for a free act. Normally human action is the spontaneous outcome of habits and of the orientation of mind and will; in emergencies this is necessarily the case, so that, as Aristotle remarks, it is not foreseen but unforeseen dangers that reveal the brave man. Nonetheless man acts freely in all such operations. Though there is little or no deliberation, still the act is not indeliberate in the sense of not free. There is a real and full consent, for the habit or orientation is in the will; it is a state of willingness with respect to an end, and such a state implies that the means will automatically yet freely be chosen whenever they present themselves unless an explicit deliberation intervene.[85]

---

tion 1870)]. Errors in principle cannot be corrected by syllogisms; St Thomas's alternative to the syllogism, *modus aestimandi quia rationabiliter et quasi collative accipit*, suggests the illative sense; finally, Newman's insistence on the importance of moral development has its counterpart in *virtus vel naturalis vel assuefactiva est causa eius quod est recte opinari circa principium*. See *De veritate*, q. 24, a. 11, ad 4m. Thus, the alleged opposition between Newman and Aristotle turns out to be merely an opposition between Newman and alleged Aristotelians. St Thomas attributes his thought on this point to Aristotle.

84 *De veritate*, q. 24, a. 12.
85 Ibid.: '... repentina sunt secundum habitum. Nec hoc est intelligendum quod operatio secundum habitum virtutis possit esse omnino absque deliberatione, cum virtus sit habitus electivus; sed quia habenti habitum iam est in eius electione finis determinatus; unde quandocumque aliquid occurrit ut conveniens illi fini, statim eligitur, nisi ex aliqua attentiori et maiori deliberatione impediatur' [sudden (acts) are according to habit. Nor is this to be understood so that an operation according to habit can be altogether without deliberation, since virtue is an elective habit; but because there is already a determinate end in the choice of the one possessing the habit; and therefore whenever something occurs as suitable to that end, at once it is chosen, unless it is prevented by some more attentive and more (intense) deliberation].

But though explicit deliberation is not needed for a free act, it is needed if the sinner is to avoid further sin. Even though the sinner in question has committed only one sin, and so has not acquired a vice, still there remains in his will a spontaneous orientation (*vis et inclinatio*) to the transitory good which he has made his end. When, then, temptation recurs, he will again succumb unless, by a special effort, he argues himself out of it.

He will succumb freely, for full advertence merely requires the reflection that the act is a sin and against God, while a consent subsequent to full advertence is of itself a free act.

But this advertence is not sufficient to restrain the sinner. It provides a motive only to the will that is actuated by charity, by love of the absolute or objective good. The sinner's will is turned away from God, and to give a sufficient motive the reason must find considerations that are deterrents from the viewpoint of self-love. Thus, for example, the sinner will have to advert to the danger of eternal punishment and to the fact that the risk is not worth running.

Now this second advertence is consequent to the first and presupposes it; moreover, it is in addition to the first, not explicitly included in it, but the fruit of further consideration.[86] It follows, then, that while the sinner can sin grievously with very little deliberation, he needs an explicit deliberation to restrain himself from sin.

At this point the third fact enters: the pressure of circumstance. The mind of man has many occupations, and nature cannot endure a perpetual strain.[87] Deliberate vigilance can succeed for a time, but not for the whole time nor even for a long time. Any mortal sin can be avoided by the sinner if only he puts his mind to it. But he cannot always put his mind to it, and, when he does not, he sins.[88] From this necessity of falling again and again into sin, the sinner is liberated only by the infusion of divine charity into the soul.[89]

---

86 Habitual 'fear of the Lord' is not to be presupposed: that is a gift of the Holy Ghost and the beginning of wisdom.
87 This is just another manner of expressing the necessity of habits in human operation: unless an indeterminate potency is determined by the habit, then it is unequal to the task of right action.
88 Note that here St Thomas is treating simply the question of the impossibility of the sinner's avoiding further sin.
89 That is the definitive liberation. But providential assistance would suffice in any particular case. See the corpus of the article, ad fin.

5.2.3 The Psychological Theory of the Need of Grace

Brilliant as is this bit of psychological analysis it is far from being the most significant element in *De veritate*, q. 24, a. 12. That article does not merely correct the error of *Super II Sententiarum*, d. 28, q. 1, a. 2. It marks the beginning of St Thomas's integration of the theory of the supernatural with the Augustinian tradition on the need of grace and the Christian tradition in the field of asceticism. Previously the theory of the habit simply stated a fact; henceforth it states a law, a complicated and delicate law, indeed, but nonetheless a law. Previously there were degrees of perfection in liberty, and between St Thomas in the commentary on the *Sentences* and the later distinction of a physical and moral potency in the will no difference can be assigned. Now, however, there are limitations to the exercise of liberty; the principle of psychological continuity has come into play; the actions of the past remain as a *vis et inclinatio*, a spontaneous force, ever tending to prejudge the issues of the present, and, in the long run, are bound to prove decisive.

Though the analysis of the sinner's impotence is the work of the scientific St Thomas, the inspiration is clearly St Augustine. *Cogenti cupiditati voluntas resistere non potest*, the latter affirms,[90] and the former shows how aversion from the incommutable good makes the possibility of sin precede the possibility of avoiding sin.[91] Augustine asserts the will of the sinner to be like a crooked leg that cannot but limp along; St Thomas points out the difference: the crooked will can avoid any sin but cannot avoid all.[92]

But not only are there these fundamental Augustinian concepts, not only is the new position itself to be attributed to a deeper study of St Augustine,[93] but the whole traditional theory of the liberation of free will by grace passes into the thought of St Thomas and forms the basis of his solution of the problem of grace and liberty.

The free will of the sinner has to be liberated. Let us take a few examples from the first series of objections. The first objection cites, 'Non enim quod volo bonum, hoc ago; sed quod odi malum, illud facio'; the solution runs:

90 [The will cannot resist a compelling cupidity] *De veritate*, q. 24, a. 12, ob. 12 (1ae ser.).
91 Ibid. c.
92 Ibid. ob. 4 and ad 4m (1ae ser.); ad 2m (2ae ser.).
93 In treating the sinner's impotence St Albert interpreted St Augustine to mean that the sinner could not merit forgiveness without grace (see Albert, *Summa de creaturis*, 2, q. 70, a. 5 [*BA* 35: 588]; *In II Sententiarum*, d. 25, a. 6 [*BA* 27: 433–34]). This position is adopted by St Thomas in his commentary

... intelligendum est, quod cum voluntas naturalis sit ad vitationem omnis mali, non potest homo peccator facere sine gratia ut vitet omnia peccata mortalia, quamvis possit vitare singula; et sic non potest sine gratia voluntatem naturalem implere; et similiter est de iusto, respectu peccatorum venialium.[94]

In this sense is interpreted the following from the *Glossa*.

Nunc homo describitur sub lege positus ante gratiam. Tunc enim homo peccatis vincitur, dum viribus suis iuste vivere conatur sine adiutorio gratiae liberantis, quae liberum arbitrium liberat, ut liberatori credat, atque ita contra legem non peccet.[95]

But not only must free will be liberated; the significance of this problem is the significance of the whole question of the relations of grace and liberty. The followers of Jovinianus make out that sin is impossible, while the Manichaeans make out that sin is inevitable. On the other hand, the Pelagians pretend that free will of itself is sufficient against temptation. But the Catholic faith holds a middle course and denies neither human liberty nor the necessity of grace.[96] The fourteen columns, the thirty-four objections, the brilliant psychological analysis of *De veritate*, q. 24, a. 12, represent St Thomas at grips with the problem of grace and liberty. His solution of

on the *Sentences* (*Super II Sententiarum*, d. 28, q. 1, a. 2). But the 22nd objection in *De veritate*, q. 24, a. 12, cites St Augustine's *De gratia et libero arbitrio* to make St Albert's interpretation untenable.

94 [for I do not perform the good that I will, but the evil that I hate, that is what I do ... (resp.) it has to be understood that, though it is natural to will to avoid all evil, a person who is a sinner cannot manage without grace to avoid all mortal sins, though he can avoid (them) singly; and so he cannot without grace fulfil the natural will; and similarly with the just person in regard to venial sins] *De veritate*, q. 24, a. 12, ad 1m (1ae ser.). Explicitly St Thomas speaks only of the indeliberate venial sins of the just both in the *De veritate* and in the *Summa theologiae* (1-2, q. 109, a. 8). Nonetheless, what he says with regard to deliberate mortal sin per se would apply to deliberate venial sin. To that one may add, He that contemneth small things, shall fall little by little.

95 [Now man is described as existing under the law before grace. For then he is conquered by sins while he strives to live justly by his own powers without the help of liberating grace, which liberates free will so that he may believe in the liberator and so not sin against the law] *De veritate*, q. 24, a. 12, ob. 3 (1ae ser.); see ob. 5, St Gregory's comparison of sin to gravitation; ob. 21, Peter Lombard's states of free will.

96 *De veritate*, q. 24, a. 12 c. init.

the problem is, at root, a limitation of human liberty: grace is compatible with liberty because of itself liberty is limited and grace enables it to transcend that limitation. He does not presuppose an unlimited liberty which grace confines to the good; he presupposes the limited liberty of psychological continuity, and makes grace an escape from the servitude of sin.

Finally, the essential liberation is operated by habitual grace, while the function of actual grace is supplementary.

To the essential liberation he alludes when he writes:

> Et ideo, supposita adhaesione liberi arbitrii ad peccatum mortale, sive ad finem indebitum, non est in potestate eius quod vitet omnia peccata mortalia ... Ab hac autem dispositione non removetur nisi per gratiam, per quam solam efficitur ut mens humana bono incommutabili per caritatem tamquam fini adhaereat.[97]

On the other hand, to actual grace there is a reference when he writes:

> ... quidam dicunt, hominem absque habituali gratia gratum faciente posse peccatum mortale vitare, quamvis non sine divino auxilio, quod hominem sua providentia ad bona agenda et mala vitanda gubernat: hoc enim verum est, cum contra peccatum conari voluerit, ex quo contingit ut possint singula vitari.[98]

5.2.4 The Maintenance of the Psychological Theory

But, it may be asked, does St Thomas maintain this psychological theory of the need of grace in his later works?

Briefly, if there is a change, the *onus probandi* lies on those who would assert it.

---

97 [And therefore, on the supposition that free will adheres to mortal sin or to a wrong end, it is not in its power to avoid all mortal sins ... And from this disposition it does not escape except through grace, which alone can bring it about that through charity the human mind adhere to unchangeable good as its end] Ibid. ad fin.

98 [some say that man without the habitual grace that makes him pleasing (to God) can avoid mortal sin, though he cannot (do so) without divine help, which by its providence governs man for doing good things and avoiding evil things; for this is true, since he has willed to struggle against sin, from which it comes about that he can avoid (sins) singly] Ibid.

Positively, one may argue as follows. The theory of the article we have been studying is that man is crooked: there is the *fomitis corruptio* that makes the avoidance of all indeliberate venial sin impossible even in the regenerate; in the sinner there is the *habitualis inclinatio voluntatis ad finem indebitum*[99] that makes the avoidance of all mortal sins impossible. The two together give an Augustinian *massa damnata*.

Now, in general, St Thomas becomes more and more Augustinian in his thought. Therefore there is a presumption against a departure from the position of the *De veritate*.

In *Prima secundae*, q. 109, a. 8, the sinner's impotence is again treated. The solution is the same, though not nearly so elaborate, as that of the *De veritate*.

The whole of 1-2, q. 109, presupposes that fallen nature has a twofold need of grace; man needs a *sanatio* as well as an *elevatio*. Article 3 affirms that the will of fallen man is egoistic, and 1-2, q. 77, a. 4, affirms self-love to be the cause of all sin.

Finally, there is the whole conception of the effect of original sin as a loss of rectitude, and of justification as a restoration of that rectitude.[100]

5.3 *The Need of Grace to Prepare for Justification*

This is a large question, and it is treated only insofar as it throws light on the nature of operative grace. Omitting the question of the supernaturalness of this grace,[101] of the development of St Thomas's thought on the subject,[102] and leaving to the next section an account of the complementary development in the theory of the will, we here are concerned solely with the general form of the ultimate solution. This is as follows.

In *Prima secundae*, q. 9, aa. 4 and 6, there is posited a further limitation of human liberty. The will does not move itself to the good in general; it does not select its end. That is the work of God, who moves the will to an end by an *instinctus divinus*. Since there is no question of freedom in the realm of ends, it follows that there can be no problem of grace and liberty with respect to the will of the end.

99 A comparison of *De veritate*, q. 24, a. 10, with a. 12 reveals that the only difference between this *inclinatio* and that which constitutes the absolute obstinacy of the demons lies in the fact that man is *in natura mutabili*. On the origin of this *inclinatio* in man see *De veritate*, q. 24, a. 12, ad 2m (1ae ser.).
100 *De veritate*, q. 28, a. 1; *Summa theologiae*, 1, q. 94, aa. 1–4; q. 95, aa. 1, 3; 1-2, q. 82, aa. 1, 3; q. 85, aa. 3, 5.
101 See above, §3.
102 See above, chapter II-2, §7.

In *Prima secundae*, q. 9, a. 6, ad 3m, the significance of this position for the theory of grace is pointed out. God moves all to the good in general, but he moves some to a determinate good, as in the case of grace.

In *Prima secundae*, q. 109, a. 6, on the preparation for grace, the same point is made in greater detail.

A general principle is first laid down from hierarchic theory.

> ... cum secundum ordinem agentium sive moventium sit ordo finium, necesse est quod ad ultimum finem convertatur homo per motionem primi moventis, ad finem autem proximum per motionem alicuius inferiorum moventium.[103]

It follows that God moves all things to their last end, each according to its capacity and proportion; and in particular, it is evident that God moves the just to their special end of God himself.

> Sic igitur, cum Deus sit primum movens simpliciter, ex eius motione est quod omnia in ipsum convertantur secundum communem intentionem boni, per quam unumquodque intendit assimilari Deo secundum suum modum ... Sed homines iustos convertit ad seipsum sicut ad specialem finem, quem intendunt, et cui cupiunt adhaerere sicut bono proprio, secundum illud Psalmi LXXII: *Mihi adhaerere Deo bonum est.* Et ideo quod homo convertatur ad Deum, hoc non potest esse nisi Deo ipsum convertente ...[104]

St. Thomas later[105] divides this conversion of the will into an imperfect and a perfect conversion: the former is prior to justification and may take place by successive stages; the latter is in the instant of justification. Both are

103 [since the order of ends is according to the order of agents or movers, it is necessary that man be converted to his ultimate end by the motion of the first mover, but to the proximate end through the motion of lower movers] *Summa theologiae*, 1-2, q. 109, a. 6.
104 [In this way, therefore, since God is the first mover simply, it is as a result of his motion that all things are converted to him according to the common intention of good, through which everything intends to be assimilated to God according to its mode ... But he converts righteous men to himself as to a special end that they intend and to which they desire to adhere as to (their) proper good, according to that text of Psalm 72: *To adhere to God is good for me.* And therefore it cannot be that man is converted to God unless God converts him] Ibid.
105 Ibid. q. 112, a. 2 c.; see ad 1m, ad 2m.

simply due to God: *Deus ad hoc quod gratiam infundat animae, non requirit aliquam dispositionem nisi quam ipse facit.*[106]

5.4 The Need of Further Grace after Justification: The Grace of Perseverance

This need may be considered absolutely or relatively; the absolute need arises from the fact that the regenerate has to live on the supernatural level in union with God, and only God can be source of such a life both in its principle, sanctifying grace, and in its fruit, the life of the Holy Spirit in us; the relative need is with respect to the danger of relapsing into sin.

St Thomas treats the former in connection with the gifts of the Holy Spirit. What the light of reason is to the natural life of man, the theological virtues of faith, hope, and charity are to his supernatural life. But though the latter are more perfect in themselves, still we have a fuller possession of the former. Just as the sun of itself gives light, but the moon only by reflecting the light of the sun, just as a doctor cures the sick in virtue of his knowledge, but his apprentice has constantly to be asking advice, so also man is proportionate to human living, but needs the instinct and motion of the Holy Spirit to be guided to everlasting life.[107]

But this active guidance of the Holy Spirit may be considered relatively; as such, it tends to the elimination of folly, ignorance, obtuseness and hardness of heart,[108] precludes relapse into sin, and if intended to continue throughout life, constitutes the grace of perseverance.[109]

Corresponding to this need of divine direction subsequent to justification, there is a third limitation of human liberty which is presented in the *Contra Gentiles.*[110] Not only does human freedom regard the choice of the means and is powerless with respect to the end; it is also true that the exercise of freedom takes place solely in each single free act. Man cannot here and now decide effectively what he is going to will for the rest of his life; his freedom is a succession of free acts, and though each by itself is free, there is no free choice with respect to the series as a whole. The argument is parallel to Aristotle's proof of a *primum se movens*: the successive *generabilia*

---

106 [For God to infuse grace into the soul, he does not require any disposition other than that which he himself causes] Ibid. q. 113, a. 7 c.
107 Ibid. q. 68, a. 2.
108 Ibid. ad 3m.
109 Ibid. q. 109, aa. 9–10.
110 *Summa contra Gentiles*, 3, c. 155 [§ 3282]. That actual grace is here conceived as external providence does not affect the use we make of the passage, namely, to point out the third limitation of human liberty.

account for a number of motions but cannot account for the terrestrial cycle or series as such: no one of them by itself, for it is not simultaneous with the whole process; nor all together, for all are not together.[111] Accordingly, just as the multiplicity of motions on earth postulates a first mover in the sky to account for their unity, so the series of human free acts as a series has its cause only outside and above the freedom of man. Now, the constancy of perseverance and the form or pattern of a development pertain not to single free acts but to a series. It follows that the first mover of the will must be the cause both of the fact of perseverance and of the relation (*ordo*) that each act in the series bears to the attainment of the final goal.

To carry this question further is to study the keystone in St Thomas's theoretical arch: *supra gubernationem qua creatura rationalis gubernat seipsam tamquam domina sui actus, indiget gubernari a Deo.*[112] This point will receive attention in the next section.

5.5 Conclusion

Preparatory to the study of St Thomas's theory of operative grace, a distinction has been drawn between the supernatural mode of acts, the existence of acts, and the specification (substance, quality, kind) of acts. God operates all three. But the study of the supernatural mode is not essential to our problem and would be too long to occupy us here. God's causation of the *esse* of acts is accounted for by the theory of God operating in the operation of the will as in the operation of nature. Thus, the specification of acts is the important matter in an examination of the theory of operative grace.

It has been shown that without habits the will does evil for the most part, that the sinner cannot always do good, and that, corresponding to this need of grace,[113] there is the limitation of liberty arising from the law of psychological continuity. Such a limitation enables God to change the will from evil to good without any interference with liberty.

Again, it has been shown that in preparation for justification there is required an orientation of the will to God himself as the will's end, that God alone can produce this orientation, and that corresponding to this need of

111 See *In VIII Phys.*, lect. 12.
112 [besides the government by which a rational creature governs itself, as having dominion over its act, it needs to be governed by God] *Summa theologiae,* 1, q. 103, a. 5, ad 3m.
113 Neither the sin of our first parents nor personal sin constitute titles or claims in justice; hence no matter what the resulting need for grace, grace remains gratuitous.

grace there is the limitation of liberty arising from the fact that freedom regards not the end but the means. Here also there can be no opposition between grace and liberty.

Finally, after justification there is a need of further grace for the realization of supernatural life and for perseverance, but, though a corresponding limitation of liberty was indicated, no detailed explanation was offered.

6   The Motion and Control of the Will

The first subsidiary investigation revealed that the theorem *Deus operatur in omni operante* did not provide either a theory of grace or the analogy for such a theory. Grace is a special divine intervention; actual grace is a motion.

The present investigation has considered, first, the nature and the possibility of human liberty (§§1–2), second, the limitations of human liberty and the need of operative grace (§§3–5). It remains that we investigate the development of the theory of special divine operations in the will, for either these are operative graces or else they supply the analogy for that conception.

After outlining the development of St Thomas's analysis of the will itself (§6.1), we draw attention to the external and purely Aristotelian theory of premotion to be found in the commentary on the *Sentences* (§6.2), the introduction of a premotion internal to the will in the *De veritate* (§6.3), the theory of the change of the will by God in the same work (§6.4), and the influence of the Eudemian Ethics (§6.5) which leads to the affirmation of a necessity of internal premotion (§6.6). Special cases of such premotions are affirmed to be graces in the *Prima secundae*, and their correlation with the need of grace is indicated (§6.7).

To bring to an end these subsidiary investigations, in which the main concern has been to winnow away the chaff, a general correlation of universal instrumentality, divine transcendence, the limitations of human liberty, and divine control of the will is attempted in an account of the grace of perseverance (§6.8). This provides the background and speculative context of St Thomas's theory of operative grace. With that context established, it will be possible in the fifth chapter [11-5] to present a detailed interpretation of the articles that deal explicitly with *gratia operans*.

6.1 Different Theories of the Will

The development of St Thomas's thought on the motion and control of the will is superposed on a development in the theory of the structure of the will itself.

According to Aristotle *appetitus movetur per bonum apprehensum*, so that the *appetibile* is a *movens non motum*, the *appetitus* a *movens motum*.[114] It is from this basis that St Thomas begins his speculation on the nature of the will.

In *De veritate*, q. 22, aa. 1–5, the nature of the *appetitus* is elaborately worked out.[115] In the twelfth article of the same question the interaction of intellect and will is studied, and the first mover of the will is said to be the intellect.[116]

Until the *De malo* it is not clear that the will moves itself except inasmuch as it moves the intellect;[117] and the theory of liberty is worked out, not in terms of the self-motion of the will, nor again in terms of the self-motion of man for the animals are also self-moving, but in terms of the self-determination of the rational creature.[118]

Corresponding to this orientation is an exteriorization of the causation of the free act of will. While in *Prima secundae*, q. 9, a. 3, the will of the end causes the act of will with respect to the means, in *De veritate*, q. 22, aa. 5–6, there is mentioned only the corresponding objective causality, namely,

114 See *Summa theologiae*, 1, q. 80, a. 2; *In III De anima*, text. 54 [lect. 15, § 830]; *In XII Metaphys.*, lect. 7.
115 The analysis proceeds as follows. First, a distinction is drawn between natural and violent motion: the former supposes an internal principle, and such a principle is termed an *appetitus naturalis*. Next, a distinction is drawn between natural and animal appetite: the former is any natural spontaneity; the latter is a distinct faculty that is exclusively a principle of appetitive acts; contrast, for instance, the spontaneity of perceptive faculties with that of appetites properly so called. Third, a distinction is drawn between sensitive and rational appetite. Finally, in rational appetite one has to distinguish between a basic tendency to happiness in general and particular acts of will: the former is to the latter as is the sense of touch in the eye to seeing in the eye.
116 *De veritate*, q. 22, a. 12, ad 2m. Attention to this position was drawn by Th. Deman, 'Le "Liber de bona fortuna" dans la théologie de S. Thomas d'Aquin' [see above, p. 101, note 47]. His thought receives important additions from Odon Lottin, 'Liberté humaine et motion divine.'
117 As Dom Lottin has noted, ibid., the formulae with respect to the motion of the will are in the passive voice: *inclinari vel non inclinari; moveri vel non moveri*; even *moveri ex se*. See *De veritate*, q. 22, a. 8 [*inclinari*]; *Summa theologiae*, 1, q. 105, a. 4, ad 2m [*moveri ex se*].
118 This is particularly evident in the long exposition of *De veritate*, q. 24, a. 1; the thought is the same in *Summa contra Gentiles*, 2, c. 48; *Summa theologiae*, 1, q. 83, a. 1. See the section on human liberty, above, § 1.

the dependence of the lower *appetibilia* on an ultimate *appetibile*. Again, the same argument that in *Prima secundae*, q. 9, a. 4, is used to prove that God is the first mover within the will is merely an objection in *De veritate*, q. 22, a. 12, and its solution is that the first mover of the will is the intellect.[119]

The difficulty against this position is that it offers no explanation of one of its most important assertions. The *appetibile* does not necessarily move the *appetitus*; the will may be either moved or not moved. But what effects the decision? If the *appetibile* is not a sufficient cause of the motion, then what is the sufficient cause?

This problem finds its solution in the *De malo* and the *Prima secundae*. A distinction is drawn between the specification and the exercise of the free act; the former is caused by the *appetibile*, the latter by the internal mover of the will. This internal mover is God with regard to the will of the end, the will itself with regard to the will of the means.

It is not improbable that there is a further development in the *Prima secundae*. The *appetitus naturalis* of the *De veritate* is, in its entitative structure, an Aristotelian accidental form, and no distinction is drawn between its limiting potency and its act. On the other hand, there are indications that in the *Prima secundae* St Thomas is perhaps thinking of the will itself as simply a limiting potency on the analogy of the *virtus operativa* of the angel in *Prima pars*, q. 54, aa. 1–3.[120]

6.2 External Premotion

By external premotion is meant the reduction of the will from accidental potency to act, either by the presentation of an object or by a change of mood, disposition, or circumstance outside the will itself.

St Thomas always recognizes the existence of this premotion but attaches quite different degrees of importance to it at different times. In the commentary on the *Sentences* it is considered a *gratia gratis data* in preparation

---

119 *De veritate*, q. 22, a. 12, ad 2m.
120 Thus, *Summa theologiae*, 1-2, q. 8, a. 2, distinguishes between the *potentia qua volumus* and the *ipse actus voluntatis*; the latter may be both with respect to the end and with respect to the means. Again, q. 9, a. 3, ad 2m, speaks of the potency of the will as always actually present, while the act of will with respect to the end is only sometimes present. Further, q. 9, a. 6, compares the *inclinatio universalis* to *materia prima*, and the response ad 3m distinguishes between God moving the will to the good in general and to some special end as is the case in the bestowal of grace.

for *gratia gratum faciens.*[121] It has the same role in the *De veritate,*[122] but in the *Quodlibetum primum* it is unequivocally rejected as insufficient for this purpose,[123] while in the *De malo* it is referred to as normally caused by the *corpus caeleste* and classified as a *motus per occasionem.*[124]

6.3   Internal Premotion

By internal premotion is meant a change in the disposition of the will itself. As was seen in the theory of physical premotion,[125] the transition from the possibility to the actuality of motion is effected either by a change in the *motivum* or by a change in the *mobile.* In the previous section, the latter type of change was considered; in the present, attention is directed to the former, to a change in the will itself.

This change is not to be confused with an essential transition from potency to act; that consists in the production of the *motivum* and is a prerequisite to the possibility of motion.[126]

St Thomas treats the internal premotion of the will, perhaps for the first time, in *De veritate,* q. 24, a. 14. The question deals with the possibility of doing good without grace,[127] and it clearly distinguishes between external premotion, conservation of the *virtus naturalis,* God operating in the operation of the creature, and finally the internal premotion. The internal premotion is alternative to an external premotion and, evidently, must remain as a mere alternative until St Thomas places in separate compartments the specification and the exercise of the act of will. Then each becomes necessary. The passage in question is as follows.

> Quamvis ... huiusmodi bona[128] homo possit facere sine gratia gratum

121 Thus *admonitio exterior, aegritudo corporis,* or anything of the kind is due to divine providence and sufficient to turn man toward God: *Super II Sententiarum,* d. 28, q. 1, a. 4. The theory of motion is derived from Aristotle's denial that, when an animal wakes up, it moves itself; it is moved by the atmosphere or something of that nature; see *In VIII Phys.,* lect. 4, § 1002.
122 *De veritate,* q. 24, a. 15. Aristotle on the animals is here mentioned explicitly.
123 *Quaestiones quodlibetales,* 1, a. 7 [q. 4, a. 2]. Cited above, p. 243.
124 *De malo,* q. 6, a. 1, ad 21m.
125 See above, chapter II-3, § 1.
126 See *In VIII Phys.,* lect. 8; *De veritate,* q. 11, a. 1, ad 12m; Stufler, *Gott, der erste Beweger aller Dinge* [see above, p. 83, note 83] 5–8 and passim. To change air into water and so give the *forma gravitatis* is an essential transition from potency to act; to let a stone fall is an accidental transition, for the stone already has the *forma gravitatis.*
127 The idea of grace is not so precise as in *Summa theologiae,* 1-2, q. 109, a. 2.
128 The usual *agros colere, domos aedificare.*

faciente, non tamen potest ea facere sine Deo; cum nulla res possit
in naturalem operationem exire nisi virtute divina,[129] quia causa
secunda non agit nisi per virtutem causae primae, ut dicitur in lib. *de
Causis*.[130] Et hoc verum est tam in naturalibus agentibus quam in
voluntariis. Tamen hoc alio modo habet necessitatem in utrisque.

Operationis enim naturalis Deus est causa, inquantum dat et
conservat id quod est principium naturalis operationis in re, ex quo
de necessitate determinata operatio sequitur; sicut dum conservat
gravitatem in terra, quae est principium motus deorsum.[131]

Sed voluntas hominis non est determinata ad aliquam unam
operationem, sed se habet indifferenter ad multas; et sic quodammodo[132] est in potentia, nisi mota per aliquid activum: vel quod ei
exterius repraesentatur, sicut est bonum apprehensum; vel quod in
ea interius operatur, sicut est ipse Deus;[133] ut Augustinus dicit in lib.
de Gratia et libero arbitrio, ostendens multipliciter Deum operari in
cordibus hominum.[134]

129 The theorem that God operates in the operation of the creature, *De veritate*,
q. 24, a. 1, ad 3m, is another early appearance of the inverse form: see
above, §2.2.2.
130 Recall that in the *Liber De causis* motions are caused not by the first cause
but by soul.
131 Note that the theorem follows simply from conservation: see *Summa
theologiae*, 1, q. 105, a. 5, where it is deduced from the fact that God is the
ultimate final cause.
132 Clearly, the potency is accidental; see the subsequent alternatives: either the
presentation of an object, or the change of the will.
133 God alone can operate within the will: *De veritate*, q. 22, a. 9.
134 [Although ... man can do good deeds of this kind without the grace that
makes him pleasing (to God), nevertheless he cannot do them without God;
since nothing can proceed to its natural operation except by the divine
power, because a secondary cause does not act except through the power of
the first cause, as is said in the book *De causis*. And this is true as much in
natural agents as in voluntary agents; still, this necessity is found in different
ways in the two cases.
   For God is the cause of a natural operation, insofar as he gives and preserves that which is the principle of natural operation in the thing, from
which by necessity a determinate operation follows; as when he preserves
gravitation in the earth, which is the principle of downward motion.
   But the human will is not determined to some one operation, but is open
indifferently to many things; and thus it is in a way in potency, unless it is
moved by something active: either something that is represented to it externally, as is the case with an apprehended good, or something that operates
in it internally, as Augustine says in the book *On Grace and Free Will*, showing
God to operate in many ways in human hearts] *De veritate*, q. 24, a. 14. The
reference to Augustine is to chapter 21, *PL* 44, 909. The same passage is
cited in the *Glossa Augustini* on Romans 1.24; see *De veritate*, q. 22, a. 8, ob. 2.

There is, then, a difference between the premotion of the will and that of a natural form. Once the latter is in act, its operation is determined, and all it needs is the right proximity to its *mobile*. But the will is naturally indeterminate, and consequently its premotion may lie either in the presentation of the object or in a modification of the will itself.

The same idea reappears in the following article,[135] in which the preparation for grace is attributed to an external admonition or to an *instinctus interior* such as God operates in the souls of men.

The precise nature of this motion of the will is perhaps the change of will discussed in *De veritate*, q. 22, a. 8.

6.4 Change of Will

In the *De veritate* the doctrine of psychological continuity is clearly implied, but its statement is obscured by the confusion already noted between freedom and noncoercion.[136] Different causes of change of will are discussed in the treatment of impeccability and fixity in evil[137] but direct action on the will itself is reserved to God alone.[138]

The nature of this change, its possibility, and its different species are explained in q. 22, a. 8, *Utrum Deus possit cogere voluntatem*. The nature of the change is the substitution of a new *inclinatio* for an old one.[139] Its possibility is that God operates in the will as in nature.[140] Finally, this change of inclination may be either simply a motion or else the introduction of a new form or habit.

The effect of the habit is that man does what is right, either always as in the case of the blessed in heaven, or for the most part as with the regenerate on earth.[141] But what precisely is the change of inclination that is simply a motion?

135 *De veritate*, q. 24, a. 15.
136 See above, §§ 1 and 5.1.
137 *De veritate*, q. 24, aa. 8–12; see *De malo*, q. 16, a. 5.
138 *Super II Sententiarum*, d. 15, q. 1, a. 3; d. 25, q. 1, a. 2, ad 5m; *De veritate*, q. 5, a. 10; q. 8, a. 13; q. 22, a. 9; *Summa contra Gentiles*, 3, cc. 85, 87, 88, 89, 90, 91, 92; *Summa theologiae*, 1, q. 105, a. 4; q. 111, a. 2; q. 115, a. 4.
139 *De veritate*, q. 22, a. 8: 'Cum igitur Deus voluntatem immutat, facit ut praecedenti inclinationi succedat alia inclinatio, et ita quod prima aufertur, et secunda manet' [When, therefore, God changes the will, he brings it about that another inclination succeeds the previous one, and in such a way that the first is taken away and the second remains].
140 See *Summa theologiae*, 1-2, q. 9, a. 6. Note that this is not an explanation of the manner in which God changes the will: see *De veritate*, q. 24, a. 1, ad 4m.
141 See the account of the function of the habit, above § 4.2.

As has already been shown,[142] there is in the will, apart from habits, the dynamic disposition that results from previous acts of will. Thus, such a *vis et inclinatio*, which is explicitly stated to result from a single mortal sin and not to be a vice, renders the sinner incapable of avoiding all mortal sins in future.

Now the change of any such disposition[143] would not be the introduction of a new habit yet would be the substitution of a new *inclinatio* for an old one. Not only does this satisfy the description given in the present article,[144] but it also is the type of internal premotion[145] spoken of in *De veritate*, q. 24. a. 14, and a sufficient explanation of the *instinctus interior* of *De veritate*, q. 24, a. 15. Further, one may note the significant fact that both in the second objection to *De veritate*, q. 22, a. 8, and in the account of the internal premotion in q. 24, a. 14, St Thomas refers to St Augustine's [*Liber De gratia et libero arbitrio* (c. 21)].

6.5 *The First Mover and the* Liber De Bona Fortuna[146]

Under the pressure of *Cor regum in manu Dei: quocumque voluerit, vertit illud* and, as well, of St Augustine's affirmation that God operates in the hearts of

142 See the presentation of *De veritate*, q. 24, a. 12, above, §5.2.2.

143 The change of the will of the sinner is, at this period, reserved to sanctifying grace (see *De veritate*, q. 24, a. 12 c. ad fin.), but the reason for this is that the *prima gratia* is justification (see chapter II-2, §7.2). But obviously there are innumerable other inclinations to be changed.

144 *De veritate*, q. 22, a. 8: 'Immutat autem voluntatem dupliciter. Uno modo movendo tantum; quando scilicet voluntatem movet ad aliquid volendum, sine hoc quod aliquam formam imprimat voluntati; sicut sine appositione alicuius habitus, quandoque facit ut homo velit hoc quod prius non volebat' [Now (God) changes the will in two ways. In one way, just by moving (it); namely, when he moves the will to will something, without imprinting some form on the will; as without the addition of some habit he sometimes brings it about that man wills what earlier he did not will].

145 Any change of disposition is a premotion. Nothing but a change of disposition could be the premotion of *De veritate*, q. 24, a. 14.

146 On this work, see Deman, 'Le "Liber de bona fortuna" dans la théologie de S. Thomas d'Aquin.' It is a medieval Latin translation of *Magna moralia* (II, 8, 1206b 30 – 1207b 19) and *Eudemian Ethics* (VII, 14, 1246b 37 – 1247b 11). The question treated is the per se and the *per accidens* of prudence: the prudent succeed because they exercise good judgment; but the lucky succeed even though their judgment is bad. Eudemus argues that the success of the prudent is also a matter of luck, for there is no possibility of taking counsel about taking counsel in an infinite regression; it follows that there is an initial impulse prior to deliberation and so prior to any exercise of prudent judgment; either, then, everything is chance or else one must acknowl-

men,[147] St Thomas in the *De veritate* added to the external premotion of the will an internal premotion which he seems to explain as a divine intervention in the stream of psychological continuity.[148] Naturally enough, when he comes across the *Liber De bona fortuna*, he cites the opinion of Eudemus with wholehearted approval.

One is not, however, to suppose that he immediately arrived at the conception of *Summa theologiae*, 1-2, q. 9, a. 4, which places the *instinctus divinus* simply in the will: that position does not arise until the specification and the exercise of the act of will have been segregated and placed in separate causal series. The Eudemian first mover accounts for the *initium consiliandi*, for a premotion that is neither from the external world nor, on the other hand, necessarily a change of will, but apparently in the intellect. The texts that impose this interpretation are as follows.

> Est igitur Deus primum principium nostrorum consiliorum et voluntatum.[149]

> ... non oportet procedere in infinitum, sed statur in intellectu sicut in primo.[150] Omnem enim voluntatis motum necesse est quod prae-

---

edge a principle higher than intellect and reason; and as God is the universal first mover, so also must he be first mover in the soul. The successful, accordingly, are divided into three classes: those that follow a principle higher than reason; those that follow reason; and the merely lucky.

The author of the *Magna moralia* seems to miss the point made by Eudemus, namely, that without a higher principle than reason even the prudent are merely lucky. He attributes good fortune to nature, refusing to attribute it to God since the wicked prosper and the virtuous are unfortunate.

The interest in the position of Eudemus is that it posits exactly the same divergence from Aristotelian theory that belief in providence requires of St Thomas. To Aristotle the *per accidens*, that is, any coincidence of unrelated predicates, any unnecessary combination of causes or conjunction of effects, does not admit explanation: it is not considered by any science, even by metaphysics, which considers all reality. St Thomas agrees with Aristotle to the extent of admitting the *per accidens* to have no natural cause, but, as was shown in treating the significance of the doctrine of *applicatio*, he attributes all coincidence, conjunction, combination to providential design. Eudemus reaches a similar conclusion on the ground that otherwise prudence is merely a matter of luck.

147　See objections [1 and 2] to *De veritate*, q. 22, a. 8; see also q. 24, a. 14 c.

148　See above, §6.4 ad fin.

149　[God is therefore the first principle of our deliberations and acts of willing] *Summa contra Gentiles*, 3, c. 89.

150　See *De veritate*, q. 22, a. 12, ad 2m.

cedat apprehensio; sed non omnem apprehensionem praecedit motus voluntatis: sed principium consiliandi et intelligendi est aliquod intellectivum principium altius intellectu nostro, quod est Deus.[151]

... agit voluntate; voluntatis autem principium est electio, et electionis consilium. Si autem quaeratur qualiter consiliari incipiat, non potest dici quod ex consilio consiliari inceperit, quia sic esset in infinitum procedere. Unde oportet aliquod exterius principium esse quod moveat mentem humanam ad consiliandum de agendis.[152]

Cum enim homo habeat potentiam ad opposita, puta ad sedendum vel non sedendum, oportet quod reducatur in actum per aliquid aliud. Reducitur autem in actum alterius horum per consilium, ex quo unum oppositorum praeeligit alteri.[153] Sed cum iterum homo habet potentiam consiliandi vel non consiliandi, oportebit esse aliquid per quod reducatur in actum consilii. Et cum in hoc non sit procedere in infinitum, oportet esse aliquod principium extrinsecum superius homine, quod ipsum moveat ad consiliandum, et hoc non est aliud quam Deus.[154]

---

151 [one must not proceed to infinity, but a stand is taken in intellect as primary. For it is necessary that an apprehension precede every motion of the will; but a motion of the will does not precede every apprehension: but the origin of deliberating and understanding is some intellective principle higher than our intellect, and this is God] *Summa theologiae,* 1, q. 82, a. 4, ad 3m.

152 [(he) acts by the will; now the principle of willing is choice, and of choice deliberation. But if it be asked in what way he begins to deliberate, it cannot be said that from deliberation he begins to deliberate, because that way would be a process to infinity. And therefore there has to be some external principle that moves the human mind to deliberating about what is to be done] *Quaestiones quodlibetales,* 1, a. 7 [q. 4, a. 2].

153 See *De malo,* q. 3, a. 3, ad 5m, ad 11m; *In IX Metaphys.,* lect. 4, §§ 1820–22.

154 [For since man has the power for opposites, for example, to sit or not to sit, he has to be brought to act by something else. Now he is brought to act in regard to one of these (opposites) by deliberation, on the basis of which he chooses one of the opposites over the other. But since man again has the power of deliberating or not deliberating, there will necessarily be something by which he is brought to the act of deliberating; and since one is not to proceed to infinity in this, there has to be some extrinsic principle higher than man, which moves him to deliberating, and this is no other than God] *In Rom.,* c. 9, lect. 3, § 773.

Hoc etiam Philosophus vult, quod numquam homo per liberum arbitrium potest quoddam bonum facere, sine adiutorio Dei. Et ratio sua est, quia in his, quae facimus, quaerendum est illud propter quod facimus. Non est autem procedere in infinitum, sed est devenire ad aliquid primum, puta ad consilium. Sic ergo bonum facio, quia consilium mihi inest ad hoc, et hoc est a Deo. Unde dicit, quod consilium boni est ab aliquo, quod est supra hominem, movens eum ad bene operandum. Et hoc est Deus, qui et homines movet et omnia, quae agunt ad actiones suas.[155]

... Pelagianos, qui dicunt principium boni operis esse ex nobis, sed consummationem ex Deo. Sed hoc non est verum: quia principium boni operis in nobis est cogitare de bono; et hoc ipsum est a Deo.[156]

However, the commentary on the next chapter of Philippians mentions solely the movement of the will,[157] a fact that can be explained by the text under discussion: *Deus est qui operatur in vobis velle et perficere.*

Other references to the Eudemian first mover are to be found in *De malo*, q. 3, a. 3, ob. 11, and in *Summa theologiae*, 1-2, q. 80, a. 1, ob. 3: both of these are colorless. On the other hand, the first objection to *Summa theologiae*, 1-2, q. 109, a. 2, is met with an appeal to Eudemus to prove that *liberum arbitrium* is in need of an extrinsic mover.

---

155 [This is also the position of the Philosopher, that man can never do any good through free will without the help of God. And his reason is that in those things which we do one must seek that on account of which we do (them). One is not, however, to proceed to infinity, but is to come to something primary, say, to deliberation. In this way, then, I do a good deed because there is deliberation in me for it, and this is from God. And therefore he says that deliberation on the good is from something that is above man, moving him to operating well. And this is God who moves both men and all things that act to their actions] *In II Cor.*, c. 3, lect. 1, §87. See the interpretation of 2 Corinthians 3.5 in *De veritate*, q. 24, a. 14, ad 4m (2ae. ser.) [Ad ea ... in contrarium]; *Quaestiones quodlibetales*, 1, a. 7 [q. 4, a. 2], Sed contra.

156 [the Pelagians, who say that the beginning of a good work is from us but the consummation is from God. But this is not true: because the beginning of a good work in us is to think about the good, and this is itself from God] *In Phil.*, c. 1, lect. 1, §12.

157 Ibid. c. 2, lect. 3, §77: 'Quia interius per instinctum movet voluntatem ad bene operandum' [Because he moves the will internally, by an impulse, to operate well].

6.6 The Necessity of Premotion in the Will

In general the necessity of premotion is the necessity of an explanation of temporal difference.[158] Granted the existence of mover and moved, of *potentia activa*[159] and *potentia passiva*; and, at the same time, granted the absence of actual motion; then the emergence of actual motion cannot be accounted for by the mere continuance of the existence of mover and moved. They already were existing and *ex hypothesi* no motion took place. When, then, motion does take place, a new factor is introduced. This introduction of a new factor is the premotion.[160]

Applying this to the will, two cases are to be distinguished: first, suppose the will is in act with respect to some end and then moves itself to act with respect to some means to that end;[161] second, suppose the will begins to be in act with respect to an end.

Now in the former case, the premotion is the *consilium rationis*.[162] The will can be in act with respect to the end and not with respect to the means simply because it does not know what means to take: the emergence of such knowledge will be the new factor that accounts for the difference between the possibility and the actuality of willing the means.

Against this position, which is not merely implicitly but explicitly the doctrine of St Thomas,[163] the followers of Bañez object that God causes not merely the possibility of willing the means but also the actual act of will with respect to the means. Commonly they appeal to *Summa contra Gentiles*, 3, c. 89, in which St Thomas affirms the truth of what they object. However, it is plain that St Thomas does not draw their conclusion. In the passage in question he begins by pointing out that some people do not understand how God can cause the act of will without prejudice to liberty; he had also pointed out that some people do not understand how the same *actio* can

---

158 God does not need premotion because he is not an *agens in tempore* (*In VIII Phys.*, lect. 2, §989). On the nature of premotion, see above, chapter II-3, §2.

159 It is defined, *In IX Metaphys.*, lect. 1, §§1776–78.

160 On *actu agit* see chapter II-3, §1.

161 *Summa theologiae*, 1-2, q. 9, a. 3; *De malo*, q. 6, a. 1.

162 *De malo*, q. 3, a. 3, ad 5m, ad 11m; see *Summa theologiae*, 1-2, q. 80, a. 1, ad 3m.

163 *De malo*, q. 3, a. 3, ad 5m: 'Ad quintum dicendum, quod voluntas, cum sit ad utrumlibet, per aliquid determinatur ad unum, scilicet per consilium rationis, nec oportet hoc esse per aliquod agens extrinsecum' [To the fifth point it has to be said that the will, since it is open to both, is determined to one by something, namely, by the deliberation of reason, nor is it necessary that this be by something acting extrinsically].

proceed both from God and from the created cause;[164] and in the present instance of contemporary obtuseness he refers back to the earlier[165] to obtain a proof that God does cause not merely the *virtus volendi* but also the *actus*. The other proofs are of exactly the same character: *Deus operatur in omni operante*.[166]

But while the *consilium rationis* supplies the premotion that releases the causation of the act of will with respect to the means, nothing but a premotion within the will itself can in the last resort account for the emergence of a new act of will with respect to an end.

The argument is as follows. Were this emergence due to a *consilium rationis*, then it would be necessary to suppose an act of will with respect to a more general end. Hence the question returns, What about that act of will? If it also is a new act, then either it is due to another *consilium rationis* or else there has been a premotion within the will itself. And since there is no possibility of an infinite regression in the matter of taking counsel, one must ultimately admit an extrinsic mover of the will.[167]

164 *Summa contra Gentiles*, 3, c. 70; cited above, chapter II-3, §6.2.
165 *Summa contra Gentiles*, 3, c. 89: 'Adhuc. Superius [c. 70] est ostensum quod Deus est causa omnis actionis, et operatur in omni agente. Est igitur causa motuum voluntatis' [Another point. It was shown above (chapter 70) that God is the cause of every action and operates in every agent. He is therefore the cause of movements of the will].
166 The nature of this operation has already been treated at length; see chapter II-3, §6. The arguments adduced in *Summa contra Gentiles*, 3, c. 89, are: first, the argument from instrumentality and universal application; second, an argument from analogy: if corporeal motion arises from the motion of the *primum mobile*, then spiritual motion arises from the first will, which is the will of God; third, the argument already cited: God is the cause of all *actio*; fourth, God is the first principle of our taking counsel and making acts of will.
167 *Summa theologiae*, 1-2, q. 9, a. 4. Observe that this argument is not valid unless one presupposes the distinction between the specification and the exercise of the act of will. Could the intellect cause not merely the specification but also the exercise of the act (as on Aristotle's theory: *appetibile apprehensum movet appetitum*), then the ultimate act of will with respect to the end could be caused by an apprehension. That this is the case is presupposed by *Summa theologiae*, 1, q. 82, a. 4, ad 3m. In the interval the theory of the will has developed (see above, §6.1).
     Further, observe that the argument presupposes a new act of will with respect to an end. But what precisely is the sense of the term 'new' is not determined: on general grounds we know that the soul has merely ordinal time ('before' and 'after' but no 'so much before or after') and only *per accidens* stands in the measurable time of the flow of sensitive consciousness.
     Finally, observe that the argument aims at proving no more than it proposes, namely, that there must be some extrinsic mover of the will. It does not prove in the general case that God must do more than move the will to the good in general.

6.7 Special Cases of Premotion within the Will

... Deus movet voluntatem hominis, sicut universalis motor, ad universale obiectum voluntatis, quod est bonum.[168] Et sine hac universali motione homo non potest aliquid velle.[169] Sed homo per rationem determinat se ad volendum hoc vel illud, quod est vere bonum vel apparens bonum.[170] – Sed tamen interdum specialiter Deus movet aliquos ad aliquid determinate volendum, quod est bonum: sicut in his quos movet per gratiam, ut infra dicetur.[171]

The purpose of this section is to correlate the doctrine of special premotion with the doctrine on the need of grace.

Such a premotion may be either the infusion of a form or habit[172] or else simply a change of inclination.[173]

If it is the infusion of a habit, it will end the state of the *agens imperfectum*, a radical egoist[174] who operates wrongly for the most part,[175] and it will be

---

168 Whether this is simply the conservation of the *appetitus naturalis* of the will or a transition from potency to act, depends on another issue, namely, Does St Thomas still think of the will as an *appetitus naturalis*? If he does, then this motion must be conservation as in *De veritate*, q. 24, a. 14. If he does not, then the will is conceived on the analogy of the angelic *virtus operativa* (see above, §6.1, note 119). In the latter case, the question of the frequency of the motion arises, and that depends on whether one goes by the ordinal time of the soul or the measurable time that pertains to the soul *per accidens* (see above, §6.6, note 167).

169 This follows from *Summa theologiae*, 1-2, q. 9, a. 4; see above, note 167 ad fin.

170 That man determines himself by his intellect to choose this or that is St Thomas's constant position. It is the very idea of *liberum arbitrium* as conceived in all his writings: *Super II Sententiarum*, d. 25, q. 1, a. 1; *De veritate*, q. 24, a 1; *Summa contra Gentiles*, 2, c. 48; *Summa theologiae*, 1, q. 83, a. 1; *De malo*, q. 3, a. 3, ad 5m, ad 11m; q. 6, a. 1; *Summa theologiae*, 1-2, q. 9, a. 3. But in the latter passages the more vague question of the freedom of man (his difference from the animals) is replaced by the precise question of the self-motion of the will.

171 [God moves the human will, as universal mover, to the universal object of the will, which is the good. And without this universal motion man cannot will anything. But man by reason determines himself to willing this or that, what is truly good or apparently good. – But nevertheless God sometimes moves some people in a special way to willing something determinate, which is a good; for example, in those whom he moves by grace, as will be said below] *Summa theologiae*, 1-2, q. 9, a. 6, ad 3m.

172 Ibid. q. 113, aa. 6–8.

173 *De veritate*, q. 22, a. 8.

174 Above, §4.3.

175 Above, §4.2.

the beginning of the *agens perfectum*, who does what is right for the most part.[176] However, only God is naturally proportionate to unfailing good action,[177] and only dynamic union with God can make the creature always do what is right.[178] Accordingly, there will remain the need of an *auxilium Dei moventis*.[179]

Simple motions may effect a turning away from sin,[180] a conversion to God, and a preparation for justification;[181] they also are necessary if fallen man, after regeneration, is to live the life of the Holy Spirit[182] and to persevere unto the end.[183]

In treating the general and special needs of operative grace, we prescinded from the question of the entitative perfection of actual graces prior to justification. Though St Thomas's position does lead to that question, it remains that he did not treat it explicitly: he distinguished between general providence and actual grace, he divided actual graces into internal and external, but he did not investigate the distinction between internal actual graces that are entitatively supernatural and those that are not. We cannot but follow him, for one must determine what St Thomas did say before attempting to meet the exigence of his thought for ulterior development.

6.8 The Grace of Perseverance

The grace of perseverance is the pattern of graces internal and external, habitual but especially actual, by which God produces the predestined unto eternal life.[184] Per se it is the cause of both merit and glory,[185] but it attains its effect infallibly only[186] because it is an instrument in the hands of the transcendent *artifex*.[187]

176 Above, §4.2.
177 *De veritate*, q. 24, a. 7; above, §4.1.
178 *De veritate*, q. 24, aa. 8–9.
179 Follow the thought from *De veritate*, q. 27, a. 5, ad 3m, through *Summa contra Gentiles*, 3, cc. 88–92, 155, to *Summa theologiae*, 1-2, q. 109.
180 *Summa theologiae*, 1-2, q. 109, a. 7; above §5.2.2.
181 Ibid. a. 6; above, §5.3, chapter II-2, § 7.
182 Ibid. q. 68, a. 2; above §5.4.
183 Ibid. q. 109, aa. 9–10; above §5.4.
184 *Summa theologiae*, 1-2, q. 109, a. 10.
185 *Summa theologiae*, 1, q. 23, a. 5.
186 *In I Peri herm.*, lect. 14, §197; *In VI Metaphys.*, lect. 3 ad fin. [§§1218–22].
187 *Summa theologiae*, 1-2, q. 112, a. 3: '... intentio Dei deficere non potest ... certissime liberantur quicumque liberantur ...' [the intention of God cannot fail ... whoever are liberated are most certainly liberated].

Corresponding to this grace is the limitation of human liberty by which man is free in his single acts but exercises no free act with respect to the series of acts as a series.[188] Since the series as a series must have a cause,[189] and since God alone operates in the will, it follows that God alone can be the cause of perseverance.[190] However, there is a notable difference between perseverance given to *natura integra* and to *natura lapsa*: the former for the most part does what is right; the latter for the most part does what is wrong, while the sinner is incapable of avoiding all sin.[191] Though this difference does not correspond exactly to St Augustine's distinction between *adiutorium sine quo non* and *adiutorium quo*, I think it can be regarded as a legitimate extrapolation of his thought.

Though predestination infallibly and the grace of perseverance per se is a cause of merit and of glory, it does not follow that reprobation is a cause of sin and damnation. The two are not parallel:[192] reprobation is *permissio culpae et praeparatio poenae*; the permission is not causal, while the *praeparatio poenae*, though causal, is itself caused by the sin that is permitted.[193]

7   Conclusion

The first subsidiary investigation ended with the conclusion that the general theorem of *Deus operatur in omni operatione* and universal instrumentality did not provide either a [theory of] grace or the analogy for a grace. In this second inquiry it has been shown how St Thomas gradually developed the idea of the necessary internal premotion of the will with respect to the end, and in this premotion found his analogy for grace which he asserted to be a special premotion to a determinate good.

Since a motion has two terms and the *terminus a quo* obviously supplies a clue to the nature of the *terminus ad quem*, we also inquired into the need for operative grace and found it to consist generally in the lack of habits of operation with a consequent ineffectualness in willing the good; more particularly it was seen that corresponding to the triple limitation of human freedom – psychological continuity, freedom with respect to the means,

---

188 *Summa contra Gentiles*, 3, c. 155.
189 See *In VIII Phys.*, lect. 12.
190 That is, the sole principal cause, for God alone is proportionate to the effect.
191 See above, §§ 4–5.
192 *Summa theologiae*, 1, q. 23, a. 3.
193 *In Rom.*, c. 9, lect. 2 [§§ 763–64]. See above, § 2.2.3, note 47; § 2.3.

freedom with respect to each single act but not the series of acts – there exists in man the need of operative grace to effect his conversion from sin, to direct him to God as a special end, to maintain him in the supernatural life on the level of the Holy Spirit's wisdom and love.

This immediate context of *gratia operans* has a remote context in the cosmic theorems of *Deus operans*. Connecting the two was the investigation of the nature of human liberty and of the prerogatives of the transcendent *artifex*.

One may legitimately infer from the gradual development of St Thomas's theory both of the structure of the will and of the nature of freedom that his theory of operative grace will attain its more general formulae prior to the explicit expression of points to which subsequent controversy lends an excessive importance. It follows that more general and earlier statements are to be interpreted by later and more precise statements.

II-5

Interpretation of St Thomas's Articles on *Gratia Operans*

The point of view established in the first chapter [II-1] by the outline of the movement from St Augustine to St Thomas enabled us in the second chapter [II-2] to interpret most of the data relevant to *gratia operans*. It was found, however, unequal to the task of eliminating all obscurity from the activity of the habit in the commentary on the *Sentences*, while the cooperative actual grace of the *De veritate* and its operative counterpart in the *Prima secundae* were plainly beyond its competence. The intervening subsidiary investigations on the idea of operation and on divine operation in the will have brought to light the nature of the materials St Thomas might have used in developing his theory of actual grace. Accordingly, we turn to consider, briefly the theory in the commentary on the *Sentences*, with greater care that of the *De veritate*, and in detail the free act in justification and the actual operative grace of the *Prima secundae*.

1   The Position of the Commentary on the *Sentences*

Only habitual grace is conceived as operative and cooperative,[1] but two aspects are distinguished. There is the function of supernatural information: accordingly, inasmuch as grace elevates man to a higher order of being, it is said to be operative; but inasmuch as it informs human acts and renders them meritorious, it is termed cooperative.[2] But grace is not merely a formal cause; it is an efficient cause as well. Through its concomi-

---

1 *Super II Sententiarum*, d. 26, q. 1, a. 6, ad 2m. See above, chapter II-2, §5.
2 See above, chapter II-2, §5.

tant virtues, it fulfils the role of a second nature and with the spontaneity of a natural principle inclines man to acts of a certain kind.[3]

Both the *De veritate* and the *Prima secundae* retain the distinction between habitual grace as a formal and as an efficient cause, but in these later works, instead of a further subdivision into operative and cooperative, the formal causality of habitual grace is said to be operative and its efficient causality is said to be cooperative.[4]

Plainly this efficient causality is to be interpreted in the light of the general theory of habits. As has been shown,[5] habits are determinations of indeterminate potencies; they make the standard and rule of rectitude an inherent form of the faculty to be ruled; without them man is, from the spiritual viewpoint, an *agens imperfectum* who for the most part fails to do what is right; on the other hand, with them man becomes an *agens perfectum*, and for the most part operates as he should.[6] Such is the efficient causality of the habit.[7]

In the commentary on the *Sentences* St Thomas attempts to divide this causality into operative and cooperative grace: inasmuch as the habit causes the internal act of will, it is operative; inasmuch as it causes the external act, it is cooperative.[8] His purpose is clear: he has found St Augustine basing the distinction between operative and cooperative grace on the difference between good will and good performance.[9] But the difficulties to the theory he presents are no less clear: first, inasmuch as grace cooperates with free will in the production of the internal act, it is said to be operative; plainly, there is no clear idea of a difference between operation and coop-

---

3 *Super II Sententiarum*, d. 26, q. 1, a. 5, ad 2m: 'operans effective' [operative effectively], 'secundum quod habitus effective causat opus' [in the way a habit causes a work effectively], 'motum meritorium voluntatis operatur eliciendo ipsum, licet mediante virtute' [(grace) operates a meritorious movement of the will, eliciting the movement, even if a virtue is mediator]; ibid. ad 3m: 'inclinat in talem actum per modum cuiusdam naturae' [it inclines to such an act in the way of a certain nature].

4 *De veritate*, q. 27, a. 5, ad 1m; *Summa theologiae*, 1-2, q. 111, a. 2.

5 Above, chapter II-4, §4.2.

6 Ibid.; see also *De veritate*, q. 22, a. 8.

7 This position of the commentary on the *Sentences* later becomes more rigid: without charity the sinner not only fails to do what is right for the most part but cannot avoid all mortal sins; the former is a statement of fact, the latter of impossibility.

8 *Super II Sententiarum*, d. 26, q. 1, a. 5 c. ad fin.

9 See above, p. [224]. [Lonergan gives no pages in the autograph; page number is supplied by the editors; the same holds wherever in this chapter page numbers are in brackets.]

eration to be found in such a statement. Further, when grace cooperates with free will in the production of the external act, it is said to be cooperative; the same difficulty recurs, nor is it alleviated by pointing out that *actus ... interiores in moralibus potiores sunt exterioribus.*[10] At the expense of dropping the Augustinian distinction between good will and good performance, this position is deserted in the *De veritate,*[11] to return under a totally different form in the *Prima secundae.*[12]

2   The Position of the *De Veritate*

In the commentary on the *Sentences* St Thomas modifies the thought of his master St Albert in two ways. He makes explicit an implicit distinction between the formal and the efficient causality of habitual grace.[13] He adverts to St Augustine's distinction between good will and good performance. On the other hand, he has no clear distinction between divine providence and actual grace;[14] the only special divine operation in the will appears to be the infusion of the virtues;[15] any absolute limitation of human liberty is denied;[16] and the theory of the preparation for justification seems inadequate.[17] On all of these points there is to be found some development in the *De veritate*, and on all except the first and the last that development is notable.

First of all, psychological theory makes great advances. The law of psychological continuity, though not explicitly stated, is consistently implied in the long treatment of impeccability and fixity in evil.[18] The analysis of the sinner's impotence to avoid sin is as fine a specimen of exquisitely balanced thought as could be imagined.[19] Cognate to both of these points is the article on God's ability to change the will,[20] and complementary to this

---

10 [in moral matters internal acts prevail over external] *Super II Sententiarum,* d. 26, q. 1, a. 5, ad 4m (cited above, p. 227).
11 At least superficially, inasmuch as both the internal and the external acts are attributed to cooperative grace.
12 See above, pp. [247–50].
13 See above, pp. [225–26].
14 See above, p. [240].
15 It alone is mentioned in *Super II Sententiarum,* d. 26, q. 1, a. 6.
16 See above, pp. [357–58].
17 See above, p. [240].
18 *De veritate,* q. 24, aa. 8-12; see chapter II-4, §5.2.
19 *De veritate,* q. 24, a. 12; see chapter II-4, §5.2.2.
20 *De veritate,* q. 22, a. 8; see chapter II-4, §6.4.

article is the theory of an internal premotion alternative to the external premotion of the will.[21]

Next, the development of psychological theory is accompanied with a development in the theory of grace. The sinner can no longer avoid sin without grace; he is dominated by cupidity, and this crookedness inevitably will result in some sin; his only liberation is by the infusion of charity.[22] Again, there is more than one grace in man, for even after the reception of grace one must pray for further divine assistance; and this special need arises from the fallen state of human nature.[23] Finally, the term *gratia gratis data* is assigned its current meaning of the charismatic gift, and any operation by which God directs man to eternal life – such as causing good thoughts and holy affections – may be termed a *gratia gratum faciens.*[24]

This coincidence of developments in psychology and in the theory of grace would by itself indicate Augustinian influence, and indeed there is no lack of specific evidence that the whole movement is predominantly indebted to St Augustine.

Thus, *De veritate*, q. 27, a. 5, ob. 3, proves from St Augustine a real distinction between prevenient and subsequent grace; the solution of the objection appeals to fallen human nature, an appeal that recalls the 'crookedness' of man in *De veritate*, q. 24, a. 12. But in that article we find a citation from St Augustine's *De gratia et libero arbitrio* which eliminates St Albert's theory of the sinner's impotence and consequently the theory held by St Thomas in the commentary on the *Sentences*.[25] Next, the acceptance of the sinner's impotence and the formulation of a psychological explanation of this fact require in turn a theory of God changing the will of man, and not only is such a theory worked out in *De veritate*, q. 22, a. 8, but there the second objection consists in another citation from the *De gratia et libero arbitrio*, which asserts divine control over the human will.[26] Finally, the same

---

21 *De veritate*, q. 24, aa. 14–15; see chapter II-4, §6.3.
22 *De veritate*, q. 24, a. 12; see chapter II-2, §6.
23 *De veritate*, q. 27, a. 5, ad 3m; see chapter II-2, §6.
24 *De veritate*, q. 27, a. 5 c.; see chapter II-2, §6.
25 See above, chapter II-1, §4.2; chapter II-2, §6; chapter II-4, §5.2.3.
26 *De veritate*, q. 22, a. 8, cites the *Glossa Augustini*, but *De veritate*, q. 24, a. 14 [c.], names the *De gratia et libero arbitrio. Summa theologiae*, 1-2, q. 79, a. 1, ad 1m, mentions both. The passage in question is (*De veritate*, q. 22, a. 8, ob. 2): 'Manifestum est Deum operari in cordibus hominum ad inclinandas voluntates eorum in quodcumque voluerit, sive in bonum pro misericordia sua, sive in malum pro meritis eorum' [It is clear that God operates in human hearts to incline their wills to whatever he wishes, either to good on account of his mercy, or to evil on account of their deserts]. Uniformly St

passage is alluded to when the theory of internal premotion of the will appears in the discussion of the need of grace to do good,[27] and the same premotion reappears in the discussion of the preparation for grace.[28]

Notable as are these developments, the position of the *De veritate* is transitional. The theory of the preparation for grace remains unsatisfactory, and the need of grace for human rectitude is more broadly stated than in the *Summa.*[29] The affirmation of psychological continuity is only implicit, and it is obscured by the traditional confusion between noncoercion and liberty.[30] Liberty itself is vaguely and inadequately conceived as the difference between rational and irrational being.[31]

The incidental treatment of the distinction between operative and cooperative grace reveals the same [lack] of definitive formulation.[32]

The second part of the division offers no difficulty: as a formal cause, habitual grace is operative; as an efficient cause, it is cooperative.[33] The only point to be noted is that now habitual grace not merely makes the difference between the *agens imperfectum* and the *agens perfectum*[34] but also liberates the will of the sinner from the impotence caused by self-love.[35]

With regard to the first part of the division, there is some difficulty in saying what precisely is cooperative grace.[36] The passage runs:

> Ex parte vero eiusdem [gratuitae Dei voluntatis] gratia cooperans dicetur secundum quod in libero arbitrio operatur, motum eius causando, et exterioris actus executionem expediendo, et perseverantiam praebendo, in quibus omnibus aliquid agit liberum arbitrium.[37]

Thomas rejects the implication that God operates evil will: *De veritate*, q. 22, a. 8 ad fin. [ad obiectiones]; *De malo*, q. 3, a. 1, ad 1m; *In Rom.*, c. 9, lect. 3, §781; *Summa theologiae*, 1-2, q. 79, a. 1, ad 1m. But what is most significant is the occurrence in this passage of the term 'inclinare voluntatem' [to incline the will].

27 *De veritate*, q. 24, a. 14. See above, pp. [371–72].
28 Ibid. a. 15. See above, chapter II-4, §6.3.
29 *De veritate*, q. 24, a. 15; ibid. a. 14; compare *Summa theologiae*, 1-2, q. 109, a. 2.
30 See above, chapter II-4, §1.
31 See above, ibid.
32 *De veritate*, q. 27, a. 5, ad 1m. See above, chapter II-2, §6.
33 *De veritate*, ibid. See above, chapter II-2, §6.
34 As in the commentary on the *Sentences*; see above, chapter II-4, §4.2.
35 See above, chapter II-4, §4.3.
36 Operative grace here is *ipsa iustificatio impii*.
37 [But from the side of the same (gratuitous will of God) grace will be called cooperative according as it operates in free will, causing its movement, and

The question that arises is, Does *motum eius causando* refer to an internal premotion of the will or to the general theorem of divine operation in all operation? Arguments can be found for both views, as follows.

The subject of the verb *operatur* in *secundum quod in libero arbitrio operatur* is, from the context, *gratuita voluntas Dei*. If this is understood in the sense that God operates in the will as in nature, then there is simply the general theorem. But it can also be understood in the sense of *De veritate*, q. 22, a. 8, ob. 2, namely, that God operates in the hearts of men inclining their wills as he pleases.

The expression *motum eius causando* clearly means that God causes the motion of free will, which is equivalent to saying that God causes the act of free will: that is the general theorem,[38] for man also causes his act of free will.[39] Further, *exterioris actus executionem expediendo* refers to general providence[40] and so does *perseverantiam praebendo*;[41] by analogy, then, *motum eius causando* also refers to general providence.

But one can argue from the parallel *De veritate*, q. 24, a. 14, to arrive at a different conclusion. There, after explaining both the general theorem and internal premotion, St Thomas sums up his position with

> Unde, si gratiam Dei velimus dicere non aliquod habituale donum sed ipsam misericordiam Dei, per quam interius motum mentis operatur, et exteriora ordinat ad hominis salutem; sic nec ullum bonum homo potest facere sine gratia Dei.[42]

Now there is a rough correspondence between *gratuita Dei voluntas* and *ipsa misericordia Dei*, between *motum mentis operatur* and *motum eius causando*, between *exteriora ordinat* and *executionem expediendo, perseverantiam praebendo*.

---

expediting the execution of an external act, and granting perseverance, in all of which free will does something] *De veritate*, q. 27, a. 5, ad 1m.

38 See the parallel remark in *Super II Sententiarum*, d. 28, q. 1, a. 4: 'etiamsi gratia gratis data dicatur ipse actus liberi arbitrii, quem Deus in nobis facit' [even if the act itself of free will, which God causes in us, be called a grace freely given].

39 *De veritate*, q. 24, a. 1, ad 3m.

40 *Summa theologiae*, 1, q. 83, a. 1, ad 4m; *De malo*, q. 6, a. 1, ob. 1 and 2.

41 *Summa contra Gentiles*, 3, c. 155 ad fin.

42 [And therefore if we wish to designate as grace of God not some habitual gift, but the mercy itself of God, through which he operates internally a movement of the mind and orders external things to man's salvation, in this sense man can do no good without the grace of God] *De veritate*, q. 24, a. 14.

But *motum mentis operatur* certainly does not refer merely to the general theorem but also to a possible internal premotion. Therefore, *motum eius causando* does so as well. Further, it would be strange if St Thomas in the corpus referred to special illuminations of intellect and inspirations of will,[43] if he defined *gratuita Dei voluntas ex parte effectuum* as anything by which God directs man to eternal life, and yet wished to exclude the internal premotion of the will when speaking of cooperative grace.

In conclusion one may say that *motum eius causando* means that God cooperates with the act of free will according to the general theorem; that it does not exclude a previous internal premotion of the will; but that it is not probable that St Thomas is thinking explicitly of such internal premotion, while it is certain that *motus liberi arbitrii* does not mean a premotion to a free act but a free act itself.[44]

It seems to us improbable that St Thomas is thinking explicitly of an internal premotion, for if he were, he would have an actual grace that is operative. So great and sudden a leap from current modes of thought was hardly possible, and in the *De veritate* the only operative grace is habitual.

3   The Position of the *Prima Secundae*: Habitual Grace as Operative

As in the *De veritate*, so also here habitual grace as a formal cause is operative, but as an efficient cause it is cooperative.

> ... habitualis gratia, inquantum animam sanat vel iustificat, sive gratam Deo facit, dicitur gratia operans: inquantum vero est principium operis meritorii, quod etiam ex libero arbitrio procedit, dicitur cooperans.[45]

The only question is, Just in what way is habitual grace the principle of the

---

43 *De veritate*, q. 27, a. 5 c.: '... sicut quod immittat nobis bonas cogitationes, et sanctas affectiones' [for example that he sends us good thoughts and holy desires].

44 Note that *in quibus omnibus aliquid agit liberum arbitrium* [in all of which free will does something] refers also to *motum eius causando* [causing its movement]; but the premotion of *De veritate*, q. 24, a. 14, precedes any free act of will.

45 [habitual grace, insofar as it heals the soul or justifies it or makes it pleasing to God, is called operative grace; but insofar as it is the principle of a meritorious deed, which proceeds from free will too, it is called cooperative] *Summa theologiae*, 1-2, q. 111, a. 2.

meritorious act? Does it merely cause the *forma meriti* [46] or does it also cause the substance of the free act?

The answer is in no way doubtful. St Thomas does not say *principium operis meritorii qua meritorii*, and there is no reason for supposing that he means something different from what he says. The theory of the habit remains the same in the *Summa theologiae* as it was in the *De veritate* and the commentary on the *Sentences*.

However, what is of special interest is that in the *Summa theologiae* the infusion of the *donum habituale* is not merely a change of will but also a premotion of the will. At the instant of justification God does not supply the grace and man the free act of will, but God by infusing grace moves the will to its free act.

In this conception three distinct lines of development converge: first, there is the development with respect to the *initium fidei*, that is, with respect to operative grace in general;[47] second, there is the development with respect to the change of the will as an internal premotion; third, there is the special character of the premotion that consists in the infusion of a habit, which is a new spontaneity, a second nature. Each of these points will be touched upon in turn, and then attention will be directed to the freedom of the consequent act of will in the instant of justification.

3.1 Development in the Analysis of Justification

The first fact to be noticed is the analysis of the process of justification in the *De veritate*.[48] Justification consists in the infusion of grace, acts of faith and contrition, and the remission of sins: all four elements are simultaneous and instantaneous.[49] Nonetheless there is a logical or 'natural' precedence among them. Thus, from the viewpoint of final and formal causality the infusion of grace precedes the remission of sins; from the viewpoint of material causality the remission of sins precedes the infusion of grace.[50] Again, the infusion of grace precedes the free acts of faith and contrition as

---

46 *Super II Sententiarum*, d. 26, q. 1, a. 5, ad 4m: '... liberum arbitrium ministrat substantiam actus, et a gratia est forma per quam meritorius est' [free will provides the substance of the act, and from grace comes the form through which it is meritorious]. See above, chapter II-2, § 5.

47 The point is that God not merely cooperates with the will but also causes its cooperation.

48 *De veritate*, q. 28. See *Super IV Sententiarum*, d. 17, q. 1.

49 *De veritate*, q. 28, a. 9.

50 Ibid. a. 7.

a formal cause; but the free acts precede as material cause.[51] Further, there is no mean position between the infusion of grace and the remission of sins.[52] Finally, it seems quite plain from the objections that, with regard to the free acts, grace supplies the *forma meriti* and free will the substance of the act.[53]

This is all quite different from the analysis in the *Summa theologiae*, where there is no mention of formal and material causality, and the infusion of grace is *motio moventis*, the free acts are *motus mobilis*, and the remission of sins is *perventio in finem motus*.[54] Plainly the whole manner of conceiving the process has been profoundly changed.

Now this change would seem to be connected with the theory of the preparation for grace. Not only are the early articles[55] that deal explicitly with this issue unsatisfactory, but one frequently comes across very significant passages in the treatment of other subjects. Thus, in discussing the possibility of fixity in sin in this life, St Thomas distinguishes between a capacity to liberate oneself from sin and a capacity to cooperate with grace towards such a liberation; the latter member is further divided into an absolute inability to cooperate with grace, and such is the obstinacy of the demons, and grave difficulty in cooperating with grace, and that is the obstinacy possible in this life.[56] Now such a definition of obstinacy is quite incompatible with the doctrine that God in giving grace makes a bad will into a good will:[57] for no matter how fixed in evil the will may be before it is changed, still the changed will is no longer obstinate. Only if one conceives

---

51 Ibid. a. 8.

52 Ibid.: '... inter gratiae infusionem et culpae remissionem nihil cadit medium' [there is nothing intermediate between the infusion of grace and the remission of guilt].

53 See the solutions to the whole second series of objections in a. 8. These are all of the type: 'illud quod est ex parte dantis, est prius formaliter: sed quod est ex parte recipientis, prius materialiter' [what is from the side of the giver is formally first, but what is from the side of the receiver is materially first] Ibid. ad 6m (2ae ser.).

54 [the motion of the moving (force) ... the movement of the movable thing ... arrival at the end of the movement] *Summa theologiae*, 1-2, q. 113, a. 6.

55 *Super II Sententiarum*, d. 28, q. 1, a. 4; *De veritate*, q. 24, a. 15.

56 *De veritate*, q. 24, a. 11; see a. 10. See also ibid. a. 14, ad 2m.

57 *De malo*, q. 16, a. 5 c.: '... puta cum Deus immutat voluntatem hominis per gratiam de malo in bonum, secundum illud *Prov.* XXI, 1: *Cor regum in manu Dei, et quocumque voluerit vertet illud*' [as when God changes a human will from evil to good through grace, according to that text of Proverbs 21.1: *The heart of kings is in the hand of God, and he will turn it wherever he will*]. Observe that though there may have been speculative difficulties against such a position in the commentary on the *Sentences*, they are certainly removed by *De veritate*, q. 22, a. 8, on the change of will.

human cooperation with grace to be simultaneous with grace and not its consequent, can obstinacy be defined as inability or difficulty in cooperation. But it is precisely such a simultaneity of grace and cooperation that is implied in the statement: grace precedes as the formal cause, the act of free will precedes as the material cause.

The full grasp of the nature of Pelagianism in the *Quodlibetum primum*, a. 7 [q. 4, a. 2],[58] necessitates a change here: not merely the supernatural form of the good act but the goodness of the will itself *quoad substantiam actus* proceeds from grace. This is reflected, delicately but clearly, in four successive responses on '*Qui creavit te sine te, non iustificabit te sine te.*'

> Deus non iustificat nos sine nobis consentientibus ... Iustificat tamen nos sine nobis virtutem causantibus.[59]

> Deus virtutes in nobis operatur sine nobis virtutes causantibus, non tamen sine nobis consentientibus.[60]

> ... virtus infusa causatur in nobis a Deo sine nobis agentibus, non tamen sine nobis consentientibus. Et sic est intelligendum quod dicitur, *quam Deus in nobis sine nobis operatur*. Quae vero per nos aguntur, Deus in nobis causat non sine nobis agentibus: ipse enim operatur in omni voluntate et natura.[61]

> ... Deus non sine nobis nos iustificat, quia per motum liberi arbitrii, dum iustificamur, Dei iustitiae consentimus. Ille tamen motus non est causa gratiae,[62] sed effectus. Unde tota operatio pertinet ad gratiam.[63]

58 See above, chapter II-2, § 7. See *Summa theologiae*, 1, q. 62, a. 2; *In Rom.*, c. 6, lect. 3; ibid. c. 9, lect. 3; *In 2 Cor.*, c. 3, lect. 1, §§ 86–87.

59 [God does not justify us without us consenting ... But he justifies us without us causing a virtue] *Super II Sententiarum*, d. 27, q. 1, a. 2, ad 7m.

60 [God effects virtues in us without us causing the virtues, but not without our consent] *De veritate*, q. 28, a. 3, ad 17m.

61 [infused virtue is caused in us by God without us acting, but not without us consenting. This is how we are to understand the words 'which God operates in us without us.' But those things that are done through us God causes in us not without our acting; for God operates in every will and nature] *Summa theologiae*, 1-2, q. 55, a. 4, ad 6m.

62 See ibid. q. 112, aa. 1-3.

63 [God does not justify us without us, because we consent to the justice of God through a movement of free will while we are being justified. But that movement is the effect of grace, not its cause. And so the whole operation pertains to grace] Ibid. q. 111, a. 2, ad 2m.

All four statements coincide inasmuch as the infused virtue or grace is caused solely by God and inasmuch as this divine action does not take place without our consent; but only the fourth adds the statement that our consent is caused by the infused virtue.[64]

The same point appears still more clearly in the account of the process of justification. Only God can cause grace, for only God can deify.[65] Only God can prepare man for grace,[66] and therefore it makes no difference whether this effect is produced gradually or instantaneously.[67] The justice of justification is the rectitude and order of the internal disposition of man; it involves the subordination of the rational element to God and of the irrational element to the rational.[68] The process of justification is a transition from the state of injustice or disorder to the state of justice.[69] In a normal human being this transmutation of the soul will not occur without acts of free will,[70] and these regard both terms of the motion, contrition for past sin and faith in God who justifies.[71] In the process the infusion of grace causes both the motions of free will and the remission of sins:[72] so that the infusion of grace is a *motio moventis*, the acts of free will are the consequent *motus mobilis*, while the remission of sin is the *consummatio motus sive perventio in finem*.[73]

3.2 Justification as a Premotion

Thus, the infusion of grace involves a premotion of the will. But one must distinguish between essential and accidental potency: air is [in] accidental potency to motion upwards, for all it requires is a *removens prohibens*; water is

---

64 Note that the definition of the infused virtue, *quam Deus in nobis sine nobis operatur*, is St Augustine's definition of the good will God causes in a stony heart. See chapter II-2, §1.4.
65 *Summa theologiae*, 1-2, q. 112, a. 1.
66 Ibid. a. 2.
67 Ibid. a. 2, ad 2m.
68 Ibid. q. 113, a. 1.
69 Ibid. See all passages on original sin, the need of the virtues.
70 Ibid. q. 113, a. 3.
71 Ibid. aa. 3–4.
72 Ibid. a. 7 c.: '... tota iustificatio impii originaliter consistit in gratiae infusione: per eam enim et liberum arbitrium movetur, et culpa remittitur' [the complete justification of the unrighteous consists originally in the infusion of grace; for by that means both free will is moved and guilt is remitted].
73 Ibid. q. 113, aa. 6–8.

in essential potency, for first it must lose the *forma gravitatis* and acquire the *forma levitatis*. Similarly, a teacher of mathematics is in accidental potency to understanding a given theorem, for all he requires is that his attention turn to it; but his pupil is in essential potency, for he must first acquire the habit of science.[74]

Note that any internal premotion of the will, involving as it does a change of will and the substitution of a new inclination for an old one, is of the type of essential premotion. It changes the agent qua agent and does not merely fulfil the conditions of his activity. Contrast the internal premotion necessary for the act of will with respect to a new end, with the external premotion, the *consilium rationis*, which fulfils the condition of the will's self-motion to an act with respect to the means.[75]

With regard to the seriation: *motio moventis, motus mobilis, perventio in finem,* compare *Summa theologiae,* 1-2, q. 23, a. 4; q. 26, a. 2. In these passages the general theory of local motion is taken as an analogy for the distinction of love, desire, joy. Just as in local motion there is first the production of the *forma gravitatis,* then the motion downwards according to the form, finally rest in the *locus connaturalis:* so also in the appetites there is first the *assimilatio appetitus,* which is love, then there is the motion following from this assimilation, which is desire, and finally there is possession of the object loved and desired, and that is joy. Observe that in these passages *appetibile movet appetitum* is presupposed: this is not quite coherent with the distinction between specification and exercise of the act of will. To understand *generans movet gravia et levia,* merely note that local motion is not an entitative change but simply a change of extrinsic denominations.

This parallel St Thomas clearly has in mind in his theory of habitual grace as operative and cooperative. Compare:

> Agens autem naturale duplicem effectum inducit in patiens: nam
> primo quidem dat formam, secundo autem dat motum
> consequentem formam; sicut generans dat corpori gravitatem, et
> motum consequentem ipsam.[76]

---

74 See *In VIII Phys.,* lect. 8. See *De veritate,* q. 11, a. 1, ad 12m.
75 See above, chapter 11-4, §6.6.
76 [A natural agent produces a twofold effect in the patient; for first of all it gives a form, and secondly it gives the movement consequent on form; as the generating (agent) gives a body gravity and the movement consequent on that (form)] *Summa theologiae,* 1-2, q. 26, a. 2.

Si vero accipiatur gratia pro habituali dono, sic etiam duplex est
gratiae effectus, sicut et cuiuslibet alterius formae: quorum primus
est esse, secundus est operatio; sicut caloris operatio est facere
calidum, et exterior calefactio.[77]

Nor is one to fancy that this is merely an extrinsic analogy: the virtue or
habit is a principle of activity; it makes the difference between the *agens
imperfectum* and the *agens perfectum*; it liberates the will from the servitude of
sin; it is an antecedent 'willingness' that inclines the will *ad modum naturae*.[78] Thus St Thomas writes:

Alio modo dicitur aliquis esse sub lege, quasi a lege coactus; et sic
dicitur esse sub lege, qui non voluntarie ex amore, sed timore
cogitur legem observare. *Talis autem caret gratia*, quae si adesset,
inclinaret voluntatem ad observantiam legis, ut ex amore moralia eius
praecepta impleret. Sic igitur quamdiu aliquis sic est sub lege, ut
non impleat voluntarie legem, peccatum in eo *dominatur*, ex quo
voluntas hominis *inclinatur* ut velit id quod est contrarium legi, sed
per gratiam tale dominium tollitur, ut scilicet homo servet legem,
non quasi sub lege existens, sed sicut liber. Gal. IV, 31: *Non sumus
ancillae filii sed liberae: qua libertate Christus nos liberavit.*

Hanc autem gratiam facientem homines libere legem implere,
non conferebant legalia sacramenta, sed conferunt eam sacramenta
Christi.[79]

77 [But if grace is taken as a habitual gift, then too there is a twofold effect of
grace as there is of any other form whatever; of these the first is being, the
second is operation, as the operation of heat is to make (something) hot,
and (to give) external heating] Ibid. q. 111, a. 2.
78 See above, chapter II-4, §4.2.
79 [Another way in which someone is said to be under the law is to be, as it
were, coerced by the law; and one who is coerced by fear to observe the law,
instead of (obeying it) voluntarily out of love, is said to be under the law in
this way. *But such a person lacks grace*, which if it were present would *incline*
the will to observance of the law, so that one would fulfil its moral precepts
out of love. Thus then, as long as one is under the law in this way, so that he
does not voluntarily fulfil the law, sin has *dominion* in him, from which a
person's will is so *inclined* that he wills what is contrary to the law. But such
dominion is removed by grace, so that he observes the law not as one living
under law but as one who is free. Galatians 4.31: '... we are children, not of
the slave but of the free woman. For by freedom Christ has set us free.'
    And the sacraments of the law did not confer this grace, which makes
men fulfil the law freely, but the sacraments of Christ do confer it] *In Rom.*,
c. 6, lect. 3 [§§ 497–98]. See *Summa theologiae*, 1-2, q. 108, a. 1, ad 2m.

Accordingly, as the sinner to avoid further sin stands in need of a notable deliberation, a marshaling of motives to counteract the spontaneous inclination of his will,[80] so also the regenerate need to be sorely tempted if their spontaneity is not to result automatically and freely in good action.[81] But the parallel goes no further: the sinner is unable to do what he really wants to do, 'for the good which I will, I do not; but the evil which I will not, that I do';[82] while the regenerate do the good that they would.[83] Again, the lack of deliberation in the sinner is a defect, for if he deliberated effectively, he would not sin; but the lack of deliberation in the regenerate is a perfection, for, no matter how great their deliberation, their choice would not be altered.[84]

But not only is habitual grace a form, a spontaneity, a second nature, that automatically leads to good action; it is also a premotion.

Recall the nature of premotion: it is a condition of activity in the *agens in tempore*. If there is action *now* and not *before*, then there is some reason for the difference. That reason is the premotion. God continuously causes habitual grace in the regenerate, but he does not continuously premove the

---

80   *De veritate*, q. 24, a. 12 c.: 'Nec hoc est intelligendum quod operatio secundum habitum virtutis possit esse omnino absque deliberatione, cum virtus sit habitus electivus; sed quia habenti habitum iam est in eius electione finis determinatus; unde quandocumque aliquid occurrit ut conveniens illi fini, statim eligitur, nisi ex aliqua attentiori et maiori deliberatione impediatur' [Nor is this to be understood so that an operation in accord with a virtuous habit can be altogether without deliberation, since virtue is an elective habit; but rather because there is already a determinate end in the choice of the one possessing the habit, and therefore whenever something occurs as suitable to that end, at once it is chosen, unless it is prevented by some more attentive and more (intense) deliberation].

81   *Super I Sententiarum*, d. 39, q. 2, a. 2, ad 4m: '...voluntas perfecta virtute iustitiae se habet ad opera iusta, sicut ignis ad motum sursum' [a will perfected by the virtue of justice has the same relation to just deeds that fire has to movement upwards]. See above, chapter II-4, §4.

82   Romans 7.19.

83   See *De veritate*, q. 24, a. 12, ad 1m. See above, chapter II-4, §5.2.3.

84   Distinguish two functions of deliberation: per se deliberation is required to attain knowledge of the course of action to be followed in a given situation; *per accidens* it is required to marshal motives that counteract the imperfection of the will without habits, the false bias of the will that has sinned. Habitual grace liberates from the accidental need of deliberation but not from the essential. But the perfection of angelic intellect, of the blessed in heaven, and of our divine Savior, dispense with the essential need of deliberation: they know at once. See *Summa theologiae*, 3, q. 34, a. 2, ad 2m; *De malo*, q. 16, aa. 5–6.

regenerate; only the infusion of habitual grace is a premotion, for only the infusion effects a change in the situation;[85] by definition (at least in Aristotle and St Thomas) a premotion is the change in the situation that accounts for the emergence of subsequent change.[86]

Two cases are to be distinguished: first, that of the normal human being; second, that of the *parvuli, amentes,* and *furiosi.*[87]

Three causal factors in the production of the free act of will are to be distinguished: first, the *appetitus naturalis,* or tendency to the good in general; second, the internal premotion of the will, a change of its inclination, whether by the introduction of a form or by a simple motion; third, the external premotion of the will, the *consilium rationis.* The first is needed for any free act.[88] The second is needed when the will is orientated to a new end.[89] The third is needed for the will to move itself from a will of the end to a will of the means, from the *actus voluntatis* properly so called to the *electio* or *consensus.*[90]

Now in the normal case the infusion of grace causes a *consensus ad detestandum peccatum et ad accedendum ad Deum.*[91] In abnormal cases it does not.[92] The reason for the difference is:

> ... in eo qui habet usum liberi arbitrii, non fit motio a Deo ad iustitiam absque motu liberi arbitrii; sed ita infundit donum gratiae iustificantis, quod etiam simul cum hoc movet liberum arbitrium ad donum gratiae acceptandum, in his qui sunt huius motionis capaces.[93]

---

85 Were the infusion of the habit a premotion in the Bannezian sense, it would be metaphysically necessary that the will always made acts of faith and contrition. See *Summa theologiae,* 1-2, q. 113, a. 3, ad 3m.

86 *In VIII Phys.,* lect. 2. See above, chapter II-3, §2.

87 *Summa theologiae,* 1-2, q. 113, a. 3 c. and ad 1m.

88 *Summa theologiae,* 1-2, q. 9, a. 6, ad 3m.

89 Ibid. a. 4; *De malo,* q. 16, a. 5; see above, chapter II-4, §5.1.

90 See above, chapter II-4, §6.6. On the terms, *Summa theologiae,* 1-2, q. 8, a. 2; qq. 13, 15.

91 [consent to detesting sin and to approaching God] *Summa theologiae,* 1-2, q. 113, a. 7, ad 1m.

92 Ibid. a. 3 c. and ad 1m.

93 [in one who has the use of free will the movement to justice is not made by God without the movement of free will; but God so infuses the gift of justifying grace that also and simultaneously with this he moves the free will to accepting the gift of grace in those who are capable of this movement] Ibid. a. 3.

Where does this second motion enter? Presumably the *parvuli, amentes,* and *furiosi* tend to the good in general. Certainly, their wills receive the internal premotion that consists in the *donum habituale.* But in normal cases there is also the illumination of the intellect, Repent and believe, and this constitutes the external premotion necessary for the self-motion of consent; in abnormal cases this is lacking.[94]

The case is parallel to the analogous motion of the *grave* and *leve*: if the *generans* gives the *forma gravitatis* to an object impeded from falling, then the object does not fall;[95] otherwise motion immediately ensues. The difference in the case of the spiritual motion is that it not merely begins immediately but also is immediately completed.

> ... in eodem instanti in quo forma acquiritur, incipit res operari secundum formam: sicut ignis statim cum est generatus, movetur sursum; et si motus eius esset instantaneus, in eodem instanti compleretur. Motus autem liberi arbitrii, qui est velle, non est successivus, sed instantaneus. Et ideo non oportet quod iustificatio impii sit successiva.[96]

There is, of course, another difference. The motion that follows the form of fire is a blind spontaneity; that following from the infusion of grace is a free act, which is caused not merely by the grace but also by the will which the grace informs. Hence:

> ... habitualis gratia, inquantum animam sanat vel iustificat, sive gratam Deo facit, dicitur gratia operans: inquantum vero est princip-

---

94 This is interpreting St Thomas on the general principles arrived at above, chapter II-4, §6.6. The only objection that might be made is that this rids Thomist thought of the 'profound' view that the greater the passivity, the greater the perfection of a free act. Such an opinion has no basis in St Thomas's writings; *liberum arbitrium* is self-determination; free will is self-motion of the will. One has only to read the first paragraphs in *De malo,* q. 6, a. 1 c., to know exactly what St Thomas thinks of such a view and of the kind of people who propose it.

95 *Summa theologiae,* 3, q. 69, a. 10 c.

96 [in the same instant in which the form is acquired, the thing begins to operate according to the form; as fire moves upward as soon as it is generated; and if its movement were instantaneous, it would be completed in the same instant. But the movement of free will, which is to will, is not successive but instantaneous. And therefore it is not necessary that justification of the unrighteous be successive] Ibid. 1-2, q. 113, a. 7, ad 4m.

ium operis meritorii, quod etiam ex libero arbitrio procedit, dicitur cooperans.[97]

It will be profitable to apply this definition of the distinction to the *motio moventis* and *motus mobilis* in the instant of justification.

It has been argued from the objection and response ad 2m, that St Thomas would attribute the meritorious and free act in justification not to cooperative grace (according to the above definition) but to operative grace. Perhaps the principal reason for this view lies in the wording of the objection in question.

> ... si gratia aliquid operetur in nobis, maxime operatur iustificationem. Sed hoc non sola gratia operatur in nobis: dicit enim Augustinus, super illud Ioan. xiv [12]: 'Opera, quae ego facio, et ipse faciet,' *Qui creavit te sine te, non iustificabit te sine te.* Ergo nulla gratia debet dici simpliciter operans.[98]

What causes confusion is to assume that this expresses the mind of St Thomas: [what he] is out to deny in his response is the conclusion *nulla gratia debet dici simpliciter operans* and not the minor premise *hoc non sola gratia operatur in nobis.* Both of these assumptions appear mistaken.

First, it is quite plain that St Thomas would not pretend any grace is *simpliciter operans.* He explicitly asserts that identically the same grace is both operative and cooperative. If, then, there is no real difference between operative and cooperative grace, to speak of a grace being *simpliciter operans* is absurd.

Next, what is quite clear from the response is that St Thomas wishes to distinguish the minor premise of the argument: *hoc non sola gratia operatur in nobis.* For first he points out that the motion of free will takes place *dum iustificamur*; he then states that this motion is not a *causa gratiae sed effectus*; finally, he concludes *tota operatio pertinet ad gratiam.*

---

97 [habitual grace, insofar as it heals the soul or justifies it or makes it pleasing to God, is called operative grace; but insofar as it is the principle of a meritorious deed, which proceeds from free will too, it is called cooperative] *Summa theologiae,* 1-2, q. 111, a. 2 c.

98 [if grace operates anything in us, above all it operates justification; but grace alone does not operate this in us, for Augustine says on that text of John 14.12, '(the one who believes) will also do the works that I do': *The One who created you without you will not justify you without you.* Therefore no grace should be called simply operative] Ibid. ob. 2.

> Ad secundum dicendum quod Deus non sine nobis nos iustificat,
> quia per motum liberi arbitrii, dum iustificamur, Dei iustitiae
> consentimus. Ille tamen motus non est causa gratiae, sed effectus.
> Unde tota operatio pertinet ad gratiam.[99]

Plainly, if the motion of free will is not a cause of grace, then the minor premise of the objection is false: *hoc non sola gratia operatur in nobis*. The point is that the free act is a condition, not a cause; the *parvuli, amentes*, and *furiosi* may be justified without any free act; hence *dum iustificamur, consentimus* and not *ut iustificemur, consentimus*. Further, the fulfilment of the condition is itself caused by grace, for it is an *effectus gratiae*: this is contrary to the earlier position which made grace prior as the formal cause and will prior as the material cause of justification; now, *tota operatio pertinet ad gratiam*.

Personally, I can find nothing in this that contradicts the very clear definition of the distinction of operative and cooperative grace to be found in the corpus. In the instant of justification, the same grace has two effects. The soul is healed, justified, made acceptable to God; this effect is caused by God alone and so is attributed to *gratia operans*. But there is a meritorious act that proceeds from free will, and this effect is caused not only by God but also by the will premoved by grace: accordingly it is attributed to *gratia cooperans*. The point of the second objection and response is simply to make clear that despite the fact that there are free acts in the instant of justification, nonetheless the grace of justification itself is an operative grace, an effect produced by God alone. Because the will cooperates in the fulfilment of the conditions of justification, it does not follow that the will cooperates in producing justification itself.[100]

3.3 The Free Act in Justification

But if it cannot reasonably be maintained either that the will does not cooperate with cooperative grace or that *gratia cooperans* refers to the *operatio*

---

99 [To the second objection it has to be said that God does not justify us without us, because we consent to the justice of God through a movement of free will while we are being justified. But that movement is the effect of grace, not its cause. And so the whole operation pertains to grace] Ibid. ad 2m.

100 The free act in justification is meritorious (*Summa theologiae*, 1-2, q. 112, a. 2, ad 1m). Hence it satisfies in all respects: 'habitualis gratia ... inquantum ... est principium operis meritorii, quod etiam ex libero arbitrio procedit, dicitur cooperans' [habitual grace ... insofar as it is the principle of a meritorious deed, which proceeds from free will too, it is called cooperative] Ibid. q. 111, a. 2.

following from the *forma*, still it may be objected that the will cannot but cooperate. Three arguments may be advanced for such a view. First, the angel cannot but do what is right in the first instant of its being; but the free act in justification seems parallel. Second, the sinner cannot but sin again; but *pari ratione*, the regenerate in the instant of regeneration cannot but consent to divine justice. Third, even though there exists an abstract possibility of the will not consenting in the instant of justification, still there is not the slightest probability for such a lack of consent, and so, practically, the will is not free.

With regard to the parallel from the angel, St Thomas holds different theories in the *Pars prima* and in the *De malo*. In the earlier work he advances that sin in the angel, though not possible through ignorance or error, is possible through exclusive attention to self;[101] but God does not create angels with such a defect. Therefore, there can be no sin in the first instant of creation.[102] It would seem that the argument presupposes the incomplete theory of liberty of the early period. In any case, in the *De malo* it is pointed out that this argument is insufficient: *malitia culpae non repugnat bonitati naturae*.[103] Accordingly, a distinction is drawn between the first act of the angel, which is in the natural order and cannot be a sin,[104] and a second act which is in reference to the supernatural order and can be a sin.[105]

To the objection, then, one may say: first, the cases are not parallel, for the angel's first act is in the natural order, while the free act in justification is with respect to the supernatural order; second, that ability to sin is not essential to freedom,[106] so it cannot be maintained that the angel is not free.

With regard to the inverse parallel of the sinner's impotence, the answer is to distinguish two interpretations of St Thomas's argument on this point.

He might be thought to argue that there is bound to be some particular case in which the sinner cannot but sin, though what or when that case will arise is not predictable. But plainly this is to interpret by the method of contradiction: what St Thomas affirms is that, though in no particular case the avoidance of sin is impossible, still avoidance in all cases is impossible.

---

101 *Summa theologiae*, 1, q. 63, a. 1, ad 4m.
102 Ibid. a. 5.
103 [the evil of guilt is not incompatible with the goodness of nature] *De malo*, q. 16, a. 4 c. init.
104 See ibid. a. 2.
105 Ibid. a. 4.
106 Ibid. a. 5.

The true interpretation should seem to be as follows. The absence of an evil orientation is necessary if sin is to be avoided over any period of time. The sinner is orientated towards evil action. Therefore, he cannot avoid sin over any period of time. Thus, the argument turns on the necessity of the absence of evil habits or evil orientation.[107] This necessity proves impossibility with regard to the general case but not with regard to any particular case.

In other words, the sinner cannot avoid all sins, not because there is bound to be some particular case in which he cannot but sin, but because he is orientated towards evil action. The former reason would imply the impossibility of not sinning in some particular case, though which one that is cannot be predicted. The latter reason has no such implication; it deduces from 'he cannot avoid all sins' not 'he cannot avoid some sin' but 'he will not avoid some sin.'

Accordingly, to the objection against the free act in justification, one may, if one chooses, affirm that the will consents, and that this affirmation is so probable as practically to amount to certitude; one cannot infer that the will cannot but consent, for it is never true that the sinner cannot but sin.

This brings us to the third objection. It is essentially superficial. For freedom does not require the slightest degree of probability that action be other than it is; it merely requires the possibility of its being different. All rhetoric is pathetically beside the point.

For an event to be contingent, it must be possible for it to be other than it is: otherwise, there is a contradiction in terms.[108] On the other hand,

---

107 The impossibility of perpetual vigilance proves this necessity, as, more generally, it proves the necessity of habits. That would seem to be the real significance of the impossibility of vigilance, and not, as the other interpretation supposes, an implication of an impossibility of not sinning in some particular case.

108 Hence St Thomas consistently rejects the possibility of certitude *in causa* with respect to a contingent event. It is worth noting that he considers not merely free acts of will but any terrestrial event to be contingent (see *In I Peri herm.*, lect. 14 [§§ 186–97]). The modern cosmic determinist says: granted knowledge of all the factors relevant to a future event, one can predict that event with certitude. To Aristotle and St Thomas this is ingenuous question begging: only an infinite mind knows with *certitude* that it knows *all* the factors relative to a future event; but to an infinite mind, nothing can be future; hence universally there is no possibility of prediction with certitude with respect to contingent future events. The exception of prophecy is by the infinite mind revealing its present to a finite mind to which that present happens to be future.

granted this possibility, contingence follows necessarily, and to pile up indefinitely a cumulation of probabilities proves nothing.[109]

4   The Position of the *Prima Secundae*: Actual Grace as Operative

This concluding section may be written in the form of a commentary on *Summa theologiae*, 1-2, q. 111, a. 2: *Utrum gratia convenienter dividatur per operantem et cooperantem.*

4.1   The Theory of Actual Grace

> Respondeo dicendum quod, sicut supra dictum est [q. 110, a. 2], gratia dupliciter potest intelligi: uno modo, divinum auxilium quo nos movet ad bene volendum et agendum; alio modo, habituale donum nobis divinitus inditum.[110]

The passage raises a single question: What precisely is St Thomas's concept of actual grace? The answer is supplied by the reference of the text to an earlier article.

> ... in eo qui dicitur gratiam Dei habere, significatur esse quidam effectus gratuitae Dei voluntatis. Dictum est autem supra [q. 109, a. 1] quod dupliciter ex gratuita Dei voluntate homo adiuvatur. Uno modo, inquantum anima hominis movetur a Deo ad aliquid cognoscendum vel volendum vel agendum. Et hoc modo ipse gratuitus effectus in homine non est qualitas sed motus quidam animae: *actus* enim *moventis in moto est motus*, ut dicitur in III *Physic.* [text. 18].
>   Alio modo adiuvatur homo ex gratuita Dei voluntate, secundum quod aliquod habituale donum a Deo animae infunditur.[111]

---

109 We do not wish to affirm that any grace makes consent so probable that consent becomes practically certain. From that question we prescind. Our contention is simply that, even were consent practically certain or anything else short of true certitude (which excludes the possibility of its contradictory), nonetheless the consent would be free.

110 [I reply that it has to be said that, as was stated above (q. 110, a. 2), grace can be understood in two ways: in one way (as) the divine help by which he moves us to willing and acting rightly; in another way (as) the habitual gift divinely conferred on us] *Summa theologiae*, 1-2, q. 111, a. 2 c.

111 [in one who is said to have the grace of God, a certain effect of God's gratuitous will is understood. But it was stated above (q. 109, a. 1) that man is helped in two ways by God's gratuitous will. In one way, insofar as man's

Thus, actual grace is any *effectus gratuitae Dei voluntatis*, apart from the *dona habitualia*, that produces a motion in the soul of man.

This is a large category, and St Thomas is quite aware of the fact. The definition was established in *De veritate*, q. 27, a. 5,[112] and is complemented by the discussion in the *Contra Gentiles* of the cognate ideas of necessity and justice.[113]

Similarly, in *De veritate*, q. 27, a. 5, ad 3m, the *divinum auxilium quod ad gratiam cooperantem pertinet* is described as a providential aid and direction of fallen man. This idea is developed against a cosmic background in *Contra Gentiles*, 3, cc. 88–92, and provides the speculative framework within which appears the *donum habituale* in the discussion of grace as *productio creaturae rationalis in finem supernaturalem* to be found in *Contra Gentiles*, 3, cc. 147–63.

The same general idea is to be found in *Summa theologiae*, 1-2, q. 109, aa. 1–5. The first of these articles takes one no further than the assertion that God is the first mover in the spiritual order as well as the material. The second distinguishes between the two functions of habitual grace, *elevatio* and *sanatio*, but merely mentions the need of an *auxilium Dei moventis* both before and after the fall. The third, fourth, and fifth articles go no further: the *gratia sanans* they mention is habitual grace.

However, the gratuitous character of this *auxilium* appears clearly in articles 6, 7, and 9.

Article 6, on the preparation for grace, distinguishes between the general motion by which all things are turned to God *secundum communem intentionem boni* and the special motion that converts man to God *sicut ad specialem finem ... cui cupiunt adhaerere sicut bono proprio.*

In article 7, on the cognate subject of conversion from sin, an *interior Dei motio* is mentioned.

In article 9, on the need of grace after justification, a distinction is drawn between the *ratio generalis* and the *ratio specialis* for the *auxilium Dei moventis*. The *ratio generalis* is that *nulla res creata potest in quemcumque actum prodire nisi virtute motionis divinae*.[114] Since this applies to the need of the heavenly

---

soul is moved by God to knowing or willing or doing something. And in this way that gratuitous effect is not a quality in man but a certain movement of the soul, for 'the act of the (actively) moving thing is a movement in the moved,' as is stated in the third book of the *Physics* (text 18).

In another way man is helped by God's gratuitous will according as some habitual gift is infused in the soul by God] *Summa theologiae*, 1-2, q. 110, a. 2.

112   See above, pp. [231–32].

113   *Summa contra Gentiles*, 2, cc. 28–30.

114   [no created thing can come to any act whatever except in virtue of a divine motion] *Summa theologiae*, 1-2, q. 109, a. 9 c.

spheres, of animals, plants, minerals, and elements, and is simply the general theorem of God operating in the operation of the creature, it is not *ratione sui* gratuitous or a grace. On the other hand, the *ratio specialis* is *propter conditionem status humanae naturae*, and clearly this in itself makes the *auxilium* gratuitous: the special needs resulting from the *culpa* of original sin constitute no claim in justice.

To conclude, actual grace is a gratuitous motion, produced in the creature, directing and aiding him to God as his special end. Nothing is said about the manner in which such a motion is produced in the soul, whether mediately or immediately. However, it would seem necessarily to be a motion and not simply God or grace operating an operation: for cooperative grace and the grace of perseverance are identified with other graces because they are not distinct motions.[115]

4.2 Operative Grace and Instrumentality

The response continues, 'Utroque autem modo gratia dicta convenienter dividitur per operantem et cooperantem.'[116] This position is in advance of the *De veritate*, where actual grace was not operative but only cooperative.

The cause of the change is quite easily assigned. As the distinction between prevenient and subsequent grace led to actual grace as cooperative in the *De veritate*, so the development of the theory of the preparation for justification necessarily implies an actual grace that operates, converts.

In the preceding section the differences between the *De veritate* and the *Prima secundae* in this respect were presented. It is now necessary to consider the intervening period, for it is the development that does most to explain the operative character of actual grace in the article we are commenting.

Theoretically, then, the whole question is resolved by *Contra Gentiles*, 3, c. 149, where it is demonstrated that all initiative pertains to God. Man cannot move himself to attain divine aid towards an end above the proportion of his nature. Man is an instrument in the hands of God. No particular cause can prevent the action of the universal cause. Were man not moved by God, then his action would not be proportionate to the end. Apprehension precedes acts of will, but knowledge of the supernatural end of man is only from God. The second last paragraph is quoted to give the tone of St Thomas's position.

115 See *Summa theologiae*, 1-2, q. 111, a. 2, ad 4m; q. 109, a. 10.
116 [And in both ways the grace we speak of is suitably divided by operative and cooperative] Ibid. q. 111, a. 2 c.

Hinc est quod dicitur *Tit.* III, 5: *Non ex operibus iustitiae quae fecimus nos, sed secundum suam misericordiam salvos nos fecit.* Et *Rom.* IX, 16: *Non est volentis,* scilicet velle, *neque currentis,* scilicet currere, *sed miserentis Dei:* quia scilicet oportet quod ad bene volendum et operandum homo divino praeveniatur auxilio; sicut consuetum est quod effectus aliquis non attribuitur proximo operanti, sed primo moventi; attribuitur enim victoria duci, quae labore militum perpetratur.

Non ergo per huiusmodi verba excluditur liberum voluntatis arbitrium, sicut quidam male intellexerunt, quasi homo non sit dominus suorum actuum interiorum et exteriorum: sed ostenditur Deo esse subiectum. Et *Thren.* IV dicitur: *Converte nos, Domine, ad te, et convertemur.* per quod patet quod conversio nostra ad Deum praevenitur auxilio Dei nos convertentis.[117]

However, as remarked above,[118] there is no clear evidence that St Thomas in the *Contra Gentiles* had thought of a conversion prior to the instant of justification. The above position will inevitably lead to it, but the citation of the passage from the epistle to Titus is not easily reconciled with an actual consideration of such an anterior conversion. Accordingly, we have not yet an actual grace that is operative.

Thus, it is perhaps in the *Pars prima* that actual grace as operative makes its first appearance. After laying down the general principle in the response to q. 62, a. 2, on the conversion of the angels, namely, that our last end is supernatural and so *nulla creatura rationalis potest habere motum voluntatis ordinatum ad illam beatitudinem, nisi mota a supernaturali agente,*[119] there

---

117 [That is why it is said (Titus 3.5): *He saved us, not because of any works of righteousness that we had done, but according to his mercy.* And (Romans 9.16): *It depends not on human will,* that is, to will, *or exertion,* that is, to run, *but on God who shows mercy* – because, namely, it is necessary for right willing and acting that man receive divine prevenient help; as in general usage an effect is attributed, not to the proximate agent, but to the first mover; for victory, which was achieved by the labor of the soldiers, is attributed to the general.

The free choice of will is not therefore excluded by words like these – as some have wrongly understood (them), as if man were not the master of his internal and external acts – but rather (free will) is shown to be subject to God. And it is said (Lamentations 5.21): *Restore us to yourself, O Lord, that we may be restored,* from which it is clear that our conversion to God is preceded by the help of God converting us] *Summa contra Gentiles,* 3, c. 149 [§ 3222].

118 See above, p. [242].

119 [no rational creature can have a movement of will directed to that beatitude, unless it is moved by a supernatural agent] *Summa theologiae,* 1, q. 62, a. 2 c.

appears in the ad 3m the recognition of an actual grace directing to this end.

> ... quilibet motus voluntatis in Deum, potest dici conversio in ipsum. Et ideo triplex est conversio in Deum. Una quidem per dilectionem perfectam, quae est creaturae iam Deo fruentis. Et ad hanc conversionem requiritur gratia consummata. – Alia conversio est, quae est meritum beatitudinis. Et ad hanc requiritur habitualis gratia, quae est merendi principium. – Tertia conversio est, per quam aliquis praeparat se ad gratiam habendam. Et ad hanc non exigitur aliqua habitualis gratia, sed operatio Dei ad se animam convertentis, secundum illud *Thren.* ult: *Converte nos Domine ad te, et convertemur* ...[120]

On the supernatural character of this act, it is not our intention to write in the present work for the reasons already given.[121] A point on which we must insist, however, is the close relation in St Thomas's thought between these three propositions: God prevents the will of man; God moves the will to the end; God operates the free act of will more than the will itself.

The logical connection of these propositions is manifest: the first and third are necessary consequents of the second. Unless God moves the will to the end, the will cannot act at all.[122] If God moves the will to the end, then clearly the divine action is prior to the human choice. Again, since the will moves itself in virtue of willing the end, then its operation is *virtute motionis divinae.*

Following up *De veritate*, q. 22, a. 8, on divine control of the will, there are chapters 88 and 89 in the third book of *Contra Gentiles.*

---

120 [any movement of the will towards God can be called a conversion to him. And so there is a threefold conversion to God. One is (conversion) by perfect love, which is the case for one already enjoying God. And for this conversion there is required the consummation of grace. – Another conversion is that of meriting beatitude. And for this, habitual grace, which is the principle of meriting, is required. – The third conversion is that by which one prepares oneself to have grace. And for this there is not required any habitual grace, but the operation of God converting the soul to himself, according to that text of Lamentations, 'Restore us to yourself, O Lord, that we may be restored'] Ibid. ad 3m.

121 See above, chapter II-2, §8 [p. 246].

122 *Summa theologiae*, 1-2, q. 9, a. 6, ad 3m. [The following sentence in the text is an interpretation. The autograph reads (p. 286), 'If God moves the will to the end, then clearly the divine action is prior to the end, then clearly the divine action is prior to the human choice.']

The first accounts for *Deus est qui operatur in nobis et velle*: for God, but no one else, can operate in the will.

The next chapter accounts for the *et perficere*: for if God causes the *virtus volendi*, it necessarily follows that he causes the *actus volendi*.[123]

The dogmatic significance of this position is very clearly presented in the commentary on Romans[124] with respect to the text, *Igitur non volentis neque currentis sed miserentis est Dei*. The passage is as follows.

> Deinde, cum dicit, *Igitur non volentis*, etc., concludit propositum ex praemissa auctoritate.
>
> Et potest haec conclusio multipliciter intelligi; uno modo sic: *Igitur*, ipsa salus hominis, *non est volentis neque currentis*, id est non debetur alicui per aliquam eius voluntatem, vel exteriorem operationem, quae dicitur cursus (secundum illud I Cor. ix, 24: *Sic currite ut comprehendatis*), *sed est miserentis Dei*, id est, procedit ex sola Dei misericordia, ut maxime sequitur ex auctoritate inducta Deut. ix, 4: *Nec dicas in corde tuo: Propter iustitiam meam introduxit me Dominus, ut terram hanc possiderem.*
>
> Potest autem et aliter intelligi ut sit sensus: Omnia procedunt ex Dei misericordia: *igitur non est volentis*, scilicet velle, *neque currentis*, scilicet currere, *sed* utrumque *est miserentis Dei*, secundum illud I Cor. xv, 10: *Non autem ego, sed gratia Dei mecum.* Et Io. xv, 5: *Sine me nihil potestis facere.*
>
> Sed si hoc solum in hoc verbo intellexisset Apostolus, cum etiam gratia sine libero arbitrio hominis non velit neque currat, potuisset e converso dicere: Non est miserentis Dei, sed volentis et currentis, quod aures piae non ferunt.
>
> Unde plus aliquid est ex his verbis intelligendum, ut scilicet principalitas gratiae Dei attribuatur.
>
> Semper enim actio magis attribuitur principali agenti, quam secundario, puta si dicamus quod securis non facit arcam, sed artifex per securim. Voluntas autem hominis movetur a Deo ad bonum. Unde supra viii, v. 14 dictum est: *Qui spiritu Dei aguntur, hi sunt filii*

123 See above, p. [379].
124 The chronological position of this work is not known with exactitude. Of interest is the fact that the theory of the will seems the same as in the *Pars prima* (see above, p. [340, note 47]). There is also the question of the origin of the development between the commentary on the *Sentences* and the *Pars prima* on the matter of reprobation (see above, pp. [340, 382], where the relevant passages from the commentary on Romans are mentioned).

Dei. Et ideo hominis operatio interior non est homini principaliter, sed Deo attribuenda. – Phil. II, 13: *Deus est qui operatur in nobis velle et perficere pro bona voluntate.*

Sed si non est volentis velle, neque currentis currere, sed Dei moventis ad hoc hominem, videtur quod homo non sit dominus sui actus, quod pertinet ad libertatem arbitrii.

Et ideo dicendum est, quod Deus omnia movet, sed diversimode, inquantum scilicet unumquodque movetur ab eo secundum modum naturae suae. Et sic homo movetur a Deo ad volendum et currendum per modum liberae voluntatis. Sic ergo velle et currere est hominis, ut libere agentis: non autem est hominis ut principaliter moventis, sed Dei.[125]

125 [Then when he says, 'So it depends not on human will,' etc., he draws his conclusion on the basis of the stated authority.

And this conclusion can be understood in many ways. One way is the following. 'So' the salvation itself of man 'depends not on human will or exertion'; that is, it is not owed to anyone because of some (act of) will or external operation, which is called 'to run' (because of that text of 1 Corinthians 9.24: 'Run in such a way that you may win') 'but on God who shows mercy'; that is, it proceeds from God's mercy alone, as follows especially from the authority adduced from Deuteronomy 9.4: 'Do not say to yourself, "It is because of my righteousness that the Lord has brought me in to occupy this land."'

But it can be understood in another way, so that the meaning is as follows: All things proceed from God's mercy: 'So it depends not on human will,' that is, to will, 'or exertion,' that is, to run, 'but' both depend 'on God who shows mercy,' according to that text of 1 Corinthians 15.10: 'Though it was not I, but the grace of God that is with me.' And (that of) John 15.5: 'Apart from me you can do nothing.'

But if the Apostle had meant only this in this word, since even grace does not 'will' or 'run' without man's free will, he could have made the contrary statement: 'It does not depend on God who shows mercy but on (human) will and exertion,' which is intolerable to pious ears.

And so something more is to be understood by these words, namely, that the principal role be attributed to the grace of God.

For an action is always attributed more to the chief agent than to the secondary; for example, if we say that the axe does not make the box, but the craftsman makes it with an axe. But human will is moved by God to the good. And so it was said above: '... all who are led by the Spirit of God are children of God' (8.14). And therefore a man's internal operation is not to be attributed principally to man but to God. – Philippians 2.13: '... for it is God who is at work in you, enabling you both to will and to work for his good pleasure.'

But if to will does not depend on the one willing, nor running on the runner, but on God moving man to this, it seems that man is not master of his act, which (mastery) pertains to the liberty of will.

The point is clear. It is not enough to say that divine mercy is a necessary condition of good will and good performance. Free will is a necessary condition, yet one cannot say, *non est miserentis Dei sed volentis et currentis.*

Therefore one must hold that the free act proceeds from God as principal cause and from man only as instrumental cause. Just as it is not the axe but the craftsman using the axe that makes the box, so it is not man's will but God using man as a tool that produces good will and good performance, *velle et currere.*

Nor is this contrary to freedom: *velle et currere est hominis, ut libere agentis, non autem est hominis ut principaliter moventis, sed Dei.*[126]

The same position reappears in the *De malo.*

> ... etiam interior voluntas movetur ab aliquo superiori principio, quod est Deus; et secundum hoc Apostolus dicit, quod *non est volentis*, scilicet velle, *neque currentis*, currere, sicut primi principii, *sed Dei miserentis.*[127]

On top of this St Thomas immediately places his theorem of the transcendent *artifex*. Because the human will is moved, its operation [is] *virtute motionis divinae.* God operates in its operation, and the *actio Dei* is infallible, efficacious, irresistible, as already explained.[128]

To conclude, the idea that actual grace is operative is contained in the fact that [there] is a conversion prior to justification. That all initiative comes from God follows from St Thomas's philosophic position that all created action is instrumental. It is in terms of this philosophic position that St Thomas interprets *Igitur non est volentis neque currentis sed miserentis est Dei,*

And so it has to be said that God moves all things, but in different ways, insofar, that is, as everything is moved by him according to the mode of its nature. And so man is moved by God to will or to run according to the mode of free will. Thus, therefore, to will and to run pertain to man as freely acting, not however to man as the one principally moving but to God] *In Rom.*, c. 9, lect. 3 [§§ 775–78].

126 [to will and to run pertain to man as freely acting, not however to man as the one principally moving but to God] Ibid. [§ 778].

127 [also the internal will is moved by some higher principle which is God; and accordingly, the Apostle says that 'it does not depend on the one willing,' that is, to will, 'nor on the one running,' that is, to run, as on the first principle, 'but on God who has mercy'] *De malo*, q. 6, a. 1, ad 1m. See *Summa contra Gentiles*, 3, c. 149; *Summa theologiae*, 1, q. 83, a. 1, ad 2m, ad 3m.

128 *De malo*, q. 6, a. 1, ad 3m. See above, chapter II-4, § 2.2.2.

in *Contra Gentiles*, 3, c. 149; in the commentary on Romans, c. 9, lect. 3; in *Summa theologiae*, 1, q. 83, a. 1, ad 2m.; in *De malo*, q. 6, a. 1, ad 1m; and in *Summa theologiae*, 1-2, q. 111, a. 2, ad 3m. The possibility of a free act of will being instrumental follows from the fact that the free act is with respect to the means while the will of the end is not a free act but a natural motion: thus, while *De malo*, q. 6, a. 1, represents the solution of the problem of freedom,[129] it would seem that the detailed study of the will at the beginning of the *Prima secundae*[130] is the culmination of the whole series of texts on divine operation in the will[131] and that its aim is to describe accurately the created mechanism on which God operates.

4.3 The Divergence from St Augustine

Operatio enim alicuius effectus non attribuitur mobili,[132] sed moventi. In illo ergo effectu in quo mens nostra est mota et non movens, solus autem Deus movens, operatio Deo attribuitur: et secundum hoc dicitur gratia operans. In illo autem effectu in quo mens nostra et movet et movetur, operatio non solum attribuitur Deo, sed etiam animae: et secundum hoc dicitur gratia cooperans.[133]

St Thomas's idea of operation has already been explained at length,[134] so that here we need only advert to the difference between St Augustine's conception of operative grace and that of St Thomas. Obviously such a difference is of considerable importance if one is to grasp what precisely St Thomas has in mind in writing this article.

---

129 See above, chapter II-4, §1.
130 *Summa theologiae*, 1-2, qq. 6–17.
131 *De veritate*, q. 22, a. 8; q. 24, a. 14; *Summa contra Gentiles*, 3, cc. 88–92; *Summa theologiae*, 1, q. 83, a. 1, ad 2m, ad 3m.
132 Note that *operatio immanens attribuitur mobili*: I will the end though I do not cause that act of will.
133 [For the operating of some effect is not attributed to the movable thing but to the (actively) moving thing. In that effect, therefore, in which our mind is moved but not (actively) moving, and God alone is the mover, the operation is attributed to God: and this is accordingly called operative grace. But in that effect in which our mind is both moved and (actively) moving, the operation is attributed not to God alone but also to the soul: and this is accordingly called cooperative grace] *Summa theologiae*, 1-2, q. 111, a. 2.
134 See above, chapter II-3, §1, §6.

St Augustine, then, does not distinguish between operative and prevenient nor between subsequent and cooperative grace. St Thomas holds a similar position in the commentary on the *Sentences* and the *De veritate* but in the *Prima secundae* introduces the following distinction.

The terms 'prevenient' and 'subsequent' are used with respect to the time series.[135] The terms 'operative' and 'cooperative' are used with respect to the causal series: causation proceeds from the first cause through the creature to the effect; inasmuch as this causation is received in the creature and effects a change in it – *mens nostra mota et non movens* – grace is said to be operative; but inasmuch as the causation is not merely received in the creature but is also causing the creature's *mens mota movens* grace is said to be cooperative.

Plainly, this is not merely a consequence of St Thomas's theory of operation and of cosmic hierarchy: it is also required by his explanation of *Non est volentis neque currentis sed miserentis est Dei* and the complementary *Deus est qui operatur in nobis et velle et perficere*. The theory of grace coincides with the philosophic theory that the creature is an instrument and with the psychological theory that the will of the end is a natural motion.

It is not surprising that such a synthesis of dogma, metaphysics, and psychology should result in a point of view that is not identical with St Augustine's.

If the reader will turn back[136] to the context of *ipse ut velimus operatur incipiens, qui volentibus cooperatur perficiens*, he will find that the example of operative grace is the initial good will St Peter had at the Last Supper when he professed his willingness to die for our Lord, but the example of cooperative grace is the perfect good will St Peter had when he did not profess and then deny but confessed Christ and underwent martyrdom. In other words, St Augustine's distinction refers to the temporal series, to successive stages in the spiritual life. The first thing needed is a desire to do what is right. Without such a desire man cannot even begin to move towards

---

135 *Summa theologiae,* 1-2, q. 111, a. 3, ad 1m: '... dilectio Dei nominat aliquid aeternum: et ideo numquam potest dici nisi praeveniens. Sed gratia significat effectum temporalem, qui potest praecedere aliquid et ad aliquid subsequi. Et ideo gratia potest dici praeveniens et subsequens' [the love of God names something eternal, and therefore it can never be called anything but prevenient; but grace means a temporal effect, which can precede something and follow something; and therefore grace can be called prevenient and subsequent].

136 See above, chapter II-2, §1.4.

eternal life: he has a heart of stone that has to be transformed into a heart of flesh. But, granted the desire, one has yet [to add] performance under difficult circumstances: St Peter professed readiness for martyrdom at the Last Supper but he was ready for martyrdom only after his apostolate. Thus, the grace of good desires is one thing, and the grace of good performance is another. But there is this difference between the two: for good desires one cannot even pray; but with good desires one can pray for good performance. Accordingly, God operates initial good will and then cooperates with this good will towards its perfection.

But St Thomas's theory of the creature as an instrument results in a far more rigid analysis. If God is principal cause, then he must operate the whole effect throughout the whole course of the spiritual life. Not merely the initial stage of the life of grace is the result of operative grace: there must always be operative grace, for the instrument must always be moved and moved in the right way. God is prevenient, not only temporally but also causally: if the former prevention can be circumscribed by a given moment in time, the latter cannot, for *sublata causa, tollitur effectus.*

Thus, just as the logic of his polemic against the Pelagians who spoke of the initial *merita bonae voluntatis* led St Augustine to point out that there is no initial *bona voluntas*, so the more exigent logic of St Thomas's philosophic interpretation of scriptural texts led him to the assertion that at no time is there *bona voluntas* without grace.

This basic difference leads to others. While for St Augustine St Peter's initial good will and his protestation at the Last Supper are attributed to operative grace, St Thomas would attribute the internal act to operative, the external act to cooperative grace. Again, while both St Peter's perfect charity in martyrdom and his endurance of the ordeal are attributed by St Augustine to cooperative grace, St Thomas again attributes the internal act to operative, the external to cooperative grace. Finally, while for St Augustine operative and cooperative denote distinct graces, for St Thomas the terms 'operative' and 'cooperative' denote one and the same grace[137] while St Augustine's different graces would be *operans et praeveniens* and *operans et subsequens.*

---

137 '... gratia operans et cooperans est eadem gratia; sed distinguitur secundum diversos effectus' [operative and cooperative grace are the same grace; but (the grace) is distinguished according to (its) different effects] *Summa theologiae*, 1-2, q. 111, a. 2, ad 4m.

4.4 The Internal and External Acts

> Est autem in nobis duplex actus. Primus quidem interior voluntatis
> ... Alius autem actus est exterior ...[138]

It will be well before considering the next phrases in detail, to determine what St Thomas usually means by the terms *actus interior, actus exterior*. As the reader is aware, such an inquiry is not decisive in the interpretation of the present article;[139] it remains that it may be useful.

Uniformly, then, St Thomas uses the term *actus interior* to denote the free act of will, the election; *actus exterior* denotes the corporeal and sensibly perceptible act. It corresponds to the difference of the *actus elicitus* and the *actus imperatus*.

This usage is found in the *De malo* in the discussion of internal and external sins;[140] in the *Prima secundae* in the analysis of human acts from the point of view of morality,[141] in the contrast between the end of divine and the end of civil law,[142] between the Old Testament and the New;[143] in the *Secunda secundae* in the treatment of the virtues.[144] It is applied to grace in the commentary on the *Sentences*[145] and in the *De malo*.[146]

Thus, if the mere number of instances and the uniformity of usage were the sole criteria, it would not be possible to have a greater antecedent probability with respect to the meaning of the terms in the article we are discussing. But a little consideration changes considerably the significance of the evidence set forth above. For when St Thomas is discussing sin, morality, law, or virtue, it is not surprising that the internal act is always the free act of will. The uniformity is determined by the matter under discussion. Again, any other meaning would hardly be possible in the commen-

---

138 [But there is a twofold act in us. The first is an internal act of the will ... But the other act is external] *Summa theologiae*, 1-2, q. 111, a. 2 c.

139 See above, chapter II-3, §1.3.

140 *De malo*, q. 2, a. 2 c. and ad 1m, ad 5m–6m, ad 8m, ad 11m–13m; a. 3; etc.

141 *Summa theologiae*, 1-2, qq. 18–20.

142 Ibid. q. 98, a. 1.

143 Ibid. q. 108, aa. 1–3.

144 *Summa theologiae*, 2-2, qq. 2–3, 24–43, in the division of questions; in text, especially q. 3, a. 1; q. 31, a. 1, ad 2m.

145 *Super II Sententiarum*, d. 26, q. 1, a. 5, ad 4m. See ibid. d. 25, q. 1, a. 3; d. 35, q. 1, a. 4.

146 *De malo*, q. 6, a. 1, ob. 2.

tary on the *Sentences* before the development of the theory of the will in the
form to be found only in the *Prima secundae*. Finally, the usage in the *De malo*
with respect to grace occurs in an objection and so may be merely the
expression of a current point of view.

Indeed in the following passage, though the *actus interior* certainly means
the election, nonetheless there is a very close approximation to the other
point of view.

> In actu autem voluntario invenitur duplex actus, scilicet actus inte-
> rior voluntatis, et actus exterior: et uterque horum actuum habet
> suum obiectum. Finis autem proprie est obiectum interioris actus
> voluntarii: id autem circa quod est actio exterior, est obiectum eius.
> Sicut igitur actus exterior accipit speciem ex obiecto circa quod est;
> ita actus interior voluntatis accipit speciem a fine, sicut a proprio
> obiecto.[147]

Now, were St Thomas not analyzing the *actus voluntarius*, the *actus humanus*,
but treating generally of the causality of the act of will, he could very easily
make the term *actus interior* the act that is with respect to the end not merely
derivatively, as is the case above, but formally.

Accordingly, we may continue our interpretation of *Summa theologiae*, 1-2,
q. 111, a. 2, without any antecedent presumption on the meaning of *actus
interior*.

4.5 *Operative Grace and the Internal Act*

> Est autem in nobis duplex actus. Primus quidem interior voluntatis.
> Et quantum ad istum actum, voluntas se habet ut mota, Deus autem
> ut movens: et praesertim cum voluntas incipit bonum velle, quae
> prius malum volebat. Et ideo secundum quod Deus movet humanam
> mentem ad hunc actum, dicitur gratia operans.
>
> ... Homo autem per gratiam operantem adiuvatur a Deo ut bonum

147 [But in the (category of) voluntary act there is found a twofold act, namely,
the internal act of the will and the external act; and each of these acts has
its object. But the end is properly the object of the internal act of the will,
and that about which the external act is concerned is the object of that act.
Therefore, just as the external act gets its species from the object about
which it is concerned, so the internal act of the will gets its species from the
end as from its proper object] *Summa theologiae*, 1-2, q. 18, a. 6.

velit. Et ideo, praesupposito iam fine, consequens est ut gratia nobis cooperetur.[148]

The meaning of the passage may be determined as follows.

(a) The act in question is an act of will, that is, not some act outside the will, nor a mere disposition in the will, nor the act of will taken simply *quoad formam meriti.*

This follows from the [phrase] *actus interior voluntatis* and from the example *praesertim cum voluntas incipit bonum velle, quae prius malum volebat.*

Against the opinion that St Thomas is thinking solely of the *forma meriti*[149] the following objections arise: the *forma meriti* is caused by habitual grace; there is no *forma meriti* when the will begins to will the good, except in the special case when this initial good will is also justification; the position overlooks the whole development of St Thomas's thought on grace.

(b) The sole efficient cause of this act is God.

Man and, in particular, man's will are the material cause: for the will is moved.

Again, man is the subject of the act of will produced: he begins to will the good.

But neither man's will nor consequently man himself is the efficient cause of this act: *voluntas mota et non movens.*

An opinion has been put forward that *non movens* means *non movens aliquid aliud,* for example, the bodily members. Such a view has its attractions. But what it lacks is evidence. St Thomas says *non movens,* and he does not say *non movens aliud.*

(c) The act of will in question is with respect to an end, not with respect to the means; it is the act of will properly so called, and not an election nor a consent.

That it is with respect to the end and not with respect to the means to an end is clearly stated in the response ad 3m. Once the will wills the end, it follows, *consequens est,* that grace becomes cooperative. But the internal act

---

148 [But there is a twofold act in us. The first is an internal act of the will; and in regard to that act the will has the role of being moved, and God the role of mover; and this is the case especially when the will, which before was willing evil, begins to will the good. And therefore, in that God moves the human mind to this act, grace is called operative ...

... But man through operative grace is assisted by God to will the good. And therefore, with the end now presupposed, the consequence is that grace cooperates with us] *Summa theologiae,* 1-2, q. 111, a. 2 c. and ad 3m.

149 See above, chapter II-2, §5.

is considered as an effect of operative grace: therefore it is not a will of the means but of an end.

Hence it is not an election: *voluntas est finis, electio autem eorum quae sunt ad finem;*[150] nor a consent: *consensus, proprie loquendo, non est nisi de his quae sunt ad finem;*[151] but an act of will in the strict sense: *Si autem loquamur de voluntate secundum quod nominat proprie actum, sic, proprie loquendo, est finis tantum.*[152]

Observe that this does not imply that the act of will in question is specified by the *bonum in genere,* for that is not the only possible end of the will. It simply means that the will tends to some object absolutely and not because it tends to some other object.

(d) Against the foregoing it will be objected: if the *actus interior* is the will of the end and the *actus exterior* is the corporeal act, then the article under discussion makes no explicit mention of the election, consent, or free act of will that mediates between the divine motion and the human external act.

To this the proper answer would seem to be: undoubtedly such a fact appears anomalous to us and if true requires an explanation; but the text of St Thomas is never explained by modifying the data or twisting them into a meaning that they do not possess. The conclusion that the internal act of will in this article is with respect to an end follows necessarily from the text; as has been shown, the more ordinary usage of the term *actus interior* does not make it impossible that *actus interior* here means the act of will with respect to the end. If anyone knows a reason for rejecting the authenticity of *praesupposito iam fine, consequens est ut gratia nobis cooperetur,* then it becomes possible to discuss theories that require the *actus interior* to be or to include the election, consent, will of the means. But as long as those words remain in the text, supported as they are by the instrumental idea of operative grace, all discussion of the matter is futile.

(e) The act of will in question is not a free act.

The opinion to the contrary is based on the response ad 2m: *dum iustificamur, Dei iustitiae consentimus.* As already remarked it can arise only from inattention to the corpus of the article: St Thomas distinguishes

---

150 [the will is of the end, but election of those things which are (means) to the end] *Summa theologiae,* 1-2, q. 13, a. 3, Sed contra.
151 [consent, properly speaking, is about only those things which are (means) to the end] Ibid. q. 15, a. 3.
152 [But if we speak of the will, according as properly it names an act, then strictly speaking it is of the end only] Ibid. q. 8, a. 2.

between *forma et operatio*; for instance, the heat by which the fire is hot, and the heat which the fire transmits to other objects. Inasmuch as grace is a formal cause, it is operative; inasmuch as it is a principle of meritorious acts of will, it is cooperative.

> ... inquantum animam sanat vel iustificat, sive gratam Deo facit, dicitur gratia operans: inquantum vero est principium operis meritorii, quod etiam ex libero arbitrio procedit, dicitur cooperans.[153]

Those who would ascribe the free act of will in justification to operative grace, and so have an analogy to justify the assertion that the *actus interior* under discussion is a free act, must either contradict the passage just cited or else maintain that the free act in justification is not meritorious, does not proceed from free will, and is a formal constituent of the regenerate, so that the *infantes, amentes, et furiosi* are not justified. For unless the free act in justification is a formal constituent of justification, then it does not pertain to *gratia operans*. And if it is a meritorious act[154] and proceeds from free will, then it does pertain to *gratia cooperans*.

Since, then, a number of writers argue from the analogy of habitual grace to the effect that habitual grace as operative produces free acts, therefore actual grace as operative produces free acts, we are quite entitled to make a right use of the analogy. Because habitual grace, as a matter of fact, simply cures and justifies the soul inasmuch as it is operative and since its function relative to free acts is defined to be cooperative, it follows that actual grace as operative has nothing to do with the free act. This position is easily confirmed. St Thomas considers that the free act is not the will of the end but the will of the means, the election, the consent. But the *actus interior* is not the will of the means nor an election nor a consent. Therefore it is not a free act.

Again, in the *actus interior* the will is *mota et non movens*. But St Thomas throughout all his works maintains that *liber est qui est sui causa* in the sense of efficient causality.[155] Therefore it is unreasonable to suppose that St Thomas suddenly changed his theory of freedom in *Summa theologiae*, 1-2, q.

---

153 [insofar as it heals the soul or justifies it or makes it pleasing to God, it is called operative grace; but insofar as it is the principle of a meritorious deed, which proceeds from free will too, it is called cooperative] *Summa theologiae*, 1-2, q. 111, a. 2 c.

154 It is meritorious: *Summa theologiae*, 1-2, q. 112, a. 2, ad 1m.

155 See above, chapter 11-4, §1. See *Summa theologiae*, 1-2, q. 108, a. 1, ad 2m.

111, a. 2, that is, in an article in which he makes no effort to discuss the nature of freedom.

Finally, if one asserts that the will *mota et non movens* elicits a free act, then one draws no distinction between the spontaneity of natural causes and the free act of will. According to St Thomas such a position is heretical, alien to philosophic thought, destructive of the principles of moral science. Indeed, what is extremely rare, he casts aspersions on the intelligence and probity of the authors of such opinions.[156]

156 *De malo,* q. 6, a. 1 c. init.: 'Ad huiusmodi autem positiones ponendas inducti sunt aliqui homines partim quidem propter proterviam, partim propter aliquas rationes sophisticas, quas solvere non potuerunt, ut dicitur in IV *Metaph.*' [Some persons were led to adopt positions of this kind, partly indeed through perversity, partly because of certain sophistical reasons which they were unable to solve, as is stated in the fourth book of the *Metaphysics*]. Among the sophistries on this subject appear to be the following.

God operates *suaviter* and *ad modum naturae;* therefore the *voluntas mota et non movens* is free. The premise is true but the supposition is Scotist doctrine, namely, that it is the nature of the act of will with respect to the end to be free.

The act is free because the will can place impediments (see *Summa contra Gentiles,* 3, c. 159). Because the will can place impediments, the placing of impediments is free, and the will is to blame if it does not receive grace. But this does not imply that when God by grace takes away the impediments without consulting the will, the will exercises another free act.

The act is free because the will can dissent. If the dissent is another act of will distinct from the *voluntas mota et non movens* then undoubtedly this possible act of dissent is free. But that does not show that the *voluntas mota et non movens* is free: to prove that Pharaoh is an Egyptian does not imply that Socrates is an Egyptian.

If, however, one means that will can dissent in and by the very act it elicits when *mota et non movens,* then one has a contradiction: for the will is both willing and not willing not merely at the same time and with respect to the same object but also by the same act.

If one means that the will can either be moved or not moved, that if it is moved, it consents, and if it is not moved, it dissents, then one is confusing the freedom of God with the freedom of the will.

If one means that the will can either produce the motion in question or not, then one is talking beside the point: there is no question of the will *qua mota et non movens* producing anything.

Finally, if one means that God can produce the necessary and the contingent at his good pleasure, the act and the mode of the act, then one appears merely to misunderstand St Thomas's theorem of divine transcendence. No doubt God can produce what he pleases. But the question is, What does it please God to produce when the will is *mota et [non] movens?* Is he executing an instance of his idea of contingence? Or is he executing an instance of his necessity? Above, three reasons were given in confirmation of the manifest implication of the text: according to St Thomas the *voluntas*

(f) Though the act of will described in the text is not a free act, St Thomas elsewhere speaks quite clearly of free internal acts consequent to the beginning of good will.

The principal example given by St Thomas of actual grace operative is the beginning of conversion: *praesertim cum voluntas incipit bonum velle, quae prius malum volebat.* Now in the *Pars tertia* the causal sequence subsequent to conversion is described as follows.

> Respondeo dicendum quod de paenitentia loqui possumus dupliciter. Uno modo, quantum ad habitum. Et sic immediate a Deo infunditur, sine nobis principaliter operantibus, non tamen sine nobis dispositive cooperantibus per aliquos actus.[157]
>
> Alio modo possumus loqui de paenitentia quantum ad actus quibus Deo operanti in paenitentia cooperamur. Quorum actuum *primum* principium est Dei operatio convertentis cor: secundum illud *Thren.* ult.: *Converte nos, Domine, ad te, et convertemur.*[158] – *Secundus* actus est motus fidei. – *Tertius* actus est motus timoris servilis, quo quis timore suppliciorum a peccatis retrahitur. – *Quartus* actus est motus spei, quo quis, sub spe veniae consequendae, assumit propositum emendandi. – *Quintus* actus est motus caritatis, quo alicui peccatum displicet secundum seipsum, et non iam propter supplicia. – *Sextus* actus est motus timoris filialis, quo, propter reverentiam Dei, aliquis emendam Deo voluntarius offert.[159]

---

mota et non movens is not a free act. On this point we are happy to be in agreement with Dominicus Bañez, who rightly advanced: *Nullus effectus cuius Deus solus sit causa, potest esse contingens* [No effect of which God alone is the cause can be contingent] (*Scholastica commentaria in primam partem Summae theologicae S. Thomae Aquinatis*, q. 19, a. 8 (Roma, 1584, p. 370 E [Madrid: Editorial F.E.D.A., 1934, p. 431]).

157 That is, the free acts in justification are cooperation.

158 This text is cited: *Summa contra Gentiles*, 3, c. 149; *Summa theologiae*, 1, q. 62, a. 2, ad 3m; *Quaestiones quodlibetales*, 1, a. 7 [q. 4, a. 2]; *Summa theologiae*, 1-2, q. 109, a. 6, ad 1m. That is, along the whole line of the development of the idea of conversion and actual operative grace.

159 [I reply that we can talk about repentance in two ways. In one way, as regards the habit, and in this way (repentance) is infused in us immediately by God without our operating as the principal agent, but not without our cooperating dispositively by certain acts. And in another way we can talk of repentance as regards the acts by which in repentance we cooperate with God in his operation. The first principle of these acts is the operation of God converting the heart, according to that text of Lamentations, 'Restore us to yourself, O Lord, that we may be restored.' – The second act is the move-

Here the subsequent acts are caused by the *primum principium*, for '... etiam ipse motus timoris procedit ex actu Dei convertentis cor ... Et ideo per hoc quod paenitentia a timore procedit, non excluditur quin procedat ex actu Dei convertentis cor.'[160]

Further, the other five acts subsequent to the conversion of the heart are internal acts: this is evident, and it is explicitly stated with respect to the act of fear.[161]

Thus, in the above passage on repentance, there is an obvious parallel between actual grace as operative and cooperative and, on the other hand, habitual grace as operative and cooperative.

Habitual grace is operative and cooperative: *paenitentia ... quantum ad habitum ... immediate a Deo infunditur, sine nobis principaliter operantibus,*[162] *non tamen sine nobis dispositive cooperantibus per aliquos actus.*[163]

Actual grace is operative and cooperative: *Alio modo possumus loqui de paenitentia quantum ad actus quibus Deo operanti in paenitentia cooperamur.*[164]

In the latter case a distinction is drawn between a *primum principium* and five other acts that are consequent to the *primum principium.*

Further, this first principle is a divine operation: *primum principium est Dei operatio convertentis cor.* Observe that this divine operation has no presuppositions: it does not presuppose an object, as does the act of faith; nor a motive, as the fear of punishment, the hope of pardon, the hatred of sin, or the resolution of amendment. It is a first principle: *hoc quod homo moveatur a Deo, non praeexigit aliquam aliam motionem: cum Deus sit primum movens.*[165]

ment of faith. – The third act is the movement of servile fear, by which one is withdrawn from sins by the fear of punishments. – The fourth act is the movement of hope, by which one in hope of gaining pardon adds the purpose of amending. – The fifth act is the movement of charity by which sin is displeasing to someone in itself and not now because of punishments. – The sixth act is the movement of filial fear, by which because of reverence for God one voluntarily offers amends to God] *Summa theologiae,* 3, q. 85, a. 5.

160 [even the movement itself of fear proceeds from the act of God converting the heart ... And therefore the fact that repentance proceeds from fear does not preclude its proceeding from the act of God converting the heart] Ibid. ad 3m.

161 Ibid. ob. 3.

162 See the texts cited above, §3.1.

163 [repentance ... so far as the habit is concerned ... is infused in us immediately by God without our operating as the principal agent, but not without our cooperating dispositively by certain acts] *Summa theologiae,* 3, q. 85, a. 5 c.

164 [In another way we can talk of repentance as regards the acts by which in repentance we cooperate with God in his operation] Ibid.

165 [the fact that man is moved by God has no other motion as a prerequisite since God is the first mover] *Summa theologiae,* 1-2, q. 109, a. 6, ad 3m.

Further, it is an act which man himself cannot cause: *liberum arbitrium ad Deum converti non potest nisi Deo ipsum ad se convertente.*[166] Clearly, then, with respect to this act, the will is *mota et non movens.* No less clearly is it an operative grace: *praesertim cum voluntas incipit bonum velle, quae prius malum volebat.*

But once the will has begun to will the good, then the intellectual premotions enable it to move itself to a number of consequent acts. The thought of religion is met with an act of faith; the truths of faith call forth fear of divine retribution; fear brings to mind divine mercy and the will hopes for pardon; quietened by such hope, the mind thinks of the objective malice of sin and the will hates it; finally, the mind turns to God whom sin offends, and the will proposes amendment.

It is with respect to these acts that man prepares his soul and does what in him lies by his own free will: *conversio hominis ad Deum fit quidem per liberum arbitrium,*[167] else there would be no meaning in the precept of repentance.

But in the production of these acts man is an instrumental cause: *cum dicitur homo facere quod in se est, dicitur hoc esse in potestate hominis secundum quod est motus a Deo.*[168] For *etiam interior voluntas movetur ab aliquo superiori principio, quod est Deus; et secundum hoc Apostolus dicit, quod* non est volentis, *scilicet velle,* neque currentis, *currere, sicut primi principii,* sed Dei miserentis.[169]

To return to the parallel between habitual and actual grace, in the former case the infusion of grace is the *motio moventis,* free acts of faith and contrition are the *motus mobilis;* the *motus moventis* as such is operative grace; the *motus mobilis* is the operation of the infused form, and so cooperative grace. But in actual grace, in the case of conversion, the *motio moventis* or *primum principium* is the divine operation that changes the heart of man, not by infusing a habit but by a simple motion; on the other hand, the *motus mobilis* are the consequent acts of faith, fear, hope, sorrow, and repentance.[170]

---

166 [free will cannot be converted to God except by God converting it to himself] Ibid. ad 1m.
167 [man's conversion to God is indeed made by free will.] Ibid.
168 [when man is said to do what is in his power, it is meant that this is in man's power insofar as he is moved by God] Ibid. ad 2m.
169 [also the internal will is moved by some higher principle which is God; and accordingly, the Apostle says that 'it does not depend on the one willing,' that is, to will, 'nor on the one running,' that is, to run, as on the first principle, 'but on God who has mercy'] *De malo,* q. 6, a. 1, ad 1m.
170 It may be objected that there is not a parallel but an identity: in both cases St Thomas is speaking of the infusion of habitual grace in *Summa theologiae,*

To such a parallel St Thomas had already adverted in the *De veritate*, when he wrote:

> Immutat autem [Deus] voluntatem dupliciter. Uno modo movendo tantum ... Alio vero modo imprimendo aliquam formam.[171]

To conclude: the parallel passages, *Summa theologiae*, 3, q. 85, a. 5, and 1-2, q. 109, a. 6, confirm the interpretation already given. The *voluntas mota et non movens* is the reception of divine action in the creature antecedent to any operation on the creature's part. So far from being a free act, it lies entirely outside the creature's power. But though not a free act in itself, it is the first principle of free acts, even internal free acts such as faith, fear, hope, sorrow, and repentance.

(g) It is now possible to meet an objection raised above: Why does St Thomas make no mention of the election, consent, will of the means, when he treats actual grace as operative and cooperative?

In the first place, his theory on actual grace as operative and cooperative was a more recent development than his theory of the free acts in justification. The same degree of explicitness is not to be expected in both cases.

In the second place, the reason why he treats actual grace as operative and cooperative is to show that his systematic thought covers all the data to be found in St Augustine. This appears from the Sed contra and the conclusion of the treatment of actual grace in the corpus of the article. The former cites: *ipse ut velimus operatur incipiens, qui volentibus cooperatur perficiens.*[172] The latter continues the citation: *Ut autem velimus operatur: cum*

3, q. 85, a. 5, but first he speaks explicitly with respect to the habit, second with respect to the acts when the habit is infused.

Such an interpretation is evidently forced. St Thomas speaks generally *quantum ad actus* and does not, in the *Pars tertia*, consider justification the *prima gratia*. Further, in the instant of justification there is no servile fear: *caritas foras expellit timorem* [1 John 4.18: *mittit timorem*; but Eccl. 1.27, quoted by Trent, *DB* 798 (*DS* 1526): 'Timor Domini expellit peccatum']. But the third act, fear of punishment, is explicitly stated to be servile fear. It is true that the fifth act is said to be a *motus caritatis* but this is qualified as *quo alicui peccatum displicet secundum seipsum* and so equivalent to the *initialis dilectio* of the Council of Trent (*DB* 798; *DS* 1526 [Trent has 'diligere incipiunt']).

171 [Now (God) changes the will in two ways. In one way, just by moving it ... in another way by imprinting some form] *De veritate*, q. 22, a. 8.

172 [the One who begins by operating so that we may will brings (the work) to completion by cooperating with those who will] *Summa theologiae*, 1-2, q. 111, a. 2, Sed contra.

autem volumus, ut perficiamus nobis cooperatur.[173] If one reflects [that] St Thomas's intention is not to give a full account of his system of thought, a thing he rarely if ever does, but to interpret St Augustine, his omission of the election is quite natural. St Augustine speaks of initial good will and effective good will: so also does St Thomas.

Before turning to the wider aspects of the point before us, it will be well to summarize what has been attained.

This amounts to a material correlation of the account of the *actus interior* with other passages in St Thomas's writings. Thus, we have shown that the *actus interior* might possibly mean the act of will with respect to the end (§4.4) and, as a matter of fact, is that act (§4.5 a–g). For it is an act of will (a), caused by God alone (b), with respect to the end (c); from this results a lack of symmetry in the response, but such a lack of symmetry cannot justify a contradiction of the text (d); accordingly, the act in question is not free (e) but simply, for example, the *conversio cordis* that is the beginning and the cause of repentance (f); finally, the lack of symmetry mentioned (d) is accounted for by the text of St Augustine which St. Thomas is interpreting.

There remains to be explained the phrase *secundum [hunc actum] dicitur gratia operans.*[174] This is considered from various viewpoints: insofar as it is motion to the good (j); insofar as it is a conversion from sin (k); insofar as it is the beginning of faith (m);[175] and in the general case of the inspiration of the Holy Spirit (n). There follows a general definition of operative grace (o).

(j) The mere fact that the will is *mota et non movens* is not, on intrinsic grounds, a grace.[176] Still, in the *Sed contra* one finds the following minor premise: *operationes Dei quibus movet nos ad bonum, ad gratiam pertinent.*[177] To the modern reader this may appear a surprising lack of precision, but such surprise will, perhaps, be largely eliminated by considering St Thomas's conception of the need of divine motion under all its aspects. It is necessary to begin with a distinction between nine different needs.

(1) There is the need of divine motion from the creature's improportion

---

173 [(God) operates that we may will; but when we will, he cooperates with us that we may perform] Ibid. c.
174 [in reference to (this act) grace is called operative] *Summa theologiae,* 1-2, q. 111, a. 2 [see freer translation above, note 133].
175 [For some reason Lonergan has no section 'l,' nor, above, sections 'h' and 'i.'
176 See above, pp. [314, 368].
177 [the operations of God by which he moves us to good pertain to grace] *Summa theologiae,* 1-2, q. 111, a. 2, Sed contra.

to produce *esse: nulla res creata potest in quemcumque actum prodire nisi virtute motionis divinae.*[178]

(2) There is the need of divine motion from the creature's natural improportion to the production of *esse supernaturale.*[179]

(3) There is the need of divine motion from the creature's natural improportion to constant good action: only God is naturally impeccable. This is the basis, it would seem, of the need of the *auxilium Dei moventis* both before and after the fall.[180]

(4) There is the need of divine motion from fallen nature's improportion to constant good action. *Natura integra* is an *agens perfectum* spontaneously doing what is right *ut in maiori parte.* But *natura lapsa* is an *agens imperfectum* for the most part doing what is wrong. This would seem to be the basis of the special need of the *auxilium Dei moventis* that arises *propter conditionem status humanae naturae.*[181]

(5) There is the need of divine motion arising from personal sin, whether the sin has generated a vicious habit or simply an evil orientation; whether the divine motion simply enables man to reflect and so react against his spontaneity[182] or effects a change of heart,[183] and in the latter case, whether the change is brought about by a motion or by the infusion of habits.

(6) There is the need of divine motion to orientate the creature to God *tamquam bono proprio.*[184] This differs from the need listed in second place as psychology differs from metaphysics.

(7) There is the need of divine motion to effect perseverance and advance in the life of the Spirit. Even in *natura integra* the supernatural life is not altogether connatural to man, for that is life living on the divine level.[185]

(8) There is the need of divine motion to effect perseverance and advance in the life of the Spirit in a member of fallen nature: for regeneration

178 [no created thing can proceed to any act whatever except through the power of a divine motion] *Summa theologiae,* 1-2, q. 109, a. 9 c.
179 The idea is common; for example, *Summa contra Gentiles,* 3, c. 47.
180 *Summa theologiae,* 1-2, q. 109, aa. 1–5; see *De veritate,* q. 27, a. 5, ad 3m; q. 24, a. 7.
181 *Summa theologiae,* 1-2, q. 109, a. 9; see a. 7, ad 3m; *De veritate,* q. 27, a. 5, ad 3m; *Summa contra Gentiles,* 3, cc. 88–92.
182 *De veritate,* q. 24, a. 12 c. ad fin.
183 *De veritate,* q. 22, a. 8; see *De malo,* q. 16, a. 5 c. med.
184 *Summa theologiae,* 1-2, q. 109, a. 6 ['sicut bono proprio']; see ibid. 1, q. 62, a. 2; *Summa contra Gentiles,* 3, c. 149.
185 See the distinction between the angels' ability to sin in the natural and supernatural order: *De malo,* q. 16. aa. 2, 4.

does not alter the disordered conditions of human life, so that the spiritual life of the justified is like the operation of an apprentice in constant need of direction and help from his master.[186]

(9) There is the same need, with at least an added nuance of gratuitousness, in the case of the converted sinner: but, in addition, the psychological effects of personal sin remain to some extent after justification; the spiritual life of a penitent is not the same as that of one who has remained innocent.

If now we turn to the Sed contra, it will be found, I think, quite adequate in its context.

> Sed contra est quod Augustinus dicit, in libro de Grat. et Lib. Arb. [cap. 17]: *Cooperando Deus in nobis perficit quod operando incipit: quia ipse ut velimus operatur incipiens, qui volentibus cooperatur perficiens.* Sed operationes Dei quibus movet nos ad bonum, ad gratiam pertinent. Ergo convenienter gratia dividitur per operantem et cooperantem.[187]

Complementing this statement in the response are

> ... divinum auxilium quo nos movet ad bene volendum et agendum,

and

> ... [gratuita Dei motio] qua movet nos ad bonum meritorium.[188]

The last of these certainly refers to the supernatural order; it can include justification, for a motion includes not merely its *terminus* but also the whole antecedent process. The second last, in which the word *bene* may have the technical sense of the *actus virtutis*, perhaps excludes so broad an interpre-

---

186 *Summa theologiae*, 1-2, q. 68, a. 2.
187 [But against that there is Augustine's statement in his book *On Grace and Free Will* (chapter 17) that in cooperating God brings to completion in us what in operating he begins; because the One who begins by operating so that we may will brings (the work) to completion by cooperating with those who will. But the operations of God by which he moves us to good pertain to grace; therefore grace is suitably divided by operative and cooperative] *Summa theologiae* 1-2, q. 111, a. 2, Sed contra.
188 [the divine help by which (God) moves us to willing and acting rightly ... (the gratuitous movement of God) by which he moves us to a meritorious good] Ibid. c.

tation; more probably it simply refers to the *auxilium Dei moventis* in the third and fourth senses of the need of divine motion; yet it certainly can be maintained that even such an aid is a grace. Finally, the Sed contra itself refers to some special divine operation: that appears not only from the Augustinian context but also from the use of the word *nos*, which refers to fallen nature.

(k) The example of operative grace given by St Thomas, *praesertim cum voluntas incipit bonum velle, quae prius malum volebat*,[189] quite clearly corresponds to St Augustine's transformation of the heart of stone into a heart of flesh.

As has already been shown, this is no incidental and isolated instance of Augustinian influence. The heart of stone is studied in detail in *De veritate*, q. 24, a. 12.[190] The theory of divine operation in the will is worked out in *De veritate*, q. 22, a. 8, in *Contra Gentiles*, 3, cc. 88–92, in *Summa theologiae*, 1, q. 105, a. 4, and in *Summa theologiae*, 1-2, q. 9, a. 6. In the last of these there appears a synthesis of several cognate ideas that hitherto had had no precise correlation, namely, God causing the *appetitus naturalis*, God moving to the good in general, God operating in the will, God changing the will, God inclining the will, God premoving the will, God directing the will, God giving grace to the will. All are reduced to two categories: either God moves to the good in general, or he moves to some determinate end; the outstanding example of the latter motion is grace.[191]

---

189 [especially when the will, which before was willing evil, begins to will the good] Ibid.

190 See above, chapter II-4, §5.2.2. On Augustinian influence, ibid. §5.2.3. An extremely interesting remark occurs in *Summa theologiae*, 1-2, q. 109, a. 7, ad 3m: *Natura integra* can repair itself after sin with respect to its connatural good but *natura lapsa* cannot. *Natura integra* is the human *agens perfectum*, endowed with habits though not with sanctifying grace (q. 109, a. 3). The difference would seem to be that while a single sin renders *natura lapsa* impotent, it does not have this effect on *natura integra* since per se a single act does not destroy a habit. The position has many implications with regard to the general theory of grace and, in particular, with regard to asceticism.

191 *Summa theologiae*, 1-2, q. 9, a. 6, ad 3m: '... Deus movet voluntatem hominis, sicut universalis motor, ad universale obiectum voluntatis ... Et sine hac universali motione homo non potest aliquid velle ... interdum specialiter Deus movet aliquos ad aliquid determinate volendum ... sicut in his quos movet per gratiam.' [God moves the human will, as universal mover, to the universal object of the will ... And without this universal motion man cannot will anything ... God sometimes moves some people in a special way to will something determinately ... for example, in those whom he moves through grace]. A different instance would be the motion of Pharaoh; see above, pp. [343–44].

Perhaps the closest parallel to the present remark on the beginning of good will occurs in the account of psychological continuity.

> ... mutabilitas seu diversitas liberi arbitrii non est de ratione eius, sed accidit ei inquantum est in natura mutabili. Mutatur enim in nobis liberum arbitrium ex causa intrinseca, et ex causa extrinseca. Ex causa quidem intrinseca, vel propter rationem, puta cum quis aliquid prius nesciebat quod postea cognoscit; vel propter appetitum qui quandoque sic est dispositus per passionem vel habitum, ut tendat in aliquid sicut in sibi conveniens, quod cessante passione vel habitu sibi conveniens non est. Ex causa vero extrinseca, puta cum Deus immutat voluntatem hominis per gratiam de malo in bonum, secundum illud *Prov.* XXI, 1: *Cor regum in manu Dei, et quocumque voluerit vertet illud.*[192]

The implication of the passage is twofold: first, a change of will requires a proportionate cause; second, underlying this law of continuity, there is the assumption that the will admits dispositions, qualities, habits, that orientate it in a given way, that specialize it and make it selective of objects of a given type. In other words, we have simply the Aristotelian theory of the habit in all its presuppositions and, consequently, the Aristotlelian law: *qualis est unusquisque, talis finis videtur ei.*[193]

From this it follows that the operative grace as such is some modification or development of existing habits and dispositions. This change results in the will receiving a new orientation, acquiring a fresh selectivity, attaining a new strength and efficacy. Combine this with the motion to the good in general, and there arises the *conversio cordis*, the *voluntas mota et non movens*, and, indeed, *ad aliquid determinate volendum.*

192 [changeableness or diversity of free will does not pertain to its nature, but is there accidentally inasmuch as it is in a changeable nature. For free will is changed in us both from an intrinsic cause and from an extrinsic cause. From an intrinsic cause, either on account of reason, as when a person did not know earlier something which he knows afterwards; or on account of desire, which is sometimes disposed in such a way by passion or by habit that it tends to something as to a thing suitable to it, which with the cessation of passion or habit is not suitable to it. And from an extrinsic cause, as when God changes a human will from evil to good through grace, according to that text of Proverbs 21.1: *The heart of kings is in the hand of God, and he will turn it wherever he will*] *De malo,* q. 16, a. 5.

193 Note that in Aristotle this remark is an objection against the freedom of the will. The solution amounts to affirming that human freedom is limited, that it is not absolutely new freedom recreated at each instant of material time.

(m) The foregoing interpretation of the idea of operative grace may be confirmed by considering St Thomas's account of *Nemo potest venire ad me, nisi Pater, qui misit me, traxerit eum.* The text occurs in the Sed contra of *Summa theologiae*, 1-2, q. 109, a. 6, on preparation for grace; it is treated at length in the commentary on St John.

The passage begins with an objection: One goes to Christ by believing; but one believes because one wills to do so. But drawing, *tractio*, involves violence. Therefore those who go are coerced.

The answer is that not all 'drawing' involves coercion.

First, man may be drawn through his intellect, whether by an internal revelation, as was St Peter,[194] or by the objective evidence of Christ's miracles.[195]

Again, a man may be drawn by the attraction exercised by the object on the will.[196] Thus, a man may be drawn to Christ by the majesty of the Father revealed in him: in such a way Arius was not drawn, who denied Christ to be [of] the substance of the Father; nor was Photinus so drawn, who affirmed Christ to be a mere man. But besides the majesty of the Father there is also the beauty of the Son.

> ... trahuntur etiam a Filio, admirabili delectatione et amore veritatis, quae est ipse Filius Dei. Si enim ... trahit sua quemque voluptas, quanto fortius debet homo trahi ad Christum, si delectatur veritate, beatitudine, iustitia, sempiterna vita, quod totum est Christus? Ab isto ergo si trahendi sumus, trahamur per dilectionem veritatis, secundum illud Ps. xxxvi, 4: *Delectare in Domino et dabit tibi petitiones cordis tui.* Hinc sponsa dicebat, Cant. I, 3: *Trahe me post te; curremus in odorem unguentorum tuorum.*[197]

194 'Beatus es, Simon Bar Iona, quia caro et sanguis non revelavit tibi ...' [(Matthew 16.17): 'Blessed are you, Simon son of Jonah! For flesh and blood has not revealed this to you ...'].
195 'Opera quae dedit mihi Pater, ipsa testimonium perhibent de me' [(John 5.36): 'The works that the Father has given me ... testify on my behalf'].
196 'Blanditiis labiorum suorum protraxit eum' [(Proverbs 7.21) 'With much seductive speech she persuades him'].
197 [they are drawn also by the Son, by the admirable delight and love of the truth which is the very Son of God. For if ... everyone's pleasure draws him, how much more strongly should a man be drawn to Christ, if he is delighted by the truth, by beatitude, by eternal life, all of which Christ is. Therefore if we are drawn by him, we are drawn by love of the truth, according to that text of Psalm 36.4: 'Take delight in the Lord, and he will give you the desires of your heart.' Therefore the spouse said, Song of Solomon 1.3: 'Draw me after you, let us make haste to the odor of your ointments'] *Super Ioannem*, c. 6, lect. 5 [§935].

But beyond the appeal to the intellect and the appeal to the will's love, there is a third way in which the Father draws to the Son.

> Sed quia non solum revelatio exterior, vel obiectum, virtutem attrahendi habet, sed etiam interior instinctus impellens et movens ad credendum, ideo trahit multos Pater ad Filium per instinctum divinae operationis moventis interius cor hominis ad credendum; Phil. II, 13: *Deus est qui operatur in vobis et velle et perficere*; Oseae II, 4: *In funiculis Adam traham eos in vinculis caritatis*; Prov. XXI, 1: *Cor regis in manu Domini: quocumque voluerit inclinabit illud.*[198]

The first and last of these texts constantly recur in St Thomas's treatment of divine control over the will, divine operation in the will. The cumulative evidence is that the *instinctus interior* is not merely a metaphysical transition from potency to act, nor simply an entitative difference between natural and supernatural, but, more prominent than either of these, a psychological modification, a new orientation, a more perfect selectivity and efficacy, the will interested in the external evidence and commensurate with, resonant to, the majesty of the Father and the beauty of the Son, who is truth.

(n) There remains the question, Why does St Thomas say *praesertim*, when he illustrates operative grace by the *conversio cordis*? We do not mean, Why was this example chosen? For it is precisely conversion that St Augustine has in mind when he writes *ipse ut velimus operatur incipiens*. The point is, Why is conversion merely an example for St Thomas, when for St Augustine it is the unique instance of *ut velimus operatur incipiens*?

To this question, the answer has perhaps already been given. While for St Augustine both the distinctions, operative and cooperative, prevenient and subsequent, refer to the time series, to different stages in the spiritual life, St Thomas gives only prevenient and subsequent this meaning; operative and cooperative he transfers to the causal series.

(n^bis)[199] On metaphysical grounds, for God alone is the proportionate

198 [But because not only external revelation, or the object, has the power of attracting, but also the internal impulse impelling and moving to believing, therefore the Father draws many to the Son through the impulse of a divine operation moving the human heart internally to believing; Philippians 2.13: 'for it is God who is at work in you, enabling you both to will and to work'; Hosea 11.4: 'In the cords of Adam I will draw them, in the bonds of love'; Proverbs 21.1: 'The king's heart is a stream of water in the hand of the Lord; he will turn it wherever he will] Ibid. On universal salvific will, see the context.

199 [Lonergan designated two sections 'n.' The second is changed here to 'n^bis.']

cause of being; on cosmic grounds, for God is the first mover of the universe and the first agent; as well, on dogmatic grounds, for Romans 9.16 cannot be inverted: [on all these grounds] it is necessary to say that human action is instrumental. Such a proposition is universal: God is always first operative and then cooperative. On the other hand, corresponding to this truth, is the structure of the human will and the limitation of human freedom, for the will is moved naturally to the end, to be free only in the consequent and implied self-motion to the means; the will is free in each single act but makes no free act with respect to the whole series of its choices; finally, the law of psychological continuity, as it enables the will to advance in perfection, so also it constitutes the possibility of a self-imprisonment from which only grace brings liberation.

Thus, grace is operative not merely in the first step along the purgative way but throughout the spiritual life. As the conversion of the purgative way presupposes the grace of conversion, so the perfection of the illuminative way presupposes the fulness of conversion, while the intimacy of mystical union is the creature, purified and perfected, yet still as much in need of divine direction and aid as any novice or apprentice. Each advance must be caused by God, for God is the principal cause of all perfection and all advancement. Nor does the attainment of the past ever make further aid in the future superfluous; it only makes it greater, for the goal is harmony with the Infinite. *Quicumque spiritu Dei aguntur, hi sunt filii Dei.*

Since in his commentary on that text St Thomas reveals with particular clarity divine domination over the will, we cite it in confirmation of the points that here have been little [more] than repeated.

> Sed quia ille qui ducitur, ex seipso non operatur, homo autem spiritualis non tantum instruitur a Spiritu Sancto quid agere debeat, sed etiam cor eius a Spiritu Sancto movetur, ideo plus intelligendum est in hoc quod dicitur *quicumque spiritu Dei aguntur.*
>
> Illa enim agi dicuntur, quae quodam superiori instinctu moventur.[200] Unde de brutis dicimus quod non agunt sed aguntur, quia a natura moventur et non ex proprio motu ad suas actiones agendas. Similiter autem homo spiritualis non quasi ex motu propriae voluntatis principaliter sed ex instinctu Spiritus Sancti inclinatur ad

200 See the three classes of men of Eudemus (above, chapter II-4, §6.5): 'those that follow a principle higher than reason; those that follow reason; and the merely lucky.'

aliquid agendum, secundum illud Is. LIX, 19: *Cum venerit quasi fluvius violentus quem spiritus Dei cogit*; et Lc. IV, 1, quod Christus agebatur a Spiritu in deserto.[201]

Were it not for the terms *principaliter, instinctu ... inclinatur*, one might be inclined to surmise that this passage dealt with something outside St. Thomas's ordinary theory of instrumentality. But he immediately continues:

Non tamen per hoc excluditur quin viri spirituales per voluntatem et liberum arbitrium operentur, quia ipsum motum voluntatis et liberi arbitrii Spiritus Sanctus in eis causat, secundum illud Phil. II, 3: *Deus est qui operatur in nobis velle et perficere.*[202]

As is plain, the passage is parallel with all the others on divine control [of] the will;[203] it sets no more a problem for freedom than the assertion of a free act in the instant of justification; it leaves true the principle *Praesupposito iam fine ... gratia cooperatur*, but it reveals the significance of control over the will of the end.

(o) [There follows a general definition of operative grace (see above, p. 425).]

201 [But because one who is led does not operate from himself, but a spiritual person is not only instructed by the Holy Spirit on what he ought to do, but also his heart is moved by the Holy Spirit, therefore more is to be understood in those words, 'All who are led by the Spirit of God.'
  For those things are said to be led which are moved by some higher impulse. And so we say of brute animals that they do not act but are acted upon, because they are moved by nature and not from their own movement to perform their actions. And likewise a spiritual person is inclined to doing something, not as if from a movement of his own will principally, but by an impulse of the Holy Spirit, according to that text of Isaiah 59.19: 'for he will come like a pent-up stream that the wind of the Lord drives on;' and Luke 4.1 (says) that Christ was led by the Spirit in the wilderness] *In Rom.*, c. 8, lect. 3 [§635].
202 [But this does not exclude (the possibility) that spiritual persons may operate voluntarily and through free will, because the Holy Spirit causes that voluntary movement itself of free will in them, according to that text of Philippians 2.3: 'it is God who is at work in you, enabling you both to will and to work]. Ibid. See *Summa theologiae*, 1-2, q. 68, a. 2.
203 See *In Rom.*, c. 9, lect. 3 (above, §4.2). Observe, however, that St Thomas's thought very gradually comes to a focus on the action of grace in the will. Even *Summa theologiae*, 1-2, q. 9, a. 6, ad 3m, is not too explicit; 1-2, q. 111, a. 2, ad 3m, and 3, q. 85, a. 5, have to be taken into account to obtain a balanced interpretation.

Est autem in nobis duplex actus. Primus quidem interior voluntatis. Et quantum ad istum actum, voluntas se habet ut mota, Deus autem ut movens: et praesertim cum voluntas incipit bonum velle, quae prius malum volebat. Et ideo secundum quod Deus movet humanam mentem ad hunc actum, dicitur gratia operans.[204]

As has been shown, the act in question is an act of the will with respect to an end, but produced solely by God and passively elicited in the will. It is illustrated by the first instant of conversion, but that is not a unique instance, for God is the principal cause of all human perfection and development and so is constantly operating. It would seem that the act itself is not the operative grace. More accurately, grace is said to be operative with respect to this act. The operative grace as such would be had by distinguishing two elements in the act: first, a universal motion to the good in general; second, some ulterior determination of this motion. The former may be found in all wills at any time. The latter under given circumstances is a grace, namely, when it is a factor in the *productio creaturae rationalis in vitam aeternam.*

4.6 Cooperative Grace and the External Act

Alius autem actus est exterior; qui cum a voluntate imperetur, ut supra habitum est [q. 17, a. 9], consequens est ut ad hunc actum operatio attribuatur voluntati. Et quia etiam ad hunc actum Deus nos adiuvat, et interius confirmando voluntatem ut ad actum perveniat, et exterius facultatem operandi praebendo; respectu huius actus dicitur gratia cooperans. Unde post praemissa verba subdit Augustinus: *Ut autem velimus operatur: cum autem volumus, ut perficiamus nobis cooperatur.*[205]

204 [But there is a twofold act in us. The first is an internal act of the will; and in regard to that act the will has the role of being moved, and God the role of mover; and this is the case especially when the will, which before was willing evil, begins to will the good. And therefore, in that God moves the human mind to this act, grace is called operative] *Summa theologiae*, 1-2, q. 111, a. 2.

205 [But the other act is external, and since this is commanded by the will, as was determined above (q. 17, a. 9), the consequence is that for this act the operation is attributed to the will. And because for this act too God helps us, both strengthening the will internally that it may come to act, and providing externally the faculty of operating, (therefore) in regard to this act, grace is called cooperative. And therefore after the words quoted above (Sed contra) Augustine subjoins: *But that we will, (God) operates; but when we will, he cooperates with us that we may perform*] *Summa theologiae*, 1-2, q. 111, a. 2.

... gratia operans et cooperans est eadem gratia, sed distinguitur secundum diversos effectus.[206]

The passage calls for a few notes.

Strictly, the *imperium* is not an act of the will but of the intellect.[207] However, since in man the intellect is the principle that directs, the will the principle that effects, the *imperium* of the reason takes place *ex virtute voluntatis*.[208] Accordingly, the statement that the external act *a voluntate imperatur* is quite natural.

There is no reason for supposing that the term *actus exterior* has any but its ordinary meaning, the act of the human body.[209]

In this act as such, there is no difficulty: St Thomas cites St Augustine on the point.

Imperat animus ut moveatur manus, et tanta est facilitas, ut vix a servitio discernatur imperium.[210]

The whole difficulty lies in eliciting an effective *imperium*, in really making up one's mind.

... animus, quando perfecte imperat sibi ut velit, tunc iam vult: sed quod aliquando imperet et non velit, hoc contingit ex hoc quod non perfecte imperat. Imperfectum autem imperium contingit ex hoc, quod ratio ex diversis partibus movetur ad imperandum vel non imperandum: unde fluctuat inter duo, et non perfecte imperat.[211]

Thus, the psychological setting reveals the significance of *interius confirmando voluntatem*. When a man is caught between two fires, then a grace in the will decides the issue in favor of the spiritual appetite.

206 [operative and cooperative grace are the same grace, but (the grace) is distinguished according to (its) different effects] Ibid. ad 4m.
207 *Summa theologiae*, 1-2, q. 17, a. 1.
208 Ibid.
209 On the usage, see above, §4.4.
210 [The will commands the hand to be moved, and so great is the facility that command is hardly distinguished from servitude] *Summa theologiae*, 1-2, q. 17, a. 9, Sed contra.
211 [when the soul perfectly commands itself to will, then already it does will; but the fact that sometimes it commands and does not will is due to this, that it does not perfectly command. And this imperfect command is due to this, that reason is moved from different sides to command and not to command; and so (the soul) fluctuates between two things and does not command perfectly] Ibid. a. 5, ad 1m.

It is to be observed, however, that this divine impulse is a *gratia operans* inasmuch as it is received in the will; it becomes a *gratia cooperans* inasmuch as with the will it causes the external act. This is clearly stated in the response ad 4m. The corpus of the article can give rise to a different impression, for there one finds St Augustine and St Thomas expressing their somewhat different views simultaneously.[212]

The objection may be raised that the introduction of an *instinctus interior* in the will when man himself is hesitating is to intrude into human liberty. But the whole force of such an objection derives from the imagination. Were this an intrusion into human liberty, then the whole of St Thomas's position on divine control of the will is an intrusion into human liberty: the only difference is that normally one represents St Thomas's theory as God first moving the will to the end and then the will moving itself within this orientation, while in this case the motion to the end may be imagined as God deciding an otherwise doubtful issue.

With respect, then, to the general case – for there is no real difference, whether God decides the issue beforehand or at the last minute – the answer is

> ... de ratione voluntarii est quod principium eius sit intra: sed non oportet quod hoc principium intrinsecum sit primum principium non motum ab alio. Unde motus voluntarius etsi habeat principium proximum intrinsecum, tamen principium primum est ab extra.[213]

> ... si voluntas ita moveretur ab alio quod ex se nullatenus moveretur, opera voluntatis non imputarentur ad meritum vel demeritum.[214]

In a word, the apex of the will which causes our free acts is, itself, not a free act. But God causes it, causes its causation, causes all that it causes. Since what it causes are free acts, divine action upon it passes through the process

---

212 On the difference, see above, §4.3.

213 [it belongs to the nature of a voluntary act that its principle be internal, but it is not necessary that this intrinsic principle be a first principle not moved by another. And hence, although a voluntary movement has its intrinsic proximate principle, still the first principle is from outside] *Summa theologiae*, 1-2, q. 9, a. 4, ad 1m; see ad 2m, ad 3m; q. 9, a. 6, ad 3m [Lonergan's 'q. 10, a. 1, ad 3m' seems erroneous].

214 [if the will were moved by another in such a way that it was not in any degree moved by itself, the works of the will would not be imputed for merit or demerit] *Summa theologiae*, 1, q. 105, a. 4, ad 3m; see q. 83, a. 1, ad 3m; *De malo* q. 6, a. 1, ad 4m, ad 17m.

of self-motion to the effect. Just as divine causation of free will does not prevent the will from being free, so also divine causation of free acts does not prevent the acts from being free. But though divine causation of free acts does not interfere with their freedom, it does mean that God governs the will above the will's self-government.

> ... creatura rationalis gubernat seipsam per intellectum et volunta-
> tem, quorum utrumque indiget regi et perfici ab intellectu et volun-
> tate Dei. Et ideo supra gubernationem qua creatura rationalis
> gubernat seipsam tamquam domina sui actus, indiget gubernari a
> Deo.[215]

Further, one is not to suppose that the greater determinateness given the will by grace is some narrowing or contraction of the universal category of the good, as though the general motion of the will were to the good in all possible forms, but the special motion of grace were to some particular species of the good. Such an opinion overlooks the fact that grace is a motion to God and God is not some particular species of the good but, transcending all differences and possibility of differentiation, he is good-ness itself. What grace does is break down the narrowing of past sin and orientate the will to what is a goodness beyond the universal good, to absolute goodness in its transcendence. Thus, grace is in every sense a liberation of the will, liberating it from the self-imprisonment of sin, and giving it the liberty of the sons of God, that is, a liberty that follows from an orientation fixed not by the abstract category of goodness but by a personal relation to the *ipsum esse separatum*.[216]

Hence after stating that grace moves the will *ad aliquid determinate vol-endum*,[217] St Thomas in the very next article writes:

> Cum igitur voluntas sit quaedam vis immaterialis, sicut et intellectus,
> respondet sibi naturaliter aliquod unum commune, scilicet bonum:
> sicut etiam intellectui aliquod unum commune, scilicet verum, vel

---

215 [a rational creature governs itself by intellect and will, both of which need to be ruled and completed by the intellect and will of God. And therefore besides the governing by which a rational creature governs itself as having dominion over its act, it needs to be governed by God] *Summa theologiae*, 1, q. 103, a. 5, ad 3m. See *Summa contra Gentiles*, 3, cc. 111–15.

216 See *Summa theologiae*, 1-2, q. 109, a. 6.

217 [to will something determinately] Ibid. q. 9, a. 6, ad 3m.

ens, vel quod quid est. Sub bono autem communi multa particularia
bona continentur, ad quorum nullum voluntas determinatur.[218]

The coherence of the two statements lies in the fact that God is not some
instance of the good. So much for *interius confirmando voluntatem*. There
remains the statement *exterius facultatem operandi praebendo*.

This idea is to be found in the account of cooperative grace in the *De
veritate*.[219] It recurs in connection with a text from Jeremias both in the *Pars
prima* and the *De malo*. Thus, to the objection

> ... homo non est dominus suorum actuum: quia ut dicitur Ierem. x,
> *Non est in homine via eius, nec viri est ut dirigat gressus suos*[220]

the answer reads

> ... dicitur *non esse in homine via eius*, quantum ad executiones
> electionum, in quibus homo impediri potest, velit nolit. Electiones
> autem ipsae sunt in nobis: supposito tamen divino auxilio.[221]

The objection and solution are substantially identical in the *De malo*.[222]

It would seem that in recalling this in the article we are commenting,
St Thomas's thought slips from *gratia operans* to *Deus operans*.

5   The Movement of Thought

In the *Prima secundae* St Thomas again had occasion to treat explicitly the
distinction between operative and cooperative grace. Since writing the

218 [Therefore since the will is a certain immaterial power, as is intellect, some
one thing corresponds to it naturally, namely, the good; just as some one
thing corresponds also to intellect, namely, the true, or being, or what a
thing is. But many particular goods are contained under the common good,
and the will is not determined to any of these] Ibid. q. 10, a. 1, ad 3m.
219 *De veritate*, q. 27, a. 5, ad 1m.
220 [man is not in control of his own acts, because, as is stated in Jeremiah
10.23, '(I know, O Lord, that) the way of human beings is not in their control, that mortals as they walk cannot direct their steps'] *Summa theologiae*, 1,
q. 83, a. 1, ob. 4.
221 ['is not in control of his own acts' is said with regard to executing choices,
in which man can be impeded, whether he will it or not. But the choices
themselves are in our power, with the supposition, however, of divine help]
Ibid. ad 4m.
222 *De malo*, q. 6, a. 1, ad 1m.

article in the commentary on the *Sentences* he had combined the Augustinian theory of grace as a liberation of will with the later more metaphysical analyis in terms of the supernatural. He had also worked into synthesis the ideas of divine prevention, creaturely instrumentality, and the natural motion of the will to the end and divine control of human freedom. Moved more by the meaning of the terms than by historical considerations he resolved to restrict the terms 'prevenient' and 'subsequent' to the time series of gratuitous effects of divine will, and refer the distinction of operative and cooperative to the causal series.

Selecting as his guiding idea St Augustine's *ipse ut velimus operatur incipiens, qui volentibus cooperatur perficiens*, he proceeded to bring together the elements of his theory of grace that were related to that statement.

Grace, then, is of two kinds: a habitual gift and a *divinum auxilium*. The former is needed to cure us of the effects of sin and raise us to the level of eternal life. The latter is necessary, too, for God alone is naturally proportionate to unfailing operation. But in the case of both of these graces it is true to say that God operates and we cooperate. For the operation referred to is the production of an effect: when, then, God alone produces an effect, grace is operative; when not only God but we as well produce an effect, grace is cooperative.

Thus, man has both internal and external acts. But with respect to the production of the former, the human will is moved but it does not itself operate: this is particularly evident when a bad will is changed into a good will. On the other hand, with regard to external acts, man's will is a cause; but God also acts, internally confirming the will and externally favoring us with opportunities. Accordingly, it is quite reasonable to say that the *divinum auxilium* is now operative and cooperative.

Again, habitual grace, like any other form, has a double function: heat, for instance, constitutes the fire as hot but it also makes other things hot. Inasmuch, then, as habitual grace cures [us] of the effects of sin and justifies us before God, it is operative; but inasmuch as it inclines free will to act in a proper fashion it is cooperative.

Certain difficulties occur. It may be thought that grace is an accident and that an accident does not operate.[223] But one has only to recall that an accident has a formal effect: whiteness makes a wall white.

Again, St Augustine's *Qui creavit te sine te, non iustificabit te sine te* may be thought incompatible with the existence of any operative grace.

---

223 The objection was treated at length by St Albert. See above, chapter II-2, §4.

But clearly St Augustine means simply that our free act in justification is a condition and not a cause of that grace; indeed our free act is caused by the grace itself, and so the whole operation belongs to grace.[224]

Further one may cite St Paul's *non volentis neque currentis*, which shows that grace is the principal cause and man instrumental,[225] and argue that grace cannot be said to cooperate.

But to say that a cause cooperates does not mean that it is subordinate. Inasmuch as grace makes man will the good, it is operative; inasmuch as man's converted will itself acts, it follows that the grace which at first was operative now becomes cooperative.

A final objection may be drawn from the logic of the issue. A good division supposes a real difference. But the same thing can both operate and cooperate, as appears from the answer to the preceding. While this is true, it remains that the same thing does not produce the same effect when it operates as when it cooperates. But the division of grace given in the article is based not on the grace itself but on its effects.

---

224 See *Summa theologiae,* 1-2, q. 55, a. 4, ob. 6 and Sed contra.
225 See *Summa contra Gentiles,* 3, c. 149; *In Rom.,* c. 9, lect. 3 [§ 775]; *De malo,* q. 6, a. 1, ad 1m.

Conclusions

(1) Though no one disputes that anachronism[1] is a fallacy, the mere admission of the point is not an efficacious antidote to its spontaneous intrusion and disastrous effects.

To depend on the indefinable 'historical sense' to hold it in check is not a scientific procedure.

What is needed is an articulate analysis of the historical process: for such an analysis can alone pass into the common and easy heritage of distinctions and arguments to establish, not as a mere matter of opinion but as a scientific conclusion, a true historical perspective.

Such a need is peculiarly manifest in a study of St Thomas's thought on *gratia operans*. For such a study is only too apt to be biased by the controversies that have raged over the question of grace and free will, and the development of St Thomas's position cannot be properly appreciated unless considered in relation to its antecedents.

(2) Dogma is one thing and speculation on dogmatic truth is quite another. Whether or not there is development of dogma, it is manifest that speculation develops. Such advance takes place between an initial and final dialectical position: first it assembles the dogmatic data relevant to a given

---

1 The outstanding example of such anachronism is Jansenism. It insisted that the categories of contemporary thought could not be valid unless found in the writings of St Augustine. From this preposterous premise, which denies all development, it was led to reject the ideas of the supernatural and of sufficient grace, while, quite arbitrarily, it transmogrified St Augustine's *adiutorium quo* into a contemporary *gratia efficax*.

point; by philosophically defining the natural element in problems and by introducing analogies for the conception of the supernatural, it elaborates theorems that explanatorily organize and correlate the body of dogmatic truths.

(3) The compound theorem that grace is both *elevans* and *sanans*, needed both because eternal life is supernatural and because man is a fallen and sinful creature, developed slowly.

The specific element appears in St Augustine's *De correptione et gratia*. It reached its full formulation in Peter Lombard's description of the states of human liberty, a formulation which precluded the development of a philo- sophic idea of liberty without being equal to the task of accounting for the idea of merit. The solution to these problems came with Philip the Chancel- lor's presentation of the idea of the supernatural, and in the *Prima secundae* of St Thomas one finds the synthesis of the functions of grace. It is to be observed that St Thomas makes this synthesis explicitly only with respect to habitual grace: he does not discuss the question, Is actual grace by itself a *gratia elevans?* It remains that his position has an obvious exigence for a discussion of this issue.

Underlying the purely theoretical movement, which regards the func- tions of grace, is the subsidiary movement with respect to the concept of grace itself. At first grace was conceived as a gratuitous gift of God; with the advent of the theorem of the supernatural, there also crystallized manifold tendencies to make the divine virtues of faith, hope, and charity habits in the Aristotelian sense. There remained the tasks of distinguishing actual grace from general providence, distinguishing internal and external actual graces, and finally discussing the functions of actual grace.

Complementary to these two movements is the development of thought on the nature of human liberty. Until the theorem of the supernatural was introduced, it was inevitable that the 'dialectical position' found its place in the very idea of liberty: such is clearly the case in St Anselm, St Bernard, and Peter Lombard. But with Philip the Chancellor speculation on the nature of liberty assumed a new vigor: according as writers were moved by philo- sophic interest or influenced by the earlier theory of the four states of human liberty, they tended to regard freedom as a potency or as a habit.

(4) The development of thought on *gratia operans* is a function of the variables enumerated above. The extremes of the movement are as follows.

In St Augustine the *donum Dei* is operative or prevenient that man may will the good, it is cooperative or subsequent lest man should will in vain.

In the *Prima secundae* of St Thomas the gratuitous effects of divine will are divided into habits and motions; both the habits and the motions may be operative or cooperative; further, the distinction between operative and cooperative is differentiated from that between prevenient and subsequent, for the latter refers to the time series of graces while the former refers to the causal series.

(5) The intermediate stages between these two extremes are, roughly, four.

In St Anselm and Peter Lombard, the former highly speculative and the latter notably positive, grace is a *donum Dei*, its function tends to be conceived as that of a *gratia sanans*, and the 'dialectical position' is in the idea of liberty. Grace is operative inasmuch as it causes the good will that brings one to eternal life; subsequently the same grace cooperates with good will to bring forth the fruits worthy of eternal life.

In the commentaries on the *Sentences* of St Albert and St Thomas, grace is a *donum habituale et supernaturale*. It is operative in two respects: first, it informs man, making him acceptable to God; second, it exerts the influence of a habit or virtue inclining the will to the good on the analogy of a natural spontaneity. Again, it is cooperative in two respects: it gives good acts the *forma meriti*, and it inclines the will in the performance of good acts. In St Thomas there is an attempt to correlate the function of the habit with the Augustinian distinction between good will and good performance.

In his *De veritate* St Thomas adverts to the inadequacy of the theorem of the supernatural to explain fully the need of grace. *Gratia gratum faciens* becomes any effect of gratuitous divine will: the direction and aid of divine providence is recognized as a *divinum auxilium quod ad gratiam cooperantem pertinet*. The division of grace into operative and cooperative is asymmetrical.

While the *Contra Gentiles* greatly develops the idea of providence and treats in detail the manifold ways in which God directs and aids the spirit of man, its most notable contribution is the speculative solution with respect to divine prevention of human liberty. Man cannot prevent God because man is an instrumental cause. In this connection is cited Romans 9.16, and it is asserted that though God is the principal cause of man's acts of choice, it remains that man is also the free cause of them. The idea recurs in the *Pars prima*, in the commentary on Romans, in the *De malo*, and in the third objection to *Prima secundae*, q. 111, a. 2.

Since man is always an instrumental cause, it follows that there is always a *motio moventis* that precedes causally the *motus mobilis*. This explains why St Thomas distinguishes between the time series of graces (reserving for them the names 'prevenient' and 'subsequent') and the causal series, with *gratia operans* predicated of the *voluntas mota et non movens, gratia cooperans* predicated of the *voluntas et mota et movens.* The same fact accounts for the anomalies of *Prima secundae*, q. 111, a. 2: St Thomas is attempting to equate his distinction in the causal series with St Augustine's temporal distinction between initial good will and the perfect charity of supremely difficult performance.

(6) Bricks are not made without straw. For a more adequate grasp of the idea of *gratia operans* in St Thomas, it is necessary to review the materials he worked into an analogy for the conception of the supernatural and the positions he modified to elaborate a satisfactory definition of the natural elements in his problem. Here it will be well to reverse the order of the inquiry, first considering the theory of liberty and then the theory of operation.

(7) St Thomas did not find a theory of *liberum arbitrium* already fashioned for him. St Bonaventure considered it a habit; St Albert considered it a potency distinct from intellect and will. Not only did he have to build from the very foundations, but the distorted speculative situation in which he began his work led to his building two structures instead of one. Thus in both the *De veritate* and the *Pars prima* he devotes separate questions to the will and to *liberum arbitrium,* but in twelve successive questions and sixty-three articles on the will in the *Prima secundae* there is not a title that includes the term *liberum arbitrium.*

Another notable point is that St Thomas did not work on the problem of liberty in isolation from the problem of its relations with grace. In the article in the *De veritate,* ten objections out of twenty proceed from the doctrine of grace; in that in the *Pars prima* there are four out of five; even in the article in the *De malo,* which was occasioned by the controversy over determinism, eight objections out of twenty-four are connected with grace.

Thus, accompanying the movement of thought from the freedom of the self-determining rational creature to the self-moving will which is determined (*quoad specificationem actus*) by no finite object, there is a complementary movement which works out the limitations of human liberty and corresponds to the idea St Bonaventure attempted to express by saying that *liberum arbitrium* is a habit.

The theory of the habit, even in the commentary on the *Sentences,* involves a distinction between the *agens perfectum* and *imperfectum*; it is complemented in the *De veritate* with a theory of psychological continuity even in simple orientations; and this development moves into the theory of grace when it is made to explain the impotence of the sinner, and again when it is correlated with the principle that God alone is naturally impeccable so that every creature, no matter what its perfection, needs for good action an *auxilium Dei moventis*.

A number of diverse influences – Avicenna's rule that the cause of the will controls the will; St Augustine's affirmation that God operates in the hearts of men and inclines their wills at his good pleasure; the idea of the *Eudemian Ethics* that, unless prudence itself is to be reduced to chance, there must be a higher cause of human counsel – are blended into a single theory when Aristotle's *appetibile apprehensum movet appetitum* is met with a distinction in the *De malo* [q.6, a. 1], and in the *Prima secundae* [q. 9, a. 4] it is argued that the will of the end *quoad exercitium actus* must, ultimately, be produced by the First Mover. The corollary that special internal premotions in the will are graces is almost immediately drawn, and later in the article on operative grace, in answer to the objection from Romans 9.16, one reads:

> Homo autem per gratiam operantem adiuvatur a Deo ut bonum velit. Et ideo, praesupposito iam fine, consequens est ut gratia nobis cooperetur.[2]

This incidental statement reveals explicitly the obvious synthesis of human instrumentality, divine operation in the will, and the Aristotelian theory that freedom lies in choosing but choosing presupposes the dynamic orientation from which free acts spring. As a man wields a whole sword though he grasps only the hilt, so God controls the whole will by grasping it beyond the limits of liberty. Complementary to this fundamental position – essentially opposed to the Scotist view which makes the will not a compound of nature and of freedom but something whose nature is freedom – is the theorem on perseverance: man has no act of choice with respect to the series of his choices, so that the series as a series must be caused by God.

It will be useful to correlate the foregoing with the general theory of the instrument. In an instrument there is the effect of the principal cause on the instrument, there is the effect produced by the instrument in virtue of the action of the principal cause, and, further, in that effect there is what is within the proportion of the instrument and what is beyond that proportion. Accordingly, in the will there is the will of the end produced by God,

2 [But man through operative grace is assisted by God to will the good. And therefore, with the end now presupposed, the consequence is that grace cooperates with us] *Summa theologiae*, 1-2, q. 111, a. 2, ad 3m.

there is the will of the means produced by the will of the end in virtue of divine action, and, further, in the will of the means there may be distinguished the free act as this single act, which is within the proportion of man, and the free act as part of a series tending to a given goal, and that is beyond the proportion of man.

This gives the immediate context of *gratia operans*: it is a special *effectus gratuitae Dei voluntatis*, a habit or a motion, that modifies the will of the end, the *voluntas mota et non movens*, and supplies the instrument by which God makes issue with the gravitation of that other instrument, fallen man, and directs its dynamism unto eternal life.

(8) It remains that *gratia operans* has its transcendental context of *Deus operans*, and no small part of the problem faced by St Thomas was to work out the distinction between the two.

Most important in this connection is the fact that while sixteenth-century thought begins with the idea of actual grace and attempts to find a satisfactory theory of divine foreknowledge and operation, St Thomas began with a satisfactory theory of divine foreknowledge and operation but had to develop the theory of actual grace.

Already in the commentary on the *Sentences* St Thomas's familiarity with Aristotelian thought on time and Platonist thought on eternity – it is equivalent to the presupposition of the Einsteinian theory of space-time – had enabled him to see that all suggestions of incompatibility between divine foreknowledge or will and created contingence were no more than anthropomorphic fallacy. Further developments occur in meeting the Aristotelian idea of contingence, in resolving the Aristotelian postulate of an eternal world, and in developing the idea of providence; but though they enrich, they do not radically modify, the position of the commentary on the *Sentences*.[3]

3 Throughout the work we have tended to treat these issues in footnotes. The subtlety of Aristotle's idea of contingence was too much for even the subtle Scotus, who dismissed it as arrant nonsense. St Thomas accepts Aristotle and then christens him by refining on his refinements. Aristotle held that the future could not be true; St Thomas that the future is not future to God. Aristotle maintained that the world must be eternal; St Thomas that divine activity is timeless but its products temporal. Aristotle held that celestial beings and events were necessary, terrestrial ones contingent; St Thomas that God produced both, making the necessary necessary and the contingent contingent. Aristotle denied providence in the terrestrial sphere; St Thomas affirmed God to be an *agens per intellectum* eternally planning and efficaciously producing a temporal and contingent world order.
    Engaged in problems on this high level, St Thomas looks upon the al-

However, this reduction of the problem of reconciling divine attributes with human liberty to the category of fallacies is equivalently a dialectical position. To assert that some things are contingent and others are necessary is no more than to admit the existence of the problem. To add that God knows infallibly, wills efficaciously, acts irresistibly, is to affirm what is self-evident in its truth yet inexplicable for the very reason that it is a first principle. To conclude that God infallibly knows, efficaciously wills, irresistibly produces both the necessary and the contingent is perfectly logical but it is not an explanation. Nor is explanation provided by arguing that the demand for an explanation involves fallacy; for even if we cannot coherently make the demand, it remains that we do not understand.

To the question, then, where does St Thomas place the mystery, it must be answered that he does not place it. He affirms nothing merely to have a theory of divine control. He affirms nothing merely to have a theory of the possibility of human liberty. He simply asserts all the truths he knows on both points and then argues that all arguments against the compatibility of these truths are fallacious. Thus his thought is properly a 'dialectical position,' and it is easily extended to the problem of *Deus causa peccati* by adverting to his three categories: positive truth, negative truth, objective falsity; good, not-good, sin; what God wills, what God does not will, what God permits. It is this subtle unfolding of his thought, like the mathematical movement into the region of complex numbers, that justifies his assertion in the commentary on Romans 9, lect. 2, that predestination is *ante praevisa merita* while damnation is *post praevisa peccata*.

It is not in this field that St Thomas found difficulty. Obviously one can possess all the foregoing and not yet have a theory of actual grace. *Deus operans* is not of itself *gratia operans*. Accordingly, we have seen that in the commentary on the *Sentences* he attempted to make the external Aristotelian premotion a grace preparatory to grace, and only gradually, through the development of the theory of the will and of the manner in which God moves and controls it, did he arrive at the motion which is the *gratia operans* of *Prima secundae*, q. 111, a. 2.

-----

leged incompatibility of divine knowledge, will, or action with human liberty as a mere frivolity (*Summa contra Gentiles*, 3, c. 94). He solves the problem as a corollary to his general solution. Conceive the existence of the stars as necessary but that of cows as contingent, eclipses as necessary but the falling of a stone as contingent; reconcile this contingence with the divine attributes; and it will become apparent why St Thomas was not perturbed by the problem of grace and free will from this point of view.

(9) There remains but a single difficulty, namely, the crux of the controversy *De auxiliis*. It is formulated by the Molinists with the question, How does God know when he causes the will of the end that the will will freely choose the means God intends to be chosen? The same question is put from a different viewpoint by the Bannezians: How can God's causing the will of the end make it true that God infallibly and irresistibly causes the will to choose the means?

To the former question the answer would seem to be that St Thomas does not explain the divine knowledge in terms of any antecedent but makes it a first principle. God knows because he is *ipsum intelligere*.

To the latter question, since it is many, the answer is more involved. God's moving the will to the end per se causes the will to choose the good, *per accidens* permits it to choose evil. God's causality is efficacious not because of the finite motion caused but because of the infinite mover: the prerogatives of divine transcendence cannot be attributed to any finite entity, not even the *praemotio physica*. Finally, by causing the will of the end God really and truly causes *ipsum actum volendi media*, because in the case of instrumental activity there are only two products (the will of the end and the will of the means) but three *actiones* (God causing the will of the end, the will of the end causing the will of the means, and God causing the causation of the will of the means by the will of the end). The third is cooperation. It is not true that Peter merely moves his rapier and the rapier kills Paul; Peter also kills Paul, and does so more than the rapier. The comparison limps, but the limping is twofold. If the will is free and so not like a rapier, it is also true that God is a transcendent *artifex* and so not like Peter.

(10) That the thought of St Thomas suggests a point of view different from that of the contending parties in the controversy *De auxiliis* is easily seen.

His *gratia operans et cooperans*, considered as a grace, does not notably differ from the *gratia excitans et adiuvans* of Molina. The difference lies in the metaphysical and psychological context in which St Thomas places his grace. He is as devoted to divine sanctity and human liberty as any Molinist, but, at the same time, he succeeds in maintaining a theory of divine dominion to which no Bannezian can take exception.

I think it may be said that Bannezian thought, point for point, corresponds to the thought of St Thomas, yet between the two there is a notable difference which arises from the arrangement of the points. St Thomas's synthesis of premotion, application, instrumental participation; his affirmation of universal instrumentality, of divine transcendence and efficacy, of operative grace as a special case of instrumental control – all these points are to be found in the Bannezian interpretation. But the difference lies in the analysis of the instrument: St Thomas posits three *actiones* but only two products; Durandus maintained that if there are only two products, there are only two *actiones*; both Molina and Bañez were out to discover a third product that they might have a third *actio*, and the former posited a *concursus simultaneus*, the latter a *concursus praevius*.

We have argued that on every point the Bannezian idea does not square with what St Thomas says: their distinction between *posse agere* and *actu agere* is not his; their idea of premotion is not his; their idea of application is not his; their idea of instrumental participation is not his; their idea of liberty is not his; their idea of divine transcendence communicated to their *praemotio* is unacceptable to him. The root of the whole trouble is that they take it for granted that a third *actio* postulates a third product.

But if we conclude that the Bannezian position is not what the Molinist has hardly claimed to be, an exact interpretation of St Thomas, we would not be thought to mean that it is a strange or surprising interpretation. That history is a science and not merely a diversion useful for the illustrations it provides for moral lessons, that the development of speculative positions is to be studied in its perspective and not telescoped into a somewhat Homeric list of allies and adversaries, these are not truths, however much admitted today, that always were taken for granted. Yet without the toil of purely historical study, St Thomas's thought on the issue treated in these pages cannot but be enigmatic. His theory of *actio* lies hidden under endless complexities. His idea of premotion finds its clearest expression in his study of Aristotle's *Physics*. The doctrine of application can be understood only as a transformation of the Aristotelian cosmic system. Universal instrumentality is a corollary from Platonist universal causes, and instrumental participation is a generalization of Aristotle's theory of the generation of animals. That God operates in the operation of the creature, initially is from the Arabic *Liber De causis*, but later is interwoven with ideas of premotion and application. Thought on liberty suffers from its starting point a distorting bifurcation. Solidary with all that precedes, the idea of divine transcendence is a 'dialectical position' that can be adequately illustrated only by later conceptions of space-time and of complex numbers. Finally, the idea of operative grace is an unsuspected compound of metaphysics and psychology that develops the pages of Aquinas through the last stages of a movement that began with Augustine.

To achieve that development I do not think that St Thomas extended himself, making it an objective as he made the reconciliation of the scientific spirit of Aristotle with the spirit of Christian faith. On the other hand, the elaboration of satisfactory theories of grace and of liberty was a long-sustained, if also a quiet, effort and concern. To one who reads the discussions of predestination and reprobation, providence and divine operation, grace and human liberty, that are to be found in the commentary on the *Sentences*, and then turns to questions 5, 6, 22, 23, 24, 27 of the *De veritate*, there is at once apparent a vast intellectual ferment: the pupil has discerned that the position of his master is not merely to be improved upon in matters of detail —such as the reduction of *liberum arbitrium* to the intellect and will and the substitution of *immediatio virtutis* for the *virtus divina creata* — but that he himself has fundamental problems to face and radical developments to achieve. Progress, however, is to the unknown and cannot be planned. The majestic sweep of the *Contra Gentiles* organizes the whole field of thought, but its detailed achievement in the theory of divine providence and government is not too relevant to the elaboration of a theory of grace. Yet the viewpoint there established will remain to provide a pattern into which all further ideas can be fitted, so that a closer analysis of human liberty, a grasp of the existence of internal graces prior to justification, a convergence of ideas on divine operation on the will and on the limitations of human freedom, all automatically combine under the theorem of creaturely instrumentality and the interpretation of St Paul's *Igitur non volentis neque currentis sed miserentis est Dei*. When, then, St Augustine's *ipse ut velimus operatur incipiens, qui volentibus cooperatur perficiens* turns up in the *Prima secundae* [q. 111, a. 2, Sed contra], no great deliberation is required for St Thomas to distinguish the causal series from the temporal series in the *effectus gratuitae Dei voluntatis* and to refine on the thought of St Augustine by making operative grace the divine grasp upon the human instrument, cooperative grace the product of God and of man guided and aided by God.

It is sometimes argued that St Thomas devoted so little attention to the problem of grace and free will that, had he lived in the sixteenth century, he would have notably altered his position. With that opinion we can hardly be expected to agree.

Appendix

[The following note was prefaced to the *excerpta* Lonergan published to fulfil the requirements for his doctorate at the Gregorian University (see p. xx above, in the Editors' Preface). It is worth salvaging, not only because it belongs to the history of his doctoral program, but also because in three paragraphs it gives us Lonergan's own very helpful abstract of his dissertation. The article from *Theological Studies* to which it refers appears in the present volume as chapters 1-5 through 1-7. – Ed.]

Note

The paging of this slim brochure may cause surprise, for the pages are numbered from 533 to 578. The fact is that, besides being an excerpt from my doctoral dissertation, what follows also is the last of a series of articles that appeared in the periodical, *Theological Studies*, in the years 1941 and 1942. To give the same matter two entirely different series of page numbers would be just ground for annoyance and a very probable cause of confusion. It seemed wiser, then, to retain in this reprint the same page numbers as are found in the article.

The reader will grasp the general nature of the argument most readily by glancing over the series of section headings appended at the end of this publication. The aim has been historical. The antecedents of Thomist thought were learnt from the well-known series of articles of Dom Lottin on the liberty of the will and of Dr Landgraf on medieval thought on grace; the latter's far-reaching work was supplemented by the monographs of Dr

Schupp on the *Gnadenlehre* of Peter Lombard and of Dr Doms on that of St Albert the Great. My own main task was to apply the method of intensive study of parallel passages propounded by the late Fr de Guibert in his celebrated *Doublets de saint Thomas d'Aquin.*

The manner in which this method worked out is, perhaps, of interest. It was soon discovered that the commentaries on the *Sentences* of Peter Lombard of the three great medieval doctors, St Albert, St Bonaventure, and St Thomas, held in common the surprising view that in one man there can be only one grace and that grace is the supernatural habit. This position seemed due to the fact that theoretical analysis of supernatural habits was of recent origin when the *Commentaries* were written and that, as yet, it had not been perceived that habitual grace along with external providence was insufficient to account for the dogmatic data. In any case in the *De veritate* of Aquinas one finds a reversal of the position of the commentary on the *Sentences*: in one man there is more than one grace in a strict sense; besides the supernatural habit, which is both operative and cooperative, there are cooperative gifts of good thoughts and holy affections. The *Summa theologiae* develops this position further by dividing both habitual and actual grace into operative and cooperative.

This general movement of thought set the problem. Within the writings of Aquinas there developed the precise notion of an operative, actual grace. What was it? Towards settling the issue, three subsidiary lines of inquiry were initiated: first, what was meant by dividing habitual grace into operative and cooperative; secondly, what seems to have been the underlying theory of operation; thirdly, what seems to have been understood by divine motions within the human will. In the light of the answers obtained to these subsidiary questions, the central issue was attacked.

The present excerpt omits the earlier parts of the dissertation on the historical background, the determination of the historical problem, the analogy from habitual grace, and the general theory of operation. It contains the subsidiary investigation on divine motions within the will, and the principal discussion of the development in the writings of St Thomas of a grace that at once is actual and operative. There seems no reason why I should summarize here the summaries that the reader will find on pages 552 f. and 572 ff. Similarly, I see no reason for repeating in a bibliography the titles of the few works drawn upon in this section of the essay. But I do wish to profit by the occasion to thank my professors at the Gregorian, and in particular Fr Charles Boyer, for their lessons and their kindness.

Bibliography of the Works of
St Thomas Aquinas

The bibliography relies on the titles in the folio volumes of the Leonine edition of
St Thomas, but then indicates the edition used in the present volume.

De operationibus occultis naturae. Opera omnia, vol. 43. Leonine ed. Rome, 1976.

De substantiis separatis. Opuscula Philosophica. Edited by R.M. Spiazzi. Turin:
Marietti, 1954.

*In Aristotelis libros De caelo, De generatione ... et Meteorologicorum. In Aristotelis libros de
caelo et mundo: de generatione et corruptione: meteorologicorum expositio*. Edited by
R.M. Spiazzi. Turin: Marietti, 1952.

*In Aristotelis libros Peri hermeneias et Posteriorum analyticorum. In Aristotelis libros Peri
hermeneias et Posteriorum analyticorum expositio*. Edited by R.M. Spiazzi. Turin:
Marietti, 1955.

In Aristotelis libros Physicorum. In octo libros Physicorum Aristotelis expositio. Edited by
P.M. Maggiolo. Turin: Marietti, 1954.

*Quaestiones disputatae de potentia, de malo, de spiritualibus creaturis, de anima, de
virtutibus in communi. Quaestiones disputatae*, vol. 2. Edited by P. Bazzi, M.
Calcaterra, T.S. Centi, E. Odetto, and P.M. Pession. Turin: Marietti, 1949.

Quaestiones disputatae de veritate. Quaestiones disputatae, vol. 1. Edited by R.M.
Spiazzi. Turin: Marietti, 1949.

Quaestiones quodlibetales. Edited by R.M. Spiazzi. Turin: Marietti, 1949. Also *Quaestiones quodlibetales*. Edited by Pierre Mandonnet. Paris: Lethielleux, 1926.

*Sententia libri De anima, librorumque De sensu et De memoria. In Aristotelis librum De
anima commentarium*. Edited by A.M. Pirotta. Turin: Marietti, 1948. And *In
Aristotelis libros de sensu et sensato: de memoria et reminiscentia*. Edited by R.M.
Spiazzi. Turin: Marietti, 1949.

Sententia libri Ethicorum. In decem libros Ethicorum Aristotelis ad Nicomachum expositio.
Edited by A.M. Pirotta. Turin: Marietti, 1934.

Sententia libri Metaphysicae. In duodecum libros Metaphysicorum Aristotelis expositio. Edited by M.-R. Cathala, revised by R.M. Spiazzi. Turin: Marietti, 1950.

Summa contra Gentiles. Summa contra Gentiles cum commentariis Ferrariensis. Opera omnia, vols. 13–15. Leonine ed. Rome, 1918–30. Also *Liber de Veritate Catholicae Fidei contra errores Infidelium, seu Summa contra Gentiles*. Edited by C. Pera et al. Turin: Marietti, 1961.

Super Epistolas Pauli Apostoli. Super epistolas s. Pauli lectura. Edited by R. Cai. 2 vols. Turin: Marietti, 1953.

Super Ioannem. Super evangelium s. Ioannis lectura. Edited by R. Cai. Turin: Marietti, 1952.

Summa theologiae. Summa theologiae cum Supplemento et commentariis Caietani. Opera omnia, vols. 4–12. Leonine ed. Rome: Ex Typographia Polyglotta, 1888–1906.

Super Librum De causis. In librum de causis expositio. Edited by Ceslai Pera. Turin: Marietti, 1955.

Super IV Sententiarum. For books 1 and 2: *Scriptum super libros sententiarum*, lib. I et II. Edited by Pierre Mandonnet. 2 vols. Paris: Lethielleux, 1929. For book 3 and part 1 of book 4: *Scriptum super sententiis*, lib. III, IV (part 1). Edited by Maria Fabianus Moos. 2 vols. Paris: Lethielleux, 1955, 1947. For remainder of book 4: *Opera omnia*, vol. 30. Edited by S.E. Fretté and P. Maré. Vivès ed. Paris: Apud Ludovicum Vivès, 1889. And Parma ed., vol. 7. New York: Musurgia, 1948.

Index of Concepts and Names

Abelard, Peter, 10, 16, 170, 210; his definition of freedom, 173–74, 177 n. 32, 186 (charity vs cupidity)

Abercrombie, N., 189–90 n. 65

Acceleration vs going faster, 15, 164

Act as one, actuating two potencies, 68

Actio: actio, factio, 271; in Aquinas, 70 n. 23, 91, 254–61, 267–74 (*actio qua actio*, 267–69; *actio, energeia*, 269–71; *actio, operatio, motus*, 271–72; *actio media, intrinseca, extrinseca*, 273–74); after Aquinas, 274–77; in Aquinas's commentary on Aristotle, 262–67; in Aristotle (seven terms: *motivum, movens, mobile, motum, motus, actio, passio*), 261–67; diverse senses, 324 & n. 25; a notional relation, 324; Platonic-Scotist view, 275, 276

Actio duplex (immanent, transient), 269, 271, 272

Actio in agente (Bañez), 74

Actio in passo, 122 n. 16, 146

Actio media, actio media intrinseca, actio media extrinseca, 70 n. 23

Actio, passio identical with *motus*, 269

Action, good vs meritorious, 353

Action does not enter into composition with agent, 71; action immanent, transient, 70 n. 23; action through contact, 68

Action and passion: agreement of Aristotle and Aquinas, with different terminology, 72 & n. 28; a. and p. one reality, 69, 261–67 passim (e.g., sound and hearing, 264); a. a relation of agent to patient, p. a relation of patient to agent (Aquinas), 72 n. 28

Acts according to nature, according to will, 279–80

Actually 'is,' 106 n. 67

Actus ab agente in aliud, 70 n. 23

Actus elicitus, imperatus, 415

Actus existentis in actu, in potentia, 129 n. 46, 272

Actus interiores in moralibus potiores sunt, 386

Actus interior et exterior, 132–42; *duplex actus* (internal, external), *triplex a.* (will of end, choice of means, bodily execution), 137–38

Actus primus, a. secundus (four senses), 253 n. 1

Aquinas's work on, 66; a. g. as *operans* and *cooperans*, 21, 30–35, chapter 1-6; a. g. and providence (divine assistance), 184 n. 41, 191, 442

Grace, cooperative: 29–30, 39–41, 117–19, 126–27; c. g. in the *De veritate*, 119–21; and external act of *Summa th.*, 1-2, q. 111, a. 2, 434–38 (*imperium*, 435)

Grace, habitual: 36 n. 50, 39–40, 41 (habit or motion), 43, 183 n. 39; efficient, 385, 390; habits and virtues, 442; habitual vs actual, 5–6 (origin of division), 246, 247, 248; as informing, 384, 390; as *operans* and *cooperans*, chapter 1-3, 384, 395; as operative, (Aquinas) 12; providence and habitual gift, 240; *sanans, elevans*, 49–58, 399–400, 405; as sanctifying, 29; as simply g., 5–6, 30 n. 31. *See also* Habit; Infused grace; Virtues

Grace, historical development: g. as actual, 19–20, 21, 42–43, 165 (new term), 183 (not yet formulated); background to Aquinas, chapter 1-1 (Augustine, 4; Anselm, 7; Peter Lombard, 11; transition to Aquinas, 14), chapter 11-1, at 181–91 (general antecedents of the development in Aquinas), 194; g. as *donum habituale*, history of, 175–78; evolution of concept of actual g. as operative and cooperative, 116; final Thomist scheme, 41; general movement of Aquinas's thought, chapters 1-2, 11-2, 11-5; medieval question on g. and infant baptism, 10, 18, 175–78 and n. 37; medieval questions on g., 171–72, 189–90; medieval terms for g. (*operans, cooperans, adiutrix, adjuvans, comitans, incipiens*, etc.), 209–10; g. as mover, 28 (Albert, *and see* 29–30), 28

n. 24 (Augustine), 29–30 (Bonaventure), 32–34 (Aquinas); g. as operative, 171, 212–16 (Peter Lombard); operative g. the fundamental problem in movement from Augustine to Aquinas, 159, 190, 349; philosophic analysis needed, 210; preparation for justification, successive treatments of, 41–42

Grace, need of: in angels, 16; in celibate, 197–98; to choose what is right, 349–50; in first parents, 16, 185–86 n. 51, 188; in Paul, 6; motion to good needed (nine reasons: improportion of man, personal sin, orientation to God, perseverance), 425–28, 431–32; need based on two theorems, 179, 181–91; need of, a compound theorem, 158; need of *divinum auxilium*, 232, 233, 235; need of, a dogma, 197; need of for good action, 352; need for g. vs need for providence, 183; to prepare for justification, 364–66; after justification, 366–67; theory of need, general (350–55), special (355–68)

Grace, operative, in chapter 11-5, by works of Aquinas: in commentary on *Sentences*, 384–86; in the *De veritate*, 37–40, 386–90 (the only operative g. is habitual); movement of thought from commentary on *Sentences* to *Prima secundae*, 438–40; in the *Summa theologiae*, 40–42; in *Prima secundae* on habitual g., 390–404; in *Prima secundae* on actual g., 404–38; in *Prima secundae*, q. 111, a. 2, 404–38; *Sentences* on, 11–12, 119; in the Three Great Commentaries (Albert, Bonaventure, Aquinas) 26–35

Grace, operative, cooperative: 224–25, 228, 233–36, 245–50; basic passages

Index of Loci in
Aquinas and Aristotle

General references to whole works (or major parts) of Thomas Aquinas

Catena aurea, 169

De caelo et mundo, 309

De malo, 59, 95, 96, 102, 121, 125, 134, 146, 159, 241 n. 168, 340, 344, 357 n. 73, 369, 370, 412, 415, 416, 438, 443, 444

De operationibus occultis naturae, 83 n. 82, 290 n. 104

De potentia, 70, 72, 76, 78 n. 59, 85, 89, 95, 159, 258, 261, 267, 268, 292, 301, 305, 309

De substantiis separatis, 291 n. 106

De veritate, 21, 22 n. 2, 33, 40, 42, 44, 45, 46, 51, 56, 57, 62, 63, 64, 65, 81, 82, 85, 89, 92, 95, 96, 98, 99, 101, 109, 119, 120, 121, 129, 132, 137, 145, 153–54, 159, 183, 184 & n. 41, 190, 229, 236, 238, 239, 241 & n. 168, 243, 246, 249, 250, 251, 294, 305, 317 n. 2, 318 n. 5, 319 n. 9, 357 & n. 73, 364, 368, 370, 375, 384, 385, 386, 388, 390, 391, 406, 413, 424, 438, 443, 444, 450

De virtutibus in communi, 353

In Aristotelis libros De caelo et mundo, 78 n. 59

In Aristotelis libros Peri hermeneias, 159

In Aristotelis libros Physicorum, 73, 159, 261, 264, 268, 275

Quaestiones quodlibetales, 143, 159

Sententia libri De anima, 261, 264

Sententia libri Metaphysicae, 159, 261, 267, 275, 281

Summa contra Gentiles, 44, 64, 65, 76, 79, 81, 82, 85, 89, 91, 98–99, 109, 119, 124, 125, 143, 145, 159, 238, 239, 241 n. 168, 242, 251, 286 n. 94, 289 n. 104, 294, 301, 305, 319 n. 9, 353, 407, 443, 450

Summa theologiae, 21, 24, 40–41, 42, 44, 47, 49, 58, 63, 64, 65, 69, 85, 86, 121, 129, 132, 143, 305, 391

– *Pars prima*, 70, 87, 89, 94, 95, 96, 97, 99, 108, 121, 124, 146, 159, 241 n. 168, 268, 289 n. 104, 292, 309, 318, 340 n. 47, 344, 353, 402, 407, 409 n. 124, 438, 443, 444

– *Prima secundae*, 21, 33, 40–41, 42, 44,

Specific references to texts of Thomas Aquinas

a. 5, 43, 127–28 n. 38, 139 n. 92, 142
n. 104, 421–22 n. 159, 423–24 n. 170,
424, 433 n. 203; c., 422 nn. 163 and
164; ob. 3, 422 n. 161; ad 3m, 422 n.
160; **q. 85, a. 6**, 127 n. 37, 128 n. 39
Summa theologiae, Supplementum: **q. 97, a.
7**, ob. 3, 45 n. 2
Super epistolas Pauli: In Phil.: **c. 1, lect. 1,**
§ 12, 101 n. 49, 377 n. 156; **c. 2**, § 77,
377 n. 157; *In Rom.:* **c. 6, lect. 3**, 393 n.
58; §§ 497–98, 61 n. 57, 396 n. 79; **c. 7,
lect. 3**, 49 n. 19; §§ 562–66, 140 n. 98;
§ 565, 354 n. 72; **c. 8, lect. 3**, § 635, 141
n. 101, 432–33 & n. 201, 433 n. 202; **c.
9, lect. 2**, 447; §§ 763–64, 116 n. 95,
340 n. 47, 382 n. 193; § 764, 333; **c. 9,
lect. 3**, 393 n. 58, 412, 433 n. 203;
§ 773, 101 n. 49, 134 n. 67, 244 n. 174,
376 n. 154; §§ 775–78, 409–11 & n.
125; § 775, 440 n. 225; § 777, 123 n. 22,
134 n. 67; § 778, 411 n. 126; §§ 780–82,
118 n. 100; § 781, 344 n. 53, 388 n. 26;
In I Tim.: **c. 2, lect. 1**, § 62, 347; *In II
Cor.:* **c. 3, lect. 1**, §§ 86–87, 244 n. 174,
393 n. 58; § 87, 101 n. 49, 377 n. 155;
c. 6, lect. 1, 121
Super Ioannem: **c. 6, lect. 5**, § 935, 141 n.
100, 149 n. 36, 430 n. 197, 431 n. 198;
§§ 937–38, 347
Super librum De causis: **prop. 1**, 88; **lect.
1**, 83 n. 80; § 13, 298 n. 128; § 14, 298
n. 128; § 24, 88 n. 104; § 26, 298 n.
128; § 29, 291 n. 106; **lect. 3**, § 80, 298
n. 127; **lect. 4**, 83 n. 80; **lect. 6**, 83 n.
80; **lect. 18**, 83 n. 80; **lect. 20–22**, 87
n. 99; **lect. 20**, 275 n. 43, 299 n. 132;
§ 366, 67 n. 4, 299 n. 131; **lect. 24**,
§ 398–99, 81 n. 71; **lect. 31**, 87 n. 99,
275 n. 43; **lect. 31**, § 456–57, 299 n.
131
Super I Sententiarum: **d. 12, q. 1, a. 3**, ad

4m, 67 n. 6, 92 n. 114, 302 n. 144; **d.
32, q. 1, a. 1**, 70 n. 23, 72 n. 26, 257 n.
11, 268; **d. 37, q. 1, aa. 1–3**, 77 n. 51;
d. 37, q. 1, a. 1, 87 n. 101, 282 n. 68;
c., 89 n. 105; ad 4m, 67 nn. 4 and 6,
87 nn. 100 and 101, 89 n. 105, 92 n.
114, 98 n. 34, 301 n. 138, 302 n. 143,
309 n. 157, 312 n. 168; **d. 37, q. 4, a.
3**, 105 n. 63, 323 n. 23; **d. 38, q. 1, a.
1**, 85 n. 87, 108 n. 72, 293 n. 115; **d.
38, q. 1, a. 5**, 110 n. 80, 326, 336 n.
41; c., 105 n. 64, 322 n. 22; ad 4m,
105 n. 64, 106 n. 68, 107 n. 70, 322 n.
22, 327 n. 27; **d. 39, q. 2, aa. 1–2**, 80
n. 69; **d. 39, q. 2, a. 1**, ad 5m, 85 n.
87, 293 n. 116; **d. 39, q. 2, a. 2**, ad 2m,
110 n. 80, 336 n. 41; ad 4m, 45 n. 3,
48 n. 16, 351 nn. 63 and 65, 397 n.
81; **d. 40, q. 1, aa. 1–2**, 80 n. 69;
d. 40, q. 1, a. 1, ad 1m, 70 n. 23, 269–
70 n. 30; **d. 40, q. 1, a. 2**, 80 n. 70; **d.
40, qq. 2–3**, 80 n. 69; **d. 40, q. 2, a. 1**,
ad 6m, 81 n. 71, 340 n. 47; **d. 40, q. 3,
a. 1**, 106 n. 69, 110 n. 80, 325 n. 26,
336 n. 41; **d. 40, q. 4, a. 1**, 80 n. 70,
340 n. 47; **d. 47, q. 1, a. 1**, ad 2m, 107
n. 71, 110 n. 80, 334 n. 37, 336 n. 41;
d. 47, q. 1, a. 2, 81 nn. 71 and 72, 340
n. 47
Super II Sententiarum: **d. 1, q. 1, aa. 1–3**,
77 n. 51; **d. 1, q. 1, a. 4** c., 89 n. 105,
90 n. 110; ad 5m, 83 n. 82; **d. 1, q. 1,
a. 5**, ad 11m (1ae ser.), 273 n. 39; **d.
1, q. 1, a. 5**, ad 13m, 105 n. 63, 323
n. 23, 324 n. 25; **d. 2, q. 1, a. 2**, 105
n. 63; **d. 13, q. 1, a. 3**, 84 n. 84, 86 n.
93, 290 n. 104; **d. 15, q. 1, a. 2**, 76 n.
49, 83 n. 82, 282 n. 69, 290 n. 104; c.,
89 n. 105; **d. 15, q. 1, a. 3**, 77 n. 51,
373 n. 138; **d. 15, q. 3, a. 1**, ad 3m,
67 n. 5, 273 n. 38, 283 n. 73, 301 n.

References to Aristotle

Lexicon of Latin and Greek Words and Phrases

Latin Words and Phrases

a voluntate imperatur: (the external act) is commanded by the will
ab aeterno: from eternity
ab intrinseco: from within
actio ... actiones: action ... actions
actio Dei: the action of God
actio divina ad extra est formaliter immanens et virtualiter transiens: divine external action is formally immanent and virtually transient
actio est motus ut ab hoc, ut ab agente: action is a movement as from this, as from an agent
actio est in passo: action is in the recipient
actio in agente ... actio in passo: action in the agent ... action in the recipient
actio media: mediate action
actio media intrinseca ... actio media extrinseca: intrinsic mediate action ... extrinsic mediate action
actio ... operatio ... motus: action ... operation ... movement
actio qua actio: action as action
actio transmutat rem exteriorem: action changes the external thing
actio voluntatis inquantum est actio: action of the will insofar as it is action
actu agere ... actu agit: actually to act ... actually acts
actualitas: actuality
actum ipsum potentiae: the act itself [accusative case] of the potency
actus ... actus ab agente in aliud: act ... act (proceeding) from an agent to another
actus elicitus ... actus imperatus: elicited act ... commanded act
actus existentis in actu ... actus existentis in potentia: act of something existing in act ... act of something existing in potency

actus existentis in potentia inquantum huiusmodi: act of something existing in potency insofar as it is in potency

actus exterior ... actus humanus ... actus imperatus: external act ... human act ... commanded act

actus interior voluntatis ... actus exterior: internal act of the will ... external act

actus moventis in moto est motus: an act of a mover is a movement in the thing moved

actus peccati: act of sin

actus primus ... actus secundus: first act ... second act

actus purus: pure act

actus virtualis ... actus virtutis: virtual act ... act of a power

actus volendi: act of willing

actus voluntarius ... actus humanus: voluntary act ... human act

actus voluntatis: act of the will

ad aliquid determinate volendum: in order to will something determinately

ad extra: to the outside

ad modum liberi ... ad modum naturae: in the way of a free agent ... in the way of a nature

adaequatio ... adaequatio veritatis ... adaequationes veritatis: equation ... equation of truth (and reality) ... equations of truth and reality

additio super esse: something added beyond being

adiutorium sine quo non ... adiutorium quo: the help without which one cannot (act) ... the help with which (one does act)

admirabili delectatione et amore veritatis quae est ipse Filius Dei: (drawn) by the admirable delight and love of the truth which is the very Son of God

admonitio exterior: external admonition

aegritudo corporis: sickness of the body

agens imperfectum ... agens perfectum: imperfect agent ... perfect agent

agens in tempore ... agens naturale: (agent) acting in time ... natural agent

agens per intellectum: (agent) acting through intellect

agere sequitur esse: action follows being

agros colere et domos aedificare: cultivate fields and build houses

alio modo possumus loqui de paenitentia quantum ad actus, quibus Deo operanti in paenitentia cooperamus: in another way we can talk of repentance as regards the acts by which in repentance we cooperate with God in his operation

aliquam intelligentiam eamque fructuosissimam: some measure of understanding and indeed very fruitful understanding

aliquid agit liberum arbitrium: free will does something

aliud esse: a different being

alterans non alteratum ... alterantia alterata: a thing changing (another) but not (itself) changed ... things that change (another and are themselves) changed

amentes: insane

amor amicitiae erga Deum: love of friendship for God

anima: soul

ante et post praevisa merita: before and after foreseen merits

appetibile (est) movens non motum ... appetitus (est) movens motum: a desirable thing (is) an unmoved mover ... desire (is) a moved mover

appetibile ... appetibilia: desirable thing ... desirable things

appetibile apprehensum movet appetitum: the desired thing which is apprehended moves the desire

appetitus movetur per bonum apprehensum: desire is moved by the apprehended good

appetitus naturalis: natural desire

applicare ... applicatur ... applicatio: to apply ... is applied ... application

applicatio potentiae ad actum: application of the potency to act

argumenta convenientiae: arguments that fit (the case but do not prove it)

artifex ... artifex divinus: artisan ... divine artisan

assimilatio appetitus: assimilation of desire (to the object)

auxilium Dei moventis ... auxilium divinum: the help of God moving (us) ... divine help

bene agere ... bonum agere: to act properly ... to do good

benedictio ... benedictio consummans: blessing ... perfect blessing

bona cogitatio praecedit fidem: a good thought precedes faith

bona voluntas: good will

bonum apprehensum: apprehended good

bonum in genere: good in general

bonum meritorium ... bonum meritorium qua meritorium: a meritorious good work ... a meritorious good work as meritorious

bonum universale: universal good

calefactio ... calefactionis causa: heating ... cause of heating

caritas foras expellit [mittit] timorem: love casts out fear

caritas se habet ad liberum arbitrium sicut sessor ad equum: charity is related to free will the way a rider is to a horse

causa actionis magis est id cuius virtute agitur quam etiam illud quod agit: that by the power of which action is taken is more the cause of an action than even that which takes the action

causa actus deformis ... causa actus peccati: cause of a deformed act ... cause of an act of sin

causa ad utrumque ... causa aequivoca: cause (effective) for either (of two) ... equivocal cause

causa defectus ... causa deformitatis: cause of defect ... cause of difformity

causa essendi: cause of being

causa impedibilis ... causa impediens: cause that may impede ... impeding cause

causa per se: a cause by or in itself

causa speciei: cause of a species

causa univoca: univocal cause

causae cognoscendi: causes of knowing

certitudo ordinis: certitude of order

cessante motu caeli: with the ceasing of the motion of the heavens

clarum-obscurum: clear-obscure

collatio aut conservatio virtutis activae: creation or conservation of active power

color in aere: color in the atmosphere

combustibile: combustible

communis doctor: common doctor (of the whole church)

concursus: concurrence

concursus divinus, generalis, indifferens, praevius, simultaneus: divine, general, indifferent, preceding, simultaneous concurrence

consensus: consent

consensus ad detestandum peccatum et ad accedendun ad Deum: consent to detesting sin and to approaching God

consensus proprie loquendo non est nisi de his quae sunt ad finem: properly speaking, consent is not (given) to anything except to means to the end

consequens est: the consequence is

consilium rationis: deliberation of reason

consummatio motus sive perventio in finem: completion of the movement or arrival at the end

contingens: contingent

contingentia in maiori et minori parte: happening in the majority of cases and happening in the minority of cases

continuator, res media: connecting link, intermediate thing

conversio cordis: conversion of heart

conversio hominis ad Deum fit quidem per liberum arbitrium: man's conversion to God is indeed made by free will

cor regum in manu Dei: the heart of kings is (like a stream of water) in the hand of God

corpus articuli: the body of the article

corpus caeleste: heavenly body

corruptibilia: things that can be destroyed

creatio: creation

crede ut intelligas: believe that you may understand

cui est actio: that to which the action pertains

culpa: guilt

cum dicitur homo facere quod in se est, dicitur hoc esse in potestate hominis secundum quod est motus a Deo: when man is said to do what is in his power, it is meant that this is in man's power insofar as he is moved by God

dabo vobis ... facite vobis: I will give you ... do (it) for yourselves

de auxiliis: (the controversy) about the helps (given by God)

de fide definita: defined as (an article) of faith

de gratia ... de gratia operante: on grace ... on operative grace

decreta praedeterminantia: predetermining decrees

defectus ... deformitas peccati: defect ... deformity of sin

Dei operatio convertentis cor: the operation of God converting the heart

determinata ad calefaciendum: determined (in the sense of orientation) to (the action of) heating

Deus agit per intellectum: God acts through intellect

Deus causa peccati: God the cause of sin

Deus est causa omnibus operantibus ut operentur: in all operating things God is the cause that they operate

Deus est qui operatur in vobis et velle et perficere: it is God who is at work in you, enabling you both to will and to work (Philippians 2.13)

Deus omnia applicat: God applies all things

Deus operans: God operating

Deus operatur in omni operante ... Deus operatur in operatione creaturae: God operates in everything that operates ... God operates in the operation of the creature

Deus sine nobis operatur: God operates without us

dilectio naturalis: natural love

dimitte debita nostra: forgive us our debts

dispositio, dispositiones: disposition, dispositions

divinum auxilium ... divinum auxilium quod ad gratiam cooperantem pertinet: divine help ... divine help that pertains to cooperative grace

divinus instinctus: divine instinct

domina sui actus ... dominium sui actus: controlling his act ... dominion over his act

dona habitualia, donum habituale: habitual gifts, habitual gift

donum Dei: God's gift

donum habituale ... donum habituale et supernaturale: habitual gift ... habitual and supernatural gift

dum iustificamur, Dei iustitiae consentimus: we consent to the justice of God while we are being justified

duplex actus ... triplex actus: twofold act ... threefold act

eadem gratia: (by) the same grace

effectus gratuitae Dei voluntatis ... effectus gratuitae divinae voluntatis: effect of the gratuitous will of God ... effect of the divine gratuitous will

electio: choice

elevans ... sanans: elevating ... healing

elevatio ... sanatio: elevation ... a healing

eminentiori modo: in a preeminent way

ens ... entia: being ...beings

entitative supernaturale: entitatively supernatural

esse ... esse ab alio: to be, being ... being from another

esse ad ... esse in: being towards ... being in

esse completum ... esse divinum ... esse incompletum: complete being ... divine being ... incomplete being

esse ... fieri: to be ... to become

esse in ... esse ad: being in (inhering) ... being (related) to

esse ... operari ... operatio: to be ... to operate ... operation

esse salubre ... esse spirituale ... esse spirituale incompletum ... esse supernaturale: healthful being ... spiritual being ... incomplete spiritual being ... supernatural being

esse vivum humanum: to be living in a human way

et peccare et non peccare posse: able to sin and able not to sin

etiam interior voluntas movetur ab aliquo superiori principio quod est Deus: also the internal will is moved by some higher principle which is God

ex aeterno: from eternity

ex falso sequitur quodlibet: anything whatever follows from a false (premise)

ex hoc ipso quod aliquid est cognoscibile cadit sub eius cognitione: by this very fact that something is knowable it falls under his knowledge

ex hypothesi: from the hypothesis

ex parte effectuum: from the side of the effects

ex virtute voluntatis: from the power of the will

exteriora ordinat: orders external things

exterioris actus executionem expediendo: expediting the execution of the external act

exterius facultatem operandi praebendo: externally providing the faculty of operating

facile mobilis ... difficile mobilis: movable with ease ... movable with difficulty

facite vobis ... dabo vobis: do for yourselves ... I will give you

factio: a making

falsitas obiectiva: objective falsity

fides quae per dilectionem operatur: faith which works through love

fides quaerens intellectum: faith seeking understanding

fomitis corruptio: corruption of yeast

forma apprehensa ... forma coloris: apprehended form ... form of color

forma et operatio: form and operation

forma gravitatis, levitatis: form of heaviness, of lightness

forma meriti: form of merit

forma per quam (actus) meritorius est: form by which (an act) is meritorious

forma quaedam habens esse firmum et ratum in natura: a certain form having in nature its stable and determined being

forma supernaturalitatis: form of supernaturality

furiosi: madmen

futura contingentia: future contingent things (or events)

futuribile, futuribilia: futurable, futurables

genera entis: genera of being

generabilia: things that can be generated

generans gravia et levia: generating heavy things and light things

gloria Dei externa: external glory of God

gratia actualis: actual grace

gratia adiutrix ... gratia adiuvans ... gratia adiuvat: helping grace ... helping grace ... grace helps

gratia aspirans ... gratia auxiliatrix: aspiring grace ... helping grace

gratia comitans ... gratia conservatrix ... gratia cooperans: accompanying grace ... preserving grace ... cooperative grace

gratia efficax ... gratia elevans ... gratia excitans et adiuvans: efficacious grace ... elevating grace ... grace that is stimulating and helping

gratia gratis dans ... gratia gratis data: grace giving freely ... grace freely given

gratia gratum faciens: grace making one pleasing (to God)

gratia incipiens: initial grace

gratia inclinans ad actum interiorem (operans) ... inclinans ad actum exteriorem (cooperans): grace inclining to an internal act (operative) ... inclining to an external act (cooperative)

gratia informans: informing grace

gratia informans hominem (operans) ... informans opus (cooperans): grace informing man (operative) ... informing a deed (cooperative)

gratia operans: operative grace

gratia operans compungit mentem et excitat: operative grace prods and arouses the mind

gratia operans et cooperans est eadem gratia; sed distinguitur secundum diversos effectus: operative grace and cooperative are the same grace; but (the grace) is distinguished according to (its) different effects

gratia perseverans: persevering grace

gratia praeparans: preparing grace

gratia praeveniens ... gratia praevenit ... gratia praeventrix: prevenient grace ... grace takes the lead ... prevenient grace

gratia salvans ... gratia sanans: saving grace ... healing grace

gratia subsequens ... gratia suscitans: subsequent grace ... arousing grace

gratia suscipit: grace accepts

gratis data ... gratum faciens: freely given ... making (one) pleasing

gratuita: gratuitous things

gratuita Dei voluntas ex parte effectuum ... gratuita voluntas divina: the gratuitous will of God from the side of the effects ... divine gratuitous willing

gratuitum ... meritum: gratuitous ... merit

gratum faciens: making one pleasing (to God)

grave ... leve: heavy ... light

gubernari ... gubernare: to be governed ... to govern

habitualis inclinatio voluntatis ad indebitum finem: habitual inclination of the will to a wrong end

habitudo: relation

habitudo ... res media ... additio super esse: relation ... intermediate thing ... addition beyond being

habitus est quo quis agit cum voluerit: a habit is that by which one acts when one wants to

haec est gratia operans et cooperans: this is operative and cooperative grace

hic et nunc: here and now

hoc idem est quod alibi dicitur praeveniens, subsequens: this is the same as what in other places is called prevenient, subsequent

hoc ipsum quod causa secunda sit causa effectus, habet a causa prima: this fact itself that the secondary cause is cause of the effect derives from the first cause

hoc non sola gratia operatur in nobis: grace alone does not operate this in us

hoc quod homo moveatur a Deo non praeexigit aliquam aliam motionem, cum Deus sit primum movens: the fact that man is moved by God has not any other motion as a prerequisite since God is the first mover

hominem semper et peccare et non peccare posse: man is always able to sin and able not to sin

honestum: upright

ideo etiam creatio significatur ut media inter creatorem et creaturam: therefore even creation is understood as mediating between Creator and creature

igitur non volentis neque currentis sed miserentis est Dei: so it depends not on human will or exertion, but on God who shows mercy (Romans 9.16)

illuminari: to be illuminated

immediatio suppositi ... immediatio virtutis ... immediatione virtutis: immediacy of the supposit ... immediacy of power ... by the immediacy of power

immittat bonas cogitationes et sanctas affectiones: (God) sends good thoughts and holy desires

imperium: command

impotentia moralis ... impotentia physica: moral impotence ... physical impotence

in causa ... in causis suis: in (its) cause ... in its causes

in genere intelligibilium ut actus: as act in the genus of intelligible things

in minori parte: in a minority of cases

in modum naturae: in the way of a nature

in natura mutabili: in a changeable nature

in nobis sine nobis: in us without us

in particulari: in particular

in quibus omnibus aliquid agit liberum arbitrium: in all of which free will does something

in re agente: in the agent thing

in se ipso: in itself

in sensu composito ... in sensu diviso: in the composite sense ... in the divided sense

in universali: universally

inclinare voluntatem: to incline the will

inclinari vel non inclinari ... moveri vel non moveri ... moveri ex se: to be inclined or not to be inclined ... to be moved or not to be moved ... to be self-moved

inclinatio universalis: universal inclination

inconveniens: unsuitable

inhaerens: inhering

initialis dilectio ... initium consiliandi ... initium fidei ... initium iustificationis: beginning of love ... beginning of deliberation ... beginning of faith ... beginning of justification

instinctu inclinatur: it is inclined by instinct

instinctus divinus ... instinctus interior: divine impulse ... internal impulse

intellectus agens et possibilis: agent intellect and potential intellect

intellectus in actu est intellectum in actu: intellect in act is the understood object in act

intentio: intention

interior Dei motio: internal motion of God

interius confirmando voluntatem ut ad actum perveniat: strengthening the will internally that it may come to act

interius motum mentis operatur: (God) produces a movement of the mind internally

ipsa misericordia Dei: God's mercy itself

ipse actus voluntatis: the act itself of the will

ipse ut velimus operatur incipiens, qui volentibus cooperatur perficiens: the One who begins by operating so that we may will brings (the work) to perfection by cooperating with those who will

ipsum actum volendi media: this act of willing the means

ipsum amare ... ipsum esse ... ipsum esse separatum ... ipsum intelligere ... ipsum intelligere separatum: love itself ... being itself ... separate being itself ... understanding itself ... separate understanding itself

lex aeterna: eternal law

liber est qui est causa sui (sui causa): he is free who is his own cause

libertas a coactione ... libertas a peccato ... libertas a miseria ... libertas a necessitate: freedom from coercion ... freedom from sin ... freedom from misery ... freedom from necessity

libertas arbitrii est potestas servandi rectitudinem voluntatis propter ipsam rectitudinem: liberty of will is the power of preserving righteousness of will for the sake of righteousness itself

libertas exercitii ... libertas specificationis: freedom of exercise (to act or not to act) ... freedom of specification (to choose this or to choose that)

libertas naturae ... libertas gratiae: freedom of nature ... freedom of grace

liberum arbitrium: free choice

liberum arbitrium ad Deum converti non potest nisi Deo ipsum ad se convertente: free choice cannot be converted to God except by God converting it to himself

liberum de voluntate iudicium: free judgment about will

locus connaturalis: natural place

malum culpae: the evil of guilt

malum culpae non repugnat bonitati naturae: the evil of guilt is not incompatible with the goodness of nature

manens: remaining

massa damnata: the masses who are damned

materia prima: prime matter

mediante virtute: with power as mediator

mens ... mens Augustini: mind ... the mind of Augustine

mens (mens nostra) mota et non movens ... mens mota et movens: mind (our mind) moved and not (actively) moving ... mind moved and (actively) moving

merita bonae voluntatis: the merits of a good will

meritum: merit

metaphorice et improprie: metaphorically and improperly

misericordia: mercy

mobile est id quod potest moveri ... mobilia ... moveri: a movable thing is that which can be moved ... movable things ... to be moved

modo eminentiori: in a preeminent way

modum actus: the way of an act

modus tollens: mode of denying

mota et movens, dicitur gratia cooperans: (when will is both) moved and (actively) moving, the grace is called cooperative

mota et non movens, solus autem Deus movens, dicitur gratia operans: (when will is) moved and not (actively) moving, but God alone moving, the grace is called operative

motio ... motio mobilis ... motio moventis ... motio moventis est motus mobilis ... motio moventis praecedit motum mobilis: motion ... movement of a thing that is movable ... motion of the mover ... the motion of the thing moving is the movement of the thing that is movable ... the motion of the mover precedes the movement of the thing that is movable

motione gratuita ... motione gratuita qua gratuita: by a gratuitous motion ... by a gratuitous motion as gratuitous

motivum est id quod potest movere: an (actively) moving thing is that which can move (something)

motor caeli ... motor immobilis: mover of the heavens ... immovable mover

motum eius causando: causing its movement

motum mentis operatur: effects a movement of the mind

motum meritorium voluntatis operatur eliciendo ipsum, licet mediante virtute: a meritorious motion of the will operates eliciting (the act), though it does so through the mediation of a power

motus (motum): moved (as past participle), movement (as substantive)

motus artis ... motus caritatis: movement of art ... movement of love

motus est actus existentis in potentia in quantum huiusmodi: movement is the act of something existing in potency insofar as it is in potency

motus huius ut ab hoc ... motus huius ut in hoc: movement of this as from this ... movement of this as in this

motus liberi arbitrii: movement of free choice

motus mobilis ... motus motivus: movement of a movable thing ... movement that moves (actively)

motus per occasionem: movement that is occasioned

motus primo-primus: the very first movement

motus secundum actionem: movement as regards action

motus ut ab hoc ... motus ut in hoc: movement as from this ... movement as in this

movens est id quod movet: a mover is that which moves (something)

movens motum: a moving (agent) that is moved

moveri ex se ... se movet: to be moved of itself ... it moves itself

multa fiunt quae Deus non operatur: many things are done which God does not operate

mysterium iniquitatis: the mystery of iniquity

natura ... natura elevata ... natura incompleta: nature ... nature elevated ... incomplete nature

natura integra ... natura lapsa: integral nature ... fallen nature

natura prius ... tempore prius: prior by nature ... prior in time

natura pura ... natura lapsa ... natura elevata: pure nature ... fallen nature ... elevated nature

natura rationalis cum potentiis suis: rational nature with its potencies

naturalia ... gratuita: things (in the order) of nature ... things (in the order) of grace

ne nos inferas in tentationem: do not bring us to the time of trial (Matthew 6.13)

necessarium et possibile sunt divisiones entis: necessary and possible are divisions of being

nemo potest venire ad me nisi Pater, qui misit me, traxerit eum: no one can come to me unless drawn by the Father who sent me (John 6.44)

nisi forte: unless perhaps

nobiscum ... nobiscum cooperatur: with us ... cooperates with us

nolite obdurare corda vestra: do not harden your hearts (Psalm 95.9)

non affirmando sed coniectando: not affirming but conjecturing

non alteratum: not changed

non bonum: non-good (as substantive), not good (as adjective)

(non) causa gratiae sed effectus: (not) the cause of grace but an effect (of grace)

non enim quod volo bonum, hoc ago; sed quod odi malum illud facio: for I do not do what I want, but I do the very thing that I hate (Romans 7.15)

non est cogens: (the argument) is not cogent

non est in homine via eius, nec viri est dirigere gressus suos: the way of human beings is not in their control ... mortals as they walk cannot direct their steps (Jeremiah 10.23)

non est miserentis Dei sed volentis et currentis: it does not depend on God who shows mercy but on (human) will and exertion

non est volentis, scilicet velle, neque currentis, currere, sicut primi principii, sed Dei miserentis; it does not depend, as on a first principle, on the one willing, that is, to will, nor on the one running, that is, to run, but on God who has mercy

non facit compositionem cum eo: does not enter into composition with it

non movens aliquid aliud: not (actively) moving something else

non posse non peccare etiam damnabiliter ... posse non peccare: not able not to sin, even to the incurring of damnation ... able not to sin

non volentis neque currentis sed miserentis est Dei: it depends not on human will or exertion, but on God who shows mercy (Romans 9.16)

nulla creatura rationalis potest habere motum voluntatis ordinatum ad illam beatitudinem, nisi mota a supernaturali agente: no rational creature can have a movement of will directed to that beatitude, unless it is moved by a supernatural agent

nulla gratia debet dici simpliciter operans: no grace should be called simply operative

nulla res creata potest in quemcumque actum prodire nisi virtute motionis divinae: no created thing can come to any act whatever except in virtue of a divine motion

nullus effectus cuius Deus solus sit causa, potest esse contingens: no effect of which God alone is the cause can be contingent

numerus stultorum infinitus: the number of fools is infinite (Ecclesiastes 1.15, Vulgate)

nunc: now

O altitudo: O depth (Romans 11.33)

occasionaliter: giving occasion

omne agens agit sibi simile: every agent produces something similar to itself

omne enim quod est dum est necesse est esse: for everything that is, as long as it is, necessarily is

omne ens agit quatenus est actu: every being acts insofar as it is in act

omne movens movetur: every moving thing is moved

onus probandi: the burden of proving

operando incipit ... cooperando perficit: by operating (God) begins ... by cooperating he completes (the good deed)

operans effective: operating effectively

operans et praeveniens ... operans et subsequens: operative and prevenient ... operative and subsequent

operans in omni operante: operating in everything that operates

operans-cooperans & praeveniens-subsequens: operative-cooperative & prevenient-subsequent

operatio attribuitur mobili: operation is attributed to the movable thing

operatio effectus ... operatio immanens: operation of an effect ... immanent operation

operatio immanens attribuitur mobili: immanent operation is attributed to the movable thing

operatio naturalis: natural operation

operationes Dei quibus movet nos ad bonum ad gratiam pertinent: the operations of God by which he moves us to good pertain to grace

operatur incipiens: beginning he operates (to make us will)

oportet reducere omnem multitudinem in unitatem: every multitude has to be reduced to unity

ordinatio divini gubernationis ... ordinatio divini intellectus: decree of divine government ... decree of the divine intellect

ordo causae ad effectum ... ordo divini intellectus: order of a cause to the effect ... order of the divine intellect

otium: leisure

pari ratione: with equal reason

pars irascibilis ... concupiscibilis: the irascible ... the concupiscent faculty

parvuli, amentes, furiosi: children, insane, madmen

passio: passion

passio est motus ut in hoc, ut in patiente: passion is a movement as in this, as in the recipient

peccata habendi dura necessitas: the hard necessity of having sins

peccatum: sin

penitus desperant: they almost despair

per accidens: accidentally (as opposed to per se)

per formam apprehensam: through an apprehended form

per modum cuiusdam defluxus ... per modum formae completae: in the way of a certain downflow ... in the way of a complete form

per modum naturae ... per modum naturae completae ... per modum naturae completae et eminentioris ... per modum naturae incompletae: in the way of a nature ... in the way of a complete nature ... in the way of a complete and preeminent nature ... in the way of an incomplete nature

per modum passionis ... per modum qualitatis inhaerentis: in the way of receiving (an effect) ... in the way of an inherent quality

per quoddam esse incompletum: through a certain incomplete being

perditio tua ex te Israel: your ruin (comes) from yourself, Israel (Hosea 13.9)

permissio culpae et praeparatio paenae: permission of guilt and preparation of punishment

perseverantiam praebendo: granting perseverance

perventio in finem motus: arrival at the term of movement

philosophia ancilla theologiae: philosophy the handmaid of theology

philosophia perennis: perennial philosophy

placitum: approved

posse agere ... actu agere: to be able to act ... to actually act

posse peccare et non posse non peccare etiam damnabiliter: able to sin and not able not to sin, even to the incurring of damnation

posse stare ... posse proficere: able to stand ... able to make progress

possibile: possible

post praevisa merita: after foreseen merits

potentia activa ... potentia passiva: active potency ... passive potency

potentia agendi ... ipsa actio: power to act ... action itself

potentia qua volumus: the power by which we will

potest agere ... actu agit: he is able to act ... he actually acts

praecedens inclinatio: previous inclination

praedeterminatio physica: physical predetermination

praemota ... praemotio ... praemotio physica: premoved ... premotion ... physical premotion

praeparatio ad gratiam: preparation for grace

praescientia culpae et praeparatio paenae: foreknowledge of the guilt and preparation of the penalty

praesertim cum voluntas incipit bonum velle quae prius malum volebat: especially when the will, which before was willing evil, begins to will the good

praestat facultatem perseverandi: furnishes the power of persevering

praesupposito iam fine, consequens est ut gratia nobis cooperetur: with the end now presupposed, the consequence is that grace cooperates with us

praeter ordinem divinae gubernationis ... contra ordinem divinae gubernationis: outside the order of divine government ... against the order of divine government

praeveniens ... praeveniens et subsequens: prevenient (taking the lead) ... prevenient and subsequent

prima bonitas ... prima gratia: first goodness ... first grace

prima individua arborum et brutorum animalium: first individuals (in the class) of trees and brute animals

primo et principaliter: first and mainly

primum alterans ... primum appetibile ... primum calefaciens: the first thing changing (another) ... the first desirable ... the primary heating thing

primum esse ... primum est esse: first being ... to be is first

primum mobile ... primum movens: first movable thing ... first moving (agent)

primum principium est Dei operatio convertentis cor: the first principle (of these acts) is the operation of God converting the heart

primum quoad nos ... primum quoad se: first from our viewpoint ... first in itself

primum se movens: first self-mover

principaliter: principally

principium actionis ... causa actionis: principle of action ... cause of action

principium operis meritorii qua meritorii: principle of a meritorious act as meritorious

prius intrat, vehementius imprimit, et tardius recedit: enters first, makes a stronger impression, and leaves more slowly

probabilior: more probable (opinion)

productio creaturae rationalis in finem supernaturalem ... productio creaturae rationalis in vitam aeternam: bringing a rational creature to the supernatural end ... bringing a rational creature to eternal life

proportio per modum naturae incompletae: proportion in the way of an incomplete nature

propositum ... praeparatio ... praescientia exitus: proposal ... preparation ... foreknowledge of the result

proprius effectus Dei: the proper effect of God

propter condicionem status humanae naturae: on account of the condition of human nature

propter principalitatem actus ad actum: because of the principal role of one act with regard to another

qua mota et non movens: as moved but not (actively) moving

qua recte vivitur: (the virtue) by which one lives rightly

qualis est unusquisque (qualis quisque est) talis finis videtur ei: such as anyone is, so does the end appear to him

qualitas per modum transeuntis: a quality in the way of something transient

quam Deus in nobis sine nobis operatur: which God operates in us without us

quandoque movens ... quandoque moventia ... quandoque moventia et mota: a thing sometimes moving (another) ... things sometimes moving (others) ... things sometimes moving (actively) and being moved

quandoque movetur, quandoque non movetur: sometimes it is moved, sometimes it is not moved

quanto virtus alicuius causae est perfectior, tanto ad plura se extendit: in the degree that the power of some cause is more perfect, in that degree does the power extend itself to more things

quantum ad actus: in what regards acts

quasi per totum in Littera: in practically the whole book

qui ab alio: who (is) from another

qui creavit te sine te, non iustificabit te sine te: the One who created you without you will not justify you without you

qui immediatius agit ... qui vehementius imprimit: who acts more immediately ... who makes a stronger impression

quibus recte vivitur: (the virtues) by which one lives rightly

quicumque spiritu Dei aguntur, hi sunt filii Dei: all who are led by the Spirit of God are children of God (Romans 8.14)

quidam calor ex virtute caelestium corporum: a certain heat from the power of the celestial bodies

quidquid movetur ab alio movetur: whatever is moved is moved by something else

quo actualiter agat: by which it may actually act

quo alicui peccatum displicet secundum se ipsum: by which sin in itself is displeasing to someone

quo nos movet ad bene volendum et agendum: by which he moves us to willing and acting properly

quo quis agit cum voluerit: by which one acts when one wishes

quoad exercitium actus ... quoad formam meriti ... quoad productionem entis: with regard to the exercise of the act ... with regard to the form of merit ... with regard to the production of being

quoad specificationem actus ... quoad exercitium actus: with regard to the specification of the act ... with regard to the exercise of the act

quoad substantiam actus: with regard to the substance of the act

quod autem attribuitur alicui ut ab eo in aliud procedens non facit compositionem cum eo: but that which is attributed to something as proceeding from it to something else does not enter into composition with it

quod Deus est causa operandi in omnibus operantibus: that God is the cause of operation in all things that operate

quod divina gratia causat in nobis fidem: that divine grace causes faith in us

quod divinum auxilium homo promereri non potest: that man cannot merit divine help

quod gratis asseritur gratis negatur: what is asserted gratuitously is denied gratuitously

quod homo indiget divino auxilio ad beatitudinem consequendam: that man needs divine help for obtaining beatitude

ratio culpae ... ratio entis ... ratio formalis ... ratio generalis: concept of guilt ... concept of being ... formal concept ... general reason

ratio gubernationis divinae: design of divine government

ratio meriti: the concept of merit

ratio ordinandorum in finem: the concept of things ordered to an end

ratio specialis: special reason

ratione adaequationis: by reason of the equation

ratione sui: by reason of itself

recepta in eo quod fit per modum passionis: received in the way of passion in that which is affected

recta voluntas ... rectificari: right will ... to be made righteous

rectitudo voluntatis propter se servata: rectitude of the will maintained for its own sake

redit quaestio: the question returns

regit liberum arbitrium, et liberum arbitrium est ut iumentum obediens: (grace) governs free will, and free will is like an obedient beast of burden

relatio rationis: mental relation

removens prohibens: removing the obstacle

res aliqua media: some mediate thing

res naturalis: natural thing

respexit Deus ad Abel et ad munera eius: God looked on Abel and on his works

sanatio: healing

scientia Dei causa rerum: God's knowledge (is) the cause of things

scientia media: middle knowledge

secundum communem intentionem boni: according to the general intention of good

secundum (hunc actum) dicitur gratia operans: in reference to (this act) grace is called operative

secundum quod habitus effective causat opus: according as a habit effectively causes the deed

secundum quod in libero arbitrio operatur: according as it operates in free will

sed communiter loquentes utuntur nomine gratiae pro aliquo dono habituali iustificante: but in common parlance they use the name of grace for some habitual justifying gift

sentire ... intelligere ... velle: to sense ... to understand ... to will

servitus peccati: the slavery of sin

si autem loquamur de voluntate, secundum quod nominat proprie actum sic proprie loquendo est finis tantum: but if we speak of the will, according as properly it names an act (instead of a potency), then strictly speaking it is of the end only

sicut ad specialem finem ... cui cupiunt adhaerere sicut bono proprio: as to a special end ... to which they desire to adhere as to (their) proper good

sicut artifex est ad artificiata, ita Deus ad naturalia: as an artisan is to artifacts, so God is to natural things

signa ... signa rationis: signs ... mental designations

similitudo per modum cuiusdam defluxus: likeness in the way of a certain downflow

simpliciter ... simpliciter implere ... simpliciter operans: simply ... simply fulfil ... simply operative

sine Deo: without God

sine gratia gratum faciente: without the grace that makes one pleasing

sine mutatione eius in quo est: without change of that in which it is

sola intentio: intention alone

solutio ad tertium: the solution to the third objection

species coloris in aere: species of color in the atmosphere

species intentionalis: intentional species

suaviter: pleasantly

sub specie aeternitatis: under the aspect of eternity

subducere se ab ordinatione divini intellectus: to withdraw themselves from the decree of the divine intellect

sublata causa, tollitur effectus: when the cause is taken away, the effect is taken away

substantia ... substantia actus ... substantia separata: substance ... substance of the act ... separate substance

subtracto autem motu ab actione et passione, nihil remanet nisi relatio: with the removal of movement from action and passion, nothing remains except a relation

supernaturale quoad modum: supernatural in the way (it is done)

tabula rasa: erased board

tamquam bono proprio: as to its proper good

tardius recedit: leaves more slowly

te tua fata trahunt: your fates draw you

terminus ... terminus a quo ... terminus ad quem: term (of a process) ... term from which ...term to which

titulus coloratus: made to appear as a title

tota operatio pertinet ad gratiam: the whole operation pertains to grace

tractio: drawing

trahit sua quemque voluptas: everyone's pleasure draws him

transitus de potentia in actum: transition from potency to act

uniri: to be united

universale principium essendi: universal principle of being

unumquodque agit secundum quod est actu: everything performs insofar as it is in act

unumquodque cognoscitur secundum quod est: everything is known insofar as it is

ut ab agente in aliud ... ut ab agente in aliud transiens ... ut ab agente in aliud procedens: as from an agent to another ... as passing from an agent into another ... as proceeding from an agent to another

ut ab hoc: as from this

ut autem velimus, operatur; cum autem volumus, ut perficiamus, nobis cooperatur: (God) operates that we may will; but when we will he cooperates with us that we may complete the work

ut bonum velit: that one may will the good

ut bonum velit, ut efficaciter velit: that one may will the good, that one may effectively will (it)

ut in maiori parte: as in a majority of cases

ut iustificemur, consentimus: we consent, that we may be justified

ut velimus operatur incipiens: (God) begins by operating so that we may will

utrum Deus operetur in operatione naturae: whether God operates in the operation of nature

utrum Deus potest cogere voluntatem: whether God can compel the will

utrum falsitas sit in rebus: whether there is falsity in things

utrum gratia convenienter dividatur per operantem et cooperantem: whether grace is suitably distinguished by operative and cooperative

utrum gratia sit multiplex in anima: whether grace is multiple in the soul

utrum homo absque gratia per solam naturalem arbitrii libertatem possit se ad gratiam praeparare: whether man, without grace by the natural liberty alone of will, can prepare himself for grace

utrum homo possit facere aliquod bonum sine gratia: whether man is able to do a good work without grace

utrum homo possit implere praecepta Dei sine gratia: whether man can without grace fulfil the precepts of God

utrum homo possit se praeparare ad gratiam sine aliqua gratia: whether man can without some grace prepare himself for grace

utrum homo sine gratia possit vitare peccatum: whether man can without grace avoid sin

utrum homo sine gratia se possit praeparare ad habendum gratiam: whether man can without grace prepare himself to have grace

utrum in uno homine sit una tantum gratia gratum faciens: whether in one man there is only one grace that makes him pleasing

utrum liberum arbitrium possit in bonum sine gratia: whether free will is capable of a good (deed) without grace

utrum liberum arbitrium sine gratia in statu mortalis peccati vitare peccatum possit: whether free will in a state of mortal sin can without grace avoid sin

vehementius imprimit: makes a stronger impression

vel ex parte motivi vel ex parte mobilis: either on the side of the motive (force) or on that of the movable (thing)

velle adiacet mihi, perficere autem (bonum) non invenio: I can will (what is right), but I cannot do it (Romans 7.18)

velle diversa: to will different things

velle et currere: to will and to run

velle et currere est hominis ut libere agentis, non autem est hominis ut principaliter moventis sed Dei: to will and to run pertain to man as freely acting, not however to man as to the one principally moving but to God

veri nominis: truly of the name

verum: truth, the true

via inventionis ... via doctrinae: way of discovery ... way of teaching

via tertia: the third way (of proving God's existence)

virtus artis ... virtus artis divinae ... virtus artis divinae in universo instrumentali: power of art ... power of divine art ... power of divine art in an instrumental universe

virtus divina creata ... virtus divina increata: divine created power ... divine uncreated power

virtus instrumentalis: instrumental power

virtus motiva efficiens ... virtus motiva imperans: a motive power effecting (something) ... a moving power commanding (something)

virtus naturalis ... virtus operativa ... virtus rei naturalis: natural power ... operative power ... power of a natural thing

virtus vel naturalis vel assuefactiva est causa eius quod est recte opinari circa principium: a power, whether natural or acquired by use, is the cause of our being able to judge rightly in regard to a principle

virtus virtutum ... virtus volendi: power of powers ... power of willing

virtute divina ... virtute motionis divinae: by divine power ... by the power of a divine motion

virtutes ... virtutes activae ... virtutes elementares: powers ... active powers ... elementary powers

vis ... vis artis ... vis et inclinatio: force ... force of art ... force and inclination

vivificari: to be vivified

volo ... ago: I will ... I act

voluntas agit: the will acts

voluntas est finis, electio autem eorum quae sunt ad finem: will is of the end, but choice is of the means to the end

voluntas mota et movens ... voluntas mota et non movens ... voluntas mota et se movens sed non movens membra corporis: will moved and (actively) moving ... will moved and not (actively) moving ... will moved and moving itself but not moving bodily members

voluntas qua reducta de potentia in actum: will as brought from potency to act

Greek Words and Phrases

autexousion: power on one's own

dunamis: force, power, action

energeia: operation, act, realization

entelekheia: perfection, attainment

pathêsis: passion, reception, undergoing change

poiêsis: a making